Lecture Notes in Economics and Mathematical Systems

Operations Research, Computer Science, Social Science

Edited by M. Beckmann, Providence, G. Goos, Karlsruhe, and H. P. Künzi, Zürich

83

NTG/GI

Gesellschaft für Informatik
Nachrichtentechnische Gesellschaft

Fachtagung „Cognitive Verfahren und Systeme"

Hamburg, 11.–13. April 1973

Herausgegeben im Auftrag der NTG/GI
von Theodor Einsele, Wolfgang Giloi und Hans-Hellmut Nagel

Springer-Verlag

Berlin · Heidelberg · New York 1973

Prof. Dr. Theodor Einsele
Institut für Datenverarbeitung
8 München 2
Arcisstraße 21

Prof. Dr. Wolfgang Giloi
Institut für Angewandte Mathematik
66 Saarbrücken
Im Stadtwald

Prof. Dr. Hans-Hellmut Nagel
Institut für Informatik
2 Hamburg 13
Schlüterstraße 70

AMS Subject Classifications (1970): 68 A 45

ISBN-13:978-3-540-06268-4   e-ISBN-13:978-3-642-80749-7
DOI: 10.1007/978-3-642-80749-7

"Cognitive Verfahren und Systeme" versucht den Kreis von Lösungsansätzen
zu umfassen, der im englischen Sprachraum unter dem - vielleicht etwas
problematischen - Begriff "artificial intelligence" subsumiert wird.

Von den unterschiedlichsten Ausgangspunkten her ist man dazu übergegan-
gen, digitale Datenverarbeitungsanlagen zur Behandlung cognitiver Fragestellungen einzusetzen. Die GI und die NTG wollen durch die gemeinsame
Veranstaltung einer Fachtagung - ihrer ersten über diesen Themenkreis -
eine Gelegenheit bieten, solche Ansätze zur Diskussion zu stellen, um
Querverbindungen zwischen den verschiedenen Fragestellungen deutlich
werden zu lassen.

Die Veranstalter begrüßen es besonders, daß auch Autoren aus den Bereichen
westeuropäischer Schwestergesellschaften der GI und der NTG sich mit Bei-
trägen an dieser Diskussion beteiligen.

"Cognitive Verfahren und Systeme" attempts to describe in German those
approaches which are referred to in English by the - not completely
unproblematical - term "artificial intelligence".

The attempts to use digital data processing to solve cognitive problems
of quite different kinds have spread considerably. The "Gesellschaft für
Informatik" and the "Nachrichtentechnische Gesellschaft" organize jointly
this special meeting - their first one for this subject - to allow the presentation of work in this area in the hope to detect common trends even in
seemingly unconnected approaches.

The organizing committee welcomes the fact that our call for papers has
been transmitted by our European Sister Societies and authors from other
countries will contribute to the discussions during this meeting.

INHALTSVERZEICHNIS

AUTORENADRESSEN

ADRIEN, F., Développement Scientifique, IBM-France, Paris-
La Défense.

BECKER, D., Institut für Datenverarbeitung, Technische Universität
München, 8000 München 2, Arcisstraße 21.

BERRINI, P.L., Istituto di Biometria e Statistica Medica
Milano/Italy.

BÖHME, J.F., c/o Fried. Krupp GmbH, Atlas-Elektronik Bremen,
2800 Bremen 44, Postfach 8545.

FINDLER, N.V., Institut für Numerische Mathematik, Technische Hochschule Wien, A-1040 Wien, Karlsplatz 13.

GELSEMA, E.S., CERN, Organisation européene pour la recherche
nucléaire, 1211 Genève 23.

GÜDESEN, A., IITB - Karlsruhe, 7500 Karlsruhe, Breslauer Str. 48.

HANAKATA, K., Universität Stuttgart, Institut für Informatik,
7000 Stuttgart, Herdweg 51.

HESS, W., Institut für Datenverarbeitung, TU München, 8000 München 2,
Arcisstr. 21.

HOLDERMANN, F., Gesellschaft zur Förderung der Astrophysikalischen
Forschung e.V., Forschungsgruppe für Informationsver-
arbeitung und Mustererkennung, 7500 Karlsruhe 1,
Engesserstraße 5.

KLEIN, H., s. N.V. Findler.

LEVINE, Z.H., s. N.V. Findler.

MARKO, H., Institut für Nachrichtentechnik, Technische Hochschule
München, 8000 München 2, Arcisstr. 21.

MEDER, H.G., IBM - Wissenschaftliches Zentrum, 6900 Heidelberg,
Tiergartenstr. 15.

NEES G., c/o Siemens AG, 8520 Erlangen 2, Postfach 325.

PAU, L.F., Institute of Mathematical Statistics and Operations
Research, Technical University of Denmark, Building 349,
Lundtoftevej 100, DK - 2800 Lyngby.

PAULUS, E., Institut für Datenverarbeitung der Technischen
Universität, 8000 München 13, Franz-Joseph-Str. 38/I.

PISTOR, P., IBM - Wissenschaftliches Zentrum, 6900 Heidelberg,
Tiergartenstraße 15.

POWELL, B.W., Genf s. Gelsema.

RAULEFS, P.G., Institut für Informatik I, Universität Karlsruhe,
7500 Karlsruhe, Postfach 6380.

REDDY, D.R., Computer Science Department, Carnegie-Mellon University,
Pittsburgh / PA 15213 / USA.

ROSENFELD, A., Computer Science Center, University of Maryland,
College Park/MD 20742/USA.

SCHADACH, D.J., Rechenzentrum der Christian-Albrechts-Universität,
2300 Kiel, Neue Universität, Olshausenstr. 40 - 60.

STIES, M., Forschungsgruppe für Informationsverarbeitung und
Mustererkennung, 7500 Karlsruhe, Engesserstr. 5.

WALCH, G., IBM - Wissenschaftliches Zentrum, 69 Heidelberg,
Tiergartenstr. 15.

WOLFERTS, K., Institut für Photogrammetrie und Topographie,
Universität Karlsruhe, 7500 Karlsruhe 1, Englerstr. 7.

EYES AND EARS FOR COMPUTERS *

R. Reddy

It is clear that all the (visual and speech) phenomena occur in both space and time. In visual signs it is the spacial dimension which takes priority, whereas the temporal dimension takes priority in auditory signs...what is the substantial difference between spacial and auditory signs? We observe a strong tendency to reify visual signs, to connect them with objects, to ascribe mimesis to such signs, and to view them as elements of an "imitative art". ... On the other hand verbal and musical signs show us two essential features. First, both music and language present a consistantly heirarchized structure, and, second, both are resolvable into ultimate, discrete, rigorously patterned components which, as such, have no existence in nature but are built ad hoc.

One should not draw the frequently suggested but over-simplified conclusion that speech displays a purely linear character or that visual perception is performed by purely simultaneous synthesis. Luria shows that in our perception of a painting, we first deploy step-by-step efforts to go over from certain selected details from parts to the whole, and for the contemplator of a painting the integration follows as a further phase, as a goal. In the fifth century, Bhartrhari, the great master of Indic linguistic theory, distinguished three stages in a speech event, conceptualization, production and audition, and comprehension. While production and audition are naturally sequential, both conceptualization and comprehension of the whole message is done at one and the same time. This conception is akin to the modern psychological problem of "short-term memory".

Jakobson (1964)

INTRODUCTION

Visual and speech perception tasks, which can be performed with no apparent effort by people, have proved to be difficult for machines. This may be in part due to the absence of cognitive models of perception of the type proposed above by Jakobson. In this paper we attempt to give a unified view of the research in machine perception of speech and vision in the hope that a clear appreciation of similarities and differences may lead to better information processing models of perception. Being active in research in both computer vision and speech, we have found it useful to look at the problems that

* This research was supported in part by the Advanced Research Projects Agency of the Department of Defense under contract no. F44620-70-C-0107 and monitored by Air Force Office of Scientific Research.

have arisen in one domain and anticipate corresponding problems in the other (Reddy, 1969). Thus, this paper represents a comparitive study of the issues, systems and unsolved problems that are, at present, of interest to visual and speech recognition research.

To distinguish from the multitude of activities that come under the all encompassing term pattern recognition (digit recognition, isolated word recognition, character recognition, etc.), this paper will be restricted to the areas of research denoted by "speech understanding systems" and "scene analysis". These terms represent attempts at machine perception of unrestricted speech and visual stimuli, e.g., spontaneous (possibly ungrammatical) connected speech from many speakers, and naturally occuring scenes such as people, rooms, trees etc. The main problem here is not one of categorization and classification but rather that of analysis and description (Narasimhan, 1966). These areas are further characterized by the notion that, to equal human performance, many sources of knowledge (possibly disjoint) have to be brought to bear on the perception task. It is also assumed that these sources of knowledge ("capsules of intelligence") must effectively cooperate with each other to achieve better perception than would be the case when some of the sources of knowledge are absent. It is appropriate to quote Newell, et al., (1971) on this subject:

> We call the type of system to be investigated a **speech-understanding** system. The inclusion of **understanding** is to distinguish the systems somewhat from speech **recognition** systems. It does not so much indicate enhanced intellectual status, but emphasizes that the system is to perform some task making use of speech. **Thus, the errors that count are not errors in speech recognition, but errors in task accomplishment.** If the system can guess (infer, deduce,...) correctly what the user wants, then its inability to determine exactly what the user said should not be held against it -- even as for you and I.

Though the eventual goal of speech understanding and scene analysis research is to accept unrestricted stimuli, we do not at present know how to design such systems. It is natural, then, to attempt to build systems which perform restricted perception tasks, e.g., recognition of isolated words from a single cooperative speaker or of a visual scene containing only rectangular parallelepipeds of different sizes and colors. However, unless these systems are designed with the eventual goal in mind, it is possible to end up with systems which are too specialized and unextendable. Thus it becomes necessary to have a global view of the problem and the many dimensions along which systems can vary. This would be helpful in designing experiments and systems which, though restricted, can provide valuable knowledge towards the ultimate system. Some of these dimensions have been discussed by Reddy (1969). A more complete list for speech was given by Newell et al., (1971). In the next section we will use many of these variables for both vision and speech.

Although there have been many papers on the subject of speech recognition, there have only been a few working systems for the recognition of connected speech. The system of Fry and Denes (1969) was hardwired and used probabilistic information to improve recognition. The system of Sakai and Doshita (1963) was hardwired to perform segmentation, phone and word recognition. Hughes and Hemdal (1965) used a computer-based feature extraction system for the recognition of vowels and some consonants.

Reddy (1967) analyzed a limited set of connected speech utterances to formulate algorithms for segmentation, phoneme grouping, and classification for many phonemes of English. The Vicens-Reddy system demonstrated the use of syntactic information (Vicens, 1969) in speech recognition. The system of Tappert and Dixon (1972) uses sequential decoding techniques in the analysis of connected speech. The Hearsay system (Reddy, Erman and Neely, 1972) is the first working connected speech recognition system using non-trivial syntax and semantics. We will describe the structure of this system in greater detail in a later section. We can expect interesting results in this area over the next several years because there are several other groups also active at present in speech understanding research (Barnett, 1972; Fant, 1970; Forgie, 1972; Walker, 1972; Woods, 1972). In addition, there is a great deal of relevant research in the areas of speech analysis, synthesis, and perception (Fant, 1960; Flanagan, 1965) and in the area of phonetics and linguistics (Lehiste, 1967; Chomsky and Halle, 1968).

The work in scene analysis has been centered mainly around robotics research at several artificial intelligence centers: Stanford, MIT, SRI, and Edinburgh. As such it has often been overly restrictive in scope. The papers by Feldman, et al., (1969 and 1971), Nilsson (1969), Fikes and Nilsson (1971), illustrate the state of the art in this area. Most of this work has produced a repertory of techniques for specific tasks, e.g., plane bounded convex objects, rooms without clutter, or, in general, subproblems whose main motivation is that they can be analyzed without too much difficulty or too many errors within the present state-of-the-art. However, there have been several advances: scene analysis by classification of types of intersections (Guzman, 1968), the use of the notion of planning in picture processing (Kelly, 1970), accommodation in computer vision (Tanenbaum, 1971), building structural descriptions from examples (Winston, 1971), analysis of curved objects (Krakauer, 1971), and so on (see Rosenfeld (1969, 1973) for a more complete survey).

FACTORS AFFECTING THE FEASIBILITY AND PERFORMANCE
OF A PERCEPTION TASK

Is speech input to computer possible? The question is not well posed. It depends on many things. Consider only the list in Figure 2.1. It seems annoyingly long. But each of the concerns is an essentially independent specification that, even with present knowledge, has a strong effect on the feasibility and performance of any proposed speech recognition system. Down towards the low performance end there are combinations that are not only feasible, but are beginning to be commercially advertised (e.g., "voice-button" systems). Up towards the high end the responsible posture is that only after other intermediate steps have been accomplished successfully should an estimate be made.

Newell et al. (1971)

The comments of Newell et al. on speech understanding systems hold for computer vision as well. The number of factors that affect the feasibility and performance are too numerous and are likely to grow as we understand the problems better. These factors can be grouped together into several general categories: characteristics of the source, environment, receiver (transducer), sources of knowledge, performance requirements, and computing system. In this section we will examine each of these categories and the factors influencing feasibility within each.

CHARACTERISTICS OF THE SOURCE

The factors influencing the characteristics of the sources are the composition of the stimulus, variability within the stimulus, and selectability and adaptability of the stimulus. Table 1 shows the possible choices for each of these factors.

Factor	Speech	Vision
Composition of the stimulus	Isolated Words? Connected Speech?	Single objects? Many (possibly occluded) objects?
Variability of the stimulus	One speaker? Many speakers? Open population? Male? Female? Child?	Variable size? Variable color? Variable texture?
Selectability of the stimulus	Carefully selected words? Slightly selected? Free?	Carefully selected objects? Slightly selected? Free?
Adaptability of the stimulus	Cooperative speaker? Casual speaker? Playful speaker? Trained speaker? Untrained speaker?	Carefully constructed scenes? Degenerate views? Impossible objects (Escher-type)?

Table I.   Factors influencing the characteristics of the Source.

Composition of the stimulus

Systems for recognition of a small set of isolated words (objects) already exist. However, when the number of words (objects) gets large or the inventory contains similar words (objects) the system performance begins to degrade significantly.

Unrestricted connected speech understanding (arbitrarily complex scene analysis) is beyond the present state of the art. The main problem here is that, depending on the context, characteristics of individual words (objects) change significantly. This may be due to coarticulation (shadows), relaxed speech (occlusion), or word boundary ambiguity (object boundary ambiguity).

Variability of the stimulus

Characteristics of a given word (object) vary depending on the speaker, sex, and physical condition (size, color, and texture). If the purpose of the perception task is to identify the word (object) independent of these variables, the system must have facilities for variability normalization. Existing systems have some variability normalization but no general schemes have emerged yet.

Selectability of the stimulus

If the words (objects) to be recognized can be preselected so as to cause minimum ambiguity resulting from similarity of structure, then the system performance can be significantly improved. While this is a useful gimmick to produce economical systems, this type of preselection can lead to unextendable systems.

Adaptability of the stimulus

If the speaker can be trained and is cooperative (if a scene composition can be carefully controlled) the system sophistication can be substantially lower than if the system has to understand casual or even playful speakers (impossible objects). However natural speech (scenes) tend to be not only ungrammatical but also not well-formed. This type of a restriction is unlikely to be useful, if the long term goal is to recognize natural speech (or scenes).

CHARACTERISTICS OF THE ENVIRONMENT

There are two factors influencing the signal quality that are independent of the source or the receiver. These are external sources of noise and the distance between the source and the receiver. Table 2 shows the possible causes affecting each of these.

Factor	Speech	Vision
Noise	Airconditioning Noise? Teletype noise? Room reverberation? Hmm, haa, and cough? Cocktail party?	Flare? Out of focus? In the shadow? Cluttered view?
Distance between source and receiver	Very close? Very far?	Very close? Very far?

Table II. Characteristics of the Environment

Noise of various forms affects the reliability of analysis. Whether a given system is useable or not depends on the environment it has to operate in. A measure of robustness of a system is how it compares with the corresponding degradation in human performance under similar noise conditions.

A microphone held too close to the lips also records the lip opening before the beginning of the utterance and the expiration at the end giving the illusion of extra sounds. When held too far, there is a loss of resolution of the signal and a decreased signal-to-noise ratio. An object too close to the camera exhibits perspective distortion and an object too far results in the loss of resolution. There is nothing much to be done except be aware and correct for the location appropriately. Note that the human being has similar limitations as well.

CHARACTERISTICS OF THE RECEIVER

There are several factors associated with the transducer that affect the performance of the system. These refer to the frequency response, amplitude response, adaptation and accomodation, and other special features. Table III indicates some of the options to be considered in the design of a system.

Factor	Speech	Vision
Transducer	Microphone? Telephone?	Vidicon camera? Image dissector?
Frequency response	50-20KHz? 300-3KHz?	10↑15Hz(400nm to 700nm)? Smallest resolvable object?
Sampling rate	6000per sec.? 10000? 20000?	256x256per frame? 512x512? 1024x1024? 4096x4096?
Dynamic range	20db? 40db? 60db? 80db? 100db?	
Adaptation and accomodation	Phase-locking to a conversation? Speaker normalization? Noise normalization?	Pan? Tilt? Zoom? Focus? Automatic gain conrol?
Special Features	Pitch extractor? Phase extractor? Timbre extractor?	Color detectors? Texture detectors?

Table III. Characteristics of the Transducer

The choice of the transducer, microphone or telephone (Vidicon or Image dissector) depends on the application, the characteristics of the digitizer (ADC), sampling rate, and so on.

To equal human performance, the microphone should have a frequency response of 50Hz-20KHz. This implies that not only should the microphone have satisfactory frequency response in that range but the analog-to-digital conversion should be at twice the rate of frequency response desired (Nyquist rate). In practice, however, it is usually adequate to digitize speech at a rate of 20,000 samples per second for a frequency response of less than 10 KHz. Further, to avoid aliasing, it is necessary to low pass filter the data so as to remove the frequency components in the signal above the frequency response. In applications where other sources of knowledge are available to compensate for the limitations of the transducer, a much more restricted frequency response may be tolerable, e.g., telephone quality response of 300 Hz-3KHz. The lower frequency response systems have difficulty disambiguating among the fricatives /f/, /θ/, and /s/.

The transducer for visual input is usually a Vidicon TV camera, an Image dissector, or a facsimile scanner. Which one is used depends on the tradeoffs within the system: real time response, accuracy of digitization, and characteristics of the stimulus, e.g., moving vs. stationary, live input vs. photograph.

There are two types of frequency responses of interest for a visual input device. One is its response to different colors, i.e., different wavelengths in the electromagnetic spectrum. The other is its response to various spacial frequencies, i.e., the smallest resolvable object within the visual field. Within the narrow fovial region the human being is able to detect objects that subtend an angle of no more than 20" of arc on the retina. Visual input systems tend to have substantially lower resolution than that unless one uses high resolution facsimile scanners.

The dynamic range of the system is probably the next most important factor affecting accuracy of the system. To equal human performance, the speech and vision transducer system must have at least a 100 db dynamic range (or 10^5 different resolvable levels of sound pressure or light intensity). This requires an 18 bit analog-to-digital converter (17 bits for vision since the values are all positive). For most practical purposes a 40 to 60db dynamic range is adequate, requiring 8 to 11 bits of resolution. For low dynamic range systems (20db), a 4 bit converter may be adequate.

Other factors affecting the system that are associated with the transducer are adaptation and accommodation. The human visual system is a classic example of the types of adaptation that may be useful. Not only does the pupil focus, expand, and contract depending on the brightness and depth of the field of view, but also there is an automatic guidance system for controlling the ballistic eye movements. In machine input systems correspondingly useful features are automatic pan, tilt, zoom, and focus mechanisms. These facilities exist on some of the current systems. For speech, corresponding facilities might also be useful for speaker, noise, and transducer normalization. At present some of the normalizaton is achieved by enhancement of high frequency components of the signal. But this is probably too primitive and too little.

Other feature extractors for measuring pitch, phase, and timbre characteristics of speech, and color and textures parameters in vision have been proposed but have not been used effectively in any speech understanding or scene analysis systems to date.

CHARACTERISTICS OF SOURCES OF KNOWLEDGE

For a given task, there are usually several sources of knowledge which can significantly enhance the performance of the system. These are usually related to the structure, number, and the interrelationship among entities (words or objects) that may appear in a given scene. The structure and interrelationships can be represented in many different ways leading to different interpretations. Table IV gives some of the main sources of knowledge available for speech and visual perception tasks.

Factor	Speech	Vision
Structure of entities	No. of different phonemes? Valid sequences of phonemes? Effect of context?	No. of different shapes that make up the objects? Strong and weak structural cues?
No. of entities	Few (<100)?　Many (<1000)?　Unrestricted?	
Probabalistic knowledge	Frequency counts?　Digram and trigram frequencies?	
Syntactic knowledge	Fixed phrases? Artificial languages? Free English?	Fixed scenes? Restricted scenes? Naturally occurring scenes?
Semantic knowledge	Task-dependent?　User and action dependent? Analysis dependent?	

Table IV.　Characteristics of Sources of Knowledge

In speech, words can be further decomposed into morphemes, syllables, phonemes, and features. For any given language, there are rules governing the morpho-phonemic structure of the words, e.g., number of different phonemes, restrictions on sequences of phonemes, effect of context on the articulation of a phoneme, digram frequencies, etc. In addition, for a given task the vocabulary used is usually constrained. This constraint may take one of two forms -- increasing the probability of occurance of words frequently used in that task, and, secondly, declaring (arbitrarily) that only a given subset of words may be used in the sentences for this task. This second constraint, when present, further restricts the morphophonemic rules of the language. As the number of words in the language increases, the complexity of the perception task increases. This increase in complexity is so great that there are no systems at present that can recognize vocabularies of a thousand or greater. Part of this is due to the fact that as the vocabulary increases the number of acoustically ambiguous words may also increase, e.g., "sit", "slit", "spit", "split", etc.

In vision, unfortunately, there is no well-defined structure, akin to morphemes, syllables, phonemes, etc., that characterizes the objects to be recognized. Surfaces and shape of surfaces that make up the object is probably the closest thing. However, as in the case of speech, a given task can provide restrictions about the number and structure of the objects that might appear in a scene. These restrictions might be probabalistic or ad hoc. Ambiguity in object perception might result if two different objects can produce the same profiles from different points of view, e.g., a cube viewed from the side would show a square profile; so would a pyramid when viewed from the bottom.

Both syntactic and semantic sources of knowledge primarily reflect the interrelationships affecting the composition of a sentence (a scene). The sentence (scene) composition may be arbitrarily constrained to minimize the problems of analysis. The problems that arise in speech at this level are word boundary ambiguities (see next section for some examples), changes in segmental and suprasegmental characteristics depending on sentence context, and non-grammaticality and non-well-formedness of sentences in spoken language. In vision, the problems are determining object boundaries in the presence of shadows, occlusions, and matched surface junctures. Availability of syntactic and semantic sources of knowledge of the type listed in Table IV helps to direct and focus the search during the perception task. We will see more on the use of syntax and semantics in the next section.

CHARACTERISTICS OF THE SYSTEM

There are several characteristics of the system which have by far the largest impact on the success or failure of a perception task, viz., the model (method of solution), the system organization, the desired performance, and the computing system used. Table V gives the choices available in each of these dimensions.

Factor	Options
Model	Hierarchical? Heterarchical? Hypothesize-and-test? Analysis-by-Synthesis?
System Organization	Simple program? Multiprocessing? Parallel processing? Pipeline? Feedback? Feed forward? Backtrack? Planning?
Performance	Real time? About real time? No hurry? No errors (<.1%)? Few errors (<)? Many errors (<20%)?
Processing power of computer	1 million instructions/sec? 10 mips? 100 mips? 1000 mips?
Size of memory	1 megabit? 10 mb? 100 mb? 1000 mb?
Cost (per second of speech or per scene) analyzed	.001$/s? .01$/s? .1$/s? 1.00$/s? 100.0$/s?

Table V. Characteristics of the System

While a hierarchical structure may be adequate for simple recognition tasks, it is not adequate for systems which have to use many diverse sources of knowledge. Analysis-by-Synthesis (Stevens and Halle, 1961) and Heterarchical Systems (Minsky and Pappert, 1972) are adequate but are either computationally expensive or do not lend themselves to systems organizations that satisfy the following requirements which we think important:

1. Contributions of syntax, semantics, context, and other sources of knowledge towards analysis should be clearly evaluatable. Exactly what and how much does each contribute towards improving the performance of the system?
2. The absence of one or more sources of knowledge should not have a crippling effect on the performance of the model.
3. When more than one source of knowledge is available, interactions between them should lead to a greater improvement in performance than is possible to attain by the use of any subset of sources of knowledge.
4. Since the decoding process is errorful at every stage, the model must permit graceful error recovery.
5. Increases in performance requirements (such as the real time requirement, increase in vocabulary, modifications to the syntax, or changes in semantic interpretation) should not require major reformulation of the model.

We have arrived at a model which is intended to satisfy the above requirements. It consists of a small set of cooperating independent processes capable of helping in the decoding process either individually or collectively and using the "hypothesize-and-test" paradigm. We will see the use of this model in the next section.

System Organization

Even when the model (the method of solution) is specified, there are several possible ways the program structure could be organized: as a single processor system, a multiprocessor system or a parallel processing system. Nonrestricted speech understanding and scene analysis tasks will probably require systems of substantially greater computational power than can be obtained by, say, a million-instruction-per-second computer. One way to achieve this power is to use several processors. Multiple processors may, in turn, require substantial reformulation of the problem solution. In addition, if each source of knowledge is to be activated as an independent process as in the model above, then the system can be programmed to run under a single processor or multiprocessor system.

A feature that characterizes all machine perception systems is that, at each stage of the processing, they make some errors while correcting others. This errorful nature of systems makes it imperative that they be fail-soft, i.e., they make no irrevocable decisions. This is achieved within a program using techniques such as backtracking, feed-forward, feed-back, etc.

Performance Requirements

The real-time requirement is probably the most difficult requirement to satisfy. To equal human performance, a system must sometimes be able to answer questions (detect motions) even before they are completed. This means that various subprocesses within the system (representing various sources of knowledge) must be able to operate on the incoming data as soon as a meaningful "chunk" of data is available without waiting for the completion of the utterance. This poses serious problems for system organization in the activation, control, and interprocess communication of the subprocesses.

The other performance requirement, accuracy, is equally demanding. By now it is axiomatic that almost any reasonable strategy for analysis will achieve 80% accuracy. Attempts at improving the performance seems to require exponentially increasing effort. The higher the accuracy requirement, the greater the tradeoffs with respect to all the other dimensions: vocabulary size (number of objects), number of speakers (colors and textures), time for analysis, and so on.

Economics of recognition

Ultimately, whether a speech understanding (scene analysis) system is used in an application or not depends on the cost of recognition. The cost in turn depends on the speed and memory requirements of the computer used in the perception task. It seems possible to build adaptive isolated word recognizers of about a 100 word vocabulary for a few thousand dollars. However, connected speech understanding systems with large vocabularies are likely to be very expensive and uneconomical for most tasks. Similarly, a simple vision system controlling a simple assembly task can be produced economically today. General purpose computer vision seems far away.

SYSTEMS FOR MACHINE PERCEPTION .

Automatic speech recognition -- as the human accomplishes it -- will probably be possible only through the proper analysis and application of grammatical, contextual, and semantic constraints. This approach also presumes an acoustic analysis which preserves the same information that the human transducer (i.e., the ear) does. It is clear, too, that for a given accuracy of recognition, a trade can be made between the necessary linguistic constraints, and complexity of the vocabulary, and the number of speakers.

J. L. Flanagan (1965)

A main focus of this paper is to suggest that, to equal human performance in perception, machines must use all the available sources of knowledge. These sources of knowledge tend to be too diverse and disjoint to be used in a uniform manner. Further, some of the sources of knowledge may be absent. Thus, the absence of useful syntax and semantics in a given task should not have a crippling effect on the performance of the system. When more than one source of knowledge is available, interactions between them should lead to greater improvement in performance than is possible to attain by the use of any subset of the sources of knowledge.

Although the use of syntax, semantics, and context in a perception task have been talked about for a long time, there have been few systems which demonstrated how these sources of knowledge may be used in a the recognition task. The focus of the report by Newell, et al, (1971) was, therefore, to propose a program for research for a class of systems in which the effect of these diverse sources of knowledge could be examined.

Rather than talk about possible organizations of systems which use many sources of knowledge, we will attempt to illustrate the point by means of two specific examples: The HEARSAY System (Reddy, Erman, Fennell, and Neely, 1973) for a speech understanding task and the image processing part of the SYNAPS System (Reddy, Davis, Ohlander and

Bihary, 1972a) performing a visual perception task. These systems were chosen because they are illustrative of the current state of the art and, more importantly, they are the systems most familiar to the author.

THE HEARSAY SYSTEM

HEARSAY is a speech understanding system presently under development at Carnegie-Mellon University. It is not restricted to any particular recognition task. Given the syntax and the vocabulary of a language and the semantics of a task, HEARSAY attempts recognition of the utterance in that language. Here we will illustrate the operation of the HEARSAY system by considering in detail the recognition process of an utterance within a specific task environment: voice chess. The task is to recognize a spoken chess move in a given board position and respond with the counter move.

Figure 1 illustrates the board position for this example at the time the move is spoken. The speaker, playing white, wishes to move his bishop on queen's bishop one to king knight five. As illustrated in Figure 2, this is one of 46 different legal moves in this position. These moves have been ordered on the basis of their goodness in the given board position. The negative rates indicate that it would be a very bad move. This judgement was based on a task dependent source of knowledge available to program (Gillogly, 1972). Note that the move chosen by the speaker was only the fourth best move in that situation.

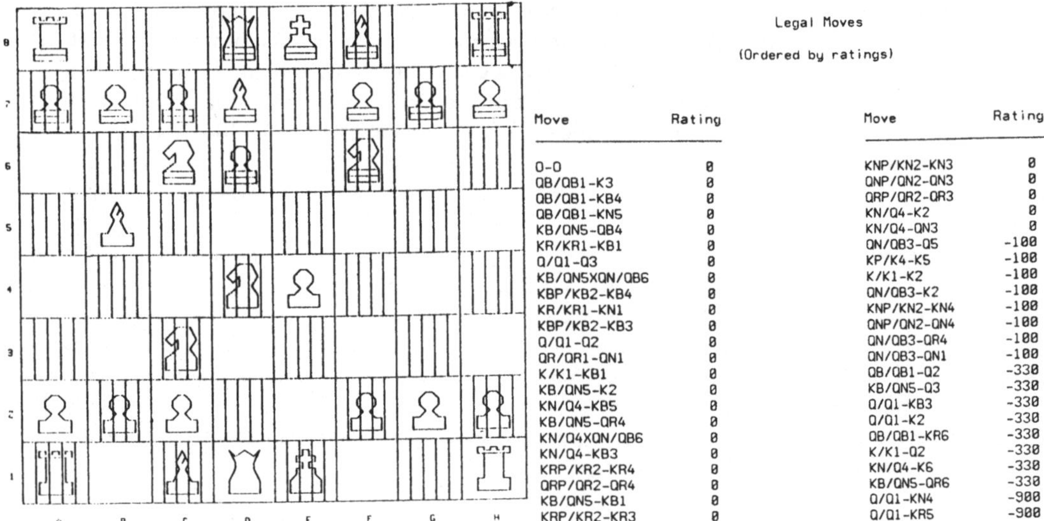

Legal Moves

(Ordered by ratings)

Move	Rating		Move	Rating
0-0	0		KNP/KN2-KN3	0
QB/QB1-K3	0		QNP/QN2-QN3	0
QB/QB1-KB4	0		QRP/QR2-QR3	0
QB/QB1-KN5	0		KN/Q4-K2	0
KB/QN5-QB4	0		KN/Q4-QN3	0
KR/KR1-KB1	0		QN/QB3-Q5	-100
Q/Q1-Q3	0		KP/K4-K5	-100
KB/QN5XQN/QB6	0		K/K1-K2	-100
KBP/KB2-KB4	0		QN/QB3-K2	-100
KR/KR1-KN1	0		KNP/KN2-KN4	-100
KBP/KB2-KB3	0		QNP/QN2-QN4	-100
Q/Q1-Q2	0		QN/QB3-QR4	-100
QR/QR1-QN1	0		QN/QB3-QN1	-100
K/K1-KB1	0		QB/QB1-Q2	-330
KB/QN5-K2	0		KB/QN5-Q3	-330
KN/Q4-KB5	0		Q/Q1-KB3	-330
KB/QN5-QR4	0		Q/Q1-K2	-330
KN/Q4XQN/QB6	0		QB/QB1-KR6	-330
KN/Q4-KB3	0		K/K1-Q2	-330
KRP/KR2-KR4	0		KN/Q4-K6	-330
QRP/QR2-QR4	0		KB/QN5-QR6	-330
KB/QN5-KB1	0		Q/Q1-KN4	-900
KRP/KR2-KR3	0		Q/Q1-KR5	-900

Figure 1.   The chess board position at the time the move is spoken

Figure 2.   A list of the legal moves for the board position in Figure 1

Having chosen the move, there are many possible ways of uttering the move. The syntax of the language permits many variations -- usually of the form <piece> <action> <position>. The piece can have qualifiers to indicate the location. The action may be of the form: "to", "moves-to", "goes-to", "takes", "captures", and so on. The position is of the form: "king three", "king bishop four", or "king knight five", and so on. The actual move spoken in this context was "bishop moves-to king knight five". Note that "queen bishop on queen bishop one" can be specified just as "bishop" because there is no ambiguity in this case.

Figure 3 shows the speech waveform of the utterance with manual segmentation showing the beginning and ending of each word and each phoneme within the word. (The manual segmentation and labelling indicated in this and succeeding figures is for our benefit only -- it is not available to the system while it is attempting recognition.) The utterance was about 2 seconds in duration and the waveform is displayed on ten consecutive rows, each row containing 200 milliseconds of the utterance. The first line of text under each row contains the word being articulated. The word is repeated for the whole duration of the word. Thus, the word "bishop" was articulated for 400 milliseconds and occupies the first two rows of the wave form. The second line of text under each row contains the phoneme being articulated. The phoneme (represented in IPA notation) is repeated for the duration of the phoneme.

Several interesting problems of speech recognition arise in the context of recognition of this utterance. The end of Row 2 of Figure 3 shows the juncture between "bishop" and "moves". Note that the ending /p/ in "bishop" and the beginning nasal /m/ in "moves" are homorganic, i.e., they both have the same articulatory position. This results in the absence of the release and the aspiration that normally characterizes the phoneme /p/. Row 6 of Figure 3 illustrates a word boundary problem. The ending nasal of "king" and the beginning nasal of "knight" tend to be articulated from the same tongue position even though in isolation they would have been articulated from two different positions. This results in a single segment representing two different phonemes in two adjacent words. Further, it is impossible to specify the exact location of the word boundary. In the manual segmentation, the boundary was placed at an arbitrary position. Another type of juncture problem appears on Row 8 of Figure 3 at the boundary of "knight five". The release and aspiration of the phoneme /t/ are assimilated into the /f/ of "five".

Feature Extraction and Segmentation

The speech input from the microphone is passed through five band-pass filters (spanding the range 200-6400 Hz) and through an unfiltered band. Within each band the maximum intensity is measured for every 10 milliseconds (the zero crossings are also measured in each of the bands but they do not play an important role in the recognition process at present). This results in a vector of 6 parameters every 10 milliseconds. These parameters are smoothed and log-transformed. Figure 4 shows a plot of these parameters as a function of time. The top line shows the utterance spoken. The second line of text indicates where the word boundaries were marked during the manual segmentation process (this will permit us to verify the accuracy of the machine recognition process in the later stages).

This vector of parameters (labeled 1, 2, 3, 4, 5, and U in Figure 4) are compared with a standard set of parameter vectors to obtain a minimum distance classification using a nearest neighbor classification technique. The line of text labeled P in Figure 4 gives the classification for every 10 millisecond unit. The standard set of parameters is obtained by selecting parameter values from a training set of utterances containing various phonemes in neutral context. When a phoneme is represented by several

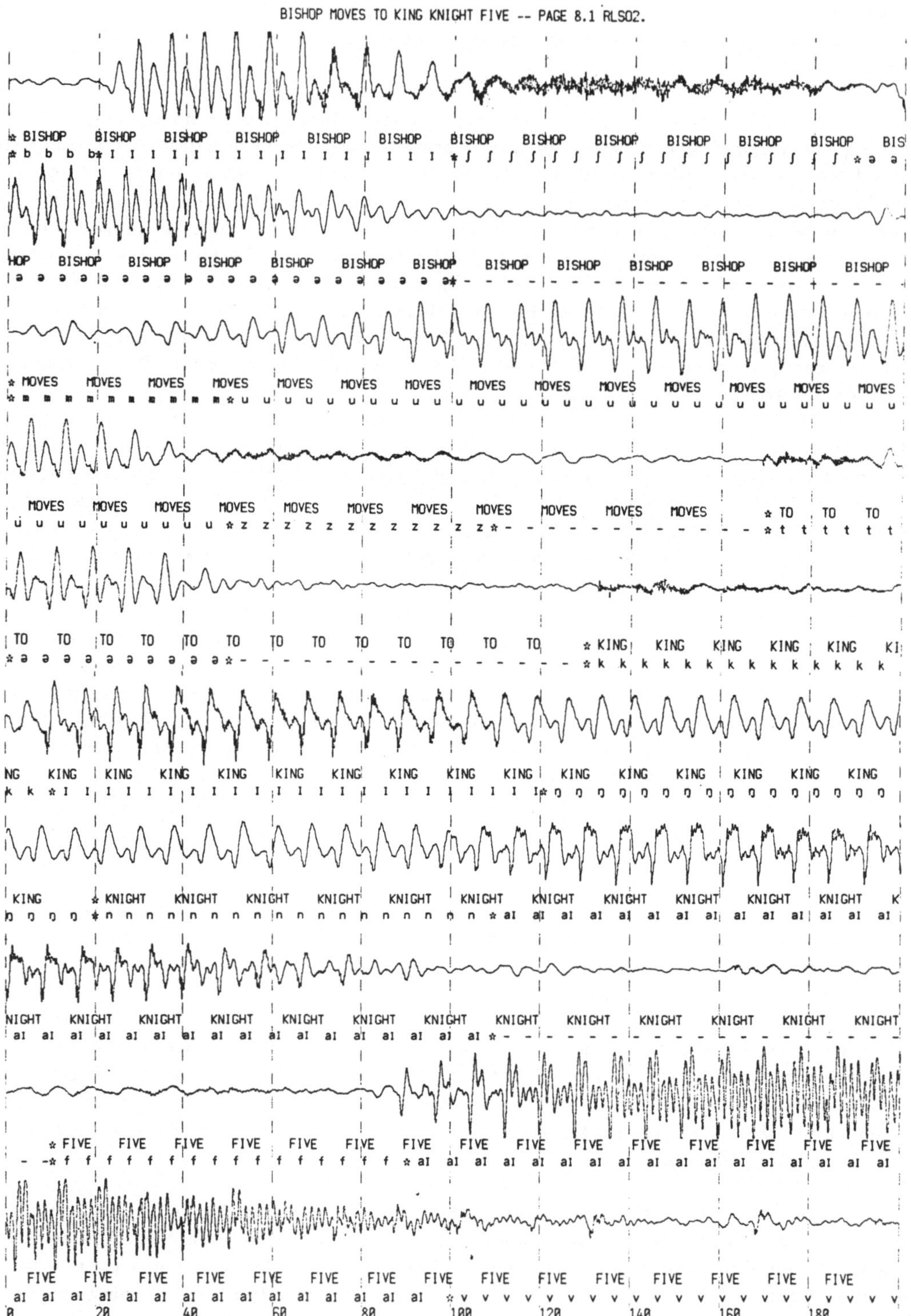

Figure 3. Waveform of the utterance showing the actual word
and phoneme boundaries

articulatory jestures more than one cluster center may be added to the standard set. This technique provides a way for correcting for the characteristics of the source (speaker variations), characteristics of the environment (noise), and characteristics of the receiver (microphone) that we discussed in the previous section.

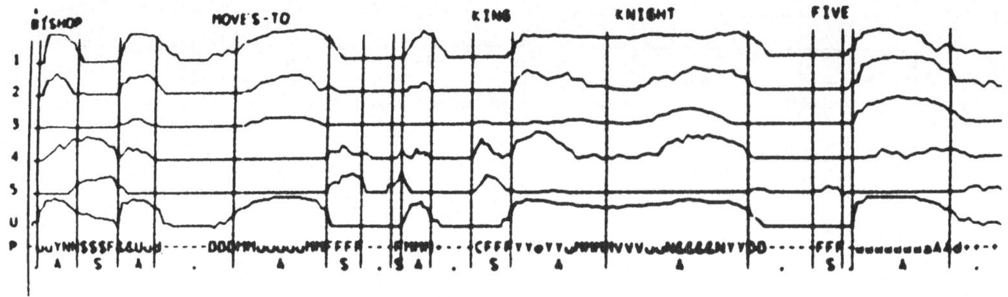

Figure 4. Parametric representation of the utterance showing the results of feature extraction and segmentation

The classification of labels so obtained (row P in Figure 4) is then used to specify a feature set, such as voicing and frication, and these features are used in the segmentation of the utterance, shown in Figure 4. The boundaries of segments are indicated by vertical lines through the parameters and the letter at the center of each segment (following the row P in Figure 4) indicates the type of segment that is present. The "A" indicates a sonorant segment, i.e., all the voiced unfricated segments. The "S" indicates a fricated segment and the period (".") indicates a silence segment. The first use of an acoustic phonetic source of knowledge can be seen in the handling of the "king knight" word boundary problem mentioned earlier. A long sonorant segment is subdivided into two segments to indicate the presence of two different syllables. The syllable juncture is determined in this case by the presence of a significant local minimum in an overall intensity plot (line labeled U on Figure 4).

The Recognition Process

The HEARSAY system has three cooperating independent processes which help in the decoding of the utterances. These represent acoustic, syntactic, and semantic sources of knowledge. The boundary between these sources of knowledge is somewhat arbitrary. What is important to know is that there can be several cooperating independent processes.

These processes cooperate by means of a hypothesize-and-test paradigm. This paradigm consists of one or more sources of knowledge looking at the unrecognized portion of the utterance and generating an ordered list of hypotheses. These hypotheses may then be verified by one or more of the sources of knowledge; the verification may accept, reject, or re-order the hypotheses. The same source of knowledge may be used in different ways both to generate hypotheses and to verify (or reject) hypotheses.

We will illustrate this recognition process by following through various stages of recognition for the utterance given in Figures 3 and 4. Figures 5 through 12 illustrate several of these stages of the recognition process. At the bottom of each figure are listed

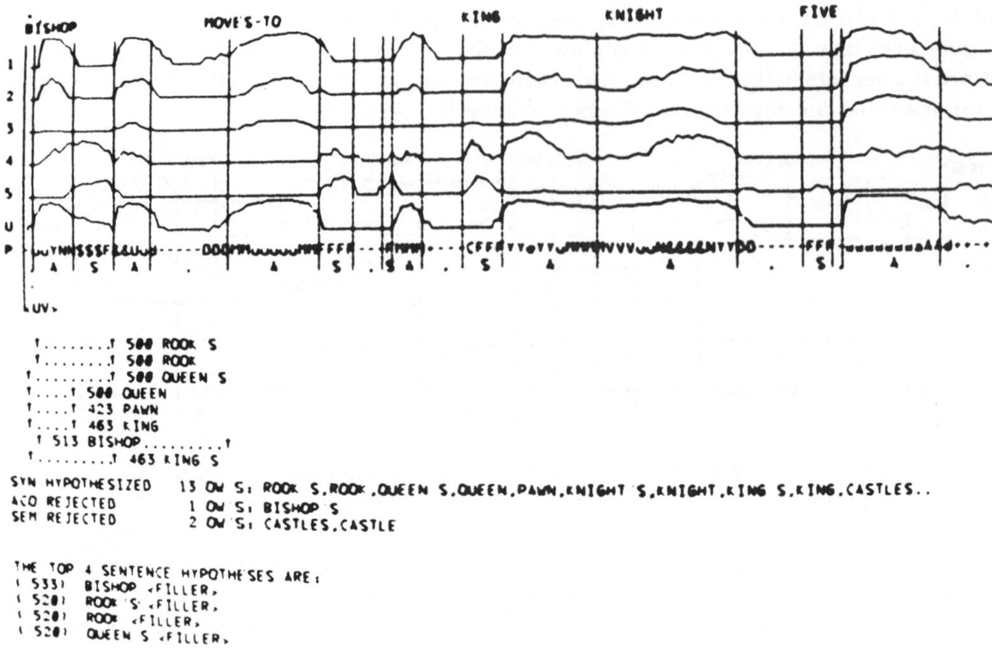

Figure 5. First stage of the recognition process

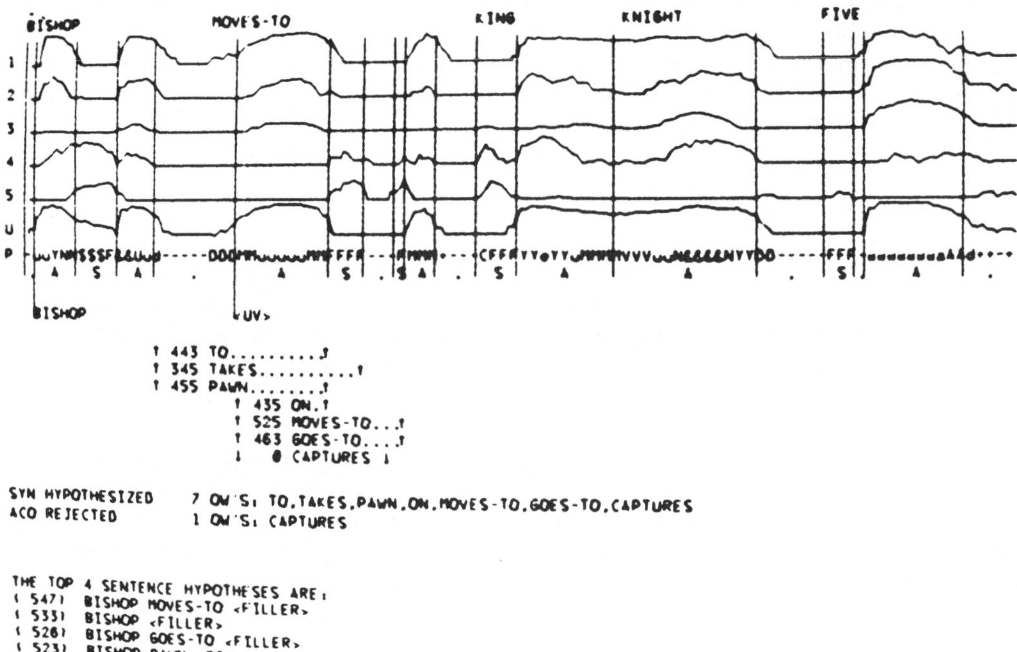

Figure 6. Second stage of the recognition process

the top four (partial) sentence hypotheses with a composite rating for each one. Above the sentence hypotheses is listed information about who hypothesized and who verified. In Figure 5, Syntax hypothesized the possible words that may follow the current sentence hypothesis and Acoustics and Semantics verified the hypothesis. The hypothesization and verification includes a rating by each module as to the goodness of match. A combined rating, along with word boundaries for the top eight words, is shown above the hypothesis and rejection information.

Figure 5 shows the first cycle of the recognition process. At this point none of the words in the sentence have been recognized and the processing begins left to right. The Syntax module chooses to hypothesize and generates 13 possible words, implying that the sentence can begin with "rook's", "rook", "queen's", etc. Of these, the Acoustics module rejects the word "bishops" as being inconsistent with the acoustic-phonetic evidence. The Semantics module rejects "castle" and "castles" as being illegal in this board position. The remaining 10 words are rated by each of the sources of knowledge. The composite rating and the word beginning and ending markers for the top 8 words is shown in Figure 5. The words "rook", "rook's", "queen's" and "queen" all get a rating of 500. "Bishop", the correct word, gets a rating of 513. These words are then used to form the beginning sentence hypotheses -- the top four of which are shown at the bottom of Figure 5.

Figure 6 shows the second cycle of the recognition process. The top sentence hypothesis is "bishop ---". An attempt is being made to recognize the word following "bishop". Again Syntax generates the hypotheses. Given that "bishop" is the preceding word, the syntactic source of knowledge proposes only 7 possible options out of the possible 31 words in the lexicon -- a reduction in search space by a factor of 4. Of these possible 7 words Acoustics rejects "captures" and Semantics rejects none. The remaining six words are rated by each of the sources of knowledge and a composite rating along with word boundaries is shown in Figure 6 for each of the acceptable words ("to" has a rating of 443, etc.). The correct word "moves-to" happens to get the highest rating of 525. The new top sentence hypothesis is "bishop moves-to ---", with a composite sentence rating of 547.

Figure 7 shows the third cycle of the recognition process. Given the top sentence hypothesis "bishop moves-to ---", the Syntax module hypothesizes 7 option words. None of these were rejected by Acoustics or Semantics. "King" and "king's" both get the highest score of 513. The first error in the recognition process occurs at this point. As new sentence hypotheses are created based on the ratings of individual words, both "bishop moves-to king's ---" and "bishop moves-to king ---" have the same rating with the former appearing at the top of the list. At this point it is instructive to see why the error was made in the first place. The phonemic description of "king's" causes a search for a stop followed by a vowel-like segment followed by a stop and fricative. This sequence of segmants occur in "king knight five" as can be seen from Figure 4 (improvements being made to the system will result in "king's" getting a much lower score). The important thing to observe is how the system recovers from errors of this type.

Figure 8 shows the system attempting to associate a meaningful word to the unverified part of the utterance, i.e., the /aɪv/ part of the word "five" in the original utterance. Syntax proposes 3 possible option words (out of a possible 31 -- factor of 10 reduction). One is rejected and the other two get very low ratings. The corresponding

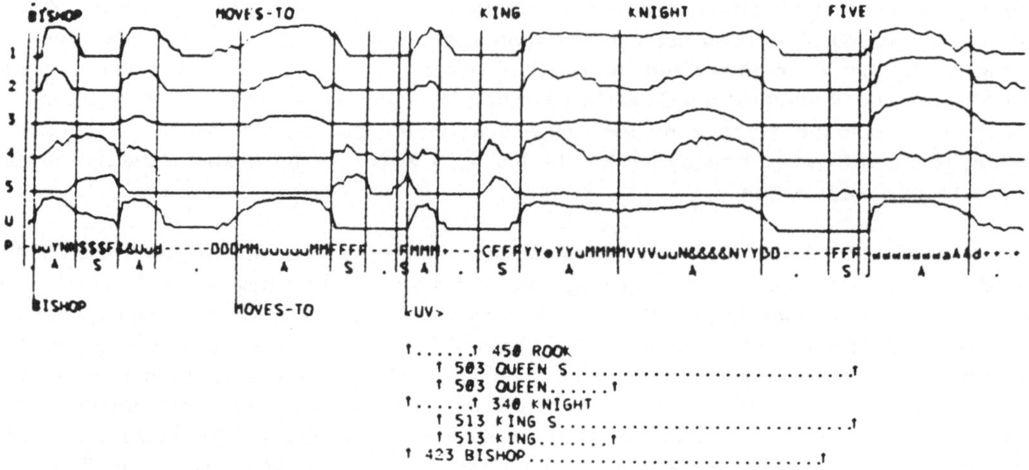

Figure 7. Third stage of the recognition process

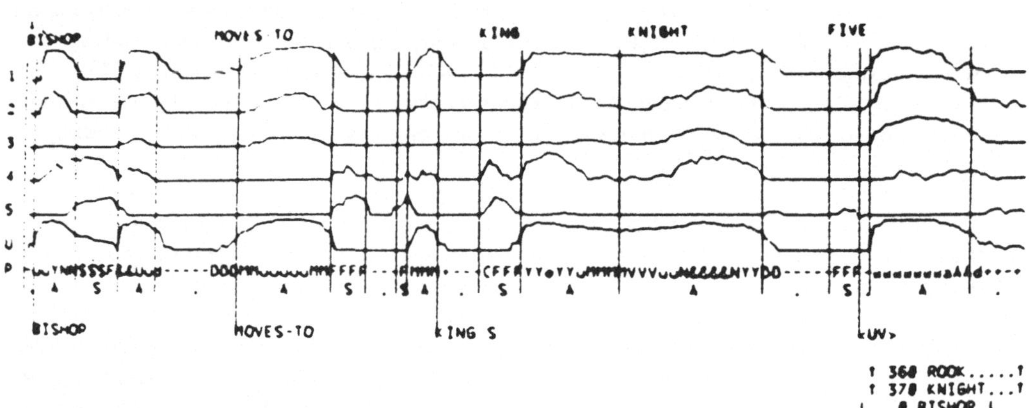

Figure 8. Fourth stage of the recognition process

sentence hypotheses also get a low composite rating and end up at the bottom of the stack (not visible in Figure 8).

Now we see an interesting feature of the system. In the preceding cycle (Figure 8) Syntax generated the hypotheses. It is possible that that source of knowledge is incomplete and did not generate the correct word as a possible hypothesis. Therefore, in this cycle (Figure 9), the Semantic module is given a chance to hypothesize. It hypothesizes 9 option words (a reduction of search by a factor of 3) all of which are rejected by Syntax and Acoustics. When both attempts to make a meaningful completion of the utterance fail, this particular sentence hypothesis "bishop moves to king's--" is removed from the candidate list.

Now the top sentence hypothesis is "bishop moves-to king--" (Figure 10). Syntax nypothesizes 11 option words. Acoustics rejects six of them and Semantics rejects two. Of the remaining words, the correct word "knight" gets the second best rating after "bishop". Again there is an errorful path, because the top sentence hypothesis now happens to be "bishop moves-to king bishop ---". This sentence hypothesis is rejected immediately in the next cycle because there is no more utterance to be recognized and "bishop moves-to king bishop" is not a legal move. Note that the correct sentence hypothesis is not at the top of the stack. Its rating of 550 is not as good as "bishop moves-to king ---" (see Figure 10).

The processing in the next cycle is illustrated in Figure 11. Note that in Figure 10, this same sentence hypothesis was used with Syntax module hypothesizing. Now Semantics is given an option to hypothesize and proposes 3 words. All of these are rejected by Syntax and Acoustics.

Finally, the correct sentence hypothesis, "bishop moves-to king knight ---", gets to the top (Figure 12). Syntax hypothesizes 17 option words. Of these Semantics rejects 16 as being incorrect leaving only "five" with a positive score. This results in the correct complete sentence hypothesis of "bishop moves-to king knight five". But the composite rating for this sentence is only 545 and there are other partial sentence hypotheses on the top. At this point, the system cycles eight more times before rejecting all of them and accepting the correct sentence hypothesis.

The HEARSAY system was demonstrated with live connected speech input in June, 1972. It is the first demonstrable system to use non-trivial syntax and semantics in the recogntion process. It is obvious from the example above that various sources of knowledge aid significantly in the reduction of search space. The system is being actively modified to increase its performance, as well as to use it as an experimental tool for studying speech understanding, recognition, and perception. More detailed descriptions of the system are given in Reddy et al. (1972), Erman (1973), Neely (1973), Reddy et al. (1973).

THE SYNAPS SYSTEM

The SYNAPS system (Symbolic Neuronal Analysis Programming System) is being developed at Carnegie-Mellon University for the three dimensional reconstruction of dye-injected serial sections of ganglia. The eventual goal of this project is to reconstruct the

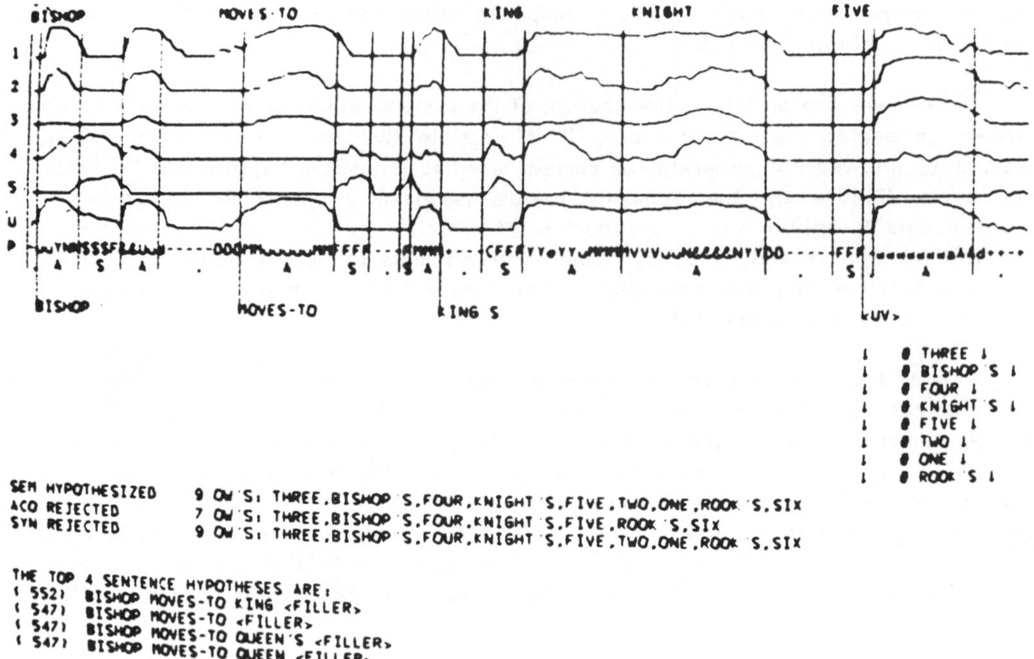

Figure 9.   Fifth stage of the recognition process

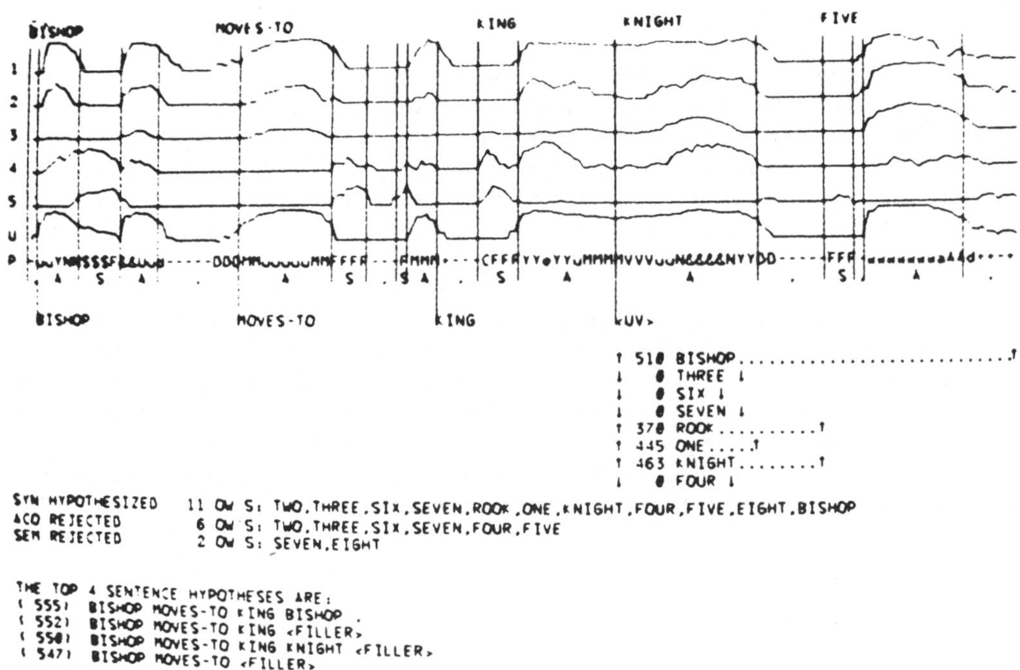

Figure 10.   Sixth stage of the recognition process

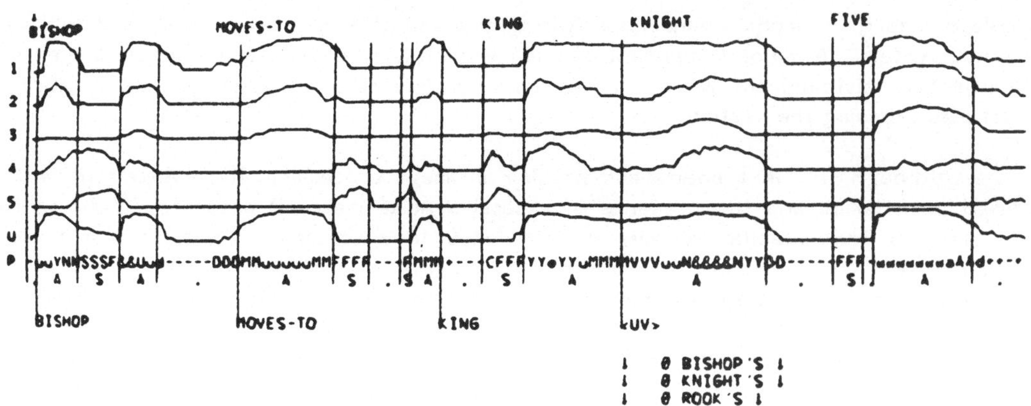

Figure 11.   Seventh stage of the recognition process

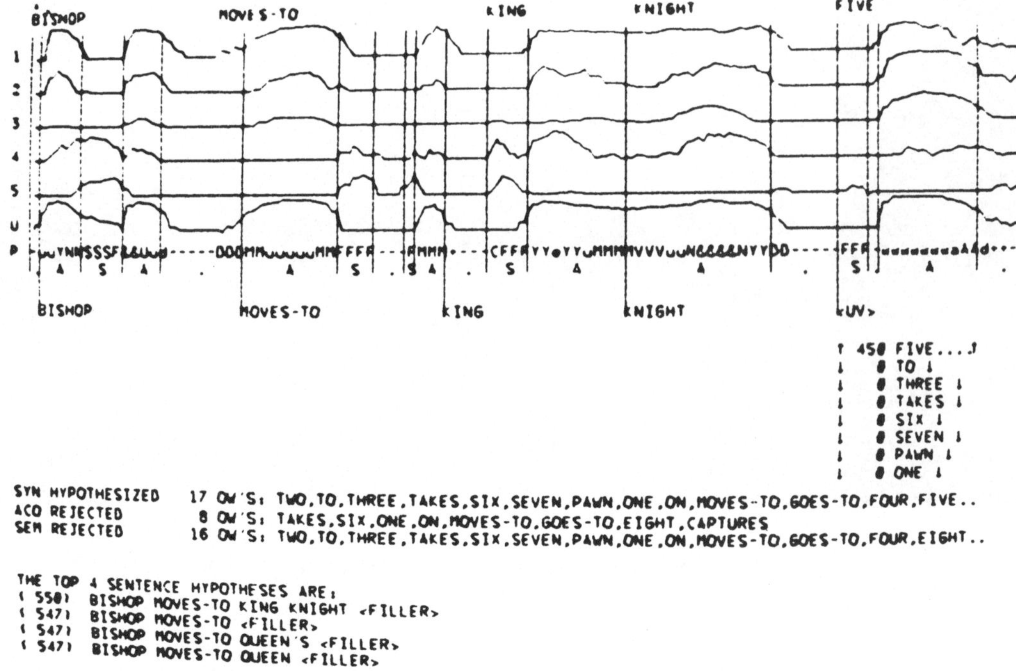

Figure 12.   Eighth stage of the recognition process

complete map of neuronal connections (wiring-diagram) of a mini-brain of an invertebrate nervous system. A major component of this research is to digitize and analyze images of dye-injected histologically-prepared sections to determine locations of all dendritic structures crossing the section.

Although this is a specialized problem in image processing, the absence of well-defined boundaries and the presence of excessive noise makes it necessary to bring to bear several task-specific sources of knowledge to successfully complete the image analysis task. The purpose of the image analysis task is to extract relevant information such as the boundary of the ganglion, dendritic profiles, and other neuronal "landmarks".

The image to be analyzed is shown in Figure 13. This image is digitized using an image dissector, resulting in a matrix of light values (densities) representing the original section. Figure 14 shows a gray-scale printout of the digitized image using a Xerox Graphic Printer (Reddy, et al., 1972b). Limitations of the paper size on the XGP make it necessary to show only a coarse resolution picture of the original image.

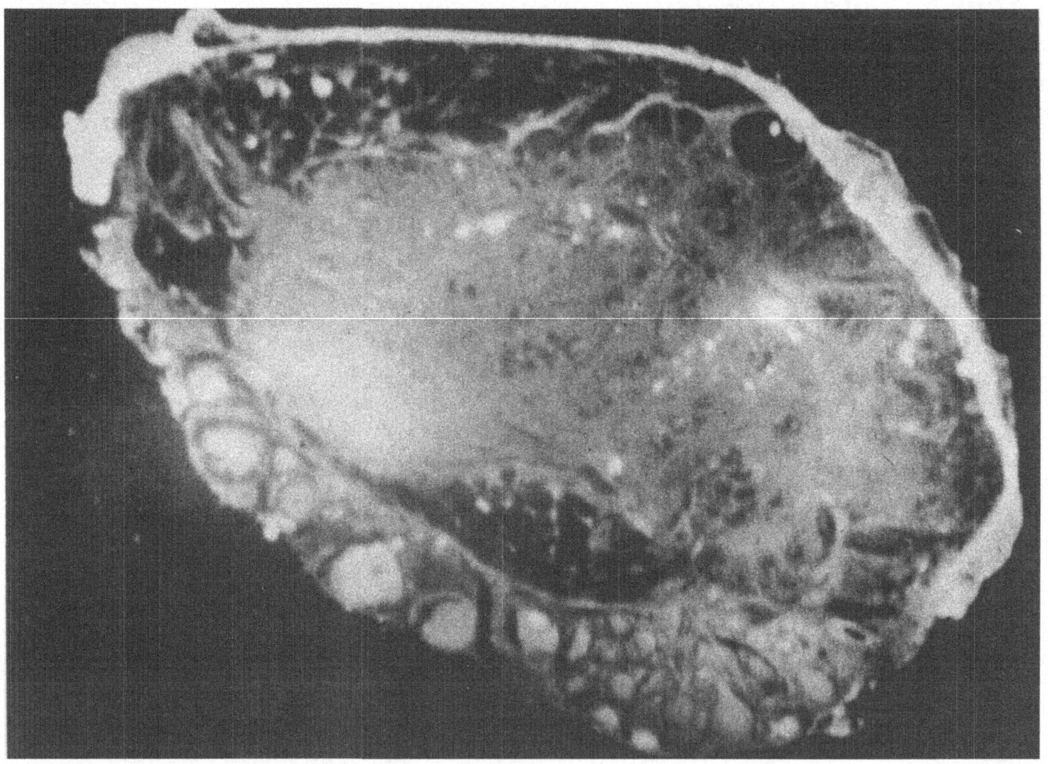

Figure 13. Photomicrograph of a section of a ganglion

Simple edge detection operations of the type used in earlier scene analysis programs results in the image shown in Figure 15. Note that many undesired regions appear in the output. This is to be expected given the noisy nature of the original image

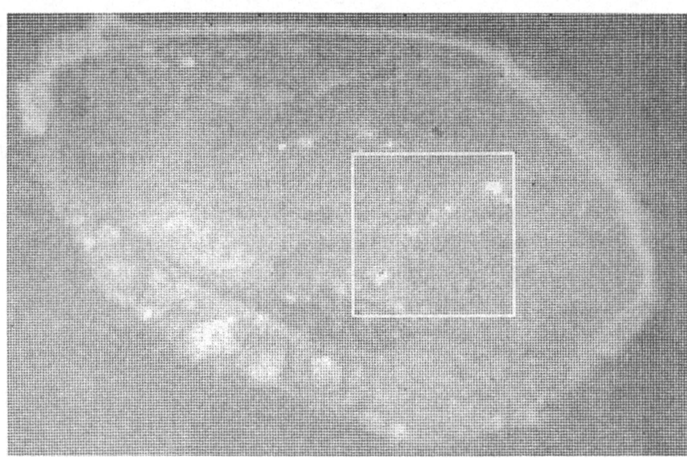

Figure 14. Gray-scale printout of the digitized image

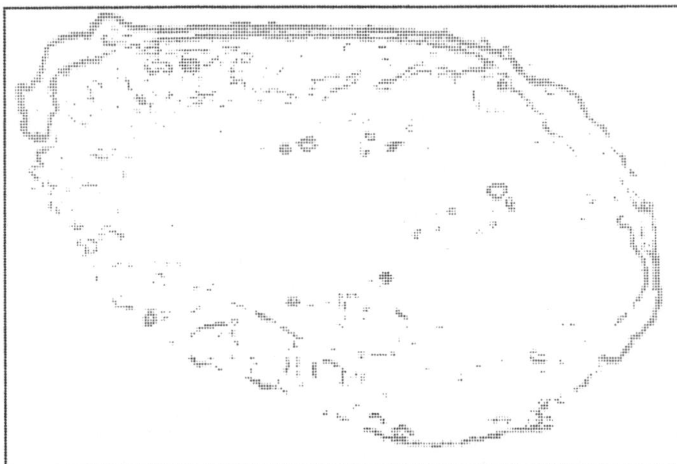

Figure 15. Result of an edge-detection operation on the digitized image

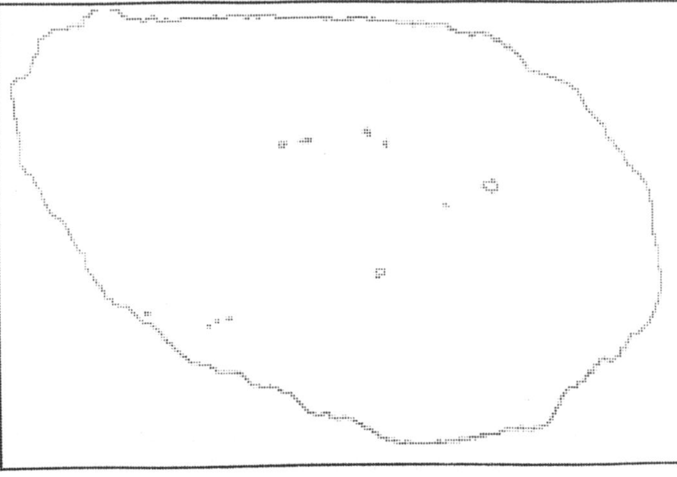

Figure 16. Noise reduction through the use of contextual information

in Figure 13.   This noise results from many sources: intensity differences caused by variable light transmission from one region to the next in a section, artifacts such as tissue or dust particles, unanticipated folds in the tissue, photographic distortions, uneven lighting of the microscopic field, undesired leakage from the injected neuron, etc.

There are, at the same time, several available sources of knowledge:
a.   We are dealing with a known species with known landmarks which can be located uniquely from experiment to experiment.
b.   The locations of desired profiles will only differ slightly from the previously analyzed adjacent section (so called continuity hypothesis).
c.   Having located one profile, it is possible to extrapolate to find other profiles in the image, based on the knowledge of the corresponding profiles analyzed in the preceding section.

The effect of these sources of knowledge is to reject uncorrelated spurious edges. Figure 16 illustrates the possible reduction in noise from the use of such techniques.

The SYNAPS system is still under development. The full impact of various sources of knowledge has not been evaluated yet in this system.   Descriptions of non-image processing parts of the system such as 3-D reconstruction, display, and pattern analysis are given in Reddy et al (1972a).

SOME UNSOLVED PROBLEMS

"...lead us to believe that performance will continue to be very limited unless the recognizing device understands what is being said with something of a facility of a native speaker (that is, better than a foreigner who is fluent in the language).   If this is so, should people continue work toward speech recognition by machine?"

Pierce (1969)

In spite of two decades of research, progress in the fields of computer vision and speech has been very limited. When one looks for reasons for this slow and unsteady progress one finds that over-optimism, inadequate technology, and incorrect models have been the prime causes. As in the case of much of artificial intelligence research, it has proved to be difficult to build on each others' research in these areas.   Significant advances in a few key problem areas could lead to rapid progress in computer vision and speech research.   These problem areas can be summarized by three keywords: tools, knowledge, and theory.

Performance Evaluation

One of the features of existing perception systems, and undoubtedly of future ones as well, is the existence of error at every level of analysis and consequent proliferation of heuristic devices throughout the system to control such error and permit recycling with improved definitions of the situation. Almost entirely missing from the literature, not only of speech and vision but elsewhere in artificial intelligence as well, are techniques for evaluating performance characteristics of proposed algorithms and heuristics.   By techniques, we mean both suitable instrumentation and experimental design to measure accuracy, response time, cost, etc., in relation to vocabulary, language, and context. Until such techniques are developed and applied to existing components of a perception system, these components should be considered of questionable value in an applied system.

Knowledge Aquisition

When one attempts to build a speech understanding or a scene analysis system, one finds that there are large numbers of unanswered questions. Although there have been large amounts of speech and vision research, much of it is defocused and not relevant to machine perception research. For example, there has not yet been a systematic acoustic-phonetic study of all the allophonic variations of phonemes of English. Thus it becomes necessary for the systems to "learn" acoustic-phonetic, syntactic, and semantic rules by abstraction from exemplars. We do not know how to build systems that can abstract such complex information. We will illustrate the issue by considering computer vision, but the comments are equally applicable to speech as well.

When the computer's vision system finds an object in the scene which has not been previously observed, then it seems reasonable to provide the system with the ability to question its master about the object, its structure, the utility, and the likelihood of occurrence. If the master is unable to provide the system with an accurate description of the object (which may be often the case) then the system would have to abstract its own set of features and characteristics about this object and its relationships to the rest of the scene. This may well require several views of the object and further abstractions about the color and texture of the object.

Systems capable of building models from several views of the object have been proposed but have proved to be of limited use so far. A recent thesis by Winston (1971) attempts to abstract structural descriptions of objects from naturally occurring scenes. This will perhaps remain a major unsolved problem for some time to come because different objects seem to require different strategies for abstraction. Abstractions of structural descriptions of people and cars and grass and water may well require assistance from a human being before they can be effectively formulated.

This raises the issue of our ability to use partial models, both in the analysis of scenes and in acquisition of knowledge from actual views of the scene. For example, the fact that only the human hand or face is visible in a scene should be sufficient to formulate a hypothesis that the rest of the person is also attached even though he is not actually visible in the scene. Scene analysis systems must be capable of recognition of partially occluded objects where only a substructure of the object (as indicated by a partial parse perhaps) is visible. Similarly, in the acquisition of knowledge, given a partial stick figure or a caricature of an object, the computer system should be capable of abstracting the rest of the relevant characteristics from the actual scene itself.

Information Processing Models

In addition to building experimental systems for perception, we need to work on the theory of perception as well. There are many theories of perception. What we mean here are the so called **information- processing** models of perception. The notion of an information-processing model reflects a current trend in cognitive psychology to view man as an information processor, i.e., his behavior can be seen as the result of a system consisting of memories containing discrete symbols, symbolic expressions, and processes which manipulate these symbols (Newell, 1970). The main advantage of this approach to perception studies is that it permits a researcher to look at the total problem of perception at a higher functional and conceptual level than is possible with stimulus-response studies and neuro-physiological models.

There is a great deal of work in cognitive psychology on memory representations (e.g., Sperling, short-term, and long-term), on attention phenomena and serial vs. parallel processing, on EPAM-like pattern matching, and on perceptual illusions (Simon and Barenfeld, 1969; Newell and Simon, 1972; Newell, 1973; Chase and Simon, 1971). But much of the work in computer vision does not seem to benefit from this work. Conversely, many of specific models of machine perception, such as cooperating independent processes, utilization of sources of knowledge, hypothesize-and-test paradigm, etc., have not found their way into information processing models in cognitive psychology. This symbiosis of the two areas seems essential for significant advances in either area.

There are many other unsolved problems in machine perception. Each of the factors discussed earlier poses an unsolved problem when all the restrictive options are removed. We chose to single out the problems of tools, knowledge, and theory here because they seem to be crucial for significant advances in machine perception.

CONCLUSION

This paper has discussed issues affecting the feasibility and performance of machine perception systems, outlined the structure of the HEARSAY speech understanding system and the image analysis part of the SYNAPS neural modelling system, and posed some unsolved problems. The main focus of the paper has been to present a unified view of the research in machine perception of speech and vision.

A main question of interest is "what is the role of computer vision and speech research in artificial intelligence?". Unlike other problems in artificial intelligence, perception problems are typified by high data rates, large amounts of data, and the availability of many diverse sources of knowledge. Contrast this to many problem solving systems in which weaker and weaker methods are used to solve a problem using less and less information about the actual task. A major problem in AI, then, is develop paradigms which can effectively use all the available sources of knowledge in problem solution. Thus, the role of perception research in AI is to address itself to the questions of task representations, data representaions, and program organizations which will permit effective use of many sources of knowledge in solving problems involving high data rates and large masses of data in close to real time.

A question to be answered eventually is how the human perceptual activity differs from other aspects of intelligent behavior. This raises several questions.
1. Why is it that man is able to see and hear without any conscious effort while requiring a great deal of intellectual effort to play chess or prove a theorem?
2. Does man use significantly different mechanisms for perceptual and intellectual tasks?

3. Why is it that machines seem to have as much (or more) difficulty with perceptual tasks as they do with intellectual tasks?

The answer to these and other similar questions is "We are not sure". Before we are sure, there will have to be several breakthroughs in artificial intelligence.

ACKNOWLEDGEMENT

The author would like to thank Lee Erman, Rick Fennell, Allen Newell, and Herb Simon for their valuable comments about this paper.

REFERENCES

Barnett, J. (1972), A Vocal Data Management System, International Conference on Speech Communication and Processing, Boston, 340-343.

Chase, W.G. and H.A. Simon (1971), Perception in Chess, CIP-182, Dept. of Psychology, Carnegie-Mellon Univ., Pittsburgh, Pa.

Chomsky, N. and M. Halle (1968), **The Sound Pattern of English**, Harper and Row, New York.

Erman, L.D. (1973), An Environment and System for Machine Recognition of Continuous Speech, Ph.D. Thesis, Computer Science Dept., Stanford Univ., to appear as a Technical Report, Computer Science Dept., Carnegie-Mellon Univ., Pittsburgh, Pa.

Fant, G. (1960), **Acoustic Theory of Speech Production**, Mouton and Company: The Hague.

Fant, G. (1970), Automatic Recognition and Speech Research, Quarterly Progress Report, 16-31, Dept. of Speech Communication, KTH, Stockholm.

Feldman, J.A., et al. (1969), The Stanford Hand Eye Project, Proc. IJCAI, May 7-9, Washington, D.C.

Feldman, J.A. et al. (1971), The Use of Vision and Manipulation to Solve the "Instant Insanity" Puzzle, Proc. Second IJCAI, London, 359-365.

Fikes, R.E. and N.J. Nilsson (1971), STRIPS: A New Approach to the Application of Theorem Proving to Problem Solving, Proc. Second IJCAI, London, 608-621.

Flanagan, J.L. (1965), **Speech Analysis, Synthesis, and Perception**, Academic Press: New York. Second edition, 1971.

Forgie, J. (1972), Personal Communication, MIT Lincoln Laboratories, Lexington, Mass.

Fry, D.B. and P.B. Denes (1959), The Design and Operation of a Mechanical Speech Recognizer, J. British IRE, 19, 211-229.

Gillogly, J.J. (1972), The TECHNOLOGY Chess Program, Artificial Intelligence, 3, 145-163.

Hughes, G.W. and J.F. Hemdal (1965), Speech Analysis, Tech. Rept, AFCRL-65-681, Purdue Univ., Lafayette, Ind.

Jakobson, R. (1964), About the Relation between Visual and Auditory Signs, **Models for the Perception of Speech and Visual Form** (Ed. Wathen-Dunn), MIT Press, Cambridge, Mass., 1-7.

Kelly, M.D. (1970), Visual Identification of People by Computers, AIM-130, Ph.D. thesis, Computer Science Dept., Stanford Univ., Stanford, Ca.

Krakauer, L.J. (1971), Computer Analysis of Visual Properties of Curved Objects, Ph.D. Thesis, Electrical Engineering Dept., MIT, Cambridge, Mass.

Lehiste, I. (1967), **Readings in Acoustic-Phonetics**, MIT Press, Cambridge, Mass.

Minsky, M. and S. Papert (1972), Artificial Intelligence, Technical Report, AI Group, MIT, Cambridge, Mass.

Narasimhan, R. (1966), Syntax-Directed Interpretation of Classes of Pictures, CACM, 9, 3, 166-173.

Neely, R.B. (1973), On the Use of Syntax and Semantics in a Speech Understanding System, Ph.D. Thesis, Stanford Univ., to appear as a Technical Report, Computer Science Dept., Carnegie-Mellon Univ., Pittsburgh, Pa.

Newell, A., J. Barnett, J. Forgie, C. Green, D. Klatt, J.C.R. Licklider, J. Munson, R. Reddy, and W. Woods (1971), Final Report of a Study Group on Speech Understanding Systems, North Holland (to be published, 1973).

Newell, A. (1970), Remarks on the Relationship between Artificial Intelligence and Cognitive Psychology, in Banerji and Mesarovic (eds.), **Non-Numerical Problem Solving**, 363-400, Springer-Verlag.

Newell, A. and H.A. Simon (1972), **Human Problem Solving**, Prentice-Hall.

Newell, A. et al. (1973), Visualization, unpublished research, Carnegie-Mellon Univ., Pittsburgh, Pa.

Nilsson, N.J. (1969), A Mobile Automaton: An Application of Artificial Intelligence Techniques, Proc. IJCAI, May 7-9, Washington, D.C.

Pierce, J.R. (1969), Whither Speech Recognition, J. Acoust. Soc. Am. 46 1049-1051.

Reddy, D.R. (1967), Computer Recognition of Connected Speech, J. Acoust. Soc. Am., 42. 2, 329-347.

Reddy, D.R., (1969), On the Use of Environmental, Syntactic, and Probabilistic Constraints in Vision and Speech, AIM 78, Computer Science Dept., Stanford Univ., Stanford, Ca.

Reddy, D.R., L.D. Erman, and R.B. Neely (1972), A Model and A System for Machine Recognition of Speech, (to be published in IEEE Trans. on Audio and Electroacoustics, 1973).

Reddy, D.R., W.J. Davis, R.B. Ohlander, and D.J. Bihary (1972a), Computer Analysis of Neuronal Structure, Technical Report, Computer Science Dept., Carnegie-Mellon Univ., Pittsburgh, Pa.

Reddy, D.R., B. Broadley, L. Erman, R. Johnsson, J. Newcomer, G. Robertson, and J. Wright (1972b), XCRIBL, A Hardcopy Scan Line Graphics System for Document Generation, Technical Report, Computer Science Dept., Carnegie-Mellon Univ., Pittsburgh, Pa.

Reddy, D.R., L.D. Erman, R. Fennell, R.B. Neely (1973), The HEARSAY Speech Understanding System, to be published.

Rosenfeld, A. (1969), **Picture Processing by Computer**, Academic Press, N.Y.

Rosenfeld, A. (1973), Progress in Picture Processing: 1969-71. Computing Surveys 5, in press.

Sakai, T. and S. Doshita (1963), The Automatic Speech Recognition System for Conversational Sound, IEEE Trans., ED-12, 835-846.

Simon, H.A., and M. Barenfeld (1969), Information Processing Analysis of Perceptual Processes in Problem Solving, Psychological Review, 76, 473-483.

Tenenbaum, J.M. (1970), Accomodation in Computer Vision, Ph.D. Thesis, Computer Science Dept., Stanford Univ., Stanford, Ca.

Vicens, P.J. (1969), Aspects of Speech Recognition by a Computer, Ph.D. Thesis, AIM 85, Computer Science Dept.ment, Stanford Univ., Stanford, Ca.

Walker, D. (1972), Personal Communication, Stanford Research Institute, Menlo Park, Ca.

Winston (1971), Learning Structural Descriptions from Visual Scenes, Ph.D. Thesis, Electrical Engineering Dept., MIT, Cambridge, Mass.

Woods, W. (1972), Personal Communication, Bolt, Beranek and Newman, Cambridge, Mass.

Nicht-Boolesche Wahrscheinlichkeitsmaße für Teilraummethoden in der Zeichenerkennung

D.J. Schadach

Bekanntlich haben sich Teilraummethoden wie CLAFIC, SELFIC, REPREX u. a. gut bewährt, wenn die Zeichenbildung (feature extraction) von .länglichen bzw. brettförmigen Clustern in einem zugrundegelegten separablen Hilbert-Raum H (pattern space) ausgeht (Kaminuma [1], Kulikowski [1], [2], Watanabe [1], [2], [4], [5], [7]). Sei ein Cluster gebildet durch die Vektoren $V^{(1)}$, $V^{(2)}$, ..., $V^{(N)} \in H$ mit dim H = n. Die oben erwähnten Methoden verwenden Vektoren mit der Norm 1; diese Normalisierung vereinfacht numerische Rechnungen, ist aber unbefriedigend, da Vektoren mit relativ kleinem Absolutbetrag, die zufällig (durch Meßfehler, Störeinflüsse etc.) in die Klasse der gemessenen Daten geraten sind und weitgehend orthogonal zu den übrigen Vektoren stehen, durch die Normalisierung einen unverhältnismäßig großen Einfluß auf die Zeichenbildung erlangen. Deshalb wird eine andere Normierung vorgeschlagen:

Sei A die Autokorrelationsmatrix der N Vektoren, also

$$A = \left[\frac{1}{N} \sum_{k=1}^{N} v_i^{(k)} v_j^{(k)} \right]_{n,n}$$

mit $V^{(k)} = \begin{bmatrix} v_1^{(k)} \\ \vdots \\ v_n^{(k)} \end{bmatrix}$ und H ein reeller Raum.

Normierung: An Stelle von $V^{(k)}$ werden die Vektoren

$$X^{(k)} = \frac{V^{(k)}}{(\text{spur } A)^{1/2}} \qquad \text{für} \quad k = 1, \ldots, N$$

verwendet. Dann ist die Autokorrelationsmatrix der Vektoren $X^{(1)}$, ..., $X^{(N)}$:

$$S = \left[\frac{1}{N} \sum_{k=1}^{N} \frac{v_i^{(k)} v_j^{(k)}}{\text{spur } A} \right]_{n,n} = \frac{A}{\text{spur } A}$$

und

$$\text{spur } S = 1 .$$

S hat also dieselben Eigenvektoren wie A und damit jeder Datenvektor dieselbe Karhunen-Loève-Entwicklung. Bei den oben erwähnten Teilraum-methoden dagegen wird eine Autokorrelationsmatrix verwendet, die andere Eigenvektoren als die aus den ursprünglichen Datenvektoren gebildete Autokorrelationsmatrix hat.

Die Elemente auf der Hauptdiagonalen von S sind Gewichte für den quadratischen Anteil der jeweiligen Koordinate zum Cluster. In einer Karhunen-Loève-Basis kann ein echter Teilraum M von H dann zur Zeichen-darstellung dienen, wenn für $\varepsilon > 0$

$$\frac{1}{N} \sum_{i=1}^{m} \sum_{k=1}^{N} |x_i^{(k)}|^2 \ = \ 1 - \varepsilon \ < \ \frac{1}{N} \sum_{i=1}^{m+1} \sum_{k=1}^{N} |x_i^{(k)}|^2$$

mit ε sehr klein und m sehr viel kleiner als n. Man kann solch ein Zeichen durch ein lokales Maximum einer Wahrscheinlichkeitsverteilung beschreiben, wenn auf dem (nicht-distributiven) orthomodularen σ-Verband aller (abgeschlossenen) Teilräume von H ein nicht-Boolesches Wahrschein-lichkeitsmaß definiert wird (mit der auf Booleschen σ-Verbänden von <u>Teilmengen</u> von H aufgebauten Maßtheorie ist dies nicht möglich).

<u>Definition</u>:   Sei L ein orthomodularer σ-Verband. Ein Wahrscheinlich-keitsmaß auf L ist eine Abbildung p von L in die Menge der reellen Zahlen mit

(1) $0 \leq p(M) \leq 1$ für alle $M \in L$,

(2) $p(O) = 0$, $p(1) = 1$,

(3) $p\left(\sum_{i=1}^{\infty} M_i \right) = \sum_{i=1}^{\infty} p(M_i)$ für jede abzählbar unendliche Menge

paarweise orthogonaler Elemente M_i aus L.

Solch eine Wahrscheinlichkeitstheorie unterscheidet sich wesent-lich von der auf Booleschen σ-Verbänden aufgebauten Wahrscheinlichkeits-theorie. Zum Beispiel gilt die bekannte Beziehung

$$p(M_1 \vee M_2) \ = \ p(M_1) + p(M_2) - p(M_1 \wedge M_2)$$

für orthomodulare σ-Verbände im allgemeinen nicht mehr.

Für die Teilraummethoden der Zeichenerkennung ist das folgende Theorem von A. Gleason sehr wesentlich:

<u>Theorem 1 (Gleason [1])</u>:   Zu jedem Wahrscheinlichkeitsmaß p auf dem vollständigen orthomodularen Verband L der abgeschlossenen Teilräume eines separablen Hilbert-Raumes H mit dim H $\geq$ 3 existiert genau ein Operator W derart, daß

$$p(M) \; = \; \text{spur} \; (P_M \, W)$$

für alle M $\in$ L (P_M = Projektionsoperator auf M); der Operator W ist positiv-semidefinit, selbstadjungiert, und spur W = 1. Umgekehrt ist für jeden Operator W mit den obigen Eigenschaften spur $(P_M \, W)$ ein Wahrscheinlichkeitsmaß auf L.

Die Operatoren W sind in der Quantenmechanik als Dichteoperatoren bekannt. Die oben definierte Autokorrelationsmatrix S erfüllt alle Eigenschaften des Operators W. Seien also r Zeichen beschrieben durch ihre Autokorrelationsmatrizen $S_1, \ldots, S_r$. Die Entscheidung, zu welchem Zeichen ein neuer Datenvektor X gehört, kann z. B. durch einen Bayes-Test für minimalen Fehler (oder minimales Risiko) getroffen werden: Sei [X] der von X aufgespannte Teilraum. Dann ist die bedingte Wahrscheinlichkeit

$$p([X] \, | \, S_i) \; = \; \text{spur} \; (P_{[X]} \, S_i)$$

für i = 1, $\ldots$, r. Sind a priori die Zeichenwahrscheinlichkeiten $p(S_i)$ gegeben, so ist die Entscheidungsregel

$$\max_{i=1,\ldots,r} \; \{p(S_i) \; \text{spur} \; (P_{[X]} \, S_i)\} \; = \; p(S_j) \; \text{spur} \; (P_{[X]} \, S_j)$$

$$\Longrightarrow \quad X \text{ gehört zum j-ten Zeichen.}$$

Es ist

$$H(S_i) \; = \; - \; \text{spur} \; (S \; \text{ld} \; S)$$

die Unbestimmtheit (Entropie) des i-ten Zeichens. Diese Größe wurde als "mikroskopische Entropie" von J. von Neumann [1] in die Quanten-

mechanik eingeführt und insbesondere von S. Watanabe [4] eingehend
untersucht. Eines der Ergebnisse ist:

Theorem 2 (Watanabe [3], [4]):   Für zwei beliebige Dichteoperatoren
W_1 und W_2 gilt

$$- \text{spur} \, (W_1 \, \text{ld} \, W_1) \; \leq \; - \text{spur} \, (W_1 \, \text{ld} \, W_2)$$

mit Gleichheit genau dann, wenn $W_1 = W_2$.

Um informationelle Beziehungen zwischen Zeichen ableiten und z. B.
Cluster von Zeichen erkennen zu können, muß der Unbestimmtheitsbegriff
verallgemeinert werden (Schadach [1]):

Sei $H \otimes H \otimes \ldots \otimes H$ das r-fache vervollständigte Tensorprodukt
von H (wird jedes Zeichen als echter Teilraum M_i in einer Karhunen-
Loève-Basis dargestellt, so kann $M_1 \otimes M_2 \otimes \ldots \otimes M_r$ nach entsprechen-
der Normierung von spur S_i genommen werden), und sei S die wie oben
normierte Autokorrelationsmatrix auf $H \otimes \ldots \otimes H$. Durch entsprechende
Summationen ergeben sich $S_1, \ldots, S_r$.

Theorem 3 :
$$H(S_1 \otimes \ldots \otimes S_r) \; = \; \sum_{i=1}^{r} H(S_i) \; .$$

Beweis: Es ist, wenn λ_{j_i} die Eigenwerte von S_i bezeichnet,

$$H(S_1 \otimes \ldots \otimes S_r) \; = \; - \text{spur} \, (S_1 \otimes \ldots \otimes S_r \; \text{ld} \, S_1 \otimes \ldots \otimes S_r)$$

$$= \; - \sum_{j_1} \ldots \sum_{j_r} \lambda_{j_1} \ldots \lambda_{j_r} \; \text{ld} \, \lambda_{j_1} \ldots \lambda_{j_r}$$

$$= \; - \sum_{i=1}^{r} \text{spur} \, (S_i \, \text{ld} \, S_i)$$

(wegen spur $S_i = 1$ für $i = 1, \ldots, r$)

$$= \; \sum_{i=1}^{r} H(S_i) \; .$$

__Theorem 4__ :

$$H(S) \;\leq\; \sum_{i=1}^{r} H(S_i)$$

mit Gleichheit genau dann, wenn $\;S = S_1 \otimes \ldots \otimes S_r\;$.

Beweis: Mit Theorem 2 ist

$$H(S) \;=\; - \operatorname{spur} (S \; \mathrm{ld} \; S)$$

$$\leq\; - \operatorname{spur} (S \; \mathrm{ld} \; S_1 \otimes \ldots \otimes S_r)$$

$$=\; - \sum_{j_1} \lambda_{j_1} \; \mathrm{ld} \; \lambda_{j_1} - \ldots - \sum_{j_r} \lambda_{j_r} \; \mathrm{ld} \; \lambda_{j_r}$$

(denn, wenn $\;S_1 \otimes \ldots \otimes S_r\;$ diagonalisiert ist, sind auch alle S_i in Diagonalform)

$$=\; \sum_{i=1}^{r} H(S_i) \;\; .$$

Damit läßt sich eine nicht-negative totale Information (Transinformation) zwischen den Zeichen durch

$$T(S_1 : S_2 : \ldots : S_r) \;=\; \sum_{i=1}^{r} H(S_i) - H(S)$$

und eine Wechselwirkung zwischen den Zeichen, die ein informationelles Maß für die irreduzible Komplexität von S im Hilbert-Raum $H \otimes \ldots \otimes H$ ist, für $r \geq 3$ durch

$$\begin{aligned}
Q(S_1 : S_2 : \ldots : S_r) \;=\; & T(S_1 : S_2 : \ldots : S_r) \\[2mm]
& - \sum_{i=1}^{r} T(S_1 : S_2 : \ldots : S_r) \, \text{(ohne } S_i) \\[2mm]
& + \sum_{\substack{i,j=1 \\ i<j}}^{r} T(S_1 : S_2 : \ldots : S_r) \, \text{(ohne } S_i, S_j) \\[2mm]
& - \ldots + (-1)^{r} \sum_{\substack{i,j=1 \\ i<j}}^{r} T(S_i : S_j)
\end{aligned}$$

definieren. Eine Reihe von Theoremen für diese Größen sind in Schadach [1] abgeleitet. Hier nur noch folgendes:

Wäre der Teilraumverband von $H \otimes \ldots \otimes H$ ein Boolescher σ-Verband, wie er der Shannonschen Informationstheorie zugrundeliegt, wäre stets $H(S) \geq H(S_i)$ für alle i. Ebenso wäre z. B. $T(S_1 : S_2) \leq H(S_1)$. Da der Verband aber nicht-distributiv ist, gelten diese Beziehungen nicht mehr (man kann dies leicht an Beispielen zeigen).

Auf eine von S. Watanabe bei der Behandlung eines Algorithmus von Fukunaga und Koontz gestellte Frage (Watanabe [6]) kann folgendes vorgeschlagen werden: Als zu minimisierende Kohäsionsfunktion der Zeichen nehme man

$$T(S_{\Delta_1} : \ldots : S_{\Delta_k}) = \sum_{j=1}^{k} H(S_{\Delta_j}) - H(S) \;,$$

wobei $\{\Delta_1, \ldots, \Delta_k\}$ eine Partition der Indexmenge $\{1, 2, \ldots, r\}$ ist und das Minimum über alle derartigen Partitionen genommen wird. Dadurch erhält man k Cluster von Zeichen.

<u>Zitierte Literatur:</u>

Gleason, A. M. [1]: "Measures on the Closed Subspaces of a Hilbert Space." Journal of Mathematics and Mechanics, Vol. 6, 885-893 (1957).

Kaminuma, T., Takekawa, T., Watanabe, S. [1]: "Reduction of Clustering Problem to Pattern Recognition." Pattern Recognition, Vol. 1, 195-205 (1969).

Kulikowski, C. A. [1]: "Pattern Recognition Approach to Medical Diagnosis." IEEE Transactions on Systems Science and Cybernetics, Vol. SSC-6, 173-178 (1970).

Kulikowski, C. A. [2]: "Discriminatory Dimensionality Reduction." IEEE Transactions on Information Theory, Vol. IT-17, 498-499 (1971).

von Neumann, J. [1]: Mathematische Grundlagen der Quantenmechanik. Springer-Verlag, Berlin, 1932.

Schadach, D. J. [1]: Grundlagen einer nicht-Booleschen Informationstheorie auf Teilraumverbänden von Tensorprodukten separabler Hilbert-Räume. In Vorbereitung.

Watanabe, S. [1]: "Karhunen-Loève Expansion and Factor Analysis."
    In: Transactions of the Fourth Prague Conference on Information
    Theory. Academia, Prague, 1967.

Watanabe, S., et al. [2]: Evaluation and Selection of Variables in
    Pattern Recognition. In: Tou, J. T. (Editor): Computer and
    Information Sciences, Vol. 2. Academic Press, New York, 1967.

Watanabe, S. [3]: "Modified Concepts of Logic, Probability, and
    Information Based on Generalized Continuous Characteristic
    Function." Information and Control, Vol. 15, 1-21 (1969).

Watanabe, S. [4]: Knowing and Guessing. John Wiley & Sons, New York,
    1969.

Watanabe, S. [5]: "Object-Predicate Reciprocity and its Application
    to Pattern Recognition." In: Information Processing 68.
    Proceedings of the IFIP Congress 1968. North-Holland Publishing
    Company, Amsterdam, 1969.

Watanabe, S. [6]: "A Unified View of Clustering Algorithms."
    Proceedings of the IFIP Congress 71, North-Holland Publishing
    Company, Amsterdam, 1972.

Watanabe, S. [7]: Pattern Recognition as Information Compression.
    In: Watanabe, S. (Editor): Frontiers of Pattern Recognition.
    Academic Press, New York, 1972.

<u>AUTOMATIC SYNTHESIS OF MINIMAL ALGORITHMS FROM SAMPLES OF THEIR BEHAVIOR</u>

P.G. Raulefs

Abstract

An efficient implementation of an exhaustive search program synthesizing a minimal representation of algorithms from samples of their behavior is presented. As finding specific machines performing given tasks crucially depends on notions of simulation assumed, concepts of operational simulation and equivalence of algorithms are given. Applications to program synthesis, describing the structure of data sets, texture recognition, systems diagnosis, and grammatical inference are indicated.

1. Introduction

Work reported here is motivated by efforts on the project KASAS [RAULEFS 73a]. The object of the KASAS-system is to synthesize representations of algorithms (resp. programs, schemata) from a finite description of their I/O-behavior. Part of this approach is generating from given I/O-relations sample computations of a machine simulating the algorithm. This is achieved by employing theorem-proving and other heuristic search techniques not being discussed in this paper.

From given records of sample computations we can infer a minimal representation of a machine performing these computations. We have implemented an efficient version [HWA-WRIGHTSON 73] of an algorithm given in [BIERMANN 71], taking Turing machines (Tm) to represent algorithms and using the number of states for given tape alphabet as complexity criterion [SHANNON 56]. Tm are taken as a convenient representation of algorithms resp. devices computing particular functions, consisting of a finite state control accessing an appropriate data storage.

Two aspects are emphasized in this note:

1. Any procedure searching for minimal algorithms performing similar tasks is based on specific definitions of simulation and equivalence of algorithms. Using the concept of mapping equivalence [WEGNER 72], we give two notions of operational equivalence. Detailed properties of a hierarchy of operational equivalence relations will be given in [RAULEFS 73b].

2. The intuitive notion of structure of a computational process is made precise by representing it in terms of an associated finite state machine. The structure of a data set is defined to be the structure of the computational process generating the set. It is expected that a more general concept of structure can be obtained from this model by applying methods of algebraic automata theory. By relating to a compu-

tational process, we obtain a uniform approach not only to program synthesis, but also to applications such as those indicated in Section 4.

2. Operational Simulation and Equivalence of Algorithms.

Rather than considering a general definition of the term "algorithm", we define a specific model for describing algorithms:

2.1 Turing machine model of algorithms: Algorithms can be specified in terms of Turing machines (Tm):

Def.: 1. A Tm $T = (Q,\Sigma,O,q_O,d)$ is given by

$Q = \{q_O,\ldots,q_k\}$ - the finite set of states, q_O being the initial state;

$\Sigma = \{a_1,\ldots,a_N\}$ - the tape alphabet containing the blank symbol;

$O = \{-1,0,+1\}$ - the set of operation symbols with $\left.\begin{array}{r}-1\\0\\+1\end{array}\right\}$ denoting the

read/write-head moving

$\left\{\begin{array}{l}\text{one square to the left}\\ \text{not at all}\\ \text{one square to the right}\end{array}\right.$

$d : Q \times \Sigma \longrightarrow Q \times \Sigma \times O$ - the next move function specifying the action of a finite state control acting on a

> tape which is infinite to both sides; we assume that the Tm initially scans the leftmost non-blank symbol on its tape and halts whenever the next move is undefined.

2. Alternatively, a Tm, T, is uniquely specified in terms of a sequence of I + 1 quintuples

$$\underline{T} = \left\langle t_i := (q_{k_i} a_{n_i} q_{1_i} a_{m_i} O_i) \;\middle|\; 0 \leq i \leq I \wedge q_{k_O} = q_O \wedge q_{k_i}, q_{1_i} \in Q \wedge a_{n_i}, a_{m_i} \in \Sigma \wedge o_i \in O \right\rangle.$$

If z is the contents of the tape after T has terminated its operation when started on initial tape x, we write $z = T(x)$.

3. Let A be an algorithm given in terms of a Tm $T_A = (Q,\Sigma,O,q_O,d)$. The <u>Tm-model, $\mathcal{M}(A)$</u>, of A consists of an infinite tape and a Mealy-machine, M_A, controlling a read/write head acting on the tape. M_A has input alphabet Σ, output alphabet $\Sigma \times O$, and the set Q of states. The next state function, δ, and the output function, λ, of M_A are defined to be projections of d on Q resp. $\Sigma \times O$: $\delta := \text{proj}_Q(d)$ and $\lambda := \text{proj}_{\Sigma \times O}(d)$.

The next set of definitions provides tools for describing the operations of Tm:

<u>Def.:</u> 1. A <u>computation $c(T,x)$</u> of a Tm T with input x is a sequence $c(T,x) :=$ $\langle c_j \mid j = 1,2,\ldots \rangle$ of quintuples $c_j \in \underline{T}$ obtained when T is started on input tape x.

2. By recording the triples $a_{n_j} a_{m_j} O_j$ of each step c_j in a computation, $c(T,x)$, we obtain the <u>record of a computation</u>
$$r(T,x) := \left\langle r_j = a_{n_j} a_{m_j} O_j \mid c_j = q_{k_j} a_{n_j} q_{1_j} a_{m_j} O_j \in c(T,x) \wedge j = 1,2,\ldots \right\rangle$$
[SHANK 71].

3. The <u>graph of a computation</u> $c(T,x)$, graph $(c(T,x))$, is given by a pair $(y,z) \in \Sigma^* \times \Sigma^*$

    s.t. y is the word being initially stored on squares

    z is the word being finally (at termination) stored on squares

    } that T scans at least

    once in the course of the computation $c(T,x)$, supposing that $c(T,x)$ is finite.

4. A string $r \in (\Sigma\Sigma O)^*$ of triples is called <u>Tm-consistent</u> iff for each segment
$$r' = \left\langle a_{n_1'} a_{m_1'} O_{j_1'} a_{n_2'} a_{m_2'} O_{j_2'} \ldots a_{n_k'} a_{m_k'} O_{j_k'} \right\rangle \text{ of } r \text{ with}$$
$$O_{j_1'} + O_{j_2'} + \ldots + O_{j_k'} = O \text{ the equality } a_{n_1'} = a_{m_{k+1}'} \text{ holds} \quad [\text{SHANK } 71].$$

Remark: Note that we do not make any assumptions about the finiteness of Tm-computations.

The connection between a Tm-model of an algorithm and records of Tm-computations is established by the following property:

<u>Theorem:</u> Let $R \subseteq (\Sigma\Sigma O)^*$ be a set of Tm-consistent strings; then, the following assertions are equivalent:

    (a) R is a set of records of Tm-computations;

    (b) R is a regular language;

    (c) there is a Mealy-machine M

s.t. (1) M accepts $W_R := \{ w \in \Sigma^* \mid \exists r \in R : r = \left\langle a_{n_j} a_{m_j} O_j \mid j = 1,2,\ldots \right\rangle$ and

$(w = a_{n_1} a_{n_2} \ldots a_{n_N}$ if r consists of N triples $\}$

(2) upon accepting $w = a_{n_1} a_{n_2} \ldots \varepsilon\, W_R$ for a record

$$r = \left\langle a_{n_j} a_{m_j} O_j \,\middle|\, j = 1,2,\ldots \right\rangle , \text{ M generates the output string}$$

$$a_{m_1} O_1 \quad a_{m_2} O_2 \quad \ldots$$

(3) if $wa_j a_k a_l,\ w' a_j a_{k'} a_{l'} \varepsilon\, R$ and $(q_o, wa_j a_k a_l) = (q_o, w' a_j a_{k'} a_{l'})$

then $a_k = a_{k'}$ and $O_l = O_{l'}$.

The proof is easily obtained from Nerode's theorem [SHANK 71].

Given a Tm-model $\mathcal{M}(A)$, we can effectively determine from M_A a regular expression, $\gamma(M_A)$, [SALOMAA 69] s.t. the associated regular language, $||\gamma(M_A)||$, is exactly the set of all records of computations of the Tm T_A. Conversely, given a regular expression $\gamma(A)$, we can determine a Mealy-machine, M_A, with minimal number of states s.t. M_A accepts exactly the language $||\gamma(A)||$.

Let γ be a regular expression on $(\Sigma \Sigma O)^*$ determining a Mealy-machine, M_γ, s.t. the set of records of computations of the associated Tm T_γ is exactly the language $||\gamma||$. From γ, we can obtain a finite set, R_γ, of words determining M_γ (see e.g. [SALOMAA 69], Thm. 2.3).
The set C_γ of computations with records R_γ is called set of <u>representative computations</u>. An initial segment of a computation in C_γ is referred to as a <u>representative subcomputation.</u> Records of representative computations can also be obtained from the state diagram of M_γ by taking all edge trains of maximal length and originating in the initial state, and then concatenating the input-output symbols labeling the edges.

2.2 Notions of operational simulation and equivalence. To talk about computations being I/O-equivalent up to differences not considered, we define f-computational equivalence:

<u>Def.:</u>   Let $f : \Sigma^* \to \Sigma^*$ be a total recursive function; two computations, c_1 and c_2, of a Tm are said to be <u>f-computationally equivalent</u>, $c_1 \overset{f}{\equiv} c_2$, iff

graph$(c_i) = (x_i, z_i)$ and $f(x_1)=f(x_2), f(z_1)=f(z_2)$ whenever $f(x_i), f(z_i)$ are defined $(i = 1,2)$.

We are now in a position to define the following relations of operational simulation between Tm-models of algorithms.

__Def.:__ Let $\mathcal{M}$ and $\mathcal{M}'$ be Tm-models of algorithms.

1. $\mathcal{M}'$ is a __strong operational f-simulator__ of $\mathcal{M}$ iff for every computation
    $c = c_1 c_2 c_3 \ldots$ of $\mathcal{M}$ there is a computation $c' = c_1' c_2' c_3' \ldots$ of $\mathcal{M}'$ s.t.
    $\forall k.\ 1 \leq k \leq L : c_1 c_2 \ldots c_k \overset{f}{\equiv} c_1' c_2' \ldots c_k'$ (L is the length of c and may be infini-
    te).

2. $\mathcal{M}'$ is a __segmentwise operational f-simulator__ of $\mathcal{M}$ iff for every computation
    $c = c_1 c_2 \ldots$ of $\mathcal{M}$ there is a computation $c' = c_1' c_2' \ldots$ of $\mathcal{M}'$ s.t. c and c' can
    be decomposed into segments $c = C_1 C_2 \ldots$ and $c' = C_1' C_2' \ldots$ with $C_1 = c_1 c_2 \ldots c_k$,
    $C_2 = c_{k_1+1} \ldots c_{k_2}$, $\ldots$ and $\forall k \geq 1 : C_1 \ldots C_k \overset{f}{\equiv} C_1' C_2' \ldots C_k'$.

3. $\mathcal{M}$ and $\mathcal{M}'$ are __strongly__ resp. __segmentwise operationally f-equivalent__ iff $\mathcal{M}$ is a
    strong resp. segmentwise operational simulator of $\mathcal{M}'$ and $\mathcal{M}'$ is a strong resp.
    segmentwise simulator of   .

Remarks: (1) Taking f to be the identity function, strong operational f-simulation is
        known to be decidable [SCHMITT 68]. Segmentwise operational f-simulation is
        decidable if the "size" of segments is __uniformly bounded__. Results on the
        decidability of various notions of operational simulation will be given in
        [RAULEFS 73b].

        (2) The notions of operational equivalence and simulation are examples of
        mapping equivalence and simulation discussed in [WEGNER 72].

3. Algorithm Synthesizing Minimal Turing Machines from Records of Sample Computations

In this section, an algorithm and its implementation [HWA-WRIGHTSON 73] is described that synthesizes Tm with minimal numbers of states (w.r.t. strong operational
equivalence) from given records of sample computations. Based on an approach of [BIER-
MANN 71], it is our strategy to search succesively the spaces of all Tm with a fixed
number of states, starting with a lower bound on the number of states initially determined from the given set of records. Consequently, the efficiency of the algorithm
crucially depends on the techniques employed to reduce the size of the space to be
searched. By preprocessing the records, dynamically reducing the space to be searched
and processing a tree-structured data set in parallel, we obtained an algorithm faster
than Biermann's. The algorithm has been implemented in ALGOL 60 on a UNIVAC 1108 computer. In addition, an approach to synthesize minimal Tm w.r.t. bounded segmentwise
operational equivalence is indicated.

3.1 Synthesis Algorithm. The algorithm consists of two phases:

(a) __Preprocessing Phase:__ Let $R = \{r_1, \ldots, r_N\}$ be the given input set of records of
    sample computations. Then, the following tasks are successively performed:

[1] Each record $r_i \in R$ is removed from R if it is a prefix of some other record $r_j \in R$.

[2] The set R of records obtained after step [1] is structured into a wood of trees:

    (i)   an arbitrary (e.g. lexicographical) partial ordering " $\angle$ " on the tape alphabet is assumed;

    (ii)   a partial ordering " $\sqsubseteq$ " is established by : $r_i \sqsubseteq r_j$ iff r_i and r_j have a common prefix $r \in (\Sigma\Sigma O)^+$, and for $r_i = ra_{n_i} a_{m_i} o_{k_i} r_i'$ and $r_j = ra_{n_j} a_{m_j} o_{k_j} r_j'$ the inequality $a_{n_i} \leq a_{n_j}$ holds;

    (iii) for each set of all records comparable under " $\sqsubseteq$ ", a tree is formed by starting at the root with the prefix common to all records and branching whenever suffixes are no longer shared by several records; an example is given in Fig. 1.

[3] By inspecting the resulting tree-structured sample computations, the minimal number (KMIN) of states is computed.

```
 F = 1   F = 5          F = 6
     |       |              |
     |       |              |                  ABL
     |       |              |                 /
     |       |      ABL - AAR - BAR
     |       |     /        |            \
ABL -|-- R -|- BAR          |              BBR                 ----- fronts
     |       |     \        |_ _ _ _ _ _ _
     |       |      BBR - ABL - BBL - AAR - BAR - BBR
     |       |_ _ _ _ _ _ _ _       |
     |                       |      |_ _ _ _ _ _
     |  ABL  -  BBL - _ R |- BAR - BBR - ABL - BBL |- AAR - BAR - BBR
     |/                   |                        |
BBR  |                    |                        |
     |\                   |                        |
     | BBR                |                        |
```

Fig. 1. Tree-structured set of records of sample computations (example).

(b) <u>Dynamic Search Phase:</u>

     In this part of the algorithm, the spaces of Tm with K = KMIN, KMIN+1,... states are exhaustively searched until a solution is found. A flow diagram is given in Fig. 2. The search proceeds along <u>fronts</u> in the wood of tree-structured records. A front delimits an initial segment of records being explained by the current model (cf. example in Fig. 1).

When searching the space of K-state Tm, the algorithm starts out assuming an initial model explaining the root triples of all trees. Using this model, the trees are run through in parallel until the current model can no longer explain the next triple, establishing the F = 1st front, thusly. Looking to the first triples beyond

the F-th front, it is decided whether they are contradicting the next-move-function
of the current model or not. If no contradiction is found, a new hypothesis supple-
menting the current model is generated and the next front is established. If a contradiction is found, however, the hypothesis generated at the previous front is deleted
from the space of admissible hypotheses, a new one is generated, and a new front is
established. If the remaining set of admissible hypotheses turns out to be empty, K
is incremented by one and the next space of Tm having one more state is searched.
Hence, a Tm with a minimum number of states is found.

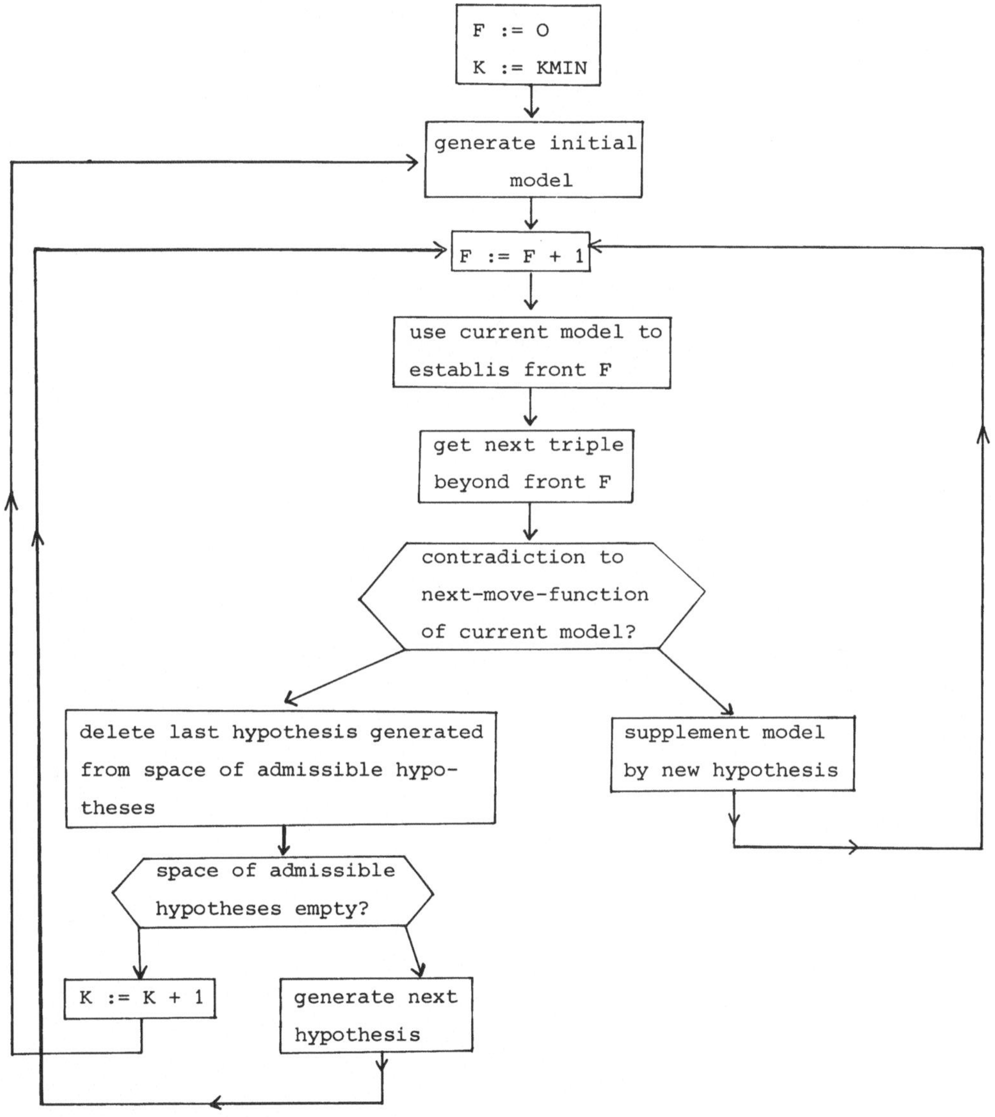

Fig. 2. Flow Diagram of Dynamic Search Procedure.

Remarks: (1) Records of sample computations could be further processed by eliminating segments repeating previous cycles on the associated Tm. However, when processing these segments, the current Tm-model does not change so that the action of the algorithm only consists in pushing the front foreward very rapidly.

(2) The uniqueness (up to renaming of states) of a resulting Tm depends on whether the associated Mealy-machine is incompletely specified or not.

(3) A formal proof that the algorithm actually has all properties desired is given in [HWA-WRIGHTSON 73].

Example: The dynamic search part of our algorithm is illustrated by showing an example also used in [BIERMANN 71]. From the preprocessed sample computations of Fig. 1, the algorithm generates a Tm that sorts strings in $\{A,B\}^+$ into lexicographical order (A´s precede B´s). As can be easily seen from Fig. 1, the minimal number of states is KMIN = 3. Fig. 3 shows the models and corresponding fronts successively generated by the dynamic search phase.

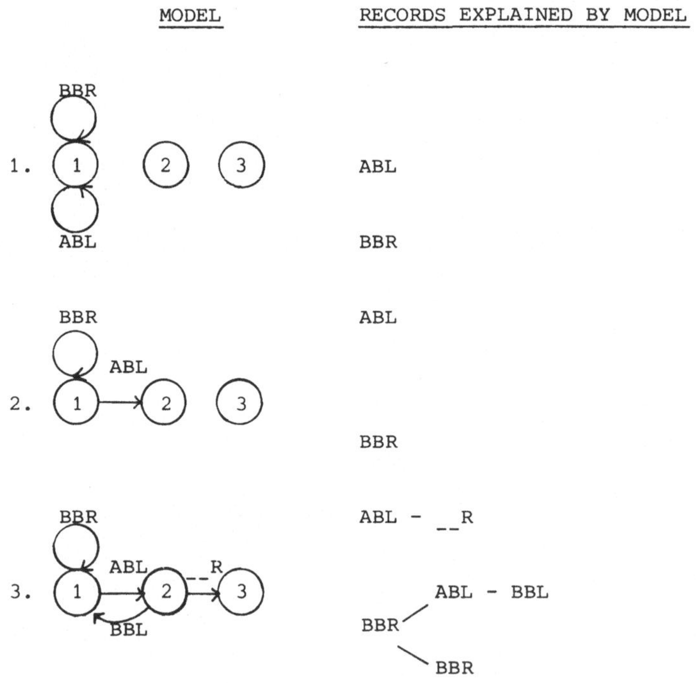

MODEL	RECORDS EXPLAINED BY MODEL

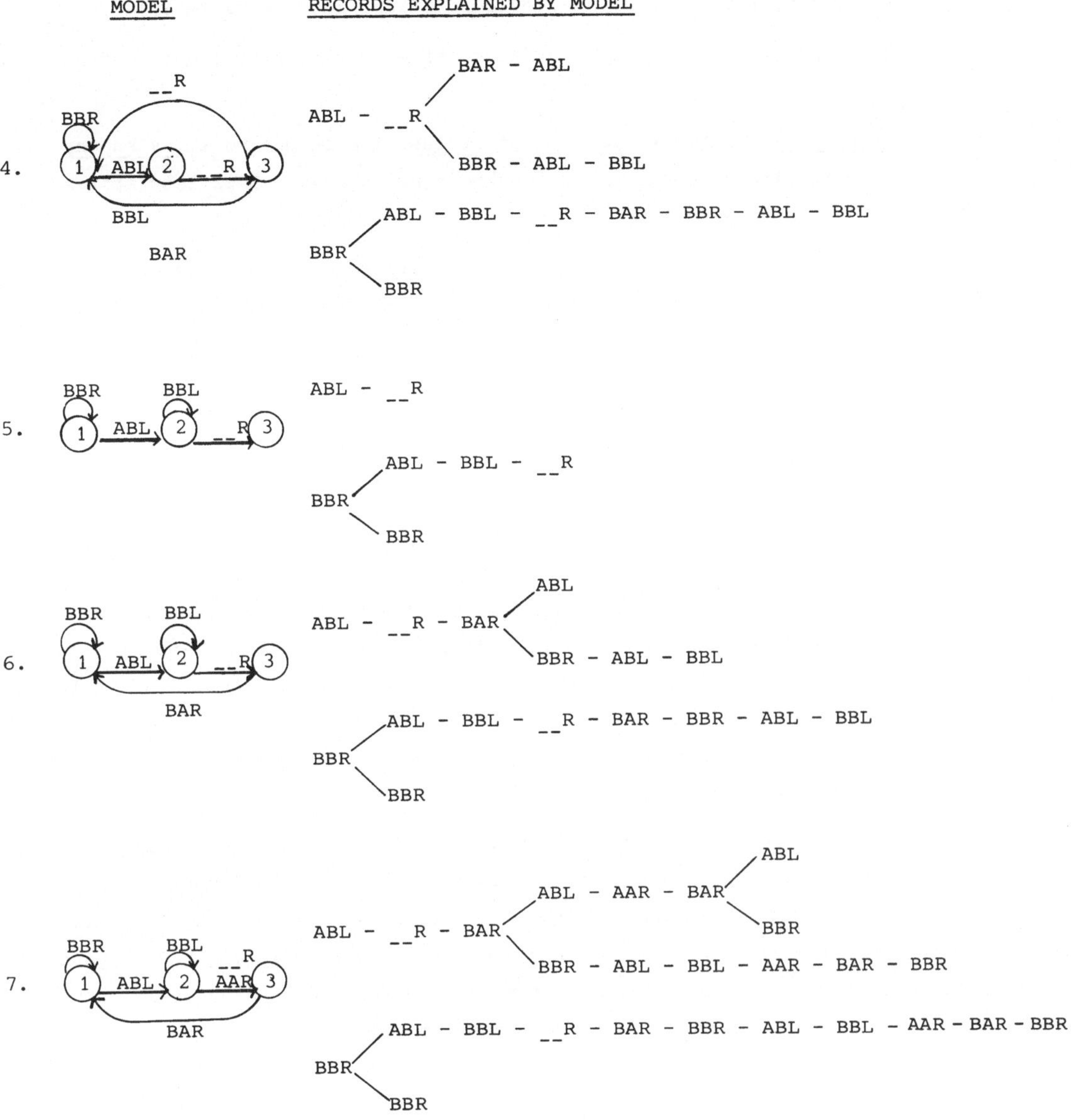

Fig. 3. Example of Dynamic Search Phase Generating a Tm from Records of Fig. 1.

3.2 Synthesis w.r.t. bounded segmentwise operational equivalence. As strong operational equivalence is a refinement of bdd. segmentwise operational equivalence, the space to be searched is significantly larger in the latter case. As we have not implemented any algorithm yet, we merely give a brief sketch of an appropriate approach to be taken after having preprocessed records of sample computations as described in Sect. 3.1:

1. Partition records of sample computations into segments $S_1, S_2, \ldots$.

2. By determining the set of graphs of each segment S_i, obtain the
   I/O-relations R_i.

3. <u>Assuming</u> that the <u>number</u> K of <u>states</u> of a resulting Tm <u>is known</u>,
   determine for segment S_i a submachine T_i having K or less states
   and satisfying R_i.

4. From the set of all submachines generated in step 3, construct a
   minimal machine being a segmentwise operational simulator of the
   given records of sample computations.

4. Applications

In this section, some applications of the algorithm described in Sect.3.1 are
briefly reviewed. It should be noted that for most applications the Tm-model is extremely inefficient. However, usually computational processes are determined by
actions of finite-state controllers operating most efficiently if they are, together
with appropriate data structures, specifically designed for particular applications.
Clearly, any such design can be coded in terms of our Tm-model exhibiting a similar
finite automaton/storage setup. In consequence, we shall be using the Tm-model when
discussing applications, to demonstrate that our approach is of general applicability
to quite different areas.

It is further remarked that synthesizing finite-state machines essentially
achieved by the above algorithm can also be accomplished by standard methods known
in finite automata theory. However, the procedure given here is intended to be incorporated in trainable systems capable of sequential learning. In the KASAS-system,
its task is to be that of hypothesis-formation to be performed interactively with
the procedure generating records of ·computations from given I/O-descriptions.

4.1 Structural description of data sets. We consider data sets consisting of (or
being encoded in terms of) strings on a finite alphabet $A : D \subseteq \{d \,|\, d \in A^*\}$. Further-
more, we assume data sets to be generated by taking snapshots in the course of the
operation of some computational process. Encoding computational process in terms of
our Tm-model, this assumption can be rephrased by considering data sets being encoded
records of sample computations. I.e., we are restricting our attention to data sets
<u>not</u> consisting the <u>output</u> of some computation. This approach can be taken to be a
deterministic variant to describing pictorial patterns in terms of stochastic processes
[e.g. BARTELS-WIED 71] or time-series analysis.

Def.: 1. A <u>presentation (D,ϕ)</u> of a data set, D, is given by D (resp. a finite description of D) and a coding function $\phi : A^* \rightarrow (\Sigma\Sigma O)^*$ mapping D to Tm-consistent records of computations.

2. Let E be an equivalence relation between Tm; then, an <u>E-structure</u> of a data
set, D, with presentation (D,ϕ) is a Tm with minimal number of states w.r.t.E.

Remark: We consider the dependency of an E-structure on a presentation and an equivalence relation, as well as the fact that an E-structure of a data set is not necessarily unique, to be an inherent property of the intuitive concept of "structure".
A generalization can be obtained by studying invariants of transformations between
E-structures.

    4.2 Texture recognition. This example illustrates structures of textures w.r.t.
strong operational equivalence, shown for two simple, one-dimensional textures.
Having been quantized to two levels (black/white), they are presented as strings of
templates of two colored cells. ϕ maps templates to triples in $\Sigma\Sigma O$. Fig. 4 gives
two closely related examples.

a) <u>PRESENTATION:</u>

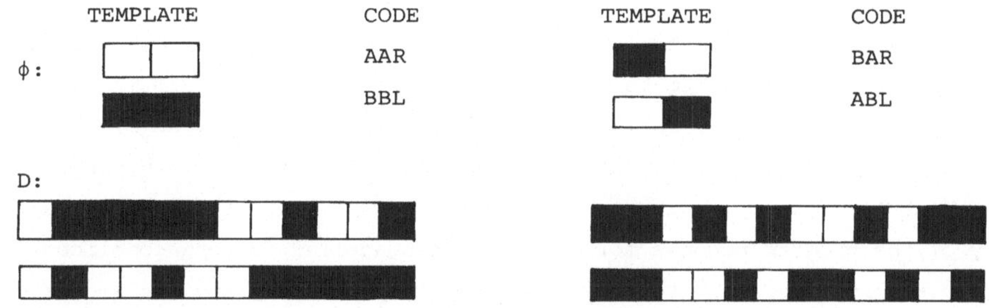

b) <u>E-STRUCTURE (E := strong operational equivalence):</u>

<u>Fig. 4.</u>   a) Presentation of Two Textures

       b) Structures

    <u>4.3 Systems diagnosis.</u> We consider the problem of making statements about systems
from observing their behavior. Specifically, suppose that measurements of values of
quantities characterizing the performance of a system are made in successive time-

-intervals. Again, by proper choice of a coding function, we obtain the collected
data represented as Tm-consistent records of computations. Taking living organisms,
a resulting Tm can be interpreted in terms of a syndrom, with records of computations
representing sequences of symptoms coming up in successive time-intervals in an order
typical for the syndrom.

4.4 Grammatical inference. The problem of grammatical inference, initially posed
by [FELDMAN 67] (for results, see [FELDMAN 69] and [BIERMANN-FELDMAN 72]), consists
in finding grammars of minimal complexity from positive or negative instances of
words of a language. Clearly, as the algorithm has been designed for synthesizing
transducers, it is not very useful for inferring grammars from terminal words. By
observing the actions of an acceptor performed on its storage device, however, the
algorithm can be applied to infer an accepting automaton. Then, there are standard
techniques constructing a grammar from automata accepting its language. For regular
languages, words can be directly taken to represent records of computations, so that
the algorithm is directly applicable (see [BIERMANN-FELDMAN 70] for an efficient
algorithm solving this problem).

5. Conclusions

(1) Procedures synthesizing minimal algorithms from samples of their behavior by
means of exhaustive search appear to be feasible and well-suited for carrying out
sequential learning and hypothesis-formation tasks in interactive systems. The algorithm implemented is quite efficient. The execution time for the example given in
Sect. 3.1 was about 1.2 sec, operating in a space of about 3.10^{12} Tm. Observe that
the efficiency of the program becomes more evident when applied to more complicated
records of computations generated by larger Tm, when preprocessing and the amount of
bookkeeping on a wood of trees really pays off.

(2) The state-symbol product used to characterize the complexity of Tm, though
having some intuitive appeal, is of questionable significance as a complexity criterion [PAGER 69]. We are currently investigating methods employing more meaningful
complexity measures, such as those satisfying the conditions of [BLUM 67a, 67 b] and
[PAGER 70].

(3) The power of any synthesis procedure is correlated to the underlying concept
of simulation of algorithms. For strong operational equivalence, the inferred machine
is minimal just by collapsing components computing the same functions in the same way.
Constructed on notions properly coarsening strong operational simulation, a synthesis
program could infer new algorithms, achieving the tasks of the observed system in a
different and more efficient way. Clearly, improved search methods are necessary to

obtain a feasible program. The significance of such programs is not only established by their inferential power, but also by the fact that they constitute a general approach applicable to a wide variety of areas.

References

[BARTELS-WIED 71]   Bartels, P.H. and Wied, G.L., "Tumor cell diagnosis based on stochastic properties of digitized images", Proc. Two-Dimensional Digital Signal Processing Conf., Columbia, Mo., Oct. 1971.

[BIERMANN 71]   Biermann, A.W., "On the Inference of Turing Machines from Sample Computations", A.I. Memo AIM-152/CS-241, Computer Science Dept., Stanford Univ., Oct. 1971. Revised version: J. Artificial Intelligence: 3 (1972), 181 - 198.

[BIERMANN-FELDMAN 70]   Biermann, A.W. und Feldman, J.A., "On the Synthesis of Finite-State Acceptors", A.I. Memo AIM-114.1, Computer Science Dept., Stanford Univ., Aug. 1970. Revised version: IEEE:C-21 (1972), 592 - 596.

[BIERMANN-FELDMAN 72]   Biermann, A.W. and Feldman, J.A., "A Survey of Results in Grammatical Inference", Proc. Conf. Frontiers of Pattern Recognition, Honululu, Jan. 1971.

[BLUM 67 a]   Blum, M., "A Machine-Independent Theory of the Complexity of Recursive Functions", JACM: 14 (1967), 322 - 336.

[BLUM 67b]   Blum, M., "On the Size of Machines", Inf. and Contr.: 11 (1967) 257 - 265.

[FELDMAN 69]   Feldman, J.A., "Some Decidability Results on Grammatical Inference and Complexity", A.I. Memo AIM-93.1, Computer Science Dept., Stanford Univ., Aug. 1969. Revised version: Inf. and Contr.: 20 (1972) 244 - 262.

[HWA-WRIGHTSON 73]   Hwa, J.C.-H. and Wrightson, G., "Synthese von Turing-maschinen aus endlichen Mengen von Beispielen", Inter-

ner Bericht, Inst. f. Informatik I, Univ. Karlsruhe, 1973
(in preparation)

[PAGER 69]   Pager, D., "On the Problem of Finding Minimal Programs
                  for Tables", Inf. and Contr.: 14 (1969) 550 - 554.

[PAGER 70]   Pager, D., "On the Efficiency of Algorithms", JACM: 17
                  (1970) 708 - 714.

[RAULEFS 73a]   Raulefs, P., "KASAS-Karlsruhe Automatic Synthesis of
                  Algorithms System. Project Specifications", Interner
                  Bericht, Inst. f. Informatik I, Universität Karlsruhe,
                  1973 (in preparation).

[RAULEFS 73b]   Raulefs, P., "Operational Simulation and Equivalence
                  of Algorithms", Interner Bericht, Inst. f. Informatik I,
                  Univ. Karlsruhe, 1973 (in preparation).

[SALOMAA 69]   Salomaa, A., "Theory of Automata", Pergamom Press, 1969.

[SHANK 71]   Shank, H.S., "Records of Turing Machines", MST: 5 (1971)
                  50 - 55.

[SHANNON 56]   Shannon, C.E., "A Universal Turing Machine with Two
                  Internal States", in Automata Studies, Princeton Univ.
                  Press, 1956.

[SCHMITT 68]   Schmitt, A., "Über die Berechnung minimaler Turing-
                  maschinen und anderer minimaler Systeme", EIK: 4 (1968)
                  318 - 326.

[WEGNER 72]   Wegner, P., "Operational Semantics of Programming
                  Languages", Proc. ACM Conf. Proving Assertions about
                  Programs, Las Cruces, N.M., Jan. 1972 (SIGPLAN Notices:
                  7.1 / SIGACT News: 14).

PATTERN DESCRIPTION AND RECOGNITION IN FORMAL LANGUAGE

K. Hanakata

Introduction

In dealing with a complicated pattern it is essential to analyse the
pattern into subpatterns, to which some information measure is to be
assigned. According to this information measure which is generated by
a certain mechanism, it is decided whether the corresponding subpattern is not worth being maintained for further processing or how
detailed it should be described or how it should be transformed. The
mechanism which generates the information measures to be assigned to
the subpatterns functions depending upon the mission for which the
given pattern is being processed.

In practice this kind of decision is made on the basis of practical
experience. For example: non critical noises which can be principally
considered as a subpattern is removed during preprocessing almost
without refering to the mission. This means that such a non-critical
noise contains the lowest pattern information in relation to the
mission. The subpattern where the most pattern information is
concentrated is usually the structure of the given pattern.

The structural information of a pattern describes the relation
between predefined picture elements, such as line element, angle
element, gray level or color, in terms of which the given pattern is
analysed. The structural description may principally take any form.
However, because of the existing method of language with extensive
descriptive power, and because of the simple symbol processing by
means of computers the structural description is formulated similarly
to the syntax of language expressed in string-like sentences[5]. Therefore, this structural description is restricted to the concatenation
of symbols.*

The problem we have when describing a multidimensional pattern in one
dimensional string-like sentence is how we convert the given multi-
dimensional pattern information into one dimensional sentence[4].

(The structural description of speech or electrical wave form is
easily achieved because of its one dimensional time dependent pattern
form).

---

* 2-dimensional language for the picture description is studied by some
researchers(Kirsch, H.-J.Schneider), but so far this looks so complicated and not developed enough to be applied to a complicated pattern
description.

The next problem is how the given pattern should be described so that the given mission is carried out in the most efficient way. The description of patterns is so crucial that the performance e.g. capacity for acceptable pattern classes, recognition time or error rate, etc. depends upon how the necessary pattern information is described in the efficient way, i.e. in compact form and in an appropriate order. In this respect the problem of pattern description involves the selection of <u>pattern primitives</u> and predicates which correspond to <u>feature selection and extraction</u> in the conventional decision-theoretic approach.[5]

Pattern primitives and feature

The selection of pattern primitives of general nature, in relation to picture processing and analysis suggested in the literature may be roughly grouped as a set of vectors of different directions, or a set of half planes of pattern space. Other selection methods are in some way related to the specific feature of pattern classes which the recognition system deals with, for instance, a set of strokes of hand-written characters,[2] or a set of primitive curves for chromosome types. These examples of primitive elements more or less depends on the specific pictorial pattern. There seems to be no formal way at present to find optimal sets of primitive elements for the description of the given pattern. Therefore it seems to be reasonable to find or synthesize an appropriate set of pattern elements on the basis of the most general primitive set, like a set of unit vectors in multi-dimensional space, e.g. in two dimensional space for pictorial patterns. The basic necessary condition for a primitive set is that (a) it includes a sufficient number of different properties, i.e. elemental directions, arcs, or elemental shapes such as circles, triangles, rectangles etc., and that (b) every primitive element of the set has a set of well-defined connecting points, similar to the bond-arm of the chemical atom etc., at which the other primitive elements can be connected to each other. It is this specification of the connecting points for each primitive element that enables us to describe the multidimensional pattern in string-like sentences. Note that according to the definition of an m-th order structure , a primitive element with m connecting points is to be referred to as an m-th order primitive element.[6]

In the following discussion we preliminarily use a set of $\underline{n}$ unit vectors which equally divide 180°. (Fig. 1). The primitive element of the arc th (Fig.2) is represented by an isosceles triangle whose

base a_{ℓ_1} is the secant of the
arc and one of the equal sides
is given by a vector $a_{\ell_2}^4$.
Once we define some kind of subpattern, feature or primitive
element as a unit, so we usually
need the additional information
which cannot be fixed as a part
of the unit but variable dependent on the situation that the
unit is placed in the pattern
complex, the information such as
magnitude or position. This kind
of information used effectively
to describe the corresponding
part of the pattern complex, is
considered as an attribute to the
unit.

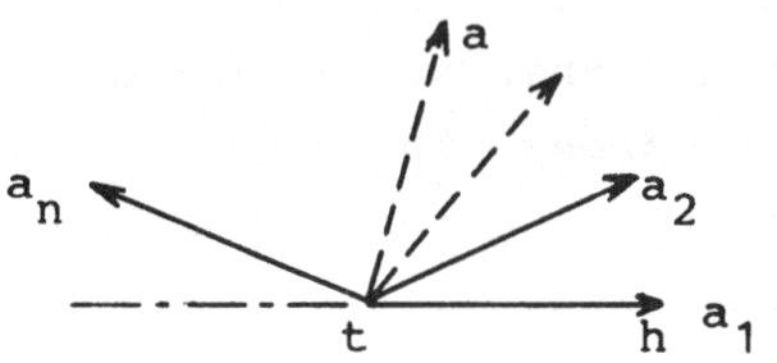

A set of n unit vectors

Fig.1

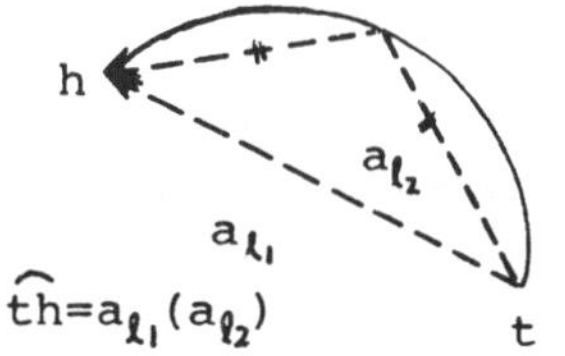

Representation of arc

Fig.2

By means of the above defined set of
vectors and arcs we can principally
describe any complicated pictorial
pattern by connecting these line
elements. However, if we describe all line elements of the pattern
complex with the corresponding unit vectors and arcs, the description
sentences would be very long.

Multilevel feature

For the compact description of patterns we introduce a hierarchical
multilevel pattern element, i.e. a feature which in general depends
upon the specific class of patterns. The features of a given level
consists of the features of the lower levels. The set of the primitive elements defined in the previous section has the lowest level.
In analysing a (complicated) pictorial pattern, we generally notice
that some regularities exist, i.e. the same small structured set of
primitive elements can be frequently found in a picture, such as an
angle containing a gray level or color, a sequence of angles along a
contour line,etc. They are simply different e.g. in position or magnitude etc. The idea is to assign to each feature a name of the
picture element with a set of parameters which specify the situation

of the feature in the given pattern complex. We use these feature
names in the pattern description with the parameter specified by the
feature situation.

If we give a different name to any combination of the primitive
elements, then we would need in practice an infinite number of
feature names. Therefore it is reasonable preliminarily to set a
restriction on the possible combinations of the primitive elements
constituting a feature, such as types or number of primitive elements.
Depending upon the degree of restriction we classify the feature
into different levels. For example, in terms of the number of
primitive elements, the primitive element itself would be the feature
of O-level. Note that the primitive element itself cannot characterise any feature since it loses its character of direction by simple
rotation.

The features of the first level consist of two primitive elements,
i.e. O-level feature.

The following table (Table 4) shows some examples of features under
4th level.

Level	Feature
O	primitive elements, attributes of gray level, color, etc.
1	angles (between two edges), arc, a contour line segment with a gray level or color on one side, parallel line segment (a special case of an angle), etc.
2	two-angle sequence of three serially connected line segments, two angles separated by a line segment, a contour line segment with gray levels or colors on both sides, an angle holding a color or a gray level.
3	three-angle sequence, e.g. triangle, two-angle sequence with color or gray level on one side, three angles separated by two line segments etc.
4	rectangle, triangle with gray level

Table   Example of features

In the definition of a feature it is to be decided what characteristic we consider as a part of the feature and what we treat as an attribute to the feature. It should be hinted here that this decision depends upon the frequency of the element found within the pattern complex in the same context relation to the feature.

Feature representation

The representation of the feature is almost the same as that of the primitive element except that it is accompanied by a set of parameters representing the attributes of the feature. A feature has its own predefined node names which are used for specifying the connection to other features or substructures.

Example

O-level feature

$$a_i(\omega, (\alpha, \beta)): t, h$$

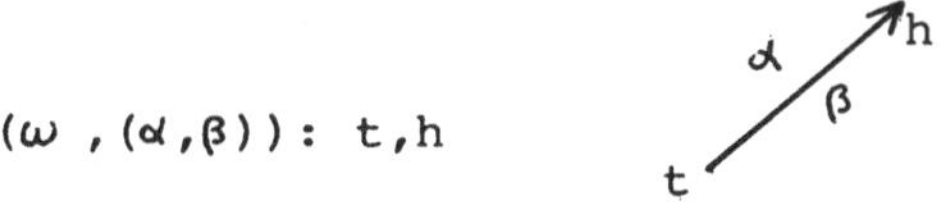

means that i-th vector has its length of ω, and left and right side of the vector are color (or gray level) of α and β, respectively. Tail and head of the vector are represented by "t" and "h" respectively.

I-level feature

$$b_i(\Theta, (2,1), (\alpha, \beta)): 1,2,3$$

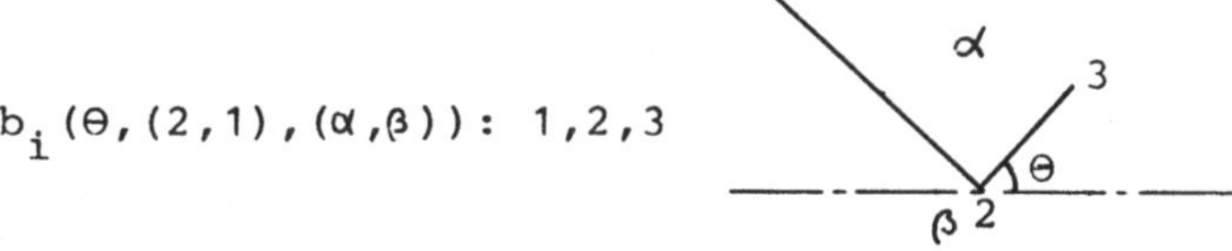

means that feature b_i is in a position Θ degrees from its originally defined position, and the magnitude of each line segment is 2,1 unit. Following a predefined node sequence from 1 to 3 we find the spatial information α and β on right and left side, respectively.

If we consider the spatial information α as a part of the feature contained between the two edges, then it is a 2-level feature

$$c_i(\Theta, (2,1), \beta): 1,2,3$$

which has only the spatial information on the right side as parameter value.

Feature entropy

The motivation of the feature definition was the compact description

of subpatterns frequently found in a pattern complex.
By counting the relative frequency $f(A)$ of a feature A contained in
a given pattern complex we can calculate its entropy $\log \frac{1}{f(A)}$ on
a given level. The conditional entropy of the feature A, given a
feature B connected to A, is:

$$\log \frac{1}{f(A \mid B)}$$

where $f(A \mid B)$ means the conditional relative frequency of A, given B.
The average feature entropy of a given pattern complex is given by:

$$H(A) = \sum_{F \supset A} f(A) \log \frac{1}{f(A)} \quad , \quad F: \text{ feature set.}$$

Our idea is to describe the given pattern complex connecting these
features found during the pattern analysis. There are features of
different levels with different entropies. In general the higher the
level of the feature is, the larger its entropy becomes. In relation
to the compact description of the pattern complex it is obviously
desirable to use features of the highest possible level. On the other
hand, however, the higher the level of features used, the larger the
feature set becomes. Here we have to find a trade-off point between
the maximal allowable entropy feature and the magnitude of feature
set, whose limit comes from the capacity of processor. Therefore, we
give some entropy limit for the possible features in order to reduce
the feature set of higher levels. The features whose entropy is
higher than this given limit, are not to be defined, i.e. not
assigned a feature name. They are, instead, represented by lower
level features whose entropy is below this limit.

Example

Following feature set is generated under the given maximum
entropes limit of 5.00 by the analysis of pattern complex shown right

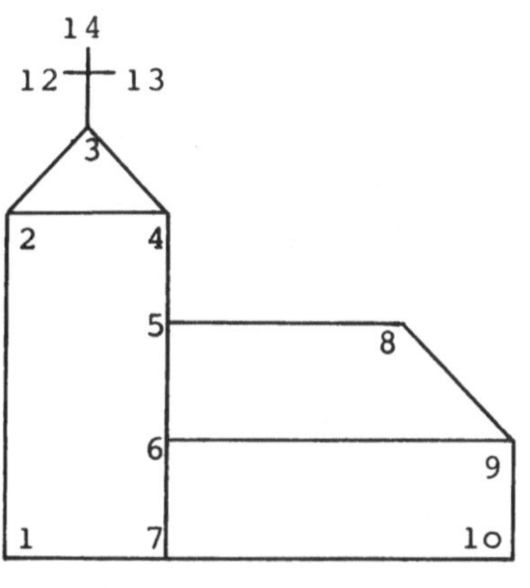

Fig.3 Pattern complex[4]

Level	Feature name	Feature	Entropy
0	a_1		
	a_2		
	a_3		
	a_4		
1	b_1		3.32
	b_2		0.81
	b_3		2.32
	b_4		2.58
2	c_1		4.52
	c_2		2.52
	c_3		3.64
	c_4		3.94
	c_5		3.64
	c_6		4.52
	c_7		4.52
	c_8		3.94
	c_9		4.52
	c_{10}		4.52
	c_{11}		4.52
	c_{12}		2.81
	c_{13}		3.45
	c_{14}		2.45
	c_{15}		3.45
3	d_1		4.49
	d_2		4.49
	d_3		4.49

Feature connection

Structures of a given pattern are described in rewriting forms
connecting multilevel features defined in the previous section. The
rewriting forms are similar to the production rules of a phrase-
structure grammar, but they only describe the given specific pattern
and not all patterns which belong to the same class as the production
rules of a grammar do. We only take the advantages of its hierarchial
pattern synthesis method building up in as many levels as needed on
the basis of the subpatterns defined in the lower levels.

We describe any relations between features or substructures exclusive-
ly with connect by using the attribute of connecting nodes which
belong to both connected objects. In case we need to describe two
disconnected subpatterns in their fixed relation as one substructure,
we use a dummy feature connecting them. Thus we understand that the
concatenation of two names (subpattern name or feature name) means in
this case their connection, and how they are connected is explained
by an attribute of a node sequence, for example:

$$\text{(i)} \quad A \longrightarrow a(\underline{\eta}) : i_1, 1; \ i_2, 2; \ldots, i_k, k$$

$$\text{(ii)} \ B \longrightarrow Ab(\underline{\alpha}) : i_1, 1; \ i_2, 2; \ldots, i_m, m$$

$$\text{(iii)} CD : i_1, j_1; \ i_2, j_2; \ldots, i_m, j_m \longrightarrow CFG : j_1 \cdot k_1; j_2, k_2; \ldots, j_m, k_m$$

In the rewriting form (i) a feature $a(\eta)$, where η denotes a set of
parameters is defined as a (sub)structure A, and in (ii) is connected
to A at the node i_1 of A with a feature $b(\alpha)$ of 1 and i_2 of A with
2 of b , thus forming a new structure B. If either i_1 or i_2 is not the
node of A, then it is understood to be a newly defined node of B.
In (iii) the substructure D in the context of C is replaced by F and
G connecting the node j_1 of F and k_1 of G etc.
The connections of features and substructures according to the above
rewriting forms are based on the general characteristics observed in
the practical patterns. In the case of the mission to find some object
contained in a given pattern complex as a substructure we generally
find that the substructures of potential objects, e.g. in a picture,
consist of a number of simple closed loops of contour lines with their
more or less uniform spatial information and open routes (which are
not parts of any closed loops). Using this general characteristic of

the pictorial information simple loops are synthesized at first in terms of features and assigned a non-terminal substructural class name. In the case of an open route, simple branches, where at most two line segments are connected at each node, are given the names. In the following, an algorithm is given which finds all simple loops and simple open routes in a contour line complex and lists their sequence of nodes, branches and angles.

(1) Start from a node i, for which degree $D(i) \geq 2$, i.e. at node i at least 2 branches are connected.
(2) Choose a branch b_{hj} connected to node i
(3) Give an arrow sign to the branch b_{hj}, in which direction we are going to trace, and keep one side (e.g. <u>right</u> side)in mind.
(4) If the next node j of the branch b_{hj} is the initial node, go to (9)
(5) If the node j is a terminal node i.e. $D(j)=1$, then initiate a sequence of nodes constituting an open route. Otherwise go to (7)
(6) Trace back the branches until the node is higher than 2, and list the nodes in a sequence of (5). Mark all branches traced with an arrow sign.
(7) At a node j for which D(j) 3, take the branch which has the <u>right</u> least angle from the last branch traced, and which is not marked with the arrow sign we are going.
(8) If the present branch has already been marked by an arrow in the opposite direction and is not registered yet as a part of a simple loop, then consider the last node j ($D(j)=1$) as a terminal node and go to (5). Otherwise go to (3).
(9) List as a simple loop the sequence of nodes, branches and angles except those which belong to an open route.
(10) If all branches are marked in both directions, then stop. Otherwise find an initial node whose branch is not marked in both directions and go to (3).

<u>Attribute feature</u>

If we connect two substructures, then there may be important features that are related to the <u>both</u> of thesesubstructures connected. The features may be very useful for the detection of some object sub-pattern. Therefore, it is necessary that each time we connect two substructures we generate a feature set which is related to that particular connection of substructures.

In the following an algorithm is given which generates attribute features. Features of two-angle sequence S are generated by a connection between two substructures F_1 and F_2 producing a sub-structure K (Fig. 4):

$$K \rightarrow F_1 F_2 : i_1, j_1; i_2, j_2; \ldots; i_k, j_k; \ldots; i_m, j_m \; / \; S$$

where node i_k (K =1,2...m) of F_1 is combined with j_k of F_2 (Fig.). We assume that F_1 has line segment $b_{(i_k)_h}$ (h=1,2...n_1) terminated at node i_k and F_2 has $C_{(j_k)_\ell}$ (ℓ =1,2...n_2^k).

A procedure to generate S is given:

(i) Find all angles at the other end node of $b_{(i_k)_h}$

(ii) Find all angles between $b_{(i_k)_h}$ and $C_{(j_k)_\ell}$ ($\ell = 1,2 \ldots n_2$):

$$\{(b_{(i_k)_1}, {}^c{}_{(j_k)_1}) , \{(b_{(i_k)_2}, {}^c{}_{(j_k)_2}) \ldots \{(b_{(i_k)_n}, {}^c{}_{(j_k)_n})$$

(iii) Take all possible two-angle pairs consisting of the first angle θ and the second $\{$ (θ , $\{$).

(iv) Give a feature name of the second level for each pair (θ , $\{$).

(v) Repeat the procedure (i) - (iv) for all $b_{(i_k)_h}$

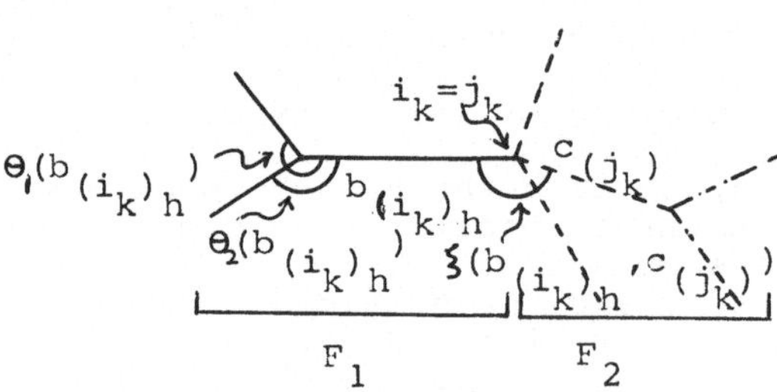

Fig.4   Connection of two substructures F_1 and F_2

Example

The example of a pattern complex given in Fig.3   is described in many different ways. In the following, one description is given in the rewriting forms with attribute feature generated by the above algorithm.

$$A_1 \rightarrow d_3 (o, (\sqrt{2}, 3, \bar{\sqrt{2}}, 3)):4,1;2,2;1,3;7,4;4,1$$

$$A_2 \rightarrow d_3 (o, (3,1,3,1)):9,1;6,2;7,3;1o,4;9,1$$

$$B_1 \rightarrow A_2 c_5 (o, (1,2,\bar{\sqrt{2}})):6,1;5,2;3,3;9,4/d_2 (o, (\sqrt{2},3,1,3):8,9,6,7,$$

$$A_3 \rightarrow b_4 (2, (o.5,2)):3,1;11,2;14,3$$

$$B_2 \rightarrow A_3 b_4 (o, (o.2,o.2)):11,2;12,1;13,2$$
$$/c_{12} (o, (o.2,o.2,o.2)):11,12,13,11$$

$$B_3 \rightarrow B_2 c_1 (1, (\sqrt{2},1,1)):3,3;2,2;4,1/c_{15} (o, (o.5,1,1)):11,2,4,3$$

$$C_1 \rightarrow A_1 B_3 :2,2;4,4/c_{13} (o, (1,3,\bar{\sqrt{2}})):3,4,1,2$$

$$D_1 \rightarrow B_1 d_1 (2, (1,1,1,\sqrt{2})):7,1;6,2;5,3;4,4;5,2/c_{12} (-2, (2,1,1):8,4$$

In the above description the unit position angle means 45°.

Pattern matching

In order to find a given object pattern which may be embedded in the
pattern complex, we describe the object pattern in terms of the same
set of features as used in the pattern complex description. Now we
compare two descriptions and decide whether the one is included in
the other. In relation to this comparison of descriptions we have
two problems.   The first problem is to restrict the region of the
pattern complex where the given object may exist. If we had to
compare piece by piece O-level features of the object pattern with
that of the pattern complex, we would repeat a great deal of unsuccessful comparison until we finally find the first corresponding
piece of O-level feature. Therefore, it is reasonable to find the
object pattern of higher level in the pattern complex description in
their connection order. That means, once we find a same feature in
the pattern complex description, then we check whether the adjacent
features of the first object pattern feature are also found in the
pattern complex description in the same adjacent manner. This
matching process continues until all connected features of the
object pattern are checked. In order to reduce the number of trial-
and-error matching, we generally start from the object pattern
feature which has the highest entropy in the description. In this
case, because the feature with the highest entropy is used least of
all in the pattern complex description, so the maximal number of
unsuccessful matchings - which turn out to be incorrect - while
checking their adjacent features are minimized. In case there are
many adjacent features to the predecessor, they should be checked in
the order of their entropy magnitude, so that the matching process
can be terminated as early as possible.
If it happens that two features have the same highest entropy, then
one idea is to select at first the one which has the highest average
conditional entropy to the adjacent features

Example

Object pattern shown right is described as follows:

$$Q_1 \longrightarrow c_{15}(-1,(o.5,1,1)):1,2;5,1;2,3;3,4$$

$$Q_2 \longrightarrow Q_1 a_3 (\sqrt{2}):1,h;2,t/c_1(-1,(\sqrt{2},1,1)):2,1,3,2$$

$$Q_3 \longrightarrow Q_2 c_{12}(-2,(o.2,o.2,o.2)):4,2;5,4;6,3;7,1$$

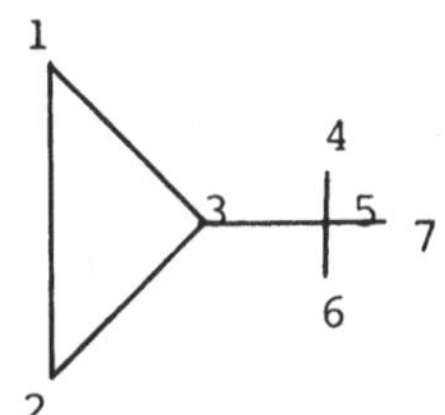

Matching process starts with the feature of the highest entropy among the foregoing description, i.e. C_1 :

Object pattern feature	pattern complex feature
c_1 :2,1,3,2	c_1 :4,2,3,4
c_{15}:2,1,3, ,5	c_{15}: 2,3,4,11
c_{12}: 5,4,6,5	c_{12}: 11,12,13,11

The second problem is related to the treatment of the object pattern whose partner substructure of the pattern complex is defective. In this case we continue the matching procedure until all corresponding parts of the substructure is matched with that of the object part. After that we check whether the defective part of the substructure of the pattern complex can be substituted by some combination of features which is to be given by the object pattern. If the ratio of the defective part to the whole object pattern is less than a certain level, then we decide that the object pattern is accepted with the given significance level.

References

1. Evans, T.G, Grammatical inference techniques in pattern analysis, <u>Software Engineering</u>, ed. by J.T. Tou, Vol.2, Academic Press,1971
2. Eden, M., Handwriting and pattern recognition, IRE.Trans.<u>Information theory</u> 8, pp 160 - 166, 1963
3. Freeman, H., On the encoding of arbitrarygeometric configuration, <u>IRE. Trans. EC.</u>10, pp 210 - 268
4. Hanakata, K.,Description-based feature analysis and recognition of pictorial pattern, Proceedings of international congress of <u>cybernetics and systems</u>, ed. by J. Rose, Gordon and Breach, 1973
5. Fu, K.S., On syntactic pattern recognition and stochastic language, <u>TR-EE 71-21</u>, Purdue University, Lafayette, Indiana
6. Pavlidis, T., Linear and context-free graph grammar, <u>J.of ACM</u> Vol. 19, No.1, Jan. 1972
7. Shaw, A.C., A formal picture description scheme as a basis for picture processing system, <u>Information and Control</u>,14 pp 9-52,1969
8. Shaw, A.C., Picture grammars and parsing, <u>NUFFIC summer course</u> on process models in psychology 1972

G. Nees

<u>Zusammenfassung</u>

Betrachtet werden zeitabhängige Systeme und ihre Beschreibung. Eine Zusatzforderung erklärt die Systeme als kognitiv: In ihrem Verhalten müssen orientierende Funktionen einerseits, agierende Funktionen andererseits unterscheidbar sein. Eine Symmetrisierung des Ansatzes faßt das kognitive System als Vereinigung von zwei Teilsystemen auf, die sich gegenseitig als Umgebung dienen. Jedes Teilsystem orientiert sich am anderen Teilsystem und wirkt auf es ein. Bezeichnet man das eine Teilsystem als Internum I, das andere als Externum E, so kann man das Verhalten des kognitiven Systems durch zwei rekursive Gleichungen

$$(1) \qquad\qquad I(u) = in(u, I, E)$$
$$(2) \qquad\qquad E(v) = ex(v, E, I)$$

beschreiben, wobei die jeweiligen Werte von u und v Aussagen über Internum und Externum machen. In (1), (2) sind die rechten Seiten aufzufassen als symbolische Abkürzungen von Ausdrücken, die im Fall von Gleichung (1) aus den Identifikatoren u, I, E und weiteren Symbolen, im Fall von Gleichung (2) aus den Identifikatoren v, I, E und weiteren Symbolen aufgebaut sind. Man kann die rechten Seiten von (1) und (2) auch als von zusätzlichen Parametern I und E abhängige Funktionen, in und ex als Funktionsnamen auffassen. Dann muß man sich jedoch im klaren sein, daß die Abbildungsgesetze für jene Funktionen erst dann bekannt sein können, wenn die rechten Seiten mit Hilfe der syntaktischen Regeln eines Kalküls, z.B. des gleich zu erwähnenden λ-Kalküls voll ausgeschrieben werden. Bei jeder solchen vollständigen Notierung gewinnt man einen Spezialfall der allgemeinen Systemgleichungen (1) und (2).

Verzichtet man auf infinitesimale Methoden, fordert man aber eine Notation, die Spezialisierungen des rekursiven Ansatzes (1), (2) zu behandeln gestattet, wobei als Werte der Verhaltensvariablen u und v beliebig komplizierte Strukturbeschreibungen zulässig sein sollen, so stößt man auf folgendes Angebot:

a) Prozedurale Programmiersprachen, z.B. Maschinensprachen, FORTRAN, ALGOL 60, ALGOL 68, PL/1 und andere.

b) Beschreibungssprachen, z.B. Wiener Definitionssprache (Lukas, Walk 69, Wegner 72), GEDANKEN (Reynolds 70, Görz 72).

c) Der λ-Kalkül (Church 41, McCarthy 60, Landin 64).

Stellt man jetzt noch die Zusatzforderungen, daß die Notation so rechenmaschinenunabhängig sein soll, als es möglich ist, daß ferner ihre Syntax und Semantik so einfach wie angängig und außerdem voll formalisierbar sein soll, so daß auch das Beweisen von Aussagen über Ausdrücke in der Notation so wenig Schwierigkeiten wie möglich macht, dann bleibt der λ-Kalkül als Beschreibungswerkzeug übrig.

Der λ-Kalkül ist insbesondere durch die Arbeiten von McCarthy und Landin zu einem attraktiven Werkzeug der Modellierung und Auswertung von Algorithmen geworden. In den vergangenen Jahren hat man den λ-Kalkül insbesondere zum Studium der Semantik von Programmiersprachen herangezogen (siehe z.B. Landin 65, McCarthy 66, Morris 68). In die angewandte Informatik hat er wenig Eingang gefunden (Nees 73). Es ist die Absicht der vorliegenden Arbeit, zu zeigen, daß der λ-Kalkül in der Gestalt der Notation, die man vor allem Landin verdankt (siehe auch Landin 66), ein leistungsfähiges Werkzeug zur Beschreibung von kognitiven Systemen im oben erläuterten Sinn ist. Zu diesem Zweck wird nach einem einleitenden Kapitel in Kapitel 2 ein verhältnismäßig einfaches Beispiel eines kognitiven Systems behandelt, das auf William M. Newman zurückgeht (Newman 68): Auf-, Um- und Abbau von Streckenkomplexen mit Hilfe eines graphischen Displaygeräts werden durch einen Spezialfall der Systemgleichungen (1), (2) beschrieben. Dabei ist die Maschine das Internum, der Benutzer das Externum.

Ein wesentlich komplizierteres Beispiel wird in Kapitel 3 besprochen. nämlich eine Erweiterung der Mustererkennungslogik von Marcel J. E. Golay auf Richtungsabhängigkeit der hexagonalen Muster und eine Anwendung der Erweiterung auf ein Regelungsproblem, bei dem ein Internum ein von einem Externum erzeugtes, verändertes und Verschiebungen unterworfenes Muster (einen Fleck) durch Zentrieren in seinem Blickfeld verfolgt. Bei diesem Beispiel wird, wiederum von einer Spezialisierung der Systemgleichungen (1), (2) ausgehend, eine Hierarchie von systembeschreibenden Funktionen angegeben, die von sehr allgemeinen zu immer spezielleren Funktionen absteigt. Deshalb kann die angegebene Problemlösung auch als Beispiel für strukturierendes Programmieren angesehen werden.

Dieser Aufsatz ist der Beschreibung von kognitiven Systemen gewidmet. Es sind jedoch weitergehende Fragestellungen denkbar, deren Bearbeitung aus der Benutzung des λ-Kalküls Gewinn ziehen könnte. Dazu gehören syntaktische Beschreibungen ganzer Systemklassen und das

Beweisen von Sätzen über die Systemklassen (siehe Burstall 69). Einen Problemkreis, der sich mit dem eben erwähnten auf jeden Fall berührt, bilden die automatischen Übertragungen von Beschreibungen im λ-Kalkül in möglichst effektiv ablaufende Programme.

1   Einleitung

1.1   Zum Begriff des kognitiven Systems

1.1.1   Iteration und Systemphasen. Internum und Externum

Unter einem System verstehen wir jede Entität, die Teile hat, wobei zwischen den Teilen Beziehungen bestehen. Bei einem zeitabhängigen System sind Struktur und Funktion zu unterscheiden. Die Funktion beschreibt das Verhalten des Systems. Neben dem eben verwendeten Funktionsbegriff benutzen wir einen zweiten, nämlich den Begriff der Funktion im Sinn einer mathematischen Abbildung. Ist ein zeitabhängiges System durch eine Abbildung f der Werte einer Variablen u auf Werte f(u) beschreibbar, so braucht u nicht die Zeit zu sein, es genügt, daß u verschiedene Modi des Systems zu unterscheiden vermag. Wir nennen diese Modi die Phasen des Systems. Eine besondere Beschreibungsmöglichkeit besteht darin, von einer Anfangsphase a auszugehen und die zeitlich aufeinanderfolgenden Phasen des Systems durch sukzessive Anwendungen der Funktion (Abbildung) f auf a, d.h. durch Iteration zu gewinnen:

$$(1) \qquad\qquad f(f(f...f(a)...))$$

An die Stelle einer Funktion f können auch mehrere Funktionen treten, z.B. die abwechselnd angewandten Funktionen f und g:

$$(2) \qquad\qquad g(f(g(f(g...f(a)...))))$$

Man kann sich die Auswertung der Funktionen f und g verbunden denken mit einer protokollierenden Aktivität, die einen Beobachter über die aufeinanderfolgenden Phasen des Systems unterrichtet. Den Ausdruck (2) kann man so deuten, daß zwei Modi f und g der Funktion (im Gegensatz zur Struktur) des Systems zu unterscheiden sind, z.B. zwei verschiedene Takte einer Maschine oder die Wach- und die Schlafphase eines Tieres.

Unter einem kognitiven System verstehen wir ein zeitabhängiges System, an dessen Funktion zwei Aspekte deutlich zu unterscheiden sind:

Rekognoszierende oder orientierende Teilfunktionen einerseits, agierende Teilfunktionen andererseits. Man kann bereits f und g in (2)
als Beschreibungen von Orientierungs- bzw. Aktionsphase eines Systems
deuten, es ist jedoch geraten, die Eingrenzung kognitiver Systeme
noch etwas weiter zu treiben: Orientierung ist Orientierung in einer
Umgebung, so daß man von der Struktur kognitiver Systeme zweckmäßig
fordert, daß sie eine Umgebung oder mehrere Umgebungen einschließt.
Hat man das vereinbart, so kann man sich überlegen, daß die Umgebung,
innerhalb dessen die Orientierung vor sich geht, selbst ein System
ist, denn sie wird nicht ungegliedert sein. Die Umgebung wird sogar
ein zeitabhängiges System sein, andernfalls bräuchte man sich nicht
(oder äußerstenfalls nur einmal) in ihr zu orientieren. Diese Überlegungen führen dazu, wenigstens eine große Klasse von kognitiven
Systemen als aus zwei Teilsystemen, z.B. I und E, bestehend anzusehen,
von denen jeweils das eine das andere als Umgebung besitzt. Diese
Situation kann man, über den einfachen Ansatz (2) hinausgehend, formal folgendermaßen beschreiben:

$$(3) \qquad I(u) = in(u, I, E)$$

$$(4) \qquad E(v) = ex(v, E, I)$$

Die zwei Teilsysteme I und E bezeichnen wir auch als das Internum
und das Externum des Systems. Der symmetrische Ansatz (3), (4) be-
günstigt keinen der beiden Teile des kognitiven Systems gegenüber dem
anderen.

Durch die Spezialisierung

$$(5) \qquad I(u) = E(f(u))$$

$$(6) \qquad E(v) = I(g(v))$$

erhält man fast Ausdrücke der Form (2), denn es ist z.B.

$$(7) \qquad E(f(a)) = I(g(f(a)))$$

$$(8) \qquad = E(f(g(f(a)))) \text{ usw.}$$

Werden die Ausdrücke (7), (8), ... von innen nach außen ausgewertet
und protokollieren die Funktionen f und g als eine ihrer Nebenwirkungen das Ergebnis ihrer Anwendung auf ein Argument, so erhält man eine
Serie

$$(9) \qquad P_0, P_1, P_2, P_3, \ldots$$

von Protokollen über die sukzessiven Phasen des kognitiven Systems,
wobei eine Beschreibung P_0 der Anfangsphase a die Serie (9) einleitet.

In den Systemgleichungen (3) bis (6) sind drei Sorten von Größen
wohl zu unterscheiden: Die Phasenvariablen u und v, die Systemteil-
bezeichnungen I und E, schließlich die Funktionsbenennungen in und
ex, bzw. f und g für die Abbildungen einer Phase auf die nächste. Da
die Größen I und E, die durch die rechten Seiten der Gleichungen erklärt werden sollen, auf den rechten Seiten wiederkehren, nennt man
ein Gleichungssystem der Form (3), (4) rekursiv.

1.1.2 Abbruchkriterien

Eine Phasenserie (1.1.1/9) kann potentiell ins Unendliche fortschrei-
ten. Bei bestimmten Systemen bricht sie jedoch mit einer Schlußphase
ab. Dieses Abbrechen kann man durch Abbruchkriterien in den Systemgleichungen wiedergeben. Wir betrachten wieder einen Spezialfall von
(1.1.1/3,4)

(1) $\qquad I(u) = (B(u) \rightarrow F(u), \sim B(u) \rightarrow E(f(u)))$

(2) $\qquad E(v) = I(g(v))$

Die rechte Seite von (1) ist umgangssprachlich folgendermaßen zu verstehen:

"Tritt die logische Bedingung B(u) ein, so ist F(u) der Wert des
 Ausdrucks,
 tritt dagegen die logische Bedingung B(u) nicht ein, so ist
 E(f(u)) der Wert des Ausdrucks"

Tritt also das Abbruchkriterium B(u) z.B. nach der ersten Anwendung
von g ein, so hat man anstatt (1.1.1/8) den Ausdruck

(3) $\qquad F(g(f(a)))$

und der Wert des Ausdrucks (3) gibt die Schlußphase wieder.

Man bezeichnet Ausdrücke der Form

(4) $\qquad (b_1 \rightarrow e_1, b_2 \rightarrow e_2, \ldots, b_n \rightarrow e_n)$

als bedingt. Die rechte Seite von (1) ist ein bedingter Ausdruck.
In (4) heißen die $b_1, \ldots, b_n$ die Bedingungen des Ausdrucks. Einen
bedingten Ausdruck wertet man aus, indem man, links beginnend, nach
der ersten Bedingung b_k sucht, deren Wert wahr (oder: das Wahre) ist.
Man erhält dann den Wert von e_k als den Wert des bedingten Ausdrucks.
Das Wahre und das Falsche, abgekürzt T und F, sind selbst logische
Bedingungen, die allerdings immer wahr bzw. falsch sind. Deshalb kann
man (1), weil $\sim B(u)=T$ genau dann ist, wenn B(u) nicht gilt, auch so
schreiben:

(5) $\qquad I(u) = (B(u) \rightarrow F(u),\ T \rightarrow E(f(u)))$

Die bedingten Ausdrücke zählen zu den formalen Beschreibungshilfs-
mitteln, es sind nur ganz wenige, die wir in diesem Aufsatz benutzen.

1.1.3 Der Puls. Zustandsvariablen und Austauschvariablen

Wir betrachten wieder die Systemgleichungen

(1) $\qquad I(u) = in(u,\ I,\ E)$

(2) $\qquad E(v) = ex(v,\ E,\ I)$

Ist a eine Anfangsphase, so liefert die Auswertung von in(a,I,E) die
nächste Phase P_1. Es ist deshalb beim betrachteten System sinnvoll,
die Anfangsphase a strukturell als vom Externum bestimmt anzusehen,
die nächste P_1 als vom Internum bestimmt, usw. Wir drücken uns auch
so auch: "Ein Puls des Internums folgt auf einen Puls des Externums,
ein Puls des Externums folgt auf einen Puls des Internums,..." Diese
Anschauung wird in vielen Fällen dem tatsächlichen Zeitverhalten des
Systems gut entsprechen, es ist z.B. allen Dialogsystemen angepaßt,
bei denen die Aktivität abwechselnd für gewisse Zeitabschnitte einmal beim einen, dann beim anderen Dialogpartner liegt. Ein solches
Problem, nämlich Tätigkeiten an einem graphischen Displaygerät, behandelt Kapitel 2. Eine andere Klasse von Systemen ist jedoch durch
ein zeitlich kontinuierliches Zusammenwirken von Internum und Externum gekennzeichnet, wie es z.B. bei einem zielverfolgenden Flugobjekt
und dem Zielsystem der Fall ist. Kapitel 3 enthält ein Beispiel aus
dieser Klasse, nämlich ein Mustererkennungs- und Musterverfolgungs-
problem.

Ungeachtet der Unterschiede der zu modellierenden Systeme aus den
beiden genannten Klassen erzwingt unser Ansatz (1), (2) eine Diskretisation der Zeitskala des Modells, wobei jeder Puls einem Zeitintervall oder Zeitpunkt zugeordnet ist. Diese Diskretisation hat jedoch
den Vorteil, daß wir mathematische Verfahren anwenden können, die auf
der diskreten Konstruktion von sukzessiven Phasen beruhen. Der Prototyp eines solchen Verfahrens ist der λ-Kalkül, den wir in Abschnitt
1.2 genauer behandeln.

Eine andere Klassifikation des zu beschreibenden Systems ist durch
die Art der Phasenvariablen in den Systemgleichungen (1), (2) bedingt.
Der Bereich, den diese Variablen überstreichen, kann systemabhängig
sehr verschieden sein. Der Wert einer Phasenvariablen kann eine Struk-
turbeschreibung von beliebiger Ausdehnung und Tiefe sein. In Kapitel
3 ist der Wert von u ein Binärmuster auf einem hexagonalen Feld. Wir

lassen anstatt einer Variablen u auch mehrere Variable oder Listen
von solchen zu (der erste Fall ist auf den zweiten reduzierbar):

$$(3) \qquad u_1,\dots,u_n \quad \text{oder} \quad (u_1,\dots,u_n)$$

Das gleiche gilt für v. Für die Beschreibung der Interaktion von
Internum und Externum durch Phasenvariablen existieren nun die beiden
in Bild 1 veranschaulichten Möglichkeiten: Entweder dienen die Variablen $u_1,\dots,u_n$ vollständig zur Unterrichtung des Internums über den
Zustand des Externums, die Variablen $v_1,\dots,v_m$ zur entsprechenden
Unterrichtung des Externums, wobei verschiedene der u_i mit Variablen
v_j zusammenfallen können (siehe Bild 1a), oder aber die Systemgleichungen nehmen im wesentlichen die besondere Gestalt

$$(4) \qquad I(s,t,u) = \text{in1}(I(s,\text{in2}(t),u),\ E(\text{in3}(t),s,\text{in4}(t,u)))$$

$$(5) \qquad E(t,s,v) = \text{ex1}(E(t,\text{ex2}(s),v),\ I(\text{ex3}(s),t,\text{ex4}(s,v)))$$

an. Protokollierende Nebenwirkungen haben jetzt zweckmäßig die Abbildungen in2 bis in4, ex2 bis ex4. Die Variable (Variablenliste) s

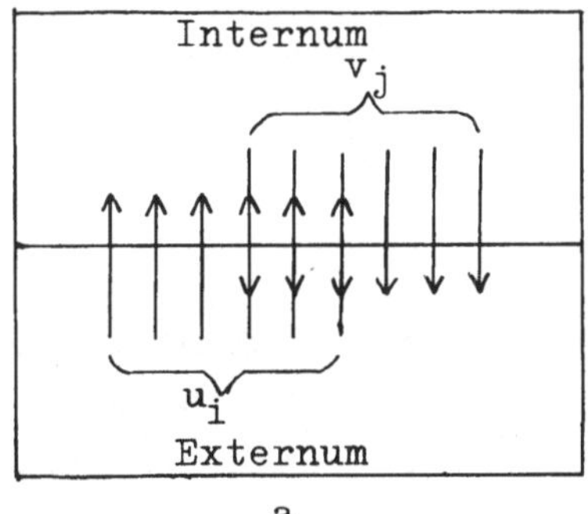

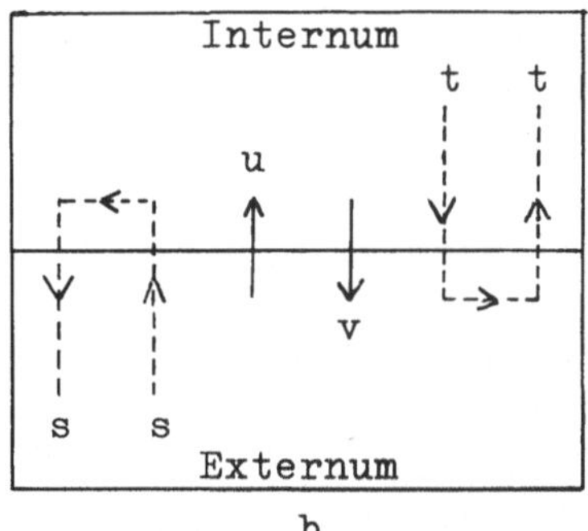

Bild 1
Modellierung ohne und mit Zustandsgrößen

kennzeichnet den inneren Zustand des Externums zu Ende eines bestimmten Pulses und taucht in I(s,t,u) aus dem einzigen Grund auf, um auf
der rechten Seite von (4) unverändert an den nächsten Puls des Externums (d.h. des übernächsten Pulses des Systems) übergeben zu werden.
Ganz entsprechend kann das Gleichungssystem (4), (5) vom Standpunkt des
Internums und seines inneren Zustands t aus betrachtet werden. Der
Unterschied zwischen Systemen vom Typ 1a und solchen vom Typ 1b
(siehe Bild 1) liegt genau darin, daß wir beim ersten Typ nur die
Vorgänge am Interface zwischen Internum und Externum modellieren und
protokollieren, beim zweiten Typ jedoch auch Vorgänge im Inneren der

beiden Teilsysteme. Nicht vergessen werden darf, daß während des Pulses des einen Teilsystems die Zeit für das andere Teilsystem stillsteht, anders ausgedrückt: Unsere Modellierung zeigt die Kollateralität von Internum und Externum nur bei Beobachtung vieler sukzessiver Pulse des Systems. Das in Kapitel 2 betrachtete kognitive System ist vom Typ 1b, weil der innere Zustand, in dem das graphische Displaygerät sich befindet, in die Modellierung einbezogen wird.

Wir bezeichnen die Variablen u, u_i, v, v_j als Austauschvariablen, dagegen die Variablen s und t als Zustandsvariablen. Austauschvariablen und Zustandvariablen sind Phasenvariablen. Für jemand, der an speicherorientiertes Programmieren gewöhnt ist, mag das Mitschleppen z.B. der Zustandsvariablen s des Externums in der Bestimmungsgleichung für das Internum seltsam erscheinen. Dieses Mitschleppen ist jedoch nichts anderes als eine Speicherung von s. Man hat hier, vom Programmierstandpunkt aus betrachtet, die Koroutinensituation vor sich, bei der der Zustand der einen Koroutine während des Arbeitens der anderen sorgfältig aufbewahrt werden muß (Knuth 68).

In Abschnitt 1.2.2 wird gezeigt werden, daß sich die Gleichungen (4), (5) auf die Form (1), (2) reduzieren lassen.

1.2 Der λ-Kalkül

Der λ-Kalkül, der ursprünglich ein Instrument der mathematischen Logik gewesen ist (Church 41, Curry 58), wurde besonders durch McCarthy und Landin in ein universales Recheninstrument für die Praxis verwandelt. Wir stützen uns ausschließlich auf McCarthy 60 und Landin 64 und benötigen auch nicht den ganzen Begriffsvorrat der zuletzt genannten Arbeit. Für weitergehende Untersuchungen sind insbesondere Landin 66 und Burstall 69 zu nennen. Die nachfolgend eingeführte Schreibweise bezeichnen wir auch als Landinnotation.

1.2.1 Funktionsdefinitionen. Landins where-Regel

Bereits in Abschnitt 1.1.2 haben wir die bedingten Ausdrücke kennengelernt. Mit ihrer Hilfe läßt sich eine Klasse von rekursiven und nichtrekursiven Funktionen definieren. Wir bringen Beispiele, vor allem solche, die in Kapitel 3 wiederkehren.

$$(1) \qquad a014(u,v) = (u=0 \wedge v=14 \rightarrow 1,\ T \rightarrow u)$$

ist eine Funktion, die für das Wertepaar u gleich 0 und v gleich 14 den Funktionswert 1 liefert, andernfalls den Wert von u unverändert weitergibt (siehe (3.1.4/2)). Die Funktion

(2)   Koll1(i) = (i=1 $\rightarrow$ 2, i=2 $\rightarrow$ 3, T $\rightarrow$ 1)

liefert für die als zyklisch geschlossen verstandene Zahlenliste
(1,2,3) den rechten Partner der i-ten Zahl (siehe (3.3.2/4)). Beide
Funktionen sind nichtrekursiv, weil der Funktionsname auf der rechten Seite nicht auftritt.

Die rekursive Funktion

(3)   . Mult(m,n) = (m=0 $\rightarrow$ 0, T $\rightarrow$ n+Mult(m-1,n))

führt die Multiplikation von positiven ganzen Zahlen auf ihre Addition zurück. Es ist z.B.

(4)   Mult(2,4) = 4+Mult(1,4) = 4+4+Mult(0,4) = 8

Unter den Argumenten einer Funktion können selbstverständlich Funktionen vorkommen. So organisiert z.B. die Funktion

(5)   Rep(n,f,x,y) = (n=1 $\rightarrow$ f(x,y),
             T $\rightarrow$ f(Rep(n-1,f,x,y),y))

die n-malige Anwendung der Funktion f(x,y) auf sich selbst und y, so
daß beispielsweise

(6)   Rep(k,Mult,m,n) = m*n^k

(siehe (3.1.3/4)).

Mit Hilfe des Symbols λ lassen sich Funktionsdefinitionen immer so
schreiben, daß der Funktionsname auf der linken Seite allein steht.
Es sind

(7)   Mult = λ(m,n).(m=0 $\rightarrow$ 0, T $\rightarrow$ n+Mult(m-1,n))

(8)   Rep = λ(n,f,x,y).(n=1 $\rightarrow$ f(x,y),
             T $\rightarrow$ f(Rep(n-1,f,x,y),y))

die auch durch (3) und (5) eingeführten Funktionen. Nichtrekursive
Funktionsausdrücke, die mit Hilfe des λ-Symbols notiert werden, verwenden wir auch im Inneren anderer Ausdrücke. z.B. ist die Zeile

(9)   Rep(k,λ(x,y).x*y,m,n) = m*n^k

bedeutungsgleich mit (6).

Einen Ausdruck
(10)   f(x)
der die Anwendung der Funktion f auf ihr Argument x angibt, nennt
Landin eine Kombination mit dem Operator f und dem Operanden x. Als

Auswertungsregel für Kombinationen gilt, daß der Operand grundsätzlich vor seiner Verwendung als Argument für den Operator ausgewertet
wird. Der Operand kann selbstverständlich selbst eine Funktion sein
(für ein Beispiel siehe (5)).

Als Landins where-Regel bezeichnen wir die Definitionsgleichung

$$(11) \qquad (\lambda x.e(x))y = (e(x) \text{ where } x=y)$$

Diese Regel für die Umformung von Kombinationen trägt sehr zur leichteren Handhabung des λ-Kalküls bei. Eine Erweiterung von (11) ist

$$(12) \qquad (\lambda(x_1,\ldots,x_n).e(x_1,\ldots,x_n))(y_1,\ldots,y_n) =$$
$$(e(x_1,\ldots,x_n)$$
$$\text{where } x_1=y_1 \text{ and } x_2=y_2 \text{ and } \ldots \text{ and } x_n=y_n)$$

Man beachte, daß die linken Seiten von (11) und (12) Kombinationen,
d.h. Funktionsanwendungen sind.

1.2.2 Listen, Konstruktoren, Selektoren, Prädikatoren

Die Bedeutung des Aufsatzes McCarthy 60 liegt vor allem darin, daß
in den λ-Kalkül als Werte von Variablen Objekte eingeführt werden,
die aus Elementen linear zusammengesetzt sind, wobei jene Elemente
selbst wieder in gleicher Weise zusammengesetzt sein können. Solche
Objekte nennt McCarthy Listen. Nicht zusammengesetzte Elemente von
Listen heißen Atome. Die Liste, die gar keine Elemente enthält, heißt
leer und wird von uns mit $\emptyset$ bezeichnet. Sie gilt als Atom.

Landin unterscheidet drei Arten von Funktionen zum Umgang mit zusam-
mengesetzten Objekten, speziell Listen: Konstruktoren setzen aus
Listen oder Atomen neue Listen oder andere Objekte zusammen. Selektoren isolieren Teile aus Listen. Prädikatoren prüfen Listen oder Atome
auf bestimmte Merkmale; der Funktionswert eines Prädikators ist also
T oder F.

Mit Hilfe von Konstruktoren, Selektoren und Prädikatoren erklären wir
jetzt die Handhabung von Listen. Zunächst dient der Doppelpunkt als
Listenkonstruktor:

$$(1) \qquad x_1:(x_2:(x_3:\ldots:(x_n:\emptyset))) = (x_1,x_2,x_3,\ldots,x_n)$$

In (1) steht rechts eine Liste, links ihre konstruktive Definition.
Es ist

$$(2) \qquad\qquad (x) = x:\emptyset$$
$$(3) \qquad x_1:(x_2,\ldots,x_n) = (x_1,x_2,\ldots,x_n)$$

In (3) heißt x_1 der Listenkopf, $(x_2,\ldots,x_n)$ der Listenrest. Zur Selektion von Kopf und Rest dienen die Funktionen

$$(4) \qquad \text{head}(x_1,\ldots,x_n) = h(x_1,\ldots,x_n) = x_1$$

$$(5) \qquad \text{tail}(x_1,x_2,\ldots,x_n) = t(x_1,x_2,\ldots,x_n) = (x_2,\ldots,x_n)$$

Es gilt

$$(6) \qquad h(x{:}y) = x, \quad t(x{:}y) = y$$

Atome haben weder Kopf noch Rest.

Der Prädikator null prüft ein Axiom, ob es gleich $\emptyset$ ist:

$$(7) \qquad \text{null}(x) = T \text{ falls } x \text{ gleich } \emptyset, \text{ d.h. null}(\emptyset) = T,$$
$$\text{null}(x) = F \text{ andernfalls}$$

Der Prädikator eq prüft Axiome auf Gleichheit:

$$(8) \qquad \text{eq}(x,y) = T \text{ falls } x \text{ und } y \text{ das gleiche Atom bedeuten,}$$
$$\text{eq}(x,y) = F \text{ andernfalls}$$

Wir schreiben jedoch in der Regel $x=y$ anstatt $\text{eq}(x,y)$.

Für die Selektion des ersten, zweiten, dritten, ... Elements einer Liste x verwenden wir die Funktionen

$$(9) \qquad \text{el1}(x), \ \text{el2}(x), \ \text{el3}(x), \ \ldots$$

die auf h und t zurückführbar sind:

$$(10) \qquad \text{el1}(x)=h(x), \ \text{el2}(x)=h(t(x)), \ \text{el3}(x)=h(t(t(x))), \ \ldots$$

Am Schluß von Abschnitt 1.1.3 hatten wir versprochen, die speziellen Systemgleichungen (1.1.3/4,5) auf die Form der allgemeinen Gleichungen (1.1.3/1,2) zu reduzieren. Dies ist mit Hilfe von (1) und (10) leicht möglich, indem man die Argumente jeder Gleichung (1.1.3/4,5) zu jeweils einer Liste zusammenfaßt:

$$(11) \quad I(x) = \text{in1}(I(\text{el1}(x){:}(\text{in2}(\text{el2}(x)){:}(\text{el3}(x){:}\emptyset))),$$
$$E(\text{in3}(\text{el2}(x)){:}(\text{el1}(x){:}(\text{in4}(\text{el2}(x),\text{el3}(x)){:}\emptyset))))$$

$$(12) \quad E(y) = \text{ex1}(E(\text{el1}(y){:}(\text{ex2}(\text{el2}(y)){:}(\text{el3}(y){:}\emptyset))),$$
$$I(\text{ex3}(\text{el2}(y)){:}(\text{el1}(y){:}(\text{ex4}(\text{el2}(y),\text{el3}(y)){:}\emptyset))))$$

Auf den rechten Seiten stehen jetzt Ausdrücke, die mit Hilfe weiterer Funktionen aufgebaut sind aus x, I, E bzw. y, E, I.

1.2.3 Der Block. Die Organisation von Nebenwirkungen

Wir benötigen die funktionenerzeugende Funktion

$$(1) \qquad \text{stat}(x) = \lambda\text{never}.x$$

In (1) ist never ein Ausnahmeidentifikator, in dessen Einflußbereich
never selbst nie vorkommt. Eine Funktionsanwendung

(2) $\qquad\qquad\qquad$ (stat(x))y

hat die Wirkung, daß zunächst das Argument y ausgewertet wird. Nach
der Auswertung von y wird der resultierende Wert in x für never eingesetzt. Da never in x nicht vorkommt, hat die Einsetzung keine Wirkung. Schließlich wird x ausgewertet, der sich ergebende Wert ist
der Wert des Ausdrucks (2). Der Wert von y wird also vergessen. Wesentlich ist jedoch, daß y vor dem Vergessenwerden eine Nebenwirkung
gezeitigt haben kann.

Der Block $[x_1;\ldots;x_n]$ ist nun definiert durch

(3) $\qquad [x_1;\ldots;x_n] =$
$\qquad\qquad$ (stat(x_n))((stat(x_{n-1}))($\ldots$((stat(x_1))$\emptyset$)$\ldots$))

In (3) bewirkt der Mechanismus von stat, daß nacheinander die Nebenwirkungen von x_1, x_2, usw. eintreten. Der Wert des Blocks ist der des
letzten Ausdrucks x_n. Dies ist in Übereinstimmung mit der Definition
des Werts eines Blocks in der Sprache GEDANKEN (Reynolds 70) bzw.
einer "range" in ALGOL 68.

In Kapitel 2 wird der Block ausgiebig angewandt werden. In Kapitel 3
kann man z.B. die Protokollierung der vom Golayoperator Golop hervorgebrachten Muster mit Hilfe eines Blocks organisieren. So ist

(4) $\qquad$ Golprot(G,a,n) =
$\qquad\qquad$ (λx.[Dump(x); x])Golop(G,a,n)

eine mit Golop hinsichtlich des hervorgebrachten Werts äquivalente
Funktion, jedoch tritt zusätzlich eine durch Dump(x) angedeutete
Nebenwirkung auf (siehe (3.1.3/2)).

2 Interaktion an einem graphischen Displaygerät

William M. Newman hat eine Systematik für die Beschreibung von interaktiven Prozessen ausgearbeitet, die besonders gut auf graphische
Programmierprobleme anwendbar ist (Newman 68). In der von uns in
Kapitel 1 eingeführten Terminologie ausgedrückt, hat man ein kogniti-
ves System vor sich, dessen Internum ein graphisches Displaygerät,
dessen Externum der Benutzer des Geräts ist. Aktionen des Externums
wirken auf das Internum ein, veranlassen es zu einem Zustandswechsel
und lösen eine vom Externum wahrnehmbare Rückmeldung auf. In Abschnitt
2.1 übersetzen wir den in Newman 68 enthaltenen Begriffsapparat in

unsere Terminologie, soweit er sich auf die Beschreibung des System-
verhaltens bezieht. Abschnitt 2.2 behandelt dann ein von Newman ange-
gebenes Anwendungsbeispiel.

2.1 Der Begriffsapparat bei Newman

Newman beschreibt das interaktive System mit Hilfe eines Diagramms,
ähnlich dem Zustandsdiagramm eines finiten Automaten (siehe Bild 2).
Dementsprechend unterscheidet er Zustände von Zweigen, die von Zustand zu Zustand führen. Der Zustand kann mit einer Aktivität verbunden sein, die Programmblock heißt (program block), wobei wir uns vor
Verwechslungen mit dem in Abschnitt 1.2.3 eingeführten Blockbegriff
hüten müssen. Gerät das System in einen bestimmten Zustand, so wird
der gegebenenfalls definierte Programmblock aktiviert. Eine zweite
Art von Aktivität ist ebenfalls dem Zustand zugeordnet, nämlich die
Rückmeldung (response). Die Rückmeldung ist ein Text- oder Bildsignal,
das dem Interaktionspartner, d.h. dem Externum zugeleitet wird und
diesem zur Orientierung über das Internum dient. Es sei daran erinnert,
daß nicht in allen Interaktionssystemen das Externum über den inneren
Zustand des Internums aufgeklärt wird. So meldet das durch Bild 2
dargestellte Beispielsystem lediglich "Press button to track", wenn
es in den Zustand 1 kommt (siehe Abschnitt 2.2).

Jeder Zweig kann mit einer bestimmten Aktivität verbunden sein, die
Newman als instruction for execution, abgekürzt IEX, bezeichnet. Er
läßt außerdem zu, daß ein Zweig sich mit Hilfe einer Testroutine vor
der Ausführung einer IEX gabelt, so daß, abhängig vom Testergebnis,
verschiedene Zustände eintreten könne. Das letzte Bestimmungsstück,
das jetzt noch benötigt wird, ist die jeweilige Aktion des Externums,
die auf das Internum übergreift, sie heißt bei Newman Kommando
(command).

Newman definiert eine Steuersprache (control language), die alle eingeführten Begriffe benutzt und lediglich dazu dient, die Übergänge
des Internums von Zustand zu Zustand zu beschreiben. Die genaue Spe-
zifikation von Programmblock- oder IEX-Aktivitäten hingegen überläßt
er besonderen Programmen, die in einer prozeduralen Sprache abzufas-
sen sind. An dieser Stelle trennen wir uns von der Behandlung des
Interaktionsproblems nach Newman und gehen zur Landinnotation über.

2.2 Ein Beispielsystem

Bild 2 veranschaulicht ein graphisches Interaktionssystem, ausgerüstet mit Bildschirm und Lichtgriffel, dessen Verhalten nur unwesentlich von dem Verhalten des in Newman 68 angegebenen Beispiels ab-
weicht. Der Kommandovorrat des Externums ist: Knopfdruck (button),
pen movement (Zeichnen mit dem Lichtgriffel), pen hit (Deuten mit dem
Lichtgriffel), "draw" (Absicht zum Zeichnen bekunden), "delete" (Absicht bekunden, eine gezeichnete Strecke zu löschen), "restart"
(Systemneustart). Über das Verhalten des Externums machen wir, auch
hier Newman folgend, weiter keine Angaben, sondern verstecken es in
einer Funktion Telos, die abhängig von den Rückmeldungen des Internums Kommandos erzeugt. Die Rückmeldungen notieren wir als Texte, d.h.
Zeichenketten, die gleichzeitig den äußeren Beobachter des kognitiven Systems informieren. Innerhalb der Landinnotation werden die
Zeichenketten wie Atome behandelt. In Abschnitt 2.2.1 beschreiben wir
das Verhalten des Internums.

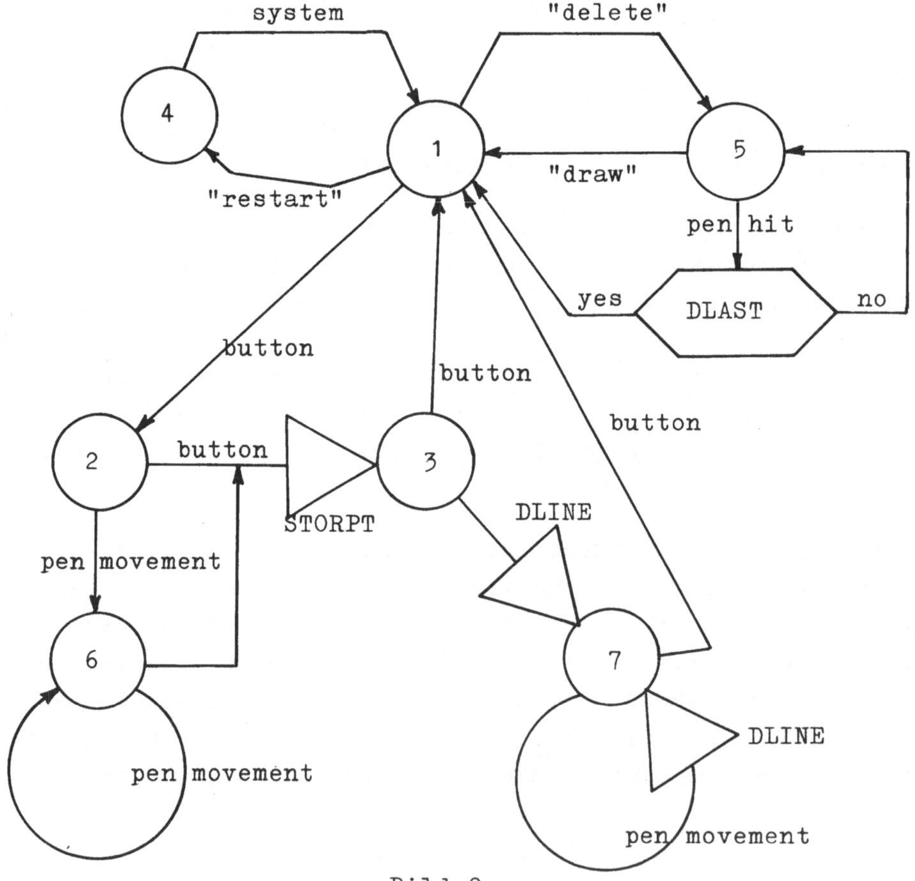

Bild 2
Diagramm des Internums im Beispiel nach Newman

2.2.1 Das Internum

Wir bringen zuerst die Systemgleichung für das Internum, danach den
Kommentar.

```
(1)   I(t,c) =
  2   (t=1 →
  3   (c=button → [go(2); E("Press button to draw",2)],
  4    c="restart" → [go(4); PBGO;
  5                      go(1); E("Press button to track",1)],
  6    c="delete" → [go(5); E("Point at line to delete", 5)],
  7    T → Special(1)),
  8    t=2 →
  9   (c=button → [STORPT; go(3);
 10                    E("Press button when complete",3)],
 11    c=pen movement → [go(6);
 12                    E("Remember: Press button to draw",6)],
 13    T → Special(2)),
 14    t=3 →
 15   (c=button → [go(1); E("Press button to track",1)],
 16    c=pen movement → [DLINE; go(7);
 17                    E("Remember: Press button when complete",7)],
 18    T → Special(3)),
 19    t=4 →
 20    c=system → [PBGO; go(1);
 21                    E("Press button to track",1)],
 22    T → Special(4)),
 23    t=5 →
 24   (c=pen hit →
 25      (DLAST → [go(1); E("Press button to track",1)],
 26       T → [go(5); E("Point at line to delete",5)],
 27    c="draw" → [go(1); E("Press button to track")],
 28    T → Special(5)),
 29    t=6 →
 30    c=button → [STORPT; go(3);
 31                    E("Press button when complete",3)],
 32    c=pen movement → [go(6);
 33                    E("Remember: Press button to draw",6)],
 34    T → Special(6)),
 35    t=7 →
 36   (c=button → [go(1); E("Press button to track",1)],
 37    c=pen movement → [DLINE; go(7);
```

```
38                    E("Remember: Press button when complete",7)],
39    T → Special(7))
40    )
```

In (1) ist t die Zustandsvariable des Internums, c die Austauschvariable, deren Wert vom agierenden Externum ans Internum gegeben
wird. Die Begriffe Zustands- und Austauschvariable haben wir in Abschnitt 1.1.3 eingeführt. Natürlich kennzeichnet t den Zustand des
Systems auch im Sinne von Newman, c das jeweilige Kommando des
Externums.

Es erweist sich als sinnvoll, das System mit dem Aufruf I(4,system)
zu starten. Dann wird gemäß Zeile 20 ein Block im Sinn von Abschnitt
1.2.3 durchlaufen, der folgende Prozesse auslöst: Der Programmblock
PBGO hat gewisse Initiierungsaktivitäten des Internums zur Folge.
Dann geht das System in den Zustand 1. Schließlich wird der Puls des
Internums beendet, indem die Funktion

$$(2) \qquad\qquad E(r,t)$$

aufgerufen wird, die das Externum mit Hilfe einer Rückmeldung r aktiviert. Im Fall von Zeile 21 wird das Externum aufgefordert, auf den
Knopf zu drücken, wenn es anschließend mit Hilfe des Lichtgriffels
eine Spurmarke auf dem Bildschirm an einen gewünschten Ort bringen
will, um den Anfangspunkt einer neuen Strecke zu setzen. Das Gesamtsystem tritt also jetzt in den Puls des Externums ein, wobei der
innere Zustand des Internums mit Hilfe der Zustandsvariablen t gespeichert wird, ein Verfahren, das wir schon in Abschnitt 1.1.3 erläutert haben. In (2) ist r eine Austauschvariable. Gleichung (1) ist
fast selbsterklärend. In Zeile 9 taucht die IEX STORPT auf, die den
Anfangspunkt einer zu zeichnenden Strecke abspeichert. Der Block in
den Zeilen (9) und (10) kennzeichnet deutlich die Maschinerie unserer
Darstellung:

$$(3) \qquad [STORPT;\ go(3);\ E("Press\ button\ when\ complete",3)]$$

Wir dokumentieren die Aktivität STORPT des Internums, erklären (und
protokollieren) dann, daß das Internum in den Zustand 3 geht. Der
nachfolgende Aufruf des Externums ist der Wert des Blocks (3). In
Zeile 16 wird ein Programmblock DLINE verwendet, der eine gezeichnete Strecke auf dem Bildschirm sichtbar macht. In Zeile 25 fragt die
Testroutine DLAST, ob alle Strecken aus einem zuvor aufgebauten Strek-
kenkomplex vom Externum gelöscht worden sind. Die Funktion Special
aktiviert hier nicht weiter dargestellte Sondermaßnahmen, falls das
Externum ein unzulässiges Kommando gibt. In Special können sich

Abbruchkriterien verbergen.

2.2.2 Das Externum. Zum Typ des Beispiels

Die Gleichung des Externums besteht aus der Zeile
$$(1) \qquad E(r,t) = I(t, \text{Telos}(r))$$
Ist also z.B.
$$(2) \qquad r = \text{"Press button to track"}, \quad t = 1$$
so kann
$$(3) \qquad \text{Telos}(r) = \text{button}$$
aber auch
$$(4) \qquad \text{Telos}(r) = \text{"delete"}$$
Benutzerkommando sein.

Die Gleichungen (2.2.1/1) und (2.2.2/1) sind im wesentlichen vom Typ
der Gleichungen (1.1.3/4,5). Man sieht das, wenn man in (1.1.3/4,5)
s mit t identifiziert, u durch c, ferner v durch r ersetzt, schließlich in (1.1.3/4) auf der rechten Seite mehr als zwei Argumente von
in1 zuläßt:

$$(5) \qquad I(t,c) = \text{in1}(E(\text{in41}(c),t), E(\text{in42}(c),t),\ldots)$$

$$(6) \qquad E(r,t) = I(s, \text{ex4}(r))$$

Eine Zustandsvariable s des Externums tritt in unserem einfachen
Modell nicht auf. Würde man von Telos verlangen, einen Entwurfsvor-
gang am Bildschirm in allen Einzelheiten zu modellieren, so bräuchte
man s, und die Gleichung (6) würde eine komplizierte und interessante
Gestalt annehmen.

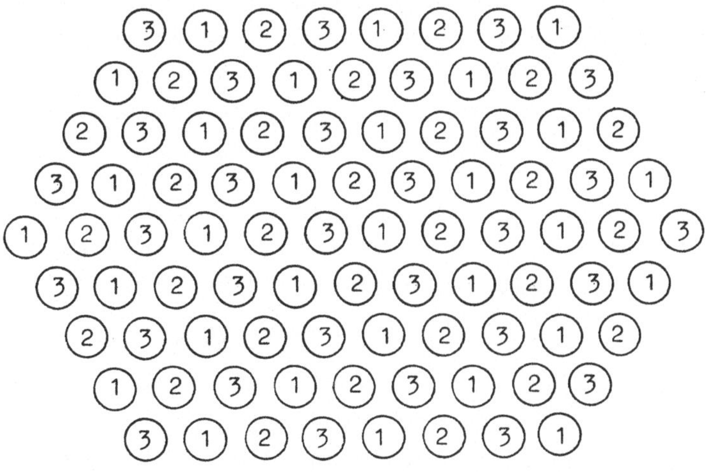

Bild 3
Ein Golayfeld

3   Erweiterte Golaylogik

M.J.E. Golay hat ein Programmiersystem angegeben, das die Transformation von Binärmustern gestattet, die auf einem hexagonalen Feld definiert sind (Golay 69). Die Golaylogik (Preston 71) ermöglicht nicht nur die Klassifikation von Mustern, sondern auch die Ableitung von Mustern auseinander. Elementare Anwendungen der Golaylogik bestehen im Aufschwellen von Flecken (blobs) bis sie konvexen Umriß zeigen, das Füllen von Löchern in Flecken, das Skelettieren von Flecken und die Fleckenabzählung. Auf kompliziertere Anwendungen führen die Wanderoperatoren (traveling operators), die zur Analyse von Fleckbegrenzungen benutzt werden können. Nachdem schon in Golay 69 ein Vorschlag zur Hardwarerealisierung der Golaylogik gemacht wird, enthält Preston 71 die Beschreibung eines Spezialrechners zur Auswertung der Golay logic language (Glol), einer Sprachfassung der Golayoperationen, die auf Golay 69 beruht. Wir stützen uns in unserer Darstellung der Golaylogik mit Hilfe der Landinnotation auf beide genannten Arbeiten.

Hardwarerealisierungen der Golaylogik streben danach, möglichst große Teile der Golayoperationen kollateral abzuwickeln. Zu diesem Zweck muß jedoch das hexagonale Feld, das wir künftig als Golayfeld bezeichnen, so in Teilfelder zerlegt werden, daß ein Ort aus einem Teilfeld i immer von Örtern aus Teilfeldern umgeben ist, die vom Teilfeld i verschieden sind (siehe Bild 3). Dann kann eine Operation, die für jeden Ort vom Zustand des Orts (Besetzung mit 0 oder 1) und von den Zuständen seiner sechs Einfassungsörter abhängt, kollateral auf alle Örter eines Teilfeldes angewandt werden, ohne daß Nichteindeutigkeit der Zustände der Einfassungsörter zu befürchten ist. Golay hat, außer der Zerlegung des hexagonalen Feldes in drei Teilfelder, auch solche in vier und sieben Teilfelder angegeben, deren Gebrauch bei manchen Problemen notwendig werden kann.

In Abschnitt 3.1 werden wir die nötige Terminologie einführen und einige Golayoperationen studieren. Dann folgt in Abschnitt 3.2 eine Spezialisierung des Gleichungssystems

(1) $I(u) = in(u, I, E),   E(v) = ex(v, E, I)$

der Interaktion auf den Fall, in dem u und v Golayfelder sind. In Abschnitt 3.3 werden alle Funktionen angegeben, die für eine in Landinnotation erfolgende Beschreibung der Golaylogik, sowie der von uns hinzugefügten Erweiterungen, benötigt werden.

3.1 Golayoperationen

3.1.1 Golayfelder und ihre Teilfelder

Bei der Einführung der Terminologie halten wir uns anschaulich an
Bild 3. Wir bezeichnen sieben Örter in einem Golayfeld, die eine Kon-
figuration wie in Bild 4 haben, als einen Stern. Der Ort p heißt die
Mitte oder der Mittelort des Sterns. Die Örter e1,...,e6 bezeichnen
wir als die Einfassungsörter des Sterns oder auch seines Mittelorts.
Zusammengenommen bilden die Einfassungsörter die Einfassung des
Sterns oder auch seines Mittelorts. Der Stern heißt auch Stern seines
Mittelorts.

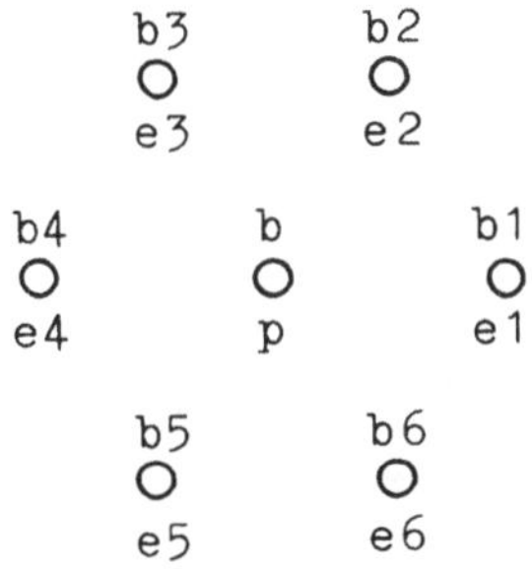

Bild 4
Ein Stern aus einem Golayfeld

Alle Örter in einem Golayfeld, die Mitte eines Sterns sind, bezeichnen wir als Innenörter, ihre Vereinigung als das Innere des Golayfeldes. Das Komplement des Inneren ist der Rand des Golayfelds, die
Örter des Rands heißen Randörter. Ein Golayfeld braucht nicht die
durch Bild 3 gezeigte Gestalt zu zeigen, es muß jedoch eindeutig in
Rand und Inneres derart zerlegbar sein, daß alle Innenörter Sterne
im Golayfeld besitzen.

Jedes Golayfeld ist (im Rahmen dieser Arbeit) Vereinigung von drei
paarweise disjunkten Mengen, die wir als Teilfeld-1, Teilfeld-2 und
Teilfeld-3 bezeichnen. Entstammt der Mittelort eines Sterns dem Teil-
feld-i, so gehören die Einfassungsörter den Teilfeldern-j und -k an,
wobei $i \neq j$, $i \neq k$, $j \neq k$. In Bild 3 ist jeder Ort markiert durch
eine Zahl, die das Feld kennzeichnet, dem der Ort angehört. Bild 5
zeigt die drei möglichen Koinzidenzen eines Sterns mit dem Golayfeld.
Den Durchschnitten der Teilfelder mit dem Inneren des Golayfeldes
geben wir einen besonderen Namen, sie heißen Innenfelder. Wir sprechen auch von den Innenfeldern-1 bis -3 des Golayfeldes.

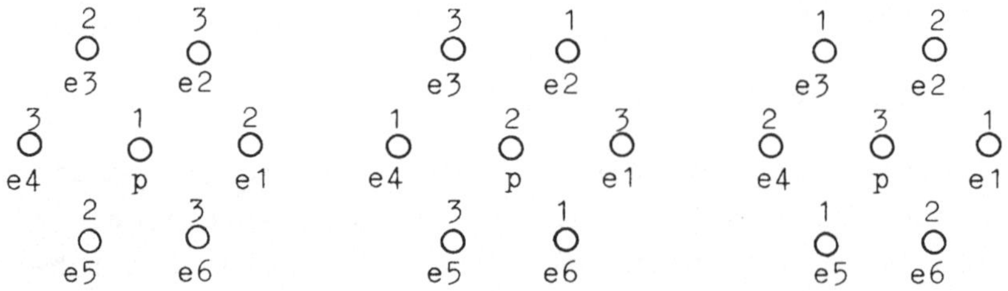

Bild 5
Die möglichen Koinzidenzen eines Sterns mit dem Golayfeld

3.1.2 Die Besetzung des Golayfelds und der Index

Zum Begriff eines jeden Golayfelds gehört eine Abbildung seiner Örter
auf die Menge der Zahlen 0 und 1. Diese Abbildung nennen wir die Besetzung des Golayfelds. Aus der Besetzung eines Golayfelds ergibt
sich die Besetzung seines Inneren, des Randes, der drei Teilfelder,
der drei Innenfelder, sowie die Besetzung eines jeden Orts und Sterns.
Für jede Besetzung eines Golayfelds jedoch gilt: Die Besetzung eines
jeden Randorts ist 0. Die Besetzung eines einzelnen Orts heißt auch
dessen Zustand.

Man kann, wenn man will, von wechselnden Besetzungen eines als unveränderlich gedachten Golayfelds sprechen. Wir setzen allerdings, wenn
von einem Golayfeld die Rede ist, grundsätzlich eine bestimmte Besetzung als gegeben voraus. Wenn wir später Flecken in einem Golayfeld
behandeln, betrachten wir sie immer als Mengen von Örtern im Zustand 1.

In Bild 6 sind die 14 Möglichkeiten der Besetzung der Einfassung
eines Sterns, abgesehen von Drehungen der Einfassung um ganzzahlige
Vielfache von 60 Winkelgraden, dargestellt; jeder Möglichkeit wird
durch Bild 6 eine Zahl zugeordnet, die als der Index des Sterns, jedoch auch als der Index der Mitte und der Einfassung des Sterns bezeichnet wird. Alle Golayoperationen, die zuerst den Zustand des
Golayfelds prüfen, führen diese Prüfung durch, indem sie nach den
Indizes und den Mittelortsbesetzungen der Sterne des Golayfelds fragen. Es sei noch einmal darauf hingewiesen, daß der Index eine In-
variante der Einfassungsbesetzung eines Sterns darstellt, so daß z.B.
allen Besetzungen aus Bild 7 der Index 3 zugeordnet wird.

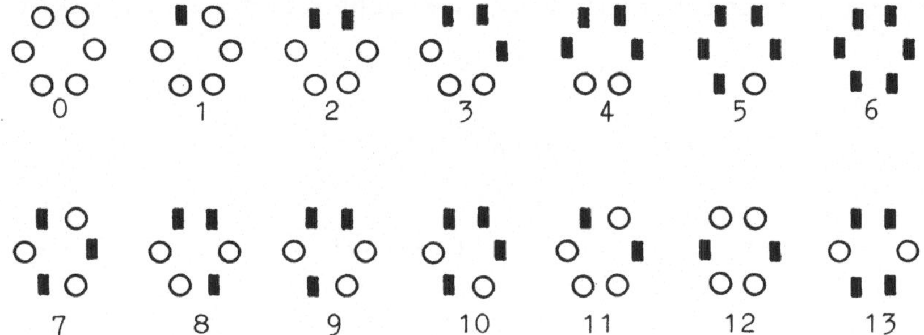

Bild 6
Die möglichen Indizes eines Sterns

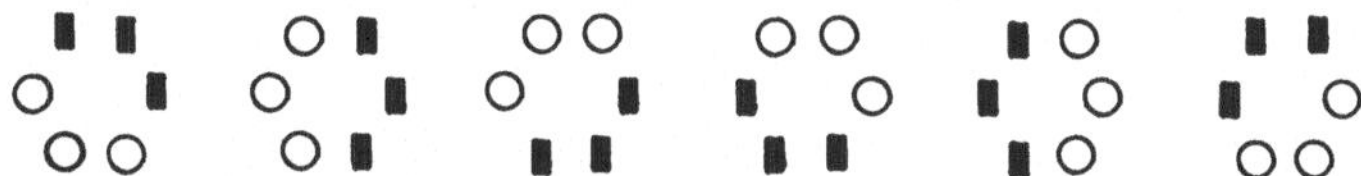

Bild 7
Die möglichen Besetzungen mit dem Index 3

3.1.3 Allgemeine Definition des Golayoperators

Die Terminologie über Golayfelder, die wir jetzt besitzen, reicht
schon aus, um Golayoperationen zu studieren. Zunächst benötigen wir
eine Hilfsfunktion

(1)   Gol(G,a)

Die Funktion Gol bildet das Golayfeld G auf ein neues Golayfeld ab.
Dabei stellt a eine Aktion dar, die auf jeden Stern des Golayfelds
angewandt wird. Es ist a eine Funktion, die zur Ermittlung ihres
Werts den Index des Sterns und dessen Mittelortsbesetzung benutzt.
Der Funktionswert ergibt die neue Besetzung des Mittelorts. Der eigent-
liche Golayoperator

(2)   Golop(G,a,n)

besteht nun aus einer mehrmaligen Anwendung von Gol auf G. Ist
$n \geq 0$, so wird Gol so oft angewandt, als die Zahl n angibt. Ist jedoch n = -1, so wird Gol so oft angewandt, bis in der Folge der
erzeugten Golayfelder zwei aufeinanderfolgende Glieder gleich sind.
Aufgrund dieser Definition läßt sich Golop mit Hilfe von Gol und

zwei Funktionen Rep und Repinf folgendermaßen formal notieren:

$$(3) \quad Golop(G,a,n) = (n=0 \rightarrow G,$$
$$n > 0 \rightarrow Rep(n,Gol,G,a),$$
$$n < 0 \rightarrow Repinf(Gol,G,a))$$

Dabei ist

$$(4) \quad Rep(n,f,G,a) = (n=1 \rightarrow f(G,a),$$
$$T \rightarrow f(Rep(n-1,f,G,a),a))$$

$$(5) \quad Repinf(f,G,a) =$$
$$(y=f(y,a) \rightarrow y, \quad T \rightarrow Repinf(f,y,a))$$
$$where \; y = f(G,a)$$

Auf der Grobheitsstufe der formalen Aufschlüsselung, auf der wir uns
momentan befinden, ist der Golayoperator Golop kollateral angewandt
zu denken auf alle Innenorte (oder Sterne) des Golayfelds G. Diese
Kollateralität bedarf jedoch einer Einschränkung, denn wir haben
schon am Anfang von Abschnitt 3 darauf hingewiesen, daß zum Zweck
der eindeutigen Bestimmung des Index die Golayoperationen hintereinander kollateral auf die drei Einzelfelder des Golayfelds angewandt
werden müssen. Das wäre noch kein Anlaß, bei der in diesem Aufsatz
erfolgenden Darstellung durch eine Sprache ebenso zu verfahren, es
sei denn zum Zweck der Dokumentation von Hardware. Der wichtigste
Grund für die Beibehaltung der Teilfelder besteht jedoch darin, daß
die später verwendeten Schwundoperationen, bei vollständiger Kollateralität, von Flecken nicht den gewünschten Rest übrig lassen, sondern
sie ganz vernichten. Leider kann das Ergebnis von Schwundoperationen
auch von der Reihenfolge der Teilfelder sowie von der Lage des Flecks
im Golayfeld abhängen, doch scheint sich die Abhängigkeit in der
Praxis nur auf Flecken auszuwirken, die aus sehr wenigen Örtern bestehen oder stellenweise sehr schlank sind (siehe auch Golay 69,
Seite 738).

3.1.4 Spezielle Golayoperatoren

Wir betrachten noch einmal den Stern in Bild 4. Die sechs Zahlen

$$(1) \qquad b, \; b1, \; b2, \; b3, \; b4, \; b5, \; b6$$

liefern eine Liste (b,I), wobei I der aus b1,...,b6 ermittelte Index
des Sterns ist. Im Golayoperator (3.1.3/2) ist nun die Aktion a immer
eine Funktion der beiden Parameter b und I mit den Werten 0 oder 1.
z.B. besetzt die Aktion

$$(2) \qquad a014(u,v) = (u=0 \wedge v=14 \rightarrow 1, \; T \rightarrow u)$$

solche Orte mit 1, die vorher im Zustand 0 waren und den Index 14
besaßen. Bei vielen Golayoperationen muß geprüft werden, ob der Index
einer vollständigen Disjunktion von Werten angehört. Dies wird durch
die Funktion

$$(3) \qquad Indor(i,x) = (null(x) \longrightarrow F, T \longrightarrow$$
$$(h(x)=i \longrightarrow T, T \longrightarrow Indor(i,t(x))))$$

bewerkstelligt.

Wir führen nun einige wichtige Golayoperatoren ein. Die Operatoren
(4) und (5) füllen ein Golayfeld (mit Ausnahme des Randes, der von
Anfang an und immer mit Nullen besetzt angenommen wird) mit dem Wert
0 bzw. 1:

$$(4) \qquad Fill0(G) = Gol(G, \lambda(u,v).0)$$

$$(5) \qquad Fill1(G) = Gol(G, \lambda(u,v).1)$$

Der Markierungsoperator markiert Örter mit bestimmten Indizes:

$$(6) \qquad Mark(G, Il) =$$
$$Gol(G, \lambda(u,v).(Indor(v,Il) \longrightarrow 1, T \longrightarrow 0))$$

Ein allgemeiner Schwundoperator:

$$(7) \qquad Shrink(G, Il, n) =$$
$$Golop(G, \lambda(u,v).(u=1 \wedge Indor(v,Il) \longrightarrow 0, T \longrightarrow u), n)$$

Ein allgemeiner Schwelloperator:

$$(8) \qquad Swell(G, Il, n) =$$
$$Golop(G, \lambda(u,v).(u=0 \wedge Indor(v,Il) \longrightarrow 1, T \longrightarrow u), n)$$

Wir beenden damit die allgemeinen Angaben über die Golaylogik und
verweisen für weitere Anwendungen auf Golay 69 und Preston 71.

3.2   Ein Regelungsproblem

Interaktionsprobleme, bei denen Muster von Bedeutung sind, existieren
in großer Anzahl. Eine wichtige Beispielklasse bildet die optische
Analyse eines Environments durch eine Maschine oder einen Organismus,
wobei der Analysator gegebenenfalls den Ort oder die Anpassung seiner
Optik wechseln muß oder sogar den Analysanden verändert. Eine Teil-
klasse dieser Klasse bildet die automatische Analyse photographischer
Aufnahmen aller Art. Eine andere Klasse liefern Brettspiele, wobei
vor allem solche mit hexagonaler Feldeinteilung in Frage kommen.

Wir behandeln ein Beispiel aus der ersten der obengenannten Klassen,
das insofern über den Umfang der Golaylogik in Abschnitt 3.1

hinausgeht, als die Verschiebung eines Flecks in einer bestimmten
Richtung im Golayfeld eine Rolle spielt. Angenommen sei ein Golayfeld von der in Bild 8 gezeigten Gestalt. Die sechs Sektoren

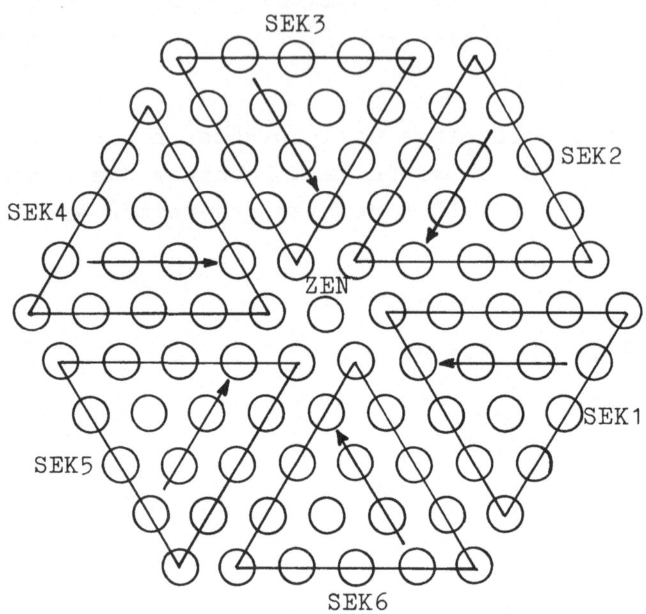

Bild 8
Ein radialsymmetrisches Golayfeld

beachten wir noch nicht. Im Golayfeld befinde sich ein einziger
Fleck, der einfach zusammenhängend ist, d.h. keine Löcher hat. Gestellt wird folgendes Problem: Das Golayfeld stelle die Retina eines
Auges dar, das den Fleck beobachtet. Das Auge gehöre dem Internum,
das die Fähigkeit hat, den Fleck im Golayfeld zu verschieben. Die
Verschiebung soll dafür sorgen, daß der Fleck ungefähr in der Mitte
des Golayfelds bleibt. Aktive Drehungen des Flecks durch das Internum
schließen wir aus. Das Externum soll die Möglichkeit haben, den Fleck
während des Regelungsvorganges zu ändern, jedoch nicht die Fähigkeit,
den Fleck in mehrere getrennte Flecken zu zerlegen.

Folgender Lösungsansatz wird gemacht:

(1) $I(g) = (bare(g) \longrightarrow fin, T \longrightarrow E(Zentrier(g)))$

(2) $E(h) = I(Change(h))$

Es sind g und h Golayfelder. Die Arbeit des Internums besteht darin,
den Fleck zu zentrieren und dann das Externum zu aktivieren, falls
nicht bare(g) eintritt, d.h. kein Fleck mehr existiert. Das Externum

ändert den Fleck und ruft wieder das Internum. Das Gleichungssystem
(1), (2) beschreibt das Problem jedoch nicht eindeutig. Außer vielleicht noch verwickelteren sind die beiden folgenden Anordnungen
denkbar:

a) Der Fleck ist ein Gebilde, zu dem Internum und Externum in gleicher Weise Zugriff haben, z.B. so, daß der Fleck durch lauter
gleiche Spielfiguren auf einem hexagonalen, wie Bild 8 aufgebauten Brett realisiert ist, wobei der Rand des durch Bild 8 dargestellten Golayfelds nicht auf dem Brett erscheint. Die Retina des
Internums besteht dann aus Sensoren, die feststellen, ob das Brett
an einer Stelle durch einen Stein besetzt ist oder nicht. Die
Zentrierung durch das Internum greift jedoch verschiebend an den
Steinen an. Dem Externum ist die Änderung der Anzahl der Steine
auf dem Brett gestattet.

b) Das Internum sieht den Fleck nur und verschiebt ihn dadurch auf
seiner Retina, daß es die Stellung der Retina zum Fleck ändert.
Also verschiebt das Internum nicht den Fleck selbst, sondern nur
sein Bild. Hat das Externum den Fleck teilweise aus dem Sehfeld
hinausgeschoben, so zentriert das Internum nur den Teil des Flecks,
den es sieht. Das braucht natürlich nicht zu einer Fehlfunktion
des Regelungsvorganges zu führen. Allerdings ist der Aufruf von E
in (1) jetzt nicht so deutbar, daß das Internum den Fleck an das
Externum zurückgibt. Vielmehr bedeutet Change(h) in (2) eine völlige Neuschaffung des Flecks durch das Externum. Der Aufruf von E
in Gleichung (1) modelliert also die Neuzuwendung der wandernden
Retina zum optisch erfaßten und als Urbild existierenden Objekt.

In beiden Fällen a und b verliert das Internum sein Objekt, wenn
dieses durch das Externum aus dem Erfassungsbereich der Retina entfernt wird, d.h. wenn bare(g) eintritt. Für die Operation Change des
Externums geben wir nur ein Beispiel:

(3)   Change(h) = Rep(J1, Shift, h, J2)

In (3) ist Rep der Wiederholungsoperator (3.1.3/4), der z.B. bei
J1 = 3 das Golayfeld

(4)   Shift(Shift(Shift(h, J2), J2), J2)

erzeugt. J1 und J2 sind Zufallsgeneratoren mit Gleichverteilung,
wobei

(5) $1 \leqq J1 \leqq Jmax, 1 \leqq J2 \leqq 6$

gilt. Die Funktion Shift wird auch im nächsten Abschnitt benötigt
werden, sie verschiebt alle im Golayfeld h vorhandenen Einsen um

eine Elementarstrecke in der Richtung J2 (siehe Bild 9). Es ist also Change, definiert man es durch Gleichung (3), ein Irrweg der Länge höchstens Jmax aller Einsen im Golayfeld.

In den Abschnitten 3.2.1 und 3.2.2 werden wir das Gleichungssystem (1), (2) weiter aufschlüsseln. Da die in Abschnitt 3.1 erläuterten Golayoperationen keine der in Bild 8 eingezeichneten Hauptrichtungen bevorzugen, muß zur formalen Lösung des Regelungsproblems zunächst ein zusätzlicher Apparat geschaffen werden.

3.2.1 Sektoreinteilung im Golayfeld. Verschiebung

Wenn wir vom Golayfeld als von einer Retina sprechen, gehen wir zu einer Auffassung über, die wir schon in Abschnitt 3.1.2 erwähnt haben: Wir betrachten wechselnde Besetzungen eines als unveränderlich gedachten Golayfelds. Der Golayoperator

$$(1) \qquad Golop(G,a,n)$$

(siehe (3.1.3/2)) werde also von jetzt an als eine Funktion interpretiert, die aus der Instanz G eines Golayfeldes eine neue Instanz des gleichen Feldes mit neuer Besetzung erzeugt. Diese Betrachtungsweise entspricht der Tatsache, daß der Golayoperator (1) die Struktur (das Substrat) von G invariant läßt, wie in Abschnitt 3.3.2 auch formal gezeigt werden wird, was wir aber auch anschaulich immer so verstanden haben.

Wir wenden uns nun der Gestaltung des zusätzlichen Apparats zur Lösung des Regelungsproblems zu. Das Innere des radialsymmetrischen Golayfelds sei Vereinigung von sieben paarweise fremden Mengen, nämlich dem Mittelpunkt ZEN und sechs kongruenten Sektoren SEK1,...SEK6 oder auch Sektor-1 bis Sektor-6 (siehe Bild 8). Es gebe einen Prädikator

$$(2) \qquad Insek(G,p,i)$$

der prüft, ob der Innenort p im Sektor-i des Golayfelds G liegt. Ist (2) wahr, so kann der Ort p (der i-te Einfassungsort in Bild 9) dem Mittelpunkt ZEN genähert werden, indem p mit dem in Richtung i gemäß Bild 9 nächstgelegenen Ort zur Deckung gebracht wird (die Mitte in Bild 9). Die Verschiebung besorge ein Operator

$$(3) \qquad Shift(G,i)$$

der eine Instanz von G erzeugt, in der alle in G mit 1 besetzten Örter um eine Elementarstrecke in Richtung i verschoben werden. Die Begriffe Elementarstrecke und Elementarabstand sind klar. Durch

wiederholte Anwendung von Shift in der vom jeweiligen Sektor vorgeschriebenen Richtung kann p nach ZEN gebracht werden (siehe Abschnitt
3.2.2).

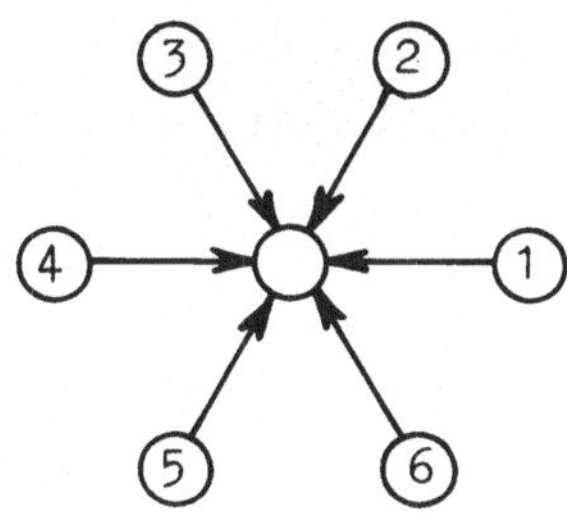

Bild 9
Die sechs Verschiebungsrichtungen

Der Operator Shift kann als Spezialfall einer allgemeinen, als Struk-
turoperator zu bezeichnenden Funktion aufgefaßt werden, die mit dem
Golayoperator Golop verwandt ist (siehe Abschnitt 3.1.3):

(4)   Strop(G,a)

Wie Golop und Gol verändert auch Strop die Besetzung b eines jeden
Ortes des Golayfelds in den Wert a. Die Besetzungsänderung durch
Strop ist jedoch nicht eine Funktion von Besetzung und Index der
Örter allein, sondern von der detaillierten Besetzung der Sterne des
Golayfelds. Anders ausgedrückt ist a eine Funktion aller sieben Werte

(5)   b, b1, b2, b3, b4, b5, b6

(siehe Bild 4), zerlegt allerdings in die beiden Größen b und
(b1,...,b6). Nun können wir Shift auf Strop zurückführen: Es ist

(6)   Shift(G,i) = Strop(G, λ(u,v).(Dortone(i,v) $\rightarrow$ 1, T $\rightarrow$ 0))

Dabei ist der Prädikator

(7)   Dortone(i,v) =
       (i=1 $\rightarrow$ el1(v)=1, i=2 $\rightarrow$ el2(v)=1, i=3 $\rightarrow$ el3(v)=1,
        i=4 $\rightarrow$ el4(v)=1, i=5 $\rightarrow$ el5(v)=1, i=6 $\rightarrow$ el6(v)=1)

wahr, wenn das i-te Element der Liste v gleich 1 ist. In Abschnitt
3.3.4 wird der formale Aufbau von Shift und Strop behandelt. Auch auf
die Funktion Insek wird dort eingegangen.

3.2.2 Nabel eines Flecks und Zentrierung

Unter Zuhilfenahme der Schwundoperation definieren wir einen in
einem einfach zusammenhängenden Fleck, der als einziger im Golayfeld
anwesend ist, zentral gelegenen Punkt, den Nabel:

(1)   Nabel(G) = Isol(Golop(G,

  λ(u,v).(u=1 $\wedge$ ~Indor(v, 1:(2:(3:(4:$\emptyset$))))) $\rightarrow$ 1, T $\rightarrow$ 0),-1))

Der Golayoperator in (1) leert das Golayfeld bis auf den Nabel aus.
Die Funktion Isol isoliert dann den Nabel aus dem durch den Golayoperator erzeugten Golayfeld (siehe Abschnitt 3.3.3, Ausdrücke (15)
bis (17)).

Mit Hilfe des Nabels und der Operation Shift kann man einen ganzen
Fleck verschieben, ja man kann ihn zentrieren, d.h. den Nabel mit
dem Mittelpunkt ZEN des Golayfelds verschmelzen lassen:

(2)   Zentrier(G) =
           (N=ZEN $\rightarrow$ G,
             Insek(G,N,1) $\rightarrow$ Zentrier(Shift(G,1)),
             Insek(G,N,2) $\rightarrow$ Zentrier(Shift(G,2)),
             Insek(G,N,3) $\rightarrow$ Zentrier(Shift(G,3)),
             Insek(G,N,4) $\rightarrow$ Zentrier(Shift(G,4)),
             Insek(G,N,5) $\rightarrow$ Zentrier(Shift(G,5)),
             Insek(G,N,6) $\rightarrow$ Zentrier(Shift(G,6)))
           where N = Nabel(G)

Jetzt fehlt nur noch die Definition von bare:

(3)   bare(G) = (Count(G,1)=0)

Die Funktion Count(G,m) gibt an, wieviele Innenörter im Golayfeld G
mit dem Wert m besetzt sind (siehe Schluß von Abschnitt 3.3.3).

3.3 Der funktionale Aufbau der Golaylogik

Zu bestimmen ist insbesondere der Aufbau der Funktion Gol (siehe
(3.1.3/1)). Wie in Abschnitt 3.1.3 erklärt, bildet

(1)   Gol(G,a)

das Golayfeld G auf ein zweites Golayfeld ab. Was wir also zuerst
benötigen, ist eine Beschreibung der Struktur des Golayfelds.

3.3.1 Das Golayfeld als Liste

Wir beschreiben das Golayfeld als eine Liste

(1)   (IF1, IF2, IF3)

Die Namen in (1) bedeuten drei Listen, die wir als Innenfeldliste-1,
Innenfeldliste-2 und Innenfeldliste-3 bezeichnen. Eine Innenfeldliste-i

enthält als Elemente die Beschreibungen aller Sterne des Teilfelds-i des Golayfelds. Dabei wird jeder Stern gemäß Bild 4 dargestellt durch den als Sternliste bezeichneten Ausdruck

$$(2) \qquad (p, b, (e1, e2, e3, e4, e5, e6))$$

In (2) bezeichnet p die Mitte des Sterns, b seine Mittelortsbesetzung, e1,...,e6 bedeuten seine Einfassungsörter. Wir zögern nicht, den Ausdruck (2) als Stern zu bezeichnen, oder eine der Innenfeldlisten als Innenfeld, oder den Ausdruck (1) als Golayfeld.

3.3.2 Die Behandlung der Innenfeldlisten

Der Ausdruck (3.3.1/1) erlaubt folgende Definition:

$$(1) \qquad Gol(G,a) = Golif(1,G,a):$$
$$(Golif(2,G,a):(Golif(3,G,a):\emptyset))$$

In (1) hat jeder Aufruf von Golif die Aufgabe, eines der drei Innenfelder von G abzutasten und dabei eines der Innenfelder von Gol aufzubauen. Die Wirkung von Golif kann als kollateral betrachtet werden. Erfaßt werden bei der Abtastung die Sterne des Innenfelds-i, wobei mit Hilfe der Einfassungsörter eines jeden Sterns (3.3.1/2) aus den anderen beiden Innenfeldern-j und -k die Information für den Index des Sterns gewonnen wird. Golif bezieht sich daher notwendig auf alle drei Innenfelder-i, -j, -k, so daß eine Hilfsfunktion Goif benötigt wird, die die drei Innenfelder berücksichtigt:

$$(2) \quad Golif(i,G,a) =$$
$$Goif(If(i,G), If(Koll1(i),G), If(Koll2(i),G),a)$$

In (2) ist If ein Selektor, der das passende Innenfeld-i von G aus dem Golayfeld auswählt:

$$(3) \quad If(i,G) = (i=1 \rightarrow el1(G), i=2 \rightarrow el2(G), T \rightarrow el3(G))$$

Die Funktionen Koll1 und Koll2 in (2) besorgen die richtigen Zahlen j und k, wenn vom Innenfeld-i ausgegangen wird:

$$(4) \qquad Koll1(i) = (i=1 \rightarrow 2, i=2 \rightarrow 3, T \rightarrow 1)$$

$$(5) \qquad Koll2(i) = (i=1 \rightarrow 3, i=2 \rightarrow 1, T \rightarrow 2)$$

Es fehlt noch die Definition von Goif:

$$(6) \quad Goif(u,v,w,a) = (null(u) \rightarrow \emptyset, T \rightarrow$$
$$(h(h(u)):(a(Sterl(h(u),v,w)):(el3(h(u)):\emptyset))):$$
$$Goif(t(u),v,w,a))$$

Hier seien u, v und w Innenfeldlisten. In der rechten Seite von (6)

scheint jetzt der Mechanismus von Gol auf. Man vergegenwärtige sich
nämlich, daß Goif die Liste u abtastet, um mit Hilfe der Listen v
und w die Indizes der Sterne von u zu bestimmen. Ist

$$(7) \qquad \text{Sterl}(s,v,w)$$

eine Funktion, deren Parameter s einen Stern und deren Parameter v
und w Innenfelder bezeichnen, hat ferner s wie bekannt die Gestalt

$$(8) \qquad (p, \ b, \ (e1,\ldots,e6))$$

und baut Sterl das Paar

$$(9) \qquad (b, \ I)$$

auf, in dem I der Index des Sterns (8) ist, so produziert der Spezialfall

$$(10) \qquad h(s):(a(\text{Sterl}(s,v,w))):(e13(s):\emptyset)$$

der zweiten Zeile von (6) aus (8) den neuen Stern

$$(11) \qquad (p, \ c, \ (e1,\ldots,e6))$$

in dem

$$(12) \qquad c = a(\text{Sterl}(s,v,w)) = a(b,I)$$

ist. Die Funktion Goif ändert also nicht die Struktur der Innenfeldliste, sondern nur die Besetzung der Innenörter.

3.3.3 Die Ermittlung des Index. Die Funktionen Isol und Count

Aus den Betrachtungen zur Funktion Sterl im vorhergehenden Abschnitt
folgt bereits, daß Sterl folgendermaßen dargestellt werden kann:

$$(1) \qquad \text{Sterl}(s,v,w) = e12(s):(\text{Index}(s,v,w):\emptyset)$$

Hier bestimmt die Funktion Index den Index des Sterns s, wobei v und
w die Innenfelder bedeuten, in denen s nicht vorkommt. Der Ansatz

$$(2) \qquad \text{Index}(s,v,w) = (\text{only}(0,j) \rightarrow 0, \ \text{only}(1,j) \rightarrow 6,$$
$$T \rightarrow \text{Ind}(\text{Canred}(j)))$$
$$\text{where } j = \text{join}(s,v,w)$$
$$\text{and only} = \wedge(x,y).(\text{null}(y) \rightarrow T,$$
$$h(y){\neq}x \rightarrow F, \ T \rightarrow \text{only}(x,t(y)))$$

beruht auf folgender Überlegung: Ist

$$(3) \qquad (b1, \ b2, \ b3, \ b4, \ b5, \ b6)$$

die Liste der Zustände der Einfassungen des Sterns s, von einem Einfassungsort aus im Gegenuhrzeigersinn abgenommen, ist ferner

$$(4) \qquad (d1, \ d2, \ d3, \ d4, \ d5, \ d6)$$

eine Liste, die aus (3) durch mehrmalige zyklische Permutation der Elemente hervorgeht, so kann man für alle Indizes außer den Indizes 0 und 6 (siehe Bild 6) die Liste (4) so bestimmen, daß sie die Gestalt

$$(5) \qquad\qquad (0,\ 1,\ g1,\ g2,\ g3,\ g4)$$

annimmt. Wir nennen die Liste $(g1,g2,g3,g4)$ eine kanonische Reduktion der Liste (3). Eine kanonische Reduktion einer Liste aus Zahlen 0 und 1 kann durch die Funktion

$$(6) \qquad\qquad Canred(x)\ =\ t(t(Zyk01(x)))$$

gefunden werden, wobei

$$(7) \qquad Zyk01(x)\ =\ (h(x){=}0\ \wedge\ el2(x){=}1\ \longrightarrow\ x,$$
$$T\ \longrightarrow\ Zyk01(Zykperm(x)))$$

und

$$(8) \qquad Zykperm(x)\ =\ append(t(x),\ h(x){:}\emptyset)$$

ist. Durch

$$(9) \qquad append(x,y)\ =\ (null(x)\ \longrightarrow\ y,$$
$$T\ \longrightarrow\ h(x){:}append(t(x),y))$$

wird die Liste y an die Liste x angehängt. Hat man nun die kanonisch reduzierte Liste $(g1,g2,g3,g4)$, so kann man anhand von Bild 6 leicht ein Entscheidungsverfahren angeben, das die Indizes des zu Liste (3) gehörigen Sterns errechnet, die ungleich 0 oder 6 sind:

$$(10) \quad Ind(a,b,c,d)\ =$$
$$(a{=}0\ \longrightarrow\ (b{=}0\ \longrightarrow\ (c{=}0\ \longrightarrow\ (d{=}0\ \longrightarrow\ 1,\ d{=}1\ \longrightarrow\ 11),$$
$$c{=}1\ \longrightarrow\ (d{=}0\ \longrightarrow\ 12,\ d{=}1\ \longrightarrow\ 9)),$$
$$b{=}1\ \longrightarrow\ (c{=}0\ \longrightarrow\ (d{=}0\ \longrightarrow\ 11,\ d{=}1\ \longrightarrow\ 7),$$
$$c{=}1\ \longrightarrow\ (d{=}0\ \longrightarrow\ 8,\ d{=}1\ \longrightarrow\ 10))),$$
$$a{=}1\ \longrightarrow\ (b{=}0\ \longrightarrow\ (c{=}0\ \longrightarrow\ (d{=}0\ \longrightarrow\ 2,\ d{=}1\ \longrightarrow\ 8),$$
$$c{=}1\ \longrightarrow\ (d{=}0\ \longrightarrow\ 9,\ d{=}1\ \longrightarrow\ 13)),$$
$$b{=}1\ \longrightarrow\ (c{=}0\ \longrightarrow\ (d{=}0\ \longrightarrow\ 3,\ d{=}1\ \longrightarrow\ 10),$$
$$c{=}1\ \longrightarrow\ (d{=}0\ \longrightarrow\ 4,\ d{=}1\ \longrightarrow\ 5))))$$

Aus (10) geht auch hervor, daß jeweils zwei verschiedene kanonische Reduktionen zu den Indizes 8 bis 11 führen.

Im Besitz der Funktion Ind befindlich kehren wir jetzt zum Ansatz (2) zurück. Da only und Canred auf eine Liste j von der Art von Liste (3) einwirken, muß join aus s, v und w eine solche Liste erzeugen. Nun hat ja s die Gestalt (3.3.2/8) und v und w sind die Innenfeldlisten, in denen der Stern nicht vorkommt. Man kann deshalb die Aufgabe so

beschreiben: join soll mit Hilfe von s, u, v die Liste (p1,...,p6)
der Einfassungsörter auf die Liste (b1,...,b6) ihrer Besetzungen ab-
bilden (siehe Bild 4). Die Bilder 3 und 5 lehren uns aber, daß join
die Liste (b1,...,b6) aus den beiden Listen (b1,b3,b5) und (b2,b4,b6)
zusammenbauen muß. Deshalb machen wir den Ansatz

(11)   join(s,v,w) = mix(blhalf(el1(q),el3(q),el5(q),v),
            blhalf(el2(q),el4(q),el6(q),w)) where q = el3(s)

in welchem

(12)   mix(x,y) =
        el1(x):(el1(y):(el2(x):(el2(y):(el3(x):(el3(y):$\emptyset$)))))

und blhalf der Lieferant der beiden Hälften von (b1,...,b6) ist:

(13)   blhalf(f,g,h,u) = sbes(f,u):(sbes(g,u):(sbes(h,u):$\emptyset$))

Es ist sbes der Selektor, der aus einer Teilfeldliste die Besetzung
eines Orts auswählt:

(14)   sbes(p,u) = (null(u) $\rightarrow$ 0,
        h(h(u))=p $\rightarrow$ el2(h(u)), T $\rightarrow$ sbes(p,t(u)))

Die rechte Seite von (14) zeigt auch, wie die Besetzung 0 der Randörter, die ja in keiner Innenfeldliste vorkommen, in die Bestimmung
des Index einbezogen wird.

Damit ist die Konstruktion des Golayoperators abgeschlossen. Ein Problem, das in diesem Aufsatz nicht gelöst wird, ist die Angabe eines
Konstruktors für das erste verwendete Golayfeld.

In Abschnitt 3.2.2 wird eine Funktion Isol benötigt, die aus einem
nur an einem einzigen Innenort mit 1 besetzten Golayfeld den so besetzten Ort isoliert. Da wir jetzt den Aufbau des Golayfelds als einer
Liste kennen, ist die Bestimmung von Isol nicht schwer:

(15)   Isol(G) =
        getort(gort(el1(G)):(gort(el2(G)):(gort(el3(G)):$\emptyset$)))

In (15) durchsucht gort je eine Innenfeldliste nach dem gewünschten
Ort. Es ist deshalb

(16)   gort(x) = (null(x) $\rightarrow$ $\emptyset$,
            el2(h(x))=1 $\rightarrow$ h(h(x)), T $\rightarrow$ gort(t(x)))

Die dreimalige Anwendung von gort in (15) erzeugt eine Liste (q,$\emptyset$,$\emptyset$)
oder eine Liste ($\emptyset$,q,$\emptyset$) oder eine Liste ($\emptyset$,$\emptyset$,q), wobei q der gesuchte
Ort ist. Schließlich isoliert

$$(17) \qquad getort(d) = (h(d){\neq}\emptyset \rightarrow h(d),$$
$$T \rightarrow getort(t(d)))$$

den gesuchten Ort aus der Hilfsliste d mit der Länge 3.

Am Schluß von Abschnitt 3.2.2 wird die Funktion

$$(18) \qquad Count(G,m)$$

verwendet, die angibt, wieviele Örter im Golayfeld G mit m besetzt sind. Wir machen einen mit (15) verwandten Ansatz:

$$(19) \qquad Count(G,m) = Con(el1(G),m)+Con(el2(G),m)+Con(el3(G),m)$$

$$(20) \qquad Con(x,m) = (null(x) \rightarrow 0, T \rightarrow$$
$$(m=el2(h(x)) \rightarrow 1, T \rightarrow 0) + Con(t(x),m))$$

3.3.4 Richtungsabhängige Erweiterung der Golaylogik

Die Konstruktion des in 3.2.1 benötigten Strukturoperators

$$(1) \qquad Strop(G,a)$$

erfolgt analog zu der von Gol:

$$(2) \qquad Strop(G,a) = Golifs(1,G,a):$$
$$(Golifs(2,G,a):(Golifs(3,G,a):\emptyset))$$

$$(3) \qquad Golifs(i,G,a) =$$
$$Goifs(If(i,G), If(Koll1(i),G), If(Koll2(i),G),a)$$

$$(4) \qquad Goifs(u,v,w,a) = (null(u) \rightarrow \emptyset, T \rightarrow$$
$$h(h(u)):(a(Sters(h(u),v,w)):(el3(h(u)):\emptyset))):$$
$$Goifs(t(u),v,w,a))$$

$$(5) \qquad Sters(s,v,w) = el2(s):(join(s,v,w):\emptyset)$$

Hier ermittelt, wie schon in Abschnitt 3.3.3 erläutert wurde, join die Liste (b1,...,b6) der Besetzungen der Einfassungen des Sterns s.

Schließlich ist noch ein Wort zur Funktion Insek zu sagen (siehe (3.2.1/2)). Wir haben in Abschnitt 3.2.1 die Innenortsmengen

$$(6) \qquad SEK1, SEK2, SEK3, SEK4, SEK5, SEK6$$

eingeführt, die man jedoch auch als Selektoren

$$(7) \qquad SEK1(G),..., SEK6(G)$$

interpretieren kann, die aus dem Golayfeld G je eine Sternmenge auswählen. Dann ist Insek der Selektor

(8)   Insek(G,p,i) =
         (i=1 → Ins(SEK1(G)), i=2 → Ins(SEK2(G)),
          i=3 → Ins(SEK3(G)), i=4 → Ins(SEK4(G)),
          i=5 → Ins(SEK5(G)), i=6 → Ins(SEK6(G)))
         where Ins = λx.(null(x) → F,
                 p=h(h(x)) → T, T → Ins(t(x)))

Literaturverzeichnis

R.M. Burstall: Proving properties of programs by structural in-
     duction. Comp. J. 12, 1969

A. Church: The calculi of Lambda conversion. Annals of mathematics
     studies 6, Princeton 1941

H.B. Curry, R. Feys: Combinatory logic, vol. 1. Amsterdam 1958

M.J.E. Golay: Hexagonal parallel pattern transformations. IEEE Trans-
     actions on Computers, vol. C-18, No. 8, 1969

G. Görz: Die Sprache GEDANKEN als Beitrag zur syntaktischen und
     semantischen Definition von Programmiersprachen (Diplomarbeit).
     Arbeitsberichte des Instituts für mathematische Maschinen und
     Datenverarbeitung. Prof. Dr. Wolfgang Händler. Friedrich-
     Alexander-Universität Erlangen-Nürnberg, Band 5, No. 6,
     Erlangen 1972

D.E. Knuth: The art of computer programming, vol. 1. Reading, Mass.
     1968

P.J. Landin: The mechanical evaluation of expressions. Comp. J. 6, 1964

P.J. Landin: A correspondece between ALGOL 60 and Church's Lambda-
     notation. CACM 8, 1965 (2 Teile)

P.J. Landin: The next 700 programming languages. CACM 9, 1966

P. Lucas, K. Walk: On the formal description of PL/1. In: Ann. Rev.
     of Automatic Programming, Vol. 6, Oxford 1969

J. McCarthy: Recursive functions of symbolic expressions and their
     computation by machine. CACM 3, 1960

J. McCarthy: A formal description of a subset of ALGOL. In: T.B.
   Steel (ed.), Formal language description languages for computer
   programming. Amsterdam 1966

J.H. Morris: Lambda-calculus models of programming languages.
   Cambridge, Mass. 1968

G. Nees: Strukturunterschiede bei graphischen Programmiersprachen.
   Berichte von der Tagung "Graphische Programmiersprachen" des
   German Chapter ACM, Erlangen, 1. Dez. 1972. Erscheint 1973

W.M. Newman: A system for interactive graphical programming. Spring
   Joint Computer Conference, 1968

K. Preston, jr.: Feature extraction by Golay hexagonal pattern transforms. IEEE Transactions on Computers, vol. C-20, No. 9, 1971

J. Reynolds: GEDANKEN - A simple typeless language based on the
   principle of completeness and the reference concept. CACM 13,
   1970

P. Wegner: The Vienna definition language. ACM computing surveys 4,
   1972

Mustererkennung durch adaptive geometrische Transformationen

H. Marko[+]

Z u s a m m e n f a s s u n g

Die bekannten mathematischen Methoden der Mustererkennung benutzen für die Signaldarstellung einen Raum hoher Dimension, den sog. Nachrichtenraum, dessen Koordinaten die Abtastwerte (oder Bildpunkte) des diskret dargestellten Signals sind. Die notwendige Vorverarbeitung (Merkmalsextraktion) und die anschließende Klassifizierung werden als Operation in diesem Nachrichtenraum durchgeführt.

In dieser Arbeit wird gezeigt, daß der Nachrichtenraum für Mustererkennungsaufgaben nicht trivialer Art, wie z.B. handgeschriebene Zeichen oder geometrische Objekte in beliebiger Lage im Raum eine ungeeignete Darstellung des Problems ist. Dies beruht darauf, daß die Verteilung der zu den verschiedenen Klassen gehörenden Muster als Punkte im Nachrichtenraum im allgemeinen durchmischt und daher nicht separabel ist. Daran ändern auch die oft angewandten linearen Transformationen nichts (z.B. Fourier-Transformation, Loève-Karhunen-Transformation, Hadamard-Transformation), da diese nur eine Translation und Rotation des Nachrichtenraumes bewirken, ohne seine innere Struktur zu verändern. Es wird daher in dieser Arbeit vorgeschlagen, anstelle des vieldimensionalen Nachrichtenraums den Raum der realen Welt zu betrachten und in diesem Koordinatentransformationen durchzuführen. Die einfachsten Transformationen dieser Art sind die geometrischen Transformationen infolge der Lageveränderung der Objekte. Sie haben 6 Freiheitsgrade, nämlich 3 Translationen und 3 Rotationen entsprechend den 3 Raumkoordinaten. Bei Einbeziehung der linearen Vergrößerung des Objekts unter Beibehaltung der Form ergeben sich 7 Freiheitsgrade, die wiederum bei Vernachlässigung der perspektivischen Verzerrungen des Objektbildes auf 6 reduziert werden können. Das nach dieser Theorie vorgeschlagene Erkennungssystem führt diese geometrischen Transformationen bzw. Rücktransformationen in adaptiver Weise durch, wobei als Indikator für die Annäherung eine Kreuzkorrelation mit einem die Musterklasse repräsentierenden idealen Prototyp vorgesehen ist. Bei räumlichen Objekten kann für diese Korrelation nur die Projektion des Objektes auf das zweidimensionale Bildfeld verwendet werden, wodurch gewisse Mehrdeutigkeiten nicht absolut auszuschließen sind, es sei denn, das Objekt wird bewegt oder von verschiedenen Seiten her betrachtet. Das Erkennungssystem führt somit eine adaptive geometrische Transformation nach 6 oder 7 Freiheitsgraden im Sinne einer Optimierung durch. Anders ausgedrückt wird ein räumlich-geometrisches Zielfindungsverfahren (tracking) durchgeführt, mit dem der Mustererkennungsvorgang untrennbar verbunden ist. Es ist zu erwarten, daß dieses Verfahren sowohl für planare Objekte, wie z.B. handgeschriebene Zeichen, als auch für räumliche Objekte bei einer relativ einfachen Realisierung zu wesentlich besseren Ergebnissen führt als die bisherigen auf Transformationen im Nachrichtenraum beruhenden Verfahren.

1. Einleitung

Seitdem es Rechenmaschinen gibt, mit der Möglichkeit, große Mengen von Daten zu verarbeiten, wird das Problem der Zeichenerkennung in der ganzen Welt untersucht.

[+] Diese Arbeit entstand während des Studienaufenthaltes des Verfassers im Image Processing Laboratory der University of Southern California in Los Angeles im Sommer 1972. Für die Ermöglichung dieses Studienaufenthaltes ist der Verfasser Herrn Professor Dr. W. Pratt (U.S.C.) sowie Herrn Dr. R. Kay (IBM) zu Dank verpflichtet.

Eine immense Menge von Literatur, die ständig zunimmt, wurde produziert. Mathematische Methoden wurden entwickelt, zum großen Teil unter Verwendung statistischer Verfahren der Entscheidungstheorie [1], [2]. Ihre Komplexität wuchs beachtlich, mit dem Ziel, sie möglichst generell anwendbar und in bezug auf bestimmte Kriterien optimal zu gestalten. Die Anwendung dieser Methoden auf praktische Probleme der Mustererkennung hat allerdings bisher recht dürftige Ergebnisse gebracht, insbesondere, wenn man diese mit den erstaunlichen Eigenschaften der Lebewesen für die Lösung von Mustererkennungsaufgaben vergleicht. Weiterhin verlangt die Realisierung dieser Methoden einen solchen Aufwand von Rechenkapazität, daß sie mit der heutigen Rechenmaschinentechnologie nicht ökonomisch durchführbar sind. Aus diesen Gründen ist zur Zeit eine große Enttäuschung in bezug auf die Anwendung von Zeichenerkennungsmethoden feststellbar, die in vielen Fällen zu einer Änderung von Forschungsprojekten geführt hat. Anstelle der Mustererkennung werden heute die Methoden der Bildverbesserung und Bildentzerrung intensiv untersucht [3], [4], [5]. Dies beruht zum Teil auch darauf, daß die bisher entwickelten Methoden der Zeichenerkennung sich eher für diese Probleme eignen. Der Zweck dieses Aufsatzes ist, zu zeigen, warum die bisher meist benutzten mathematischen Methoden, die in der Regel Transformationen im Nachrichtenraum behandeln, wenig geeignet sind, um das Problem der Mustererkennung zu lösen. Dies ist insoweit ein pessimistisches Resultat, aber es erklärt wenigstens, warum die Mustererkennung heute so weit von einer ökonomischen Lösung entfernt ist. Freilich existieren bereits auch mathematische Methoden und Vorschläge, die sich auf eine intensivere Vorverarbeitung der Muster beziehen und daher eine Verbesserung versprechen [6], [7]. Im vorliegenden Aufsatz wird eine Behandlung der Mustererkennung vorgeschlagen, die nach Meinung des Verfassers dem Problem besser angepaßt ist, im Hinblick auf die inneren Gesetze, nach denen Muster entstehen. Dies führt dazu, daß die Mustererkennung nicht als eine sukzessive Abfolge von Vorverarbeitung und Klassifizierung aufgefaßt wird, sondern als ein Regelprozeß. Die Regelung bezieht sich hierbei auf eine Veränderung von zweckmäßig gewählten Parametern des Erkennungssystems, so daß ein adaptiver Vorgang entsteht. Es ist zu hoffen, daß mit dieser Methode auch komplizierte Probleme der Mustererkennung mit heutigen Rechenanlagen in Verbindung mit speziell dafür entwickelten Zusatzgeräten ökonomisch gelöst werden können.

Der nächste Abschnitt behandelt die Konzeption des Nachrichtenraumes, der als unzweckmäßig für die Lösung komplexer Mustererkennungsaufgaben erkannt wird. Dies wird im einzelnen diskutiert mit dem Ergebnis, daß man zwei verschiedene

Probleme unterscheiden muß, nämlich: Erkennung gestörter Signale (wofür die Darstellung im Nachrichtenraum gut geeignet ist) und Erkennung von Mustern (wofür die Darstellung im Nachrichtenraum schlecht geeignet ist).

In den nächsten beiden Abschnitten wird eine Theorie geometrischer Verzerrungen entwickelt, die sich auf den dreidimensionalen Raum der realen Welt bezieht. Diese Theorie soll den Entstehungsprozeß der Muster beschreiben. Sie wird für planare Objekte (z.B. Schriftzeichen) sowie für dreidimensionale Objekte (Körper der realen Welt) entwickelt. Verschiedene Blockschaltbilder von Erkennungssystemen nach dieser Theorie werden vorgeschlagen. Ihr wesentliches Kennzeichen ist die Benutzung adaptiv geregelter geometrischer Transformationen. Diese Schemata sind optimal für den Fall, daß die Entstehung der Muster durch die hier dargestellten Prinzipien beschrieben werden kann, was vermutlich in vielen praktischen Fällen zutrifft.

Im letzten Abschnitt wird eine Dekompositionstheorie entwickelt, bei der angenommen wird,daß die Muster aus Teilen bestehen, die getrennt behandelt werden können. Dafür wird ebenfalls ein Blockschaltbild des Erkennungsschemas angegeben.

Der Verfasser hofft, daß mit den hier dargestellten Methoden eine bessere Einsicht in den Entstehungsprozeß der Muster und die diesem Prozeß eigenen Gesetze gewonnen werden kann und daß damit eine effektivere und ökonomischere Realisierung von Mustererkennungssystemen möglich wird.

2. Der Nachrichtenraum und seine Unzweckmäßigkeit für die Lösung von Mustererkennungsproblemen

Das Konzept des Nachrichtenraumes (manchmal auch Signalraum benannt) ist eine seit langem bekannte nützliche Methode für die Behandlung von Signalerkennungsauf-

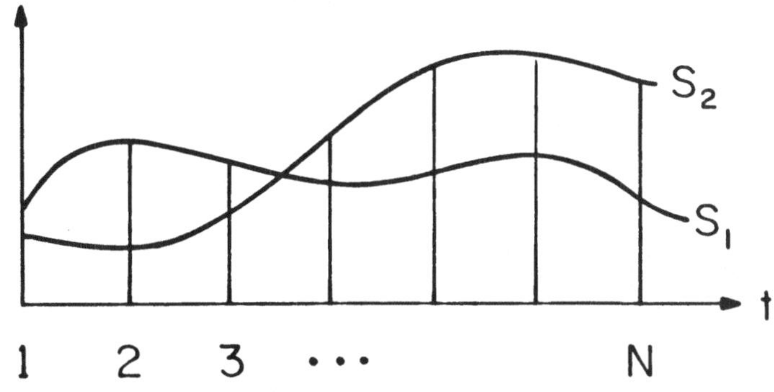

Bild 1: Zwei zeitdiskrete Signale mit N Abtastwerten

gaben, bei denen es sich um durch Rauschen gestörte Signale handelt. Bild 1 zeigt zwei Signale S_1 und S_2, die nach dem Abtasttheorem durch ihre Abtastwerte (1...N) gekennzeichnet sind. Diese Signale können als Punkte in einem n-dimensionalen Raum, dem Nachrichtenraum, dargestellt werden, wobei jede Dimension einem Abtastwert entspricht. Dies ist in Bild 2 für drei Signale aber mit nur zwei Dimensio-

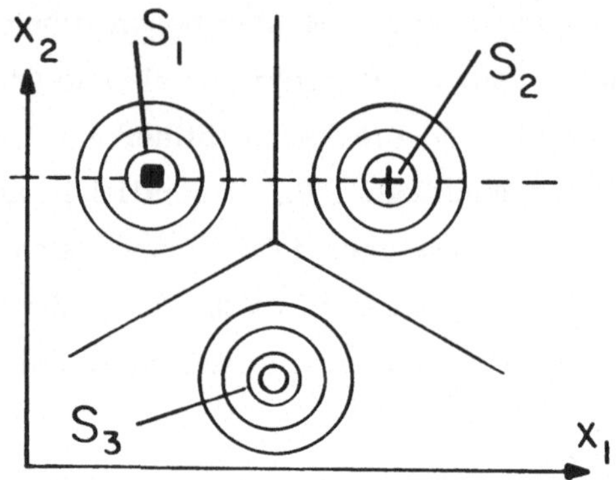

Bild 2: Drei Signale im Nachrichtenraum mit zwei Dimensionen

nen gezeigt. Normalerweise ist die Zahl der Dimensionen sehr groß (z. B. mehr als hundert), aber dies bedeutet keine grundlegende Schwierigkeit in der mathematischen Behandlung. Bei einem Bild sind die Abtastwerte gleich den Bildpunkten. Wird nun ein Signal durch additives Rauschen gestört, so resultieren daraus Abweichungen in den Koordinaten, die durch ein Wahrscheinlichkeitsgesetz beschrieben werden können. Das Ergebnis ist eine Wahrscheinlichkeitsverteilung im Nachrichtenraum (s. Bild 2), wobei Linien gleicher bedingter Wahrscheinlichkeit $p(X|S)$ angezeigt sind. Man sieht, daß die exakte Separabilität nun verlorengegangen ist, weil ein Signal S_1 mit einer bestimmten Wahrscheinlichkeit in das Signal S_2 übergehen kann. Bild 3 zeigt die bedingten Wahrscheinlichkeitsdichten $p(X_1|S_1)$ und $p(X_1|S_2)$

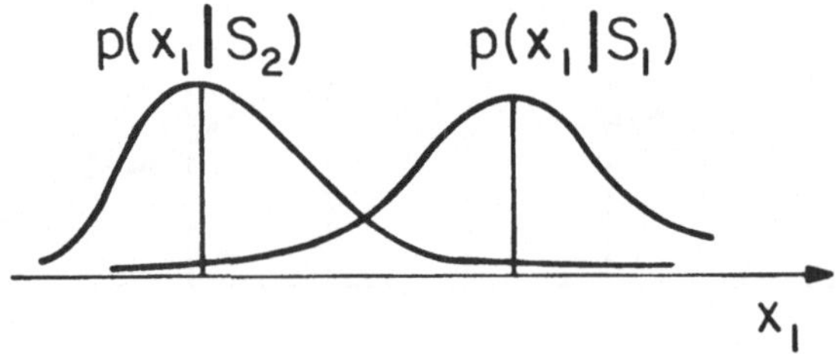

Bild 3: Bedingte Wahrscheinlichkeitsverteilungen von S_1 und S_2 in bezug auf X_1

in Abhängigkeit von X_1 (wobei sowohl das Signal S_3 als auch die Dimension X_2 vernachlässigt wurde), die eine Projektion der zweidimensionalen Verteilungen von Bild 2 auf die X_1-Achse sind. Das Wahrscheinlichkeitsverhältnis (likelihood ratio)

$$\lambda(X_1) = \frac{p(X_1 \mid S_1)}{p(X_1 \mid S_2)} \tag{1}$$

gibt ein Maß für die beste Detektion. Nach dem Bayes'schen Gesetz

$$p(X_1 \mid S_1) \cdot p(S_1) = p(S_1 \mid X_1) \cdot p(X_1) \tag{2}$$

und

$$p(X_1 \mid S_2) \cdot p(S_2) = p(S_2 \mid X_1) \cdot p(X_1) \tag{3}$$

folgt nämlich

$$\frac{p(S_1 \mid X_1)}{p(S_2 \mid X_1)} = \lambda(X_1) \cdot \frac{p(S_1)}{p(S_2)} \tag{4}$$

Dies bedeutet, daß, wenn X_1 beobachtet wird, im Falle

$$\lambda(X_1) \cdot \frac{p(S_1)}{p(S_2)} > 1 \tag{5}$$

das Signal S_1 und im Falle

$$\lambda(X_1) \cdot \frac{p(S_1)}{p(S_2)} < 1 \tag{6}$$

das Signal S_2 wahrscheinlicher ist.

Dies ist die bekannte Bayes'sche Entscheidungsregel. Ähnliche optimale Entscheidungsregeln können bestimmt werden, wenn bestimmte Fehlerwahrscheinlichkeiten oder beliebig festlegbare Kostenfunktionen zugrundegelegt werden. Diese Entscheidungsregeln teilen den Nachrichtenraum in Gebiete ein. Im Falle von Gauss'schem Rauschen sind die Begrenzungen lineare Funktionen (lineare Separabilität) und bilden Hyperflächen der Dimension N-1 im N-dimensionalen Nachrichtenraum. Diese Begrenzungen kann man erhalten, wenn man Abstandsmaße aufgrund der bedingten Wahrscheinlichkeiten definiert, wie z.B. die Battagharyy-Distanz oder die Divergenz [1]. In dieser Weise kann das Signalerkennungsproblem optimiert und gelöst werden, und dafür ist der Nachrichtenraum ein sehr geeignetes Werkzeug. Dies führte zunächst zur Vermutung, daß auch Mustererkennungsprobleme im Nachrichtenraum behandelt und gelöst werden können.

Muster sind definiert als Signale, die bestimmten Klassen zugehören, wie S_1 oder S_2 oder S_3 usw. Dies ist in Bild 4 dargestellt, wo die zu den einzelnen Klassen zu-

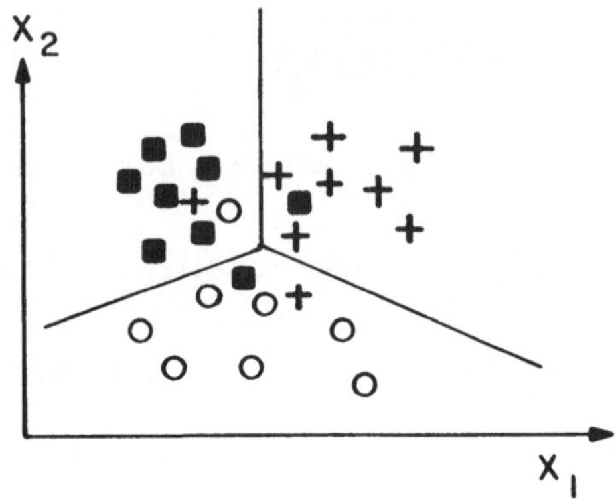

Bild 4: Prototypen dreier Musterklassen im 2-dimensionalen Nachrichtenraum und Entscheidungsgrenzen

gehörigen Muster als Punkthaufen dargestellt sind. Die verschiedenen Realisierungen der Prototypen aller Klassen können mit verschiedenen Wahrscheinlichkeiten auftreten. Wenn wieder die Klasse 3 und die Dimension X_2 vernachlässigt werden, kann man, wie Bild 5 zeigt, die diskreten bedingten Wahrscheinlichkeiten für das

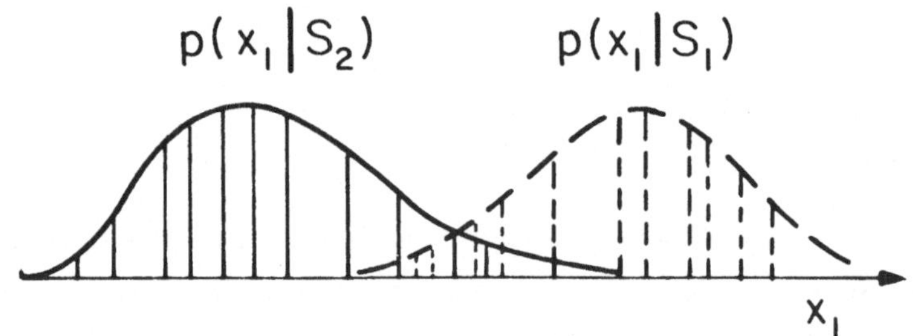

Bild 5: Diskrete bedingte Wahrscheinlichkeiten und die sie annähernde Wahrscheinlichkeitsdichtefunktionen für die Musterklassen S_1 und S_2 in Abhängigkeit von X_1

Auftreten von S_1 oder S_2 in Abhängigkeit der Koordinate X_1 angeben. Nähert man die diskreten Wahrscheinlichkeiten durch eine Wahrscheinlichkeitsdichtefunktion an, so läßt sich dieses Problem auf das vorher diskutierte Signalerkennungsproblem zurückführen. Dies entspricht der Annahme, daß man sich die Signale entstanden denken kann aus einem idealen Prototyp, der durch additives Rauschen gestört ist in Analogie zum Signalerkennungsproblem. Allerdings ist auf diese Weise die vorher existierende komplette Separabilität (die durch die Definition der Muster gegeben war) verlorengegangen. Die Muster sind jetzt nur noch mit einer gewissen Fehlerwahrscheinlichkeit separabel, in gleicher Weise wie die durch Rauschen gestörten Signale. Dieser Fehler wurde durch die Beschreibungsmethode eingeführt, tritt aber auch in der Praxis auf, wenn ein Erkennungssystem nach diesem Prinzip gebaut wird. Er könnte nur vermieden werden, wenn man zu den diskreten Wahrscheinlichkeiten zurückgeht und die damit verbundene Komplexität in Kauf nimmt. Dieser Einwand ist allerdings weniger bedeutend als der im folgenden zu diskutierende, der sich auf typische Eigenschaften praktisch vorkommender Muster bezieht.

Wir betrachten im folgenden handgeschriebenen Schriftzeichen, wie den Buchstaben "P" von Bild 6. Das Bildfeld wird mit 12 x 16 = 192 Bildelementen gerastert. Jedes Bild ist daher ein Punkt in einem Nachrichtenraum mit 192 Dimensionen. Bei Schwarzweißbildern können die Koordinaten nur binäre Werte annehmen. Das originale Muster ist in Bild 6a dargestellt. Verschiebt man dieses um einen Bildpunkt diagonal schräg nach rechts oben, so erhält man Bild 6b. Man erkennt nun, daß 19 Punkte von weiß auf schwarz gewechselt und 19 Punkte von schwarz auf weiß gewechselt haben. D.h. insgesamt 38 Punkte sind nun in bezug auf das Bild 6a fehlerhaft. Dies entspricht einer Fehlerwahrscheinlichkeit von 20 %. Wenn eine solche Fehlerwahrscheinlichkeit mit statistischer Unabhängigkeit auf das Bild einwirkt, so kann daraus das Muster von Bild 6c entstehen. Diese Störung wäre also der Translation des Bildes um einen Bildpunkt äquivalent. Sowohl die Translation als auch die zufällige Störung würde zu Punkten im Nachrichtenraum führen, die denselben Abstand vom originalen Bild haben. Dieser Abstand kann gemessen werden durch die Hamming-Distanz, die in unserem Fall 38 ist, oder die Euclidische Distanz, die in unserem Fall $\sqrt{38}$ ist. Wir sehen daher, daß eine einfache Translation des originalen Musters zu einer schweren Störung im Nachrichtenraum mit einer entsprechend großen Verschiebung führt. (Hier könnte man einwenden, daß normalerweise eine Bildzentrierung in der Vorverarbeitung vorgenommen wird. Aber abgesehen davon, daß eine solche Zentrierung meistens nicht auf einen Bildpunkt genau erfolgen kann, würden andere natürliche Mustertransformationen, wie z.B. eine leichte Rotation, zu ganz ähnlichen Effekten führen.) Betrachten wir nun nach Bild 6d die Umwandlung eines P in ein R. Sie erfolgt dadurch, daß lediglich fünf Punkte von weiß auf schwarz wechseln, was einer Hamming-Distanz von 5 oder einer Euclidischen Distanz von $\sqrt{5}$ entspricht. Die entsprechende Fehlerwahrscheinlichkeit ist 2,5 %; sie würde im Sinne einer Zufallsstörung ein Muster nach Bild 6e erzeugen. Wir erkennen daraus, daß die Interklassen-Transformation P → R einer kleineren Störung

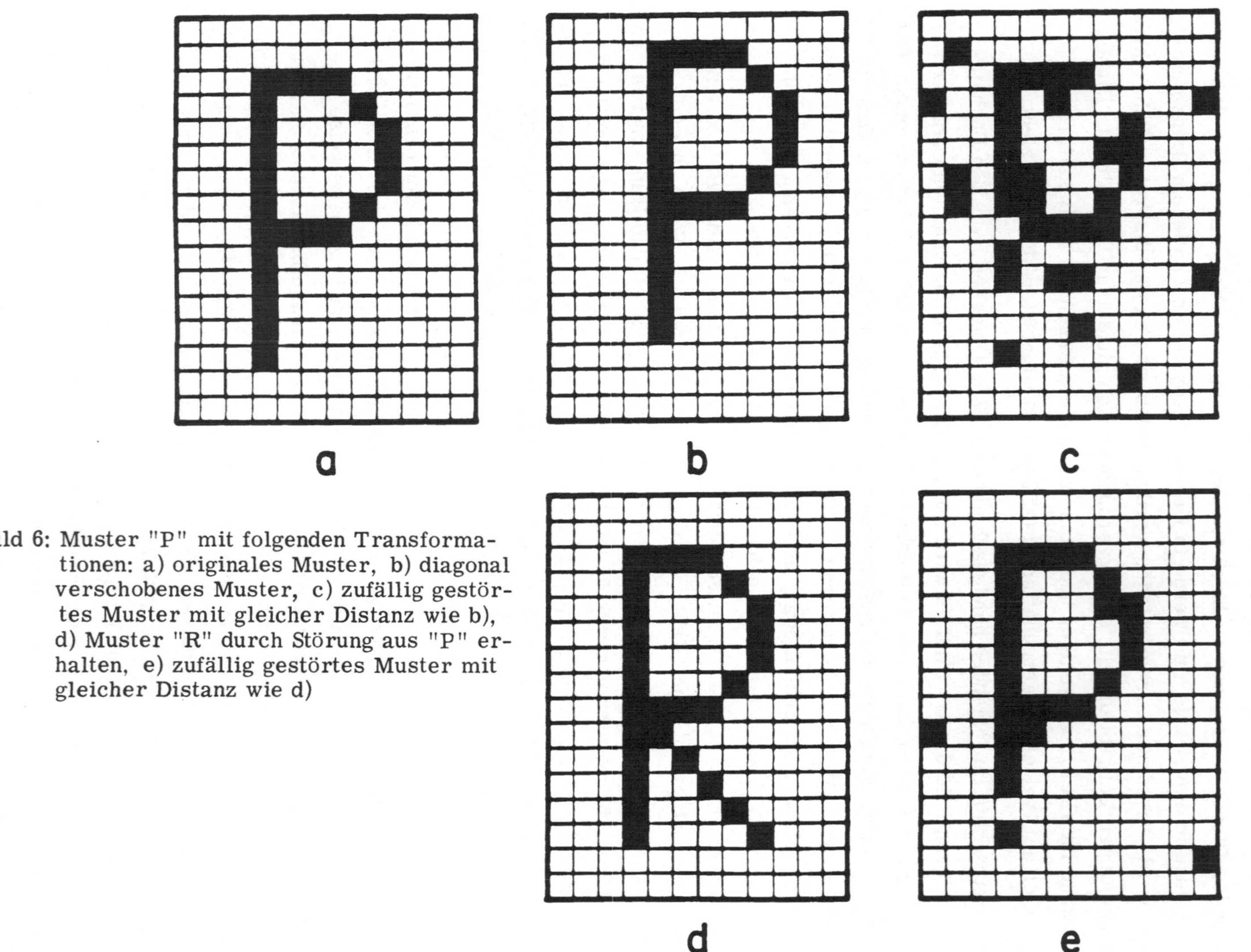

Bild 6: Muster "P" mit folgenden Transformationen: a) originales Muster, b) diagonal
verschobenes Muster, c) zufällig gestörtes Muster mit gleicher Distanz wie b),
d) Muster "R" durch Störung aus "P" erhalten, e) zufällig gestörtes Muster mit
gleicher Distanz wie d)

entspricht und zu einem kleineren Abstand im Nachrichtenraum führt als die Intraklassen-Transformation $P \rightarrow P_{trans}$. Dies führt auf eine typische Struktur des Nachrichtenraumes, wie Bild 7 zeigt, mit den entsprechenden in Bild 8 dargestellten

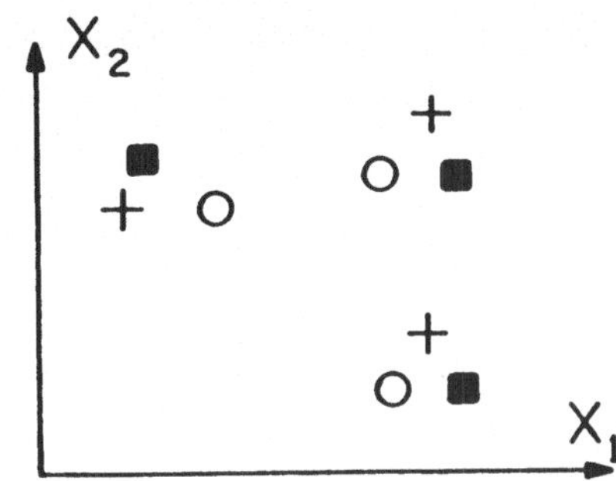

Bild 7: Typische Struktur des Nachrichtenraumes bei Mustererkennungsaufgaben

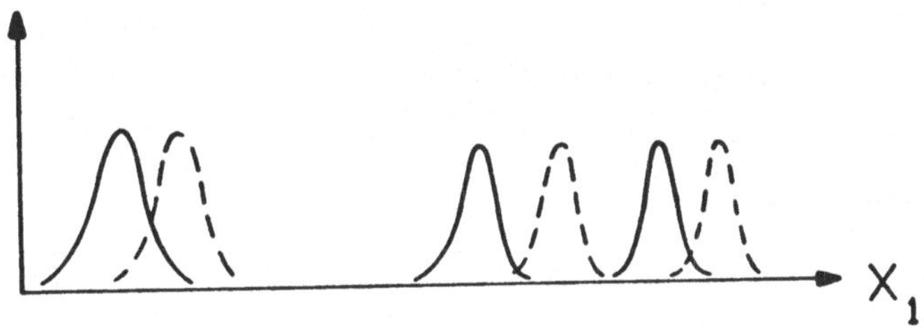

Bild 8: Typische bedingte Wahrscheinlichkeitsverteilungen bei Mustererkennungsaufgaben

Wahrscheinlichkeitsverteilungen. Die Prototypen aller Musterklassen sind über den ganzen Nachrichtenraum verteilt und bilden durchmischte Punktmengen. Es ist daher hoffnungslos, sie durch Hyperebenen separieren zu wollen. Dies trifft zumindest für die linearen Klassifizierungsmethoden zu (Schwellwertlogik). Aber auch von den nichtlinearen Methoden, die kompliziertere Trennflächen liefern können, ist wenig Gewinn zu erwarten, wenn nicht Funktionen sehr hohen Grades mit dem entsprechenden Komplexitätsaufwand benutzt werden. Aus diesem Grunde ist der Verfasser der Ansicht, daß der Nachrichtenraum sehr hoher Dimension nicht die geeignete Darstellungsmethode für Mustererkennungsprobleme ist. Er ist nur geeignet für Musterklassen geringer Variabilität, in welchem Falle das Problem auf ein Signalerkennungsproblem mit additiver Störung rückführbar ist. Komplexere Muster weisen aber eine starke Variabilität der zu einer Klasse gehörenden Prototypen auf. In diesen Fällen ist der Nachrichtenraum mit den Mustern aller Klassen durchmischt, und die Distanz kann nicht mehr als ein Entscheidungskriterium dienen. Es ist also wenig sinnvoll, das Problem im Nachrichtenraum darzustellen, wenn die Distanz in diesem Raum keinen rechten Sinn mehr hat. Auf der anderen Seite wird verständlich, warum die mathematischen Methoden, die auf einer Problemdarstellung im Nachrichtenraum beruhen, in praktischen Fällen bisher so wenig erfolgreich waren. Die meisten dieser Methoden benutzen nämlich lineare Transformationen im Nachrichtenraum, die gut erforscht sind und Optimierungen verschiedenster Art gestatten. So werden z. B. häufig die Loève-Karhunen-Transformation, die Fourier-Transformation oder die Hadamard-Transformation u. a. angewendet. Solche lineare Operationen bewirken aber lediglich eine Translation oder eine Rotation des Koordinatensystems des Nachrichtenraumes. Es ist offensichtlich, daß dadurch die innere Struktur, insbesondere die Durchmischung des Nachrichtenraums, nicht verändert werden kann. Daher können solche Methoden auch das Wesen der Mustererkennung (nämlich die Entmischung des Nachrichtenraumes) nicht erfassen. Nichtlineare Transformationen im Nachrichtenraum könnten zwar das Problem prinzipiell lösen (z. B. durch Definition komplizierter Trenngrenzen), dies führt aber zu einer - nach Meinung des Verfassers - nicht unbedingt notwendigen Komplizierung des Problems.

Im folgenden wird deswegen vorgeschlagen, anstelle des vieldimensionalen Nachrichtenraumes den dreidimensionalen Raum der realen Welt zu betrachten, in dem die Muster tatsächlich vorkommen. Dies führt zu der Theorie der geometrischen Transformationen, die in den beiden folgenden Abschnitten beschrieben wird.

3. Geometrische Transformationen für planare Objekte

In der im folgenden erörterten Theorie wird zunächst angenommen, daß die Menge aller zu einer Klasse gehörenden Muster durch geometrische Verzerrungen oder Transformationen ineinander überführbar sind. Später wird dann gezeigt, daß diese Annahme nur näherungsweise gültig sein muß. Wir betrachten im folgenden den Raum der realen Welt mit drei Dimensionen (x, y, z) oder möglicherweise vier Dimensionen, wenn die Zeit mit eingeschlossen ist (x, y, z, t). Dieser Raum darf nicht mit dem im vorigen Abschnitt besprochenen vieldimensionalen Nachrichtenraum verwechselt werden. Betrachten wir nun verschiedene planare Muster, wie z. B. die Zahl "8" von Bild 9 oder das Segelboot nach Bild 10. Wie kann das Gesetz, das diese Prototypen ineinander überführt, beschrieben oder angenähert werden? Objekte der realen Welt sind durch ihre Formkonstanz gekennzeichnet. Aber sie können von verschiedenen Richtungen oder Entfernungen aus betrachtet werden.

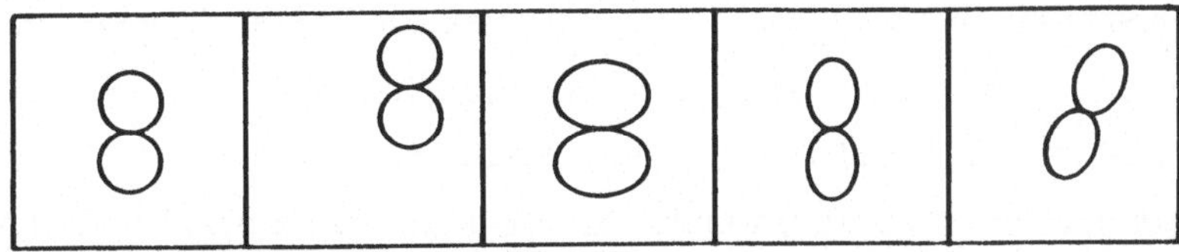

Bild 9: Verschiedene Prototypen der Klasse "8" bei handgeschriebenen Ziffern

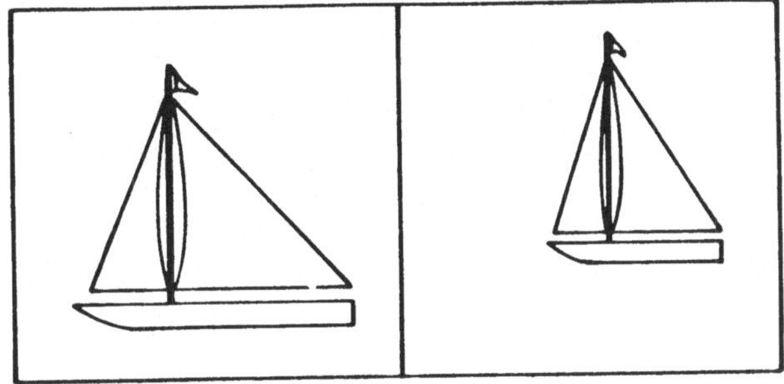

Bild 10: Zwei Prototypen der Klasse "Segelboot"

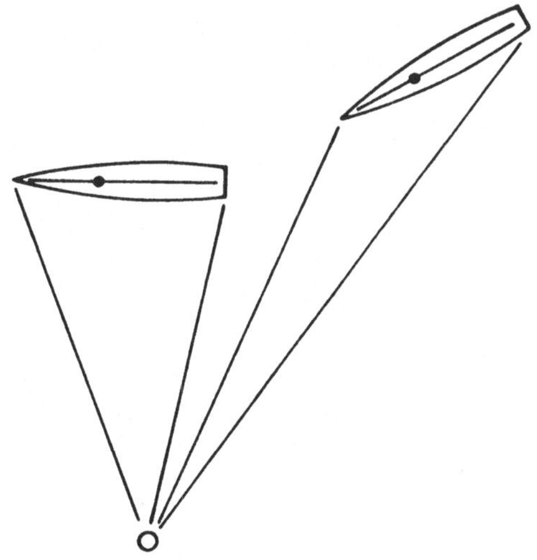

Bild 11: Die Entstehung der beiden Prototypen von Bild 10

Zum Beispiel kann das Segelboot (das als flaches Objekt betrachtet wird) nach Bild 11 von zwei verschiedenen Positionen aus betrachtet werden, was zu den zwei Bildern von Bild 10 führt. Wieviele Transformationen dieser Art sind möglich? Im dreidimensionalen Raum haben wir exakt 6 Freiheitsgrade, nämlich 3 Translationen in orthogonalen Richtungen (x, y, z) und 3 Rotationen des Objekts (um die Achsen x, y, z). Die Transformationen von Objekten nach diesen 6 Freiheitsgraden folgen

den Gesetzen der sphärischen Geometrie. Die Projektion dieser Objekte auf das Bildfeld ist von Interesse. Diese Projektionen bilden die Vielfalt der zu einer Klasse gehörigen einzelnen Muster. Es hat den Anschein, daß solche geometrische Transformationen für viele praktisch vorkommende Musterklassen relevant und von Bedeutung sind. Es wird deshalb sinnvoll sein, solche Transformationen zu untersuchen
und sie bei einem Mustererkennungsverfahren auszunutzen. Sie sind für zweidimensionale Objekte, wie handgeschriebene Buchstaben (Bild 9) oder flache Objekte,
wie ein Segelboot (Bild 10) relativ einfach durchzuführen. Bild 12 veranschaulicht
diese Transformationen mit Hilfe einer Anordnung, bei der das flache Objekt in
einem divergenten Lichtstrahl bewegt wird. Das Objekt ist durch eine Transparenzfunktion definiert und wird durch eine Punktlichtquelle beleuchtet. Auf Schirm 1 erscheint das transformierte Objekt, wobei 3 Translationen und 3 Rotationen des ursprünglichen Objekts infrage kommen. Hierbei ist festzustellen: Die Translation
in z-Richtung hat zwei Effekte. Erstens ändert sich die Vergrößerung und zweitens

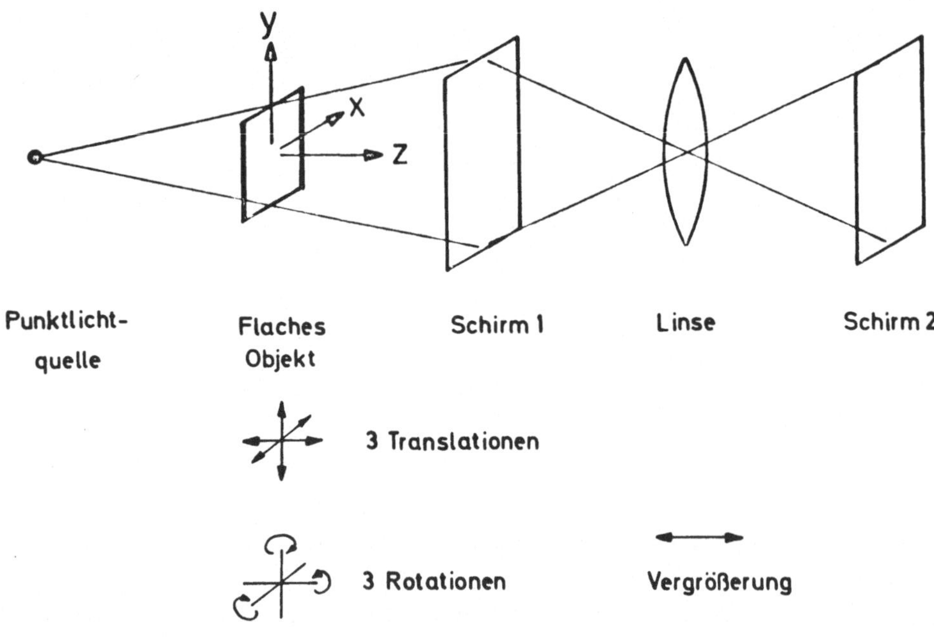

Bild 12: Geometrische Transformationen planarer Objekte variabler Größe im
divergenten Licht (Fall mit perspektivischer Verzerrung)

111

hat sie einen Einfluß auf die perspektivische Verzerrung durch die Divergenz des Lichtstrahles, die umso größer ist je näher das Objekt an der Lichtquelle ist. Die Vergrößerung kann allerdings unabhängig davon verändert werden mit Hilfe einer Linse und eines zweiten Schirmes. Durch die Position der Linse wird ein siebenter Freiheitsgrad eingeführt. Dadurch kann man durch die Translation des Objektes in z-Richtung nur die perspektivische Verzerrung verändern und die Vergrößerung mit Hilfe der Linse regeln. Wenn die Dimensionen des Objekts klein in bezug auf den Abstand zur Lichtquelle sind, kann die perspektivische Verzerrung vernachlässigt werden. Dies ist gleichbedeutend damit, das Objekt in einem parallelen Lichtstrahl zu betrachten, wie dies Bild 13 zeigt. Jetzt ist eine Translation in z-Richtung irrelevant. Die Transformationsparameter sind nun auf 6 reduziert, näm-

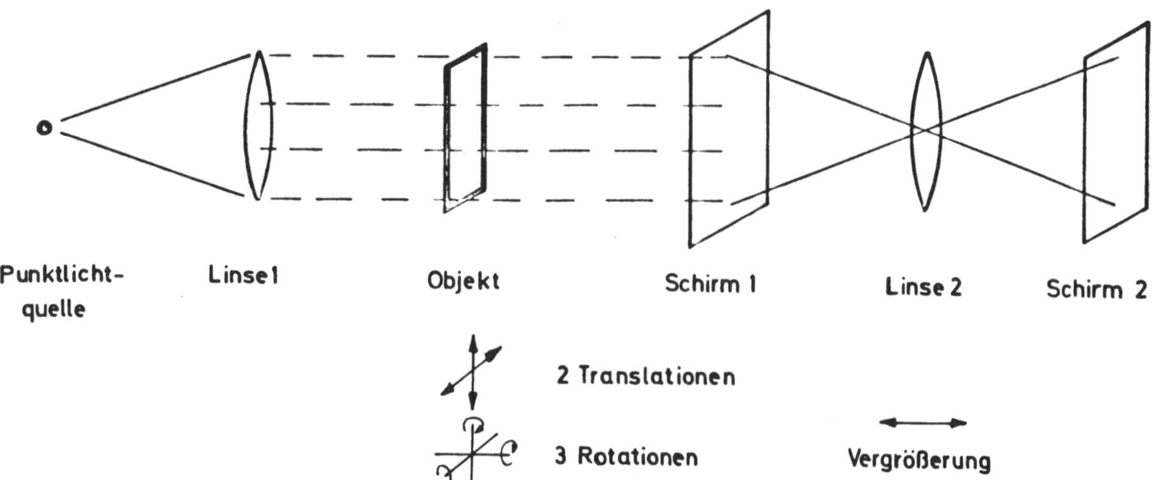

Bild 13: Geometrische Transformationen planarer Objekte variabler Größe im parallelen Licht (Fall ohne perspektivische Verzerrung)

lich Translation in x und y, Rotation in x, y, z und Vergrößerung. Man kann deshalb entweder 7 Transformationsparameter anwenden und damit die perspektivische Verzerrung berücksichtigen (Bild 12), oder, was einfacher ist, die perspektivische Verzerrung vernachlässigen, womit man 6 Transformationsparameter erhält (Bild 13).

Wir berechnen nun die möglichen Transformationen planarer Objekte nach dem Schema von Bild 13 (ohne perspektivische Verzerrung). Das Objekt kann beschrieben werden durch eine Helligkeitsfunktion $g(x, y)$. Weiterhin wird angenommen, daß diese Helligkeitsfunktion unabhängig ist von der Position des Objektes. Dies ist äquivalent mit der Annahme, daß die Beleuchtung des Objekts durch diffuses Licht erfolgt (s. z.B. Bild 11). Wenn Farben mitbetrachtet werden sollen, muß man drei Funktionen $g_R(x, y)$, $g_G(x, y)$ und $g_B(x, y)$ aufstellen, die den drei Farben rot, grün und blau entsprechen. Die durch die Anordnung von Bild 13 hervorgerufenen geometrischen Transformationen führen auf eine lineare Verzerrung des Bildes in jeder gewünschten Richtung, sowie auf eine Translation und eine Rotation in der Bildebene. Dies kann in der Bildebene selbst beschrieben werden, wobei folgende Operationen anzuwenden sind:

Nr.	Art der Operation	Eingeführte Parameter
1	Translation in x, y	x_0, y_0
2	Rotation der Bildebene zur Festlegung der Richtung der linearen Verzerrung	$\emptyset_1$
3	Lineare Verzerrung in x, y entsprechend einer Vergrößerung	ξ, η
4	Endgültige Drehung der Bildebene	$\emptyset_2$

Eine Rotation der Bildebene führt auf folgende Koordinatentransformation:

$$x' = x \cos \emptyset + y \sin\emptyset \qquad (7)$$

$$y' = y \cos \emptyset - x \sin \emptyset$$

Eine lineare Verzerrung in x oder y führt auf folgende Transformation:

$$x' = \xi\, x$$
$$y' = \eta\, y \qquad (8)$$

was die Vergrößerung einschließt.

Führt man diese Operationen nacheinander aus und ersetzt die alten Koordinaten x', y' jeweils durch die neuen Koordinaten x, y, so wird g(x, y) wie folgt transformiert:

$$g_1 = g\left[x + x_0,\ y + y_0\right] \qquad (9)$$

$$g_2 = g\left[x\cdot\cos\emptyset_1 + y \sin\emptyset_1 + x_0,\ y \cos\emptyset_1 - x \sin\emptyset_1 + y_0\right] \qquad (10)$$

$$g_3 = g\left[\xi\, x\cdot\cos\emptyset_1 + \eta y \sin\emptyset_1 + x_0,\ \eta y \cos\emptyset_1 - \xi x \sin\emptyset_1 + y_0\right] \qquad (11)$$

$$g_4 = g\Big[\xi\, (x\cdot\cos\emptyset_2 + y \sin\emptyset_2) \cos\emptyset_1 + \qquad (12)$$

$$+ \eta(y\cdot\cos\emptyset_2 - x \sin\emptyset_2) \sin\emptyset_1 + x_0,$$

$$\eta(y \cdot \cos\phi_2 - x \sin\phi_2) \cos\phi_1 -$$

$$-\xi(x \cdot \cos\phi_2 + y \sin\phi_2) \sin\phi_1 + y_o\Big] =$$

$$= g\Big[x \cdot (\xi \cos\phi_1 \cos\phi_2 - \eta\sin\phi_1 \sin\phi_2) +$$

$$+ y (\xi \cos\phi_1 \sin\phi_2 + \eta\sin\phi_1 \cos\phi_2) + x_o,$$

$$- x (\xi \sin\phi_1 \cos\phi_2 + \eta\cos\phi_1 \sin\phi_2) +$$

$$+ y (-\xi \sin\phi_1 \sin\phi_2 + \eta\cos\phi_1 \cos\phi_2) + y_o\Big]$$

Das Ergebnis von Gl. (12) ist eine lineare Transformation der Koordinaten von $g(x, y)$ gemäß

$$g_T(x, y) = g_4 = g(ax + by + c, \ dx + ey + f) \tag{13}$$

Hierbei sind die Koeffizienten von Gl. (13):

$$a = \xi \cos\phi_1 \cos\phi_2 - \eta \sin\phi_1 \sin\phi_2 \tag{14}$$

$$b = \xi \cos\phi_1 \sin\phi_2 + \eta\sin\phi_1 \cos\phi_2 \tag{15}$$

$$c = + x_o \tag{16}$$

$$d = - \xi \sin\phi_1 \cos\phi_2 - \eta\cos\phi_1 \sin\phi_2 \tag{17}$$

$$e = -\xi \sin\phi_1 \sin\phi_2 + \eta\cos\phi_1 \cos\phi_2 \tag{18}$$

$$f = + y_o \tag{19}$$

Die hier durchgeführten Transformationen sollen auf ein Muster führen, das die größtmögliche Ähnlichkeit mit einem idealen Prototyp $\hat{g}(x, y)$ hat. Wird die Ähnlichkeit im Sinne des quadratischen Fehlers gemessen, so gilt:

$$\iint \big[g_T(x, y) - \hat{g}(x, y)\big]^2 \, dxdy \longrightarrow \min \tag{20}$$

Das Minimum muß dadurch erreicht werden, daß die Koeffizienten a, b, c, d, e, f in einer geeigneten Weise justiert werden. Die Veränderung der Koeffizienten bedeutet, daß die geometrischen Transformationen variabel und adaptiv sein müssen und vom erhaltenen Ergebnis abhängig sein müssen. Dies bedeutet wiederum, daß ein Regelprozeß für die Justierung der Transformationsparameter notwendig ist. In dieser Weise wird die Zeichenerkennung zu einem adaptiven Regelungsprozeß unter Verwendung geometrischer Transformationen. Wenn wir Gl. (20) entwickeln, erhalten wir:

$$\iint g_T^2(xy)\,dxdy + \iint \hat{g}^2(x,y)\,dxdy - 2 \iint g_T(x,y)\hat{g}(x,y)\,dxdy \longrightarrow \min \tag{21}$$

Daher ist die Zielvorstellung, nämlich die Minimisierung des quadratischen Fehlers, äquivalent mit dem Maximum der Kreuzkorrelationsfunktion.

$$\iint g_T(x,y)\hat{g}(xy)\,dxdy \longrightarrow \max \tag{22}$$

Um das System zu optimieren, muß noch der ideale Prototyp $\hat{g}(x,y)$ gefunden werden. Da die Zielvorstellung das Maximum der Kreuzkorrelation mit allen möglichen einer Klasse zugehörigen Prototypen $g_\nu(x,y)$ ist, wird im Mittel das beste Ergebnis erreicht, wenn $\hat{g}(x,y)$ so gewählt wird, daß die folgende Gleichung erfüllt ist

$$\sum_\nu \iint p_\nu g_{\nu T}(x,y)\hat{g}(x,y)\,dxdy \longrightarrow \max \tag{23}$$

Hierbei ist p_ν die Wahrscheinlichkeit des Prototyps $g_\nu(x,y)$. Wird die Musterenergie normiert, so ist die Autokorrelation das Maximum der Kreuzkorrelation. Deshalb gilt:

$$\hat{g}(x,y) = \sum_\nu p_\nu g_{\nu T}(x,y) \tag{24}$$

Wenn alle Prototypen $g_\nu(x,y)$ durch die beschriebenen geometrischen Transformationen aus einem idealen Muster $g(x,y)$ entstanden sind, können sie auch auf genau dieses Muster wieder zurückgeführt werden, und dann gilt einfach:

$$\hat{g}(x,y) = g(x,y) \tag{25}$$

Ist dies jedoch nur näherungsweise der Fall, so muß Gl. (24) angewendet werden. Wenn $g(x,y)$ unbekannt ist - wie im Fall des unüberwachten Lernens - dann muß eine Annahme über $\hat{g}(x,y)$ gemacht werden, z. B.

$$\hat{g}(x,y) = g_\nu(x,y) \tag{26}$$

wobei dasjenige ν gewählt wird, für welches $p_\nu \to \max$.

Aufgrund der besprochenen Theorie wird das Mustererkennungsschema von Bild 14 vorgeschlagen. Hier bezeichnet $g_{\mu\nu}(x,y)$ den ν-ten Prototyp der μ-ten Klasse, der dem System angeboten wird. T ist die geometrische Transformation, die von sechs

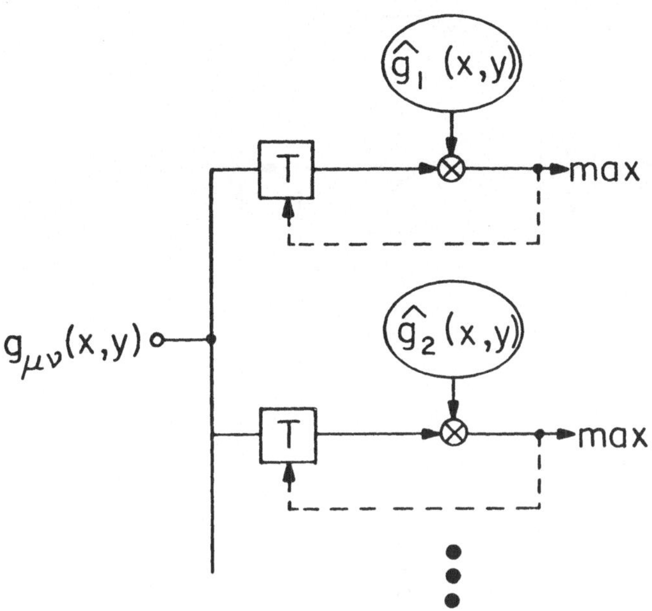

Bild 14: Schema eines Mustererkennungssystems mittels adaptiver geometrischer Transformationen und Korrelation (Maximum-Detektion)

Freiheitsgraden abhängt (a, b, c, d, e, f). $\widehat{g}_\mu$(x, y) ist der ideale Prototyp der Klasse μ. Die sechsparametrige Transformation wird bei jedem angebotenen Muster optimiert, im Hinblick auf maximale Korrelation mit den verschiedenen Prototypen. Nach dieser Optimierung zeigt das absolute Maximum die Musterklasse an. Dies kann durch einen Maximumdetektor festgestellt werden. Wenn ein solcher benutzt wird, muß eine Energienormierung der transformierten Muster vorgenommen werden. Will man dieses vermeiden, so kann ein Minimumdetektor gemäß Bild 15 benutzt werden. Hier wird anstelle der Korrelation der quadratische Fehler als Abstandsmaß verwendet. Die Justierung der Transformationsparameter entspricht einer Optimierungsprozedur. Alle bekannten Optimierungsmethoden können für diesen Zweck Anwendung finden. Die Schwierigkeit von lokalen Maxima tritt hier auf wie bei allen Optimierungsprozeduren. Jedoch ist hier die Größe des absoluten Maximums bekannt, wenn man annimmt, daß nur geometrische Transformationen die Musterklasse definieren. Dies erleichtert das Verfahren. So kann z.B. der Regelungsprozeß abgebrochen werden, wenn eine ausreichende Annäherung an die maximale Korrelation erreicht ist. Die Dauer des Optimierungsprozesses ist natürlich von den Anfangsbedingungen abhängig. Hier entsteht aber ein Vorteil, wenn ähnlich

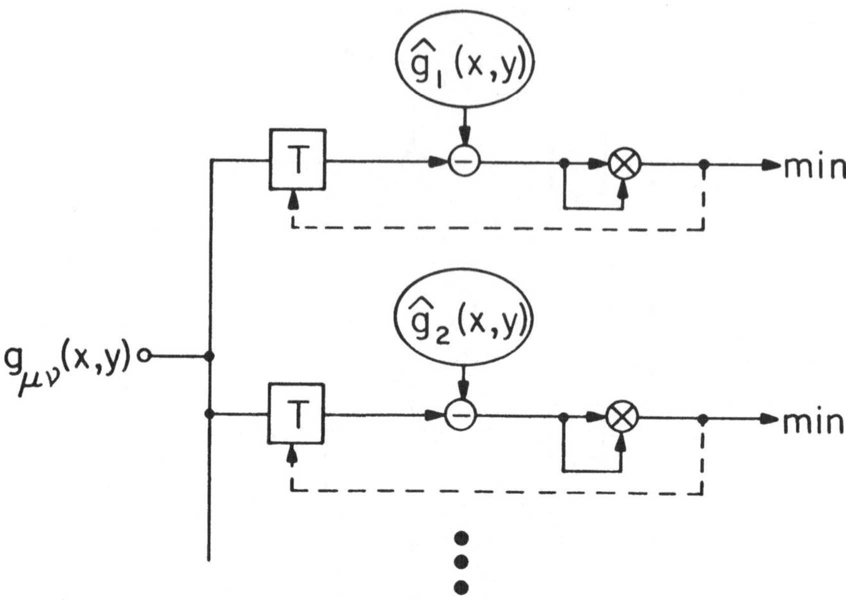

Bild 15: Äquivalentes Schema zu Bild 14 bei
Messung des quadratischen Fehlers (Minimum-Detektion)

verzerrte Muster nacheinander angeboten werden. Dies ist z. B. der Fall beim Lesen handgeschriebener Buchstaben eines Schreibers, weil dessen graphologische Eigenheiten zu für ihn typischen geometrischen Verzerrungen Anlaß geben (z. B. sind die Buchstaben in einer Richtung geneigt). Weiterhin muß gesagt werden, daß in vielen praktischen Fällen die Parameter nur in Grenzen zu variieren sind (z. B. bei den Rotationen $\pm$ 20 Grad). In Bild 14 und 15 wurde die Korrelation bzw. der Vergleich mit transformierten Eingangsmustern vorgenommen. Stattdessen kann man jedoch auch die idealen Prototypen transformieren, wie dies Bild 16 (entsprechend Bild 14) und Bild 17 (entsprechend Bild 15) zeigen. Da die vorgeschlagenen geometrischen Transformationen eindeutig und umkehrbar sind, kann die Korrelation oder der Vergleich auf jeder Stufe der transformierten Muster vorgenommen werden. Die Realisierung eines Erkennungsschemas aufgrund der Bilder 14 - 17 kann durch optische oder elektronenoptische Verfahren, wie sie z. B. Bild 13 zeigt, vorgenommen werden. Alternativ lassen sich Computerprogramme verwenden, die in der Lage sind, Koordinatentransformationen bei Bildern durchzuführen, wie z. B. VICAR [13]. Es kann erwartet werden, daß für eine große Menge möglicher Muster die hier beschriebenen geometrischen Transformationen den Musterentstehungsprozeß mit genügender Genauigkeit beschreiben. Eine exakte Gültigkeit der gemachten

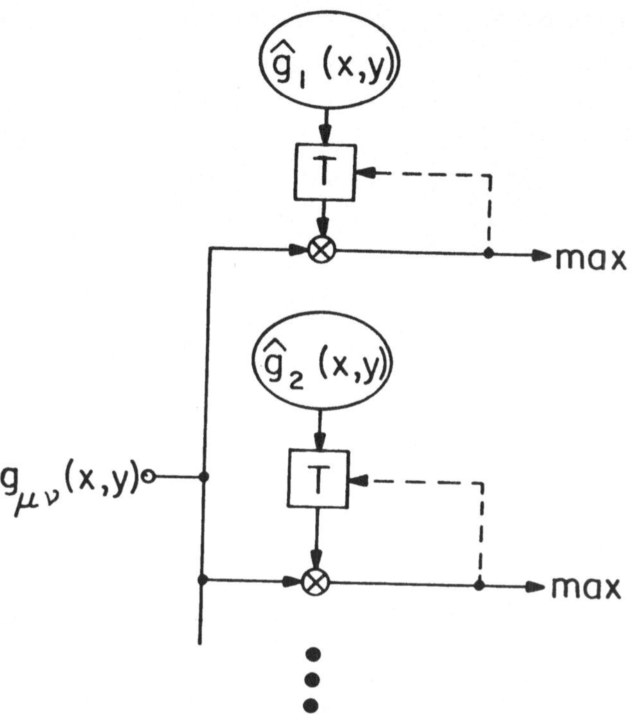

Bild 16: Äquivalentes Schema zu Bild 14 bei Transformation der idealen Prototypen

Annahmen ist nicht notwendig, denn es ist völlig ausreichend, wenn die hier vorgeschlagenen geometrischen Transformationen zu einer Verbesserung der Struktur des
Nachrichtenraumes führen,so daß die transformierten Muster linear separabel werden. D.h. aber, es können kleinere Deformationen der Muster sowie additive Störungen noch zusätzlich zugelassen werden. Wenn andererseits die Voraussetzungen gut
erfüllt sind, kann das System unter Umständen nur näherungsweise ausgeführt werden. So wäre es möglich, die Rotationen zu vermeiden und nur eine Translation in x
und y sowie eine lineare Verzerrung in x und y zuzulassen. Dann führt die Transformation von g(x, y) auf

$$g_T(x, y) = g(ax-x_o,\ by-y_o) \tag{27}$$

mit den vier Parametern a, b, x_o, y_o.

Weiterhin soll erwähnt werden, daß die Theorie und das vorgeschlagene Erkennungsschema auch für bewegte planare Objekte gilt. In diesem Fall ändern sich die Transformationsparameter mit der Zeit. Der Regelungsprozeß muß diesen Änderungen folgen. D.h. die Zeitkonstanten der Regelkreise von Bild 14 - 17 müssen entsprechend

gewählt werden. Zu schnell bewegte Objekte können nicht erkannt werden, aber dies scheint eine natürliche Begrenzung jedes Erkennungssystemszu sein.

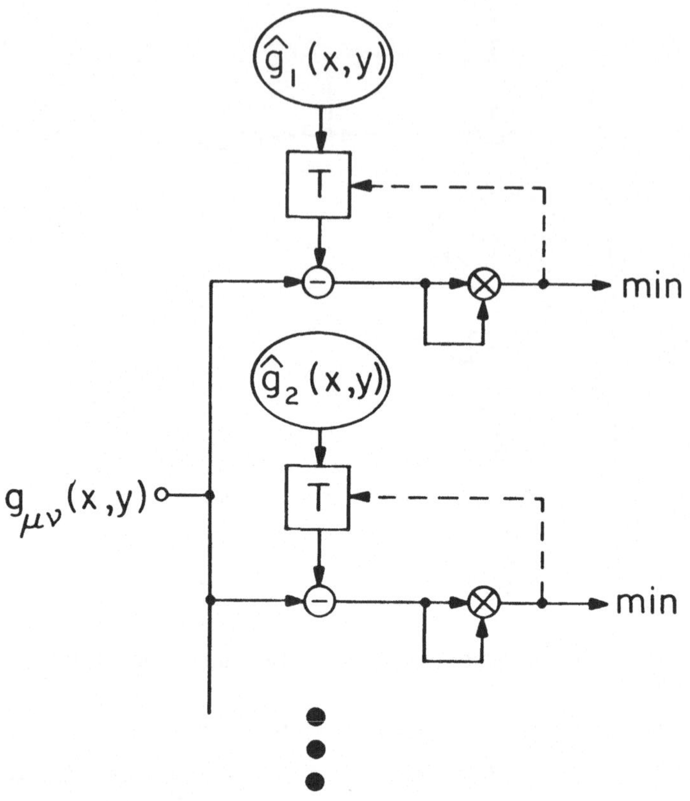

Bild 17: Äquivalentes Schema zu Bild 15 bei Transformation der idealen Prototypen

4. Geometrische Transformationen für dreidimensionale Objekte

Bisher wurde die Theorie der geometrischen Transformationen nur für zweidimensionale (planare) Objekte dargestellt, obwohl alle Freiheitsgrade des dreidimensionalen Raumes betrachtet wurden (drei Translationen und drei Rotationen). Im folgenden soll die Theorie auch auf dreidimensionale Objekte, also Körper, ausgedehnt werden. In diesem Falle treten jedoch Schwierigkeiten hinsichtlich von Mehrdeutigkeiten bei der planaren Projektion des Objekts in das visuelle Feld auf. Im folgenden sei nur ein einziges visuelles Feld bzw. monokulares Sehen (Zyklopenauge) betrachtet.

Betrachten wir z.B. das Rechteck von Bild 18a. Dieses kann ein planares Objekt sein oder aber z.B. aus dem Quader von Bild 18b entstanden sein. Ohne die Sichtposition zu ändern, kann dieses nicht entschieden werden. In ähnlicher Weise kann bei Bild 18c nicht entschieden werden, ob es sich um drei oder zwei Objekte handelt, wie Bild 18d

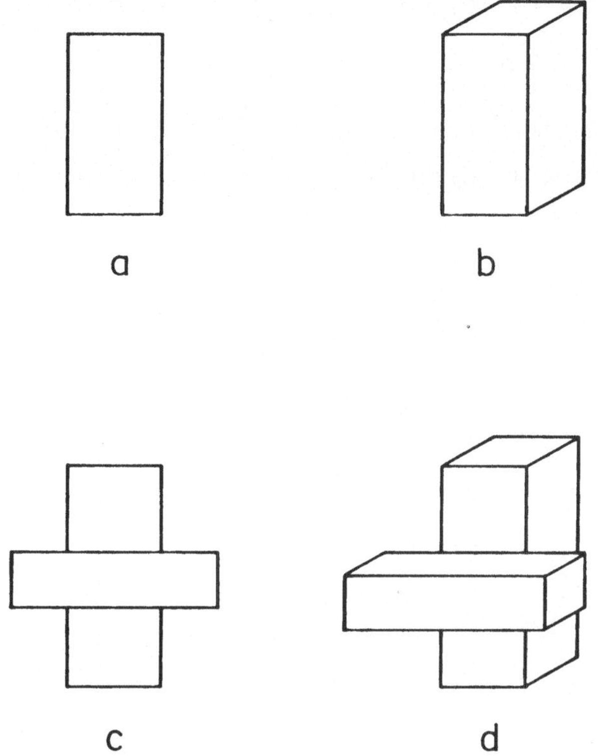

Bild 18: Mehrdeutigkeiten bei der planaren Projektion 3-dimensionaler Objekte

zeigt. Aus diesem Grunde haben wir Mehrdeutigkeiten zu erwarten, wenn wir dreidimensionale Objekte im monokularen Gesichtsfeld erkennen wollen. Solche Mehrdeutigkeiten können nur durch verschiedene Sichtpositionen (was einer Bewegung
zwischen Objekt und Beobachter entspräche) beseitigt werden. Betrachten wir nun
die möglichen geometrischen Transformationen dreidimensionaler Objekte in das
visuelle Feld. Wieder gibt es zwei Fälle: Mit perspektivischer Verzerrung (sieben
Freiheitsgrade) und ohne perspektivische Verzerrung (sechs Freiheitsgrade). Wir
betrachten im folgenden den einfacheren Fall ohne perspektivische Verzerrung,
was einer Drehung und Translation des dreidimensionalen Objektes im parallelen
Licht entsprechend Bild 13 gleichkommt. Das Objekt kann aber jetzt nicht mehr
durch eine Transparenzfunktion charakterisiert werden, wenn wir es mit festen
Körpern mit strahlenden oder reflektierenden Oberflächen zu tun haben. Einen solchen festen Körper können wir durch zwei Funktionen charakterisieren, nämlich
eine Helligkeitsfunktion $h(x, y, z)$, die aber nur auf der Oberfläche des Objekts existiert, die wiederum durch die Oberflächenfunktion $w(x, y, z) = 0$ definiert ist. Die
Lösung z_w der Oberflächenfunktion muß in die Helligkeitsfunktion eingesetzt werden.

Somit ist die Helligkeit auf der Oberfläche des Körpers durch den Ausdruck

$$h(x, y, z_w(x, y))$$

gegeben. Hierbei muß beachtet werden, daß, wie Bild 19 zeigt, mindestens zwei Lösungen für z_w existieren, womit die Funktion h mehrwertig wird.(So entspricht

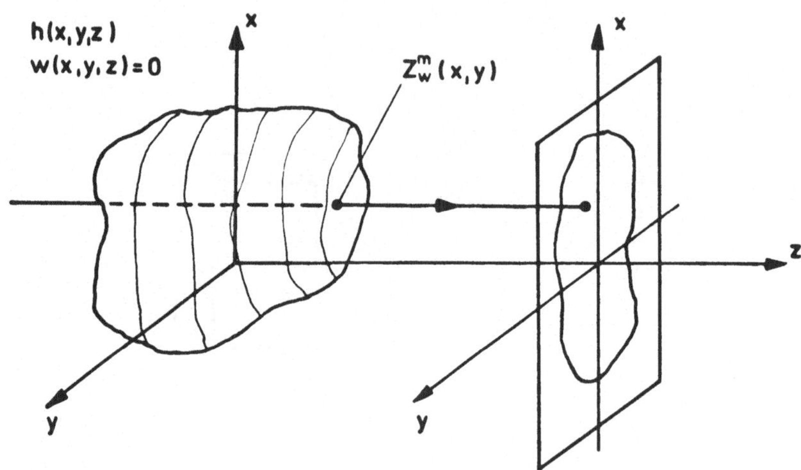

Bild 19: Darstellung des 3-dimensionalen festen Körpers und seiner Projektion in das visuelle Feld

jedem Punkt (x, y) ein Wert z_w auf der Rückseite und ein Wert z_w auf der Vorderseite des Körpers. Um die Projektion in das visuelle Feld durchzuführen, muß nun einfach der Wert der Vorderseite, d.h. der maximale Wert $z_w^m(x, y)$ genommen werden. Auf diese Weise wird der Abschattungseffekt berücksichtigt und es kommt nur die dem visuellen Feld zugewendete Seite des Körpers zur Wirkung.

Es gilt also:

$$g(x, y) = h\left[x, y, z_w^m (x, y)\right] \tag{28}$$

g(x, y) ist das Muster der Körper im visuellen Feld, welches aus den beiden den Körper charakterisierenden Funktionen h(x, y, z) und w(x, y, z) = 0 gemäß Gl.(28)berechnet werden kann. Es sei bemerkt, daß für farbige Objekte drei Helligkeitsfunktionen h_R, h_B und h_G aber nur eine Oberflächenfunktion w definiert werden muß, was dann zu drei Funktionen g_R, g_B und g_G im visuellen Feld führt.

Wir haben nun den Entstehungsprozeß der Muster im visuellen Feld durch die Anwendung von geometrischen Transformationen des Körpers zu studieren. Bei einer

Anordnung entsprechend Bild 13 (ohne perspektivische Verzerrung) haben wir zu betrachten: Translation in x- und y-Richtung, Vergrößerung, Rotation um x, y, z. Dies ergibt sechs Freiheitsgrade. Diese geometrischen Transformationen sind auf beide Funktionen $h(x, y, z)$ und $w(x, y, z)$ anzuwenden. Das Ergebnis dieser Transformationen ist eine transformierte Helligkeitsfunktion $h_T(x, y, z)$ sowie eine transformierte Oberflächenfunktion $w_T(x, y, z)$. Diese Funktionen hängen von den ursprünglichen Funktionen h und w in der folgenden Weise ab:

$$h_T(x, y, z) = h(a_{11}x + a_{12}y + a_{13}z, a_{21}x + a_{22}y + a_{23}z, a_{31}x + a_{32}y + a_{33}z) \quad (29)$$

$$w_T(x, y, z) = w(a_{11}x + a_{12}y + a_{13}z, a_{21}x + a_{22}y + a_{23}z, a_{31}x + a_{32}y + a_{33}z) \quad (30)$$

D.h. die Koordinaten des neuen Systems ergeben sich durch eine Lineartransformation des alten Systems. In vektorieller Schreibweise kann man mit

$$k = \begin{pmatrix} x \\ y \\ z \end{pmatrix} \quad \text{und} \quad k_o = \begin{pmatrix} x_o \\ y_o \\ 0 \end{pmatrix}$$

kürzer schreiben:

$$h_T(k) = h(k_T) \quad (31)$$

$$w_T(k) = w(k_T) \quad (32)$$

Hierbei ist der transformierte Koordinatenvektor durch

$$k_T = Ak + k_o \quad (33)$$

gegeben, wobei für die Matrix A von Gl. (33) gilt:

$$A = \begin{Vmatrix} a_{11} & a_{22} & a_{23} \\ a_{21} & a_{22} & a_{23} \\ a_{31} & a_{32} & a_{33} \end{Vmatrix} \quad (34)$$

Die neun Matrix-Elemente von Gl. (34) sind teilweise voneinander abhängig, da nur sechs Freiheitsgrade existieren. Um diese Elemente zu berechnen, führen wir folgende Transformationen durch:

1. Vergrößerung m
2. Drehung um die z-Achse ($\emptyset_1$)
3. Drehung um die neue x-Achse ($\emptyset_2$)
4. Drehung um die neue z-Achse ($\emptyset_3$)
5. Translation in x-Richtung (x_o)
6. Translation in y-Richtung (y_o)

Damit ergeben sich die Matrix-Elemente wie folgt:

$$a_{11} = + m\cos\emptyset_1 \cos\emptyset_3 + m\cos\emptyset_2 \sin\emptyset_1 \sin\emptyset_3 \tag{35}$$

$$a_{12} = + m\cos\emptyset_1 \sin\emptyset_3 + m\cos\emptyset_1 \sin\emptyset_1 \sin\emptyset_3 \tag{36}$$

$$a_{13} = + m\sin\emptyset_1 \sin\emptyset_2 \tag{37}$$

$$a_{21} = + m\sin\emptyset_1 \cos\emptyset_3 - m\cos\emptyset_1 \cos\emptyset_2 \sin\emptyset_3 \tag{38}$$

$$a_{22} = + m\sin\emptyset_1 \sin\emptyset_3 + m\cos\emptyset_1 \cos\emptyset_2 \cos\emptyset_3 \tag{39}$$

$$a_{23} = - m\cos\emptyset_1 \sin\emptyset_2 \tag{40}$$

$$a_{31} = - m\sin\emptyset_2 \sin\emptyset_3 \tag{41}$$

$$a_{32} = \quad m\sin\emptyset_2 \cos\emptyset_3 \tag{42}$$

$$a_{33} = \quad m\cos\emptyset_2 \tag{43}$$

In dieser Weise wird das transformierte Objekt erhalten und in gleicher Weise wie
das ursprüngliche Objekt durch die beiden transformierten Gleichungen $h_T(x, y, z)$
und $w_T(x, y, z)$ beschrieben. Die Projektion in das visuelle Feld wird nun in gleicher Weise wie vorhin durchgeführt und ergibt das transformierte Muster $g_T(x, y)$.
D.h. es muß die Gleichung $w_T(x, y, z) = 0$ gelöst werden, und die maximale Lösung
$z_{wT}^m(x, y)$ in $h_T(x, y, z)$ eingesetzt werden. Das transformierte Muster im visuellen
Feld ist daher:

$$g_T(x, y) = h_T\left[x, y, z_{wT}^m(x, y)\right] \tag{44}$$

Gl.(44)ist die allgemeine Formel für die Durchführung geometrischer Transformationen dreidimensionaler Objekte und ihre Projektion in das visuelle Feld ohne
Berücksichtigung der perspektivischen Verzerrung. Sie kann in zwei Operationen
aufgespalten werden, nämlich:

1. eine Koordinatentransformation, T, entsprechend

$$k_T = A \cdot k + k_o$$

2. eine Projektion, T_p, entsprechend der Lösung von

$$w_T(x, y, z) = 0 \text{ und Ermittlung von } z_{wT}^m(x, y).$$

Die erste Operation ist entsprechend den sechs Freiheitsgraden von sechs variablen Parametern abhängig. Die zweite Operation ist dann bestimmt und hat keinen
weiteren Freiheitsgrad. Wird der Musterentstehungsprozeß in dieser Weise verstanden, so kann das dafür am besten geeignete Erkennungssystem unschwer angegeben werden. Die zur Verfügung stehende Information ist durch die Projektion
$g_T(x, y)$ gegeben. Auf ihr muß die Entscheidung basieren. Wenn alle Werte von
$g_T(x, y)$ gleich gewichtet werden, muß eine Korrelation durchgeführt werden. Das
Schema des entsprechenden Mustererkennungssystems zeigt die rechte Seite von
Bild 20. Im linken Teil von Bild 20 ist der Musterentstehungsprozeß dargestellt.

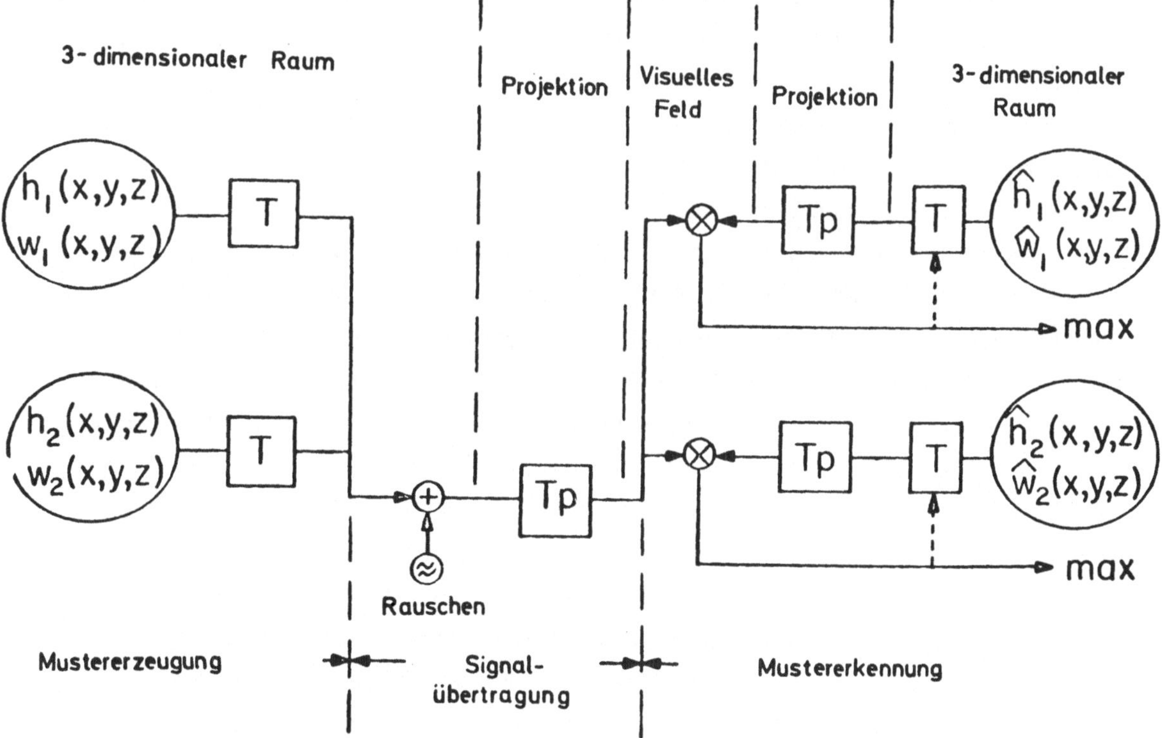

Bild 20: Schema der Mustererzeugung und der Mustererkennung bei 3-dimensionalen
Objekten

Hierbei wird angenommen, daß im dreidimensionalen Raum der realen Welt feste Körper vorhanden sind, die durch Helligkeitsfunktionen $h_\mu(x, y, z)$ sowie durch Oberflächenfunktionen $w_\mu(x, y, z) = 0$ gekennzeichnet sind. Durch geometrische Transformationen T nach sechs Freiheitsgraden dieser idealen Prototypen erhält man die Objekte der realen Welt, die durch die Funktionen $h_{\mu T}(x, y, z)$ und $w_{\mu T}(x, y, z) = 0$ gegeben sind. Mehrere Objekte können gleichzeitig im Raum vorhanden sein (wobei eine gegenseitige Durchdringung sowie eine Abschattung zweier Objekte ausgeschlossen sei). Außerdem können die optischen Signale durch additives Geräusch gestört werden. Nun muß die Projektionstransformation T_p in das visuelle Feld des Beobachters durchgeführt werden. Sie führt auf Funktionen $g_{\mu T} = h_{\mu T}(x, y, z^m_{\mu T}(x, y))$ entsprechend Gl. (44). Nach dem in Bild 20 vorgeschlagenen Mustererkennungsschema wird diese Funktion korreliert mit Vergleichsfunktionen $\hat{g}_{\mu T} = h_{\mu T}(x, y, z^m_{\mu T}(x, y))$, die in ähnlicher Weise abgeleitet werden. D.h. es müssen Vergleichsfunktionen (Schätzwerte) des idealen Prototyps $\hat{h}_\mu(x, y, z)$ und $\hat{w}_\mu(x, y, z) = 0$ bekannt und im Erkennungssystem gespeichert sein. Diese werden dann geometrische Transformationen T mit sechs Freiheitsgraden unterworfen, wobei ein Regelungs- oder Optimierungsprozeß mit dem Ziel einer maximalen Korrelation erfolgt. (Diesen Prozeß kann man auch als generalisierte Korrelation unter Verwendung geometrischer Transformationen bezeichnen.) Nach der Anwendung der Projektionstransformation T_p wird damit die Vergleichsfunktion $\hat{g}_{\mu T}$ erhalten. Die parallel arbeitenden Regelungs- oder Optimierungsprozesse von Bild 20 sind auf die Auffindung des absoluten Maximums programmiert. Nach einer Energienormierung ist die Größe dieses Maximums ein Maß für die Wahrscheinlichkeit des Auftretens eines Objektes im Raum. Das System kann daher auch mehrere Objekte gleichzeitig erkennen. Wird aber nur ein Objekt zugelassen, so liefert die Höhe der erreichten Maxima die Entscheidung (Maximum-Detektion). Aus Bild 20 ist ersichtlich, daß der Mustererkennungsprozeß zusammengeht und nicht trennbar ist von einem Zielfindungsverfahren (tracking) des Objekts in bezug auf seine Translation und Rotation im Raum. Dieser Vorgang scheint auch für die Mustererkennung durch den Menschen typisch zu sein. Mit der Erkennung eines Objekts ist die Ortung seiner Lage im Raum untrennbar verbunden. Schließlich muß noch erwähnt werden, daß auch bewegte Objekte prinzipiell durch dasselbe Schema erkannt werden können. Dies bedeutet, daß die Zeitkonstanten der Regelkreise so bemessen sein müssen, daß sie den Schwankungen der Parameter während der Bewegung folgen können. Das Schema von Bild 20 kann daher auch als ein Zielverfolgungsverfahren nach allen geometrischen Freiheitsgraden angesehen werden. Es ist dem Musterentstehungsprozeß angepaßt und unter der Voraussetzung, daß dieser durch geometrische Transformationen beschreibbar ist, optimal.

5. Dekompositionsverfahren

Die dargelegte Theorie der geometrischen Transformationen behandelt das Muster
als Ganzes. Sie führt daher globale Operationen im Bildfeld aus. Kompliziertere
Muster kann man sich jedoch auch aus Teilen zusammengesetzt denken. Wenn die
geometrischen Verzerrungen dieser Teile nicht die gleichen sind, kann eine Dekomposition des Musters zweckmäßig sein, um die erwähnten Teile getrennt zu behandeln. Prinzipiell gibt es zwei Arten zur Durchführung einer solchen Dekomposition:

   a) Dekomposition durch Aufteilung des Bildfeldes und

   b) Dekomposition nach Merkmalen.

Bild 21 zeigt beide Methoden am Beispiel des Musters "P". Bei der Methode a)
wird das Bildfeld in eine obere und eine untere Hälfte aufgeteilt. Natürlich kann

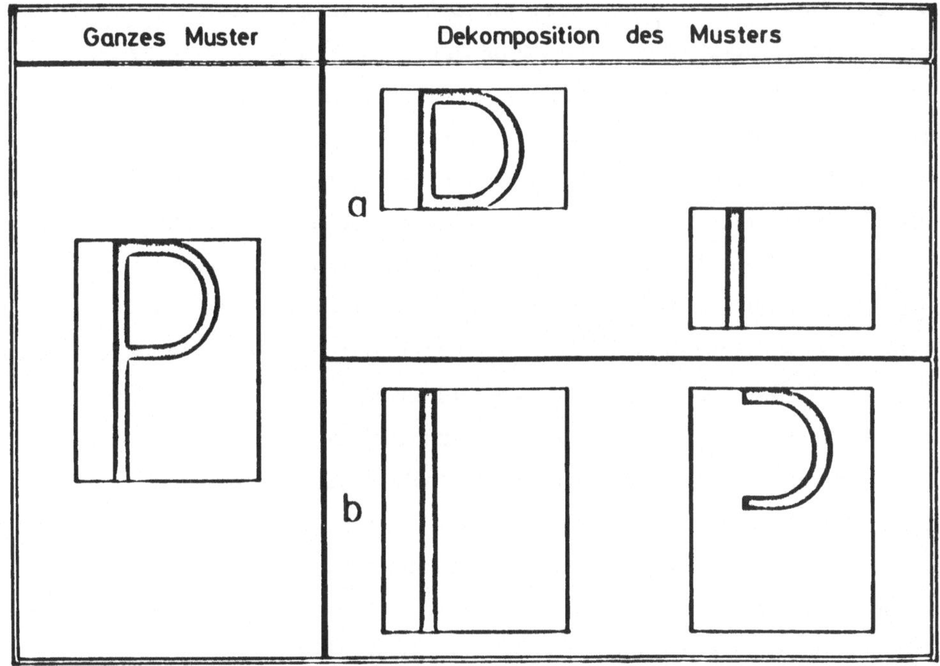

Bild 21: Dekomposition eines Musters
  a) durch Aufteilung des Bildfeldes (obere und untere Hälfte)
  b) durch Merkmalsextraktion (Linien und Krümmungen)

auch eine weitere Aufteilung vorgenommen werden. Für jeden Teil der Bildebene
kann das Verfahren der räumlichen Verzerrungen getrennt angewendet werden. Bei

der Methode b) werden typische kompositorische Elemente des Bildes extrahiert, die Merkmale genannt werden. Solche Merkmale sind z.B. für handgeschriebene Buchstaben: Linien von verschiedener Richtung, Krümmungen, Endpunkte, Kreuzungen usw. Bild 21b zeigt die Extraktion von Linien und Krümmungen. Für jedes so gewonnene Merkmal ist eine weitere Bildebene notwendig. Dies bedeutet aber nicht notwendig einen Zuwachs an Komplexität, weil die Zahl der Bildelemente in den Merkmalsebenen im Sinne einer gröberen Rasterung kleiner gewählt werden kann. Diese Merkmalsebenen können nun wieder verschiedenen Transformationen unterworfen werden. Mit beiden Methoden wird eine Dekomposition des Musters wie folgt vorgenommen:

$$g_\mu (x, y) = \sum_\mu g_{\mu\nu}(x, y) \tag{45}$$

Hierbei bezeichnet μ die Klasse und ν das Teilmuster, also entweder einen Teil des visuellen Feldes oder ein bestimmtes Merkmal. Deshalb kann das gleiche prinzipielle Erkennungsschema in beiden Fällen benutzt werden, das in Bild 22 dargestellt ist. Hier bezeichnet F_1, F_2 .... die Dekompositionsoperation (Bildfeldaufteilung oder Merkmalsextraktion). Es muß erwähnt werden, daß beide Operationen nichtlinear sind und einen Entscheidungsprozeß beinhalten. So muß im Fall der Merkmalsextraktion durch räumliche Filterung eine Schwellwertoperation auf das gefilterte Ergebnis angewendet werden. Dieser Vorgang ist vermutlich im Nervensystem der Säugetiere realisiert. Ein danach entwickeltes Erkennungssystem ist in $\lceil 5 \rfloor$ - $\lceil 8 \rfloor$ beschrieben. Für das zerlegte Bild kann nun das Erkennungsschema mittels geometrischer Transformationen angewendet werden. Dies zeigt Bild 22, wobei T die adaptive räumliche Transformation und $g_{\mu\nu}$ den idealen Prototyp des Musters μ und Teils oder Markmals ν bezeichnet. Ein adaptiver Regelungsprozeß wird für jeden Teil $g_{\mu\nu}$ gesondert verwendet mit dem Ziel einer maximalen Korrelation. Die korrelierten Ausgänge werden für alle Teile ν summiert und ergeben die Anzeige der Klasse μ. Es wird zweckmäßig sein, eine globale geometrische Transformation durchzuführen, bevor das Dekompositionsschema angewendet wird. Auf diese Weise kann ein an die kompositorischen Elemente der Zeichen gut angepaßtes Erkennungssystem gebaut werden. Es gibt freilich viele Arten, solche kompositorischen Elemente zu definieren, und es ist keine einheitliche mathematische Lösung dafür bekannt. Insoweit könnte die Konstruktion des besten Erkennungssystems eher als Kunst denn als Wissenschaft bezeichnet werden. Freilich, die bestgeeignete Lösung für ein kompliziertes Problem zu finden, hat immer schon zur Aufgabe des Ingenieurs gehört und insoweit ist die Mustererkennung ein typisches Problem, dessen Lösung der Ingenieurskunst bedarf.

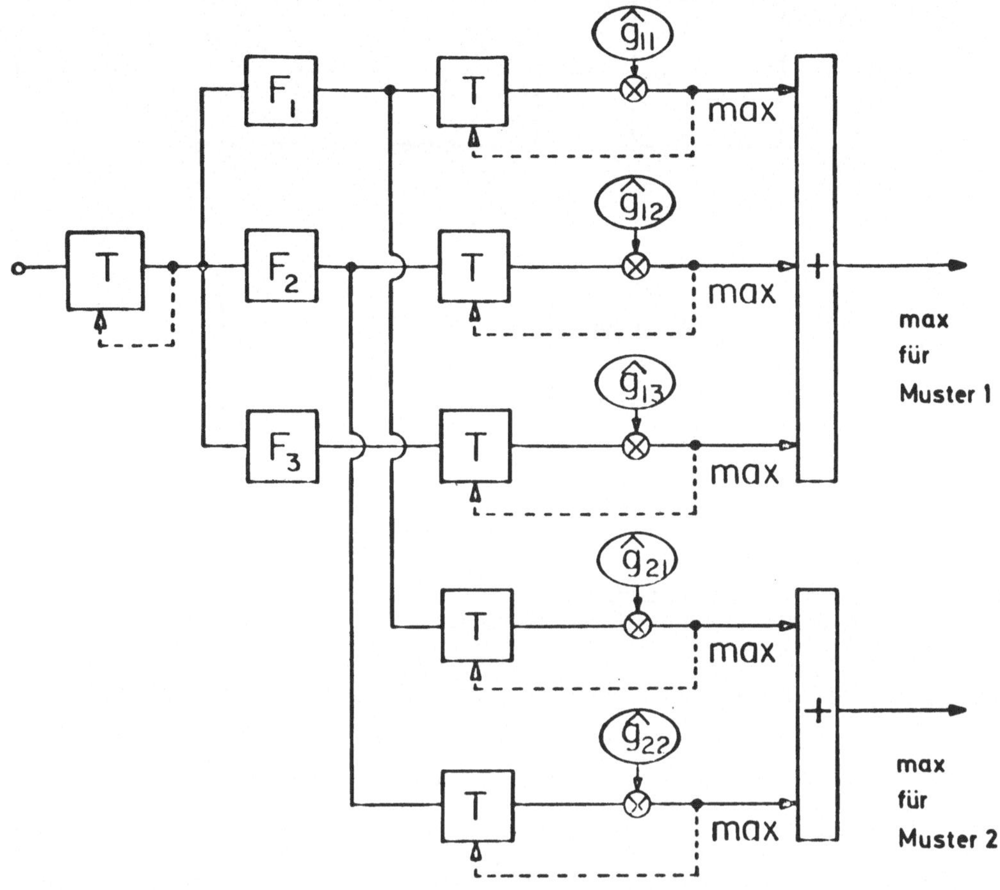

Bild 22: Schema der Mustererkennung nach dem Dekompositionsverfahren

6. Ergebnis

Das Ergebnis der vorliegenden Arbeit läßt sich wie folgt kurz zusammenfassen: Die meisten heute bekannten Verfahren für die Mustererkennung basieren auf einer Darstellung des Problems im Nachrichtenraum und auf Klassifizierungsmethoden nach den Regeln der Entscheidungstheorie. Diese Methoden sind - wie gezeigt wurde- für stark variable Musterstrukturen ungeeignet. Sie führen zu einem Erkennungsschema, das in der Regel die folgenden hintereinander geschalteten drei Stufen gem. Bild 23a enthält: Zentrierung, Merkmalsextraktion und Klassifikation. (Bei der Zentrierung wird zwar ein Teil der vorgeschlagenen geometrischen Transformationen, nämlich

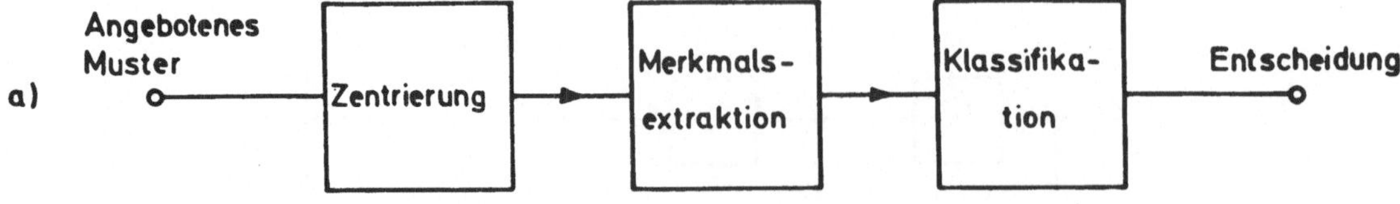

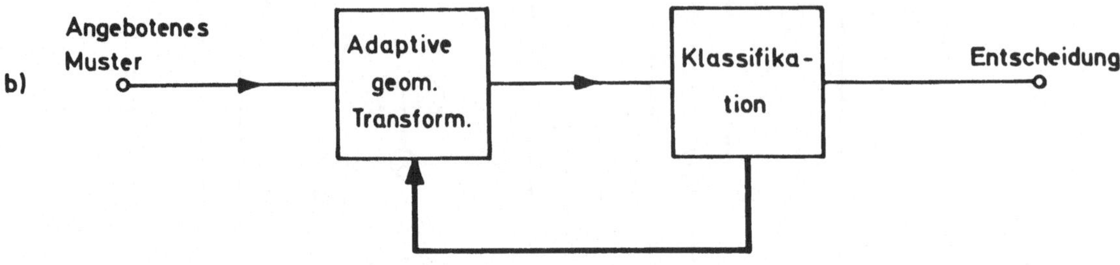

Bild 23: Prinzipielles Erkennungsschema
  a) nach den herkömmlichen Methoden, b) nach dem Vorschlag dieser Arbeit

die Translation, durchgeführt, jedoch in nicht adaptiver Weise. Außerdem fehlen die wichtigsten Transformationen, nämlich die Rotationen um drei Achsen, die geometrische Musterverzerrungen in beliebiger Richtung bewirken können.)

In der vorliegenden Arbeit wird der Entstehungsprozeß der Muster untersucht, was zur Idee der geometrischen Transformationen nach 6 oder 7 Freiheitsgraden führt. Ein darauf basierendes Erkennungssystem gem. Bild 23b benutzt diese Transformationen in der Vorverarbeitungsstufe, wobei eine vom Ausgang her gesteuerte Regelung stattfindet. Diese Regelung wirkt im Sinne einer Optimierung (z. B. Maximierung der Kreuzkorrelation) und macht das System adaptiv. Auf diese Weise kann die Zeichenerkennung als ein Zielverfolgungsverfahren aufgefaßt werden, das zusammen mit der Erkennung auch die Position des Musters bzw. Objektes im Raum ermittelt. Es kann erwartet werden, daß dieser adaptive Regelungsprozeß die Klassifizierung der Muster erheblich erleichtert und Muster mit großer Variabilität linear separierbar macht. Es ist zu hoffen, daß damit ein leistungsfähiges und zugleich wirtschaftliches Erkennungssystem realisierbar wird.

Schrifttum

[1]   Andrews, H.C.: An Introduction to Mathematical Techniques in Pattern Recognition. John Wiley and Sons, New York, 1972

[2]   Nagy, G.: State of the art in pattern recognition. Proc. IEEE, Vol. 56, S. 836-862, Mai 1968

[3]   Bibliography on digital image processing and related topics. USCEE Report 410

[4]   Huang, T.S.; Schreiber, W.F.; Tretiak, O.J.: Image Processing. Proceedings of the IEEE, Vol. 59, No. 11, S. 1586 1610, Nov. 1971

[5]   Pratt, W.K.: A comparison of digital image transforms. Proceedings of the Mervin J. Kelly Communications Conference, Universität von Missouri, Rolla, 1970

[6]   Bremermann, H.J.: What mathematics can and cannot do for pattern recognition. In: Tagungsbericht des 4. Kongresses der Deutschen Gesellschaft für Kybernetik, Berlin-Heidelberg-New York, Springer 1971

[7]   Hoffman, W.C.: The Lie algebra of visual perception. J. Math. Psych. 3, S. 65-98, 1966, 4, S. 348-349, 1967

[8]   Marko, H.: Die Anwendung nachrichtentheoretischer Methoden in der Biologie. In: H. Marko, G. Färber (Hrsg.) Kybernetik 1968, S. 21-44, R. Oldenbourg, München, 1968

[9]   Marko, H.: Die Systemtheorie der homogenen Schichten. Kybernetik 5, S. 221-240, 1969

[10]   Marko, H.: The Biological Approach of Pattern Recognition. (In Vorbereitung)

[11]   Marko, H.; Giebel, H.: Recognition of Handwritten Characters with a System of Homogeneous Layers. Nachrichtentechnische Zeitschrift, S. 455-459, 1970

[12]   Platzer, H.: The simulation of a system of homogeneous layers with coherent light. In: Tagungsbericht des 4. Kongresses der Deutschen Gesellschaft für Kybernetik, Berlin-Heidelberg-New York, Springer 1971

[13]   Vicar Image Processing System: Guide to System Use. Jet Propulsion Laboratory, Pasadena, California, Ref. 324-IPG/1067, Oct. 1, 1968.

Ein Algorithmus zur störsicheren Gruppierung von Mustern

E. Paulus

Zusammenfassung

Die Arbeit behandelt einen Algorithmus zur Unterteilung einer Auswahl von beobachteten
Merkmalmustern in verschiedene Untermengen, die geeignet sind, Kategorien für die Klassifizierung zukünftiger Beobachtungen zu begründen. Eine solche Unterteilung sollte
weitgehend unabhängig von zufälligen Schwankungen oder Störungen der Merkmale sein
und dürfte daher nur "signifikante" Untermengen ergeben. Der Algorithmus liefert eine
große Zahl von kleinen Untermengen und zeigt an, auf welche Weise diese zu größeren
Untermengen vereinigt werden können, um die zufälligen Einflüsse auf die resultierende Unterteilung zu verringern. Dadurch kann der Anwender über eine gewisse Vielfalt
verschiedener Unterteilungen verfügen, die zwischen zwei Extremen liegen. Auf der
einen Seite gibt es sehr viele Untermengen von geringer Signifikanz und auf der anderen
Seite ist die vorgegebene Musterauswahl die einzige Untermenge und die Signifikanz ist
am höchsten. Zu jeder Untermenge (und zu jeder zweckmäßigen Vereinigung von mehreren
Untermengen) wird ein besonderes Maß angegeben, das dem Anwender eine abschließende
Beurteilung der Signifikanz ermöglichen soll.

Außer einer Metrik zur Bestimmung des Abstandes zwischen zwei beliebigen Mustern sind
für die Anwendung des Algorithmus keinerlei Annahmen (z.B. über die Wahrscheinlichkeitsverteilung der Muster) notwendig. Für eine erste Erprobung wurden neben Modell-
versuchen auch Versuche mit Frequenzspektren von Sprachlauten durchgeführt.

1. Einführung

Bei der Beobachtung von Merkmalmustern aus einer bestimmten Grundgesamtheit werden im allgemeinen Annahmen über die Unterscheidung zwischen relevanter und irrelevanter Information benötigt. Solche Annahmen sollen eine wirksame Informationsreduktion ermöglichen und damit den Austausch von Beobachtungsergebnissen zwischen verschiedenen Beobachtern erleichtern. Für die Informationsreduktion ist es zweckmäßig, eine bestimmte Anzahl von Musterkategorien zu vereinbaren und die Vielfalt der Muster innerhalb jeder einzelnen Kategorie als zufalls- oder störbedingt und damit als irrelevant anzunehmen. Dann wird durch das Einordnen eines beobachteten Merkmalmusters in eine der Kategorien die relevante Information voll ausgeschöpft.

Um ein beobachtetes Merkmalmuster zu klassifizieren, das heißt in eine der vereinbarten Kategorien einzuordnen, wendet der Beobachter Entscheidungsregeln an, die ihm auf Grund seiner Erfahrung geeignet erscheinen, die Übereinstimmung mit anderen Beobachtern soweit wie möglich sicherzustellen. Das Risiko für Mißverständnisse wird sich im allgemeinen aber nicht ganz vermeiden lassen. Dafür gibt es vor allem zwei Gründe: Einerseits kann die Erfahrung noch mangelhaft sein, und andererseits können die beobachteten Merkmale zur sicheren Unterscheidung zwischen den vereinbarten Kategorien teilweise unzureichend sein.

Zur Senkung des Risikos kann versucht werden, die Erfahrung zu erweitern und zusätzliche Merkmale in den Entscheidungsprozeß einzubeziehen. Meist sind diese Maßnahmen aber nur dann möglich, wenn genau bekannt ist, auf welche Weise zusätzliche Beobachtungen zu verarbeiten sind, und durch welche zusätzlichen Merkmale die Merkmalmuster ergänzt werden sollen. Schwierigkeiten ergeben sich insbesondere dort, wo die Rolle des lernenden und klassifizierenden Beobachters zumindest teilweise von einem Maschinenprogramm übernommen wird. Aber auch der menschliche Beobachter kann durch mangelhafte Vorkenntnisse daran gehindert sein, weitere nützliche Erfahrungen zu sammeln und neue wirksame Merkmale zu finden.

Das Risiko für Mißverständnisse kann aber auch bei begrenztem Erfahrungsschatz und ohne die Berücksichtigung zusätzlicher Merkmale günstig beeinflußt werden. Dazu ist es notwendig, solche Kategorien zu vereinbaren, deren Unterscheidbarkeit auf Grund der vorliegenden Erfahrung als besonders sicher gelten kann. Im folgenden wird ein Algorithmus behandelt, der die Grundlagen für eine derartige Vereinbarung liefern kann. Ausgangspunkt ist eine Auswahl von beobachteten Merkmalmustern, die als "Lernstichprobe" bezeichnet wird und durch die der begrenzte Erfahrungsschatz gegeben ist. Der Algorithmus führt zu einer Unterteilung der Lernstichprobe in verschiedene Untermengen, die geeignet sind, Kategorien für die Klassifizierung zukünftiger Beobachtungen zu begründen. Dabei werden - vereinfacht ausgedrückt - verschiedene Muster, zwischen denen auf Grund der vorliegenden Lernstichprobe "fließende Übergänge" angenommen werden können, zu einer Untermenge zusammengefaßt. Demgegenüber erscheinen Muster aus verschiedenen Untermengen im Idealfall deutlich getrennt.

Für eine derartige Unterteilung könnten auch einige der bereits bekannt gewordenen Algorithmen zum "nichtüberwachten Lernen" oder "Selbstlernen" (auf Englisch "nonsupervised learning" oder "clustering", siehe /1/) eingesetzt werden. Allerdings erfüllt keiner von diesen Algorithmen eine Anforderung, die hier für wesentlich gehalten wird. Bei praktischen Anwendungen läßt es sich nämlich im allgemeinen nicht vermeiden, daß die Unterteilung von zufälligen Schwankungen oder Störungen der Merkmale mitbestimmt wird. Um aber das Risiko für Mißverständnisse gering zu halten, dürfen Kategorien nur auf "signifikante" Untermengen gestützt werden, bei denen der zufällige Einfluß gering ist. Daher ist zu verlangen, daß der eingesetzte Algorithmus auch eine Möglichkeit zur Beurteilung der Signifikanz jeder der resultierenden Untermengen bietet.

Der hier behandelte Algorithmus liefert eine große Zahl von kleinen Untermengen und zeigt an, auf welche Weise diese zu größeren Untermengen vereinigt werden können, um die Signifikanz zu erhöhen. Dadurch kann der Anwender über eine gewisse Vielfalt verschiedener Unterteilungen verfügen, die zwischen zwei Extremen liegen. Auf der einen Seite gibt es sehr viele kleine Untermengen von geringer Signifikanz und auf der anderen Seite ist die Lernstichprobe die einzige Untermenge und die Signifikanz ist am höchsten. Als vorteilhafte Besonderheit ist auch hervorzuheben, daß diejenigen Muster festgestellt werden, welche die Signifikanz einer bestimmten Untermenge drücken, indem sie "Übergänge" zu anderen Untermengen bilden. Außer einer Metrik zur Bestimmung des Abstands zwischen zwei beliebigen Mustern sind für die Anwendung keinerlei Annahmen (z.B. über die Wahrscheinlichkeitsverteilung der Muster) notwendig.

2. Wirkungsweise des Algorithmus

2.1 Vorbereitende Schritte

Der Algorithmus beginnt damit, die Lernstichprobe T in zwei unabhängige, gleich große Unterstichproben A und B zu unterteilen. Um zu einer großen Zahl von kleinen vorläufigen Untermengen zu gelangen, wird jedes Muster mit demjenigen Muster vereinigt, das ihm am nächsten liegt und das im folgenden "nächster Nachbar" genannt werden soll. Bei diesem Vorgehen werden A und B getrennt unterteilt. Wenn ein Muster zu A gehört, wird demnach auch der nächste Nachbar in A gesucht. Ebenso wird jedes Muster von B mit seinem nächsten Nachbarn in B vereinigt. Jede vorläufige Untermenge enthält mindestens zwei Muster, kann aber ebensogut mehr als zwei umfassen. In Fig.1 sind beispielsweise die Muster der Stichprobe A als Punkte in einer Ebene dargestellt. Jedes Muster ist mit seinem nächsten Nachbarn verbunden. Der dadurch entstandene Graph zerfällt in drei Teilgraphen, die untereinander nicht verbunden sind und drei vorläufige Untermengen von A darstellen.

2.2 Kriterium für die Gruppierung

Auf Grund von zufälligen Einflüssen werden die Unterteilungen von A und B einander nicht voll entsprechen. Indem nun vorläufige Untermengen zu größeren Untermengen ver-

einigt werden, wird versucht, die Entsprechung zu verbessern. Diese Versuche haben
das Ziel, die zufälligen Einflüsse auf die resultierende Unterteilung der Lernstichprobe T soweit wie möglich auszuschalten. Dementsprechend soll die Signifikanz einer
Untermenge von T danach beurteilt werden, in welchem Ausmaß einander die beiden auf
zwei unabhängige Unterstichproben A und B entfallenden Anteile entsprechen. Im folgenden wird ein Maß für diese Entsprechung beschrieben, mit dem es möglich erscheint,
die genannten Versuche durchzuführen und das angestrebte Ziel zu erreichen.

Als Maß für die Entsprechung zwischen einer Untermenge i von A und einer Untermenge j
von B dient der aus der mathematischen Statistik bekannte Vierfelderkorrelationskoef-
fizient, der hier mit C_{ij} bezeichnet werden soll. Um diese Größe bestimmen zu können,
ist es zunächst notwendig, zu jedem Muster von A ein entsprechendes Muster in B und
ebenso zu jedem Muster von B ein entsprechendes Muster in A zu bestimmen. Als entsprechendes Muster wird wieder der nächste Nachbar verwendet. Für ein Muster von A wird
diesmal aber der nächste Nachbar nicht in A sondern in B gesucht und für ein Muster
von B muß der nächste Nachbar in A bestimmt werden. Neben der Unterteilung in die beiden disjunkten Untermengen i und A-i ergibt sich für A eine weitere bedeutsame Unterteilung in zwei disjunkte Untermengen, von denen die eine alle Muster mit nächsten
Nachbarn in j und die andere alle Muster mit nächsten Nachbarn außerhalb von j (d.h.
in B-j) umfaßt. Bei vollständiger Entsprechung zwischen i und j sind die beiden Unterteilungen von A identisch und i umfaßt alle Muster von A mit nächsten Nachbarn in j
und darüber hinaus keine weiteren Muster. Dem steht die völlige Unabhängigkeit der
beiden Unterteilungen gegenüber, wo der relative Anteil der Muster mit nächsten Nachbarn in j bei i nicht signifikant höher ist als bei A insgesamt. Ebenso läßt sich B
nicht nur in j und B-j unterteilen, sondern auch in eine Untermenge von Mustern mit
nächstem Nachbarn in i und eine dazu disjunkte Untermenge von Mustern mit nächstem
Nachbarn in A-i. Auch hier liegen die Extreme für die Entsprechung bei der Identität
der beiden Unterteilungen einerseits und der völligen Unabhängigkeit andererseits.
Die Entsprechung zwischen i und j ist also gleichbedeutend mit der Korrelation zwischen den jeweils zwei Unterteilungen von A und B und kann durch den schon erwähnten
Vierfelderkorrelationskoeffizienten quantitativ erfaßt werden.

Die bei der Bestimmung von C_{ij} maßgebenden vier Größen sind:

$$n_{11} = a(i,j) \quad + b(j,i) \qquad n_{12} = a(i,B-j) \quad + b(B-j,i)$$

$$n_{21} = a(A-i,j) + b(j,A-i) \qquad n_{22} = a(A-i,B-j) + b(B-j,A-i).$$

Wenn dabei x eine der Untermengen i oder A-i von A und y eine der Untermengen j oder
B-j von B bezeichnen, dann bedeuten a(x,y) die Anzahl der Muster von x mit nächsten
Nachbarn in y und b(y,x) die Anzahl der Muster von y mit nächsten Nachbarn in x. Mit
dieser Vereinbarung gilt

$$C_{ij} = \frac{n_{11}\,n_{22} - n_{12}\,n_{21}}{\sqrt{(n_{11} + n_{12})\,(n_{11} + n_{21})\,(n_{22} + n_{12})\,(n_{22} + n_{21})}}$$

und die Summe $n = n_{11} + n_{12} + n_{21} + n_{22}$ ergibt den Umfang der Lernstichprobe T.

Bei vollständiger Entsprechung zwischen i und j ergibt sich $C_{ij} = 1$. Demgegenüber ergibt sich aus der Unabhängigkeit von i und j der Erwartungswert $E(C_{ij}) = 0$. Die Größe C_{ij} kann für jede Untermenge von T bestimmt werden, die sowohl Muster von A als auch Muster von B enthält. Wenn sie aber entweder nur Muster von A oder nur welche von B enthält, dann wird $C_{ij} = 0$ vereinbart. Damit ist insbesondere für jede der schon erwähnten vorläufigen Untermengen $C_{ij} = 0$.

2.3 Hierarchie von Untermengen

Um C_{ij} schrittweise zu vergrößern, werden die vorläufigen Untermengen zu immer grösseren Untermengen zusammengefaßt bis einige wenige endgültige Untermengen erreicht sind. Die dabei resultierenden Untermengen genügen zunächst den folgenden Bedingungen: Je zwei beliebige Untermengen sind entweder disjunkt oder die eine ist vollständig in der anderen enthalten, und zu jeder noch nicht endgültigen Untermenge gibt es eine andere, sodaß die Vereinigung von beiden zu einem Anwachsen von C_{ij} führt. Die Vereinigungsmenge genügt dann entweder selbst der zuletzt genannten Bedingung oder sie ist eine endgültige Untermenge. Unter Umständen ist die Lernstichprobe selbst die einzige endgültige Untermenge, doch kann es ebensogut mehrere disjunkte endgültige Untermengen geben. Die resultierenden Untermengen können durch die Knoten in einem Baum graphisch dargestellt werden, wie in Fig. 2 gezeigt ist. Jeder Wurzel des Baumes entspricht eine endgültige Untermenge und jedem Endknoten eine vorläufige Untermenge. An jedem dazwischen liegenden Knoten verzweigt sich der Baum in zwei Zweige. Verfolgt man einen Pfad von einem Endknoten, wo $C_{ij} = 0$ ist, zu einer Wurzel, wo C_{ij} seinen Höchstwert annimmt, dann steigt C_{ij} jedesmal, wenn ein Knoten passiert wird.

2.4 Verarbeitungsstufen

Durch die bisher genannten Bedingungen sind die resultierenden Untermengen noch nicht eindeutig festgelegt. Daher sind Maßnahmen notwendig, um unter mehreren möglichen Vereinigungsmengen jeweils besonders günstige auszuwählen. Der Algorithmus schreitet von kleinen Untermengen zu immer größeren fort und durchläuft verschiedene Verarbeitungsstufen. Auf jeder Stufe ist die Vereinigung einer bestimmten Anzahl von vorläufigen Untermengen zu einer einzigen Untermenge zulässig. In dem in Fig. 3 gezeigten Flußdiagramm ist diese Anzahl als "zulässige Größe" bezeichnet. Für die Vereinigung werden jeweils zwei Untermengen vorgesehen, die das Ergebnis vorangegangener Verarbeitungsstufen sind und die bisher noch nicht in einer umfassenderen Untermenge enthalten sind. Unter allen möglichen Paarungen zwischen solchen Untermengen wird eine Vorauswahl getroffen, um nur diejenigen für die weitere Verarbeitung bereitzuhalten, welche zur zulässigen Größe und zu einem Anwachsen von C_{ij} führen. Wenn bei der Vorauswahl alle Paarungen ausgeschieden werden, wird die Verarbeitungsstufe ohne Ergebnis sofort abgeschlossen. Für die erste Verarbeitungsstufe ist die zulässige Größe zwei, und jede in die engere Wahl gezogene Paarung umfaßt genau eine vorläufige Untermenge von A und eine von B.

Für die weitere Verarbeitung werden die bereitgehaltenen Paarungen nach fallenden Werten von C_{ij} angeordnet. Nach diesem Sortiervorgang wird als erstes die Paarung mit dem größten Wert von C_{ij} ausgewählt. Danach werden die übrigen Paarungen der Reihe nach überprüft, um diejenigen auszuwählen, welche disjunkt zu allen vorher ausgewählten sind. Dabei wird zusätzlich gefordert, daß C_{ij} kein "lokales Minimum" annimmt. Diese Bedingung ist dann verletzt, wenn jeder der beiden Bestandteile auch zu einer Paarung mit größerem C_{ij} gehört, die deshalb verworfen wurde, weil sie nicht disjunkt zu allen jeweils schon vorher ausgewählten Paarungen ist. Durch diese zusätzliche Bedingung soll die voreilige Vereinigung von zwei Untermengen vermieden werden, die besser auf nachfolgenden Verarbeitungsstufen verschiedenen Untermengen zugeschlagen werden können. Ohne diese Bedingung könnte es zum Beispiel passieren, daß eine "Brücke" zwischen zwei signifikanten Untermengen nicht aufgeteilt, sondern zunächst als eigene Untermenge gebildet und dann als Ganzes einer der beiden Untermengen zugeschlagen wird.

Jede ausgewählte Paarung wird als Ergebnis der Verarbeitungsstufe festgehalten und liefert einen Knoten zu dem angestrebten Baum. Nach Abschluß einer Verarbeitungsstufe wird die zulässige Größe um eins erhöht. Wenn mindestens zwei Untermengen mit $C_{ij} < 1$ für weitere Vereinigungsversuche zur Verfügung stehen, wird die nächste Verarbeitungsstufe begonnen. Andernfalls ist die Verarbeitung insgesamt abgeschlossen und alle Untermengen, die noch nicht Bestandteil einer umfassenderen Untermenge sind, gelten als endgültige Untermengen. Die schrittweise Vereinigung von jeweils nur zwei Untermengen und die dabei angewendete Auswahlstrategie gewährleisten, daß C_{ij} möglichst rasch anwächst, während gleichzeitig eine Vielzahl von Untermengen erhalten bleibt. Auf diese Weise werden die distinktiven Details der Merkmalmuster gründlich ausgewertet.

3. Hierarchie von Musterkategorien

Es bleibt dem Anwender überlassen, den resultierenden Baum auszuwerten, um zu einer Hierarchie von Kategorien zu gelangen, von denen keine mit einem unerwünscht hohen Risiko für Mißverständnisse verbunden ist. Dieses Risiko ist am kleinsten, wenn nur endgültige Untermengen berücksichtigt werden, aber es kann auch vorteilhaft sein, einige der weniger umfassenden Untermengen heranzuziehen. Andererseits können aber auch endgültige Untermengen dazu ungeeignet sein, die Einrichtung von Musterkategorien zu rechtfertigen. Um die Frage der Signifikanz einer Untermenge zu entscheiden, muß vor allem C_{ij} überprüft werden. Dabei ist zu berücksichtigen, daß die hier geübte Anwendung des Vierfelderkorrelationskoeffizienten in einem Gruppierungsalgorithmus nicht unmittelbar mit normalen Anwendungsfällen verglichen werden kann. Daher kann auch der übliche Signifikanztest, bei dem für nC_{ij}^2 eine χ^2 - Verteilung mit zwei Freiheitsgraden anzunehmen ist, nicht ohne weiteres übernommen werden. Das Ergebnis eines solchen Tests, bei dem C_{ij} praktisch mit einer bestimmten Schwelle zu vergleichen ist, wird nämlich nicht nur von der Grundgesamtheit der Merkmalmuster, sondern auch von der Wirkungsweise des Algorithmus wesentlich mitbestimmt. Die Frage, welche Rückschlüsse auf die Grundgesamtheit dabei tatsächlich möglich sind, konnte noch nicht befriedigend geklärt werden. Es muß aber von vornherein ausgeschlossen werden, daß sich für C_{ij} eine Schwelle finden läßt, die in gleicher Weise für alle Untermengen gilt und dabei nur vom gewünschten Signifikanzniveau und vom Umfang der Lernstichprobe T abhängt. Vielmehr ist zu erwarten, daß jede Untermenge nach einer eigenen Schwelle verlangt, die z.B. vom Umfang der Untermenge und von ihrer Aufteilung auf die beiden Unterstichproben A und B mitbestimmt wird.

Die bisherigen Erfahrungen bei der Erprobung des Algorithmus führen jedoch zu der Annahme, daß es in vielen Fällen auch ohne Bezugnahme auf eine Schwelle für C_{ij} möglich ist, zwischen signifikanten und nichtsignifikanten Untermengen zu unterscheiden. Eine solche Möglichkeit besteht immer dann, wenn an dem resultierenden Baum (oder wenigstens an Teilen davon) ein bestimmtes Kennzeichen festgestellt werden kann. Dazu ist es notwendig, die von den einzelnen Endknoten ausgehenden Pfade zur Wurzel hin zu verfolgen und das Anwachsen von C_{ij} zu beobachten. Dabei zeigt es sich häufig, daß C_{ij} nur an einem einzigen der durchlaufenen Knoten stark ansteigt, während der Zuwachs an den übrigen Knoten vergleichsweise gering ist. Unter den Knoten des Baumes lassen sich dann einige "Randknoten" feststellen, bei denen jeweils der Übergang von kleinen Werten von C_{ij} zu einem Wert nahe an dem erreichbaren Höchstwert erfolgt. Durch Fig. 4 soll die Rolle der Randknoten deutlich gemacht werden.

Bei Bäumen mit ausgeprägten Randknoten läßt sich in einfacher Weise eine brauchbar erscheinende Grenze zwischen signifikanten und nichtsignifikanten Untermengen finden. Zu diesem Zweck sind die von der Wurzel ausgehenden Pfade zu den einzelnen Endknoten zu verfolgen, und die Grenze ist jeweils dort anzunehmen, wo erstmals einer der Randknoten erreicht wird. Die jeweils noch nachfolgenden Knoten stellen dann Untermengen dar, die zurückzuweisen sind. Nach der Entfernung dieser Knoten werden die meisten Randknoten zu Endknoten E des verbleibenden Baumes (siehe Fig. 4), der die gesuchte Hierarchie von Musterkategorien darstellt.

Bei ausgeprägten Randknoten kann die Existenz signifikanter Untermengen als ausreichend sicher angenommen werden. Demnach wird bei dem zuletzt beschriebenen Vorgehen eher eine signifikante Untermenge zurückgewiesen als eine nichtsignifikante Untermenge beibehalten. Zukünftige Untersuchungen sollen die Möglichkeiten zur Beurteilung der Signifikanz erweitern.

4. Demonstrationsbeispiele

Der Algorithmus und die Auswertung des resultierenden Baumes werden gegenwärtig noch erprobt. Daher dienen alle im folgenden erwähnten Ergebnisse von Anwendungsbeispielen nur zur Demonstration und haben darüber hinaus keine wesentliche Bedeutung.

Als erstes wurde eine Grundgesamtheit von Mustern betrachtet, die durch Störung zweier gleich wahrscheinlicher Muster S_1 und S_2 entsteht. Die beiden Muster werden dabei als zwei bestimmte Punkte in einem m-dimensionalen euklidischen Raum aufgefaßt, zwischen denen eine Entfernung d besteht. Die einzelnen Koordinaten von S_1 und S_2 werden unabhängig voneinander von einer normalverteilten Störung mit der Streuung 1 betroffen. Als Lernstichprobe wurde eine Auswahl von je 200 (gestörten) Mustern S_1 und S_2 verwendet. Bei m = 10 und d = 3,16 ergaben sich 86 vorläufige Untermengen (45 von A und 41 von B) und die Lernstichprobe selbst war die einzige endgültige Untermenge. Der resultierende Baum hat zwei ausgeprägte Randknoten mit C_{ij} = 0,88, die zur Annahme von zwei signifikanten Untermengen berechtigen. Dabei umfaßt die eine Untermenge 186 Muster S_1 und 29 Muster S_2 und die andere 14 Muster S_1 und 171 Muster S_2. Dieses Ergebnis steht im Einklang mit den vorgegebenen Eigenschaften der Grundgesamtheit von Merkmalmustern. Zu Vergleichszwecken wurden eine gleichverteilte und eine normalverteilte Grundgesamtheit betrachtet, wo keine signifikanten Untermengen erwartet werden dürfen. In beiden Fällen umfasste die Lernstichprobe wiederum 400 Muster. Im ersten Fall ergaben sich 93 vorläufige Untermengen (46 von A und 47 von B) und 11 endgültige Untermengen. Im zweiten Fall wurden 68 vorläufige Untermengen (32 von A und 36 von B) und ebenfalls 11 endgültige Untermengen gebildet. Bei den meisten endgültigen Untermengen ist C_{ij} deutlich näher an 0 als an 1, und in keinem Fall konnten bei den resultierenden Bäumen ausgeprägte Randknoten festgestellt werden. Daher führt auch der Ausnahmefall von C_{ij} = 0,62 bei einer 39 Muster umfassenden endgültigen Untermenge nicht zur fälschlichen Annahme einer signifikanten Untermenge.

Das nächste Beispiel soll zeigen, daß der Algorithmus auch für Aufgaben eingesetzt werden kann, die weitaus schwieriger sind als der Nachweis von nur zwei verhältnismäßig deutlich unterscheidbaren Musterkategorien. Zu diesem Zweck wurde eine Lernstichprobe von 402 Frequenzspektren von Sprachlauten verarbeitet. Die Einzelheiten über diese Spektren sind hier nicht weiter interessant und wurden bereits an anderer Stelle behandelt (E. PAULUS: Automatische "Cluster" - Analyse von Sprachdaten. Beitrag zum Speech Symposium, Szeged 1971). Es sei lediglich darauf hingewiesen, daß jedes Spektrum als Punkt in einem 22-dimensionalen euklidischen Raum aufgefaßt werden kann. Der Algorithmus ergab 102 vorläufige Untermengen und 7 endgültige Untermengen. Ausgeprägte Randknoten führen zu der Annahme von 13 signifikanten Untermengen, die in Fig. 5 dargestellt sind. In der Darstellung fehlen zwei sehr kleine endgültige Untermengen (mit 6 bzw. 12 Spektren), die trotz hohem C_{ij} (1,0 bzw. 0,8) nicht geeignet erscheinen, die Annahme signifikanter Untermengen zu unterstützen. Die signifikant erscheinenden Untermengen sind durch Dreiecke dargestellt, die jeweils den Umriß des

Baumes andeuten, der von einem Randknoten ausgeht. An der Basis der Dreiecke ist der Umfang der jeweiligen Untermenge vermerkt. Darüber hinaus ist in phonetischer Schrift angegeben, welche Sprachlaute hauptsächlich in der betreffenden Untermenge vertreten sind. Diese Angaben umfassen zwei Zeilen. Eine Eintragung in der ersten Zeile bedeutet, daß der angegebene Sprachlaut nur in einer einzigen Untermenge vertreten ist. Dementsprechend ist jeder der in der zweiten Zeile eingetragenen Laute in mindestens zwei Untermengen vertreten. Es ist zu sehen, daß die Sprachlaute bei der Unterteilung der Lernstichprobe in nur 13 Untermengen, nicht vollständig getrennt werden. Es scheint aber, daß auch der menschliche Zuhörer die Sprachlaute auf ähnliche Weise unvollständig unterscheidet, wenn ihm die Hinweise versagt werden, die normalerweise aus dem sprachlichen Zusammenhang folgen. Daher kann auch das mit den Spektren von Sprachlauten erzielte Ergebnis als wirklichkeitsnah gelten. Für eine endgültige Bewährung des Algorithmus müssen aber noch weitere Anwendungsfälle untersucht werden.

Literatur

/1/   G. NAGY: State of the Art in Pattern Recognition. Proc. IEEE 56 (1968),836-862.

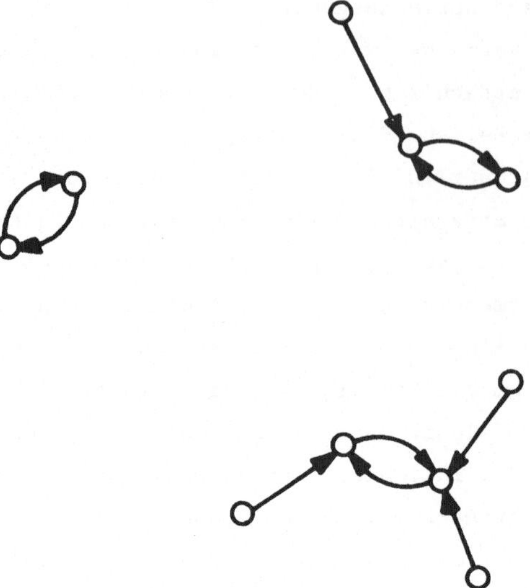

Fig. 1.   Beispiel für die Unterteilung einer Auswahl von Mustern in vorläufige Untermengen

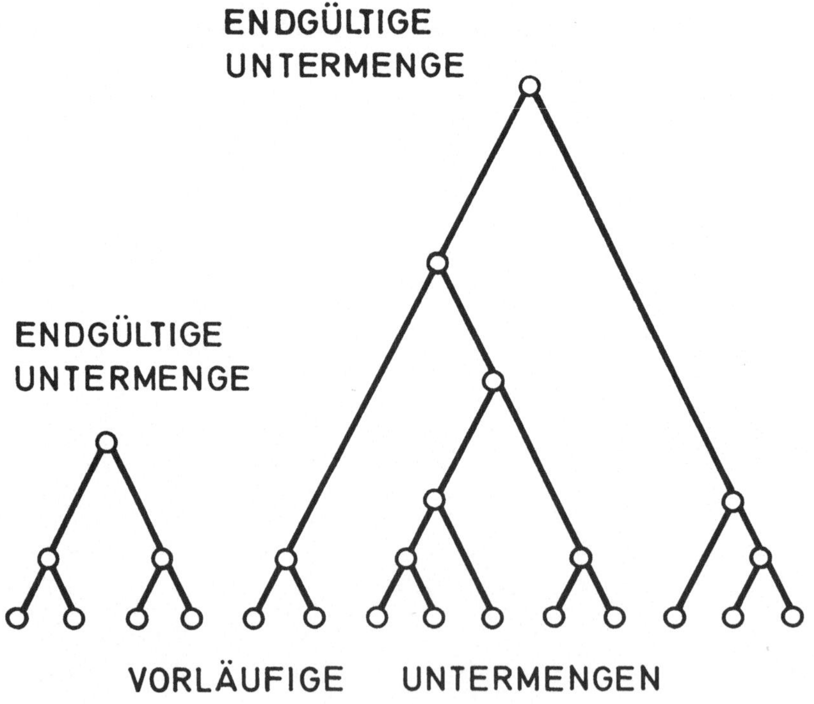

Fig. 2.   Hierarchie von Untermengen der Lernstichprobe

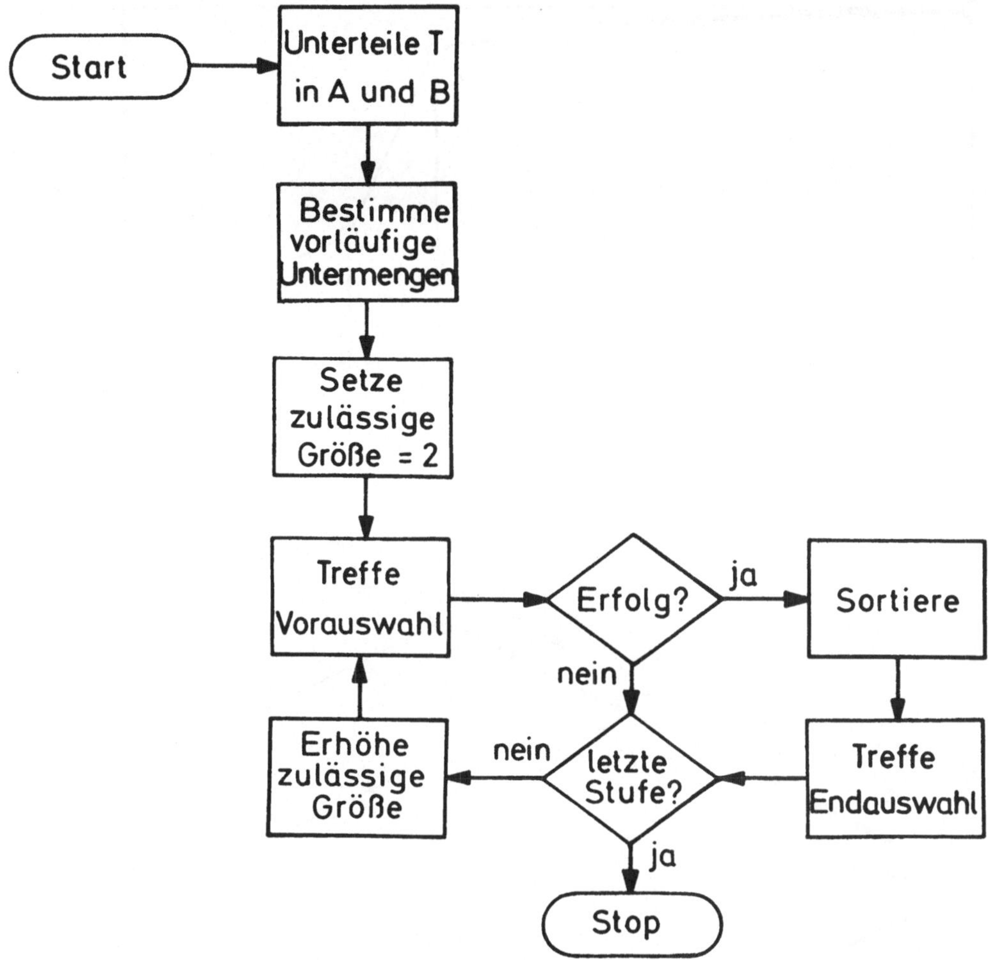

Fig. 3.   Operationsfolge bei der Gruppierung von Merkmalmustern

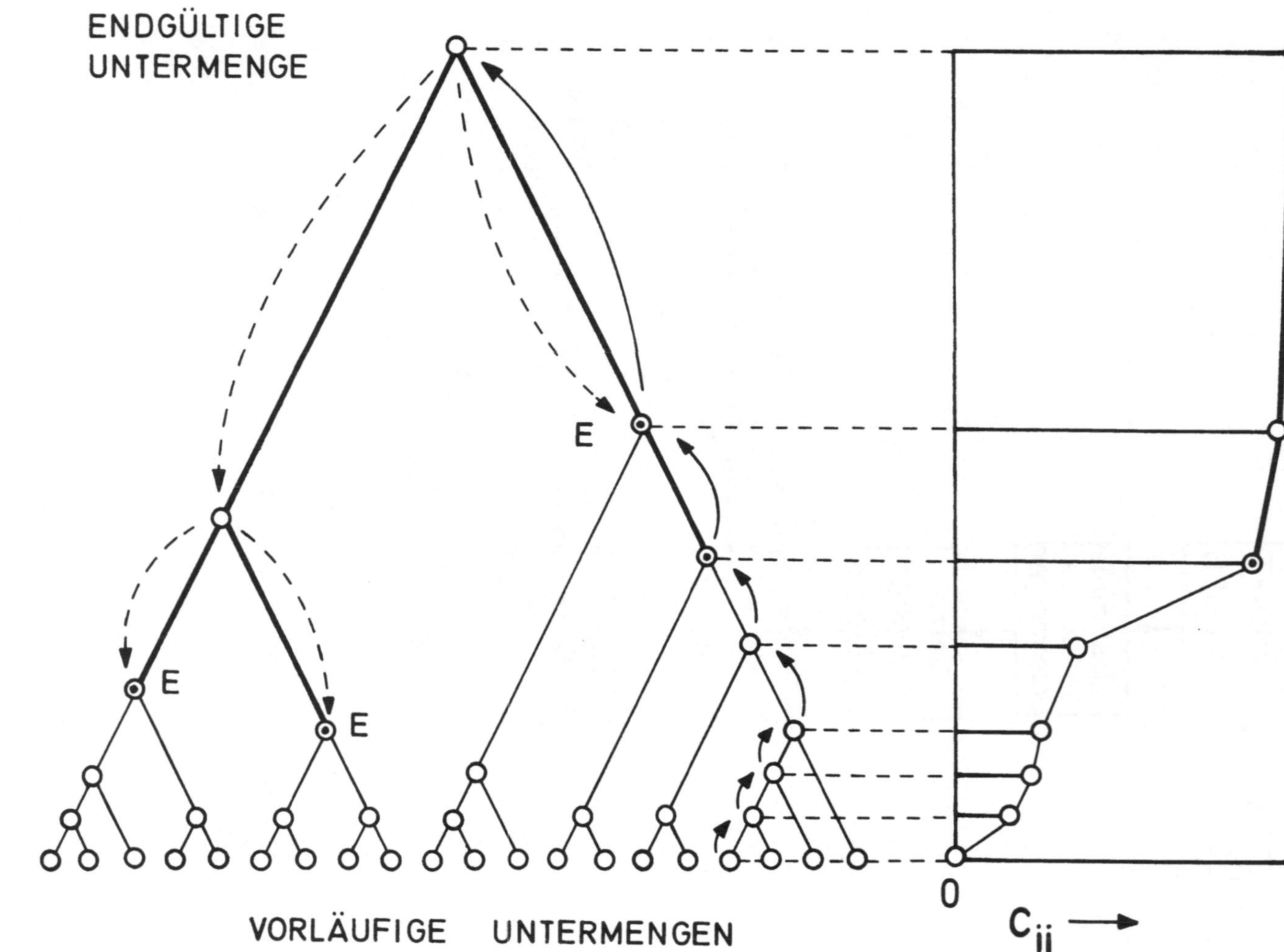

Fig. 4.   Randknoten und Grenze zwischen signifikanten und nichtsignifikanten Untermengen

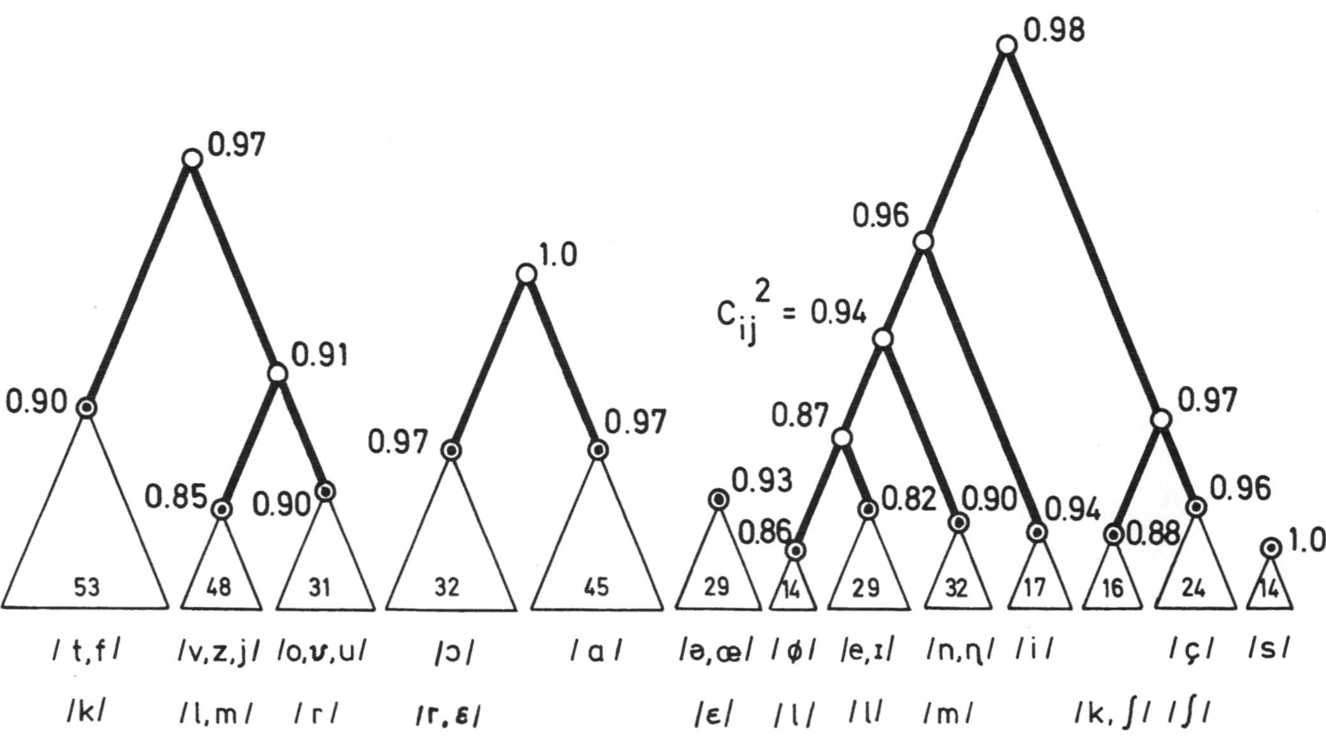

Fig. 5.   Gruppierung von 384 Frequenzspektren von Sprachlauten

D. Becker

1. Einleitung

Ein Spracherkennungssystem ist eine spezielle Art von Informationswandler. Aus den angebotenen akustischen Eingaben muß eine Entscheidung über die mutmaßliche Bedeutung "des Gesprochenen", über die Klassenzugehörigkeit hergeleitet werden. Aufgabe des Spracherkennungssystems ist vorerst nur das Klassifizieren von getrennt gesprochenen Worten mit einem beschränkten Wortvorrat.

Da es sich im wesentlichen darum handelt, die bei der Zeichenerkennung bewährte Methode der Regressionsanalyse $\underline{/}\,1\,\underline{/}$, $\underline{/}\,2\,\underline{/}$ auf das Spracherkennungsproblem anzuwenden, liegt die Klassifikatorstruktur und die mathematische Optimierungsmethode fest. Man kann das Spracherkennungssystem in eine Folge von Verarbeitungsstufen zerlegen, in denen die Entscheidung Schritt für Schritt vorbereitet wird.

- Erzeugung der Daten,
- Vorverarbeitung,
- Schätzfunktion,
- Entscheidung.

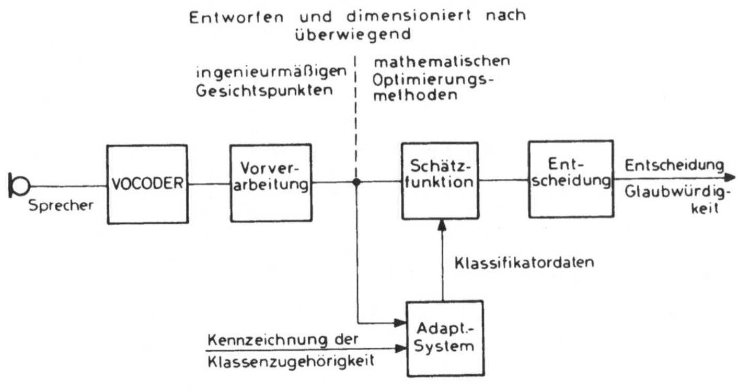

Bild 1: Spracherkennungssystem

In Bild 1 ist das Spracherkennungssystem dargestellt. Entwurf und Dimensionierung des Systems stehen unter dem Einfluß zweier Prinzipien, die man am besten durch die Stichworte

- ingenieurmäßige Methoden,
- mathematische Optimierungsmethoden

charakterisieren kann. Durch die Systemmitte verläuft eine Grenze, die die beiden Prinzipien voneinander trennt. Während Erzeugung der Daten und Vorverarbeitung überwiegend nach ingenieurmäßigen Gesichtspunkten konzipiert und konstruiert werden, dominieren in der zweiten Hälfte des Systems die mathematischen Optimierungsmethoden.

Zuerst soll aufgezeigt werden, welche Vorverarbeitung notwendig ist, damit die mathematischen Optimierungsmethoden angewendet werden können. Im Zusammenhang mit Spracherkennungsaufgaben tritt uns "das Gesprochene" mit zwei Aspekten entgegen, und es ist wichtig, begrifflich zwischen ihnen zu unterscheiden. Auf der einen Seite haben wir die "akustische Äußerung", die je nach Gewohnheiten des Sprechenden ganz verschieden klingen wird, und auf der anderen Seite haben wir die "Bedeutung" der akustischen Äußerung, die z. B. bei den 10 gesprochenen Ziffern nur 10 diskrete Werte annehmen kann. "Akustische Äußerung" und Bedeutung gehören zusammen.

Um das Sprachmaterial reduzieren und verarbeiten zu können, verwenden wir zur Aufnahme einen Vocoder, der eine beträchtliche Datenreduktion durchführt. Die Bedeutung der "akustischen Äußerung" muß durch den Menschen mitgeteilt werden.

2. Die Stichprobenaufnahme

Ausgehend von einem Frequenz-Zeit-Energiemuster, dem VISIBLE SPEECH Diagramm, wie es in Bild 2 analog dargestellt ist, versuchen wir innerhalb dieser Darstellung die Merkmale zu bestimmen, die den größten Beitrag zur Worterkennung liefern. In Bild 2, das mit einem Sonagraphen erzeugt wurde, ist das gesprochene Wort "eins" dargestellt, und zwar nach oben die Frequenzachse, nach rechts die Zeitachse und, ausgedrückt durch die Schwärzung, die Energie.

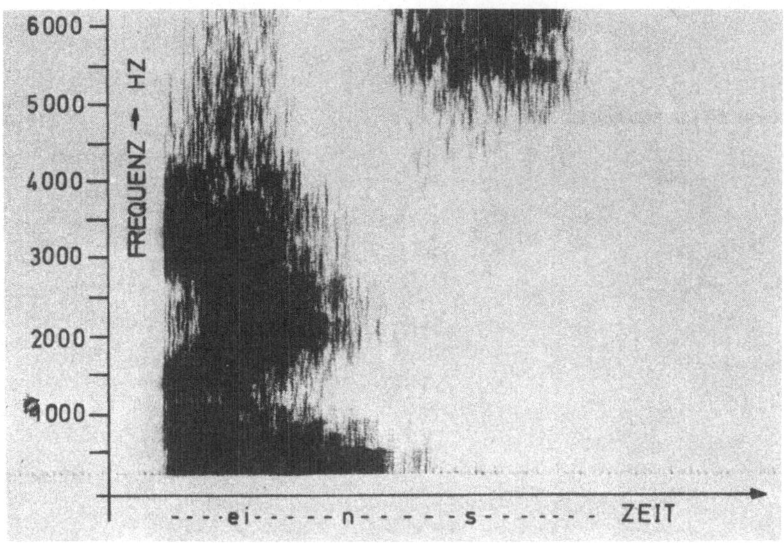

Bild 2: Visible Speech Diagramm des Wortes "eins" (Sonagraph)

Durch Quantisierung dieses Frequenz-Zeit-Energiemusters gewinnen wir unser Datenmaterial. Dazu verwenden wir das im Forschungsinstitut von AEG-TELEFUNKEN in Ulm vorhandene Simulationssystem $\boxed{3}$. Dieses besteht aus einem Digitalrechner und einem Kanalvocoder mit 16 Kanälen. Von den 16 Kanälen überträgt Kanal 1 den Wert der PITCH-Frequenz, Kanal 2 die Gesamtdynamik des Eingangssignals und die Kanäle 3 bis 16 die Ausgangsdynamik von 14 Terzfiltern, die ein Frequenzband von 0,25 bis 5 kHZ umfassen. Die Eingabe des Sprachmaterials erfolgt mit Hilfe eines Programmes, das es ermöglicht, die Bedeutung des Gesprochenen gleichzeitig mit der vom Vocoder durchgeführten Spektralanalyse in einen Digitalmagnetbandblock unterzubringen. Durch Drücken eines Knopfes am Vocoder wird die Rechnereingabe gestartet. Danach wird in das Mikrofon gesprochen - nachdem "das Gesprochene" zu Ende ist, wird der Knopf losgelassen und dadurch die Eingabe beendet. Nachdem dieses Wort mit seiner Bedeutung auf ein Digitalmagnetband geschrieben ist, kann mit der nächsten Eingabe fortgefahren werden.

Das Wort, das uns schon in Bild 2 begegnete, wurde nach der Methode auf ein Digitalmagnetband gespeichert und mit Hilfe des Schnelldruckers in Bild 3 ausgedruckt.

An diesem Frequenz-Zeit-Energiemuster, dem "quantisierten Wort eins", werden verschiedene Normierungsoperationen betrachtet, deshalb soll Bild 3 ausführlich erklärt werden. Die Zeitachse erstreckt sich jetzt nach unten, die Frequenzachse nach rechts, und die Energie wird durch Zahlenwerte dargestellt.

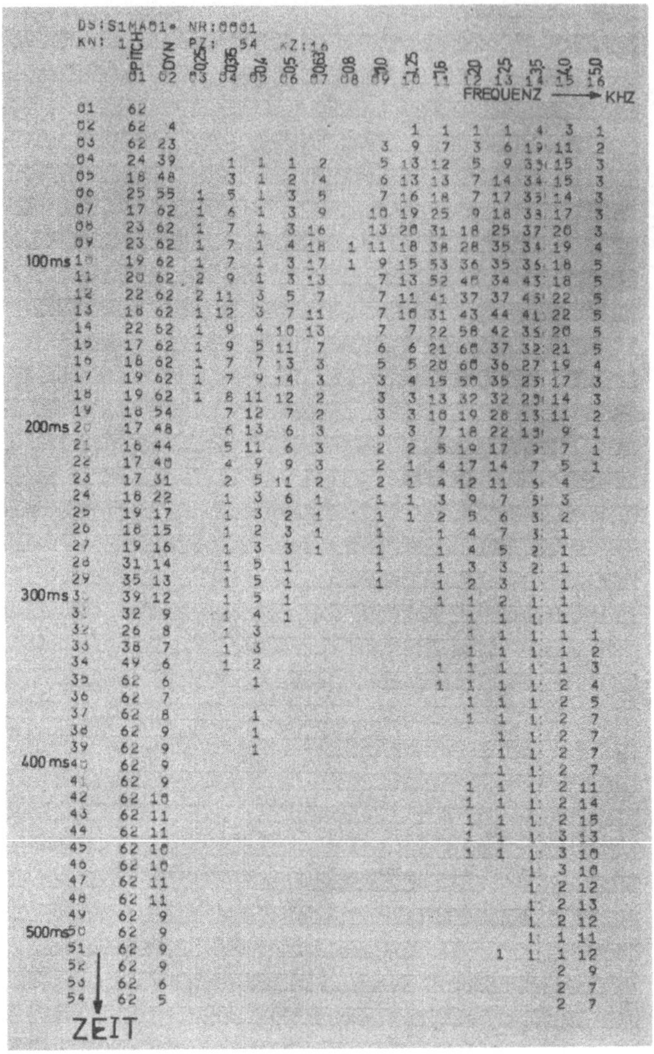

Bild 3: Frequenz-Zeit-Energiemuster des gesprochenen Wortes "eins"

● Zeitachse

Bei 100 Hz Abtastfrequenz werden alle 10 ms 16 Werte dem Rechner angeliefert,
jeweils 16 Werte bezeichnen wir als Probe, und jede Probe bekommt eine aufstei-
gende Numerierung. In Bild 3 sind 54 Proben angeliefert worden. d. h. der Rechner war 540 ms aufnahmebereit.

● Frequenzachse

Die Kanäle wurden von links nach rechts numeriert, wobei Kanal 1 den Wert der
Pitchfrequenz, Kanal 2 die Gesamtdynamik des Eingangssignals und die Kanäle 3
bis 16 die Ausgangsdynamik von 14 Terzfiltern darstellen. Außerdem wurden die

Mittenfrequenzen der Vocoderfilter festgehalten.

● Energie

Bei 6 BIT-Quantisierung liegt die Zahlendarstellung der Energie im Bereich von
$0 \leq X_i \leq 2^6 - 1 = 63$. Nur in Kanal 2 wird innerhalb des Aufnahmeprogramms die
Summe über die Kanäle 3 bis 16 gebildet, so daß dort die Zahlendarstellung
$0 \leq X_i \leq 99$ beträgt. Die Darstellung auf dem Schnelldrucker wurde so gewählt,
daß der Wert 0 durch Leertasten dargestellt wird.

● Bedeutung

Daß es sich bei dem in Bild 3 dargestellten Frequenz-Zeit-Energiemuster um das
Wort "eins" handelt, wird durch das Zeichen hinter KN: (Kennung) festgehalten.

3. Vorverarbeitung

3.1. Operation KÜRZEN

Nachdem die wortweise Eingabe mit Hilfe des Rechners erklärt wurde, ist klar,
daß die Energiewerte vom Zeitpunkt des Eingabeknopfdrucks bis zum Beginn der
"akustischen Äußerung" Null sein werden. Ebenso hängt das Ende der Rechnereingabe von der Reaktionszeit des Sprechers ab. Die Energiewerte am Ende der "akustischen Äußerung" bis zum Loslassen des Eingabeknopfes sind auch Null. Es ist
klar, daß die Meßwerte, die am Beginn und am Ende eines Wortes Null sind, nichts
zur Unterscheidung der Klassen untereinander beitragen werden. Man muß also die
"akustische Äußerung" zentrieren, d. h. die Meßwerte, die am Anfang und Ende
des Wortes Null sind, weglassen.

Es liegt nahe, alle Proben (eine Probe = 16 Werte), die im Dynamikkanal (Kanal
2) kleiner gleich als ein anzugebender Dynamik-Schwellwert sind, am Beginn und
Ende des Wortes wegzulassen.

Diese Operation entspricht einer Kantenzentrierung, und es wird sich zeigen,
ob man in diesem Punkt noch weitere Zentrierkriterien einführen muß. Hier soll
noch die grundsätzliche Schwierigkeit bei der richtigen Wahl des Schwellwertes
aufgezeigt werden. Wählt man den Schwellwert zu klein, dann täuschen Störungen
"Beginn der akustischen Information" vor. Wählt man den Schwellwert zu groß,
werden Teile der akustischen Information weggeschnitten, die zum Erkennen einen
Beitrag leisten. Als Beispiel möge das Zahlwort "sechs" stehen. Ist das "s" am
Schluß des Wortes zu leise artikuliert und die Dynamik-Schwelle zu hoch gewählt, wird dieses "s" weggeschnitten.

In den Fällen, in welchen Information durch "Kürzen" am Anfang oder Ende weggeschnitten wird, oder bei einer unkorrekten Eingabe durch zu frühes Loslassen
des Eingabeknopfes am Rechner wird dieses Wort durch das Kantenzentrierverfahren falsch zentriert.

Im Zusammenhang mit diesem Problem sei angeführt, daß an dieser Stelle noch
weitere Untersuchungen angestrebt werden müssen, um herauszufinden, ob das
Schwerpunktzentrierverfahren $/\overline{4}\_/$ dem Kantenzentrierverfahren überlegen ist.

Nachdem die Operation "Kürzen" erklärt ist, soll anhand von Bild 3 die Wirkungsweise aufgezeigt werden. Bei einer Dynamikschwelle = 8 würden die Proben 1, 2,
53 und 54 wegfallen.

3.2. Operation LAUTSTÄRKE

Lautstärkeunterschiede sollen durch diese Operation beseitigt werden, außerdem
wird dadurch der Zahlenbereich der Frequenzkanäle, die mit 6 BIT quantisiert
werden, auf $0 \leq X_i \leq 99$ erweitert.

In Kanal 3 bis Kanal 16 wird das Maximum gesucht, mit diesem wird der Normie-
rungsfaktor nach folgender Vorschrift gebildet

$$\text{FAKTOR} := \frac{\text{Normlautstärke}}{\text{Maximum}}$$

Danach werden alle Energiewerte mit diesem FAKTOR multipliziert und gerundet.
Ausgenommen aus dieser Operation sind die Meßwerte, die zum PITCH-Kanal (Kanal 1) gehören.

3.3. Operation ZEITNORMIERUNG

Außer der verschiedenen Artikulation, verschiedenen Stimmhöhen, unterschiedli-
chen Lautstärken, Dialekteinflüssen, Störgeräuschen usw. tritt bei der Worterkennung als erschwerender Faktor die unterschiedliche Sprechgeschwindigkeit bei
verschiedenen Sprechern hinzu. Verfahren zu finden, die durch eine geschickte
Behandlung eines Wortes, aus einem schnell gesprochenen Wort und aus einem langsam gesprochenen Wort gleicher Bedeutung, ähnliche Merkmalsbeschreibungen liefern, wird eine Aufgabe sein, die noch mehrere intensive Untersuchungen innerhalb dieses Problemkreises erfordert. Außer aus den eben erwähnten Gründen ist
es für den mathematischen Optimierungsprozeß erforderlich, daß alle Worte unabhängig von den Klassen gleiche Anzahl von Meßwerten haben.

Als Beispiel soll die kürzeste und längste Sprechdauer bei den Worten "eins" bis "null" angegeben werden. Das kürzeste Zahlwort liegt in der Klasse "sechs" mit einer Dauer von ca. 180 ms, das längste Zahlwort in der Klasse "sieben" mit ca. 720 ms.

Ein sehr naheliegendes Verfahren, die Zeitnormierung durchzuführen, besteht darin, kanalweise den vorhandenen Verlauf über der Zeit zu approximieren. Man wird das Zeitnormierungsverfahren so wählen, daß die

$$\left.\begin{array}{c}\text{Energie im}\\\text{neuen Intervall}\end{array}\right\} = \left\{\begin{array}{l}\text{der mittleren Energie über die}\\\text{Dauer des neuen Intervalls ist.}\end{array}\right.$$

Mit dieser Forderung kann man die akustische Information kürzen, d. h. auf die gleiche Anzahl von Meßwerten normieren. Ebenso kann man die Zahl der Meßwerte erhöhen, obwohl dadurch die Information nicht genauer dargestellt wird. Mathematisch formuliert lautet das Problem

$$\text{neue Intervallänge} \cdot \text{Wert in Intervall} = \int\limits_{\text{neues Intervall}} \text{Treppenkurve } dt$$

Programmtechnisch läßt sich die Zeitnormierung einfach durchführen. Wir kennen die Probenzahl PZ, die bei jedem Wort nach der Operation "Kürzen" verschieden sein wird, und nennen sie Variable Probenzahl = VP. Außerdem muß man angeben, auf welche Probenzahl man das Wort normieren will, diese Zahl nennen wir Normprobenzahl NP. Mit diesen Festlegungen läßt sich eine neue Abtastzeit $\Delta t'$ berechnen:

$$\Delta t' = \frac{VP}{NP}$$

Hat man die neue Abtastzeit berechnet, kann man die Energie innerhalb dieses neuen $\Delta t'$ aufaddieren, durch $\Delta t'$ dividieren, und bekommt dadurch den mittleren Energiewert in dem neuen Intervall. Jedes Wort ist nach Durchlaufen dieser Operation gleich lang, d. h. die Anzahl seiner Meßwerte ist gleich.

Führt man die Zeitnormierung nach diesem Verfahren mit einer Normprobenzahl = 25 an unserem Wort von Bild 3 durch, bekommen wir als Ergebnis dieses Rechenprozesses Bild 4.

152

DS:ZZZZZZ* NR:0001
KN: 1   PZ: 25   KZ:16

FREQUENZ ——► KHZ

Nr.	PITCH 01	DYN 02	0.25 03	0.315 04	0.4 05	0.5 06	0.63 07	0.8 08	1.0 09	1.25 10	1.6 11	2.0 12	2.5 13	3.5 14	4.0 15	5.0 16
01	61	37							2	5	4	2	4	12	7	2
02	21	98		2	1	2	3		6	13	13	6	12	32	15	3
03	21	99	1	6	1	3	8		9	18	22	9	18	37	16	3
04	23	99	1	7	1	3	17	1	12	19	36	24	31	35	19	4
05	20	99	2	8	1	3	14		8	14	51	38	35	49	18	5
06	20	99	1	11	3	7	10		7	10	34	42	41	42	22	5
07	19	99	1	9	5	11	9		6	6	21	59	39	33	20	5
08	19	99	1	7	9	13	3		4	4	16	51	35	25	17	3
09	18	99		7	12	8	2		3	3	10	23	28	15	12	2
10	17	89		5	11	7	3		2	2	5	18	18	9	7	1
11	17	60		2	6	9	2		2	1	4	13	11	5	4	
12	18	30		1	3	3	1		1	1	2	6	7	4	2	
13	22	21		1	3	2	1		1		1	4	5	2	1	
14	35	16		1	5	1			1		1	2	3	1	1	
15	32	10		1	4	1						1	1	1	1	
16	39	10		1	3							1	1	1	1	2
17	60	11			1						1	1	1	1	2	4
18	62	12			1							1	1	1	2	7
19	62	12			1								1	1	2	7
20	62	17										1	1	1	2	12
21	62	19										1	1	1	2	14
22	62	15										1	1	1	3	10
23	62	15												1	2	12
24	62	14												1	2	12
25	62	13												1	1	11

ZEIT

Bild 4: Operation Zeitnormierung - Normprobenzahl = 25

Man sieht im Vergleich mit Bild 3, daß die grobe Struktur des Wortes "eins" erhalten bleibt.

4. Schätzung der Klassenzugehörigkeit

Wir haben die Operationen des Spracherkennungssystems bis in die Systemmitte
hinein verfolgt (Bild 1). Die durch die Vorverarbeitung standardisierten Daten
treten jetzt aus dem Bereich, in dem die ingenieurmäßigen Methoden dominieren,
in den Teil des Systems ein, der von der mathematischen Optimierungsmethode be-
herrscht wird. Im weiteren soll aufgezeigt werden, wie der Klassifikator an die
vorliegende Aufgabenstellung adaptiert wird. Ausgangspunkt ist dabei eine gegebene Menge von Beispielsworten, die die zu erkennenden Worte in allen zulässigen Variationen enthält.

Optimierungsziel ist, das Spracherkennungssystem durch die Adaption dahin zu bringen, daß es angesichts der gegebenen Aufgabenstellung möglichst wenig Fehler macht.

● Definition der Variablen

$\mathcal{X}$ = Merkmalsvektor

Nach der Operation "Kürzen", Lautstärkenormierung und Zeitnormierung betrachten wir nur noch die Meßwerte der Frequenzkanäle. Die Menge dieser Meßwerte fassen wir als Komponenten eines Merkmalsvektors $\mathcal{X}$ auf. Dieser Merkmalsvektor repräsentiert das durch die Vorverarbeitung standardisierte Wort.

Im weiteren soll die Zuordnung zwischen dem Komponentenindex, der von O bis m zählt, und den beiden Indizes für Zeit und Frequenz aufgezeigt werden.

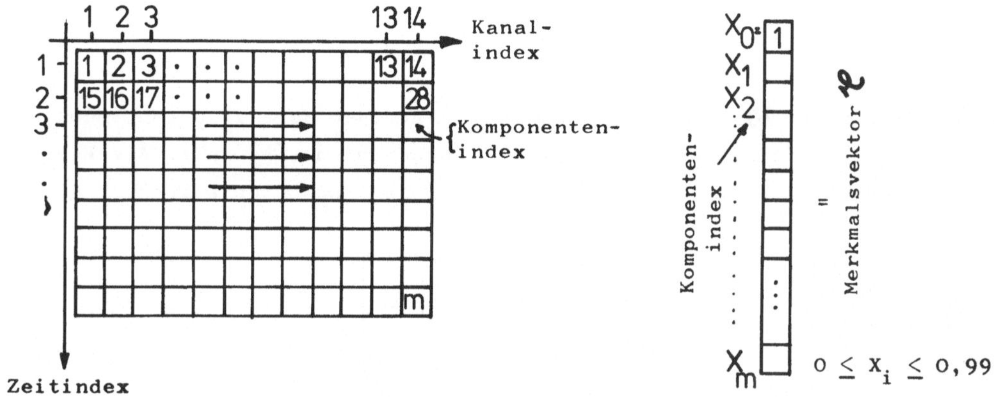

<u>Bild 5</u>: Der Merkmalsvektor $\mathcal{X}$

Die Werte, die zu einem bestimmten Abtastzeitpunkt abgetastet wurden, haben wir schon als Probe definiert. Da die Mittenfrequenzen der Kanalausgänge durch Terzfilter festliegen, sprechen wir von dem Kanalindex, so daß das Produkt aus Kanalzahl x Probenzahl + 1 = Anzahl der Vektorkomponenten ergibt.

Zusammenfassend sei wiederholt: Ein Wort wird repräsentiert durch den Merkmalsvektor $\mathcal{X}$. Durch die Probenzahl wird etwas über die zeitliche Dauer des gesprochenen Wortes und durch die Kanalzahl etwas über die Frequenzen ausgesagt.

● PZ = Probenzahl,

● KZ = Kanalzahl.

Die Anzahl der Vektorkomponenten ergibt sich aus

$$n = PZ \cdot KZ + 1$$

Und schließlich sagt die Vektorkomponente X_i etwas über die Energie zu einem
ganz bestimmten Frequenzzeitpunkt aus. In unserem Beispiel ist die Probenzahl
= 20 und die Kanalzahl = 14, so daß sich eine Vektorlänge von n = 281 ergibt.
Wir fassen das Spracherkennungsproblem als eine Prognoseaufgabe auf, nämlich
nur aus den Messungen, die wir zu dem Merkmalsvektor $\boldsymbol{x}$ zusammengefaßt haben,
die wahre Klassenzugehörigkeit zu schätzen.

Das Ziel der Schätzung, die wahre Klassenzugehörigkeit drücken wir durch einen
Zielvektor $\boldsymbol{y}$ aus.

$$
\boldsymbol{y}_G = \begin{bmatrix} y_{1G} \\ y_{2G} \\ \vdots \\ y_{jG} \\ \vdots \\ y_{KG} \end{bmatrix}
\qquad
y_{jG} = \begin{cases} 1 & \text{wenn } j = G \\ 0 & \text{wenn } j \neq G \end{cases}
$$

$$
K = \text{Klassenanzahl}
$$

Bei unserem Zielvektor $\boldsymbol{y}$ hat genau eine Komponente den Wert 1, deren Index mit
der wahren Klasse übereinstimmt, die anderen Komponenten sind null. Als Beispiel
sollen für die drei Klassen F, G, H die Zielvektoren angegeben werden.

$$
\boldsymbol{y}_F = \begin{bmatrix} 1 \\ 0 \\ 0 \end{bmatrix}
\qquad
\boldsymbol{y}_G = \begin{bmatrix} 0 \\ 1 \\ 0 \end{bmatrix}
\qquad
\boldsymbol{y}_H = \begin{bmatrix} 0 \\ 0 \\ 1 \end{bmatrix}
$$

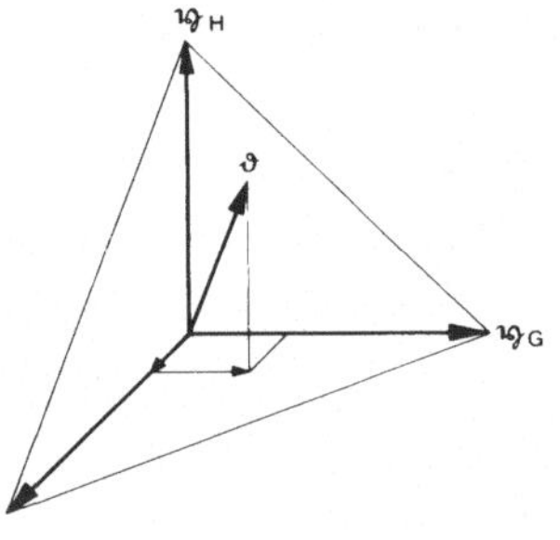

Bild 6: Die Zielvektoren bei 3 Klassen

Die Aufgabe ist jetzt, nur aus Kenntnis des Merkmalsvektors $\boldsymbol{x}$ eine Schätzung
für den Zielvektor $\boldsymbol{y}$ abzugeben. Wir suchen dafür eine vektorielle Funktion $\boldsymbol{v}(\boldsymbol{x})$
so daß

$$
E\left\{|\boldsymbol{y} - \boldsymbol{v}(\boldsymbol{x})|^2\right\} \stackrel{!}{=} \text{Minimum wird.}
$$

Wir wollen also eine Schätzung im quadratischen Mittel optimieren.

Die beste Funktion $\vartheta(\mathfrak{r})$ ist die sogenannte Regressionsfunktion $\underline{/1\_/}$, die aber bei einer so großen Zahl von Merkmalen (in unserem Fall = 281) nicht ermittelt werden kann. Wir machen deshalb für die Schätzfunktion $\vartheta(\mathfrak{r})$ einen besonders einfachen in den Merkmalen linearen Ansatz

$$\vartheta = \begin{bmatrix} d_1 \\ d_2 \\ \cdot \\ \cdot \\ \cdot \\ d_K \end{bmatrix} = \begin{bmatrix} a_{11} & \cdots & a_{1n} \\ \cdot & & \cdot \\ \cdot & & \cdot \\ \cdot & & \cdot \\ \cdot & & \cdot \\ a_{K1} & \cdots & a_{Kn} \end{bmatrix} \cdot \mathfrak{r} = A \cdot \mathfrak{r}$$

Die noch unbekannten frei wählbaren Koeffizienten a_{ij} fassen wir zu einer Matrix A zusammen.

Die Koeffizientenmatrix A wird aus der Forderung bestimmt, den Erwartungswert für die Abweichung zwischen der Zielgröße und der Schätzung zu einem Minimum zu machen. Das Kriterium, kleinstes mittleres Fehlerquadrat, deckt sich nicht vollständig mit dem Kriterium "kleinste Fehlerrate", doch bekommt man durch diesen Ansatz den Vorteil, daß die Bestimmung der Koeffizientenmatrix A auf ein lineares Gleichungssystem führt, dessen Lösung keine grundsätzlichen Schwierigkeiten bereitet $\underline{/1\_/}$. Außerdem ist gewährleistet, daß wenn das mittlere Fehlerquadrat verschwindet, auch die Fehlerrate Null ist.

Mit den aus der Mathematik bekannten Methoden, d. h. Ableiten und Nullsetzen der Gleichung $S^2 = E\{|\vartheta - A \cdot \mathfrak{r}|^2\}$ kann man die gesuchte Koeffizientenmatrix A berechnen. Eine anschauliche Interpretation soll helfen, die Lösung zu verstehen.

Die Menge aller möglichen Merkmalsvektoren bildet den Merkmalsraum R. Die Unterscheidungsfunktion $\vartheta(\mathfrak{r})$ bildet den gesamten Merkmalsraum in den Entscheidungsraum ab, wobei sich jetzt die Vektoren der gleichen Klasse in der Nähe ihres Klassenzielpunktes versammeln. Zusammenfassend sei wiederholt: Aus einer Stichprobe, bei der jedes Element mit seiner Klassenzugehörigkeit gekennzeichnet ist, wird ein lineares Gleichungssystem aufgestellt. Aus der Auflösung dieses linearen Gleichungssystems erhalten wir die Klassifikatordaten, die Koeffizientenmatrix A.

Hat man die Koeffizientmatrix berechnet, so werden die Schätzungen für die einzelnen Worte wie folgt berechnet:

$$\vartheta(\mathfrak{r}) = A \cdot \mathfrak{r}$$

Die Komponenten des Schätzvektors ϑ kann man auch als Wahrscheinlichkeiten interpretieren.

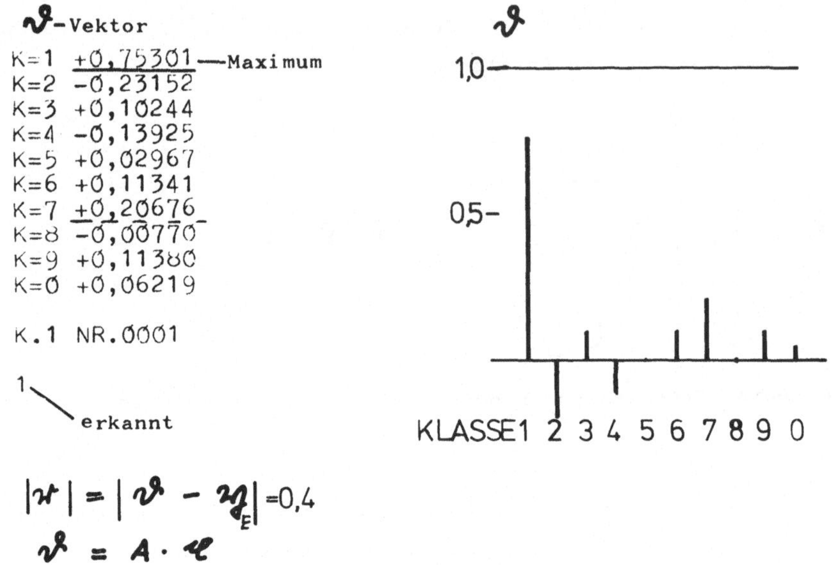

Bild 7: Die Worterkennung, Schätzvektor ϑ , Maß für die Sicherheit $|\mathit{u}|$

In Bild 7 sind die geschätzten Wahrscheinlichkeiten für das Wort "eins" festgehalten. Dabei wurde für die Bildung des Schätzvektors ϑ eine aus 2000 Worten berechnete Koeffizientenmatrix A verwendet.

Aus den in Bild 7 graphisch dargestellten ϑ-Komponenten wird klar, daß es sich um das Wort "eins" handelt, denn das Maximum der geschätzten Wahrscheinlichkeit beträgt 0,75 für die Klasse eins.

Nach der Bildung des Schätzvektors wird das Wort der Klasse j zugeordnet, deren Schätzwert am größten ist.

$$d_j = \max (d_k) \qquad k = 1 \ldots K$$

Hat man diese Entscheidung gefällt, interessieren wir uns für die Sicherheit dieser Zuordnung. Ein gutes Maß für die Sicherheit der Entscheidung ist der Betrag des Fehlervektors $|\mathit{u}|$ zwischen dem Schätzvektor ϑ und dem Zielvektor z.

$$|\mathit{u}| = |\vartheta - \mathit{z}|$$

Im Klassifikator meßbar ist jedoch nur die maximale Komponente d_{max}, deshalb bilden wir

$$|\mathbf{w}| = |\mathbf{v} - \mathbf{v}_E|$$

Die wahre Klassenzugehörigkeit ist prinzipiell unbekannt, und $\mathbf{v}_E$ (E für Entscheidung) ist die vom Klassifikator geschätzte Klassenzugehörigkeit. Eine Klassifikation gilt als sicher, solange $|\mathbf{w}|$ unter einem vorgegebenen Wert (z. B. R = 0,5) bleibt. Dies läßt sich folgendermaßen deuten: Um die Spitzen der Zielvektoren $\mathbf{v}$ werden im K-dimensionalen Raum Kugeln mit dem Radius R gelegt. Nur wenn der Schätzvektor $\mathbf{v}$ in das Innere einer solchen Kugel zeigt, ist die Zuordnung eindeutig. In unserem Beispiel Bild 7 ist der Betrag des Fehlervektors $|\mathbf{w}|$ = 0,4. Das Spracherkennungssystem (Bild 1) liefert uns bei der Eingabe eines Merkmalsvektors $\mathbf{v}$ die Klassenzugehörigkeit j des Wortes und ein Maß $|\mathbf{w}|$ für die Sicherheit der Aussage.

5. Beurteilung der Klassifikatorleistung

Berechnet wurde der zugrunde gelegte Klassifikator aus 2000 Worten, gesprochen von 2 verschiedenen Sprechern. Bei den Worten handelt es sich um die Zahlworte von eins bis null. Mit jedem Wort wurde die Operation Kürzen, Lautstärke und Zeitnormierung durchgeführt. Jedes für die Berechnung der Klassifikatordaten verwendete Wort wurde auch bei der Simulation der Erkennung verwendet. Bei den eigegebenen 2039 Worten wurden 26 Worte falsch klassifiziert. Nimmt man Worte von den gleichen Sprechern, die nicht bei der Berechnung verwendet wurden, erhält man ähnliche Ergebnisse. Die Anzahl der Fehler bei der Erkennung gibt nur ein grobes Maß über die Qualität eines Klassifikators. Besseren Aufschluß erhält man jedoch, wenn man statistische Daten über den Entscheidungsprozeß bildet. Aus diesem Grunde führen wir eine Häufigkeitsstatistik über den Betrag des Fehlervektors $|\mathbf{w}|$, und zwar getrennt nach richtigen und falschen Entscheidungen. Bild 8 zeigt diese Verteilungen.

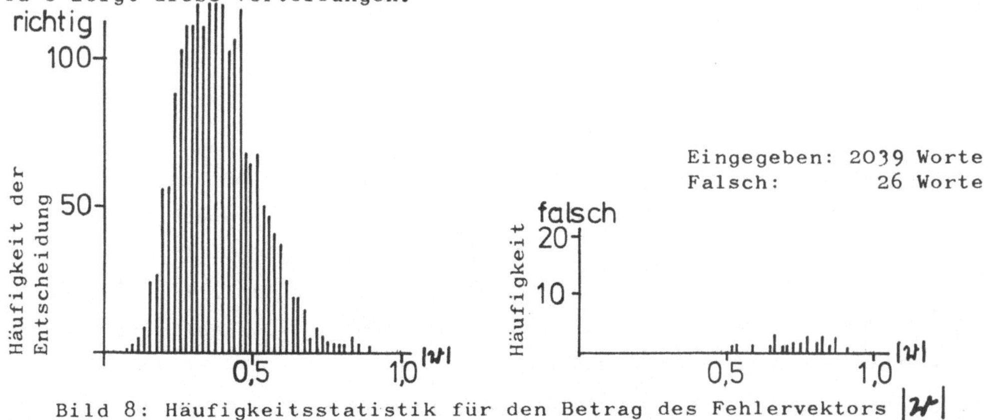

Bild 8: Häufigkeitsstatistik für den Betrag des Fehlervektors $|\mathbf{w}|$ getrennt nach richtigen und falschen Entscheidungen

158

In praktischen Andwendungen sieht man immer die Möglichkeit einer Zurückweisung
vor. Mit dem Maß $|\varkappa|$, das für die Sicherheit einer Aussage steht, als Zurück-
weisungskriterium, kann man das Zurückweisungsverhalten angeben. Aus der Häufig-
keitsverteilung von Bild 8 konstruieren wir das Zurückweisungsverhalten unseres
Klassifikators.

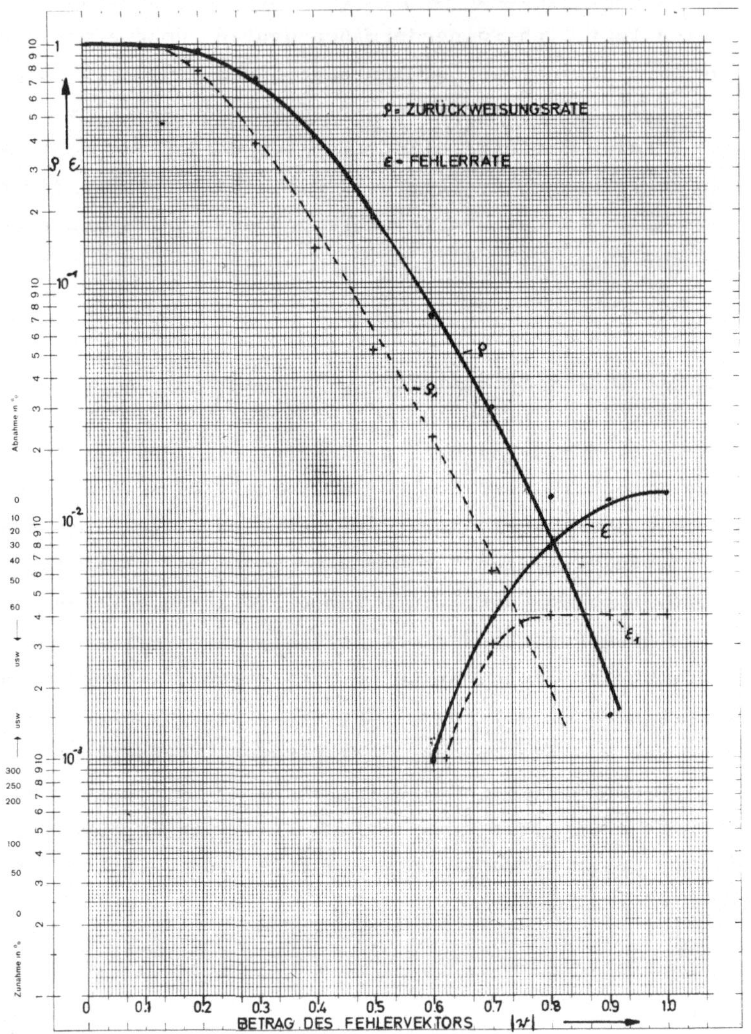

Bild 9: Zurückweisungsverhalten des Klassifikators mit dem
Betrag $|\varkappa|$ des Fehlervektors als Zurückweisungskriterium

Bild 9 zeigt den Verlauf der Zurückweisungsrate $\wp$ und der Fehlerrate $\mathcal{E}$ über dem
Betrag $|\varkappa|$, der als Gütekriterium für eine Entscheidung verwendet wird. Je klei-
ner die Zurückweisungsschwelle R gesetzt wird, um so höher steigt die Zurückweisungsrate, während die Fehlerrate zurückgeht. In Bild 9 ist noch eine Kurve $\wp_1$

und ε_1 gestrichelt eingezeichnet. Bei diesen Kurven handelt es sich um die Ergebnisse, die mit einem Sprecher erreicht wurden, und man sieht, daß diese Ergebnisse besser sind.

Abschließend sei erwähnt: ist die Anzahl der zu unterscheidenden Worte klein, und sind die Benutzer eines Spracherkennungssystems vorher bekannt, kann man mit der hier aufgezeigten Methode die Klassifikatordaten automatisch berechnen und so zu einem wirtschaftlich einsetzbaren Spracherkennungssystem kommen.

Literatur:

$\sqrt{1\_7}$ J. Schürmann

Über die Anwendung der Regressionsanalyse auf das Zeichenerkennungsproblem

Dissertation, TH Berlin, 1968

$\sqrt{2\_7}$ G. Meyer-Brötz, J. Schürmann

Methoden der automatischen Zeichenerkennung

Oldenbourg Verlag, 1970

$\sqrt{3\_7}$ H. Mangold

Der Einsatz elektronischer Rechner für Aufgaben der nachrichtentechnischen Systemforschung

Telefunken-Zeitung, Heft 1/2, Jahrgang 40, 1967

$\sqrt{4\_7}$ J. Schürmann

Experimenteller Vergleich verschiedener Schwerpunktzentrierverfahren für die Zeichenerkennung

NTZ, 21, 1968

DIGITALE SEGMENTATION VON SPRACHSIGNALEN IM ZEITBEREICH.

W. Hess

Das beschriebene digitale Segmentationsverfahren unterteilt das Sprachsignal im Zeitbereich in einzelne diskrete Abschnitte, die die zeitliche Lokalisierung der meisten gesprochenen Phoneme im Sprachsignal zulassen. In zwei Vorbereitungsschritten werden zunächst die Pausen sowie die stimmlosen Abschnitte im Verlauf des Signals ausgesondert. Der folgende eigentliche Segmentationsschritt versucht, die Artikulationsgeschwindigkeit des Vokaltrakts an Hand einiger globaler Sprachsignalparameter zu beschreiben. Da der Vokaltrakt sich beim Sprechen nicht konstant bewegt, sondern versucht, die zu jedem Phonem gehörige artikulatorische "Zielstellung" zu realisieren, lassen sich Abschnitte mit geringen Änderungen der Vokaltraktstellung ("stationäre" Segmente) von solchen mit grösseren Änderungen ("dynamische" Segmente) trennen. Berücksichtigt man die Richtung der Änderungen im Parameterverlauf während der dynamischen Segmente, so lassen sich diese noch weiter aufteilen. Das Verfahren wurde auf isoliert gesprochene Wörter angewendet (insgesamt 7 Sprecher); die Fehlerrate - sofern sich eine solche hier überhaupt bestimmen lässt - lag, verglichen mit einer aus der Lautschrift des gesprochenen Textes gewonnenen "Idealsegmentation", für alle Sprecher bei etwa 3,5%.

1. EINLEITUNG

Im akustischen Sprachsignal sind im Gegensatz zum geschriebenen Text die Bausteine (Wörter, Laute) nicht getrennt, sondern gehen fliessend ineinander über. Trotzdem ist der Hörer in der Lage, das akustische Signal und die diskrete schriftliche Form zueinander in Beziehung zu bringen. Er führt also eine Segmentierung des Sprachsignals durch, d.h. die Einteilung in diskrete, zeitlich aufeinanderfolgende Abschnitte. Wie bereits die geschriebene Form zeigt, ist die Handhabung der in der Sprache enthaltenen Information um so ökonomischer, je elementarer die verwendeten Bausteine sind (z.B. besitzt die englische Sprache nach OLSON et al. /3/ bei einem erfassten Anteil von 97% aller Sprachäusserungen ungefähr 10000 Wörter, 1500 Silben, aber nur etwa 50 Phoneme). Der im folgenden beschriebene maschinelle Segmentierungsalgorithmus versucht daher, das Sprachsignal in eine Folge von Segmenten bzw. Bausteinen zu zerlegen, aus denen sich die gesprochenen Phoneme (eindeutig) lokalisieren lassen.

Der erste Ansatz einer Segmentation ist bereits in der Sprachsignalübertragung mittels Vocoder zu finden. Dieser im folgenden als "Vorsegmentation" bezeichnete und in zwei Teilschritte zerfallende Verarbeitungsschritt umfasst die Feststellung zweier binärer Merkmale des Sprachsignals, die beide die Schallquellen des menschlichen Sprachorgans betreffen und die folgenden Aufgaben mit sich bringen:

1) Feststellung der Abschnitte, in denen ein Sprachsignal vorkommt, und ihre Abgrenzung gegen die Pausen.

2) Lokalisierung aller Abschnitte des Sprachsignals mit periodischer Anregung und ihre Abgrenzung gegen Sprachsignalabschnitte, deren Anregung eine Turbulenz im Vokaltrakt ist ("stimmlose" Abschnitte).

Die Lösung dieser Aufgaben führt zur Bestimmung der Merkmale "PAUSE", "STIMMHAFT" und "STIMMLOS".

Eine andere Art der Segmentation ergibt sich, wenn man nicht die Quelle, sondern den Vokaltrakt betrachtet. Dieser versucht, für jede akustische Realisierung eines Phonems eine bestimmte Zielstellung zu realisieren /1/, /2/. Für die weiteren Untersuchungen ist daher von den folgenden Voraussetzungen auszugehen: /5/

a) Für die Realisierung eines Phonems stellt sich der Vokaltrakt zunächst auf die zugehörige Zielstellung ein, verweilt dort eine bestimmte Zeit und geht dann auf die nächste zu realisierende Zielstellung über. Daher wechseln schnelle Bewegungen des Vokaltrakts ab mit Zeitabschnitten, in denen der Vokaltrakt seine Stellung nur unwesentlich ändert.

b) Jede Artikulationsänderung bewirkt eine Änderung des Sprachsignals und seiner wesentlichen Parameter.

Man erhält daher zu jedem gesprochenen Phonem zunächst einen dynamischen Anlaut, einen stationären Mittelteil und einen wiederum dynamischen Auslaut, der in der Regel mit dem Anlaut des nächsten Phonems zu einem Übergang verschmilzt (Bild 1).

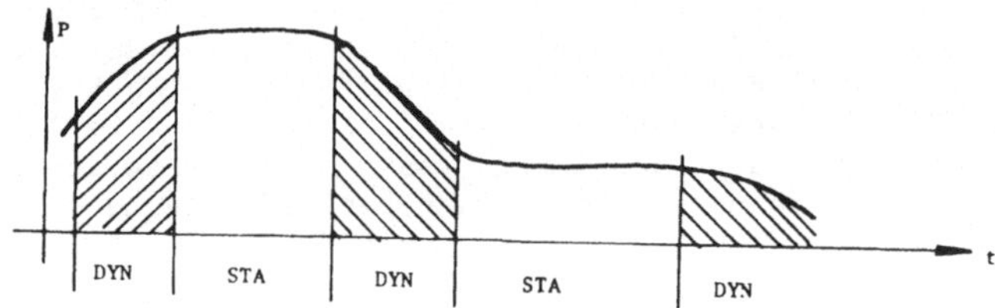

Bild 1: Aufbau der gesprochenen Phoneme aus (dynamischem) Anlaut, stationärem Mittelteil und Auslaut sowie Verschmelzung von An- und Auslaut bei Übergängen zwischen zwei gesprochenen Phonemen.

P   Parameterverlauf
STA   stationärer Abschnitt
DYN dynamischer Abschnitt

Ausnahmen bilden die Diphthonge, die zwei stationäre Abschnitte besitzen können, sowie die Verschlusslaute, bei denen der stationäre Abschnitt wegfällt.

Gelingt es also, **diese** stationären **und** dynamischen Abschnitte zu lokalisieren, so ist eine (eindeutige) Zuordnung der Sprachsignalabschnitte zu den gesprochenen Phonemen möglich. Daher lautet die dritte und wesentlichste Aufgabe der Segmentation:

3) Trennung der Abschnitte, während derer sich der Vokaltrakt in relativer Ruhe befindet, und die den Zielstellungen des Vokaltrakts entsprechen ("stationäre" Abschnitte), von den Übergangsabschnitten ("dynamische" Abschnitte), während derer sich der Vokaltrakt in schnellerer Bewegung befindet.

2. VORSEGMENTATION

Die Lokalisierung der Sprachsignal- und der Pausenabschnitte bzw. das hierfür angewendete Verfahren hängt wesentlich vom Ziel des gesamten Verarbeitungssystems ab. So werden z.B. die Anforderungen an diese Stufe in einem Spracherkennungssystem höher sein als in einem blossen Übertragungssystem mit reduzierter Kanalkapazität (wo es nicht so viel ausmacht, wenn Pausen gelegentlich als "Sprachsignal" mit übertragen werden und man ggf. auf einen Pausendetektor ganz verzichten kann). Ebenfalls eine Rolle spielen der Störabstand des Signals und die sonstigen Aufnahmebedingungen. Im vorliegenden Verarbeitungssystem, das als Vorstufe eines automatischen Spracherken-

nungssystems arbeitet /10/ und für Sprachsignale guter Qualität ausgelegt ist,reicht
z.B. eine feste Pegelschwelle, wie sie REDDY /7/ verwendet, zur Trennung der Sprach-
signal- und Pausenabschnitte nicht aus.

Deshalb wird während der Verarbeitung die Pegelver-
teilung des Signals in Form eines Histogramms aufgenommen (Bild 2). Dieses weist an der Stelle des
- als langsam veränderlich anzunehmenden - Störpe-
gels ein scharfes Maximum auf; da der Pegel L_S in
Sprachsignalabschnitten sehr viel stärker schwankt,
kann der mittlere Pegel in Pausenabschnitten auf
diese Weise einfach bestimmt werden; die aus diesem
Wert L_{OS} berechnete Schwelle L_{PS} trennt Sprachsig-
nal- und Pausenabschnitte. Zur besseren Erkennung
der schwachen Frikativlaute wird dieses Verfahren
zusätzlich noch auf den Pegel L_D des digital differenzierten Sprachsignals angewendet und eine weitere

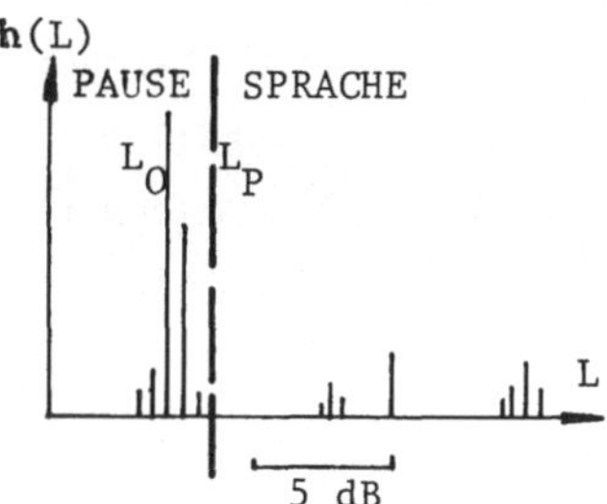

Bild 2:
Trennung Sprachsignal -
Pause
Messung alle 5 ms
Jeweils betrachtetes
Zeitintervall: 25 ms
L_P: Pegelschwelle zur
Trennung

Schwelle L_{PD} bestimmt. Ein Signalabschnitt ist demnach dann als "PAUSE" zu betrachten, wenn die gemessenen Pegelwerte beide Schwellen unterschreiten:

$$\text{"PAUSE"} = (L_S < L_{PS}) \wedge (L_D < L_{PD}) \tag{1}$$

Da der Störpegel als langsam zeitveränderlich angenommen ist, wird das gesamte Hi-
stogramm in bestimmten Zeitabständen mit einem Faktor kleiner 1 multipliziert, so
dass zeitlich zurückliegende Werte allmählich in den Hintergrund treten.

Die zweite Stufe der Vorsegmentation trennt stimmhafte und stimmlose Signalabschnitte. Von allen im Zeitbereich gemessenen Parametern ist hierfür der Quotient Q_S der
beiden als Betragsmittelwert des Signals bzw. des differenzierten Signals berechneten und im weiteren Verlauf als "Pegel" bezeichneten Werte L_S und L_D am ehesten geeignet:

$$L_S = \frac{1}{N} \sum_{i=n}^{n+N} |a_i| \qquad\qquad L_D = \frac{1}{N} \sum_{i=n}^{n+N} |a_{i+1} - a_i| \tag{2}$$

$$Q_S = \frac{L_D}{2 \cdot L_S} \tag{3}$$

Hierbei sind a_i die (mit 20 kHz) abgetasteten) digitalsierten Signalwerte. Durch den
Faktor 2 im Nenner wird Q_S auf den Maximalwert von 1 festgelegt. Dieser Parameter
bietet nun eine grobe Aussage über das Frequenzverhalten des Signals. Neben Q_S ist
auch noch die relative Nulldurchgangshäufigkeit

$$ND = \frac{1}{N} \sum_{i=n}^{n+N} \left[ND_i = (\text{sgn}(a_i) \neq \text{sgn}(a_{i+1})) \right] \tag{4}$$

als Parameter bedingt geeignet,wenn die Aufnahmebedingungen keinen grösseren Schwankungen unterworfen sind. Durch N ist das jeweils für die Messung verwendete Zeitintervall bestimmt.

An Hand dieser Parameter wird das Sprachsignal mit zwei experimentell ermittelten Schwellen in "sicher stimmhafte" und "sicher stimmlose" Abschnitte eingeteilt. Die dazwischenliegenden Abschnitte werden im Verlauf der nachfolgenden Grundfrequenzbestimmung /10/ klassifiziert.

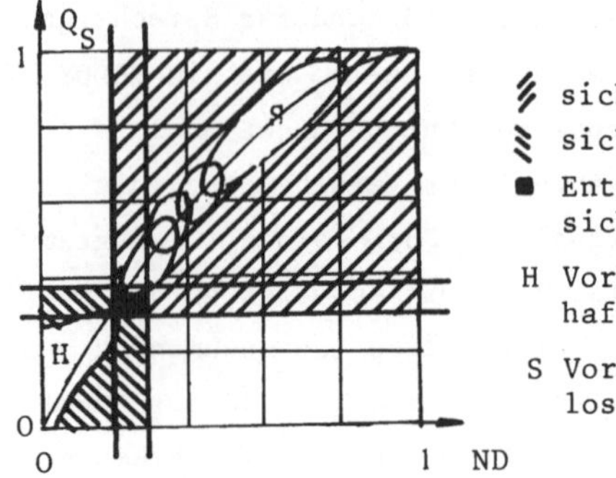

Bild 3: Trennung "stimmhaft/stimmlos".

3. PARAMETERWAHL, SEGMENTLÄNGENFUNK-
TION, MINIMALSEGMENTE

Sind die im eigentlichen Segmentationsschritt zu bestimmenden stationären Segmente "stationär" bzw. die dynamischen "dynamisch" genug, um in einem automatischen Klassifizierungsalgorithmus mit ausreichender Sicherheit bestimmt werden zu können? Welche Parameter sind hierzu zu wählen? Wichtig ist zunächst dies: das Merkmal "stationär" oder "dynamisch" ist im Unterschied zur Vorsegmentation keine physikalisch genau bestimmbare Eigenschaft des Signals wie z.B. das Vorhandensein einer Periodizität. Deshalb ist hier eine nichtlineare Behandlung des Signals bzw. der für die Segmentation selektierten Parameter vonnöten, mit deren Hilfe die Entscheidung "stationär/dynamisch" erfolgen kann; diese kann in einem adaptiven oder auch in einem fest programmierten Algorithmus stattfinden. Wie frühere Versuche, insbesondere von REDDY und VICENS /8/ zeigen, scheint die Segmentation des Signals in stationäre und dynamische Abschnitte bereits mit wenigen sehr globalen Sprachsignalparametern und einem fest programmierten Algorithmus möglich zu sein.

Reddy und Vicens verwenden als Segmentationsparameter den Scheitelwert des Signals sowie die relative Nulldurchgangshäufigkeit. Wie sich jedoch zeigt, ist den Betragsmittelwerten L_S und L_D wegen der (trotz des grossen mittleren Störabstandes) häufigen Knackstörungen der Vorzug zu geben; dass der Pegelquotient Q_S ein zuverlässigerer Parameter ist als die stark schwankende Nulldurchgangshäufigkeit ND, hat bereits die Vorsegmentation ergeben. Deshalb werden neben den binären Merkmalen der Vorsegmentation im folgenden die drei Parameter L_S, L_D und Q_S als Segmentationsparameter verwendet. Diese Parameter werden grundfrequenzsynchron gemessen und auf einen Abstand von 5 ms interpoliert /10/. Das Sprachsignal ist daher zu Beginn der Segmentation als aufgeteilt in Mikrosegmente von 5 ms Dauer zu betrachten; diese kurze Zeitspanne wurde gewählt, um auch schnelle Übergänge noch richtig zu erfassen; sie erscheint durch die Genauigkeit der grundfrequenzsynchronen Messung gerechtfertigt.

Was die Segmentationsstrategie angeht, so erscheint es ratsam, sie auf eine genaue Ermittlung der dynamischen Abschnitte hin abzustimmen. Wie Versuche u.a. von ÖHMAN /12/ ergeben haben, sind die dynamischen Abschnitte für das Verstehen der Sprache wichtiger als die stationären. Weiterhin erscheinen in einem Verarbeitungssystem, das einen Klassifikator ansteuern soll, Segmentierungsfehler dann als besonders schwerwiegend, wenn dadurch mehrere gesprochene Phoneme in einem stationären Segment zusammengefasst werden. Aus diesem Grund werden im folgenden primär die dynamischen Segmente bestimmt.

Im ersten Schritt werden die Mikrosegmente zu grösseren Einheiten, den Minimalsegmenten, zusammengefasst. Hierzu wird für jeden Parameter P die relative Änderung zwischen zwei (nicht unbedingt benachbarten) Mikrosegmenten M_i und M_k bestimmt (Bild 4):

$$r_{P_{i,k}} = \frac{P_i - P_k}{|P_i + P_k|} \qquad (5)$$

Diese relative Änderung r_p sei dann "wesentlich", wenn ihr Betrag eine Schwelle q_p überschreitet:

$$\text{"WESENTLICHE ÄNDERUNG"} = |r_p| > q_p \qquad (6)$$

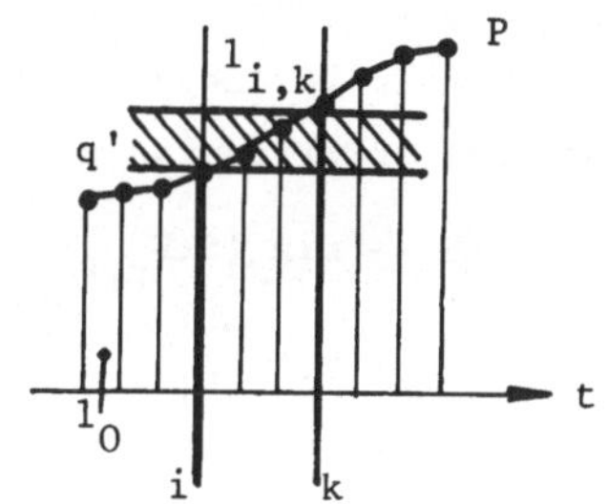

Bild 4:
Zur Definition des Minimalsegments (MS)

i   Beginn des MS
k   Ende des MS
$l_{i,k}$ Länge des MS
P   Parameterverlauf
q' Toleranzbereich entsprechend (6)
l_0 Länge eines Mikrosegments (5 ms)

Das Minimalsegment ist damit definiert als Folge benachbarter Mikrosegmente; seine Länge ist so festgelegt, dass zwischen Anfangs- und Endmesspunkt der massgebende Parameter P seinen Wert gerade einmal "wesentlich" ändert.

Bildet man aus den Mikrosegmenten die Minimalsegmente zeitsequentiell,so ist festzustellen, dass die Verarbeitungsrichtung noch eine wesentliche Rolle spielt (Bild 5). Um diesen Einfluss auszuschalten - er stellt sonst eine erhebliche Fehlerquelle dar - können die Minimalsegmente nicht zeitsequentiell ermittelt werden. Vielmehr ist ein Umweg über die "Segment-Längenfunktion" (genauer: Minimalsegment-Längenfunktion) SLF zu wählen; diese sei nach Bild 6 für den Zeitpunkt n wie folgt definiert:

$$SLF_n = \min (l_{i,n}, l_{n,k}) \qquad (7)$$

Hierbei ist $l_{i,n}$ die Länge des nach (6) zu bestimmenden Minimalsegments, das an der Stelle n endet, während $l_{n,k}$ die Länge des an der Stelle n beginnenden Minimalsegments darstellt. Auf diese Weise werden Beginn und Ende jeder wesentlichen Änderung und damit alle dynamischen Segmente zeitlich genau festgelegt.

Die SLF (für deren Zahlengrösse

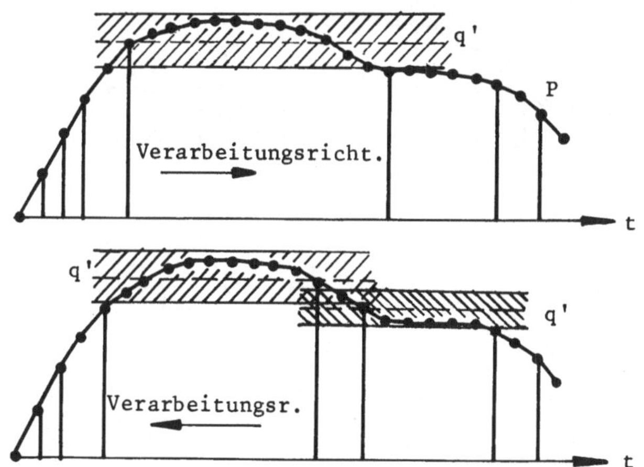

Bild 5: Der Einfluss der Verarbeitungsrichtung auf die Bildung der Minimalsegmente. Bezeichnungen wie in Bild 4

im folgenden die Einheit "Mikrosegment" gelten soll)
ist zunächst nur für einen Parameter definiert. Sind
nun, wie im vorliegenden Fall, mehrere Parameter beteiligt, so wird eine gemeinsame SLF definiert zu:

$$SLF_n = min\ (SLF_{n,P_i}),\ i = 1\ ...\ k \qquad (8)$$

Hierbei ist SLF_{n,P_i} die gemäss (7) für einen Parameter P_i an der Stelle n definierte SLF. Die kombinierte SLF berechnet sich als Minimum der Segment-
Längenfunktionen für die einzelnen Parameter P_i. Für
die mit hinzugezogenen binären Merkmale lässt sich
eine "SLF" dann angeben, wenn jede Änderung eines
dieser Merkmale als "wesentlich" angesehen wird. Auch aus der kombinierten SLF gehen die dynamischen Segmente eindeutig hervor, da bereits die wesentliche   Änderung
eines einzelnen Parameters den Wert der SLF bestimmt.

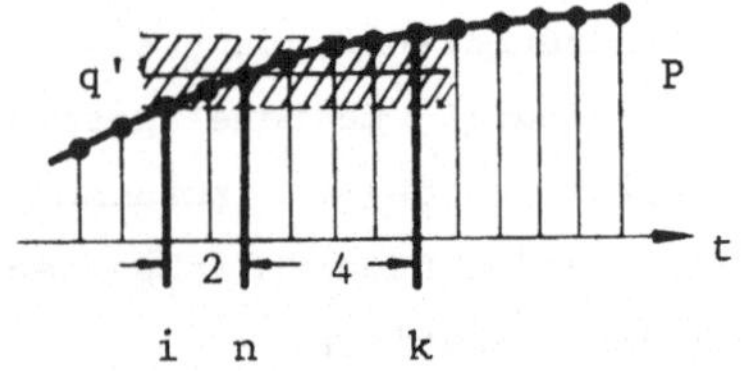

Bild 6:
Zur Definition der Segment-
längenfunktion SLF.

P Parameterverlauf
q' Toleranzbereich um P_n
   entsprechend (6)
Im Bild: $SLF_n = 2$

Die Bildung der Minimalsegmente aus der SLF erfolgt nun längensequentiell, d.h. zuerst werden alle Mikrosegmente mit SLF=1 zu Minimalsegmenten verknüpft, dann die Mikrosegmente mit SLF=2 usw. Vorher noch wird die SLF so "geglättet", dass sich ihre
Werte für benachbarte Mikrosegmente nur um 1 unterscheiden können. Um den dynamischen
Segmenten keinen Abbruch zu tun, darf die SLF ihren Wert im Verlauf der Glättung an
keiner Stelle vergrössern.

Der Schritt vom Mikrosegment zur SLF bzw. zum Minimalsegment macht die weitere Segmentation unabhängig von den verwendeten Parametern und - mit Hilfe der Schwellen
q_P - auch unabhängig vom jeweiligen Sprecher. Die individuelle Einstellung von q_P
ist unkritisch, da sie nur die Lage, nicht aber die Struktur der SLF wesentlich be-
einflussen kann.

4. DIE BILDUNG DER "SEGMENTE"

Aus den Minimalsegmenten werden
nun schrittweise dynamische und
stationäre Segmente gebildet. Minimalsegmente, die nur ein Mikrosegment umfassen, sind mit
Sicherheit als "dynamisch" zu
klassifizieren. Andererseits ergibt sich aus dem Experiment sowie aus der Literatur /7/, dass
auch in langsamen Übergängen so
gut wie nie Minimalsegmente von
mehr als 25 ms Dauer auftreten,
die nach dem Signalverlauf dyna-

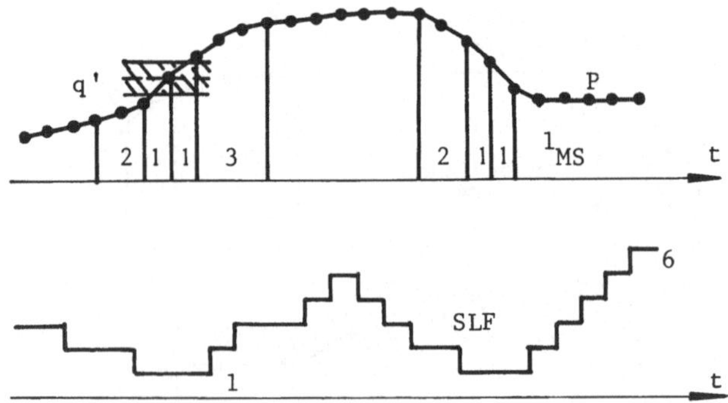

Bild 7: Segment-Längenfunktion SLF und Minimalsegmentfolge, gewonnen aus dem
Parameterverlauf P

q' Toleranzbereich um jeden Wert
    von P entsprechend (6)
l_{MS} Länge der Minimalsegmente

mischen Segmenten zugeordnet werden müssten. Die Berechnung der SLF kann daher auf Werte unter 30 ms (6 Mikrosegmente) beschränkt bleiben; alle Mikrosegmente mit SLF-Werten über 5 sind als "stationär" zu klassifizieren.

Die Minimalsegmente, die nicht unter eine dieser Bestimmungen fallen, werden zunächst als "undefiniert" bezeichnet und sind weiter zu untersuchen. Benachbarte gleich klassifizierte Minimalsegmente werden zu grösseren Zeitabschnitten zusammengefasst, die im folgenden als "Segment" bezeichnet sind. Die Klassifizierung in dynamische, undefinierte und stationäre Segmente wird im folgenden nur für stimmhafte Signalabschnitte durchgeführt; schliesst man zunächst die (relativ seltenen) Fälle aus, dass zwei stimmlose Phoneme unmittelbar benachbart sind, so genügt es, die stimmlosen Signalabschnitte durchweg als "stimmlose" Segmente zu klassifizieren. In Pausenabschnitten ist die SLF nicht definiert; diese Abschnitte gehen als "Pause"- -Segmente in die Klassifikation ein.

5. VOM DYNAMISCHEN ZUM "TRANSIENTEN" SEGMENT

Ein dynamischer Abschnitt im Verlauf des Sprachsignals ist stets der Übergang von einer Stellung des Vokaltrakts zu einer anderen. Dieser Übergang kann genauer charakterisiert werden, wenn es gelingt, ein Mass oder eine Aussage für die Richtung des Übergangs zu finden und insbesondere anzugeben, ob er monoton verläuft oder nicht. Zu diesem Zweck werden in allen dynamischen (und auch in den undefinierten) Segmenten für alle drei Parameter folgende Hilfsgrössen bestimmt:

$$a_m = \frac{1}{K} \sum r_{i,i+1} \qquad b_m = \frac{1}{K} \sum \left| r_{i,i+1} \right| \qquad c_m = \frac{a_m}{b_m} \qquad (9)$$

Hierbei ist K die Zahl der Mikrosegmente im betrachteten dynamischen oder undefinierten Segment, über welches sich auch die Summierung erstreckt. a_m ist der Mittelwert und b_m der Betragsmittelwert der relativen Änderungen des Parameters P, gemessen für jeweils benachbarte Mikrosegmente. b_m ist demnach ein Mass für die Grösse der Änderungen jedes Parameters im Segment. Aus dem Quotienten c_m lässt sich sowohl die Richtung der Änderung als auch das Mass ihrer Gleichförmigkeit ablesen; bei monoton steigendem oder fallendem Verlauf des betrachteten Parameters P liegt der Betrag von c_m nahe bei 1. Verläuft P dagegen schwankend oder oszillierend, so wird sich c_m um den Wert 0 herum bewegen. Aus der Hilfsgrösse c_m können daher zwei Richtungsmerkmale abgeleitet werden: das "Richtungsprädikat" sowie die "Richtungscharakteristik" (siehe hierzu Bild 9).Auf diese Weise werden aus den dynamischen Segmenten "transiente" Segmente mit Angabe der Richtung des Übergangs.

Wirklich "transiente" Segmente, also direkte Übergänge von einem gesprochenen Phonem zum nächsten, sollten eine monotone Richtungscharakteristik aufweisen. Ist die Richtungscharakteristik jedoch "unbestimmt", so nimmt der Algorithmus an, dass in dem betrachteten transienten Segment mehrere Übergänge ohne stationäres Zwischensegment vorliegen (was z.B. auf einen Verschlusslaut hindeuten kann), und zerlegt das transiente Segment in die kleinstmögliche Zahl monoton verlaufender Teilsegmente.

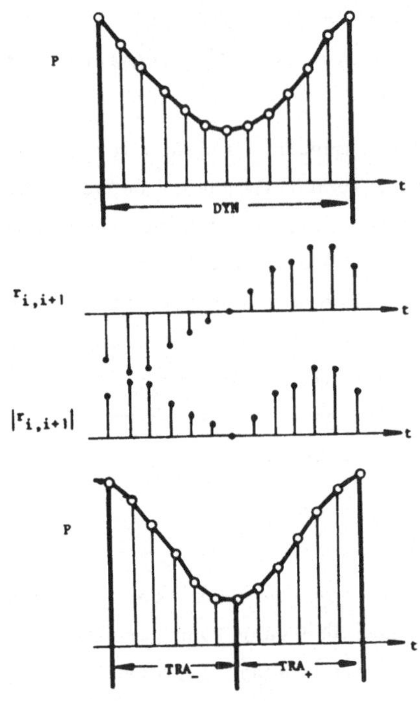

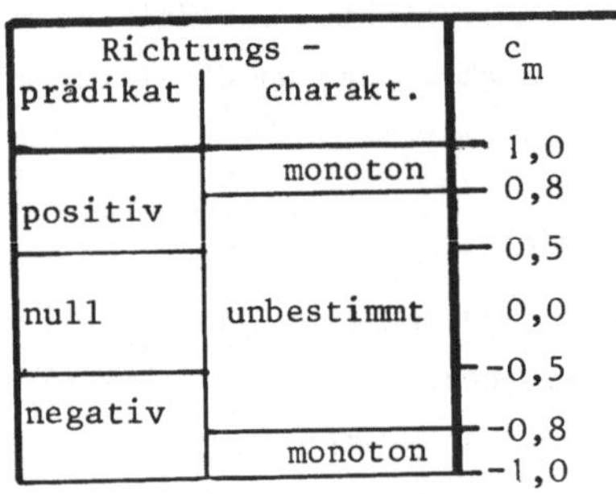

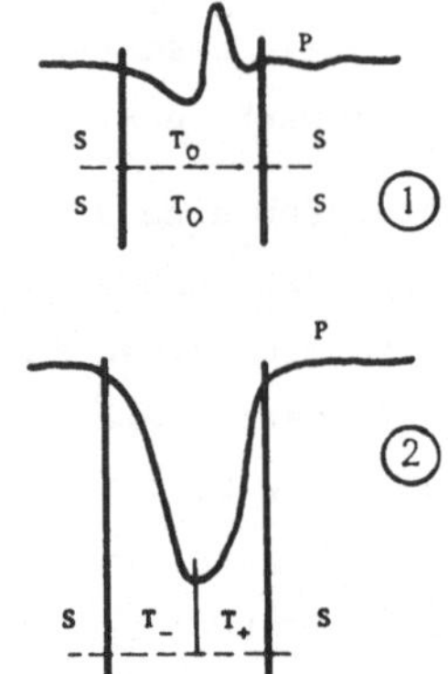

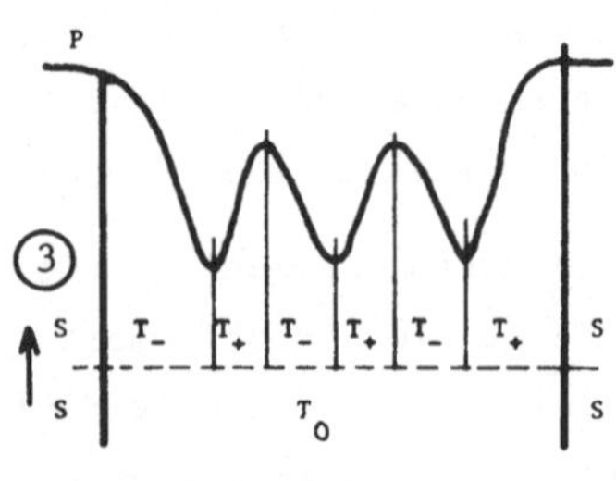

Bild 8b: Teilung transienter Segmente mit
unbestimmter Richtungscharakteristik

Bild 8a: Zur Bestimmung der Richtungseigenschaften dynamischer Segmente.

	S	Stationär	−	"negativ"
TRA, T		Transient	+	"positiv"
DYN		Dynamisch	O	"null"

Richtungs –		c_m
prädikat	charakt.	
positiv	monoton	1,0
		0,8
	unbestimmt	0,5
null		0,0
		−0,5
negativ		−0,8
	monoton	−1,0

Bild 9: Definition der beiden
Richtungseigenschaften
transienter Segmente

Die Bruchstücke bleiben als selbständige Segmente erhalten, sofern sie nicht zu kurz sind und
somit nur auf einen gestörten Parameterverlauf
hinweisen (Bild 8b).

Etwas komplizierter liegt der Fall, wenn an der
Bildung der Richtungseigenschaften mehrere Parameter und/oder binäre Merkmale beteiligt sind.
Um auch hier eindeutige Verhältnisse zu schaffen, wird für jedes dynamische Segment ein Parameter selektiert, nach dem dann die Richtungseigenschaften ermittelt werden. Dies geschieht
nach den folgenden, experimentell ermittelten Regeln:

1) Grenzt das betrachtete dynamische Segment an ein stimmloses oder ein
   Pausensegment an, so ist das Richtungsprädikat stets negativ, wenn man
   sich auf das stimmlose bzw. Pausensegment zu bewegt, auch wenn die Parameter anders verlaufen. Sollte ein derartiges dynamisches Segment
   wegen nichtmonotonen Parameterverlaufs geteilt werden, so ist die Teilung an Hand des Signalpegels L_S vorzunehmen.

2) Ist Regel 1 nicht anwandbar, und ist der Quotient c_m für einen der
   drei Parameter wesentlich grösser als für alle übrigen, so bestimmt
   dieser Parameter die Richtungseigenschaften.

3) In allen anderen Fällen werden die Richtungseigenschaften vom Pegel L_D
   des differenzierten Signals bestimmt.

6. ABBAU DER "UNDEFINIERTEN" SEGMENTE

Nach der ersten Klassifizierung der Minimalsegmente in transiente und stationäre

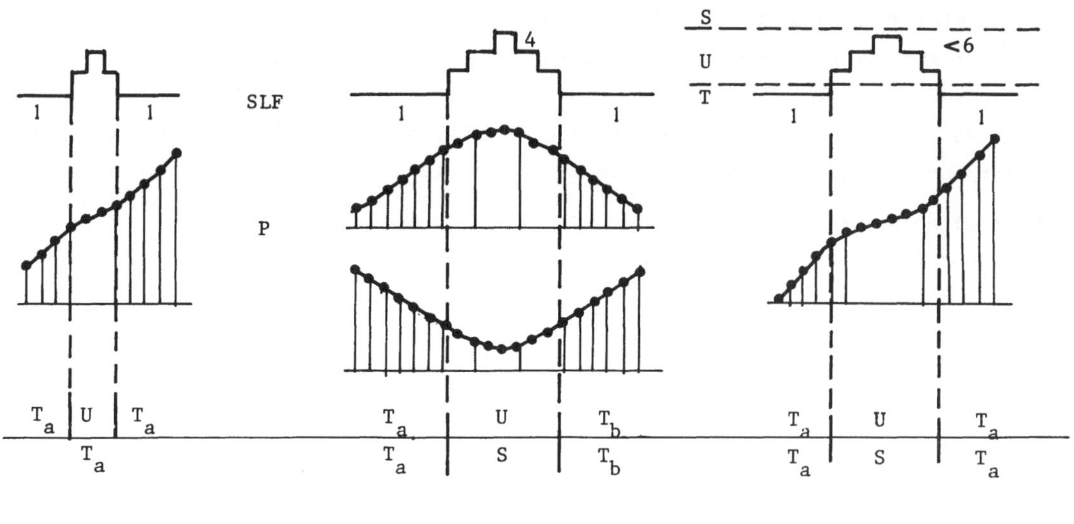

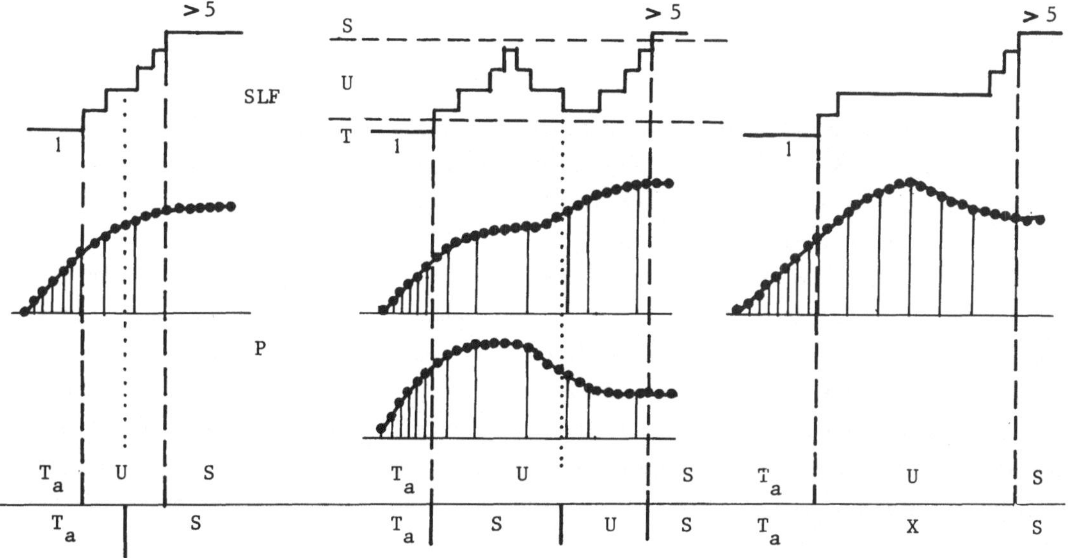

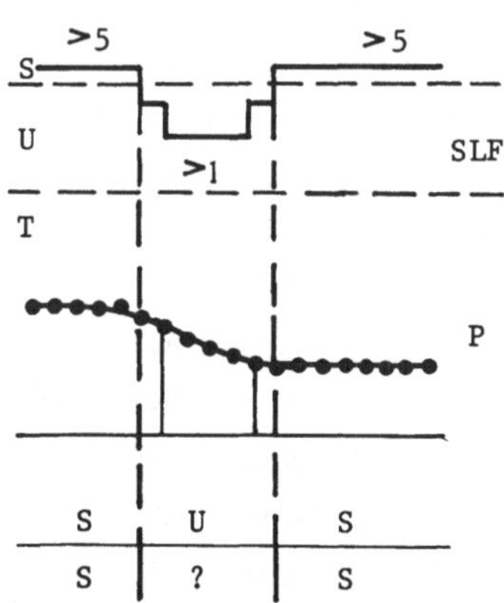

Bild 10:
Abbau der undefinierten Segmente.

T	Transient	?	Segmentation unsicher
U	Undefiniert	X	SLF mit veränderten
S	Stationär		Schwellen neu bilden

SLF   Segment-Längenfunktion
P   Parameterverlauf, Mikro- und Minimalsegmentfolge

Segmentationsergebnis $\dfrac{\text{VOR}}{\text{NACH}}$ der Korrektur

In allen Diagrammen kann die Zeit t sowohl von links nach rechts als auch von rechts nach links laufen. Die Zahlenangaben beziehen sich auf die Werte der SLF (in Mikrosegmenten).

a   Richtungsprädikat (positiv oder negativ)
b   Richtungsprädikat (entgegengesetzt zu a)

Segmente bleiben noch ungefähr 30% des Sprachsignals in Form von "undefinierten" Segmenten zurück; diese Segmente sind entstanden aus Minimalsegmenten von 10 bis 25 ms Dauer. Diese Segmente können nur in Verbindung mit den Nachbarsegmenten weiterbehandelt werden. Soweit dabei stationäre bzw. transiente Segmente neben gleichartigen Nachbarn entstehen, werden sie mit diesen zusammengefasst.

Die einzelnen Segmentkombinationen gliedern sich in drei Gruppen:
1) Kombination "transient"-"undefiniert"-"transient"
2) Kombination "stationär"-"undefiniert"-"transient" und umgekehrt
3) Kombination "stationär"-"undefiniert"-"stationär"

Eine Zusammenstellung dieser Fälle und der getroffenen Massnahmen zeigt Bild 10.

Liegt ein undefiniertes Segment zwischen transienten Segmenten, so besitzt die SLF an dieser Stelle ein lokales Maximum, das freilich zur Bildung eines stationären Segments nicht ausreicht. Der Algorithmus geht jedoch davon aus, dass in der Regel ein schnell ausgesprochener Laut vorliegt, und klassifiziert das undefinierte Segment als stationär, wenn es nicht zu kurz ist. Dies gilt besonders dann, wenn die Richtungseigenschaften der beiden transienten Nachbarsegmente verschieden sind.

Liegt ein undefiniertes Segment zwischen einem transienten und einem stationären Segment, so ist die Struktur der Segment-Längenfunktion im Bereich des undefinierten Segments ausschlaggebend. Verläuft die SLF in diesem Bereich monoton, so ist lediglich eine Verlangsamung des Übergangs eingetreten; die beiden Nachbarsegmente werden auf Kosten des undefiniertes Segments erweitert. Liegen jedoch Extremwerte der SLF im Bereich des undefinierten Segments, so ist anzunehmen, dass dieses zumindest ein stationäres sowie ein weiteres, wahrscheinlich transientes Segment beinhaltet. Im Bereich des Maximums der SLF wird von dem undefinierten Segment ein stationäres Teilsegment abgespaltet; der Rest des undefinierten Segments bleibt zunächst undefiniert. Ein Sonderfall liegt vor, wenn im undefinierten Segment die SLF über eine längere Zeitspanne konstant bleibt (40 ms oder mehr). In diesem Fall wird die SLF mit Parameteränderungsschwellen q_p^*, die gegenüber den sonst verwendeten Schwellen q_p erhöht oder erniedrigt sind, auf einen der beiden erstgenannten Fälle zurückgeführt.

Am wenigsten eindeutig ist das undefinierte Segment zwischen zwei stationären Segmenten weiterzuverarbeiten. Das undefinierte Segment in dieser Stellung bedeutet ein lokales Minimum der SLF, das jedoch zur Bildung eines transienten Segments nicht ausreicht. Es kann sich hierbei ebenso gut um eine kurzzeitige Parameterschwankung wie um einen Übergang zwischen zwei gesprochenen Phonemen handeln. Mit Sicherheit kann das undefinierte Segment dann als "transient" klassifiziert werden, wenn die Änderung des bestimmenden Parameters in diesem Segment wesentlich grösser ist als in den stationären Nachbarn. In unsicheren Fällen wird ausserdem versucht, das undefinierte Segment so lange zu verkürzen, als sich dadurch eine Vergrösserung der relativen Änderungen b_m in diesem Segment erreichen lässt. Ist die Entscheidung dann immer noch nicht eindeutig, so wird das undefinierte Segment als "potentiell transient" klassifiziert und damit für die nachfolgenden Verarbeitungsstufen angedeutet, dass an dieser Stelle die Segmentation nicht sicher arbeitet.

Bis auf einige Spezialfälle (Zungen-/r/, das Pegelschwingungen verursacht;schlecht ausgesprochene Vokale oder Gleitlaute) ist die Segmentation mit diesem Schritt abgeschlossen.

Verschiedene Autoren, z.B. HUGHES und HEMDAL /4/ oder REDDY /7/,schliessen an dieser Stelle eine Weiterklassifizierung der stationären Segmente in Vokale und Nichtvokale an. Dieses Problem scheint jedoch noch ungelöst; entweder ergibt sich eine hohe Fehlerrate oder eine hohe Rückweisungsrate (so dass ein beträchtlicher Teil der stationären Segmente nicht weiterklassifiziert wird), oder die gebildeten Phonemgruppen weichen vom Vokal-Konsonant-Schema ab und weisen eine starke Überlappung auf /7/. Im vorliegenden Verarbeitungssystem wird die Weiterklassifizierung in vokalische und konsonantische Segmente an Hand der Richtungseigenschaften und einiger einfacher experimentell ermittelter Regeln versucht. Bei einer Fehlerrate von 2,5% lassen sich rund 80% der stationären Segmente weiterklassifizieren, wobei dieser Anteil bei den vokalischen Segmenten geringfügig höher liegt als bei den konsonantischen.

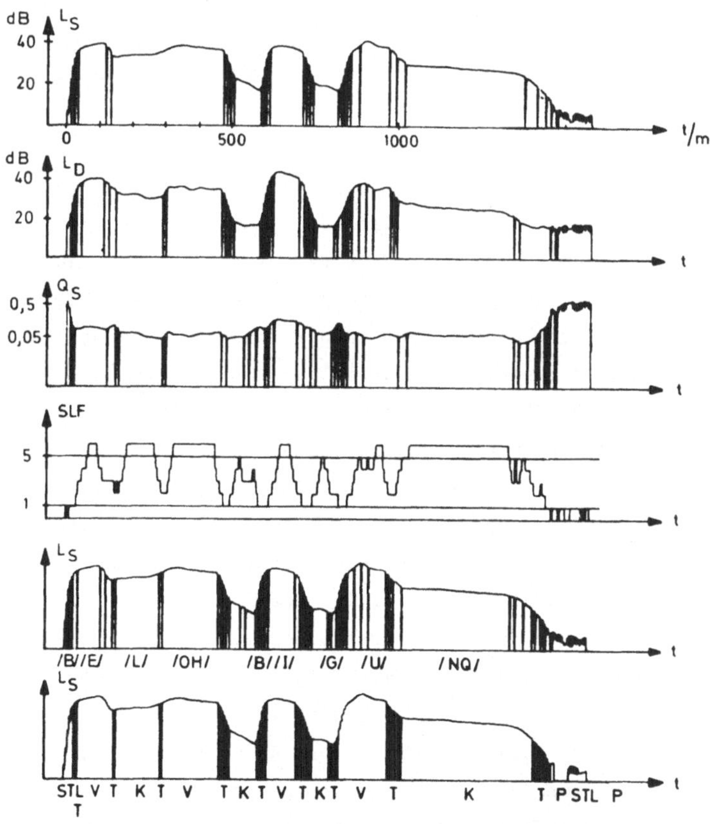

Bild 11: Segmentation des Wortes "Belobigung".
Sprecher: NOK.

7. ERGEBNISSE

Bild 11 zeigt als Beispiel die Segmentation des Wortes "Belobigung". Aufgezeichnet sind die Minimalsegmentfolgen für jeden der drei Parameter allein samt dessen Verlauf, die kombinierte SLF, die kombinierte Minimalsegmentfolge sowie die endgültige Segmentfolge. Aus diesem Bild wird auch die Wirkungsweise der drei Parameter deutlich. Der Signalpegel L_S (also der zeitliche Betragsmittelwert des direkten Sprachsignals) weist den grössten Störabstand auf; die grössten Änderungen und damit die beste Lokalisierung dynamischer Segmente ergeben sich bei Verschlusslauten und beim Übergang von und nach Pausen und stimmlosen Lauten. Änderungen dagegen, wie sie bei Übergängen zwischen Vokalen und Semivokalen, Nasalen oder Gleitlauten auftreten,werden hier weniger gut registriert (siehe die fehlende Grenze zwischen /L/ und /OH/ in der Minimalsegmentfolge für L_S). Der Pegel (Betragsmittelwert) L_D des differenzierten Signals betont dagegen bei insgesamt etwas schlechterem Störabstand die Übergänge zwischen stimmhaften stationären Lauten. Der Pegelquotient Q_S indes reagiert von allen Parametern auf Änderungen im Frequenzverhalten am empfindlichsten, z.B. zeigt er eindeutig an der Stelle des Verschlusslautes /G/ eine Turbulenz an und arbeitet auch beim Übergang Vokal-stationärer Konsonant (Nasal oder Semivokal) recht zuverlässig.

Das beschriebene Segmentationsverfahren wurde auf eine aus 200 isoliert gesprochenen Wörtern mit insgesamt 826 Phonemen bestehende Sprachstichprobe und insgesamt sieben Sprecher angewendet. Das Ergebnis (ohne die Weiterklassifizierung der stationären Segmente) ist in Bild 12 zusammengestellt. Bei der Auswertung der Ergebnisse war zunächst davon auszugehen,inwieweit sich die eingangs geforderte eindeutige Zuordnung von Segment einerseits und gesprochenem Phonem andererseits, wie sie sich aus der Lautschrift und der Definition des stationären und dynamischen Segments als Zielstellung bzw. Übergang als "Idealsegmentation" herleitet, in der Praxis überhaupt realisieren lässt. Wie sich zeigt, müssen für einige Laute, so den Laut /R/ und die Diphthonge, Allophone zugelassen werden. Die Diphthonge z.B. werden von den meisten Sprechern so realisiert, dass zunächst die Anfangsstellung des Vokaltrakts eine Zeitlang gehalten wird; hier liegt also sicher ein stationärer Abschnitt vor. Auf diesen Abschnitt folgt ein mehr oder weniger langsamer Übergang zur Zielstellung des Vokaltrakts für den Endlaut des Diphthongs, die zum Grossteil ebenfalls eine Zeitlang beibehalten wird. Artikulationsmässig zerfällt der Diphthong also in der Regel in zwei stationäre Segmente, die bei einer Segmentation im Frequenzbereich auch recht gut lokalisiert werden. Da aber zumindest bei zwei deutschen Diphthongen ein divergierender Formantverlauf vorliegt, bleibt für die Dauer des Diphthongs die Energieschwerpunktsfrequenz des Spektrums und damit auch der ihr nahe verwandte Pegelquotient Q_S nahezu konstant. Da sich auch die Pegel L_S und L_D im Verlauf des Diphthongs nur sehr wenig ändern, ist der dynamische Teil des Diphthongs bei einer Segmentation im Zeitbereich nur schwer lokalisierbar; der Diphthong wird grösstenteils als einzelnes stationäres Segment angezeigt. Allgemein ist die Un-

Sprecher ...	GRR	KAG	HRS	WGH	THS	KSC	IGH	Gesamt	Rel.
1. Schwere Segmentierungsfehler.									
Fehlende transiente Segmente (Phonemgrenzen)	9	16	11	9	11	15	6	77	1,33
fehlende stationäre Segmente	2	8	10	11	4	14	6	55	0,95
fehlende (isolierte) Verschlusslaute	1	8	10	1	2	15	10	47	0,81
stimmhaft/stimmlos falsch getrennt	5	3	1	3	4	1	2	19	0,32
Gesamt	17	35	32	24	21	45	24	198	3,42
2. Leichtere Segmentierungsfehler.									
Zuviel vorhandene transiente Segmente	18	13	18	24	31	5	16	125	2,16
Zuviel vorhandene "potentiell" stationäre oder transiente Segmente	23	23	14	29	27	9	16	141	2,43
Gesamt	41	36	32	53	58	14	32	266	4,60

Bild 12: Ergebnis der Segmentation für 7 Sprecher und eine Sprachstichprobe, bestehend aus 200 isoliert gesprochenen Wörtern mit insgesamt 826 Phonemen. Die relativen Angaben (in Prozent) beziehen sich auf die Gesamtzahl der gesprochenen Phoneme.

empfindlichkeit der verwendeten Segmentationsparameter gegen divergierende Formantverläufe die grösste Schwäche aller Segmentierungsverfahren, die Pegel oder Amplitude als alleinige Segmentationsparameter benutzen. Diese Unempfindlichkeit ist weitgehend verantwortlich für das Fehlen mancher Phonemgrenzen im Ergebnis.

Bei den Segmentierungsfehlern ist zu unterscheiden zwischen "schweren" Fehlern, die in einem Erkennungssystem aufgrund der eingangs genannten drei Aufgaben der Segmentation notwendig bei der Erkennung Klassifizierungsfehler nach sich ziehen, sowie den leichteren Segmentierungsfehlern, die dies nicht tun. Die Fehlerrate beträgt für alle 7 Sprecher 3,4% für die schweren und 4,6% für die leichteren Segmentierungsfehler, bezogen auf die Zahl der segmentierten Phoneme. Hierbei ist zu bedenken, dass alle Fehler dem Verfahren angelastet werden, auch wenn sie signal- oder sprecherbedingt sind. Wie stark Sprechereigenschaften an solchen Fehlern beteiligt sind, mag daraus hervorgehen, dass sich z.B. die fehlenden isolierten Segmente (Verschlusslaute am Wortende) mit 90% ihres Vorkommens auf drei der Sprecher konzentrieren.

Die Ergebnisse erscheinen zunächst recht ermutigend; sie dürfen jedoch nicht darüber hinwegtäuschen, dass die Segmentation noch am Anfang steht. Auch bei Verwendung isoliert gesprochener Wörter als Sprachmaterial bleiben bei Betreiben der Segmentierungsstufe in Verbindung mit einem Klassifikator zur automatischen Spracherkennung auf Phonembasis   noch Fragen offen. Dies betrifft vor allem die Lokalisierung von Lauten ohne stationäres Segment, wie z.B. von Verschlusslauten. Im übrigen müssen die gesamten Versuchsbedingungen als noch nicht hart genug angesehen werden. Die eigentliche Bewährungsprobe für ein Segmentationsverfahren ist die Anwendung auf grössere sprachliche Einheiten, wie z.B. Sätze oder zusammenhängenden Text. Neuere Versuche auf diesem Gebiet mit amerikanischem Sprachmaterial zeigen, dass dabei offensichtlich die Sprechereigenschaften mit einem derartigen Anteil von "Fehlern",also Abweichungen des ausgesprochenen Textes von der vorgeschriebenen Aussprache, in das Segmentationsergebnis eingehen, dass die Anwendbarkeit eines Segmentierungsverfahrens überhaupt in Frage gestellt ist /13/. Was die Anwendung auf isoliert gesprogesprochene Wörter allerdings bereits zeigt, ist dies: Die Struktur des Sprachsignals erlaubt die Segmentierung in stationäre und dynamische Abschnitte bereits bei Verwendung weniger Segmentierungsparameter. Demnach lassen sich die Phoneme, soweit sie im Verlauf einer sprachlichen Äusserung überhaupt ausgesprochen werden, in den meisten Fällen auch im Sprachsignal lokalisieren.

<u>Schrifttum</u>

/1/   J.L.Flanagan: <u>Speech Analysis, Synthesis, and Perception.</u> Springer-Verlag,Ber-
      lin, Heidelberg, New York, 2. Aufl. 1972.

/2/   G. Fant und B. Lindblom: Studies of Minimal Speech Sound Units. STL-QPSR 1961,
      Heft 2, S. 1 ... 10

/3/   H.F.Olson et al: Speech Processing Techniques and Applications. IEEE Trans-
      actions on Audio and Electroacoustics 15(1967), S. 120...126

/4/   G.W.Hughes, J.F.Hemdal: <u>Speech Analysis.</u> Purdue Res. Found. Techn. Reprt.
      TREE 65-9, 1965.

/5/   B.V.Bhimani: <u>Multidimensional Model for Speech Recognition.</u> Defense Document.
      Center, Alexandria (Virg.), USA, 1963.

/6/   K.W.Otten:.Segmentation of Continuous Speech into Phonemes. Report Nr.
      RTD-TDR-63-4005, Part 2, U.S.Army, 1964.

/7/   D.R.Reddy: Segmentation of Speech Sounds. Journ.Ac.Soc.Am. 40(1966),S.307...312
      <u>   </u>: Phoneme Grouping for Speech Recognition. Journ.Acoust.Soc.Am.
      41(1967), S.1295...1300

/8/   P.B.Denes, T.von Keller: Articulatory Segmentation for Automatic Recognition of
      Speech. Proceedings of the 6th International Congress on Acoustics, Tokyo 1968:
      American Elsevier Publ.Comp. 1969.

/9/   D.R.Reddy und P.Vicens: A Procedure for the Segmentation of Connected Speech.
      Journ.Audio Eng. Soc. 16(1968), S.404...411

/10/ W.Hess: Digitale grundfrequenzsynchrone Analyse von Sprachsignalen als Teil
      eines automatischen Spracherkennungssystems. Diss. TU München 1972.

/11/ P.Delattre: From Acoustic Cues to Distinctive Features. Phonetica 18(1968),
      S.198...230

/12/ S.E.G.Öhman: Perceptual Segments and Rate of Change of Spectrum in Connected
      Speech. Proceedings of the Speech Communication Seminar, Stockholm 1962.

/13/ W.A.Lea: An Approach to Syntactic Recognition Without Phonemics. Conference
      Record, 1972 Conference on Speech Communication and Processing, Boston, Mass.:
      AFCRL, Bedford, Mass. 1972, paper F2.

A Method of Description and Classification of Line Drawings

M.Sties

Abstract. Research on automatic picture interpretation includes work
on the description and classification of line drawings. In this
approach, scanning of the pictures and information preprocessing are
considered to be seperate problems. Starting point for the considerations to be presented here are contour lines which have to be extracted from the pictures by appropriate methods.

Special lists are set up which serve as description of contour line
pictures. The lists comprise metrical properties of the basic elements and topological relations between the basic elements of the
picture. Points, lines and regions are excepted as basic elments. The
lines may be straight or circularly curved. Two criteria are given
which aim at the removal of certain distortions.

Classification is based on the sequential comparison of the description of an unknown picture with the descriptions of several known models. The compilation of many local decisions allows a global classification. The delimitation of classes is treated with special interest.

Simulation of the method has shown its capability of successfully
processing line drawings. Examples are shown and results are discussed.

Zusammenfassung: Im Rahmen der Untersuchung eines Systems zur automatischen Bildverarbeitung wurde ein Verfahren zur Beschreibung und Klassifizierung von Linienmustern entwickelt. Bildabtastung und -vorverar-
beitung wurden als davon getrennte Probleme betrachtet. Ausgangspunkt
der Überlegungen sind die durch geeignete Methoden aus dem Bild extra-

hierten Konturlinien.

Zur Beschreibung eines solchen Linienmusters werden Listen aufgebaut,
die die metrischen Eigenschaften der Grundelemente sowie die topologischen Relationen zwischen den Grundelementen angeben. Als Grundelemente einer Linienstruktur gelten Punkte, Strecken und Flächen. Es sind
gerade und kreisförmig gekrümmte Strecken zugelassen. Zur Beseitigung
von "Störungen" werden Kriterien angegeben, die mehrere aneinander-
grenzende Flächen zu größeren Flächeneinheiten zusammenfassen.

Die Klassifizierung beruht auf einem sequentiellen Vergleich der Beschreibung eines fremden Linienmusters mit den Beschreibungen bekannter Modelle. Durch die Zusammenfassung einer Vielzahl von lokalen Entscheidungen wird die globale Klassifizierung ermöglicht. Dabei wird
dem Problem der Klassenabgrenzung besondere Bedeutung beigemessen.

Das entwickelte Verfahren wurde durch Simulation getestet. Ergebnis-
beispiele werden gezeigt und diskutiert.

1. Introduction

In the past, efforts in picture processing have been concentrated on
the classification of complete, discrete patterns belonging to a finite set of classes. The concept for many solutions of this problem is
based on decision theory: define a certain number of features; partition the feature space into mutually disjoint subspaces and assign
each subspace to one of the classes; evaluate the features of a given
token and determine to which subspace it belongs.

Emphasis is put on the fact that within this concept the number of
features is fixed. All features are always processed in parallel.

When applied to complex pictures such as line drawings or photographs,
which will be called scenes subsequently, this concept was not very
successful. One of the main reasons for this deficiency results from
the fact that the whole pattern is always treated as a unity - as an
atom. A scene, however, represents a complicated structure. A scene
as a whole is composed of several parts, each of which in turn may be
broken into several elements. Each element may consist of a number of
atoms, the elements of the lowest level, which cannot be broken down

any more. The number of structural levels need not be predetermined.
Attributes may be assigned to the elements of each level. The elements
as well as the attributes will therefore be ordered in a specific way.
Consequently, efforts in processing complex pictures imply the finding
of a proper organization of the picture. This organization is found by
describing the elements of each structural level together with their
assigned attributes and by describing the relations between the elements of the different levels.

2. The scene

For the purpose of developing methods of describing scenes the two
main problems of scanning of hardcopy and preprocessing the derived
picture, which are essential parts of a complete system for picture
processing, have been disregarded. Line drawings are generated instead
by means of a CAD system (computer plus display terminal in combination with a rolling ball system). These line drawings are regarded as
ideally preprocessed and undistorted scenes. The generative elements
composing the scenes are straight lines, circles and arcs of circles.
The high resolution of the display screen of about 1600 x 2000 points
allows the user to draw scenes of a considerable complexity with great
accuracy. The input data for the following scene analysis and description are given by the unordered list of coordinates of the endpoints
of each line, subsequently termed as head and tail of a line. In the
case of a circle or an arc the coordinates of the centre of the circle
are added. Examples of scenes are shown in figures 1 and 2.

3. Analysis of the scene and topological attributes

It is evident that, in a scene generated as described above, the lines,
the endpoints and crossing points of the lines, and the areas which are
separated by the lines form the essential elements of the picture. The
aim of the algorithm will be to describe the scene in terms of these
elements under special consideration of the topological relationships
between them and their geometrical properties. The choice of the elements - point, line, area - at once suggests the use of fundamentals
of graph theory as a basis for the analysis of the scene. With the
following correspondences the 1:1 transformation between a scene and
a directed graph becomes obvious:

$$point \longrightarrow vertex;$$
$$line \longrightarrow edge;$$
$$area \longrightarrow region.$$

A plane, directed graph is defined by a set of vertices $V = \{v_1, v_2, \ldots \ldots v_k\}$, a set of directed edges $E = \{e_1, e_2, \ldots e_1\}$ and a set of regions $R = \{r_1, r_2, \ldots r_m\}$ with the following conditions:

(i) Each directed edge has one vertex as head and one vertex as tail. Both vertices may also be identical.

(ii) Each vertex is head or tail of at least one edge (which means that there are no isolated vertices).

(iii) There are no points of intersection of edges other than the vertices.

(iv) Each edge is incident to at least one, at most two, regions.

(v) In the case of a connected graph there is only one closed boundary which correlates with each region. In the case of a disconnected graph there are more than one. (A graph is disconnected if it can be divided into at least two subgraphs which are not connected by any edge.)

(vi) In the total number of closed boundaries each edge is included twice.

The consequent realization of these conditions provides the means for developing an algorithm which sets up three ordered incidence tables:

(i) the incidence table of edges which comprises 1 rows (1 being the number of edges) and two columns. The first column gives the name of the edge's head while the second names the tail.

(ii) the incidence table of vertices which comprises k rows (k being the number of vertices). For each vertex the ordered sequence of edges starting or ending at that specific vertex is given.

(iii) the incidence table of closed boundaries which includes q rows (q being the number of closed boundaries). For each boundary the name of the attached region and the ordered sequence of edges forming this boundary are given.

These tables represent the complete topological description of the graph by means of the incidences between its elements. Because of the 1:1 transformation these tables represent the topology of the scene as well. The following rules are meant to evaluate topological relationships between new elements on a higher level.

Consider a simple line drawing as shown in figure 3(a). There are indications that region A may be regarded as a distorted triangle. Thus merging the regions A, B and C would allow the reconstruction of a meaningful new closed boundary. In order to unite two regions A and B the following conditions must be satisfied:

(i) Let M be the number of edges of the closed boundary of region A, N the number of edges of the boundary of region B, P the number of edges common to both (two edges meeting at an angle of 180° are taken as a single one). Extensive tests have shown that both regions could be merged if

$$P > M/2 \qquad \text{or} \qquad P > N/2 \, .$$

(ii) Neither of the two regions belongs to the background. The outermost region surrounding the whole line drawing is called the background.

(iii) The shape of the resulting region is meaningful (see section 4 for details).

The second rule is found by considering a simple line drawing as shown in figure 3(b). Merging the three regions A, B and C would allow the reconstruction of a meaningful new closed boundary namely that of a rectangle. In this case the following conditions must be satisfied:

(i) Compile a possible sequence of edges which always meet one another at an angle of 180°. This sequence of edges is called a continuous line (see edges a, b and c in figure 3(b)). Group all regions to the left and to the right of the continuous line and which are bounded by it into two subsets of regions.

(ii) Disregard any subset of regions which is included in another one.

(iii) Disregard any subset of regions if the background is included.

(iv) Merge all regions of a subset if the shape of the resulting boundary proves to be meaningful (see section 4 for details).

Any new closed boundary which can be found according to one of these two rules is added to the existing incidence tables.

4. Geometrical attributes

It is clear that topological attributes as outlined above are not sufficient for an unambiguous characterization of a scene. The geometrical attributes which have already been used in order to set up the incidence tables are:

(i) The coordinates of the vertices which are used to determine whether disconnected parts of a graph are located inside or outside one another.

(ii) The angle between any edge and the horizontal axis which is used to set up the counterclockwise ordered sequence of edges starting or ending at each vertex.

(iii) The coordinates of the centres which are used to distinguish straight lines and circles.

Beside these the following geometrical attributrs are evaluated and added to the elements.

(i) The length of the edges. In case of a part of a circle the length of the radius is given.

(ii) The angle between any two edges.

(iii) The shape of any region is classified according to the number and shape of the edges of the corresponding boundary and according to the angles between any two adjacent edges of the boundary. Thus a number of meaningful shapes is categorized beginning with the triangle up to a hexagonal shape for boundaries composed of straightlined edges only and continuing with the circle and 'lenses' up to 'doors' for boundaries composed of two arcs and one straight edge or composed of one arc and three straight edges at most. Any boundary comprising more edges than outlined before is categorized as undefined. All specified kinds of shapes are divided further into certain types, for example general triangle, triangle with a right angle, equilateral triangle, rectangle, parallelogram, etc.

In conclusion the complete list of elements and their attributes is given below:

Elements	Attributes
vertex:	coordinates
	head, tail, centre

<pre>
edge: shape
                             length
                             4 adjacent edges (AE)
                             4 angles with the 4 AE's
                             region to the left
                             region to the right (see figure 4)

closed boundary: corresponding region
                             kind of shape
                             type of shape

continuous line: same as for edges

unified closed boundary: same as for closed boundary.
</pre>

The description based on these elements and the relations between them
and their attributes provides a characterization of a scene which is
well suited for the localization of objects (see section 5). The description does not vary with

- variation in size, if the attribute "length of an edge" is disregarded

- rotation of the scene

- translation of the scene.

It has to be noted however that these invariances also apply to parts
of the scene. This means that disconnected parts of the scene may be
translated or rotated relative to each other without any change of
description.

5. Localization of objects

An object is a specific part of a scene or a scene as a whole.

A model is a special scene whose name is known.

The questions usually to be answered by the method described above
for scene analysis are posed as follows:

Can an object identical with model no. 3 - a house - be found in a
specific scene ?

Does any object within a certain scene resemble a specific model ?

Can any model at all be found in a certain scene ?

The description of a scene as outlined above is not yet equivalent to
the denomination of objects in that scene. The basic idea, however, is
that this description of an object remains widely unchanges with respect to variation of size and with respect to rotation and translation and that the description is independent of all surrounding parts
of the scene. Thus the algorithm for the localization of objects con-
centrates on the comparison of the description of an unknown scene with
the description of a known model in order to determine whether the model can be retraced identically or whether it can be recognized up to
a certain degree of similarity. The description of a model is obtained
by applying the same algorithms but the evaluation of the additional
elements (continuous line and unified closed boundary) is dropped.
Figure 5 shows a rough block diagram of the complete processing system.

The comparison of the two descriptions is based on the framework of
edges. Consider the graph of a model and that of a scene shown in figures 6(a) and 6(b) respectively. The first edge b within the lists of
the model's graph (the edges a, c and e are disregarded because they
belong to the closed boundary of the background) is compared with all
edges of the subset $\{e', f', g', h', i', k'\}$ of the scene's graph
(the remaining edges of the scene's graph are again disregarded because they bound the background). In fact the comparison applies to
the attributes of the edges. Coincidences of angles are weighted as
well as coincidences of shapes. The number of successes is evaluated
by summing the weights of successful comparisons. If the number of
successes reaches a certain threshold a match for edge b is said to be
found (edge i' in the example shown in figure 6(b)). If no match is
found the same test is applied to the next edge of the model's graph.
If a starting match is found the four possible adjacent edges of both
partners are compared respectively and the number of successes are
evaluated (edge f is compared with edge h' as well as edge d to edge
k' (see figures 6(a) and 6(b)). As the algorithm proceeds lists of
suspected correspondences of edges and regions between the model's
graph and that of the scene are established and continually updated.
The procedure stops when no more edges of the model's graph are available. The reconstructed object within the scene is said to be identical with the model if, in the course of comparison, the number of
successes always reached the largest possible value. There are three
further possibilities:

(i) Angles and shapes of compared elements do not always match exactly
(tolerances of $\pm$ 5° to 10° are admitted when comparing angles).

(ii) The neighbourhood of edges and regions does not always correspond.

In both cases a reconstructed object is said to be similar to the model if the great majority of all compared geometrical attributes as well as the great majority of all compared topological attributes correspond. Certain tolerances are allowed for successful comparison of angles but no tolerances are allowed for all other attributes.

(iii) No starting match is found at all or the number of mismatches surpasses the given threshold. In this case the model is not to be found within the scene.

Large numbers of examples having been tested, this criterion of similarity did not contradict human estimation. These statements apply fully to models with connected graphs. In the case of disconnected graphs some minor modifications have to be introduced into the comparison. In all cases where the number of inner edges (edges not bounding the background) is below a certain threshold or where these edges do not form a connected framework, all edges of the graph are allowed to participate in the procedure of comparison. All attributes applying to the background are disregarded here. The localization of an object is terminated by denominating the respective edges and vertices of the scene.

6. Discussion

Because of the chosen kind of description the following statements can be pointed out:

(i) The method described above is capable of describing scenes depicting line drawings and of denominating objects within the scenes by means of comparison with known models. Model and object need not be identical. A certain degree of variance is covered as well.

(ii) The method is well suited to handle scenes which are highly structured and have connected graphs. A certain amount of complexity may not be exceeded with respect to the limitations of the simulation facilities.

(iii) The method has difficulties in handling extremely simple scenes. Models consisting of one or two regions only do not offer enough relations and attributes in order to allow reliable comparisons. They are easily confused with arrangements which really do not resemble each other.

(iv) The method is capable of separating and denominating more than one object within one scene.

(v) The method is not prepared to handle distortions caused by perspective projections and completely different views of the same object. There is a chance of success if the changes are minor. In general different views of three-dimensional objects will produce differently structured pictures and will therefore need different models.

Extensive tests of the method have proved its capability of successfully processing line drawings within the outlined limits (see figures 7 and 8). The dotted lines indicate a scene to be processed. The models to be looked for are depicted in small size to the left of the scenes. In case of success the objects within the scenes are retraced with heavy lines.

The integration of this method into a complete system for picture processing, presumably under the aspects of feedback systems, presents many more problems to be solved.

Acknowledgment

This work was sponsored by the German Ministry of Defence. The author gratefully thanks his colleagues for many valuable discussions.

References

Barrow H.G. and Popplestone R.J., 1971 Machine Intelligence 6

Busacker R. and Saaty T.L., 1968, Endliche Graphen und Netzwerke
        (München: R. Oldenbourg)

Clowes M.B., 1971 Artif. Intelligence 2

Guzmán A., 1967 MSc Thesis

Narasimhan R. 1970 Proc. Conf. on Picture Language Machines, Canberra
        1969 Ed. S. Kaneff (London: Academic Press)

Reidemeister K., 1951, Einführung in die kombinatorische Topologie
        (Braunschweig: Vieweg)

Stanton R.B., 1970 Proc. Conf. on Picture Language Machines, Canberra 1969 Ed. S. Kaneff (London: Academic Press)

Sties M., Forschungsbericht aus der Wehrtechnik 71-25, Bundesministerium für Verteidigung Bonn

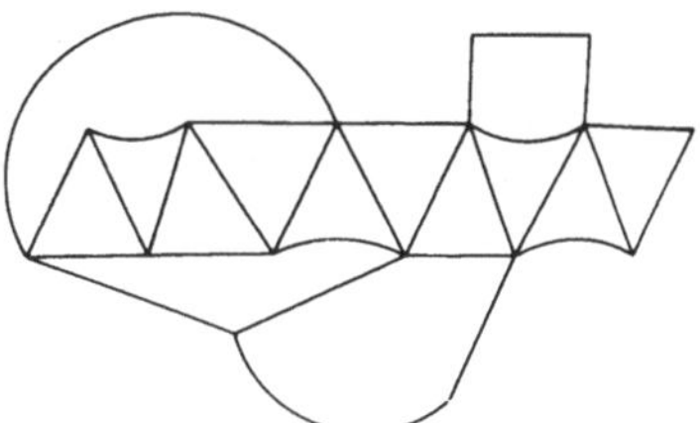

Fig.1: Example of a scene

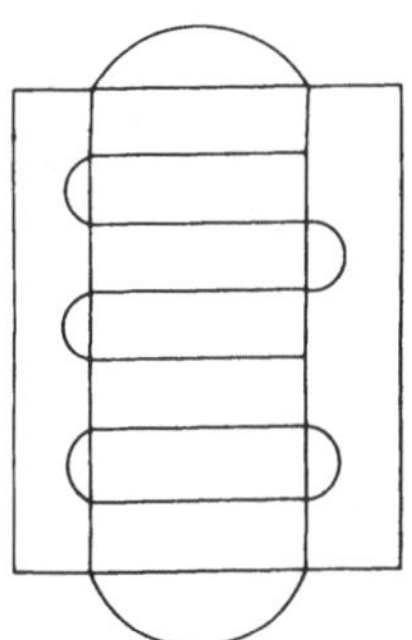

Fig.2: Example of a scene

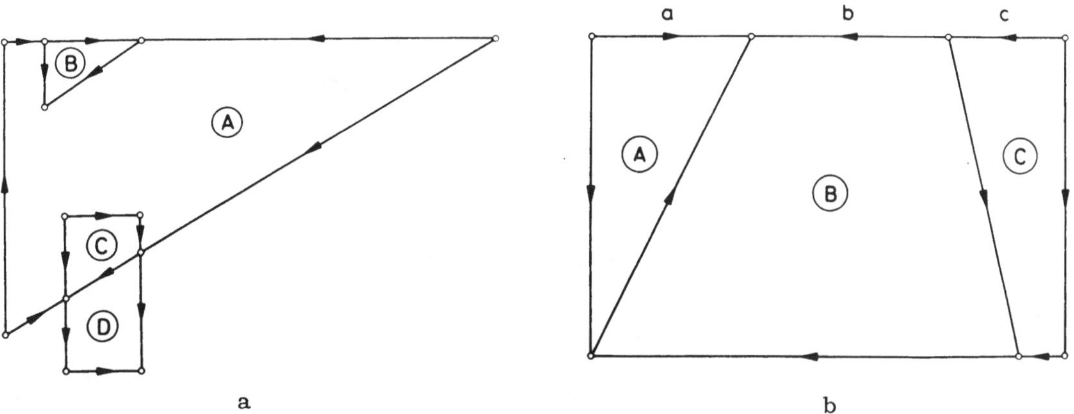

a

b

Fig.3a: Distorted Triangle b: Distorted Rectangle

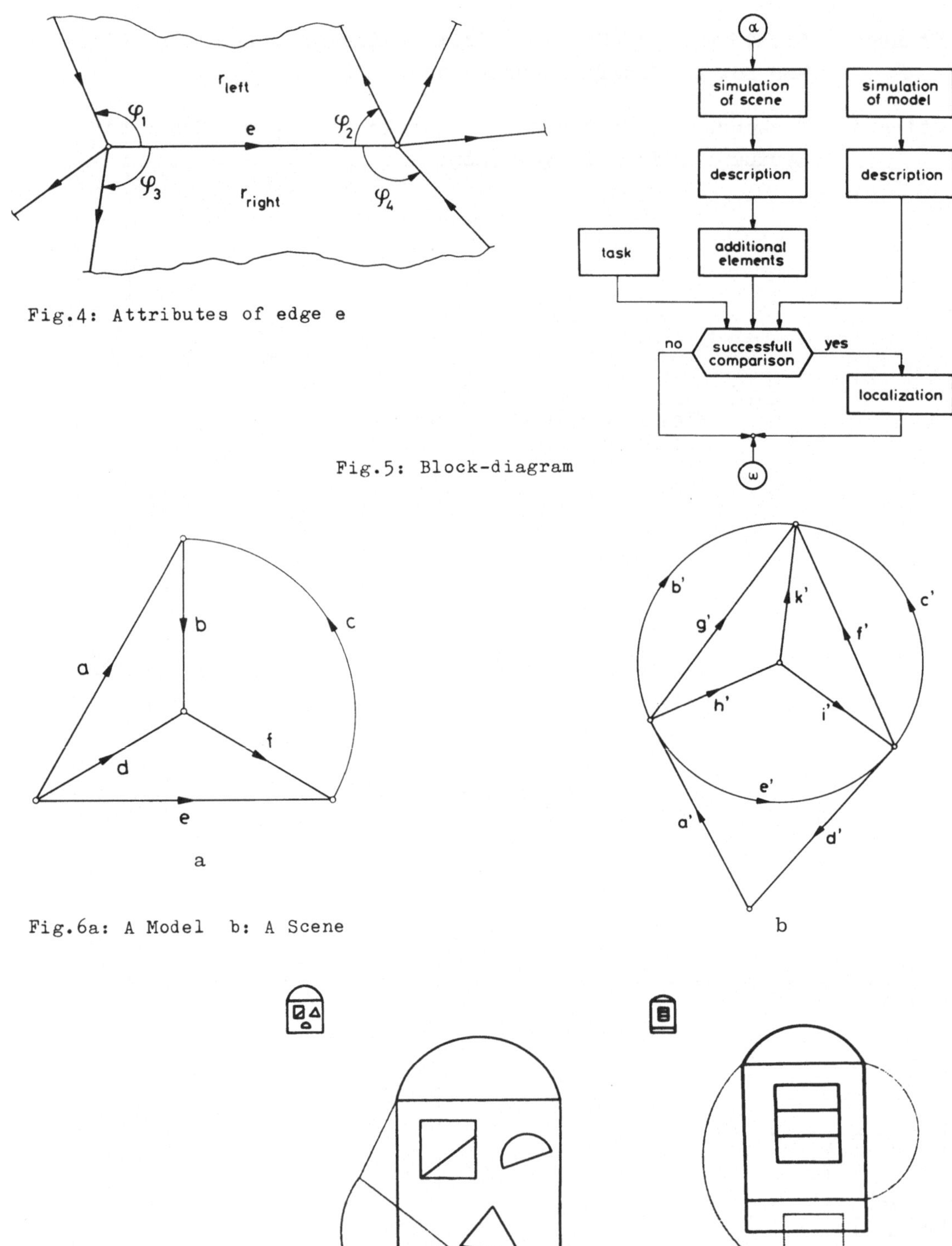

Fig.4: Attributes of edge e

Fig.5: Block-diagram

Fig.6a: A Model b: A Scene

Fig.7 und 8:
Processed scene

PROCESSING OF GREY SCALE PICTURES

F. Holdermann

1. Introduction

Picture processing with the aim of object recognition may be subdivided into 4 functional groups:

1) Picture scanning
2) Picture preprocessing
3) Contour- and scene-analysis
4) Classification

During the scanning process, the digitized grey values of a picture are transmitted to a computer and stored in a twodimensional picture matrix. In a next step the grey information of a picture must be preprocessed in such a way that areas with a reasonably uniform distribution of intensities and their boundaries may be extracted. This preprocessed information serves as input data for a contour and scene analysis, regarding the special structure of the objects to be recognized. The output information of this analysis may then be used as input criteria for a classification algorithm.

In general an object extraction from a grey-scale picture could be achieved by a comparison with representative object masks. Since however position, size, orientation and intensity of the objects may vary strongly, a large number of masks would be needed to identify even one object, that means that such an automatic processing would be unrealistic [1].

It is therefore an important task of picture processing algorithms to reduce the picture information and to generate suitable invariants. The most important features of an object are its boundaries and the contour-lines which separate its different surfaces and not the grey values of the surfaces themselves. Considering these facts, a first step in picture processing consists in generating all the contourlines of a grey scale picture.

In the simplext case such a contour line picture could be represented
as a binary matrix, where elements which belong to a boundary are
marked by 1. Using this kind of presentation, the following difficulties and disadvantages would arise:

1) In certain cases the reduction of information would be too
   strong. A separating boundary between two areas with slightly
   differing grey value, e.g., would be presented in the same way
   as a boundary between considerably differing grey areas. This
   fact could lead to unnecessary ambiquities in contour tracing
   algorithms.

2) In generating the binary contours, noise may arise because of
   the unavoidable thresholds which must be implemented.

3) A contour tracing algorithm basing on this information would be
   rather time consuming.

If an additional characterization of a boundary is introduced, e.g. a
measure of the difference of the grey values on both sides of the
contour element, then problems 1 and 2 are diminished but not problem
3. A moderation of problem 3 can be reached by additionally characterizing the contour elements with a differential direction of the
contour, because a searching algorithm may define an area by these
means where in all probability neighbouring elements may be found
[2,3].

In the following chapters three methods for generating differential
directions are presented and discussed. Two of these methods start
from a scanned grey scale picture and extract the directions of the
line elements by local preprocessing of the picture. These routines
should be regarded as simulation of peripheral pipeline processors
which are able to perform the same task in parallel. The third method
allows a detection of direction elements by preprocessing the analog
scanning signal by hardware during the scanning process.

2. Generation of differential directions

2.1 Generation of direction elements by comparision with different
    masks

A digitized picture B is given by its elements B_{pq}, (p,q = 1...N). All
the operations to be described are local operations [4] which must be

performed in each picture element B_{pq}. For this reason the surrounding elements $B_{p\pm i,q\pm j}$, $(i,j = 1...(n-1)/2)$, of B_{pq} are summarized in a submatrix b of size $n \times n$, with elements b_{ij}, $(i,j = 1...(n-1)/2)$, so that the central element b_{oo} of b coincides with each element B_{pq} of B, (figure 1a).

The method to be described is based on a comparison of the local picture information of a submatrix b with the information of different masks m^k. In order to keep the necessary number of masks as small as possible, the algorithm starts from the first derivative ΔB of a picture B. The evaluation of the elements ΔB_{pq} of ΔB is given by equ. (1), (figure 1b).

$$\Delta B_{pq} = \frac{1}{2}(\left| b_{-1,o} - b_{1,o} \right| + \left| b_{o,-1} - b_{o,1} \right|) \tag{1}$$

$$p,q = 1 \ldots N$$

Since only the amount of the differences in equ. (1) is used, the number of direction masks could be reduced by factor 2. The result of this operation is shown in the display output pictures of figure 2, where the different values of the elements ΔB_{pq} are displayed with different intensity levels.

The algorithm to determine the differential directions R_{pq} compares the differential boundaries within ΔB with idealized line elements in 8 different orientations, which are marked by the numerals 0 ... 7, (figure 3). The masks m^k $(k = 0...7)$, representing the idealized line elements, are numbered according to the orientation of the line elements. The number k of that mask m^k is taken as differential direction R_{pq}, which delivers the best value of comparison. The procedure to describe the comparison is given by equ. (2)...(4), the exact shapes of the 8 masks is shown in figure 4.

$$d_k = \sum_{i=-n1}^{i=+n1} \sum_{j=-n1}^{j=+n1} (\Delta b_{ij} - u) \cdot m^k_{ij} \tag{2}$$

$$k = 0...7$$

with: $n1 = (n-1)/2$

and: $u = \frac{1}{n^2} \sum_{i=-n1}^{i=+n1} \sum_{j=-n1}^{j=+n1} b_{ij}$

Maximum detection:

$$d_{max} = \max_{k=0}^{k=7} (d_k) \tag{3}$$

$$R_{pq} = k \,|\, (d_k = d_{max}) \tag{4}$$

$$p,q = 1 \ldots N$$

The importance of the evaluated direction elements R_{pq} can be expressed by weights W_{pq}. In the simplest case the values of the weights W_{pq} may be derived from the values of the first derivative ΔB_{pq}, equ. (5), if the corresponding value of d_{max} is beyond some threshold, figure 5c. But the results

$$W_{pq} = \Delta B_{pq} \tag{5}$$

are not very satisfactory. An other way to generate the weights is to derive them from the values of d_{max}, equ. (6)

$$W_{pq} = \frac{1}{const} \cdot d_{max} \tag{6}$$

const must be determined experimentally, so that the values of the W_{pq} are within a prescribable range (0...7), figure 5d. This manner of determination of the weights represent a compromise between a pure valuation of the shape of the differential contour line on the one hand and a pure valuation of the gradient value ΔB_{pq} on the other hand. A third method to determine the weights is to normalize the values of the d_{max} and to take these normalized values as weights, equ. (7), figure 5e.

$$W_{pq} = \frac{d_{max}}{\displaystyle\max_{i=-n1}^{i=+n1} \max_{j=-n1}^{j=+n1} (\Delta b_{ij} - u)} \tag{7}$$

This method represents a pure valuation of the shape of a contour line and fully disregards the value of the gradient in a position (p,q). The results of the three methods do not differ too much among each other, which method really should be used cannot generally be told. To some degrees it depends upon the specific application.

The display outputs in figure 5c,d,e show combined representations of

direction and weight matrices. The detected directions (0...7) are
presented as small line elements in the given orientation, whereas
the detected weights (0...7) are displayed by intensity modulation
of the corresponding line elements.

2.2 Evaluation of Direction elements by plane approximation

This method extracts the direction elements R_{pq} and the weights W_{pq}
starting from the grey scale picture B without using the differentia-
ted picture ΔB. If the grey information of each submatrix is regarded
as a three-dimensional surface $f(x,y)$, equ. (8), it is the task of an
algorithm to find a plane, equ. (9), which approximates the given
surface as good as possible.

$$b = f(x,y) \tag{8}$$

$$z = ex + fy + g \tag{9}$$

The resulting normal vector $\mathcal{N}$ of this plane then gives information
about slope and direction of boundary elements. The inclination μ of
the plane against the vertical axis corresponds directly to a weight,
characterizing the slope of the surface and the inclination ν against
the x- or y-axis corresponds to the orientation in the x-y-plane (figure 6).

The criterion to define the best position of a plane is the volume V
which is built by plane and surface. The orientation of the plane must
be determined in such a way that this volume comes to a minimum, equ.
(11).

$$V = \int_{-x_1}^{+x_1} \int_{-y_1}^{+y_1} \left| b-z \right| \, dydx \stackrel{!}{=} \text{Min.} \tag{11}$$

For computational reasons, the following function, equ. (12), which
leads to the same result, has been minimized.

$$V' = \int_{-x_1}^{+x_1} \int_{-y_1}^{+y_1} (b-z)^2 \, dydx \stackrel{!}{=} \text{Min.} \tag{12}$$

x_1, y_1 determine integration limits. Equ. (13) formulates the same
problem in a quantized form.

$$V' = \sum_{i=-n1}^{i=+n1} \sum_{j=-n1}^{j=+n1} (b_{ij} - z_{ij})^2 \overset{!}{=} \text{Min} \tag{13}$$

The solution of this problem delivers equations to define the variables e,f and g of a plane in a general way, equs. (14...16).

$$e = c \cdot \sum_{i=-n1}^{i=+n1} \sum_{j=-n1}^{j=+n1} b_{ij} \cdot (i + n1 + 1) \tag{14}$$

$$f = c \cdot \sum_{i=-n1}^{i=+n1} \sum_{j=-n1}^{j=+n1} b_{ij} \cdot (i + n1 + 1) \tag{15}$$

$$g = \frac{1}{n^2} \cdot \sum_{i=-n1}^{i=+n1} \sum_{j=-n1}^{j=+n1} b_{ij} \tag{16}$$

with: $\quad c = \dfrac{12}{n^2 \cdot (n^2 - 1)} \qquad n = 2n1 + 1$

By table look up a weight W_{pq} in the range 0...7 may be derived from the angle μ, equ. (17), which defines the inclination of the plane against the vertical axis.

$$\mu = \text{arc cos} \left(\frac{1}{\sqrt{e^2 + f^2 + 1}}\right) \tag{17}$$

$$0 \leq \mu \leq 90^\circ$$

Similarly the direction R_{pq} results from the angle ν against the y-axis, equ. (18).

$$\nu = \text{arc tg} \left(\frac{e}{f}\right) \tag{18}$$

$$0 \leq \nu \leq 180^\circ$$

2.3 Detection of differential directions during scanning

A suitable control of the scanning light spot and a corresponding preprocessing of the analog scanning signal allows, to detect differential directions during the scanning process (figure 7).

This requires that in each scanning position the light spot must be deflected on a circle. Whereas in homogeneous grey areas, the scanning signal will have no characteristic shape, sinelike shapes of different amplitudes will result provided, that the light spot crosses a boundary (figure 8). The shape of the scanning signal may also vary according to the ratio η/ϱ of the radii of light spot and scanning circle (figure 8a,b) and according to the relative positions of scanning circle and boundary (figure 8c). The phase of this signal determines the direction of the scanned boundary. The only condition is, that the light spot must start from an exactly defined position [5]. In this case the detection takes place online during the scanning processs and needs no additional computer time.

2.4 Discussion of the results

All the 3 presented methods supply direction and weight matrices which contain all the essential contour lines of a grey scale picture. The results only differ somewhat as to the sensitivity of the detection of weak contrast boundaries and as to noise manipulation in homogeneous grey areas.

The pictures 9c,d,e show the display outputs of direction matrices, which were received by the application of the three methods to a grey scale picture (picture 9a). The detected directions $R_{pq}(0...7)$ and weights $W_{pq}(0...7)$ are displayed in the same manner as in figure 5.

Using equ. (6) or (7) to evaluate the weights, the mask comparison method allows to detect rather weak contrast boundaries (figure 9c). For better discrimination of the directions, represented by the 8 masks m^k (k = 0...7) it is reasonable to use submatrices of size 7 × 7 or 9 × 9. But this fact has some negative consequences concerning small objects in a picture. To some extend, their boundaries are destroyed.

In contrast to the mask comparison method the plane approximation method (figure 9d) allows to detect the directions (0...7) using smaller submatrices (3 × 3 or 5 × 5), since the directions to be discriminated must not be stored in different masks. Because of the smaller submatrices, the resulting picture has a better resolution than a picture generated by the mask comparison method. But on the other hand com-

pared to the plane approximation method, the mask comparison method
has a better discrimination power between weak contrast boundaries
and noise in homogeneous grey regions.

The generation of directions using special hardware devices can be
accomplished within a rather short processing time, (10 μsec/element).
The results, (figure 9e), are similar to those, obtained with the
plane approximation method.

3. Thinning of contour lines

Contour lines generated by one of the methods described in chapter 2,
have the disadvantage that they are rather broad bands of direction
elements. The aim of the procedure to be described is to thin these
bands to a thickness of one or two elements, using the direction information of the band. As an example, a section of such a band of directions is illustrated in the submatrix r, figure 10a. The task of
the thinning algorithm is to determine whether the direction of the
central element r_{oo} may be deleted or not. This can be decided for all
elements R_{pq} (p,q = 1,...N) within one run through the matrix R, if
it is possible to determine the relative position of an element R_{pq}
with regard to the remaining elements of a band. Only those elements
R_{pq} of the matrix R are taken into consideration, the corresponding
weights of which are $W_{pq} \neq 0$.

In a first step a binary matrix br is defined, according to equ. (19).

$$br_{ij} = \begin{array}{c} 1 \\ 0 \end{array} \quad if \quad \left| (r_{ij}-r_{oo})\bmod 8 \right| \begin{array}{c} \leq \\ > \end{array} 1 \tag{19}$$

$$i,j = -n1 \ldots +n1$$

This means, that in the matrix br (figure 10b) only those elements
are marked, the direction values of which do not differ too much from
the value of the central element.

In order to find out, whether the central element r_{oo} of the submatrix
r is a marginal or a central element of a direction band representing
a contour line within R, the distance transform of br is evaluated,
equ. (20), (figure 10c).

$$dr = D(br) \tag{20}$$

D is an operator, performing the distance transformation. The procedure has been described elsewhere [6].

The values of the elements dr_{ij} exactly reflect the positions of the corresponding elements r_{ij} within a band of similar directions.

In order to determine whether the direction of the central element r_{oo} may be deleted or not, the value of dr_{oo} must be compared with the values dr_{ij} of surrounding elements, especially with elements in a direction k perpendicular to the direction specified by r_{oo}, equ. (21), figure 10d.

$$k = (r_{oo} + 4)\bmod 8 \tag{21}$$

In order to be able to address the elements r_{ij} within a specific direction k, the following definition is used: The transition from one element in a submatrix to one of its neighbours shall be expressed by elementary steps, denoted by lower case signed letters $\pm\alpha$, ..., $\pm\delta$, according to the chain encoding scheme [7], figure 11.

By this definition an element $\varepsilon_{ij\mid a}$ of a submatrix may be referenced by addressing a neighbouring element ε_{ij} in combination with an additional specification of an elementary step a, $(a \in \{\pm\alpha, ..., \pm\delta\})$, equ. (22).

$$\varepsilon_{ij\mid a} = \varepsilon_{i\pm\sigma, j\pm\lambda} \tag{22}$$
$$0 \leq \sigma \leq 1$$
$$0 \leq \lambda \leq 1$$

Elements which may not be reached within one step, starting from ε_{ij}, shall be referenced by a sequence of steps, equ. (23).

$$S_k = a_1, a_2, ..., a_k \tag{23}$$
$$\varepsilon_{ij\mid s_k} = \varepsilon_{i\pm\sigma, \, j\pm\lambda}$$
$$0 \leq \sigma \leq k$$
$$0 \leq \lambda \leq k$$

In order to determine the relative position of r_{oo} within the direction band, the algorithm starts from the central position in dr and determines the maximum value dr_{max} of the elements $dr_{oo\mid S_k(\pm k)}$,

($0 \leq k \leq n1$) in both directions +k and -k. The search in each of the
two directions terminates at the first element ϑ ($\pm$k) with value zero
or if not existing, at the margin (n1) of the submatrix dr., equ. (24,
25, 26).

$$\vartheta (K) = \min(k \mid dr_{oo}\mid_{S_k}(K) = 0) \tag{24}$$

$$K \in \left\{+k, \ -k\right\}$$

$$drm(K) = \max_{k=0}^{k = \min(\vartheta(K),n1)} (dr_{oo}\mid_{S_k}(K)) \tag{25}$$

$$K \in \left\{+k, \ -k\right\}$$

$$dr_{max} = \max(drm(+k), \ drm(-k)) \tag{26}$$

In a next step the distance ξ of the element with maximum value dr_{max}
to the center of the submatrix must be determined, equ. (27).

$$\xi = k\mid(dr_{oo},S_k(K) = dr_{max}) \tag{27}$$

The distance ξ allows an estimation of the relative position of the
submatrix center element r_{oo} to the center of a contour line. If the
distance is large, the element r_{oo} belongs to the marginal regions of
the band and can be deleted, if it is small or even zero, the element
is a center element of a band and must be preserved, equ. (28).

$$r_{oo} = \begin{array}{l} oo \\ r_{oo} \end{array} \quad \text{if } \xi \begin{array}{l} \geq \\ < \end{array} lim \tag{28}$$

Since the value r_{oo} = 0 corresponds to the vertical direction, the
notification "no direction" must be expressed by a special symbol "OO".

The value of lim determines the final thickness of the processed contour lines, in the given example, figure 12, it was chosen to lim = 1.
In order to get a better impression of the efficiency of this procedure,
only the weights corresponding to the directions are displayed.

4. Contour-tracing

Further processing of contour lines, generated and processed by methods
described in chapters 2 and 3, may exist in contour tracing, in order

to get coordinate lists of connected elements. This requires search algorithms which are able to make use of the direction- and weight-information of the preprocessed pictures.

4.1 Contour tracing, not object oriented

It is the task of such a tracing algorithm to follow a given band of directions straight forward, not regarding any branches, connected to this band.

The given direction information of each element of a band determines a region where neighbouring elements may be expected (figure 13). The tracing algorithm must consider the following cases:

1) If there is more than one element in the selected region, that element is selected, which agrees best in weight and direction with earlier found elements of this direction band. If there are more than one element with these properties, the element with the greatest distance to the center element of the region is selected. In figure 13, the regions are presented as small sections of circles. The selected element of a region is always the center element of the next region.

2) If there is no element in the predetermined region, fitting with elements selected before, neighbouring regions must be searched for connected elements. This fact may happen in edge points and curves (regions 5,6,7 and 9,10 in figure 13).

3) If there is no continuing element at all, the line has to be terminated.

By this means, straight lines can be traced very quickly (steps 1...4 in figure 13), and the speed of the search will only be diminished at strongly curved boundaries (steps 5...11). Some results of such tracing runs through different pictures are given in figure 14. Detected contour lines, the length of which were bellow a given threshold, have been suppressed.

4.2 Contour tracing, object oriented

An object oriented tracing algorithm is specialized to recognize certain objects, the data structure of which is implemented in the search algorithm. As an example an algorithm was developed to search for parallel contour lines of a given distance (figure 15) [10].

The algorithm works in the following manner:
Perpendicular to the given direction of a starting position, elements of similar direction are searched for (rectangular regions in figure 15). If such an element can be found, search regions, denoted by 1 and 1' are defined tentatively and the elements are selected according to chapter 4.1 for both regions. The only modification is, that the algorithm has to proceed simultaneously on both direction bands.

This procedure was applied to some pictures in order to find out streets. Some results are demonstrated in figure 16.

As a second example of an object oriented tracing algorithm, the probelm to find out closed areas, was treated [11]. In this case the algorithm has to look for branching elements of a direction band and has to follow them (figure 17). A new center element is determined as an element on a circle around the position of the center element of the step before. The starting position of the search is perpendicular to the given direction of the center element. Normally, if no branching elements are touched, the search terminates near the center of the direction band (steps 1...4). If branching elements can be located, the search terminates earlier, steps 5 and 6, follows the branch and tries to close a loop. This procedure was used to extract houses from pictures. Some results are shown in figure 18.

5. Conclusion

The results of chapter 4 show that the preprocessing routines and search principles applied, represent a first step towards on object extraction and scene analysis. They also show, that the applied search principles are not yet sufficient. It seems to be absolutely necessary to formulate more structural features of the objects to be searched for and to use this additional information besides the weight-direction- and grey level information of a preprocessed picture.

Bibliography

/1/ Harley, T.J. et al.: System considerations for automatic imagery
    screening. Pictorial Pattern Recognition, Thompson Book Com.,
    1968, pp. 15-33

/2/ Macleod, I.D.: On finding structure in pictures, Picture Langua-
    ge Machines, Academic Press, 1970, pp. 231-257

/3/ Simon, J.C. et. A. Checroun: Procedes de filtrage digital d'une
    image de lignes, Proceedings of the AGARD Avionics XXI techn.
    Symp. on Artificial Intelligence, Rome, Italy 1971, to be
    published.

/4/ Rosenfeld, A.: Picture processing by computer, Academic Press,
    1969

/5/ Kazmierczak, H. and F. Holdermann: The Karlsruhe system for
    automatic photointerpretation, Pictorial Pattern Recognition,
    Thompson Book Comp., 1968, pp. 45-63

/6/ Kazmierczak H. et al.: Informationsverarbeitung mit Rechenanla-
    gen, Nicht-numerische Informationsverarbeitung, Springer-Ver-
    lag, 1968, pp. 400-432

/7/ Freemann, H.: On the encoding of arbitrary geometry configura-
    tions, IRE Trans. EC-10, 1961, pp. 260-268

/8/ Pfaltz, J.L. and A. Rosenfeld: Computer representation of planar
    regions by their skeletons, Comm. ACM 10, 1967, pp. 119-123

/9/ Pfaltz, J.L. et al.: Local and global picture processing by com-
    puter, Pictorial Pattern Recognition, Thompson Book Comp.,
    1968, pp. 353-373

/10/ Enderle, G., F. Holdermann: Ermittlung von parallelen Konturen
     in einem vorverarbeitenden Grauton-Bild, Diplomarbeit am In-
     stitut für Nachrichtenverarbeitung und Nachrichtenübertra-
     gung, Universität Karlsruhe, 1970

/11/ Bär, H., W. Zorn: Ermittlung einfacher Objekte aus Grauton-Bildern, Diplomarbeit am Institut für Nachrichtenverarbeitung und Nachrichtenübertragung, Universität Karlsruhe, 1970

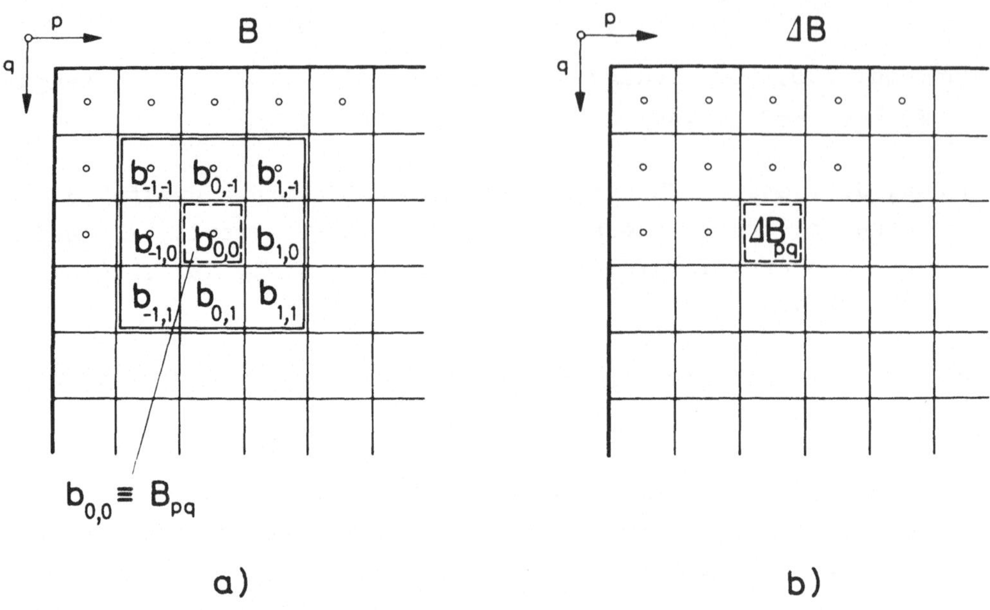

Fig. 1 Local processing with submatrix b, a) position of the submatrix in the original matrix, b) position of the processed element in the resulting matrix

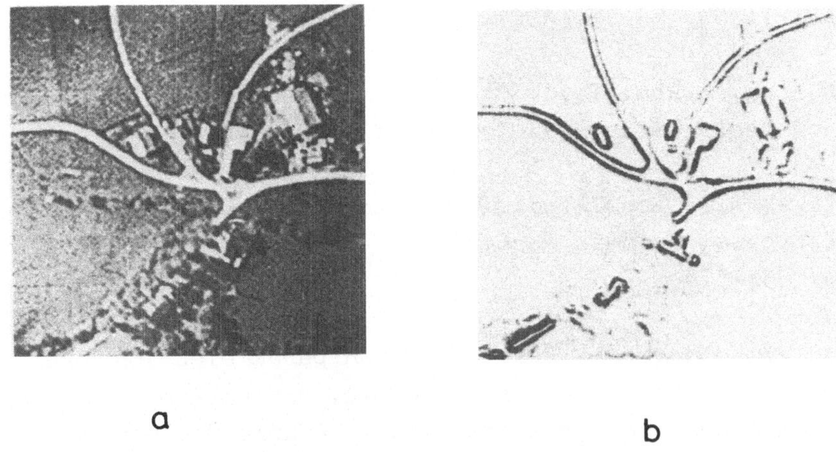

Fig. 2 Display outputs, a) of an areal photo (scanning resolution 256 x 256,64 grey levels), representation with 8 grey levels,b) first derivative of a)

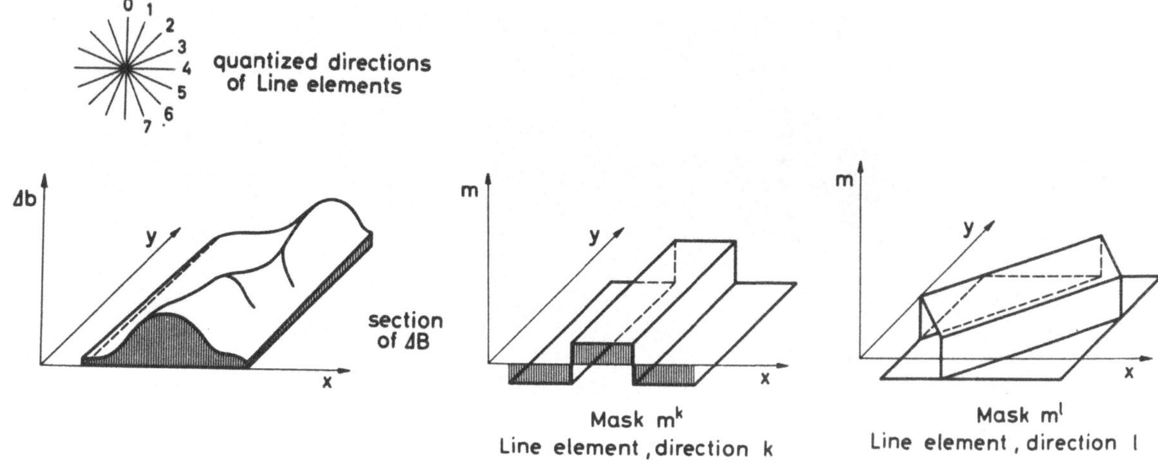

Fig. 3 Comparison of contour line elements with masks m^k

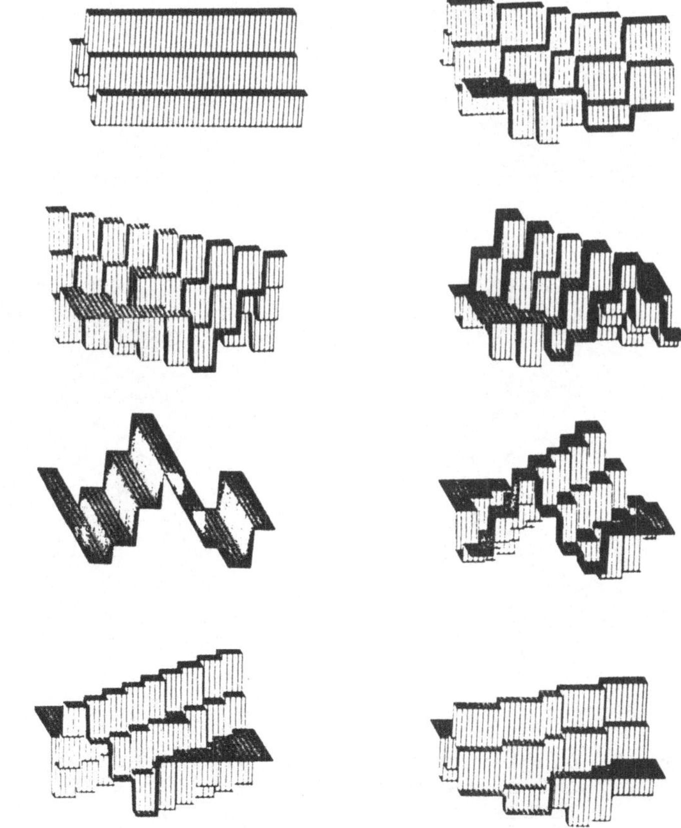

Fig. 4 Three-dimen-
sional display-
outputs of the
8 masks represen-
ting an idealized
line element in 8
orientations

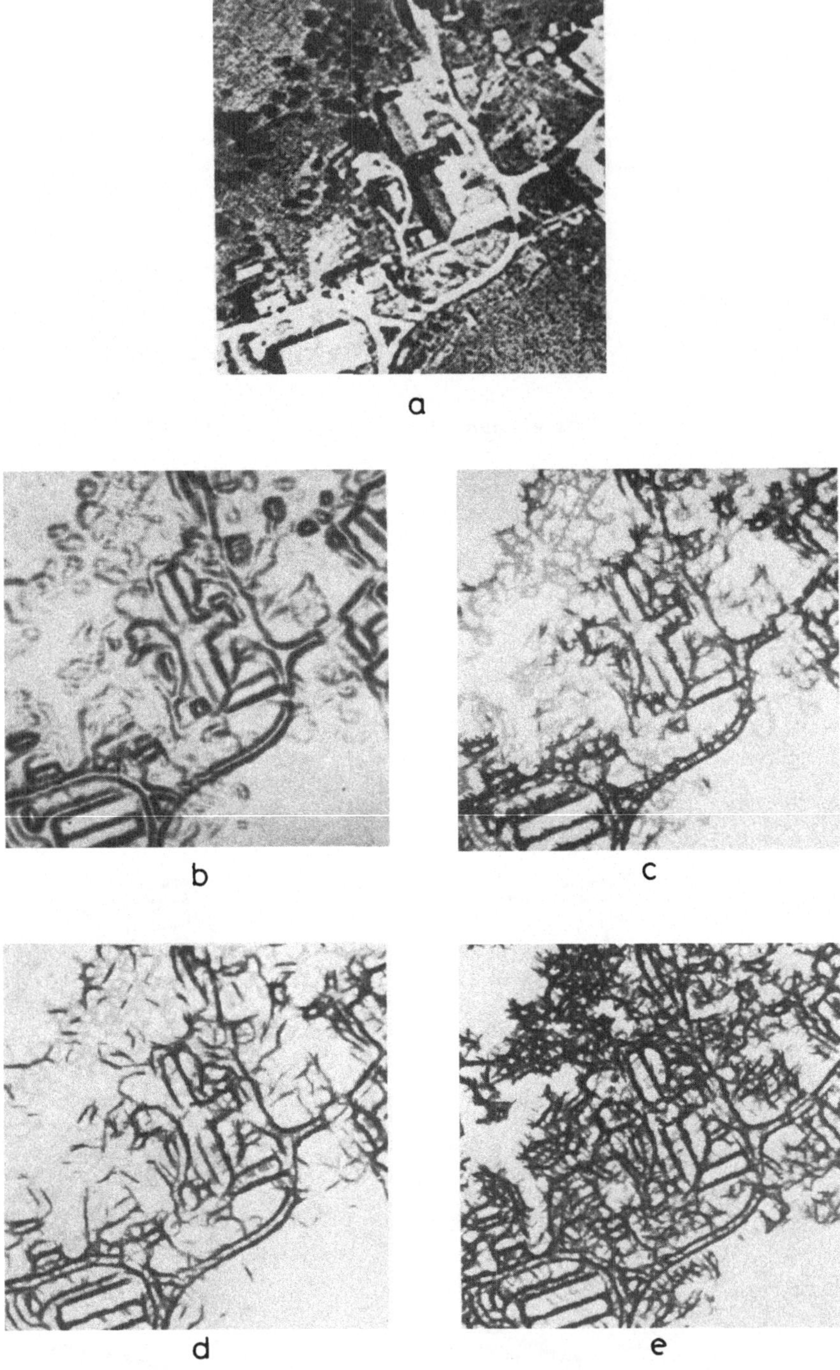

Fig. 5 Display outputs of a) areal photo (scanning resolution
256 x 256 points, 64 grey levels), presented with 8 grey
levels, b) first derivative, c) combined presentation of direction and weight information using equ. (5), d) using equ. (6),
e) using equ. (7)

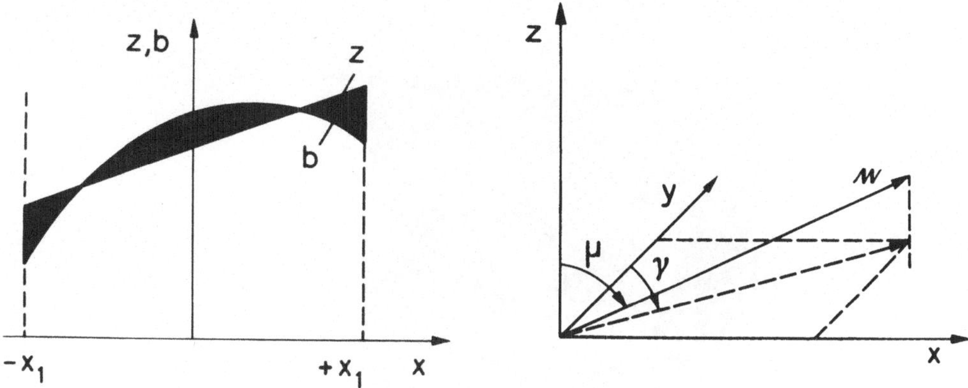

Fig. 6   Position of picture surface b and plane z

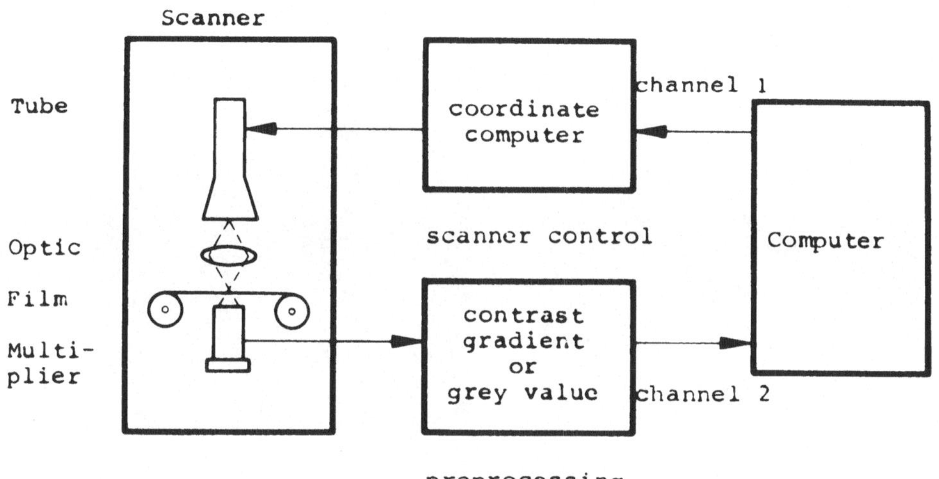

Fig. 7   Organization of the scanning system

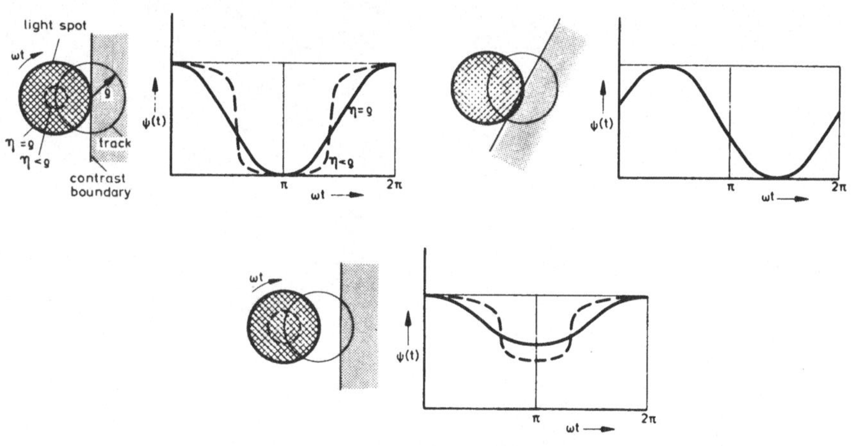

Fig. 8   Scanning method, a) scanning signal, vertical direction of
         a contrast boundary, b) scanning signal, inclined boundry,
         c) displacement between scanning position and boundry

a

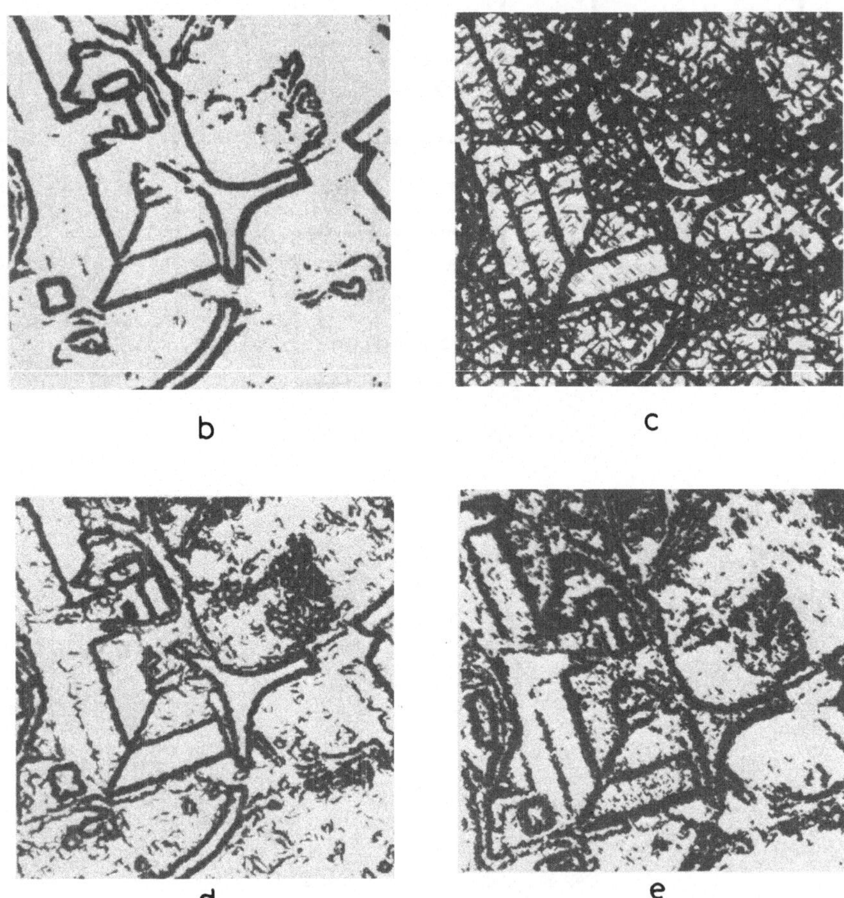

b

c

d

e

Fig. 9   Display outputs of direction matrices,
         a) areal photo after scanning (resolution 256 x 256 points,
         64 grey levels), 8 grey level presentation, b) first derivative,
         c) after application of the mask comparison algorithm (weights
         evaluated according to equ. (6), submatrix size 9 x 9), d) after
         application of the plane approximation method (submatrix
         size 5 x 5), e) hardware generated directions

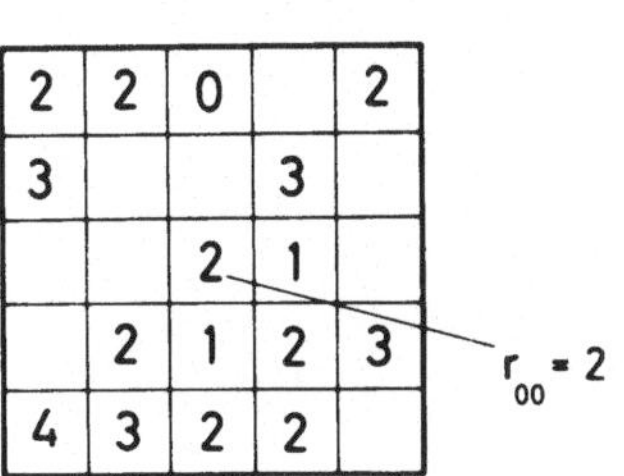

a) direction matrix r

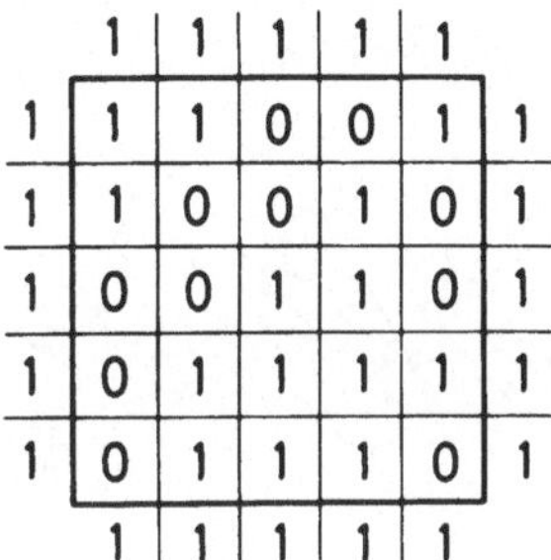

b) binary matrix br

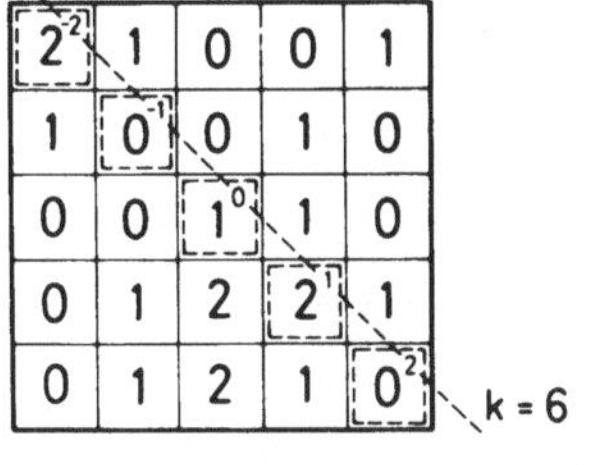

c) distance transform
dr = D(br)

D ≡ distance transform operator

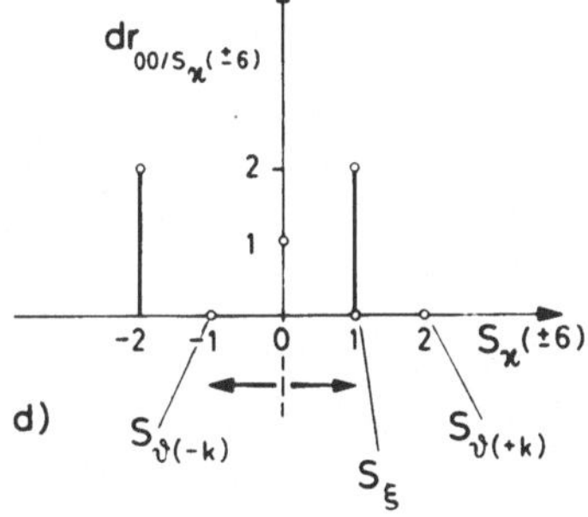

d)

Fig. 10 Line thinning by distance transformation

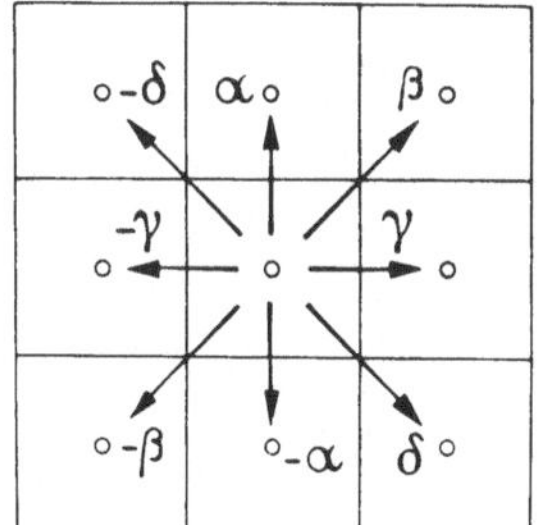

Fig. 11 Elementary step definition

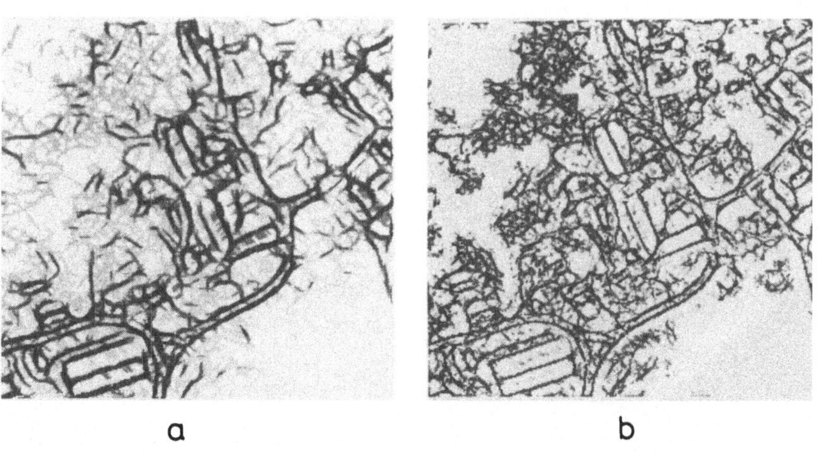

a

b

Fig. 12 Display outputs of a) weight matrix corresponding to the direction matrix in figure 5e, b) weight matrix after application of the thinning procedure

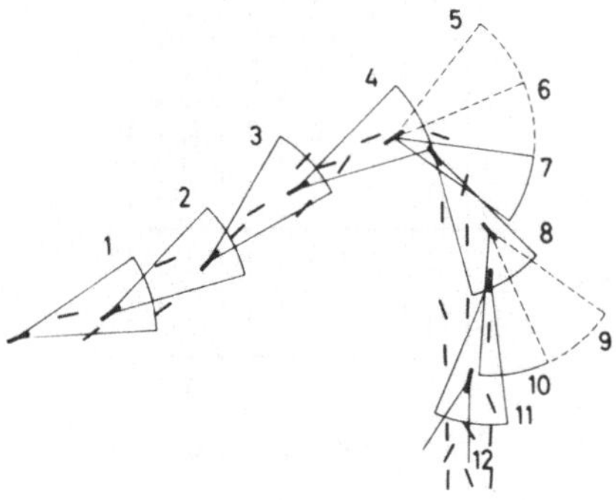

Fig. 13 Tracing of a direction band,
        search principal

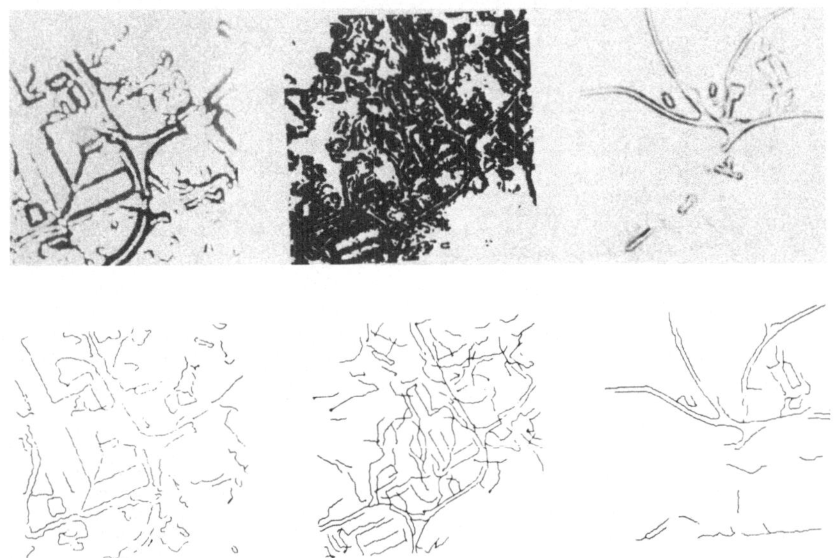

Fig. 14 Display outputs of the contour tracing algorithm, a) applied
        to picture 9a, b) applied to picture 5a, c) applied to
        picture 2a

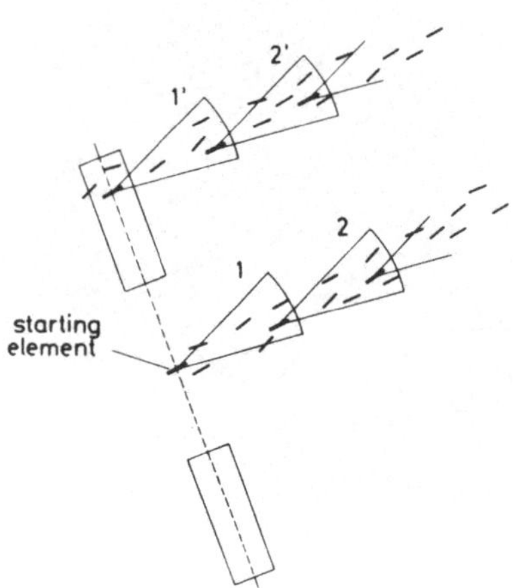

Fig. 15 Tracing of parallel
         contours,
          search pricipal

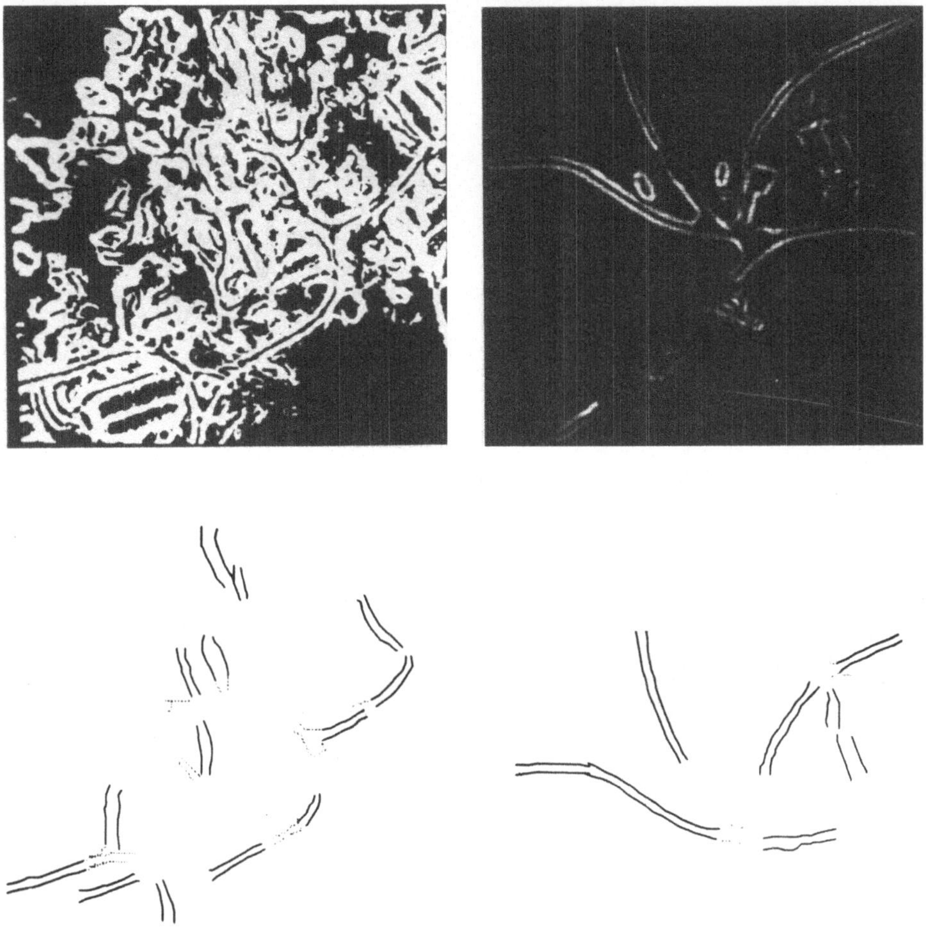

Fig. 16 Tracing of parallel contours, results

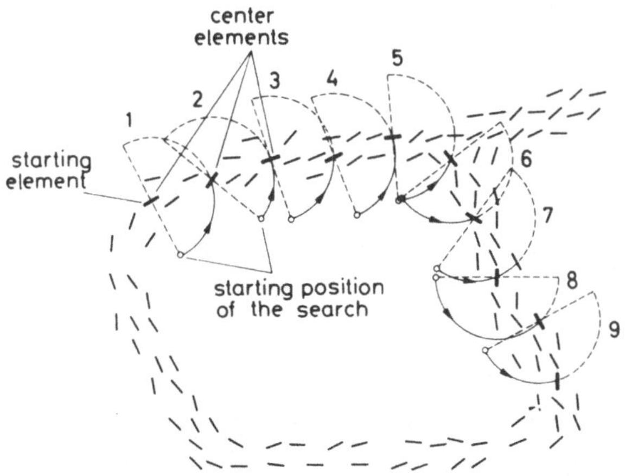

Fig. 17 Tracing of closed areas, search principal

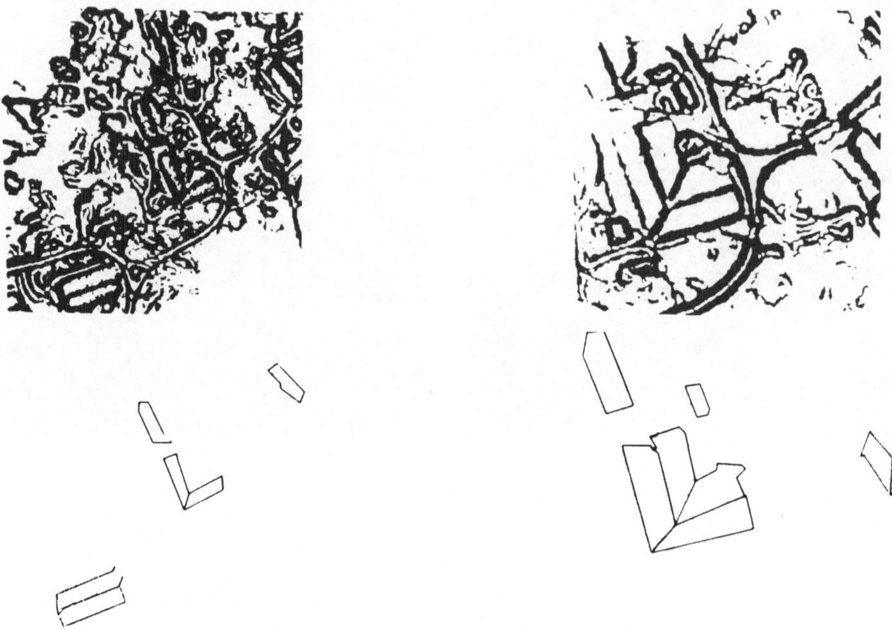

Fig. 18   Extraction of houses, results

Vorverarbeitung handgeschriebener gerasterter Ziffern

A. Güdesen

Abstract: Handprinted characters have to be rastered before processing in
a digital computer. Classifications of these data give poor results without
preprocessing methods. Different techniques have been tested to find out
what could lead to an improvement in recognition rate with a given classification system consisting of Loève-Karhunen feature extractor and Bayes clas-
sificator. Non linear preprocessing by local operations has been investigated as well as global techniques using geometric transformations. All methods
have been tested with a character set of 560 members per class. Combinations
of different techniques will also be discussed.

Die hier erläuterten Techniken zur Mustervorverarbeitung sind ein Teilprob-
lem aus dem Entwurf eines Verfahrens zur Klassifikation handgeschriebener
Ziffern und Buchstaben. Endziel der Arbeiten soll die Realisierung der direkten Eingabe von handgeschriebenen Formularen in den Digitalrechner sein.
Es wird davon ausgegangen, daß die dabei zumutbaren Fehlerraten bei fehlen-
dem Kontext in der gleichen Größenordnung liegen dürfen, wie sie gegeben ist,
durch manuell zu bedienende Eingabemedien. In jedem Falle soll aber zunächst
von Zeichen in Blockschrift ausgegangen werden. Das Problem des Segmentierens
fließender Schrift wird hier noch nicht weiter verfolgt.

Entscheidend für jede Aussage über die Leistung eines Klassifikationsverfah-
rens ist die Art des verwendeten Testmaterials. Es soll deshalb zunächst ein
Eindruck von der Qualität des Ausgangsmaterials gegeben werden (Bild 1). Die
Schreiber wurden gebeten, jeweils einen ganzen Bogen vollzuschreiben und dabei die Kästchengröße und die zur Unterscheidung der einzelnen Zeichenklassen
getroffenen Auflagen zu beachten. Diese Auflagen sind aus der Musterzeile ersichtlich. Die Ergebnisse zweier Stichproben sind ebenfalls abgebildet. Man
erkennt, wie stark die individuellen Abweichungen der Schreiber sind trotz
der getroffenen Konventionen. Der gewonnene Schriftsatz ist im Raster 9 x 14
abgetastet worden und auf Magnetplatten gespeichert. /1/

Die Verarbeitung der Proben erfolgte bisher allein nach einem mathematischen
Modell, das an anderen Stellen mehrfach in Einzelheiten erläutert wurde. /2/,
/3/. Grundvoraussetzung ist die Annahme, daß der Vorgang des Schreibens ein
stochastischer Prozeß ist und die Klassifikation der Schriftzeichen als ein

Beispiel für die multiple Detektion gestörter Empfangsvektoren angesehen werden kann. Das Bild 2 erläutert die grundlegenden mathematischen Zusammenhänge. Demnach besteht das System aus zwei Hauptteilen, der Extraktorstufe und dem nachgeschalteten Klassifikator. Die Muster, die grundsätzlich in diskreter oder kontinuierlicher Form vorliegen können, werden in der Extraktorstufe der Loève-Karhunen-Reihenentwicklung unterworfen. Die Koeffizienten dieser Reihe sind die systematisch erhaltenen Merkmale, die ein jeweils eingegebenes Muster charakterisieren. Die Koeffizientenzahl kann dabei zwischen 5 und 40 schwanken. Der so erhaltene Merkmalsvektor, von dem nachgewiesen werden kann, daß seine Komponenten weitgehend gaußisch verteilt sind, wird einem quadratischen Klassifikator angeboten. Es werden Prüfgrößen ermittelt, die ein Maß für die mutmaßliche Zugehörigkeit zu einer Klasse darstellen. Entschieden wird zu Gunsten der Klasse mit der größten aposteriori-Wahrscheinlichkeit. Die Rückweisung unsicher erkannter Zeichen ist zunächst nicht vorgesehen.

Der genaue Ablauf der Simulation dieses Verfahrens auf dem Digitalrechner ist im Bild 3 erläutert. In der Bildhälfte oberhalb der gestrichelten Linie ist der Ablauf der Extraktion der statistischen Parameter für die Dimensionierung des Klassifikators dargestellt, also die Ermittlung klassenbedingter Mittelwerte und Kovarianzmatrizen. Außerdem wird noch das optimale Basissystem für die Loève-Karhunen-Transformation ermittelt. Sind diese Kenngrößen bekannt, so kann im nächsten Schritt die eigentliche Klassifikation durchgeführt werden. Sie ist in der unteren Bildhälfte kurz dargestellt.

Über die Leistungsfähigkeit dieses ursprünglichen Systems ist berichtet worden /4/. Durchgeführte Untersuchungen haben jedoch gezeigt, daß eine starke Reduzierung der Fehlerraten zu erwarten ist, wenn der bisherigen Anordnung eine Vorverarbeitungsstufe vorgeschaltet wird. Diese Stufe macht in unserem Falle keine Reduktion der Dimensionalität der zu verarbeitenden 126-komponentigen Mustervektoren. Die gesamte zur Verfügung stehende Stichprobe von 560 Repräsentanten pro Klasse wird vorverarbeitet und anschließend in 2 Hälften aufgeteilt. Die erste Hälfte dient als Lernstichprobe, d. h. es werden daraus die statistischen Parameter extrahiert. Anschließend wird klassifiziert mit dem anderen Teil als unbekannter Teststichprobe. Die noch zu erläuternden Klassifikationsergebnisse für unterschiedliche Verarbeitungstechniken beziehen sich nur auf das Zehnklassenproblem, also die Erkennung von Ziffern. Wie diese ursprünglich gerastert waren, zeigt das Bild 4. Man erkennt deutlich die sehr stark schwankenden Zeichenhöhen anhand der aus jeder Klasse ausgewählten Repräsentanten und die starken Variationen in der Zeichengestalt. Diese Muster wurden nach jedem Vorverarbeitungsschritt von einem Speicheroszillographen abfotographiert, so daß die Einflüsse der Verarbeitung sichtbar werden.

Wenn man sich entschließt, eine Mustervorverarbeitung durchzuführen, so geht
man in der Regel von Zeichen aus, die nach einem starren Schema abgetastet
wurden und nun in gerasterter Form vorliegen. Alle vorgenommenen Techniken beziehen sich dann auf dieses vorgegebene Ausgangsfeld. Sollen Abbildungen ir-
gendwelcher Art durchgeführt werden, so muß man bei den Transformationen zum
Teil erhebliche Fehler in Folge der Quantisierung und Rasterung in Kauf nehmen. Günstiger erscheint in jedem Falle eine Vorverarbeitung im On-Line-Ver-
fahren zu sein. Hierbei wird das Zeichen zunächst einmal probeweise abgetastet und zwischengespeichert. Die Kenngrößen durchzuführender Transformationen werden dann mittels schneller Algorithmen errechnet. Diese Größen steu-
ern in einem zweiten und endgültigen Abtastvorgang Schwellen und Ablenkspan-
nungen im Lesegerät in geeigneter Art und Weise. Aus rein technischer Sicht
ist dies zweifellos die optimale Vorgehensweise, braucht es aber unter Berücksichtigung anderer Aspekte (Kosten) nicht immer zu sein. Entscheidend ist in
jedem Falle der Grad der Anpassung der Vorverarbeitungstechniken an in der Regel schon früher vorhandene Klassifikations- und Merkmalsextraktionsverfahren.
Hier muß man nun grundsätzlich unterscheiden zwischen der Gewinnung der Merkmale mittels globaler Verarbeitung eines Musters oder der Extraktion von Merkmalen aus örtlich begrenzten Bereichen des Gesamtfeldes (z. B. Endpunkte, Bö-
gen, Winkel, etc.). Das Ziel jeder Vorverarbeitung muß sein, die für die Unterscheidung der Zeichenklassen wesentlichen Merkmale adaptiv herauszuarbei-
ten. Demzufolge muß bei den Vorverarbeitungstechniken auch unterschieden werden zwischen globalen Transformationen und lokalen Operationen.

Obwohl wir Muster global verarbeiten, soll zunächst über Ergebnisse lokaler
Operationen berichtet werden /5/. Auf günstige Weise lassen sich diese Techniken z. B. verwenden, um einfache Störstellen in Linienzügen zu beseitigen.
Grundsätzlich wird so vorgegangen, daß jeder unbesetzte Rasterpunkt auf seine
acht Nachbarn hin abgefragt wird, um dann zu entscheiden, ob ein leeres Feld
gefüllt wird oder weiterhin unbesetzt bleibt. Das Bild 5 soll die Vorgehensweise erläutern. Die Umgebung eines leeren Feldes wird zu einem Codewort von
acht Bit zusammengefaßt und mit den Codewörtern vorgegebener Matrixmasken in
einer "UND"-Bedingung verknüpft. Aus dem Ergebnis dieser Maskenvergleiche
wird die Entscheidung zum Auffüllen abgeleitet. In dem gezeigten Beispiel
wird die Übereinstimmung zweier Fehlstellen mit vorgegebenen Prüfmatrizen
festgestellt. Demzufolge werden beide Löcher aufgefüllt. Ein Auffüllen an un-
erwünschten Stellen findet nicht statt. Unterbrechungen in Linienzügen, die
länger als ein Feld sind, sollten tunlichst nicht mit 3 x 3-Matrizen aufgefüllt werden. Um sicher zu sein, daß man keine unvorhersehbaren Effekte erhält, müßte man zu größeren Prüfmatrizen übergehen. Dies empfiehlt sich aber
wiederum deshalb nicht, weil die Zahl der dann vorzusehenen Prüfmatrizen sehr

groß werden würde, was eine sehr lange Rechenzeit für jeden einzelnen Rasterpunkt bedingt. Die Technik des Auffüllens von Störstellen hat keinen signifikanten Einfluß auf die Reduktion der Fehlerraten. Immerhin läßt sich aber
feststellen, daß die Fehlerrate von vorher 1,7 % auf 1,6 % reduziert wird.
Das liegt daran, daß in Folge von schlechter Schreibqualität oder Quantisierungsfehlern Störstellen doch relativ häufig auftreten. Das Bild 6 vermittelt einen Eindruck von der Wirkung der Operation. Aufgefüllt werden z. B.
in der vierten Zeile die Ziffern 4 und 7 und in der zweiten Zeile die 6. Un-
erwünschtes Auffüllen findet bei der 5 in der ersten Zeile statt.

Ging es bisher darum, unbesetzte Felder mittels Information aus der Umgebung
aufzufüllen, so kann man in einem weiteren Schritt natürlich mit den gleichen
Methoden auch besetzte Felder bereinigen, wenn ihr Vorhandensein als irrelevant erachtet wird. Dies gilt insbesondere für isolierte Flecken ohne Verbindung zum Zeichenrumpf. In einem weitergehenden Schritt können Knospen an Linienzügen eliminiert werden. In letzter Konsequenz ist es sogar möglich, Zeichen zu skelettieren, d. h. auf Linienzüge mit einer Rasterfeldbreite zu reduzieren. Das Problem ist die Auswahl geeigneter Prüfmatrizen. Der Versuch,
den Einfluß einer weitgehenden Skelettierung der Zeichen auf die Erkennungsrate zu ermitteln, ist durchgeführt worden. Knospen, isolierte Störstellen
und nicht vollständig vorhandene doppelt oder mehrfach breite Linienzüge
sind dabei sukzessive eliminiert worden. Dies kann auf einfache Weise dadurch
realisiert werden, daß fortlaufend jeder Rasterpunkt abgefragt wird und das
Löschen eines vorhergehenden Feldes für das jeweils abgefragte Feld schon berücksichtigt wird. Das Skelettieren kompakter gerader Linienblöcke gelang dabei allerdings deshalb nicht, weil keine Information darüber zu erhalten ist,
ob es günstiger ist, obere oder untere Linien abzutragen. Das Ergebnis der
Skelettierung zeigt das Bild 7. Die Zeichen machen auf den menschlichen Be-
trachter einen sehr befriedigenden Eindruck. Das rechnerische Klassifikationsergebnis ist jedoch ausgesprochen unbefriedigend. Die Fehlerrate von 1,7 % erhöht sich auf über 4 %. Die Ursache für diese Verschlechterung ist aus den
statistischen Parametern der Stichprobe zu entnehmen. Man stellt fest, daß
sich die Abstände der Mittelwertvektoren verringern, während die Streuungen
der Merkmalskomponenten beträchtlich zunehmen. Es ist also festzustellen, daß
für das vorgegebene Klassifikationsschema eine Zeichenskelettierung nicht an-
gebracht ist.

Erfolgversprechender sind bei globaler Musterverarbeitung Methoden, die sich
auf eine Transformation des Gesamtmusters stützen. Diese Transformationen
sind der Struktur der Zeichen entsprechend im wesentlichen von geometrischer
Art. Es soll bei allen Verfahren keine apriori-Information über die jeweilige Zeichenklasse verwendet werden.

Eine sehr einfach zu realisierende Vorverarbeitungstechnik ist das Zentrieren
der Muster. Der Schwerpunkt eines Musters wird ermittelt. Anschließend wird
das Zeichen so verschoben, daß sein Schwerpunkt auf einen vorgegebenen Zielpunkt fällt. Die Auswahl des Zielpunktes ist insofern etwas problematisch,
als seine Lage entscheidet, wieviel Information eines Musters dadurch verloren gehen kann, daß einzelne Zeichenteile über den Bildrand hinausgeschoben
werden und damit nicht weiter berücksichtigt werden können. Dieser Vorgang
wird umso bedenklicher, wenn dabei signifikante Musterteile verlorengehen.
Das Zentrieren ist also durch zwei gegenläufige Tendenzen gekennzeichnet. Auf
der einen Seite wird eine geometrische Angleichung der Schwerpunktslagen erzielt, auf der anderen Seite geht aber Information verloren. Das Bild 8 zeigt,
wie die Muster nach dieser Transformation in ihren Feldern stehen. Man erkennt deutlich, daß in manchen Fällen wesentliche Musterteile verlorengegangen sind. Trotzdem läßt sich mit dem Zentrieren eine Verbesserung erzielen.
Die Fehlerrate sinkt von 1,7 % auf 1,0 % ab.

Nun ist der Schwerpunkt natürlich nicht die einzige mögliche geometrische
Kenngröße, auf die ein Muster zentriert werden kann. Denkbar wäre insbesondere eine Zentrierung bestimmter Musterteile auf definierte Feldbereiche oder
aber eine Verschiebung dergestalt, daß ein Muster mit einer geometrischen Mas-
ke möglichst weitgehend übereinstimmt. Gemeint ist damit zum Beispiel ein
waagerechter Balken oder auch ein Bogenstück am oberen Bildrand, die als Zie-
le dienen können. In der Praxis wirft dieses Vorhaben allerdings erhebliche
Probleme auf. Es ist deshalb in dieser Form noch nicht realisiert worden. Man
kann dieses Verfahren versuchen zu approximieren, indem man die Muster z. B.
auf eine der 4 Ecken des Bildfeldes so zentriert, daß ein Zeichen jeweils die
beiden Begrenzungslinien des rechten Winkels berührt. Die Klassifikationsergebnisse sind für die vier Ecken durchaus unterschiedlich. Zentriert man auf
die rechten Ecken, so erhält man bessere Ergebnisse als auf den linken, während auf der rechten Seite selbst eine Verschiebung in die obere Ecke die besten Resultate ergibt. Die Fehlerrate läßt sich von 1,7 % immerhin auf 1,2 %
reduzieren. Das Bild 9 zeigt den Zentriereffekt sehr deutlich bei den Einsen
und Dreien.

Bei der Durchsicht der gesamten Lernstichprobe stellt man fest, daß die Muster sehr unterschiedliche Breiten und Höhen aufweisen. Genauere Untersuchungen haben ergeben, daß die Variation in der Höhe sich etwa auf den Faktor 2
beläuft trotz vorgegebener Schreibfelder. Diese Tatsache ·fordert eine Normierung der Zeichenabmessungen geradezu heraus. Für die Realisierung dieses Vorhabens sind nun mehrere Wege gangbar. Zunächst wäre eine zentrische Streckung
des Zeichens aus einem zu definierenden Ursprung heraus möglich. Der Strek-
kungsfaktor wäre dann zu ermitteln als der Quotient aus möglicher Höhe zu

tatsächlicher Höhe. Für die Breite müßte analog verfahren werden. Wenn man keine Zeichenverzerrung in Kauf nehmen möchte, ist von beiden Faktoren der kleinere auszuwählen und als gemeinsamer Streckungsfaktor einzusetzen. Im allgemeinen ist die mögliche Vergrößerung in der Höhe kleiner als in der Breite. Deshalb kann bei dieser Art der Vergrößerung die Feldbreite fast nie ausgenutzt werden. Es hat sich als günstiger erwiesen, trotz der Verzerrungen, alle Zeichen über das ganze Feld zu expandieren. Allerdings läuft man hierbei Gefahr, einige schmale Zeichen, vornehmlich Einsen, derart stark zu strecken, daß das gesamte Feld geschwärzt erscheint. Es muß deshalb durch eine automatische Abfrage der Zeichenbreite dafür Sorge getragen werden, daß ein solcher Fall nicht eintritt und eine Sonderregelung abgerufen wird. Wie das Bild 10 zeigt, stellt das Ergebnis einer solchen Normierung für einen menschlichen Beobachter ein ziemlich unbefriedigendes Bild dar. Die meisten Zeichen sind sehr viel dicker geworden und haben auch in ihrer Struktur erhebliche Veränderungen erfahren. Das rechnerische Klassifikationsergebnis zeigt jedoch eine signifikante Reduktion der Fehlerrate um mehr als den Faktor zwei. Die Fehlerrate ist von 1,7 % auf 0,8 % gesunken und liegt damit erstmals unter der 1 %-Grenze. Die Analyse der statistischen Parameter zeigt, daß die Verteilungskurven für die einzelnen Klassen auseinanderrücken und gleichzeitig auch noch schmäler werden. Offensichtlich bewirkt die Verteilung der Bildpunkte und damit die Ausbreitung der im Muster enthaltenen Information über das gesamte zur Verfügung stehende Feld diesen positiven Effekt.

Man kann feststellen, daß viele Schreiber eine gewisse Schräglage ihrer Zeichen bevorzugen. Leider sind die Neigungswinkel durchaus nicht einheitlich und liegen etwa zwischen $- 40^{0}$ und $+ 50^{0}$, wobei über die Häufigkeit gesagt werden kann, daß Rechtslagen im vorliegenden Schreiberkollektiv dominieren. Es stellt sich daraus die Frage, ob nicht bessere Klassifikationsergebnisse dann zu erwarten wären, wenn alle Muster eine einheitliche Schräge, bzw. keine Schräge hätten. Die Realisierung dieser Idee beinhaltet ganz erhebliche Probleme. Zunächst muß der Neigungswinkel eines Zeichens ermittelt werden. Das geschieht am günstigsten durch Errechnen der Hauptträgheitsachsen des Musters. Zu diesem Zweck muß der Zeichenschwerpunkt ermittelt werden, weil die Trägheitsachsen sich in diesem Punkt schneiden. Die Steigung der Achsen erhält man aus der Berechnung der drei Flächenträgheitsmomente. Daraus läßt sich ein Winkel ableiten, um den das Zeichen um seinen Schwerpunkt gedreht werden muß. Die Auswahl der Drehrichtung ist einigermaßen problematisch, weil sichergestellt werden muß, daß die Trägheitsachse mit dem minimalen Moment senkrecht zu stehen kommt. Das Hauptproblem liegt aber in der Ausführung der Drehung. Im kontinuierlichen Fall ist die Drehung eine leicht auszuführende geometrische Transformation. Das ist aber nicht der Fall, wenn eine Figur

nur in binärer und gerasterter Form vorliegt. Es ist dann die kreisförmige Bewegung eines jeden einzelnen Rasterpunktes zu ermitteln und abzufragen, ob
ein Zielpunkt in einem neuen Rasterpunkt so liegt, daß er mehr als zur Hälfte
geschwärzt wird. Dabei treten natürlich ganz erhebliche Quantisierungsfehler
auf, die ein Zeichen zerreißen können und beträchtliche weitere Strukturver-
änderungen mit sich bringen. Das Ergebnis einer durchgeführten Drehung zeigt
das Bild 11. Man erkennt die starken auftretenden Verunstaltungen der Zeichen
sehr deutlich. Besonders negativ wirken sich auch noch Verschiebungen in Folge von Quantisierungsfehlern aus. Das Klassifikationsergebnis ist dementsprechend sehr schlecht. Es ergibt sich eine Fehlerrate von über 6 %. Daraus muß
man folgern, daß eine geometrische Drehtransformation in dem vorliegenden Raster von 9 x 14 nicht vernünftig zu realisieren ist, da gemessen an den wenigen Rasterpunkten zu viele Quantisierungsfehler begangen werden müssen.

Da eine echte Drehung nicht sinnvoll durchführbar ist, kann versucht werden,
eine solche Transformation wenigstens zu approximieren. Eine **der** Drehung
verwandte affine Abbildung ist das Scheren. Es ist zunächst untersucht worden, was eine Scherung in x-Richtung, also entlang der Zeilen des Rasterfel-
des, als Ergebnis liefert. Es ist zu erwarten, daß eine Scherung in dieser
Richtung den größten Effekt zeigt, weil die Absolutwerte der Verschiebung infolge des weiteren Abstandes der oben und unten liegenden Zeilen vom Schwerpunkt ihre größten Werte annehmen. Geschert wurde jeweils um den Schwerpunkt
herum, d. h. oberhalb davon in eine Richtung und unterhalb des Schwerpunktes
in die entgegengesetzte. Das Bild 12 zeigt das Ergebnis dieser Operation. Es
wurde eine Verbesserung der Fehlerrate erzielt. Sie sank von 1,7 % auf 1,3 %
ab. Die Fehlerreduktion ist also nicht signifikant und rechtfertigt vielleicht gerade den relativ hohen Rechenaufwand. Die Quantisierungsfehler in
Folge von zu grober Rasterung für diesen Zweck treten schon bei der Vorstufe
zur Drehung klar zu Tage. Das ist insbesondere an dem Zerreißen gerader Linienzüge zu erkennen.

Im nächsten Schritt kann nun auch noch in y-Richtung geschert werden. Damit
ist eine Drehung noch weitergehend zu approximieren. Der verwendete Algorithmus bleibt der gleiche. Es wird nach dem Scheren in x-Richtung nun auch in
Richtung der Spalten aufwärts oder abwärts geschoben, je nach Ablage der Spalte von der Spalte, in der sich der Schwerpunkt befindet. Die Muster erfahren
noch weitergehende Quantisierungsfehler und ergeben eine schlechtere Erkennungsrate. Im Bild 13 wird das Ergebnis dieser Operation dargestellt. War
die Fehlerrate nach dem Scheren in x-Richtung abgesunken, so ist sie nun wieder angestiegen und liegt mit 1,6 % nur sehr knapp unter der Rate des unver-
arbeiteten Ausgangsmaterials. Offensichtlich dominieren auch hier die Quantisierungsfehler über die Egalisierungstendenzen. Als Folgerung daraus kann

nur festgehalten werden, daß diese Dreh- und Scherverfahren für ein Raster
von 9 x 14 nicht günstig zu sein scheinen.

Schon aus dem Skelettierungsversuch war klar geworden, daß das System auf
eine relative Verringerung der von einem Muster belegten schwarzen Punkte mit
einer Verschlechterung der Erkennungsrate reagiert. Dieses Ergebnis legt die
Hoffnung nahe, daß die Erhöhung der vorhandenen Punktzahlen zu einer Verbesserung führen könnte. Zweckmäßigerweise müßte man dazu so vorgehen, daß alle
Kurvenzüge in Richtung senkrecht zu ihrer Tangente schlauchartig aufgebläht
werden. Als mögliches Werkzeug zur Durchführung des Verdickens von Zeichen
kämen natürlich auch lokale Operationen in Betracht. Aufgrund der gemachten
schlechten Erfahrungen beim Skelettieren ist aber darauf verzichtet worden,
dieses Konzept weiter zu verfolgen. Stattdessen ist versucht worden, das Ver-
dicken in einer globalen Verarbeitung zu erledigen. Als beste Möglichkeit zur
Realisierung des Vorhabens hat sich das Aufdoppeln von Zeichen erwiesen. Zu
diesem Zweck wird das zu verarbeitende Zeichen um ein Feld in vertikaler oder
horizontaler Richtung aus seiner Originallage verschoben. Das auf diese Weise
erhaltene Bild wird nun in einer ODER-Bedingung Punkt für Punkt mit dem Origi-
nalzeichen verknüpft. Das Resultat ist also ein Muster, das überall dort geschwärzt ist, wo mindestens eines der beiden Ursprungsbilder geschwärzt war.
Insgesamt ergeben sich vier einfache Möglichkeiten des Aufdoppelns gemäß den
vier möglichen Verschiebungen nach links, rechts, oben und unten. Die Ergebnisse weichen stark voneinander ab. Es stellt sich heraus, daß Verschiebungen
in der Horizontalen ungünstiger sind als in der Vertikalen. In der Horizontalen selbst wirkt sich eine Linksverschiebung positiver aus als eine Rechtsver-
schiebung. Im ersteren Fall erhält man 1,6 % Fehler, während es im zweiten
Fall noch etwas mehr sind. Betrachtet man die Vertikale, so stellt man fest,
daß hier eine Verschiebung nach oben den Wert 1,25 % Fehler ergibt, während
eine Verschiebung nach unten die Fehlerrate auf 1,2 % reduziert. Das Bild 14
vermittelt einen optischen Eindruck von den erhaltenen Ergebnissen. Das Bild
zeigt das Resultat einer Aufdoppelung nach Verschiebung um ein Feld nach oben.

Sobald Techniken gefunden worden sind, die sich als geeignet erwiesen haben,
die Fehlerrate des Klassifikators zu reduzieren, kann daran gedacht werden,
geeignete Kombinationen mehrerer Schritte zu finden, um damit eine noch weitergehende Reduktion zu erreichen. Die Hauptschwierigkeit liegt hierbei in
der kombinatorischen Vielfalt der Möglichkeiten und dem Fehlen eines eindeutigen theoretischen Hinweises, in welche Richtung gegangen werden muß. Eine
kleine Einschränkung erfährt die Vielfalt dadurch, daß sich einige Techniken nicht sinnvoll kombinieren lassen, z. B. eine Zentrierung und sich anschließende Größenordnung. Andererseits liegt eine Erschwernis aber besonders

darin, daß es sich bei fast allen Operationen um mehr oder weniger stark
nichtlineare Abbildungen handelt, voraus insbesondere folgt, daß die Reihenfolge vorzunehmender Schritte nicht mehr gleichgültig ist oder mit anderen
Worten, die Kommutativität nicht gilt. Es würde den Rahmen dieses Berichtes
sprengen, sollten alle durchgeführten Kombinationen erwähnt werden. Zwei
wichtige Ergebnisse sollen dennoch mitgeteilt werden. Das erste Ergebnis betrifft die absolut beste Erkennungsrate bis dato. Die Sequenz: Auffüllen von
Löchern, Aufdoppeln durch Verschiebung nach oben und Zentrieren aller Muster
in einem gemeinsamen Schwerpunkt hat als Fehlerrate nur noch 0,57 % ergeben.
Die vormals gegebene Fehlerrate von 1,7 % ohne Vorverarbeitung konnte damit
um den Faktor drei reduziert werden. Das Bild 15 vermittelt einen Eindruck
von diesem Datensatz. Auch der Mensch als "Klassifikator" würde an der Klassifizierung dieser Daten sein Wohlgefallen finden.

Ein sehr wichtiges weiteres Ergebnis ist die durch die Mustervorverarbeitung
zu erzielende Aufwandsreduktion. Der Aufwand ist im wesentlichen gegeben
durch die Anzahl der zum Klassifizieren verwendeten Merkmale, sprich Koeffizienten der Loève-Karhunen-Reihenentwicklung und dem Quadrat dieser Zahl proportional. Es ist z. B. gelungen, mit nur fünf Merkmalen eine Fehlerrate von
4,7 % zu erzielen. Das ist eine Reduktion um den Faktor 2,5 gegenüber dem Ergebnis ohne Vorverarbeitung und deutet darauf hin, welch erhebliche Bedeutung
einer geeigneten Vorverarbeitung zukommt. Der Rechenaufwand dafür wird durch
die erzielten Reduktionen jedenfalls mehr als gerechtfertigt.

War bisher von globalen Techniken ohne apriori-Wissen berichtet worden, so
soll doch die mögliche Anwendbarkeit spezieller Operationen bei vorhandenem
Wissen wenigstens kurz gestreift werden. Apriori-Wissen ist z. B. dann vorhanden, wenn man es nur mit einer sehr kleinen Klassenzahl zu tun hat, im
Idealfall also mit einem Zweiklassenproblem. Das kann bei hierarchisch struk-
turierten Klassifikatoren der Fall sein.

In all diesen Fällen empfiehlt sich eine klassenspezifische Vorverarbeitung
in Form von speziellen Zentrierungen oder z. B. auch durch Aufdoppeln der in
Frage kommenden Mittelwertvektoren. Es sind Voruntersuchungen durchgeführt
worden, abschließende Ergebnisse liegen jedoch noch nicht vor.

Es wurde schon erwähnt, daß es für die Mustervorverarbeitung keinen von der
Theorie vorgezeichneten Weg zu beschreiten gibt. Die Auswahl und Kombination
der möglichen Operationen bleibt der Intuition des Suchenden überlassen. Das
zu erwartende Ergebnis der Bemühungen ist in keinem Falle vorherzusagen, Enttäuschung und vergebliche Rechenzeit sind die Resultate. Um diesem unbefrie-
digenden Zustand Abhilfe zu schaffen, ist versucht worden, Kenngrößen zu er-

mitteln, die eine brauchbare Aussage über zu erwartende Fehlerraten ermöglichen. Anzustreben wäre natürlich eine deterministische Vorhersagemöglichkeit.
Zufrieden sein sollte man aber auch schon mit dem Nachweis einer stochastischen Abhängigkeit zwischen Fehlerrate und Kenngröße, da es schwerlich jemals
gelingen wird, über den komplexen Verarbeitungsprozeß hinweg eine deterministische Aussage zu machen. Zunächst wurden Güteziffern aus den klassenbeding-
ten Mittelwertvektoren und Kovarianzmatrixen errechnet und mit der Fehlerrate in Zusammenhang gebracht. Es ist weiterhin versucht worden, direkt aus
den Mustern Gütewerte abzuleiten. Beide Versuche haben aber nur unbefriedi-
gende Ergebnisse erbracht. Ein Ziel weiterer Untersuchungen wird die Ermittlung der wesentlichen Einflußgrößen des Mustersatzes auf die Fehlerrate sein.

Als wesentliches Ergebnis der bisher durchgeführten Arbeiten zur Mustervor-
verarbeitungverarbeitung kann zusammenfassend festgehalten werden, daß es gelungen ist, bei einem vorgegebenen Musterkollektiv eine vormals gegebene Fehlerrate um den Faktor 3 zu reduzieren. Gleichzeitig konnte durch eine Gestalt-
adaption der Mustersatz in sich ähnlicher gemacht werden, was sich durch ver-
minderten Aufwand im Klassifikator bemerkbar machte. Ein Teil der Ergebnisse
ist in der Tabelle 1 zusammengefaßt. Es sind noch nicht alle Techniken voll
ausgeschöpft worden. Weitere Verbesserungen erscheinen deshalb als reali-
stisches Ziel.

	Art	Koeffizientenzahl	Fehler
0	Keine Vorverarbeitung	30	1,7 %
1	Auffüllen von Löchern	30	1,6 %
2	Skelettieren	30	4,2 %
3	Schwerpunkt zentrieren	30	1,0 %
4	Schieben	30	1,2 %
5	Größennormieren	20	0,8 %
6	Drehen	20	6,7 %
7	Scheren (x)	30	1,3 %
8	Scheren (x,y)	30	1,6 %
9	Verdicken	20	1,25%
10	Bisher günstigste Kombination	20	0,57%

Tabelle 1: Ergebnisse der Mustervorverarbeitung (10 Klassen)

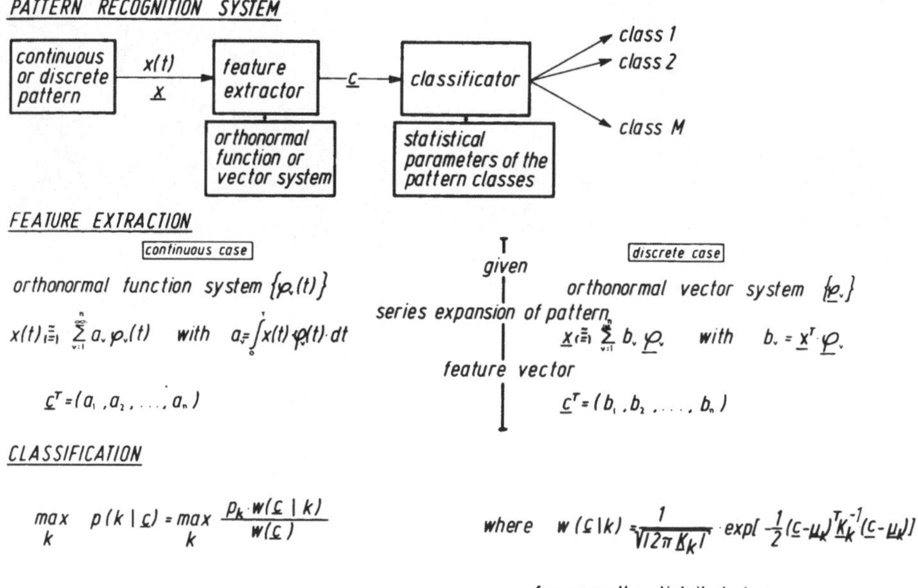

Bild 2: Das Mustererkennungssystem

Scheme of Pattern Processing

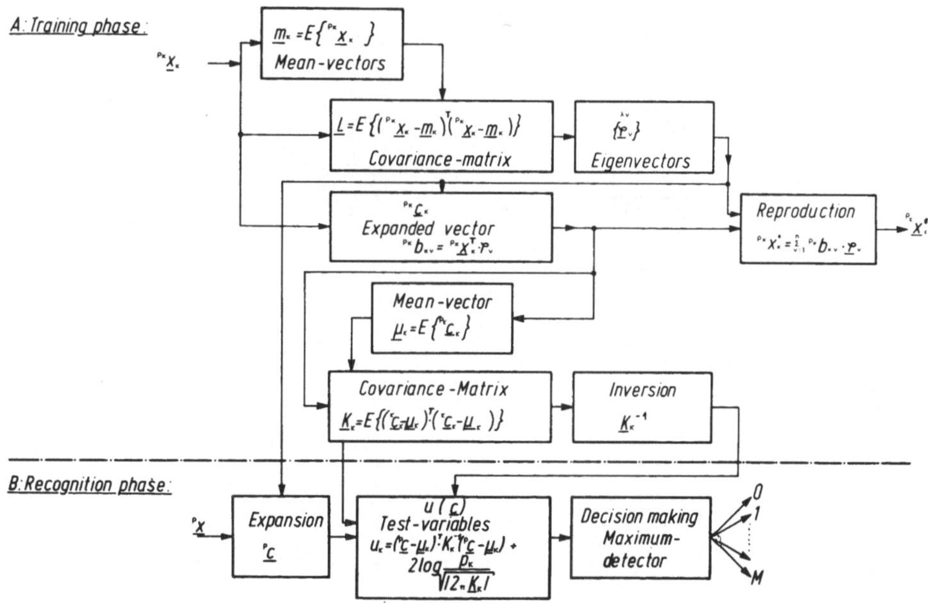

Bild 3: Schema der rechnerischen Simulation

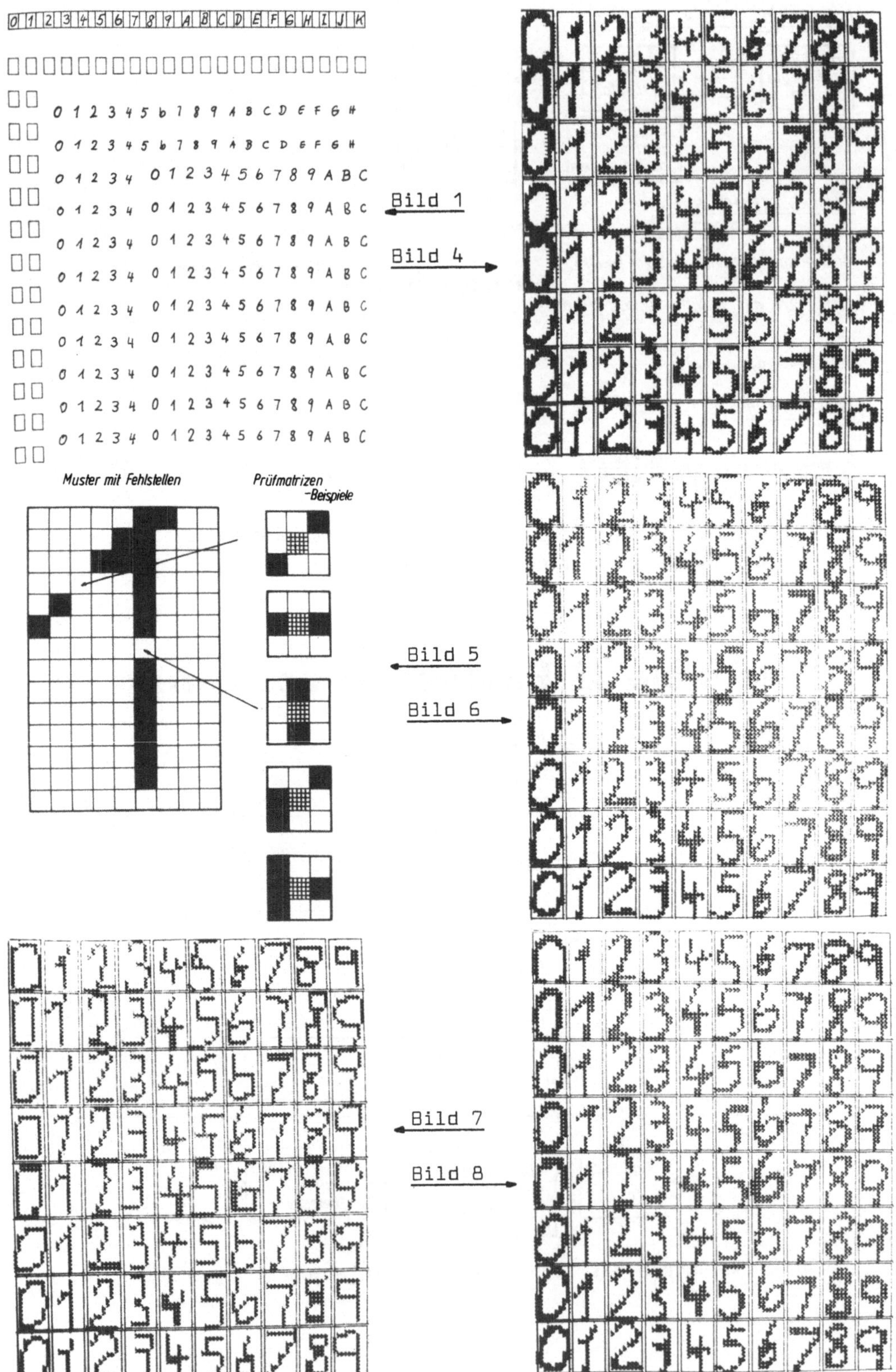
Muster mit Fehlstellen
Prüfmatrizen
-Beispiele
Bild 1
Bild 4
Bild 5
Bild 6
Bild 7
Bild 8

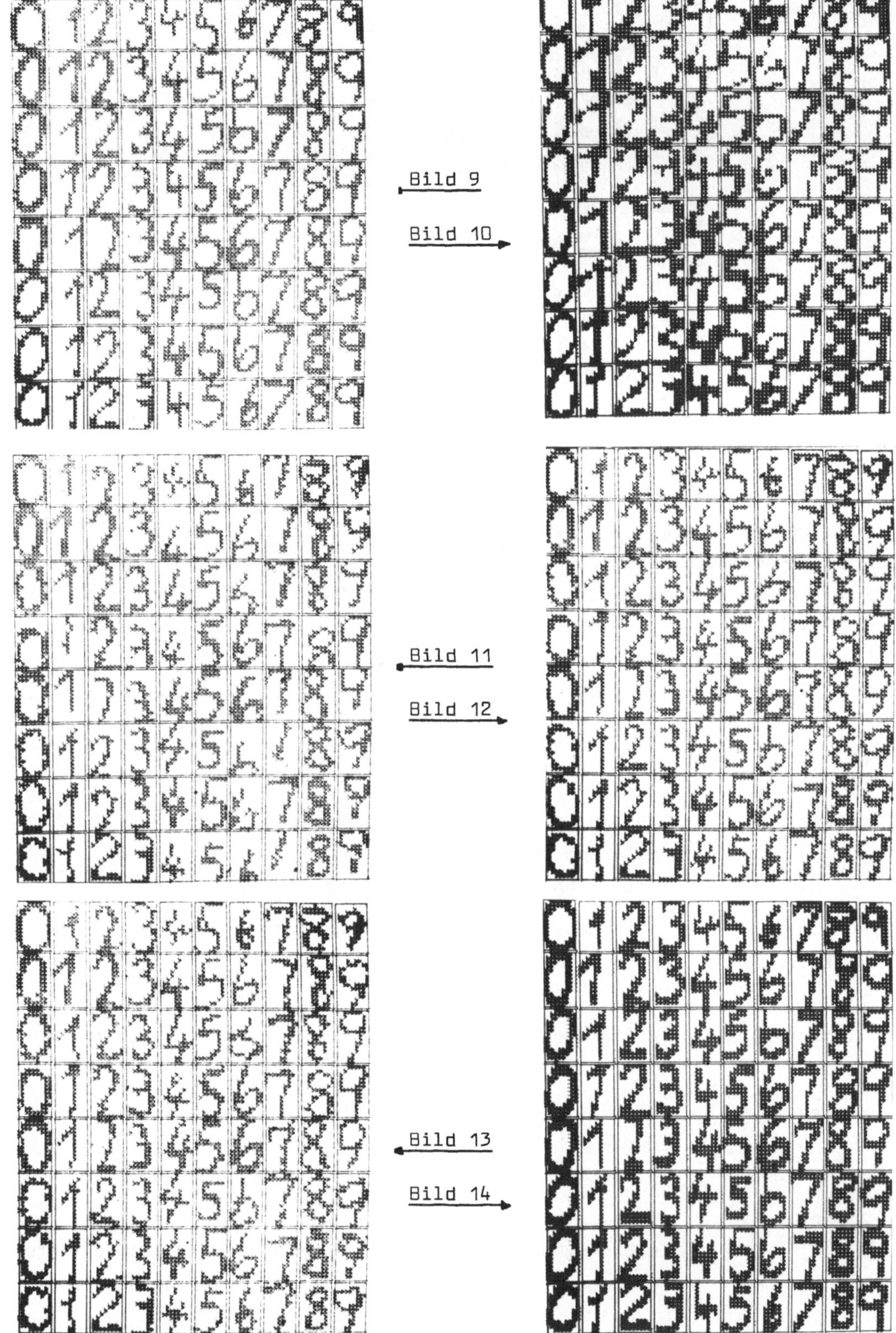

Bild 9
Bild 10
Bild 11
Bild 12
Bild 13
Bild 14

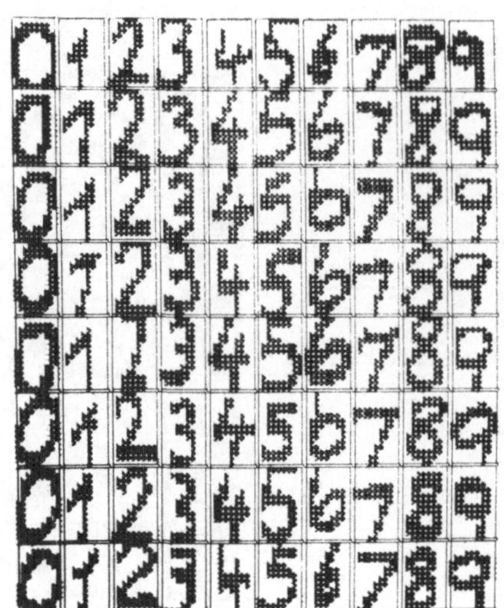

← Bild 15

Bild 1: Ausgangsdaten auf Schreibbögen
Bild 2: Das Mustererkennungssystem
Bild 3: Schema der rechnerischen Simulation
Bild 4: Gerasterte Ausgangsdaten
Bild 5: Auffüllen von Störstellen
Bild 6: Ausgangsdaten aufgefüllt
Bild 7: Skelettieren der Muster
Bild 8: Zentrieren der Muster

Bild 9: Schieben der Muster
Bild 10: Größennormierte Muster
Bild 11: Drehen der Muster
Bild 12: Scheren (x) der Muster
Bild 13: Scheren (x,y) der Muster
Bild 14: Aufdoppeln der Muster
Bild 15: Bisher günstigste Vor-
         verarbeitung

<u>Literatur:</u>

/1/ Krause, P.:   Eingabe von Ziffern und Buchstaben in Digitalrechner mit
                    optischem Lesekopf.
                    Mitteilungen aus dem IITB 1970, S. 28 ... 29

/2/ Niemann, H.,   Eine Theorie zur quantitativen Beschreibung und Erken-
    Winkler, G.:   nung von Mustern.
                    NTZ 1969, Nr. 22, S. 94 ... 100

/3/ Niemann, H.:   An Improved Series Expansion for Pattern Recognition.
                    NTZ 24, 1971, S. 94 ... 100

/4/ Krause, P.:   Informationsverarbeitung bei automatischer Erkennung mit
                    Loève-Karhunen-Entwicklung durch Rechenanlagen.
                    Bericht zum Forschungsvorhaben: T/0230/02340/01006

/5/ Triendl, E.:   "Bildmustererkennung mit lokalen Operationen" in:
                    Zeichenerkennung durch biologische und technische Systeme.
                    Herausgeber: Grüsser, O. J., Klinke, R., Springer Vlg.
                    S. 241 ... 247

<u>ERKENNUNG VON ANOMALIEN IN SZINTIGRAMMEN</u>

G. Walch, H. G. Meder, P. Pistor

1. Problemstellung

In Zusammenarbeit mit dem Institut für Nuklearmedizin im Deutschen
Krebsforschungszentrum in Heidelberg befasst sich eine Arbeitsgruppe
des Wissenschaftlichen Zentrums der IBM seit einiger Zeit mit einem
Spezialgebiet der digitalen Bildbearbeitung, nämlich der computer-
unterstützten Interpretation von Szintigrammen.

In der Nuklearmedizin werden zur Diagnose von Krebserkrankungen radio-
aktive Stoffe injiziert, die auf Grund des veränderten Stoffwechsels
in Tumoren dort entweder besonders stark gespeichert oder im Vergleich
zur gesunden Umgebung geringer angelagert werden. Hat man eine Möglichkeit, die Verteilung der inkorporierten Aktivität zu messen, so
kann man durch Vergleich mit der Verteilung in gesunden Individuen Rückschlüsse auf das Vorhandensein von Tumoren ziehen. Eine Möglichkeit zur
Messung der Verteilung bietet neben dem bewegten Scanner die sogenannte
γ-Kamera, wobei in einem NaJ-Kristall absorbierte γ-Quanten zu Licht-
blitzen (Szintillationen) führen. Vor dem Kristall befindet sich an
Stelle einer Linse ein Parallel-Loch-Kollimator als abbildendes Element.
Das Licht eines absorbierten γ-Quants wird durch eine zweidimensionale
Anordnung von Photomultipliern erfasst, der Ort des Ereignisses durch
Bildung zweier gewichteter Summen ihrer Ausgangssignale bestimmt, anschließend auf einem Oszillographenschirm sichtbar gemacht und eventuell
in digitaler Form gespeichert. Die so gewonnenen Bilder werden Szintigramme genannt. Die Genauigkeit der Ortsbestimmung ist durch die Ortsauflösung im Kristall von etwa 10 mm und Streueffekte im Kollimator auf
insgesamt etwa 15 mm begrenzt. Diese Ortsverschmierung setzt natürlich
auch die Erkennbarkeit von kleinen Anomalien in einer strahlenden Umgebung herab, da sowohl der Zerfall der Radioaktivität als auch ihr Nachweis statistische Prozesse sind und infolgedessen starken statistischen
Schwankungen (Rauschen) unterliegen. Das Signal-Rausch-Verhältnis läßt
sich weder durch Erhöhung der injizierten Aktivität wegen der Strahlen-
schäden im gesunden Gewebe, noch durch Verlängerung der Meßzeit wegen
der erforderlichen Ruhigstellung des Patienten beliebig verbessern.

Die Bilder sind also gekennzeichnet durch hohes statistisches Rauschen und geringe Ortsauflösung. Um kleine Tumore und Metastasen früher zu erkennen - und erfolgreicher zu behandeln - ist eine Bildverbesserung dringend erwünscht.

2. Filtermethode

Einer mathematischen Bildbearbeitung mit digitalen Filtern [1] liegen folgende Vorstellungen zu Grunde:

Das abbildende System wird durch die ortsinvariante Abbildungsfunktion (Bild einer Punktquelle) a beschrieben. Das unverrauschte Bild $\hat{b}$ (Erwartungswert) ist die Faltung der Objektverteilung o mit dieser Abbildungsfunktion:

$$\hat{b} = o * a \tag{1}$$

oder

$$\hat{b}_{ij} = \sum_{kl} a_{kl} \cdot o_{i-k,j-l} \tag{1'}$$

Das gemessene Bild b ist die Summe von Idealbild und Rauschen r

$$b = \hat{b} + r = o * a + r \tag{2}$$

und r ist statistisch unabhängig von der Objektverteilung. Wir suchen nun einen Filteroperator f, der angewandt auf das Bild b das Ergebnis e liefert (e = b * f), und stellen an ihn die Forderung, daß der Erwartungswert der Quadratsumme I der Abweichungen von einem gewünschten Ergebnis d minimiert wird:

$$I = E(\sum_{ij} (d_{ij} - e_{ij})^2) = E(\sum_{ij} (d_{ij} - \sum_{kl} f_{kl}\, b_{i-k,j-l})^2) \tag{3}$$

(Wiener-Kriterium).

Das gewünschte Ergebnis ist die gesuchte Objektverteilung, aber bei der Auswertung des Ausdrucks (3) wird nicht die Objektverteilung selbst benötigt, sondern nur ihre Autokorrelation oder deren Fouriertransformierte, und diese läßt sich an Hand von Modellen abschätzen.

Die Bildung der partiellen Ableitungen des Ausdrucks (3) nach den zu bestimmenden Filterkoeffizienten führt zu einem linearen Gleichungssystem, welches das zweidimensionale, diskrete Analogon zur Wiener-Hopf-

Gleichung für kontinuierliche Vorgänge ist.

Nach dem Faltungstheorem kann die Faltung im Ortsraum ersetzt werden durch eine Multiplikation im Frequenzraum. Führt man auch die Bestimmung des Filters im Frequenzraum aus, so erhält man für seine Fouriertransformierte F:

$$F = \frac{1}{A(u,v)} \cdot \frac{|O(u,v)|^2 \cdot |A(u,v)|^2}{|O(u,v)|^2 \cdot |A(u,v)|^2 + R(u,v)} \qquad (4)$$

Dabei ist $A(u,v)$ die Fouriertransformierte der Abbildungsfunktion a, $|A(u,v)|$ = Modulationsübertragungsfunktion, $|O(u,v)|$ ist das Amplitudenspektrum der Objektverteilung o, $R(u,v)$ die spektrale Rauschenergiedichte, u,v sind die Frequenzvariablen in x-und y-Richtung.

Das Filter in Gleichung (4) kann in zwei Stufen errechnet und ausgeführt werden. Man erhält den zweiten Term

$$F_2 = \frac{|O|^2 \cdot |A|^2}{|O|^2 \cdot |A|^2 + R} \, , \qquad (5)$$

wenn man in (3) als Zielfunktion d das unverrauschte Bild $\hat{b}$ einsetzt. F_1 besorgt durch Unterdrückung der hohen Frequenzen die Unterdrückung des Rauschens. Der Faktor

$$F_2 = \frac{1}{A(u,v)} \qquad (6)$$

ist die Inverse der Abbildungsfunktion und würde aus einem störungsfreien Bild die unverzerrte Objektverteilung regenerieren. F_2 verstärkt die mittleren und hohen Frequenzen, welche die Information über Objektdetails enthalten.
Das Filter $F = F_2 \cdot F_1$ liefert einen optimalen Kompromiß zwischen den beiden sich widersprechenden Zielen mit einer mäßigen Verstärkung der mittleren und Unterdrückung der hohen Frequenzen. Einen typischen Frequenzgang gibt Bild 1 wieder. Die Lage und Größe der maximalen Verstärkung und der Übergang zur Unterdrückung der hohen Frequenzen wird beeinflusst durch gewisse Parameter, die aus der Kenntnis über das zu untersuchende Organ und der statistischen Qualität des Bildes bestimmt werden.

Zur Abschätzung von O wird als einfaches Modell [2] angenommen, daß die Objektverteilung aus der Summe einer konstanten Aktivitätsbelegung und regelmäßig verteilten Objektdetails einfacher geometrischer Gestalt,

z.B. Kugeln, besteht. Das Verhältnis der Aktivitäten von Detail und
Umgebung wird aus der Kenntnis des Speicherverhaltens von Organ und
Tumoren abgeschätzt. In diesem Modell ist R frequenzunabhängig und
wird aus der mittleren Quantendichte im interessierenden Gebiet er-
mittelt.
Die Betrachtung der Filter im Ortsfrequenzbereich bietet neben der
Unterstützung des Verständnisses und der einfacheren mathematischen
Form auch rechentechnische Vorteile, da für die Fouriertransformation
schnelle Algorithmen zur Verfügung stehen (FFT). Während die Berechnung
eines 25x25-Filters im Ortsbereich (Lösen eines Gleichungssystems mit
625 Unbekannten) 20 Minuten, seine Anwendung auf ein Bild von 128x128
Elementen etwa 5 Minuten beansprucht, erfordert die Erstellung des
Filters im Frequenzbereich etwa 25 Sekunden, seine Anwendung mit zwei-
maliger Transformation des Bildes etwa 30 Sekunden.

Die mit diesen Filtern bearbeiteten Szintigramme weisen gegenüber den
unbearbeiteten drei qualitative Verbesserungen auf: 1. geringere Halb-
wertsbreite von Bildern kleiner Objekte, 2. vergrößerter Kontrast,
3. verbessertes Signal-Rausch-Verhältnis.

3. Interaktive Auswertung

Nicht zu trennen vom Problem der Bildbearbeitung ist das Problem der
Darstellung, einerseits weil gewisse Darstellungsmethoden selbst eine
Bildfilterung beinhalten, andererseits weil durch ungünstige Darstellung
der Vorteil einer guten Filterung zunichte gemacht werden kann.

Neben der Wiedergabe der Szintigramme auf dem Schnelldrucker in Grautö-
nen durch Übereinanderdrucken mehrerer Zeichen und in einer Darstellung
mit 19 Symbolen für 19 Intensitätsstufen haben wir ein interaktives
Bildschirmprogramm entwickelt, das dem Benutzer, nämlich dem Arzt, der
die Diagnose stellen muß, den Umgang mit der EDV sehr erleichtert, wenn
nicht überhaupt erst praktisch brauchbar gemacht. Unter anderem sind
folgende Möglichkeiten vorhanden:

1) Setzen oberer und unterer Abschneidegrenzen zur Auswahl
   des dargestellten Intensitätsbereiches,
2) Wahl von Bildausschnitt und Bildmaßstab,
3) Darstellung von Intensitätprofilen längs Zeile und
   Spalte durch einen mit dem Lichtstift ausgewählten
   Punkt oder längs der Verbindungslinie zweier beliebiger Punkte,

4) Eingrenzung von sogenannten Regions of Interest und Bestimmung derer Mittelwerte und Maximalwerte,
5) Drucken von Szintigrammen und Profilen mit den am Bildschirm gewählten Parametern auf dem Schnelldrucker.

Der Arzt hat somit die Vorteile, qualitativ bessere Bilder als die bisherigen Polaroidaufnahmen vom Oszillograph zur Verfügung zu haben, die
Darstellungsparameter variieren zu können und neben der bildhaften Darstellung weitere quantitative Informationen abrufen zu können.

4. Likelihood-Ratio-Test

4.1. Allgemeine Überlegungen

In Grenzfällen schwacher Abweichungen vom Normalmuster bleibt natürlich
immer die Frage, ob diese auf statistische Fluktuationen oder biologi-
sche Ursachen zurückzuführen sind. Um den Arzt bei seiner Entscheidung
zu unterstützen, die er unbedingt fällen muß, wurde ein statistischer
Test für dieses Problem formuliert, der Likelihood-Ratio-Test [3,4].
Bei einem statistischen Test besteht die Aufgabe darin, eine vorliegende
Gruppe von Meßwerten einer von zwei oder mehreren möglichen Hypothesen
zuzuordnen. Als Nullhypothese H_0 werde formuliert, daß das vorliegende
Szintigramm das Bild einer bekannten "normalen" Objektverteilung ist.
Die Alternative H_1 besteht in der Annahme, daß die Objektverteilung zusätzlich an einer bestimmten Stelle durch eine Anomalie bekannter Form
verändert ist, z.B. Kugelform, wobei jedoch Kugelradius und Aktivitäts-
konzentration noch als unbestimmte Parameter auftreten können. Die Alternative H_1 wird dann als zusammengesetzt bezeichnet. Die Parameter werden
nach der Maximum-Likelihood-Methode geschätzt, d.h. es werden diejenigen
Werte der Alternativ-Hypothese zu Grunde gelegt, für welche die Wahrscheinlichkeit, gerade die vorliegende Stichprobe zu erhalten, maximal
wird. Somit ist die zusammengesetzte Alternative auf eine einfache Alternative zurückgeführt, die nun gegen die Nullhypothese getestet werden
soll.

Es liegt nahe, als Testgröße das Verhältnis Λ der a posteriori Wahrscheinlichkeiten L_0 und L_1 zu betrachten, und die Nullhypothese zu verwerfen, wenn dieses Verhältnis kleiner als eine vorgegebene Konstante K
ist:

$$\Lambda = \frac{L_0(x_1,\ldots,x_n)}{L_1(x_1,\ldots,x_n)} < K. \qquad (7)$$

$X = (x_1, \ldots, x_n)$ sind die Beobachtungsgrößen (Stichprobe), $L_0(x)$ und $L_1(x)$ sind die Wahrscheinlichkeiten, daß die vorliegende Stichprobe gemessen wird, wenn die Hypothese H_0 bzw. H_1 gilt. Das kritische Gebiet, der Teil des Ereignisraumes, der zur Ablehnung der Nullhypothese führt, wird durch die Ungleichung (7) definiert. Die Teststärke oder Gütefunktion Π ist die Wahrscheinlichkeit, daß die Stichprobe im kritischen Gebiet liegt, mit anderen Worten, die Wahrscheinlichkeit, daß H_0 verworfen wird. Sie ist eine Funktion des Parameters Θ, der die statistische Gesamtheit beschreibt. $\Pi(\Theta) = P(H_0 \text{ verworfen } | \Theta)$.

Im Falle einfacher Hypothesen kann Θ nur zwei Werte Θ_0 und Θ_1 annehmen. $\alpha = \Pi(\Theta_0) = P(H_0 \text{ verworfen } | \Theta_0)$ ist der Fehler 1. Art (Signifikanzniveau). $\Pi(\Theta_1) = P(H_0 \text{ verworfen } | \Theta_1)$ ist die Güte (Stärke) des Tests, die Wahrscheinlichkeit H_1 zu akzeptieren, wenn H_1 wahr ist.
$\beta = 1 - \Pi(\Theta_1) = P(H_0 \text{ nicht verworfen } | \Theta_1)$ ist der Fehler 2. Art, d.h. die Wahrscheinlichkeit, daß H_0 nicht verworfen wird, obwohl H_1 richtig ist.

Nach dem Neyman-Pearson-Lemma ist ein Test, dessen kritisches Gebiet durch Ungleichung (7) definiert ist, "most powerful", d.h. es gibt keinen Test größerer Stärke, der bei gleichem Signifikanzniveau α einen kleineren Fehler 2. Art β hätte.

Statt durch $\Lambda < K$ kann das kritische Gebiet auch durch

$$T = -2\log\Lambda > K' \tag{8}$$

definiert werden. Von dieser Teststatistik weiß man, daß sie asymptotisch, d.h. für großen Stichprobenumfang, eine Verteilung vom χ^2-Typ hat, und zwar ist der Index der χ^2-Verteilung gleich der Anzahl der Parameter, die zur Fixierung der Alternativhypothese aus der Stichprobe geschätzt werden. Diese Kenntnis kann u.U. zur Festlegung des kritischen Wertes K' bei gegebenem Signifikanzniveau benützt werden. Außerdem bietet die Logarithmierung rechentechnische Vorteile, wie aus dem folgenden ersichtlich ist.

4.2. Spezialisierung auf den Fall eines Szintigramms

Eine Bildfläche sei in k Zellen aufgeteilt, die Zahl der in der i-ten Zelle registrierten Quanten sei x_i, $n = \sum_{i=1}^{k} x_i$ ist die Gesamtzahl der Quanten. Die erwartete Verteilung der Quanten sei durch die a priori

Wahrscheinlichkeiten p_i beschrieben, so daß die erwartete Häufigkeit in der i-ten Zelle $p_i \cdot n$ ist. Die x_i sind poisson-verteilt mit den Mittelwerten $p_i \cdot n$, die Poisson-Verteilung werde durch eine Normalverteilung mit dem Mittelwert $\mu_i = p_i n$ und der Varianz $\sigma_i^2 = \mu_i$ ersetzt. Da die beobachteten Häufigkeiten in den einzelnen Zellen statistisch unabhängig sind, erhält man für die Wahrscheinlichkeit, die vorliegende Stichprobe X zu ziehen,

$$L(X) = \prod_{i=1}^{k} \frac{1}{(2\pi p_i n)^{1/2}} \; e^{-\frac{(x_i - p_i n)^2}{2 p_i n}} \tag{9}$$

und

$$-2\log L(X) = k \log (2\pi n) + \sum_{i=1}^{k} \log p_i + \sum_{i=1}^{k} \frac{(x_i - p_i n)^2}{p_i n} \tag{10}$$

Die letzte Summe in (10) ist gerade die bei Anpassungstest verwendete Größe χ^2.

Unterscheidet man jetzt die Verteilungen unter H_0 und H_1 durch die Indices $_0$ und $_1$ an den Größen p_i und χ^2, so erhält man für die Prüfgröße T:

$$T = \sum_{i=1}^{k} \log \left(\frac{p_{0_i}}{p_{1_i}}\right) + (\chi^2)_0 - (\chi^2)_1 \tag{11}$$

Wie aus (10) und (11) ersichtlich, benötigt man zur Bestimmung der Testgröße die Größen p_{0_i} und p_{1_i}, d.h. man muß sowohl das Normalszintigramm, hier Trend genannt, als auch die Form der Störung als bekannt voraussetzen; die Kenntnis des Trend kann sich allerdings auf die Umgebung der Störung beschränken. Ferner muß zur Anwendung des Tests der kritische Wert der Testgröße fixiert sowie nach Möglichkeit eine Aussage über die Fehler 1. und 2. Art gemacht werden. Nun ist zwar die Verteilung von T unter H_0 bekannt, aber sie gilt nur unter der Annahme, daß die Stichprobe vollkommen zufällig entnommen wird, d.h. der Bildausschnitt, an dem der Test ausgeführt wird, muß zufällig gewählt sein. Macht man jedoch den Test, wie es in der Anwendung naheliegt, nur an den Bildbereichen, die im gefilterten Bild eine besonders starke Abweichung vom Normalmuster erkennen lassen, so wird die Wahrscheinlichkeit, eine relativ große Prüfgröße zu finden, mit zunehmender Ausdehnung des Gesamtbildes anwachsen, d.h. die Verteilung der ermittelten Prüfgröße wird nicht mehr durch die theoretische χ^2-Verteilung beschrieben. An ihrer Stelle wird eine empirische Verteilung benützt, die durch Simulation von

Szintigrammen gewonnen wird.

4.3. Simulation und Diskussion der Ergebnisse

Zur Simulation wird der Erwartungswert der Bildintensität vorgegeben,
sodann für jedes Bildelement eine Zufallszahl aus einer normalverteilten
Population, deren Mittelwert gleich diesem Erwartungswert ist, gezogen,
und der Erwartungswert durch diese Zufallszahl ersetzt. Es wird dann
ein Filter angewendet, dessen Parameter dem Aufsuchen eines Objekts
bestimmter Größe und Stärke angepasst sind, und in einem Bildausschnitt
definierter Größe nach der Maximalabweichung des gefilterten Bildes vom
vorgegebenen Erwartungswert gesucht. Am Ort der Maximalabweichung wird
sodann die Prüfgröße T errechnet (selbstverständlich am ungefilterten
Bild, da nur hier die Voraussetzung der statistischen Unabhängigkeit
gilt). Bei der Errechnung von T nach Gleichung (11) wird der erste
Term vernachlässigt, da gezeigt werden konnte, daß er für kleine Anomalien (Störungen) klein gegen $(\chi^2)_0 - (\chi^2)_1$ ist.

Die Verteilung der Testgröße unter diesen Voraussetzungen (H_0) gestattet
nun, bei vorgegebenem kritischen Wert T_k Aussagen über α, den Fehler
1. Art, zu machen, oder umgekehrt bei gegebenem α den Wert T_k zu fixie-
ren (siehe Bild 2, Kurve $P_0(T>X|H_0)$). Will man außerdem Aussagen über
den Fehler 2. Art machen, so sind weitere Simulationen von Szintigrammen,
welche die gesuchten Anomalien enthalten, erforderlich. Es werden dabei
zu dem Trend vor der Erzeugung von Zufallszahlen noch die Bilder kleiner
Objekte (Anomalien) addiert. Am Ort der Störung wird die Prüfgröße wiederum berrechnet. Aus ihrer Verteilung kann man die Wahrscheinlichkeit ablesen, daß trotz Gültigkeit von H_1 der Wert T_k unterschritten, also H_0
nicht verworfen wird (siehe Bild 2, Kurve $P_1(T<X|H_1)$).

4.4. Entscheidung

Es ist noch die Frage zu stellen, wie der kritische Wert T_k zu wählen
ist, bei dessen Überschreitung H_0 verworfen wird. Eine Möglichkeit besteht darin, das Signifikanzniveau α vorzugeben und T_k der Kurve P_0
zu entnehmen (z.B. $\alpha=5\%$, $T_k=16$). Im Fall $\alpha=\beta$ ist es ebenso wahrscheinlich, H_0 zu verwerfen, wenn H_0 wahr ist, als H_1 zu verwerfen, wenn H_1
wahr ist. Will man die Summe der Fehler $\alpha+\beta$ minimieren, so wählt man
jenes α, bei dem die Gerade $\alpha+\beta=$const die Kurve $\beta(\alpha)$ berührt. In unserem Beispiel von Bild 3 ergibt dies $\alpha=11\%$, $\beta=14\%$ und $T_k=13$.
Nun können aber die Konsequenzen einer falsch-positiven und einer falsch-

negativen Entscheidung sehr verschieden sein, einerseits indem sie verschiedene Kosten verursachen, andererseits indem gerade in unserer Anwendung medizinische und menschliche Probleme mit einer falschen Entscheidung verknüpft sind. Es geht ja um die Frage, ob man eher bereit ist, einen gesunden Menschen mit einer falschen Krebsdiagnose zu belasten, oder eine Krebserkrankung im Anfangsstadium zu übersehen. Nun beruht natürlich die Krebsdiagnose nicht nur auf dem Szintigramm, es können sich weitere Untersuchungen anschließen, wodurch die oben erwähnte Kostenfrage ins Spiel kommt. Diese Überlegungen werden dadurch berücksichtigt, daß man die Fehler 1. und 2. Art mit verschiedenen Risikofaktoren R_1 und R_2 gewichtet und das Gesamtrisiko

$$R = R_1 \cdot \alpha \cdot p(H_0) + R_2 \cdot \beta \cdot p(H_1)$$

zu minimieren trachtet. $p(H_0)$, $p(H_1)$ sind die a priori Wahrscheinlichkeiten, daß H_0 bzw. H_1 zutrifft.

Zur Darstellung der Verknüpfung der Fehler 1. und 2. Art kann auch die sogenannte Empfängercharakteristik herangezogen werden. Sie zeigt die Güte des Tests $\pi = 1 - \beta$ als Funktion von α (Bild 4). Man sieht, wie mit zunehmender Wahrscheinlichkeit der richtig-positiven Aussagen (π) auch die Wahrscheinlichkeit falsch-positiver Aussagen (α) zunimmt. Die Kurven in den Bildern 2 und 3 gelten jeweils für ein Objektdetail bestimmter Größe und Stärke im Fall H_1 und für eine bestimmte Größe des simulierten Bildes im Falle H_0. Sie sind durch Ausführung von jeweils 500 Tests gewonnen. Von Interesse ist außerdem die Operationscharakteristik, das ist die Stärke des Tests als Funktion der Objektstärke bei festem α bzw. T_k.

Man kann fragen, ob nicht ein anderes Kriterium ebenso gut für eine Entscheidung benützt werden kann, z.B. das Verhältnis der Signalamplitude zur Standardabweichung des Rauschens nach der Filteranwendung. Bei einer Simulationsreihe wurde deshalb an derselben Stichprobe sowohl die Verteilung des Signal-Rausch-Verhältnisses unter den Hypothesen H_0 und H_1 als auch die Verteilung der Prüfgröße T aufgenommen. Die gestrichelte Kurve im Bild 3 stellt diesen Fall dar. Wie zu erwarten, da der Likelihood-Ratio-Test "most powerful" ist, ist das Signal-Rausch-Verhältnis als Prüfgröße wesentlich ungünstiger.

4.5. Anwendung im IAEA-Test

Wir haben dieses Verfahren entwickelt und erstmals angewandt im Zusammenhang mit einem von der Internationalen Atomenergiebehörde (IAEA) unternommenen Untersuchung, bei der geprüft werden sollte, ob digitale Techniken die Erkennbarkeit kleiner Anomalien verbessern. Es wurden 24 simulierte Szintigramme an 16 teilnehmende Arbeitsgruppen versandt und für jeden Quadranten dieser Szintigramme war eine Ja-Nein-Entscheidung zu fällen, ob eine solche Anomalie vorhanden ist, insgesamt also 96 Entscheidungen. In diesem Fall kam uns die Tatsache zustatten, daß der Trend in allen Szintigrammen gleich war und leicht ermittelt werden konnte. Wir waren daher in der Lage, vollautomatisch nach vorhergehendem Filtern in jedem Quadranten die maximale Abweichung vom Trend zu suchen und an ihrem Ort den Test auszuführen. Wir konnten auf diese Weise 48 von den echten Anomalien erkennen, ohne falsch-positive Entscheidungen zu fällen, während ohne Bildbearbeitung von uns nur 26, nach Anwendung eines Filters und interaktiver Auswertung etwa 40, sicher erkannt wurden. Dabei ist allerdings zu berücksichtigen, daß bei der Simulation nicht nur der Ort der Anomalie, sondern auch ihre Stärke zufallsmäßig festgelegt wurden. Daher war es möglich, wie später anhand der nach der Auswertung bekanntgegebenen Daten festgestellt wurde, daß 10 der Anomalien so schwach waren, daß keine Chance für eine Entdeckung bestand, während andererseits 26 ohne Bearbeitung erkennbar waren. Im Übergangsbereich von schwachen zu mittleren Störungen, wo dieser Trend den anderen Verfahren überlegen ist, enthielt das Testmaterial nur wenige Exemplare.

4.6. Interaktive Anwendung auf klinische Beispiele

Will man den Likelihood-Ratio-Test auf klinische Szintigramme anwenden, so hat man zwei Schwierigkeiten zu überwinden: erstens kennt man den Verlauf des Normalszintigramms über das ganze Bild nicht mit hinreichender Genauigkeit, da große individuelle Unterschiede auftreten und bei manchen Organen, z.B. Leber, die Form außerdem von der Lagerung des Patienten abhängt, zweitens kennt man auch nicht die Form der Störung, Tumor oder Metastase. Was diesen zweiten Punkt angeht, wollen wir die Näherung einer Kugelform für kleine Anomalien für eine brauchbare Hypothese halten. Bezüglich der ersten Schwierigkeit ist zu bedenken, daß die Kenntnis des Trend nur über die Fläche der Störung benötigt wird, und diese kann gewonnen werden aus der Fortsetzung des in der Umgebung der Störung ermittelten Trend. Es ist nun nur noch festzulegen, welche Umgebung zur Ermittlung des Trend benützt werden soll. Dies geschieht am besten und leichtesten auf interaktivem Wege, da je nach Lage der Anomalie, z.B. am Rande eines Organs oder - allgemein gesprochen - in der Nähe einer starken Trendänderung, Größe und Form der benützten

Umgebung verschieden gewählt werden müssen.

Das weiter oben beschriebene Interaktivprogramm wurde deshalb ergänzt durch einige Routinen mit folgenden Funktionen:

1) Definition von Untersuchungsgebiet und Umgebung,
2) Berechnung des Trend als Ausgleichsfläche 2. Grades in der Umgebung,
3) Ausführung des Likelihood-Ratio-Tests,
4) Darstellung der Ergebnisse von 2. und 3.

Das Verfahren wurde an dem Datenmaterial des IAEA-Tests überprüft. Anschließend wurde eine Nachauswertung einer Serie von archivierten Leberszintigrammen vollzogen. In Zukunft soll die Methode für die Beurteilung der aktuellen Daten im Krebsforschungszentrum mit herangezogen werden.

5. Schlussfolgerung

Während früher die Wirkung des Filterns stark auf die Seite der Rauschunterdrückung gelegt wurde, um nicht durch Verstärken des Rauschens künstlich Anomalien zu produzieren, kann jetzt die Auflösungsverbesserung etwas mehr berücksichtigt werden, da diese falschen Anomalien durch den Test größtenteils erkannt werden. Wie durch Simulation und an Hand des IAEA Testmaterials gezeigt wurde, ist der Likelihood-Ratio-Test nach Anwendung des Filters der Filteranwendung allein in Fällen schwacher Anomalien deutlich überlegen.

Wir hoffen, mit unserer Arbeit einen bescheidenen Beitrag zur früheren Erkennung von Krebserkrankungen geleistet zu haben.

Literatur

1. P. Pistor, G. Walch, H. G. Meder, W. A. Hunt, W. J. Lorenz,
   A. Amann, P. Georgi, H. Luig, P. Schmidlin, H. Wiebelt: "Digital
   Image Processing in Nuclear Medicine", Kerntechnik 14, 299 (Teil 1)
   und 353 (Teil 2), 1972

2. P. Pistor, P. Georgi, G. Walch: "The Heidelberg Scintigraphic Image
   Processing System", Proc. of Second Symposium on Sharing of Computer
   Programs and Technology in Nuclear Medicine, Oak Ridge National
   Laboratory, 1972

3. B. W. Lindgren: "Statistical Theory", Sec. Ed. Macmillan, London,
   1968

4. E. L. Lehmann: "Testing Statistical Hypotheses", Wiley, New York,
   1959

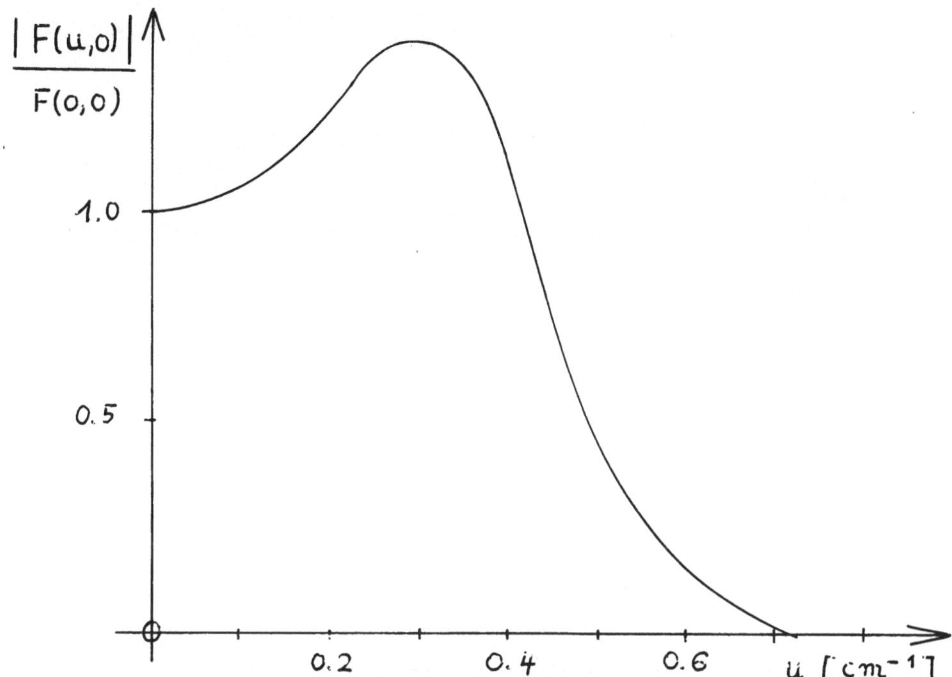

Bild 1: typische Filtercharakteristik

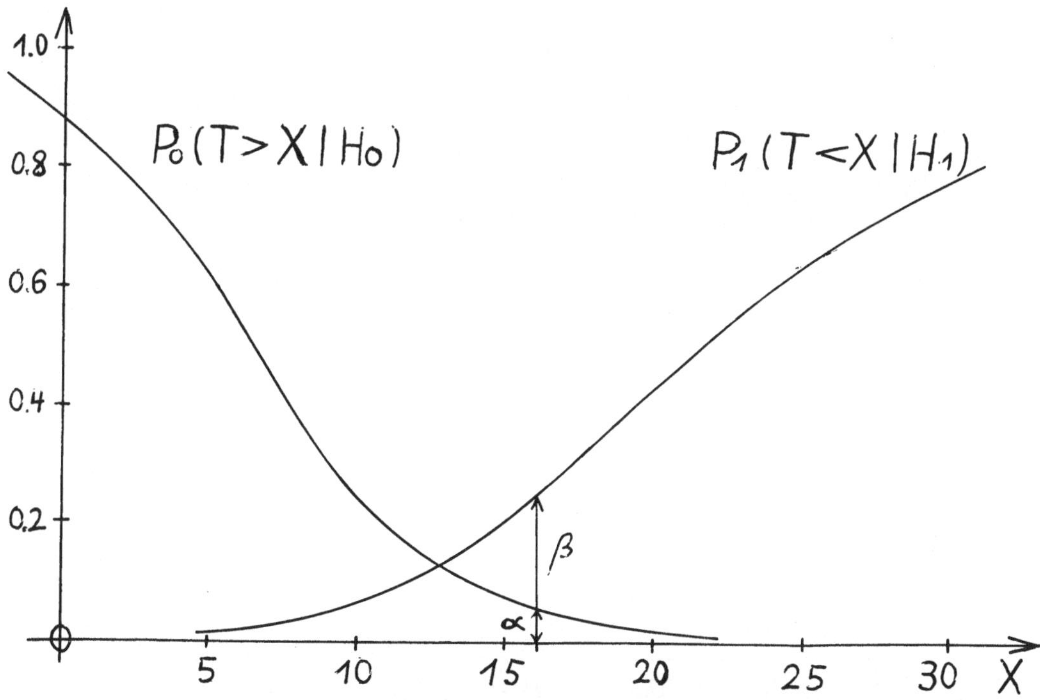

Bild 2: Verteilung der Prüfgröße T

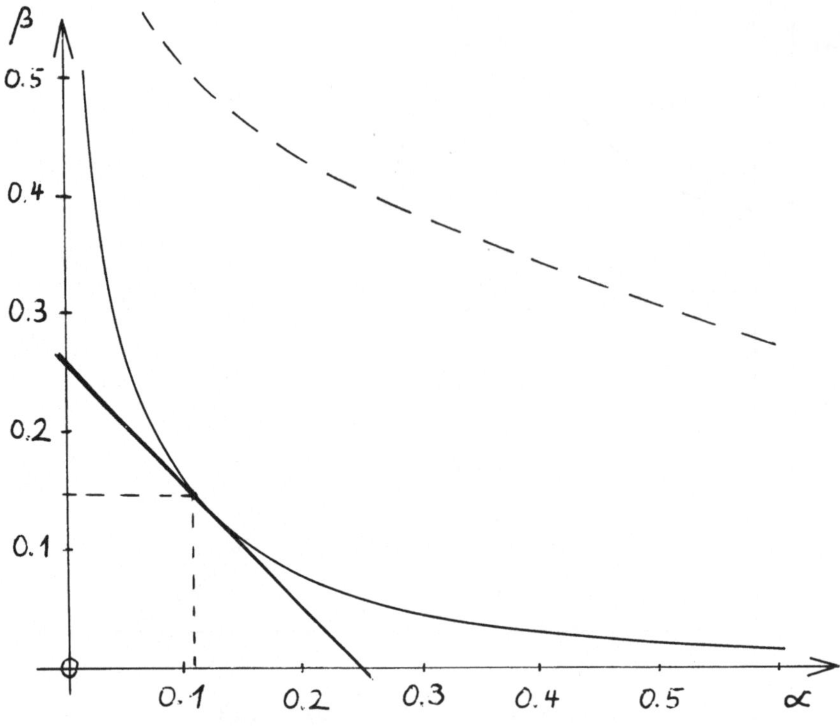

Bild 3: Fehler 2. Art

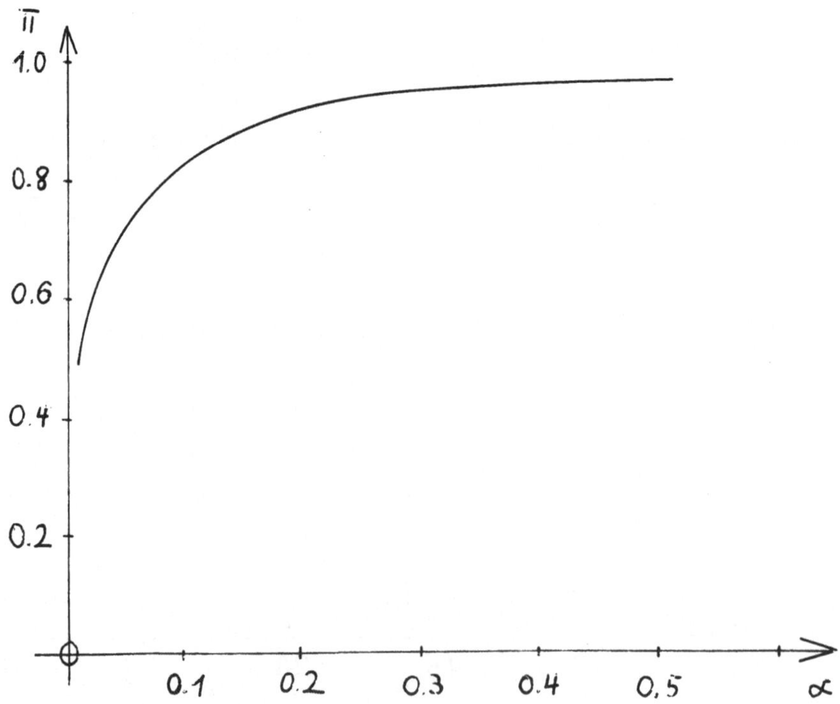

Bild 4: Empfängercharakteristik

<u>PROCEDURES FOR THE AUTOMATION OF THE WHITE BLOOD CELL DIFFERENTIAL COUNT</u>

E.S. Gelsema, B.W. Powell, P.L. Berrini

1. <u>INTRODUCTION</u>

The complete clinical examination of a blood sample comprises a number of tests of which one is the white blood cell differential count. This test consists of examining a suitably prepared blood smear under the microscope to establish the percentage of occurrence of the five normal types of white cell and to see whether any abnormal or immature cells are present. Typical values would be:

Neutrophils	(including band cells)	65%
Lymphocytes		27%
Monocytes		5%
Eosinophils		2%
Basophils		1%

A complete description of the various hematological tests has been given by Wintrobe (cf (11)).

When done by a trained technician, the average time required to find and classify the customary 100 cells is in the region of ten minutes. A large hospital, with some 2000 beds, would do in the region of 100.000 differential counts per year and thus need several technicians for this purpose alone. Given the repetitive nature of such work and the importance of recognising the occasional anomalies, maintaining a uniformly high standard of work is difficult and automation would be desirable if the required level of performance could be reached.

Although other approaches are being tried too by Kamentsky (cf (7)) and Saunders (cf(10)), publications by Bacus (cf (2)), Ingram (cf (5)), Prewitt (cf (9)) and Young (cf (11)) suggest that most of the work on automatic white blood cell recognition has been based on the "pattern recognition" approach, meaning: the analysis by digital computer of a digitised grey-scale image. This is not surprising in that many of the features thought to be used by the eye can in principle be extracted by the computer from such an image and on the other hand there are not many other properties of these cells which could be exploited for recognition purposes and which would also reveal the anomalies which may occur.

Of the work published to date, only the groups of Bacus (cf (2)) and Ingram (cf (5)) have presented results based on as many as a thousand cells and although some manufacturers have announced their intention to market scanners suitable for routine use, it has still to be demonstrated that one can do as well as a competant technician. This is particularly true with regard to recognising immature cells.

The work described in the present paper has been done in collaboration with the group of Neurath at the New England Medical Center Hospitals (NEMCH) in Boston who are engaged in a project aimed at the development of an instrument suitable for routine use. From NEMCH we have received cell images digitised using their existing CRT scanner PIQUANT which has been described by Neurath (cf (8)). The results presented here have been obtained by analysing this data using the CDC 6600/6500 system at CERN.

2. DATA ACQUISITION

For normal use, a blood smear is prepared by placing a drop of blood on a glass microscope slide and then smearing it out into a thin layer by pressing another slide over it. It is then stained either by hand or with an automatic staining machine using Wright's stain or an equivalent. More uniform preparations can be obtained by using a "slide-spinner" to spread out the drop of blood but these are not in general use. Most of the cells present are red cells since they are about one thousand times more numerous than the white ones. The white cells seldom overlap one another but do sometimes appear in contact with one or more red cells. In a good preparation this is relatively rare.

Staining gives the white cell nucleus a bluish-purple appearance which varies somewhat with cell type. The outer part of the cell (or cytoplasm) stains differently and less heavily and may range from blue-grey through blue to pink in colour. This colouring serves to define the boundaries of both the cell and the nucleus as well as providing important information about the cell type (figures 1a and 1b). Further information about the cell can come from the presence of granules in the cytoplasm which stain differently and thus stand out clearly. Also in the nucleus, in addition to its variation in shape, some internal structure or texture is usually visible and this too contributes to the recognition process. Even from this very brief description it is easy to see that recognition by eye uses some combination of features such as cell area, nuclear area, nuclear shape, contrast between nucleus and cytoplasm, cytoplasm colour, nuclear colour, nuclear texture, presence and colour of granules, etc. In the present work one tries to evaluate similar features with the computer and to classify a sample of cells using the values obtained.

The PIQUANT scanner measures a 35 mm photograph rather than operating directly through a microscope. Thus each cell is first photographed at high magnification using coloured filters. The resulting black-and-white negatives (one for each filter) are then scanned in turn using PIQUANT. In this way the optical density of the images is digitised into 64 levels over an area which on the slide corresponds to 96 x 64 microns using a nominal resolution of 0.1 microns. Though such a procedure would be unsuitable for routine use, for the purpose of acquiring data with which to develop the recognition programs it is entirely adequate and in fact produces higher quality data than one would have from a scanner optimised to this specific application.

The absorption spectra of the cells after staining do not show a great deal of structure. For the present data two coloured filters (Kodak 44 and 22) have been used corresponding to the regions 440 - 550 nm and 560 - 700 nm respectively. Other tests have indicated that the red cells can be more reliably rejected by using an additional blue filter for the region 400 - 470 nm (Kodak 47B) but it is not yet clear whether this additional complication is necessary when one uses well-prepared slides. Moreover the results of Gelsema (cf (4)) suggest that the additional filter does not contribute much to the colour measurement of the areas within the cell.

3. PREPROCESSING

The raw data for a cell consists of two sequences of grey-scale values (one for each filter image). The work described in the following sections is done on a (3 x 3) reduced image, i.e. only one point out of 9 in the original raster is used. The nominal resolution is therefore 0.3 μm and a typical cell image has 60x60 raster points. Fig.1c is a computer printout of a cell image, where the grey-scale information is represented by 16 different printer characters.

The purpose of preprocessing is to distinguish three areas of interest in such a picture, i.e. background, cytoplasm and nucleus. Also, any touching red cells should be removed from the white cell. They must not be included in the background either, because, as will be seen later, the background density is used as a reference for the colour determination.

In order to achieve this, a grey-scale histogram is constructed, in which the frequency of occurrence of all density values is plotted versus the density. Fig.1d shows such a histogram for the cell in fig.1c.

Ideally such a histogram has three peaks, roughly corresponding to the

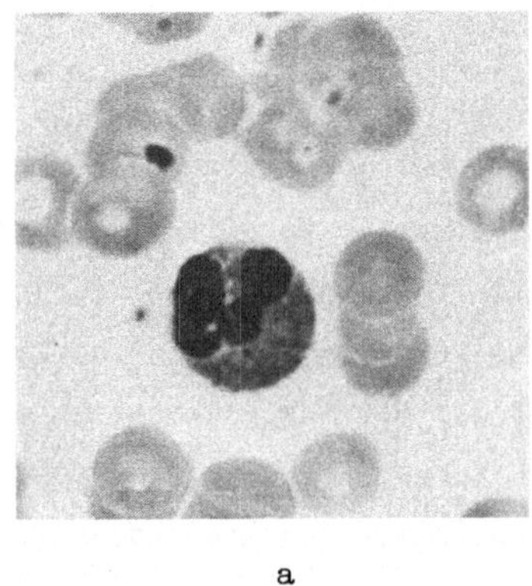

a

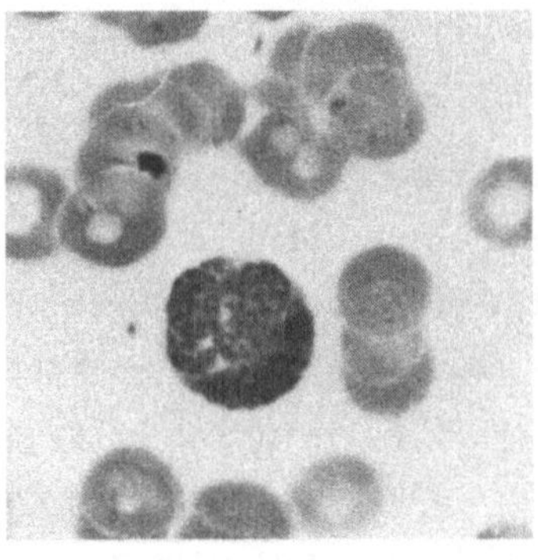

b

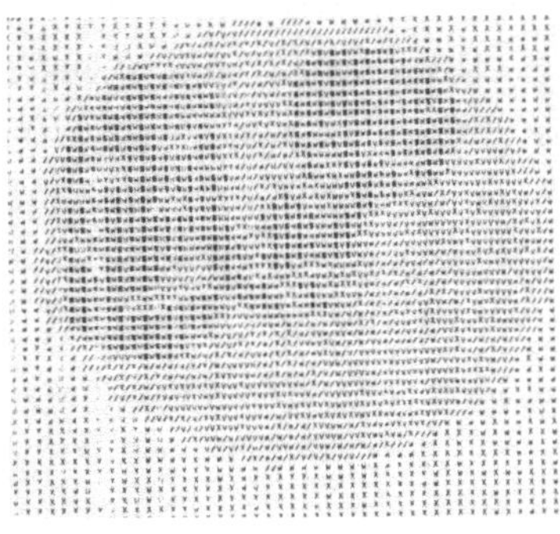

c

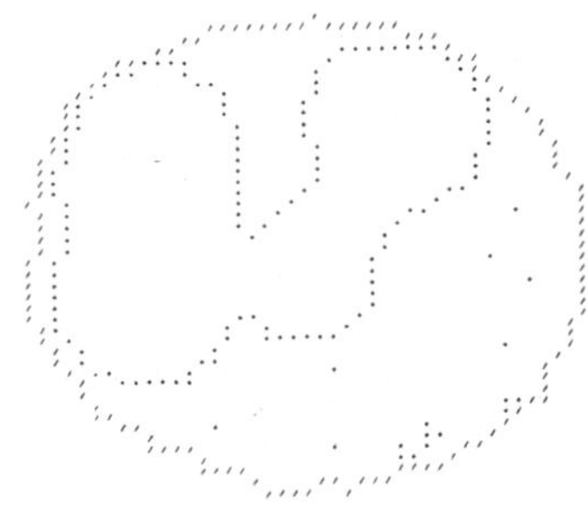

e

Figure 1

a and b: eosinophil as registered on black and white film through a red and a green
filter, respectively. c: computer print-out of the red image of the same cell with
16 levels of grey. The horizontal dimension is slightly expanded with respect to
the vertical one. d: histogram showing the number of points in the field of fig. 1c
with a given density versus the density. From this histogram threshold values for
the separation into background, cytoplasm and nucleus are obtained. e: boundaries
of cytoplasm and nucleus as obtained in the preprocessing phase.

three areas mentioned above. The background density value d_{bg} is defined as the density corresponding to the maximum in the first peak. The threshold value for the cytoplasm is then defined as the integer value nearest to $d_{bg} + 3$. This has proved to be a simple and adequate estimate for a large number of cells.

The threshold value for the nucleus is more difficult to obtain, because to some extent the shape of the right hand side of the grey-scale histogram depends on the cell type. For a histogram as in fig.1d, where there is a clear minimum between the peaks corresponding to cytoplasm and nucleus a simple and stable estimate for the threshold level is the integer value nearest to the value for which the frequency is minimum. This is stable in that if an error of one unit in the threshold value occurs, it will cause little change to the boundaries computed. The situation is more difficult in cases where the nuclear peak is only a shoulder on the cytoplasm peak or when the cytoplasm peak degenerates to a shoulder on the nuclear peak. It was therefore decided to determine the nuclear threshold not from the grey-scale histogram but from its derivative. The threshold level is then set at the integer value nearest to the minimum in the derivative curve, (having first excluded that due to the maximum of the histogram itself). It was shown on a large sample of cells that this is an adequate estimate. In "shoulder cases" the determination is of course more critical, since a small error in the threshold value may have a large effect when applied to the image.

The procedure described above having been applied to both histograms of a cell, the cytoplasm threshold on the red image t_c is then taken as the final one and the nuclear threshold on whichever image gives the smallest nuclear area, t_n, is retained, this yielding the best approximation to the real morphological nucleus.

A process of contour following is then initiated on the red picture to locate the cell boundary. This is done on the red image because there the red cells are more transparent than on the green image and are therefore less likely to distort the boundary. The process consists of: starting at a given point with density $\geq t_c$ on the cell boundary, moving to a neighbouring point on the scan raster with:

i)   density $\geq t_c$ and

ii) colour angle greater than a preset minimum value, keeping all neighbouring points with density $< t_c$ to the left (our units of colour measurement are defined in the next section).

This process is repeated until one returns to the original starting point. In the area enclosed by the cell contour a search for nuclear material (points with density $\geq t_n$ on the appropriate image) is then initiated and when one has found a nuclear point a nuclear contour is traced in the same way as described above. One must then

make sure that all nuclear material is enclosed by the contour as some cells may
have nuclei consisting of apparently distinct fragments. Once all nuclear fragments
have been found and contoured in this way, the areas corresponding to cytoplasm and
nucleus are easily obtained in the form of segment tables, i.e. tables giving the
starting point and end point of the area on each scanline. In this form the areas
of interest are in the most suitable form for the process of feature extraction.
The cell and nuclear contours for the cell in fig.1c , as obtained in the way described above are given in fig. 1e.

4. FEATURE EXTRACTION

The properties or features that the eye uses in recognising the different
cell types may be subdivided into three general categories:

i)   geometry

ii)   colour

iii)   texture.

In this work similar features are extracted. The three categories are
described below:

Geometry

Once one has the segment table representation of the image (section 3)
parameters such as total cell area, total nuclear area, nuclear perimeter, etc. are
readily obtained. Two other parameters, based on these and which are thought to
contribute considerably to the separation between the various types are the ratio of
nuclear to cell area and the nuclear shape. The shape factor was defined as the
ratio of the square of the circumference to the nuclear area.

It is already clear at this point that there will exist strong correlations between the parameters. They cannot therefore be expected to contribute
equally to the separation. This problem will be dealt with in the next section.

Other geometrical features are total extinction, average transmission for
both the cytoplasm and the nucleus, and contrast between the cytoplasm and the nucleus.
Through the density vs.illumination curve of the film these parameters can be defined
on the smear rather than on the film, assuming that one always works in the linear
part of the curve and assuming $\gamma = 1$. Total extinction is defined as the area of a
completely black disk of the same absorption. These parameters are classified in
the category of geometry rather than of colour because they can be extracted from
both colour images independently. This is in fact done because it is not known a
priori which image will yield the more powerful descriptor. Here again, of course,

strong correlations between the parameters occur. In total 19 geometrical features are extracted.

Colour

The colour properties of a cell (for a given light source) are completely described by its absorption spectrum (fig. 2). Even the eye is unable to exploit all the information contained in such a curve. What the eye sees can be simulated by combining the information contained in three suitably colour-filtered images. In this way each possible colour may be represented as a point in a chromaticity diagram as described e.g. by Judd (cf (6)). Young (cf (11)) and Gelsema (cf (4)) have studied the use of three filters for this application. Using only two filters, it is not possible to represent colours in this way. By measuring the transmission through the object using each of the two filters in turn one can, however, characterise the colour by using the ratio of the two values. This is a degenerate form of colour representation with respect to the chromaticity coordinates but it is still powerful when the two filters are suitably chosen.

Transmission, being directly related to film density, a colour may be represented as a point in a diagram with the two axes corresponding to the two film densities. Shifting the origin in this diagram to the point corresponding to both background densities (the two-filter representation of white), the colour represented by a point in the diagram may then be measured as the angle between the radius vector to that point and one of the axes. The "red axis" was taken as the reference direction. Absorptivity is defined as the absolute value of the radius vector.

In the process of extraction of the colour parameters the colour and absorptivity of a sufficient number of uniformly distributed points in the cytoplasm and in the nucleus were determined. Points near the boundaries were not taken into account in order to minimize the propagation of errors from the preprocessing phase. Average values and standard deviations of the distributions for cytoplasm and nucleus are the final colour parameters. In order to have colour parameters that are completely free from errors in the nuclear boundary definition, averages of colour and absorptivity for the whole cell were also retained. Finally, colour contrast was defined as the vector in the colour diagram joining cytoplasm and nucleus of each cell. A total number of 12 colour parameters were extracted.

Texture

The approach to texture presented here should be regarded as a preliminary one, liable to indicate ways to possibly better solutions.

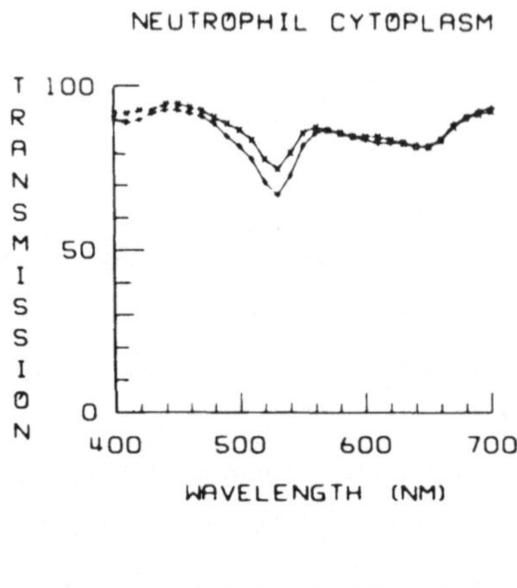

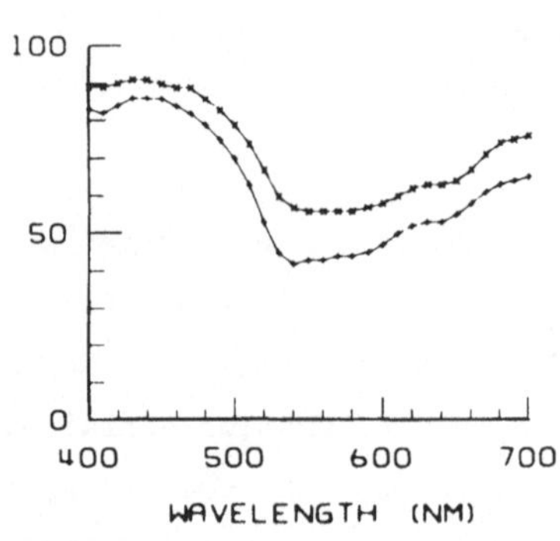

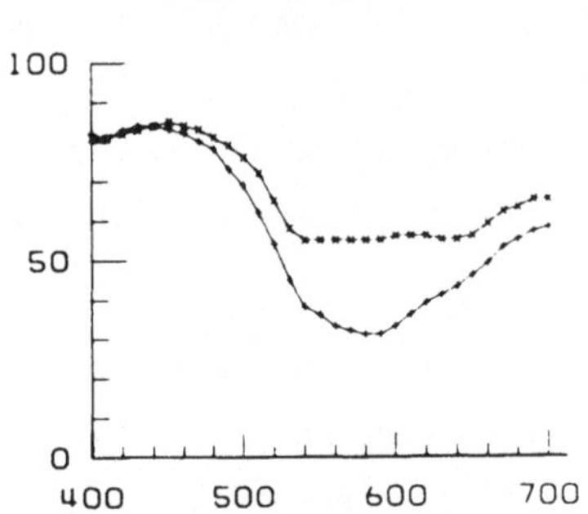

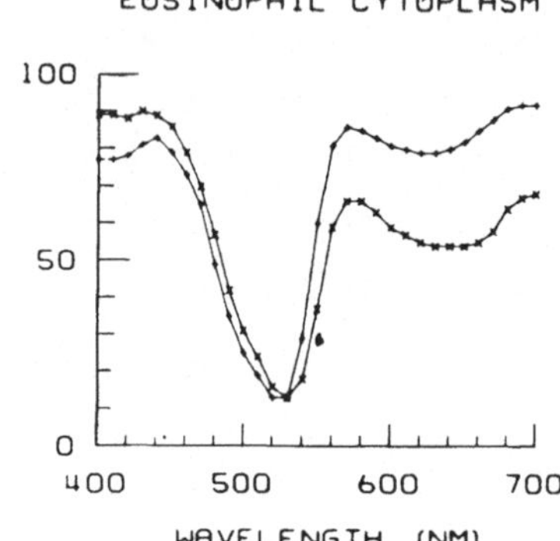

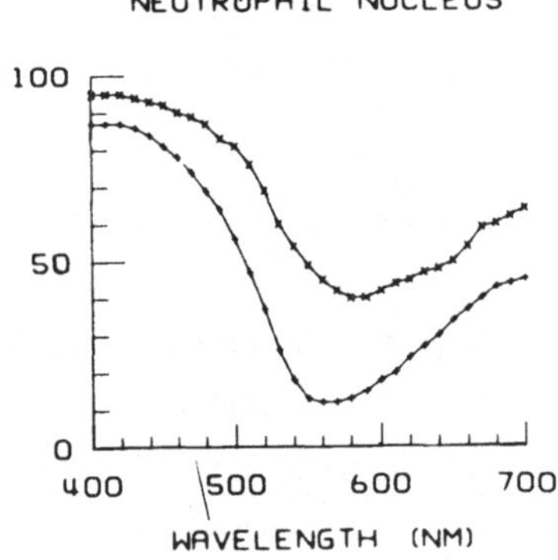

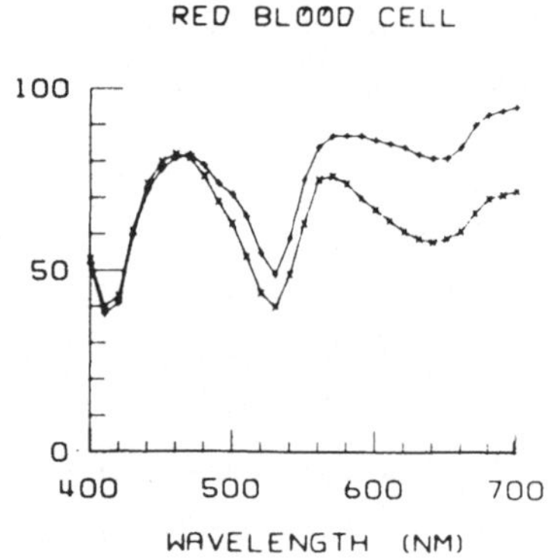

<u>Figure 2</u>

Absorption spectra as obtained using a microspectrophotometer. Each curve shows
the transmission as a function of wavelength for a region of the cell approximately
1 μm in diameter.

In the cell three types of object were defined:

1) very high density objects ($d_{max}-4 \leq d \leq d_{max}$, where d_{max} is the highest non-empty bin of the frequency distribution)

2) low density objects (holes) in the cytoplasm ($d < d_c$, where d_c is the cytoplasm threshold level)

3) low density objects (holes) in the nucleus ($d < d_n$, where d_n is the nuclear threshold level).

For these three types of objects the following five parameters were obtained:

a) chance of hit (i.e. following all scan lines the number of transitions from non-object points to object points divided by the total number of non-object points)

b) total area (i.e. the total number of object points)

c) mean length (i.e. the average number of consecutive object points)

d) average colour

e) average absorptivity.

If a certain type of object was not found the last two parameters were set to the colour and absorptivity of the area in which it was defined (i.e the surrounding area being either cytoplasm for type 2 or nucleus for types 1 and 3). Thus a total of 15 texture parameters were transferred to the classification process.

5. CLASSIFICATION

For the classification of the white cells on the basis of the 46 features described in the previous section two methods have been used, one being in a way complementary to the other. Both methods consist of two phases. In the learning phase cells of known type are used to establish for each type mean values and standard deviations of all parameters as well as the correlations between them. In the classification phase these values are then used to assign unknown cells to one or other of the classes thus defined. Textbooks on multivariate analysis are e.g. Anderson (cf (1)) and Cooley (cf (3)).

Linear Discriminant Analysis

With this procedure one finds the linear combination of all parameters which best separates the different classes by optimizing the ratio of differences amongst the different classes to the within group differences. The coefficients for

the discriminant function represent the weights assigned to the different parameters
and may be used to list them in order of decreasing separation power. In this way
the problem of singular dispersion matrices in the case of completely dependant parameters is avoided. Also, if strong correlations between pairs of parameters exist,
the better one will have the larger weight, the weight of the second one decreasing
with increasing correlation coefficient. This ranking of parameters will in general
depend on the classes being considered. The linear discriminant model used is based
on two assumptions about the different populations:

i)   all parameters are normally distributed and

ii) have the same dispersion matrix.

For the majority of parameters the first condition is probably fulfilled, the second,
however, is not. For this reason only the learning part of the discriminant procedure was used. Classification was then achieved using a least chi-square method,
using the best parameters as obtained from the discriminant model.

Least Chi-Square Analysis

In the least chi-square procedure the learning phase is repeated in order
to calculate a dispersion matrix for each class. By taking the most powerful parameters from the preceding analysis one is relatively sure that problems with singular
matrices will not occur.

In the classification phase the following quadratic form is evaluated for
each class j:

$$\chi_j^2 = (\vec{x}-\vec{\bar{x}}_j)^T D_j^{-1} (\vec{x}-\vec{\bar{x}}_j)$$

where $\vec{x}$ is the vector of parameters, $\vec{\bar{x}}_j$ is the vector of group means for class j and
D_j is the dispersion matrix for class j (the superscript T indicating transposition
of the column vector). This function has a χ^2 distribution with N degrees of
freedom, where N is the dimension of $\vec{x}$ (= the number of parameters used).

For each unknown cell the expression:

$$\chi_j^2 + \log_e |D_j|$$

is then evaluated, where $|D_j|$ is the determinant of the dispersion matrix. The cell
is assigned to the class for which this expression is minimum. When the dispersion
matrices are different for the various classes, the second term serves to minimize
the number of misclassifications by drawing the boundaries between classes through
points of equal population densities rather than through points of equal χ^2. The
only assumption underlying this classification procedure is the assumption of multivariate normal distributions.

A priori probabilities are sometimes included in the expression to be minimized. This is not done here as the objective of the present work is to demonstrate the classification power of a set of parameters, independently of relative sample sizes.

6. RESULTS

When comparing a computed classification with that of a hematologist, disagreements may arise from both machine misclassification and human classification errors. Bacus (cf (2)) has shown that for the five normal cell types a human error rate as low as 1.5% can be expected.

However, when a subdivision of these classes is attempted, the number of disagreements between humans rises rapidly. This is not surprising since different hematologists use slightly different criteria to decide, for example, when a band cell has developed into a neutrophil. A given hematologist may, however, be quite self-consistant in applying his own criteria. For this particular subdivision Bacus finds that for a group of nine people, individuals disagreed with the consensus in at least 15% of the cases. In the comparison of the machine classification against that of a hematologist these systematic differences may not be so important. If there is no clear transition between two successive states, the machine will merely show the same biases as the hematologist who provided the initial classification.

For the present work a total of 1146 cells were available in digitised form. These consisted of 483 normal cells (including band cells) and 663 immature cells. This very large proportion of immature cells was chosen deliberately so that one could study the probability of immature cells being misclassified as normal ones and also attempt the classification of the various immature forms. In table 1 the sample sizes in the training set and in the test set are given according to the hematologist's classification. It should be noted that the total sample consists of white blood cells and other nucleated cells that may occur in a smear. In the present work the cell types indicated with an (N) are considered as normal cells, all other types being referred to as immature cells.

With a training set of 243 cells and a testing set of 240 cells, 15 parameters have been used to classify normal cells into their six types. The confusion matrix for the testing set is shown in table 2. The percentage of correct classifications is 87%. Apparently better results than these can be obtained with more parameters and by using the same cells for both the training and the testing set. Indeed, with 30 parameters and using the whole set, a 99% correct confusion matrix was obtained. This results from using too many parameters for the statistics avail-

TABLE 1

Class Name	Sample size in training set	Sample size in testing set
Myeloblast	33	32
Promyelocyte	31	30
Myelocyte	34	34
Metamyelocyte	34	33
Band cell (N)	44	44
Neutrophil (N)	38	37
Monocyte (N)	36	35
Lymphoblast	34	34
Atypical lymphocyte	41	41
Lymphocyte (N)	37	37
Eosinophil (N)	38	38
Basophil (N)	50	49
Plasma cell	35	35
Nucleated Red cell A	25	24
Nucleated Red cell B	40	39
Nucleated Red cell C	27	27
Total	577	569

Composition of the total sample according to the hematologist's classification.

TABLE 2

Cell Type	Total No.	Computer Classification						
		Bands	Neutrophils	Lymphocytes	Monocytes	Eosinophils	Basophils	% correct
Bands	44	36	7	0	1	0	0	82
Neutrophils	37	5	29	0	1	1	1	78
Lymphocytes	37	0	0	30	2	0	5	81
Monocytes	35	0	1	0	31	0	3	89
Eosinophils	38	0	1	0	0	35	2	92
Basophils	49	0	0	0	1	0	48	98

15 parameters
Percentage correct 87%

Training set: 243 cells
Testing set: 240 cells

Confusion matrix for six class machine classification of the cells of normal type.

TABLE 3A

	Number of cells in testing set	Number of parameters	% correct for six classes	% correct for five classes
Bacus	518	8	80	93
NEMCH	197	10	85	91
CERN	240	8	88	93
CERN	240	15	87	92

Summary of the results for five and six class recognition compared to similar results obtained by other groups. (Sample consisting of normal cells only).

TABLE 3B

	Number of cells in testing set	Number of parameters	% correct for 16 classes	% correct for 10 classes
CERN	569	8	60	75
CERN	569	15	64	77

Summary of results of recognizing normal and abnormal cells.

TABLE 4

Cell type	No. cells	Computer Classification						
		Bands	Neutrophils	Lymphocytes	Monocytes	Eosinophils	Basophils	Immatures
Bands	44	32	10	0	2	0	0	0
Neutrophils	37	4	29	0	1	2	0	1
Lymphocytes	37	0	0	26	1	0	0	10
Monocytes	35	1	0	0	17	0	2	15
Eosinophils	38	0	0	0	0	36	0	2
Basophils	49	0	0	1	1	2	40	5
Immatures	329	0	6	3	8	3	11	298

15 parameters

percentage correct   84%

false negatives   9.4%

false positives   13.8%

Training set: 577 cells

Testing set: 569 cells

Reduced confusion matrix for machine classification of normal and abnormal cells.

TABLE 5

Cell type	No. of cells	Myeloblast	Promyelocyte	Myelocyte	Metamyelocyte	Band cell	Neutrophil	Monocyte	Lymphoblast	Atypical Lympho	Lymphocyte	Eosinophil	Basophil	Plasma cell	Nuc. Red Cell A	Nuc. Red Cell B	Nuc. Red Cell C
Myeloblast	32	13	8	1	2	0	0	1	1	2	0	2	0	2	0	0	0
Promyelocyte	30	2	14	4	2	0	0	0	3	1	0	0	1	3	0	0	0
Myelocyte	34	0	2	14	10	0	1	1	3	0	0	1	2	0	0	0	0
Metamyelocyte	33	1	1	7	15	0	1	5	0	0	0	0	3	0	0	0	0
Band cell	44	0	0	0	0	32	10	2	0	0	0	0	0	0	0	0	0
Neutrophil	37	0	0	0	0	4	29	1	1	0	0	2	0	0	0	0	0
Monocyte	35	0	0	1	6	1	0	17	0	7	0	0	2	1	0	0	0
Lymphoblast	34	3	1	5	0	0	0	0	18	0	0	0	3	4	0	0	0
Atypical Lymph.	41	2	1	0	1	0	0	0	1	26	3	0	1	6	0	0	0
Lymphocyte	37	2	0	0	0	0	0	1	2	4	26	0	0	1	1	0	0
Eosinophil	38	2	0	0	0	0	0	0	0	0	0	36	0	0	0	0	0
Basophil	49	0	1	0	2	0	0	1	1	1	1	2	40	0	0	0	0
Plasma cell	35	1	0	0	0	0	0	1	2	1	0	0	1	28	1	0	0
Nuc. Red Cell A	24	0	0	0	0	0	1	0	0	4	0	0	0	0	13	6	0
Nuc. Red Cell B	39	0	0	0	0	0	1	0	0	0	0	0	0	0	4	32	2
Nuc. Red Cell C	27	0	0	0	0	0	2	0	0	0	0	0	0	0	2	12	11

The column header "Computer Classification" spans all sixteen classification columns.

15 parameters

Percentage correct for 16 classes: 64%

Percentage correct for 10 classes: 77%

Training set: 577 cells

Testing set: 569 cells

Confusion matrix for machine classification of normal and abnormal cells.

able. With a separate testing set misleading results such as these are unlikely.

In order to make a comparison with the results of Bacus and with an early result obtained by the NEMCH group who used a subset of the present data, classification on the basis of 8 parameters was also performed. With 15 as well as with 8 parameters a testing set different from the training set was used. The results, given in table 3A, are for both five and six types – the five being obtained by adding the band and neutrophil types together. From these results, in view of the sample sizes, it is concluded that comparable performance has been obtained by the three groups. Even when the band cells and neutrophils are combined the performance is not as good as that of a human though with the statistical errors normally present in a differential count the additional errors due to the machine would be small. The effect of using 8 or 15 parameters has been considered (see also table 3B where a greater variety of cell types has been used) and as can be seen the benefit is rather small. The reasons for misclassification have still to be studied in detail but a first look suggests that when errors occur in the location of the cell and nuclear boundaries many of the parameters are affected and the classification will often depend on the particular choice of parameters.

When all cell types are being considered the testing set consists of 569 cells. The confusion matrices shown in tables 4 and 5 show the result of trying to classify these cells using the best 15 parameters chosen by the discriminant analysis program. From table 4 one sees that a total of 9.4% of the immature cells were confused with normal cells. Similarly 13.8% of the normal cells were classified as immature. Since the former figure corresponds to the proportion of "false negatives" it may seem the more important of the two. Though we do not have figures on this, hematologists expect to miss only a few percent of immature cells. However, this is assuming that there will be more than one immature cell present in the sample. With a 90% probability of recognition for each immature cell, the probability of recognising that some are present will normally be high and a greater problem is that of getting rid of the false positives which would be numerous and which could only be checked by visual inspection. These numbers are therefore marginal because they imply a machine which requires too much help rather than because it cannot find the immature cells with sufficient reliability.

In table 5 the complete classification is shown. The order in which the cells are listed has been chosen so that cells of a given type in different stages of evolution occur in the correct sequence. The boxes indicate categories which are not very well separated in nature and which one could reasonably merge together. With the full sixteen types 64% are correctly classified and this rises to 77% when only ten categories are used. Table 3 shows the numbers obtained when using only 8 parameters.

As above, tests using 30 parameters and the whole set of cells have been made giving 91% correct classification for the sixteen cell types. We do not, however, believe that a separate test sample would confirm this result.

At this stage the estimation of performance seems of greater importance than the prediction of the cost and speed of a device to do routine differential counts However, it is estimated that the extraction of 15 parameters and the subsequent classification of a cell take respectively in the region of 0.9 and 0.04 CP seconds on the CDC 6600. This figure can certainly be improved upon by optimizing those parts of the procedure that are most time consuming. This has not been studied so far. On the other hand it is not clear how much additional computation would be needed to get a significant improvement in performance and this can only be found out by further study.

7. CONCLUSION

The results presented in the previous section confirm that the five commonly occurring cell types can be recognised with a reliability slightly better than 90%. They also show that immature cells and other similar cells which are sometimes present in a sample can be recognised as such with 90% probability, while some 14% of normal cells are incorrectly classed as immature. The classification of the immature cells has also been tried with an overall success of between 64% and 77% depending upon the degree of subdivision attempted.

For the classification of white cells into the five normal types, the present results, together with those of Bacus and the unpublished results of the NEMCH work show that one is approaching the recognition efficiency of the trained technician. The present results also show with good statistics that on the crucial point of recognising whether immature cells are present, the performance is adequate but the rate of false positives, being 14% of the normal cells present, is too high for an automatic device.

Since the normal differential count is based on only 100 cells the statistical accuracy would only be slightly modified by the additional errors of the automatic system (even if the standard sample became 200 cells this would still be true). It is therefore mainly in the reduction of the probability of getting false positives without loss of efficiency in recognising genuine immature cells that there is the most need for improvement.

Further study of the present data is likely to show that some improvement is possible. This study needs to cover the whole sequence starting with the hematologist's classification and then looking for reasons for misclassification by the computer, for systematic effects in the data, for incorrect extraction of features etc. Finally a reconsideration of the statistical methods of classification would be desirable. The choice of parameters also deserves more thought. In particular, it has emerged very clearly that increasing the number of parameters does not necessarily improve performance. Better parameter evaluation may be more important and since colour seems to be one of the most significant areas, detailed study of how to evaluate it more effectively would be desirable. There is also reason to think that a more careful procedure for defining the boundaries would help significantly in the parameter extraction.

The white blood cell differential count may prove to be one of the first successful medical applications of image processing techniques. The results now available show that on statistically significant samples one is coming close to the performance required for a working device. There is a need to improve the recognition performance still further and the studies should be extended to even larger samples so that as far as possible one meets with the full range of biological variability.

Acknowledgements

We would like to thank Dr. G.R. Macleod, head of the Data Handling Division at CERN, for encouraging us to persue this work. We are also very much indebted to Dr. P.W. Neurath and his group at NEMCH in Boston for their help and for providing us with the data on which this work is based.

We would also like to thank Dr. R. Anner of the Hopital cantonal in Geneva, Dr. G. Gallus of the Istituto di Biometria e Statistica Medica in Milan, Dr. J.M. Howie of CERN, Mr. W. Selles of NEMCH and Dr. H.P. Wagner of the Tiefenauspital in Bern for their contributions to this work.

<u>References</u>

1. Anderson, T.W., An Introduction to Multivariate Statistical Analysis (John Wiley, 1958).

2. Bacus, J.W. and Gose, E.E., IEEE Transactions on Systems, Man and Cybernetics, SMC-2, 513, (1972).

3. Cooley, W.W. and Lohnes, P.R., Multivariate Data Analysis, (John Wiley, 1971).

4. Gelsema, E.S. and Powell, B.W., Colour Measurement and White Blood Cell Recognition, CERN Data Handling Division Report DD/72/24 (1972).

5. Ingram, M. and Preston Jr, K., Scientific American, 223, 5, p. 72 (November 1970).

6. Judd, D.B., Colour in Business, Science and Industry (John Wiley, 1963).

7. Kamentsky, L.A. and Melamed, M.R., Proceedings IEEE, 57, 2007 (1969).

8. Neurath, P.W., Brand, D.H. and Schreiner, E.D., Annals of New York Academy of Sciences, 157, 324, (1969).

9. Prewitt, J.M.S. and Mendelsohn, M.L., Annals of the New York Academy of Sciences, 128, 1035, (1966).

10. Saunders, A.M., Groner, W. and Kusnetz, J., A Rapid Automatic System for Differentiating and Counting White Blood Cells. Paper presented at the Technicon International Congress in New York, (November 1970).

11. Wintrobe, M.M., Clinical Hematology (Lea and Febiger, 1967).

EXPERIMENTS WITH INDUCTIVE DISCOVERY PROCESSES LEADING TO HEURISTICS IN A POKER PROGRAM*

N.V. Findler, H.K.Klein, Z.H. Levine**

ABSTRACT

Inductive reasoning relies on a limited data base, say D, to produce hopefully universally true statements expressed as hypotheses, say H. In decision making, control is sought over certain events that are affected by some variable(s) or by some relation(s). The hypotheses concern the values of these variables and the structure of these relations. As Pólya has formulated it, the inductive inference embodied in H is valid if D is true and H implies D.

An earlier report described results with a computer model that plays Poker at the level of an experienced (but not professional) human player. Now the above principle has been used in constructing various adaptive Poker playing programs. Here, D consists of the betting and drawing behavior of the opponents as observed in past games up to the current situation. H is with reference to the value of the opponents' current hands and their expected future decisions in the current game. The inferred information is then used towards maximizing (long-term) monetary gains.

Experimental designs for the evaluation of three different strategies to construct and exploit H are discussed and empirical results are presented. Finally, we draw conclusions with regard to a behavioral theory of decision making in situations that share the main characteristics of the Poker environment.

---

*The work reported here was supported by NSF Grant GJ-658.

**Nicholas V. Findler's address during the 1972-73 academic year is: Institut für Numerische Mathematik, Technische Hochschule Wien, A-1040 Wien, Karlsplatz 13, Austria.

Zachary H. Levine is now a student at the Massachusetts Institute of Technology, Cambridge, Massachusetts.

"Poker hands are man-made but the
probabilities of winning are divine."
(Anonymous Poker player - own collection)

INTRODUCTION

One of the fundamental questions facing behavioral scientists
is how humans make decisions relying only on partial information.
Researchers in Artificial Intelligence have joined the quest for
knowledge in this area, with the additional objective of automating
such decision making processes. We would like to use computers in
highly complex task environments that are characterized by uncertainty and/or risk. It is hoped, with good reason, that simulation studies
should contribute valuable information towards the above goal.

A complex expandable programming system was first created [see
Findler, Klein, Gould, Kowal and Menig (1971), and Findler (1973)],
which was to serve as a framework for various gaming experiments. It
performs the banker's role and does the housekeeping duties, such as it
    shuffles and deals cards (or reads in pre-dealt cards),
    calls players for opening bets,
    takes bets,
    calls for draw cards,
    carries out the showdown.
It also posts certain public information:
    the state of the game (opening, betting before draw, draw, opening
    after draw, betting after draw, evaluation),
    the general betting sequence (the betting history of each player
    in the current game),
    the size of the pot, etc.

Monte Carlo calculations provided probability values from which
the partitioning of possible hands and some basic, qualitative heuristic rules of playing could be derived. The refinement of these
heuristic rules and the establishing of new ones would depend on the
game environment represented by
    the ratio of people staying in the game after paying the ante,
    the seating arrangement (number of players before and after the
    player in question),
    the number of raisers and checkers,
    odds offered by the pot,
    the nature of selected opponents and of the games played so far
    (conservative, fair, liberal, wild, etc.), and so on.

In order to study these problems, the executive routine was so constructed that it could generate decision trees (incorporating various heuristic rules) for 0-7 players, and accept 1-8 strategies provided by "outsiders". This, in fact, was done and the so obtained machine players' performance was measured by different statistical techniques. The latter aspect of exact evaluation procedures is emphasized, particularly in view of the various learning processes incorporated in the computer experiments.

A large number of studies have been carried out and planned for future investigations. The following describes some experiments along a certain line of thought.

THREE "BAYESEAN" PLAYERS MAKING INDUCTIVE INFERENCES

In general, we call a "Bayesean" player a computer program that readjusts its playing strategy, based on estimated values of probability of winning, by comparing the actual outcome of events with the ones previously anticipated. The changes in the strategy can be accomplished in two, not mutually exclusive, ways. First, by systematically modifying parametric values built in the contributing heuristics, and by ordering the heuristic rules in a hierarchy according to their frequency of successful employment. Second, by automatically generating, testing and, when successful, incorporating new heuristics.

In fact, the program in question generalizes -- it derives conclusions from available, and growing, amounts of data concerning "absolute truth", i.e. it makes inductive inferences of improving quality.

A Base Line Player

The experiments were carried out by having the strategy under study play against six machine players. This fact represented both some advantages and some disadvantages. On one hand, the speed of interaction between players and of the evaluation and record keeping activities is of immense value. On the other hand, most of the presently available machine players have certain idiosyncratic tendencies, not necessarily all deterministic, that one would not like to influence the learning performance of the new machine players, such as our "Bayesean" novices, with.

In the spirit of experimental control, a Poker player was programmed, which did not incorporate learning of any sort. It goes on with the strategy each "Bayesean" player starts out with, namely it calls any bet, regardless of the hand it holds.

As expected, this player did very poorly. In 500 games, with 9 raises per betting round, the player lost 31,500 units, or an average of
63 units per turn.

The First "Bayesean" Player

This player acts in one of three ways - folding, calling or raising - depending on the value of his hand. It takes no other variable
of the Poker situation into account, except for the fact that it will
not call a bet greater than the raise limit. After the game is over,
a table containing the strength of the hand (independent variable)
versus the proper action (dependent variable) is readjusted. Further,
the running sum of winnings and a table of frequency counts of game
situations are updated.

When it is time to make a bet, two averages - one for calling
and one for raising - are computed. (The financial outcome of folding is known: the loss of the ante.) The player averages the winnings
so far with the current hand and the winnings of one type better and
one type worse hands. The action leading to maximum win (or minimum
loss) is then followed.

The above approach of averaging three types of hands takes reasonable care of statistical fluctuations and, also, false estimates
get corrected faster, as the following example indicates. Suppose,
the player's current strategy tells him to fold on all hands except
three of a kind or better, and to raise in the latter cases. It would
win money consistently and the effect would be felt on one category
lower, on hands with two high pairs. The player would then start
raising on two high pairs and if this is still successful, the effect
would be transmitted to even one lower category by this domino reaction
until losing hand types are reached.

Figure 1 shows the results of 800 games against six machine players, with 5 raises per betting round. As time went on, the program
developed better estimates of the best action with a given hand. We
note that in order to gather data more quickly initially, the program
was instructed to play each hand type with each action at least once
before the above described method is started.

At the end of 800 games, the player would fold on anything less
then two pairs, it would raise with any two pairs, and call with better

than two pairs -- a strategy not unusual among professional Poker
players.

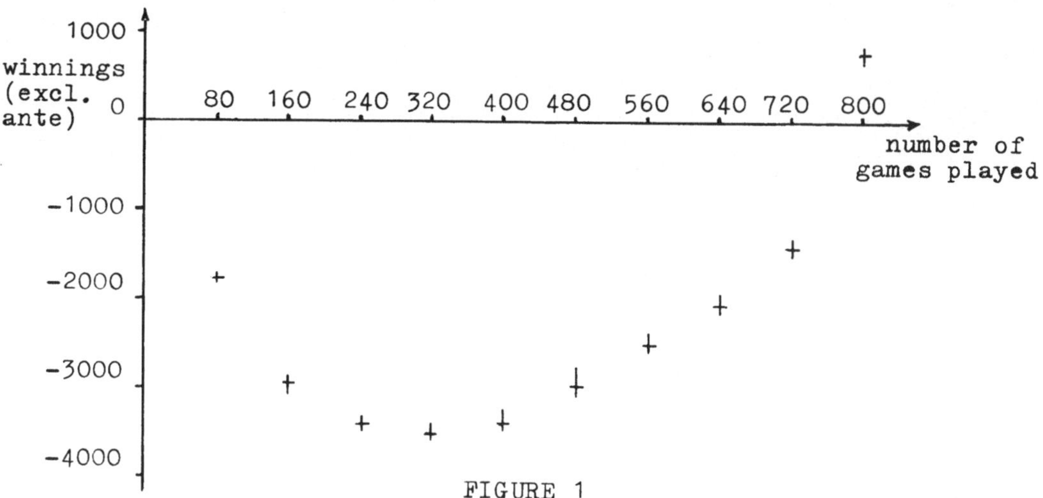

FIGURE 1

The above results looked promising and, also, some interesting
side effects appeared. So, we decided to play 2,000 more games, continuing the strategy obtained so far. As Figure 2 indicates, the
total winnings increase roughly linearly with the game number, after
the first few hundred games. The graph also contains a distinct sinusoidal component. The latter is due to the fact that the player
will tend to play the hands a bit lower when it is winning, and only
the hands a bit higher when it is losing. For example, a pair of
aces or kings were clear winners when it raised with them, but a pair
of queens or jacks were clear losers. When winning, however, the player would start playing with queens and jacks - whereupon it would
begin to lose. Eventually, it would stop playing queens and jacks
and, again, it would win.

After 2,000 games, the first "Bayesean" player would raise on
anything better than a pair of queens and fold on queens or worse.
This pattern was, in fact, reached after 500 games (checking every
50), and its gross characteristics stayed constant ever after.

An additional set of 2,900 games were played with five raises
per betting round, instead of the nine allowed until now. This run
was to be used for comparison with the third "Bayesean" player (see
Figure 4 later). The general characteristics of the winnings versus
the-number-of-games-played relation was preserved but the absolute
value of winnings decreased. Also, the sinusoidal component of the
curve was greatly damped.

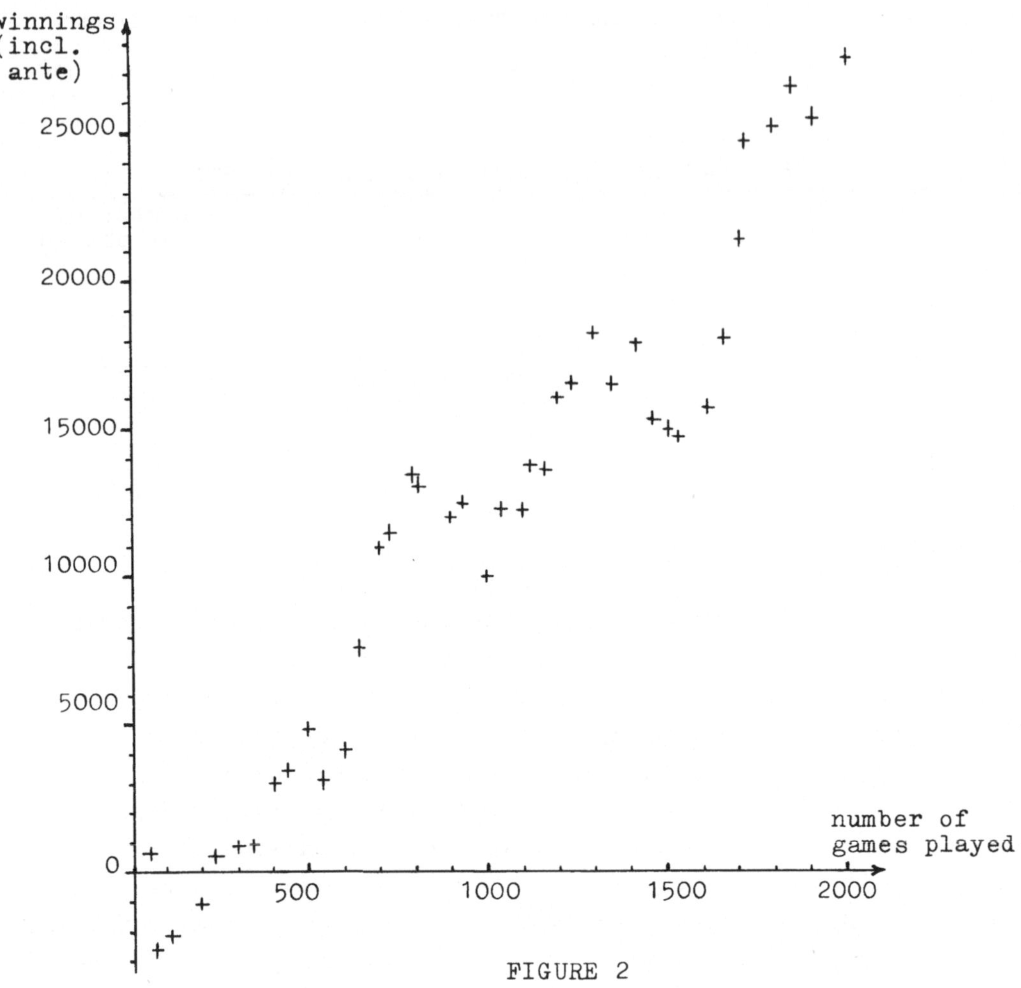

FIGURE 2

The Second "Bayesean" Player

The method of inference was made more complex in this instance by also recording and making use of the information as to which opposing player has opened or called first. (Since in most cases, Poker games are two-person interactions, it seemed unnecessary to make provisions for different triplets, quadruplets, etc. of the opponents.)

Obviously, if one were to have accurate data on players individually, rather than on "opponents" as an aggregate, one could play against each individual player at least as well, if not better, as against the aggregate. However, to have the same "tolerance limits" of the quality of the first "Bayesean" player's strategy, we could expect number-of-opponents-squared times as many games to be played to gather information. This would have required prohibitively much machine time (6^2x300=10,800 games). Instead, only 5,000 games were played and analyzed (Figure 3). After the first 2,000 games or so, there is a slight recovery from heavy losses.

It seems certain that the initial (wrong) estimates had prevailed too long and did not allow for a self-correcting trend to develop -- the second "Bayesean" player did not dare to play practically any hands for a longtime.

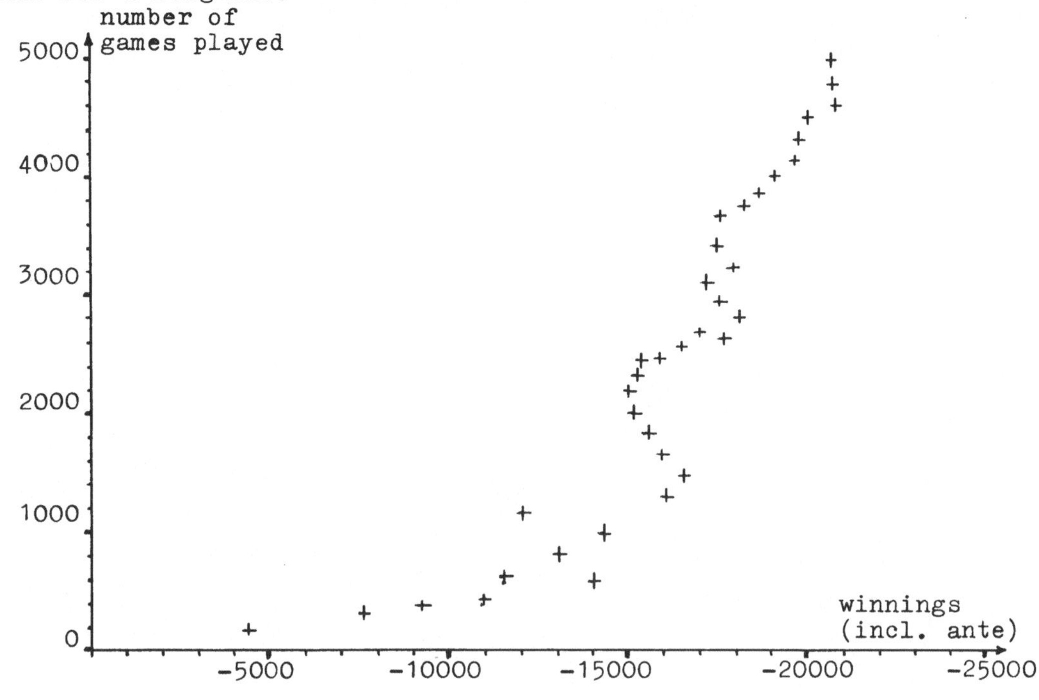

FIGURE 3

The Third "Bayesean" Player

After the relative failure of the previous strategy, we could see that better use had to be made of the total experience, more information has to be collected per game.

The third "Bayesean" player updates tables similar to those of the first "Bayesean" player but the tables are more refined -- they contain information as to whether the decisions were made in the pre-draw or post-draw betting round and in which raising cycle.

Three-thousand games, with five raises per betting round, were played. Figure 4 shows a comparison between the first and the third

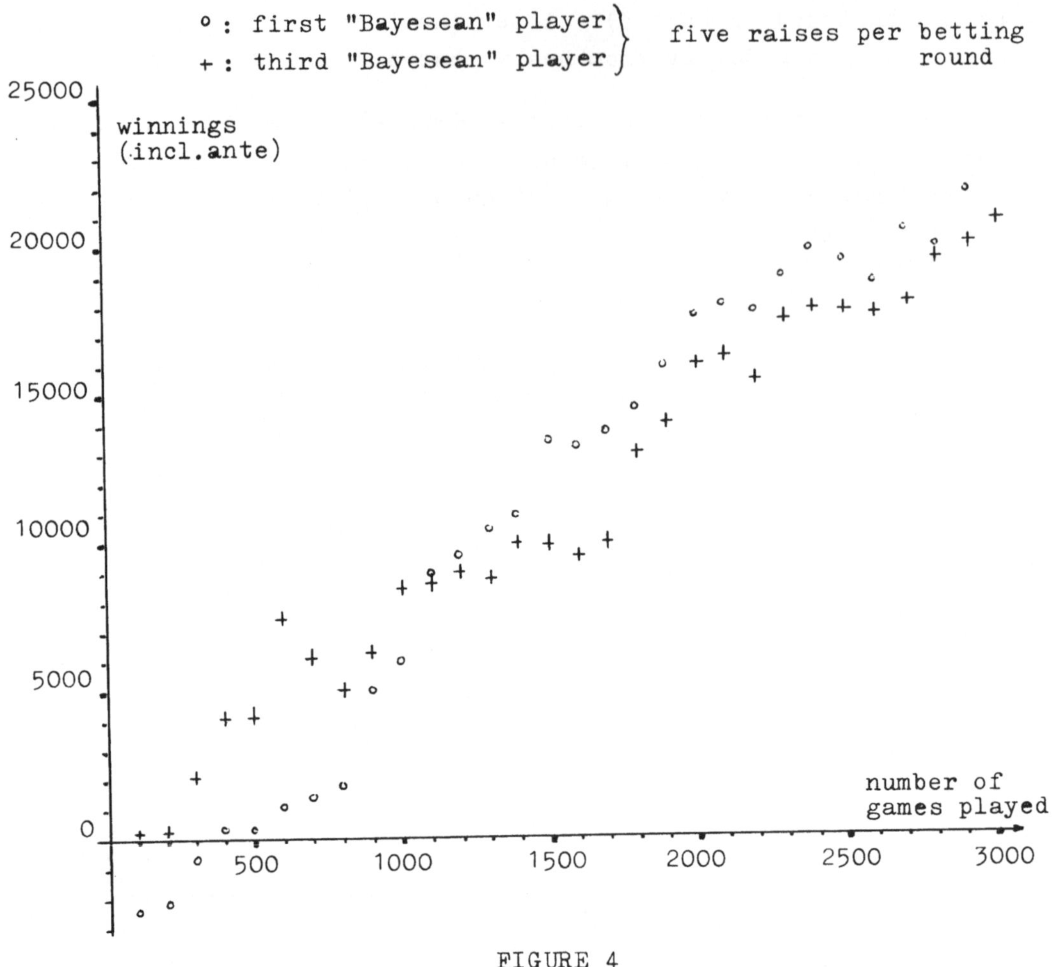

FIGURE 4

"Bayesean" players. The latter is better in the first 1,100 games or
so -- several hundred games after the heuristics of the first "Bayesean" player were essentially complete. The relative drop in the quality of the third "Bayesean" player's strategy is due to the fact
that it did not venture to go beyond three raises in the pre-draw
betting round and beyond four raises in the post-draw betting round
for lack of experience, even at the end of 3,000 games.

The heuristic rules formed were quite involved. Hence, it could
afford to play poorer hands than the first "Bayesean" player. In particular, it would call opening bets if it held a pair of jacks or
better, as opposed to kings or better for the first "Bayesean" player.
It would fold if another player raised before the draw unless it had
at least two pairs, in which case it would re-raise. It would call if
it had another pre-draw decision to make. It would open or call with

a pair of jacks or better after the draw. However, if the opponent
raised, it would re-raise with a pair of kings or better and would
call with a pair of jacks or queens. It would re-raise again on the
second re-raise of the opponent. One more re-raise would provoke his
calling.

We have to evaluate this strategy and its results in the context
of the "wild and woolly" games played by the six machine opponents.
Some of the players will bluff rampantly. The biggest winnings come
from staying in with these bluffs. The third "Bayesean" player, like
the first one most of the time, does call these bluffs when its cards
are high enough. The two "Bayesean" players will not necessarily perform equally well against all possible opposing players. In fact, the
third "Bayesean" player is expected to do better than the first one
against more sophisticated and more responsive opponents. It also
tends to be more conservative and its initialization is also better -
it did not lose money at first.

CONCLUSIONS

In this work, we have tried to establish and to compare three
machine players that make inductive inferences. It was shown that
even a rich information environment cannot provide sufficient data
for certain, much too refined, decision making processes -- the second
"Bayesean" player failed to perform well.

A certain extension of our program could result in an even richer
source of information. After showdown, each known hand and its performance could be recorded -- an act similar to the one followed by
human players.

Also, a more timid approach in the initial information gathering
phase could lead to the same quality of playing strategy without having to pay for the lesson with a few thousand units of money.

Human learning in the game of Poker can be broken down concept-
ually into two processes. First, there is the learning to play the
game itself. Presumably, this happens over a period of time and in a
number of different game environments. This process should yield:

(a) A set of evaluation routines (own hand, own hand with respect to game position, style of other players);
(b) Storage of information (rules, probabilities, response
routines to common situations);

(c) Adequate structures for storing information about the game in progress and the actual players;

(d) Decision making routines that draw together (a), (b) and (c).

The second learning process constitutes the acquisition of the knowledge to operate in the specific game environment. This process seems to depend upon the evaluation of the style of other players and the storage of other information about that style.

If a group of experienced Poker players, who had never before played together, were brought together, it might be expected that the initial strategies would be characterized by responsiveness to own hand and to the game situation, and by the attempts to search out for and to purchase information. Later strategies may be weighted by paying more attention to the stored information about the other players. In other words, the style of play should change somewhat during the course of the evening.

An attempt to incorporate these ideas into our "Bayesean" players in our future research activity seems to be a challenging and useful task.

<u>ACKNOWLEDGEMENTS</u>

We wish to express our gratitude for numerous simulating discussions to the other members of our study group on human decision making (affectionately called, the 'Poker Group'), especially to John Menig, Ryder C. Johnson and Alex Kowal.

<u>REFERENCES</u>

Findler, N. V., H. Klein, W. Gould, A. Kowal and J. Menig: Studies on Decision Making Using the Game of Poker (<u>Proc. IFIP Congress 71</u>, Book TA-7, pp. 50-61, Ljubljana, Yugoslavia, 1971)

Findler, N. V.: Computer Experiments on Forming and Optimizing Heuristic Rules (Proc. of NATO Symposium on Human Thinking - Computer Techniques for Its Evaluation, St. Maximin la Ste. Baume, France, 1971; Published as Elithorn and Jones (Eds.): <u>Artificial and Human Thinking</u> by Elsevier, Amsterdam, 1973)

UNE EXPERIENCE D'INTERROGATION EN FRANCAIS D'UNE BANQUE DE DONNEES A
L'AIDE D'UNE GRAMMAIRE NON CONTIGÜE (JUXTAPOSITION DE GRAMMAIRES).

F. ADRIEN

PRESENTATION

La plupart des analyseurs du langage naturel traitent les textes
séquentiellement : un terme n'est pris en compte et intégré à un
arbre qu'une fois reconnus tous ceux qui sont à sa gauche.

Cela entraîne des traitements de portions de phrases qui pourront
s'avérer inutiles lorsque sera lue la phrase entière, et que s'effor-
cent d'ailleurs d'éviter les systèmes récents.

Dans les systèmes documentaires, l'analyse ne suppose pas cette contiguïté des termes : elle se contente en effet généralement de relever
la présence de mots-clés (ou de représentants d'ensembles de mots-
clés) dans le texte. Outre les perspectives théoriques et épistémolo-
giques qu'il ouvre, ce type de traitement présente l'intérêt d'une
grande légèreté. Il paraît à peu près suffisant dans certains contex-
tes.

Dans la communication homme-machine en langage naturel, cependant,
une telle approche est souvent incomplète. Ainsi l'interrogation
d'un ensemble de données structurées, tel qu'une base de données, met
en jeu des liaisons syntaxiques et sémantiques qui ne peuvent être
ignorées dans la mesure où elles expriment la structure des informations, à laquelle on se réfère.

Pour garder les caractéristiques de la non contiguïté, le repérage de
l'occurrence de termes-clés doit s'accompagner d'outils plus précis
tels que :

   a) la relation d'antériorité entre 2 ou plusieurs termes, qui
      permet notamment l'utilisation d'écrans, de connecteurs.
      Un tel indicateur est utilisé depuis longtemps en documentation
      automatique.

   b) un ordre de précédence dans l'application des règles de recon-
      naissance des liaisons.

Un texte en langage naturel peut alors être analysé par une superposi-
tion partiellement ordonnée de grammaires portant sur tout ou parties
(non contigües) du texte.

Le problème est alors de définir les catégories syntaxiques et sémantiques et les règles d'analyse correspondantes, adaptées au sous-en-
semble du langage naturel que l'on considère et au traitement que l'on
veut en déduire.

N.B. An English version is available

Dans cette optique, le présent rapport indique les grandes lignes d'une expérience d'interrogation en français d'une banque de données du personnel d'une entreprise. Cette expérience a été menée dans sa première partie avec MM. G. LAFIEVRE, C. RIVOALLAN, A.ROLLAND, de l'Institut d'Informatique d'Entreprise de Paris.

INTRODUCTION

1.   On considère une base de données, contenant par exemple les informations afférentes au personnel d'une entreprise.

On désire interroger cette base en langage spontané; poser par exemple la question : "Liste des P3 qui ont 2 enfants et entre 30 et 50 ans".

Pour traiter une telle question, le système devra au préalable la traduire sous une forme normalisée telle que :

```
            Liste employés
dont        qualification = P3
et          nombre d'enfants = 2
et          30 ans ≤ age ≤ 50 ans
```

Cette interprétation suppose que soient reconnues correctement

- les notions

- la (les) transactions à appeler

- la façon dont celles-ci s'imbriquent

- les paramètres sur lesquels elle(s) porte(nt)

- les contraintes qui délimitent "extérieurement" l'ensemble des enregistrements à retenir auxquels se rapporte(nt) la (les) transaction(s).

Ces contraintes apparaissent comme des relations dont il faut dégager

- l'élément de gauche (la variable)

- l'élément de droite (la valeur)

- l'opérateur (=, $>$, $<$ ..)

- les relations logiques entre les contraintes.

Cette analyse permet d'éviter les interprétations suivantes de l'exemple cité :

"Liste des employés qui ont 2 ans et entre 30 et 50 enfants"
"Liste des âges des employés qui ont 2 enfants et entre 30 et 50 ans".
"Liste de 2 employés qui ont 2, 30 ou 50 ans et des enfants"
"Liste de 2 enfants des employés qui ont entre 30 et 50 ans"
etc.
../..

2.   Les méthodes généralement utilisées pour ce type de problèmes commencent par une analyse syntaxique de la question. Celle-ci suppose que tous les termes puissent être analysés séquentiellement et s'intégrer dans des formes grammaticales avec les termes qui leur sont contigüs (quitte à appliquer ensuite des règles transformationnelles).

La valeur d'un terme, son rôle dans l'interprétation de la phrase, se déduit alors de la place prise dans cette analyse.

Dans l'interrogation d'une base de données telle que celle évoquée plus haut, la structure des données à laquelle se réfère la question (1) tend à diminuer, parfois dans des proportions importantes, l'ambiguïté que pourrait avoir la question si on considérait dans le désordre les mots (2) qui la composent. Si "qualification" et "employé" ne sont liés que par un type de liaison "qualification de l'employé", dans la banque, il peut ne pas y avoir lieu d'analyser grammaticalement les portions de question :

      employés dont la qualification
      qualification des employés
      qualification qu'ont les employés
      employés ayant comme qualification
      ...

à seule fin de dégager la-dite liaison. La désambiguisation peut alors se baser sur une analyse réduite ne portant éventuellement pas sur tous les mots du texte.

3.   Dans la présente étude, seront donc définis successivement :

     o des termes et notions autorisés et leur groupement en catégories.

     o des liaisons entre ces catégories, et à partir de cela :

        - une base de données
        - les questions qui peuvent lui être posées
        - les règles d'analyse

---

(1) et mentalement le questionneur
(2) non grammaticaux

../..

<u>LES DONNEES</u>

<u>DEFINITIONS PRELIMINAIRES ET NOTATIONS</u>

- Termes : ce sont les mots ou expressions des questions posées en langage naturel. Dans les règles, ils figurent entre côtes.

- Notions : ce sont des ensembles de mots ayant une même valeur sémantique.

- Catégories: ce sont des ensembles de notions. La plupart d'entre elles groupent les notions intervenant dans une même liaison.

Notions et catégories s'expriment par une suite de caractères alphanumériques ne commençant pas par L. Les relations entre termes et notions et notions et catégories ne sont pas biunivoques : à un même terme peut correspondre plusieurs notions et à une même notion plusieurs catégories.

A tout terme, notion ou catégorie intervenant dans un texte est affecté un ordre qui est le rang dans le texte du terme correspondant : si deux termes A_1 et A_2 sont respectivement des notions B_1 et B_2, de catégories C_1 et C_2, on dira que B_1 précède B_2 et C_1, C_2 si A_1 précède A_2

- Liaisons : ce sont des relations entre n catégories : elles sont définies par le nom de la liaison et les catégories qu'elles relient. Elles s'expriment par une suite de caractères alphanumériques commençant par L ou PL (cf. paramètres), suivie des catégories entre parenthèses :

  LA (BC) indique une liaison entre B et C.
  Si on a LA (BC) et LA (DE).. LA désignera l'ensemble de ces liaisons.

- Paramètres: ils seront utilisés pour simplifier l'écriture. Ils s'expriment par une suite de caractères alphanumériques commençant par P.

- X : désigne une suite quelconque de caractères. Dans une suite AXB, X ne contient ni A ni B.

- $\bar{A}$: indique que A ne figure pas dans un texte donné.

- $\longleftarrow$ ou $\longrightarrow$ désignent l'implication logique.

<u>N.B.</u> Plus généralement, on peut définir des catégories et liaisons de notions, catégories, liaisons et implications. De telles catégories peuvent de plus avoir de rang.

../..

- Si A, B et C sont des termes, notions ou catégories (non généra-
lisées)

AB   exprime que A précède B dans le texte et lui est contigü.

A,B   "   "   "   " sans lui être forcé-
                                                 ment contigü.

A et B   "   A et B figurent dans le texte, mais dans un
                                  ordre quelconque.

A ou B   "   A ou B figurent dans le texte dans un ordre
                                  quelconque.

A {B}   "   A ou AB. De même A {,B} exprime A ou A,B. A {et B}
             exprime A ou (A et B).

N.B. 1) L(AB) indique une liaison entre A et B contigüs.
     2) (A et B) ← (A,B) ← AB

De même L (A et B) ← L (A,B) ← L (AB)
On se contentera d'indiquer les relations les plus strictes.

On peut définir de même des ordres partiels sur des groupes de
catégories, et par suite sur les liaisons. Pour des couples de
catégories ils peuvent se définir par les conditions suivantes :

(AB) (CD)   suppose BC

(A,B) (C,D)   "   BC

(A et B) (C et D)   "   (AC) ou (BC) ou (AD) ou (BD) et (AC) et
                                                    (AD) et (BC)
(A ou B) (C ou D)   "   (AC) ou (BC) ou (AD) ou (BD)   et (B,D)

(AB), (CD)   "   B,C

(A,B), (C,D)   "   B,C

(A et B), (C et D)   "   (A,C) et (A,D) et (B,C) et (B,D)

De même

(A,B),,(C,D)   suppose A,D et BD et C,B

(A,B),,,(C,D)   "   A,C et D,B

De la même façon, LA(BC) LD(EF) supposera CE et ainsi de suite.

- Un ensemble de liaisons dont chacune a une catégorie commune
  avec une autre est dite une chaîne de liaisons.

  Une chaîne de n liaisons identiques peut s'écrire $L(A\ B)^n$; sauf
  précision contraire, n sera quelconque.
  Dans une chaîne, LO indique une chaîne quelconque de liaisons
  autres que celles qui figurent explicitement dans la chaîne.

       ../..

<u>LES CATEGORIES</u>

Un terme d'une question désigne une notion appartenant à l'une des catégories suivantes :

- Un vecteur

    N1 ⟵ employé | conjoint | enfant | expérience profession-
               nelle | état civil |

- Une variable ou paramètre d'un vecteur

    Avec valeur numérique:

    N2 N ⟵ date de naissance | âge | salaire |

    Avec valeur alphanumérique:

    N2 AN ⟵ numéro de sécurité sociale | adresse | qualification|
            numéro matricule |

    Avec valeur alphabétique:

    N2 A ⟵ situation de famille | nationalité | sexe | métier |
          langue parlée|

    N2 AM ⟵ nom | prénom   (1)

- Une valeur d'un paramètre

    . numérique:

    VN ⟵ 1 | 2 | 3 | ... "tout nombre"
         un | deux| trois| ...

    . alphanumérique:

    VAN ⟵ "les valeurs que peuvent prendre les paramètres:
        elles sont définies par un format.
        ex. : N° de sécurité sociale : 13 chiffres".

    . alphabétique:

    <VA> ⟵ célibataire | marié | veuf | divorcé | séparé |
        masculin | féminin | français | française | anglais/
        anglaise| ...

    <VAM> ⟵ "Tout mot commençant par une majuscule"

    <V > ⟵ <VN> | <CVAN> | <VA>

- Une unité dans laquelle est exprimée une valeur.

    <N3> ⟵ ans | francs | %

---

(1) On a : N2 ⟵ <N2N> | <N2AN> | <N2A> | <N2AM>

../..

```
-           NB        nombre
```
- Un déterminant

$$D \longleftarrow du \mid de \mid des$$

- Un terme d'affectation

$$E \longleftarrow est \mid sont$$

- Un terme d'appartenance

$$A \longleftarrow a \mid ont \mid dont \mid \text{"verbes actifs terminés par -ant"} \mid$$
$$leur \mid son$$

- Un terme anaphorique

$$I \longleftarrow en \mid il$$

- Un coordonnant

$$K \longleftarrow et \mid ou \mid , \mid mais \mid ni$$

- Des séparateurs

$$S1 \longleftarrow ; \mid . \mid , \mid et \mid ou \mid sauf \mid I$$

- Une comparaison de valeurs

$$RO \longleftarrow plus \mid au\ plus \mid$$
$$moins \mid au\ moins \mid$$
$$maximum \mid au\ maximum \mid maximum\ de \mid$$
$$minimum \mid au\ minimum \mid minimum\ de \mid$$

$$RI \longleftarrow plus\ de \mid moins\ de \mid égal\ à$$

```
        Q         que
```
- Une fonction sur des ensembles de valeurs

$$F \longleftarrow total \mid somme \mid différence \mid moyenne$$

- Un rang

$$OC \longleftarrow premier \mid deuxième \mid troisième$$

- Une relation logique

$$RL \longleftarrow et \mid ou \mid sauf$$

- Une négation

$$NG \longleftarrow ne \mid non$$

- Une transaction

$$T \longleftarrow Liste\ de$$

- Un temps

$$TP \longleftarrow en$$

```
../..
```

<u>Remarques</u>

1.   Les guillemets indiquent une explication.

2.   Les termes situés à droite des formules indiquent non pas des
     mots utilisés dans la question, mais des notions.

3.   Les mots figurent dans un dictionnaire, où est indiqué notam-
     ment la(les) notion(s) à laquelle/auxquelles ils appartiennent.

     Les notions figurent également au dictionnaire; on y indique
     notamment pour les notions N2 les caractéristiques des va-
     leurs correspondantes:

     la nature de la valeur : numérique
                               alphanumérique
                               alphabétique

     le format éventuel

     la présentation typographique (1er terme commençant par une
     majuscule).

4.   On ne peut cependant pas mettre dans un dictionnaire tous les
     mots admissibles. Par exemple, les noms propres des employés
     d'une entreprise peuvent être trop nombreux et changer trop
     souvent.

     Ils sont alors considérés comme des valeurs réparties selon
     leur format, leur nature et leur typographie dans la catégo-
     rie correspondante.

     S'ils n'entrent dans aucune catégorie, ils sont considérés
     comme vides et purement et simplement effacés. Ils sont donc
     admis - dans la mesure où leur présence ne modifie pas le
     sens de la phrase (certains mots vides fréquents sont décla-
     rés tels dans le dictionnaire).

../..

<u>LES LIAISONS</u>

Les catégories peuvent être reliées par les liaisons suivantes,
illustrées par des textes en langage naturel :

L1(N1,N1)   ⟵   Les enfants des employés
                   N1   N1

L2(N2,N1)   ⟵   Les prénoms des employés
                   N2   N1

L3(V,N2)   ⟵   Le nom est Untel
                   N2   V

L4(TP et V) ⟵   En 1972
                   TP V

L4(N3,VN)   ⟵   40   ans
                   VN N3

L5(N3,N1)   ⟵   Employés de 40 ans
                   V   N3

L6(VN,N1)   ⟵   Deux enfants
                   VN   N1

L6(VN,N2)   ⟵   Deux prénoms
                   VN   N2

L7(RO,VN)   ⟵   Plus de 20
                   RO   VN

L7(RO,N1)   ⟵   Plus d'enfants
                   RO   N1

L7(RO,N2)   ⟵   Plus âgés que leur conjoint
                   RO   N2

L7(RO,OC)   ⟵   Egal au troisième
                   RO   OC

L8(F,N2)   ⟵   Total des salaires
                   F   N2

$L8(F^1,F^2)$ ⟵   Total des moyennes
                   F   F

L8(F,N1)   ⟵   Total des employés
                   F   N1

L8(F,OC)   ⟵   Total des premiers salaires
                   F   OC

L9(OC,N1)   ⟵   Le troisième enfant
                   OC   N1

L9(OC,N2)   ⟵   Le troisième prénom
                   OC   N2

../..

L10(RL,V) ⟵ ou 40
              RL V

L10(RL,N1) ⟵ ou les enfants
               RL   N1

L10(RC,N2) ⟵ et les prénoms
               RL   N2

L11(T,N2) ⟵ Liste des âges
              T   N2

L11(T,N1) ⟵ Liste des employés
              T   N1

L11(T,F) ⟵ Liste de la moyenne des salaires
             T   F

L11(T,OC) ⟵ Liste des troisièmes salaires
              T   OC

L11(T,VN) ⟵ Liste de 3 enfants
              T   VN

L11(T,I) ⟵ Listez - en
             T   I

L12($N1_1$,$N1_2$) ⟵ Les enfants qui sont employés
                           $N1_1$ $N1_2$

L12($N2_1$,$N2_2$) ⟵ Les noms qui sont des prénoms
                           $N2_1$ $N2_2$

L13(NG,V) ⟵ Les gens qui n'ont pas 40 ans
                                     NG V

L13(NG,OC) ⟵ Sauf le troisième
               NG   OC

L13(NG,RO) ⟵ Pas plus de trois
               NG   RO

L13(NG,N2) ⟵ Pas de diplômes
               NG   N2

L13(NG,N1) ⟵ Pas d'enfants
               NG   N1

L14(N1,I) ⟵ L'employé a 2 enfants; le premier en a 1
                          N1   I

L15(N2,I) ⟵ L'employé est âgé de 50 ans; le fils en a 20
                          N2   I

L16(I,V) ⟵ Le fils en a 20
             I   V

L17(V^1,V^2) ⟵ Untel a 20 ans
                     V   V

L6 (VN et NB) ←— enfants en nombre de 2
                 NB   VN

L7 (R1 et N1) ←— plus d'enfants
        R1   N1

L7 (R1 et N2) ←—plus de prénoms
       R1   N2

L7 (R1 et NB) ←— nombre supérieur à
        NB   R1

L7 (RO et Q) ←— plus agé que
        RO   Q

L7 (NB et V) ←— Le nombre de Dubois
        NB   V

L8 (F et NB) ←— Total du nombre
        F   NB

L8 (F et V) ←— Total des Dubois
        F   V

L9 (OC et V ←— Le troisième Dubois
        OC   V

DEFINITION DE LA BANQUE DE DONNEES ET DES QUESTIONS A PARTIR DES LIAISONS.

DEFINITION DE LA BANQUE DE DONNEES

1. La Structure

La structure d'une banque de données peut être définie comme un ensemble de restrictions apportées aux liaisons possibles L1 et L2 entre les termes ou notions des catégories N1 et N2.

Relations L1

Ainsi, la liaison L1 ne peut pas exister entre toutes les notions N1.

On supposera que les liaisons possibles ont une structure arborescente, les notions N1 étant les sommets et les liaisons, les arcs.

On indiquera par un index haut le rang dans cette structure:

$N1^0$ sera le vecteur origine

$N1^1$ "   "   conjoint..

$N1^2$ "   "   enfant ...

Ainsi, tout N1 est relié par une chaîne de L1 à $N1^0$.

Relations L2

De même, certaines liaisons L2 seulement existent entre les notions N1 et N2.
Exemple : seuls les employés (N1) peuvent avoir une qualification professionnelle (N2).

Cependant,
- pour tout N2, il y a au moins une liaison L2.
(il peut y en avoir plusieurs. Exemple : le prénom (N2) peut être celui d'un enfant (N1) ou d'un employé (N1) ou d'un conjoint (N1).

- donc, tout N2 est relié par une chaîne de L2 et L1 à $N1^0$.
- pour tout N1, il y a au moins une liaison L2. On en privilégie une. Pour le niveau $N1^0$ on appellera le N2 correspondant ' la clé' et on la notera $N2^0$.

D'une façon générale, N1 peut se définir par l'ensemble des N2 qui lui sont liés par la relation L2.

../..

2. <u>Les Enregistrements</u>

- Tout paramètre N2 est affecté d'au moins une valeur. En général, il y en a plusieurs.

- Si on appelle V^0 la valeur liée à $N2^0$ par L3, un 'enregistrement' sera l'ensemble des valeurs V reliées par L18 (VV^0) à un V^0 donné.

Il y a donc autant d'enregistrements que de V^0.

- Tout V relié à un V^0 par L18 (VV^0) est relié à un N2 par L3 (N2,V)

- Si pour un même N2, on a des valeurs V_1, V_2,...V_n et une valeur V^0 telles que

$$L3 \ (N2 \ V1)$$
$$L3 \ (N2 \ V2)$$
$$...$$
$$L3 \ (N2 \ Vn)$$

et

$$L18 \ (V1 \ V^0)$$
$$L18 \ (V2 \ V^0)$$
$$L18 \ (Vn \ V^0)$$

on dit qu'il y a plusieurs occurences de N2 dans l'enregistrement défini par V^0. Ces occurences sont supposées ordonnées selon un "rang d'arrivée" et ne peuvent être distinguées dans la question que par un terme OC ("premier", "deuxième"..)

<u>DEFINITION D'UNE QUESTION</u>

Une question Q peut être définie par

$Q \longleftarrow$ (ensemble de transactions)　　(ensemble de contraintes)

(ensemble de transactions)$\longleftarrow$ L11 et C1 et L2 $\{$ etL6 $\{$ et L7 (RO etV) $\}\}$ $\{$ et L8 $\}$ $\{$ et L9 $\}$ $\{$ et L10 $\{$ et L13 (NG et OC) $\}$ $\{$ et L13 (NG et RO) $\}$ $\{$ et L13 (NG et N2) et L13 (NG et N1) $\}$

(ensemble de contraintes)$\longleftarrow (L3)^n$ et C1 et $(L2)^h$ et $\overline{L11}$ $\{$ et LO $\}$

$C \ 1 \longleftarrow (L1)^n$ et L1 (Ni et Ni^0)

n indique le nombre des contraintes.

On délimite les ensembles de contraintes et les contraintes en ne permettant à un N1 ou un N2 de prolonger les chaînes qui les compose que par des liaisons L1 et L2.

../..

Il y a autant de questions que de chaînes L2 et C1.

Dans le traitement d'une question, les contraintes sont supposées être reliées par la relation 'et', sauf

- s'il y a dans une contrainte une chaîne L10 et L3 et L2 et
  L1, la relation logique est alors celle exprimée par L10.

- s'il y a deux contraintes L3(V1 et N2) et L7(RO et V1) d'une
  part, L3(V1 et N2) et L7 (RO et V2) d'autre part avec RO ⟵
  égal à, et le même N2, c'est la relation 'ou' qui relie les
  deux contraintes correspondantes. La relation 'et' est supposée
  distributive par rapport à la relation 'ou'.

../..

L'ANALYSE

La recherche de la réponse dans une banque de données à partir
de questions telles qu'elles ont été définies sont du ressort
des "query languages" (comme G1S ou IQF). Cette partie du traitement n'est pas évoquée ici; on remarquera juste que la structure
physique des données dans la banque peut être différente de celle
à laquelle se réfère mentalement le questionneur, différence qui
rejaillit évidemment sur les procédures de recherche.

Outre l'analyse lexicologique (1), le traitement comporte deux
étapes:

- l'analyse des liaisons explicitées dans le texte;

- le passage des liaisons explicites à la question.

   La nécessité de cette deuxième étape tient au caractère
   elliptique ou redondant du langage.

LES LIAISONS EXPLICITEES

Les règles ci-dessous s'appliquent de haut en bas; toute la phrase
est passée en revue avant de passer à la règle suivante.

A,B, en partie droite, signifie A,$\overline{A}$,$\overline{B}$,B : pour que deux termes
de catégories A et B soient liés, il ne doit pas y avoir de tels
termes entre eux.

A,B,B signifie qu'on considère la liaison entre A et le B le plus
à droite.

Ce qui est entre deux ";" indique les catégories qui ne peuvent
plus intervenir dans certaines règles ultérieures, et les règles
correspondantes (repérées par un n° de règle ou de ligne). Il est
clair qu'on peut écrire cette condition en introduisant de nouvel-
les catégories; une telle façon de faire a paru moins parlante.

<u>Liste des règles</u>

1   L4(VN,N3)$\longleftarrow$ VN,$\overline{\overline{K}}$,N3   ;VN,L6;VN,L3

2   L4(N3,VN)$\longleftarrow$ N3,$\overline{K}$,VN   "   "

3   L4(TP,VN)$\longleftarrow$ TP VN   "   "

4   INT1 $\longleftarrow$ N1 ou N2

5   L6(VN,INT1)$\longleftarrow$ VN $\{OC\}$ INT1   ;VN,L3;VN,L16;

6   L6(INT1,VN)$\longleftarrow$ INT1,$\overline{K}$,VN   "   "

____

(1) cf. Réf.2

```
7    L16(I,V)      ⟵— I {A}  {RO} V              ;VN,L3;

8    L9(OC,INT1)⟵— OC {OC}{D} N2

9    INT2          ⟵— VN ou INT1 ou OC'

10   L7(RO,INT2)⟵— RO   INT2

11   L7(INT2,RO)⟵--- INT2   RO

12   INT3          ⟵— INT2 ou RO

13   L13(NG,INT3)⟵—   NG,K̄,INT3

14   L13(INT3,NG)⟵--   INT3 {N3} NG

15   INT4          ⟵— INT2 ou F

16   L11(T,INT4) ⟵— T,K̄,INT4                 ; INT4,81

17   PL2           ⟵--L4 ou L6 ou L7 ou L9 ou L11 ou L13

18   INT5          ⟵--N3 ou TP ou INT3 ou NG
```

$$21 \quad PL2(INT5_1,INT5_2),PL2(INT5_1,INT5_3)$$
$$\Longleftarrow PL2(INT5_1,INT5_2)\text{')'}INT5_3;\ INT5_1,22;VN,L3;INT4,81;$$
$$INT4,82$$

$$22 \quad PL2(INT5_1,INT5_2),PL2(INT5_1,INT5_3)$$
$$\Longleftarrow PL2(INT5_1,INT5_2)\ K\ INT5_3;VN,L3;INT4,81;INT4,82$$

$$23 \quad PL2(INT5_1,INT5_2),PL2(INT5_3,INT5_1)$$
$$\Longleftarrow INT5_3\text{', '}PL2(INT5_1,INT5_2);INT5_2,24;VN,L3;INT4,81;$$
$$INT4,82.$$

$$24 \quad PL2(INT5_1,INT5_2),PL2(INT5_1,INT5_3)$$
$$\Longleftarrow INT5_3\ K\ PL2(INT5_1,INT5_2);VN,L3;INT4,81;INT4,82$$

On appelle R(PL2 et INT5) la suite des 4 implications précédentes
avec ;INT5, 22;INT5$_2$,24;

```
31   L3(N2,V)      ⟵—N2,K̄,V

32   L3(V,N2)      ⟵—V,K̄,N2

33   PL2           ⟵—L3

34   INT5          ⟵—V ou N2

35   R(PL2 et INT5)
```

../..

```
41   L5(N1,N3)   ⟵── N1,N̄2,N3

42   PL2          ⟵── L5

43   INT5         ⟵── N1 ou N3

44   R(PL2 et INT5)

46   L16(INT1,I) ⟵── INT1,'en'

47   L15(INT1,I) ⟵── (INT1,)ⁿ I

51   L2(N2,N1)    ⟵── N2,K̄,N1

52   PL2          ⟵── L2

53   INT5         ⟵── N2 ou N1

54   R(PL2 et INT5)

55   L2(N1,N2)    ⟵── N1,N2

56   R(PL2 et INT5)

61   L1(N1,N1)    ⟵──N1,(D et K̄ et N̄2),N1

62   L1   (N1,N1) ⟵──N1,K̄,N1

63   PL2          ⟵──L1

64   INT5         ⟵──N1

65   R(PL2 et INT5)

66   L8(F,INT4)  ⟵──F,(K̄ et D),INT4            ; INT4,83

67   L8(F,V)      ⟵──F,(D et INT4‾)

68   INT6         ⟵──INT1 ou F ou 'en'

69   L8(INT6,F)  ⟵──INT6,F

70   PL2          ⟵──L8

71   INT5         ⟵──INT4 ou V

72   R(PL2 et INT5)

73   INT7         ⟵──INT3 ou INT4 ou V

74   L10(RL,INT7)⟵──RL, INT7

75   L12(N1,N1)   ⟵──N1,E,N1

81   L11(T,INT4) ⟵──T, { AX INT2 }, INT4

82   L11('en',T) ⟵──'en',T

83   L8(F,INT4)  ⟵─F, { AX INT2 },INT4
```

Ces règles de liaison s'appliquent sous ^{des} conditions générales
d'accord (de genre, de nombre.. et des conditions sémantiques par-
ticulières (un âge ne peut être inférieur à une ancienneté, par
exemple.

LE PASSAGE DES LIASONS EXPLICITES A LA QUESTION

Le texte du questionneur fait référence à la banque de données et
définit la question de façon incomplète (certaines chaînes de
liaison sont juste signalées, de façon non ambiguë, mais certaines
liaisons manquent pour le traitement) ou de façon redondante (plusieurs liaisons indiquent la même chose). On ne peut réduire cette
étape en raison de la possibilité d'exprimer la même chose de dif-
férentes façons.

Le tableau suivant se lit de haut en bas.

../..

Commentaires

$L2(N1$ et $N2)$ et $L3(N2$ et $V)$ et $L4(V$ et $N3)$ ⟵ $L5(N3$ et $N1)$ et $L2(N1$ et $N2)$ et
$L3(N2$ et $V)$ et $L4(V$ et $N3)$

Tous les N2 compatibles avec N1 et N3

$L2(N1$ et $N2)$ et $L3(N2$ et $VN)$ et $L4(VN$ et $N3)$ ⟵ $L5(N1$ et $N3)$ et $L4(N3$ et $VN)$

RO ⟵ égal à
Tous les N2 compatibles avec N3

$L4(N3$ et $VN)$ et $L7(VN$ et $Q)$ et $L7(Q$ et $RO)$ ⟵ $L4(N3$ et $VN)$ et $\overline{L7(VN\ et\ RO)}$
et $L7(RO$ et $N2)$

$L11(T$ et $N1)$ et $L6(VN$ et $N1)$ ⟵ $L11(T$ et $VN)$ et $L6(VN$ et $N1)$
$L11(T$ et $N2)$ et $L6(VN$ et $N2)$ ⟵ $L11(T$ et $VN)$ et $L6(VN$ et $N2)$

$L6(N1$ et $V)$ ⟵ $L16(N1$ et $I)$ et $L17(I$ et $V)$
$L6(N2$ et $VN)$ et $L6(N2$ et $VN_2)$ ⟵ $L16(N2$ et $I)$ et $L17(I$ et $VN2)$ et
$L6(N2$ et $VN_1)$

$L3(N2$ et $V)$ ⟵ $L16(N2$ et $I)$ et $L17(I$ et $V)$ et
$\overline{L6(N2\ et\ V)}$

RO ⟵ égal à
$N2_d$: option par défaut(1)

$L7(VN$ et $Q)$ $L7(Q$ et $RO)$ et $L7(RQ$ et $NB)$
et $L(NB$ et $V)$ et $L3(V$ et $N2_d)$ et $L2(N2_d$ et $N1)$
⟵ $L6(VN$ et $N1)$

RO ⟵ égal à

$L7(VN$ et $RO)$ et $L7(RO$ et $NB)$
et $L6(V$ et $NB)$ et $L3(V$ et $N2)$
⟵ $L6(VN$ et $N2)$

$L2(N1_1$ et $N2_d)$ et $L7(N2d$ et $RO)$ et ⟵ $L12(N1_1$ et $N1_2)$
$L7(RO_1$ et $Q)$ et $L7(Q$ et $N2_d)$ et $L2(N2_d$ et $N1_2)$

$L7(N2_1$ et $RO)$ et $L7(RO$ et $Q)$ et $L7(Q$ et $N2_2)$ ⟵ $L12(N2_1$ et $N2_2)$

$L2(N1_1$ et $N2_1)$ et $L7(N2_1$ et $RO)$ et $L7(ROetQ)$ ⟵ ⎡ $L2(N1_1$ et $N2_1)$ et $L7(N2_1$ et $RO)$
et $L7(RO$ et $Q)$ et

$L7(Q$ et $N1_2)$ et $L2(N1_2$ et $N2_1)$ ⎦ $L7(Q$ et $N1_2)$ et $\overline{L2(N1_2\ et\ N2)}$

$L2(N1_1$ et $N2_1)$ et $L7(N2_1$ et $RO)$ et $L7(RO$ et $Q)$ ⟵ ⎡ $L2(N1_1$ et $N2_1)$ et $L7(N2_1$ et $RO)$
⎣ et $L7(RO_1$ et $Q)$

____
(1) La notion par défaut n'est pas forcément la 'clé'

et L7(Q etN2$_2$) et L2(N1$_1$ et N2$_2$)   ⎫⎧ et L7(Q et N2$_2$) et $\overline{\text{L2(N2}_2 \text{ et N1)}}$

L2(N1 et N2$_d$) et L3(N2$_d$ et V) et L7(V et NB)←L7(R1 et N1) et $\overline{\text{L2(N1 et N2)}}$
et L7(NB et R1)

L3(N2 et V) et L7(V et NB)et L7(NB et R1) ←L7(R1 et N2)

L3(N2 et V) et L7 (V et RO)   ←L7(RO et N2) ·et $\overline{\text{L3(N2 et V)}}$

L8(F et V) et L3(V et N2)   ←L8(F et N2)

L8(F et NB) et L7(NB et V) et L3(V et N2$_d$) ←L8(F et N1)

L8(F et V) et L3(V et N2) et L9(OC et V)   ←L8(F et OC) et L9(OC et N2)

L9(OC et V) et L3(V et N2$_d$) et L2(N2$_d$ et N1)← L9(OC et N1)

L9(OC et V) et L3(V et N2)   ← L9(OC et N2)

L2(N1 et N2$_d$) et L3(N2$_d$ et V) et L11(T et V)← L11(T et N1)

L3(N2 et V) et L11(T et V)← L11(T et N2)

L2(N1 et N2$_d$) et L3(N2$_d$ et V) et L9(OC et V)←L11(T et OC) et L9(OC et N1)
et L11(T et V)

L3(N2$_d$ et V) et L9(OC et V) et L11(T et V) ←L11(T et OC) et L9(OC et N2)

L18(V$_1$ et V$_2$)   ←L2(N1 et N2$_1$) et L3(N2$_1$ et V$_1$)
et L2(N1 et N2$_2$) et L3(N2$_2$ et V2)

CONCLUSION

1.

Une question posée en français à une banque de données exprime des
liaisons entre notions qui permettent de définir la-dite banque.

La structure - hiérarchique comme ici ou autre - se traduit par
des restrictions sur les types de liaisons possibles. Ces restrictions permettent d'interprêter une question partiellement implicite
comme le font les dernières règles indiquées.

D'ailleurs, dans la mesure où ces règles parviennent à traduire une
question sous une forme normalisée, on peut vérifier si une structure de données prédéterminée y est sous-jacente.

2.

L'analyse a été présentée à l'aide d'une grammaire non-contiguë.
Le concept de grammaire non contiguë n'est pas lié à une structure
de données particulière. L'intérêt pratique qu'il présente est de
réduire le traitement lorsque l'on veut isoler une des grammaires
(linguistique, psychologique..) qui sillonnent un texte.

Pour le situer brièvement, on peut rappeler que dans une grammaire
classique, A◄——BC indique que dans le texte, il y a :

        A   et   B

        A   avant B

        A   contigu à B

Comme les deux dernières conditions entraînent la première, on peut
définir trois "grammaires" moins structurées en prenant un sous-
ensemble de ces conditions :

        A   et   B   : "grammaire documentaire"

        A   avant   B   : "grammaires non contiguës"

        A   contigu à B : "grammaires non temporelles"

Les grammaires classiques correspondent assez bien à la syntaxe du
français, où les structures sont emboitées, mais moins à la sémantique où interviennent des imbrications du .type

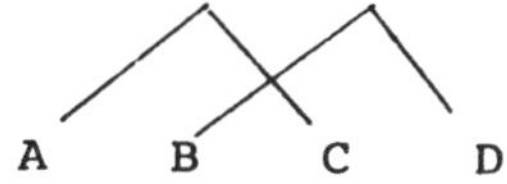

dues notamment aux anaphores. Des règles non contiguës peuvent
alors être un outil souple d'analyse.

../..

Une grammaire non contiguë dissocie également une certaine précédence implicite liée à la contiguité dans les grammaires classiques:

Ainsi, les règles

$$A \longleftarrow BC$$

$$D \longleftarrow B\ E\ C$$

appliquées à un texte B E C donnent D

Par contre,

$$A \qquad B,C$$

$$D \qquad B,E,C$$

peuvent donner A + D ou A et D selon que l'on établit ou non une précédence entre les règles, et laquelle.

Indiquer une précédence, c'est donner une hiérarchie entre les liaisons reconnues par la grammaire. Dans une grammaire non contiguë, c'est supposer que cette hiérarchie n'est pas toujours liée à la syntaxe : on remplace l'inventaire complet des suites de caractères par des conditions paramétrées.

$$A \longleftarrow B,C \quad \text{est équivalent à} \quad A \longleftarrow B\ X\ C, \forall X$$

(Cela conduit à dresser des règles négatives du type $A \longleftarrow B,\overline{E},C$)

$A \longleftarrow B\ X\ C \quad \forall X$ n'est pas choquant si on considère que toute grammaire reconnaît un ensemble fini de liaisons et que certaines liaisons peuvent devoir se faire (telles que   valeur numérique - unité). Aussi bien, une telle règle se prête assez bien à un apprentissage. (1)

Cette précédence permet également une interaction entre plusieurs grammaires, (ce à quoi se réfère, par exemple, l'expression courante : "Ça dépend de la façon dont c'est dit")

Signalons enfin qu'en plus de la place et du sens (qu'il soit un concept ou une adresse) des mots, la grammaire non contiguë s'adapte bien à l'analyse de la forme des mots nécessaire pour des analyses telles que celle des règles d'accords.

---

(1)   Dans un processus d'apprentissage basé sur des statistiques, des règles provisoires telles que
$$A \qquad B\ \overline{C}\ D$$
$$A \qquad B, \{C\}, D$$
peuvent ne pas être oiseuses pour marquer des configurations probables.

ELEMENTS DE BIBLIOGRAPHIE

 Aux travaux très connus de BAR-HILLEL, BLACK, BOBROW, GREEN,
HEWITT, KELLOG, LANDSDALE, QUILLIAN,SIMMONS, THOMPSON, WEISENBAUM,
WINOGRAD, WILKS, WOODS,...
on peut ajouter ceux d'auteurs français.

ADRIEN: CIG, une expérience d'interrogation d'une banque
            d'informations en langage naturel. Revue "Automa-
            tisme", Juillet 1972

ADRIEN, LAFIEVRE, RIVOALLAN, ROLLAN: Interprétation du lan-
            gage naturel en vue de l'interrogation d'une base
            de données. Développement Scientifique, IBM France.

COLMERAUER, KANONI, PASERO, ROUSSEL: Un système de communi-
            cation homme-machine en français . Groupe de
            Recherche en Intelligence Artificielle. U.E.R. de
                 Université d'Aix - Marseille.

D. COULON et D. KAISER : Analyse de réponses rédigées en
            français courant. A.F.C.E.T. Revue Française d'Au-
            tomatique, Informatique, Recherche Opérationnelle,
            Juin 1972.

M. PEUCHOT : Contribution à la recherche en méthodologie de
            l'enseignement assisté sur ordinateur.

APPLICATIONS OF PATTERN RECOGNITION TO THE DIAGNOSIS OF EQUIPMENT FAILURES*

L.F. Pau

Abstract: The theory of a feature extraction method, called correspondence analysis, is given. It is applied to learning datas made of all available informations about a given type of equipment, as stored in a reliability and maintenance data bank.

Correspondence analysis is a variant of principal component analysis, based upon a CHI-square distributional metric wherein patterns and observations play symmetrical roles. A simultaneous graphical representation of both patterns and observations helps in analyzing the operational behaviour of the equipment for design review and maintenance control; two examples hereof are given for an airborne equipment, and for resistor components.

Real time diagnosis and fault localization have been achieved, thanks to a real time data compression into the reduced feature space generated by correspondence analysis, and by a sequential recognition procedure. This procedure is the generalized nearest neighbour rule, applied sequentially to learning sets of increasing size; the stopping rule uses a compromise between recognition time and the misclassification probability. An example of automated real time testing is given, showing a 92% true recognition rate for acceptable items produced by machine-tools, and a mean correct diagnosis rate of 81% for non-accepted items. 16 references.

---

* This paper is part of a course in Technical Diagnosis at the Ecole Nationale Supérieure de l'Aéronautique et de l'Espace, France.

1. INTRODUCTION

The purpose of any diagnosis searching procedure is to recognize a failure, or a set of failures (also called syndrome), on the basis of:

. informations about the past history of the equipment, including maintenance and operational utilization, alltogether called learning data; these learning data are stored in a reliability and maintenance data bank, with permanent updating.

. informations about the circumstances of the failure (s), visual observations of the equipment, and results of non-destructive tests, alltogether called pattern coordinates.

The "correlation" of the present symptomas described by the pattern parameters, with the learning data, yields a classification of the ill-working equipment into some few classes of possible failure causes. A final decision is made regarding the class membership of the observed equipment by a stored decision rule.

Such a diagnosis searching procedure can be formalized as a pattern recognition problem, the unknown patterns being the equipments described by pattern coordinates. Some research has been reported since 1968 on testing methods which were automated to varying degrees and which utilize pattern recognition. HANKLEY and MERRILL[5] consider the error analysis problem in an inertia platform; BECKER[1] and PAGE[8] detect up to three faults on the basis of jet engine vibrations; CORTINA[3] reports operational results on truck motors and PAU[9] on airborne electromechanical equipments.

Our discussion will be centered around the practical applications of a pattern recognition technique designed in order to contribute to the solution of following problems P1-P3:

P1:   eliminate all redundant tests and observations, and select those synthetic observations yielding the best discrimination between the failure causes: this is the feature extraction or data compression problem;

P2:   how to build a satisfactory list of a few relevant diagnosis assumptions, and to display the relations among these on some drawings;

P3:   automation of the diagnosis or test procedure, through a minimization of the misclassification probability.

2. REDUCTION OF THE LEARNING DATAS AND DESIGN REVIEW

This part is devoted to the description of the data used, and to a short development of the feature extraction algorithm to be applied.

2.1. Description of the learning datas $k(I,J)$

Assume that all learning datas $k(I,J) = \{k(i,j) \geq 0, i \in I \ j \in J\}$ about equipments $j \in J$ of the same type, are coded and stored in a data bank:

$$k(i,j) = \begin{cases} 1 & \text{symptoma } i \text{ present} \\ 0 & - \quad i \text{ absent or missing information} \end{cases}$$

and/or

$$k(i,j) = \text{measured value } i \text{ concerning the equipment } j,$$
$$\text{i.e. time since last overhaul } TBO_j,$$
$$\text{operational circumstances,...}$$

In the coding, at most N different types of information c = 1,N are given about each equipment j, due to the content of the failure/ maintenance reports. Each information "c" has a fixed set of alternatives "i", corresponding for example to a fixed partition of the intervals "i" of variations of the time since last overhaul "c".

2.2. Transformations of the tableau k(I,J)

The past experiments have shown that misleading conclusions may be drawn from once compressed learning data, either because of too small learning samples, or because of uncarefully filled reports. Methods to account for these phenomenons have been thoroughly tested in practice and justified theoretically (PAU[9]). Other transformations may be done, in order to study the learning datas from specific viewpoints:

a) the learning data k(I,J) are called explicit if one of the sets I, J designates equipments, and the other observations about these (as in 2.1).

b) the learning data k(I,J) are called implicit if both sets I, J are observations; such a tableau is deduced from an explicit tableau by aggregating some observations with respect to all equipments, or by classifying all equipments with respect to some observations. For example, if J has become the set of TBO intervals, we may define:

$$k(i,j) = \text{number of learning equipments having had a failure}$$
$$\text{in the TBO-interval "j", and on which the symptoma}$$
$$\text{"i" was present.}$$

Design review uses generally learning data in the implicit form (2.4, 2.5), while automated diagnosis uses the explicit form (3.).

2.3. Feature extraction by the means of correspondence analysis

Assume that the tableau k(I,J) of non-negative numbers is given. The feature extraction procedure used herein, is a special form of principal component analysis, characterized by the following additional properties demonstrated in BENZECRI[2] and PAU[10]:

- no a priori hypothesis is made about the nature of the elements in the sets I (failures) and J (observations or equipments), and all interactions are considered;in other words, we do not care for the labels in the sets I and J.

- all elements in both sets I and J may be displayed simultaneously in the same reduced feature space, because they play symmetrical roles in a tableau; in this reduced pattern space, the euclidean distance between any two elements of I-J, I-I, or J-J, is an overall statistical measure of the correspondence between those elements, independently of all scale effects.

It can be shown that the principal component analysis, factor analysis, and the present correspondence analysis are all special forms of the KARHUNEN-LOEWE expansion or Varimax principle, for different choices of the metrics on I, J and/or of the criterion used (see KULIKOWSKY[6], WATANABE[15]). We will therefore describe correspondence analysis according to the common guidelines:

a) The non-negative learning datas k(I,J) are transformed into an estimated contingency table p(I,J):

$$p(i,j) = k(i,j) \Big/ \Big(\sum_{\substack{\ell \in I \\ m \in J}} k(\ell,m) \Big)$$

with estimated marginal probability density functions as in a contingency table:

$$p^I = \{p(i,.) = \sum_{j \in J} p(i,j)/i \in I\} \quad \text{Prob}(j|i) = p(i,j)|p(i,.)$$

$$P_J = \{p(.,j) = \sum_{i \in I} p(i,j)/j \in J\} \quad \text{Prob}(i|j) = j(i,j)|p(.,j)$$

b) The metric on I is the distance function d_I, while the metric on J is the distance function d_J:

$$d_I^2(i_1,i_2) = \sum_{j \in J} [\text{Prob}(j|i_1)-\text{Prob}(j|i_2)]^2/p(.,j)$$

$$d_J^2(j_1,j_2) = \sum_{i \in I} [\text{Prob}(i|j_1)-\text{Prob}(i|j_2)]^2/p(i,.)$$

c) The element i has the weight p(i,.), while j has the weight p(.,j). The element i has Card (J) coordinates

$$(\text{Prob}(j|i)) \quad j = 1, \text{Card (J)}.$$

The element j has Card (I) coordinates

$$(\text{Prob}(i|j)) \quad i = 1, \text{Card (I)}.$$

d) Let be given a constant $r <$ Inf(Card (I), Card (J)). We want to minimize, in the sense of the d_I or d_J metric, the dependence between I,J defined as $||p(I,J) - P^I P_J||^2$.

It can be shown that the r-dimensional vector basis of basic features which minimizes this dependence after transforming Card (I) - or Card (J) - dimensional patterns in k(I,J) into r-dimensional feature vectors, can be constructed as follows (see PAU($9,10$)).

- for I the r base vectors f_ℓ ℓ = 1,r are the r first principal axes of inertia of the solid body made of the discrete Card (J) dimensional elements $i \in I$ having the weight p(i,.); this inertia is computed for the d_I distance; let $\lambda(f_\ell)$ be the inertia of axis f_ℓ ℓ = 1,r ordered by $\lambda(f_1) > \lambda(f_2) >...> \lambda(f_r)$; the f_ℓ's are normed to the unit length with respect to d_I. And $f_\ell(\lambda_\ell)$ is the (ℓ+1)'st eigenvector (resp. eigenvalue) of the S = $\left[s_{j_1 j_2} \right]$ matrix:

$$\left[\begin{array}{l} s_{j_1 j_2} = \sum_{i=1,\text{Card}(I)} p(i,j_1)p(i,j_2)/p(i,.) \sqrt{p(.,j_1)p(.,j_2)} \\ \\ j_1,j_2 = 1, \text{Card (J)} \end{array} \right.$$

- for J, we have equivalent definitions and relations for the r basis vectors g_ℓ ℓ = 1,r.

f_ℓ, g_ℓ ℓ = 1,r are here row vectors, i.e. linear mappings.

- or: the failure mode i_1 may systematically be the main cause of the failure i_2, or conversely.

b) It can be shown that, when the sample size $\sum_{I,J} k(i,j)$ becomes infinite, the asymptotic distributions of d_I, d_J, d, are CHI-square distributions with (Card (I)-1)(Card (J)-1) degrees of freedom; we do therefore obtain a natural clustering and discrimination between failures, quite equivalent to CHI-square partitions in a contingency table.

Moreover, the interpretation phase suggests a simple answer to problem P2 with applications to design review and maintenance control. We will use the natural clustering obtained in the data compression process, and the meaning of the metrics d_I, d_J, d; the goal will be to express in the physical terms used for the definitions of the i's and the j's, the associations corresponding to the geometrical proximities observed on the maps of decreasing weights.

a) In the first phase, we will interpret the natural clusters obtained; if any two points are:

- d-very close, those points will be very strongly associated with respect to the d_I, d_J similarity measures: one point is very probably the cause of the other one, or conversely;

- d-close, these points will often have a similar behaviour with respect to d_I, d_J and there exists a causality relation between them at a medium level;

- d-distant, those points will often have different behaviour, and the causality association is weak in the sense of d_I, d_J.

Once an association has been detected, i.e. between certain failures and maintenance operations, the maintenance department will have to give technical reasons herefore, or demonstrate why it is meaningless.

b) In the second phase, which is the confirmation of the first one, the d-distances measured on the map, and CHI-square tables are used to compute the probabilities that two vectors p(J/i) or p(I/j) are identical.

c) In the third phase, we want to select those observations or failures having effectively an influence upon the extracted features. This is done by a study of the contributions to the r features, as illustrated below in the case of I:

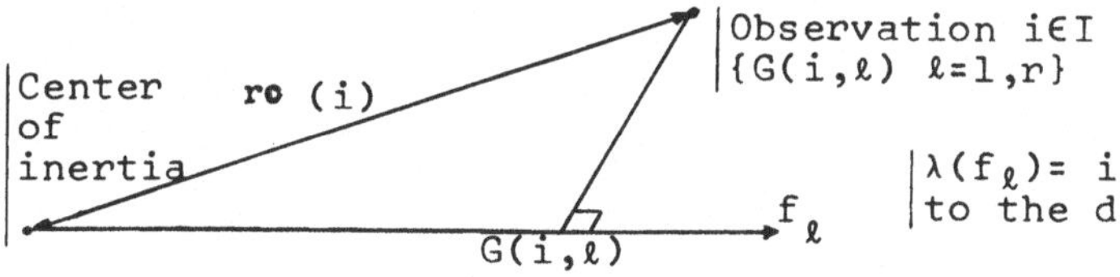

Center of inertia — ro (i) — Observation $i \in I$ — $\{G(i,\ell)\ \ell=1,r\}$ — $\lambda(f_\ell)$ = inertia with respect to the direction f_ℓ. — $G(i,\ell)$ — f_ℓ

$$p(i,j) = p(i,.)p(.,j)(1 + \sum_\ell F(j,\ell)G(i,\ell)\sqrt{\lambda(f\ell)})$$

$$\lambda(f_\ell) = \sum_{i \in I} p(i,.)G(i,\ell)^2$$

$p(i,.)ro(i)^2$ = absolute contribution of i
$p(i,.)G(i,\ell)^2$ = absolute contribution of i to $\lambda(f_\ell)$
$G(i,\ell)^2$ = absolute contribution of feature ℓ to i
$G(i,\ell)^2/ro(i)^2$ = relative contribution of feature ℓ to i

Figure 1: Study of the contributions in the extracted feature space for I.

e) The coordinates of the learning patterns projected into the
    r-dimensional feature space, are computed as follows:

    - for I, the feature ℓ=1,r of learning pattern i∈I on the axis f_ℓ,
    originated in the center of inertia of all elements in I, is
    given by (see Figure 1):

$$G(i,\ell) = f_\ell \cdot [\text{Prob}(j|i) \; j = 1, \text{Card}(J) \; \text{vector}] \qquad [1]$$

    - for J, the feature ℓ of learning pattern j∈J on the axis g_ℓ,
    originated in the center of inertia of all elements in J, is
    given by:

$$F(j,\ell) = g_\ell \cdot [\text{Prob}(i|j) \; i = 1, \text{Card}(I) \; \text{vector}] \qquad [2]$$

f) I can be shown that $\lambda(f_\ell) = \lambda(g_\ell)$ ℓ = 1,r, and that it is
    sufficient to compute either the f_ℓ's or the g_ℓ's because:

$$\left[\begin{array}{l} g_\ell \quad = \dfrac{1}{\sqrt{\lambda(f_\ell)}} \quad f_\ell \left[\text{Prob}(j/i) \begin{array}{l} i = \text{column} \\ j = \text{row} \end{array} \right] \\[2em] G(i,\ell) = \displaystyle\sum_{j=1,\text{Card}(J)} F(j,\ell)\,\text{Prob}(i|j) / \sqrt{\lambda(f_\ell)} \qquad \ell=1,r \end{array} \right. \qquad [3]$$

Moreover, the latter formula transforms biunivocally a d_I -
orthonormal vector base into a d_J - orthonormal vector base of
same dimension r and with the corresponding unit lengths.
Consequently, all elements of I and J may be displayed
simultaneously in this feature space f_ℓ ℓ = 1,r, thanks to
formulas [1][2][3]. In this space, the euclidean distance d
between any two elements of I or J being proportional to d_I, we
may also measure mixed d_I distances between an element of I
and an element of J (see BENZECRI([2]), PAU([10])).

g) The best two-dimensional (r=2) approximation of the learning data
    (see BENZECRI([2]), PAU([10])),is obtained by displaying all elements
    of I and J on the (f_1, f_2) plane which contains the largest
    inertia, namely ($\lambda(f_1)$ + $\lambda(f_2)$). Such a 2-dimensional
    approximation will be called a map, and any pair of vectors
    f_ℓ, f_m yields such a map of weight $\lambda(f_\ell)$ + $\lambda(f_m)$.

2.4. Application to design review and control of maintenance

The correspondence analysis used as indicated is an answer to the
problem P1:

a) All redundant observations can be identified: the distance d_I,
    and thus d, of any two observations i_1,i_2 in I will be small
    if they are conditionally associated in the same way to all
    observations of J:

$$\forall j \in J \quad \text{Prob}(j|i_1) = \text{Prob}(j|i_2) \Rightarrow d_I(i_1,i_2) = 0 \Rightarrow d(i_1,i_2) \neq 0$$

Thus, if two failures i_1,i_2 are represented almost by the same
point in the feature space:

    - either: one of the observations i_1,i_2 is redundant, i.e.
    because of the coding, or because one of these observations can
    only be done by taking down a module connected to the other one
    (this is a maintenability question);

If the absolute contribution of the observation $i \in I$ is large, it contributes significantly to $||p(I,J) - P^I P_J||$, which means that an observation i, located far away from the center of the map, and having a small weight $p(i,.)$, does not have much meaning. The relative contribution of the feature ℓ to $i \in I$, indicates whether this feature explains correctly the location of this obsertation.

The main goal of this interpretation procedure is to draw attention upon causality relations among failures, maintenance, modifications, operating conditions and times; it has been applied to both electronic and mechanical airborne equipments in order to:

- detect systematic coding errors;

- criticize maintenance operations and their real time schedule;

- detect subsystem or operating conditions which may be responsible forfailures because of uncareful design, fabrication, maintenance, eventually in some special time intervals.

These preoccupations, as related to specifications and test organizations, are discussed by YOUNG([16]). Our view is that the learning phase must be conducted in parallel with the analysis of experts' special reports, in order to compare them both.

2.5. Example 1: airborne equipment

We will interpret some associations between observations and/or time intervals in the Fig. 2 relative to a radiocompass RNA 26 C. Our main concern will here be to criticize the coding of the learning data of the implicit type 1 explained in Fig. 3.

All observations of class c=1 (physical failure cause) are, except 1DV, 1TR, lined up on the first axis f_1 in the following order: 1TE, 1EM, 1EL, 1ME. The latter classification, obtained through a natural discrimination, is feasible from the technical point of view, namely:

- electromechanical lies halfwaysbetween electrotechnical and passive component failures;

- electrotechnical and mechanical failures are strongly dissociated.

In the same way, the failures of active components are clearly discriminated: these components have quite specific failure causes, mostly between 50 h and 100 h. The other failures are very strongly dissociated from 1TR; which means that there is no ambiguity from the point of view of those people who classify failures as being of the 1TR type. We will almost never find among "other failures" some 1TR failures.

The failures 1TE, 1EM, 1EL are approximately equidistant of 1DV: there is an indifferent tendency to classify the named failures as miscellaneous in case of ambiguity. The failures 4 CO, 4 CC are also fairly frequently classified as "miscellaneous", or the opposite. There seems therefore to be an ambiguity about all these failures, especially 1EL. The measure taken was to modify the maintenance handbook in order to avoid this kind of coding ambiguity, and a success was noted.

Many other failure diagnoses may be formulated, and are left as an exercise to the reader. It should for example be noted that 1EL, and 1EM, are the failures to be investigated most thoroughly by the designers in order to improve the life-time up to around 400-800 h.

2.6. Example 2: common and high-stability resistors

An implicit learning data set is being used in order to investigate
the actual drift failures J, as related to other characteristics of
the resistors announced by the manufacturers. Correspondence analysis
yields the map of highest inertia given in Fig. 4 while the data sets
are reported in GOARIN[4].

Note that the axis f_1 is ranking the drifts so that the other
observations may be classified with respect to the drift reliabilities.
This is why the socalled "high-stability resistors" FHS and "common
resistors" FUC are located diametrally in the f_1-direction, and have
high absolute contributions to f_1. We do also remark that metal film
resistors behave better than metal oxide resistors, and even better
than carbon film resistors.

The negative drifts DMO are well explained by f_2 and by the
manufacturer F of carbon film resistors having this property. The
connection mode, welded or set, has a significant effect. Though,
F is not the only manufacturer to produce carbon film resistors, and
the technology alone cannot explain his criticable position. In the
same way, the manufacturer E has an enviable position on f_1 and f_2,
even if he produces both carbon and metal film resistors with very
different drift properties; it is therefore proved that the
manufacturer has a big influence upon this kind of reliability, and
that this influence is not due to the technology used.

3. REAL TIME DIAGNOSIS BY PATTERN RECOGNITION

Real time diagnosis has been achieved, yielding a simultaneous
solution to the problems P2 and P3. The pattern recognition technique
which has been used, includes first the learning stage, next the real
time feature extraction, and lastly the recognition procedure wherein
the r features characterizing the observed failures are compared to
the learning datas.

3.1. Learning stage

The learning patterns are defined as being the explicit tableau
$k(I,J) = \{k(i,j) > 0, i \in I \ j \in J\}$ defined in 2.1. They are obtained by
gathering all informations $i \in I$, and moreover TBO_j and others, about a
large number of equipments $j \in J$, for which the failure cause $d(j)$ has
been determined by the quality control or maintenance personnel. We
assume that the total number of different failure causes $d \in D$ is small
with respect to the total number of equipments observed. Assume that
the probability distribution $\{P(d) \mid d \in D \ P(d) > 0 \ \sum_D P(d) = 1\}$ of the
failure causes has been estimated within the learning datas or by
other means.

The learning features, which will be used during the recognition
phase, are the images of the learning patterns in a reduced feature
space having a fixed dimension r. The feature extraction procedure
used is the correspondence analysis of paragraph 2.3 applied to the
tableau $k(I,J)$.

3.2. Real time feature extraction for a failed equipment

Assume that troubleshooting has just been observed on an equipment $\bar{j}$
of the type investigated in 2.1, and that it has been possible to
gather all informations $\{k(i,\bar{j}), i \in I\}$ about $\bar{j}$. We may consider $\bar{j}$ as a
supplementary learning pattern belonging to an unknown class $d(\bar{j})$;

but, since the correspondence analysis of $k(I,J)$ is made without taking into account the knowledge of $d(j)$ $j\in J$, we may locate $\bar{j}$ in the feature space thanks to the formula [2]:

$$\left[\begin{array}{l} F(\bar{j},\ell) = g_{\ell}\cdot[\,\mathrm{Prob}(i|\bar{j})\ i = 1,\ \mathrm{Card}\ (I)]\quad \ell=1,r \\[2mm] \mathrm{Prob}(i|\bar{j}) = k(i,\bar{j})/(\sum_{I} k(i,\bar{j})) \end{array}\right. \qquad [4]$$

where $F(\bar{j},\ell)$ is the coordinate of the equipment $\bar{j}$ on the ℓ-th feature axis g_{ℓ}; it is assumed that the numerical values of $\{k(i,\bar{j}),i\in I\}$ do not perturbate the earlier calculation of the vectors g_{ℓ} $\ell=1,r$. Here again, the failed equipment may be displayed on maps as those discussed in 2.4, and we look for associations, either with the learning equipments $j\in J$ for which $d(j)\in D$ is known, or with the observations $i\in I$. These associations may help in formulating some precise experimental hypothesis about the mechanism of the failure detected in 3.3 on the equipment $\bar{j}$.

3.3. Recognition procedure

We will consider one single recognition procedure, applied sequentially, and yielding at each step a classification of the observed equipment pattern $\bar{j}$ into the most probable failure class $d(\bar{j})\in D$. The nearest neighbour rule has been generalized as follows (see LOFTSGAARDEN[7], PAU[8] and Fig. 5):

$$\bar{j} \in \text{class } d(\bar{j}) \leftrightarrow \frac{n_{d(\bar{j})}{}^{PP}{}_{d(\bar{j})}}{(N_{d(\bar{j})}+1)V_{d(\bar{j})}} = \mathop{\mathrm{Max}}\limits_{d\in D} \frac{n_d\,P_d}{(N_d+1)V_d}$$

$$\left[\begin{array}{ll} d & = \text{class of failure causes selected in D.} \\ N_d & = \text{number of "reference patterns" in class d, as defined below.} \\ P_d & = \text{estimated probability of occurence of a random failure} \\ & \quad\ \text{cause d in the set D, as introduced in 3.1.} \\ n_d & = \text{integer parameter, determined for each class d.} \\ V_d & = \text{minimal volume of a neighbourhood of the newly observed} \\ & \quad\ \text{equipment } \bar{j}, \text{ so that } (n_d-1) \text{ reference patterns of the} \\ & \quad\ \text{class } d\in D \text{ are interior to this neighbourhood, while one} \\ & \quad\ \text{single reference pattern is on the boundary hereof; the} \\ & \quad\ \text{neighbourhoods have statistically independent shapes as} \\ & \quad\ \text{those of } \text{TUKEY's}[14] \text{ tolerance regions.} \end{array}\right.$$

The named "reference patterns" are N_d points, i.e. learning equipments, projected into the feature space, and representing a single class of failure causes $d\in D$; for each cause $d\in D$ they are:

a) the center of gravity of all the learning equipments j belonging to the class d because $d(j) = d$: then $n_d = N_d = 1$;

b) the extremities of r dipoles approximating the cloud of all projected learning equipments j belonging to the class d: then $N_d = 2r,\ n_d \# r$;

c) all the projected learning equipments j belonging to the class d: their number is again called N_d, and n_d is determined in order to minimize the probability of misclassification; n_d is of the size 3 to 20.

Our nearest neighbour rule is then used sequentially as follows (see PAU([12])): given an observed failed equipment $\bar{j}$ for which we need a diagnosis, we do apply this rule successively from a) to c) to different types of "reference patterns" so that the ratio (global recognition time for $\bar{j}$/ estimated probability of good classification) is minimized. The computation time at each step, and the approximation of the probability of good classification, will probably both increase with the N_d's. Therefore, if a quick procedure such as 3.3 a) yields a high recognition rate thanks to a good experimental discrimination of $\bar{j}$, it will be useless to continue to step b).

The final diagnosis is made by computing the product of the probabilities of misclassification yielded by each step we have been through, and for all classes in D, when taking into account the apriori recognition rates. The best classification decision $d(\bar{j})$ minimizes this global misclassification probability within the set D of alternatives, even if conflicts may appear between successive steps. The two or three best alternatives, including $d(\bar{j})$, may also be obtained. We will only put down and repair those few subsystems which are the failure causes of highest probability.

Though, it is clear that this procedure would be misleading if the actual failure had not been included in the catalog D; if the result $d(\bar{j})$ happens frequently to be absurd, one has to examine thoroughly the learning data and the set D of alternative failures.

3.4. Example of automated testing

We have considered a stationary fabrication process of complex electro-mechanical systems with very stringent specifications and small dimensional tolerances. The 82 observations on each equipment $j \in J$ in the process were the measurements made by the quality control department at the input of the process, and the operational characteristics of the machine tools when used on each specific system (settings, cumulated time of operations, time since servicing, type of tool, air flow, temperature, oil flow, rotation speeds, workers operating the machines,...). The 21 classes of failures included the special class d_0 of all equipments for sale fulfilling all quality control requirements.

a) During the learning phase, data were collected on Card (J) = 2000 items (20 days of production), among which 800 non-acceptable items were identified at the final quality control and received a diagnosis each (chosen among the 21 classes of failures). These learning datas were processed on a general purpose IBM 370-65 computer (12 min CPU). The computation of the f_ℓ $\ell=1,r$ ran into some numerical diagonalization problems. Through the review process described in 2.4, it became possible to pinpoint those systematic aspects of the production process having indirectly the strongest contributions to the named failures, in this case the oil flows.

b) During the testing phase, a true recognition rate of 92% was achieved for the items classified into the class d_0 by the final quality control, still working. The mean true diagnosis rate for the 20 types of actual failures was 81% when r=10; mean unitary diagnosis computing time: 0,46 s.

c) During the operational phase under final implementation, all 82 observations will be monitored in real time for each equipment in the production line; most non-destructive tests and the final quality control will be suppressed. Some few specialists will play a supervisor role for the automatic diagnosis system, including the small on-line data-logging and computing unit. Considerable economical benefits may be obtained, as evaluated on the basis of the testing phase b). These specialists will perform design reviews, modify and enlarge the learning data bank.

The case of a non-stationary fabrication process, has been investigated by POKROWSKY[13] along with accelerated testing. The mean result is that the number of observations by item, here 82, must be increased as the process stabilizes.

The author has at a certain moment been uncertain on the wisdom of using reduced features whithout reference to the learned diagnosis $d(j)$ $j \in J$, when the features are to be used for diagnosis. Therefore a canonical correlations analysis and discriminant analysis were used, but performed very badly; the reason is that the "natural" clusters obtained by the non-parametric correspondence analysis do not usually fit well with the classifications determined by the coding (see again 2.5).

4. CONCLUSION

The conclusion is that pattern recognition techniques can help providing the designers and the maintenance specialists with a set of assumptions, and in making repairs more efficient through a rationalization of the inductive and sequential diagnosis formulation processes.

The results will be all the more realistic than the individual equipments will be numerous to be monitored during their whole life or during the production process. But even more important is the quality requirement for these datas. It is indeed a very actual problem to define properly the reliability or maintenance parameters to be monitored, to control the data-logging process, and to make the data files compatible. These are very lengthy, costly and even risky steps, and the manufacturer should beforehand be aware of it. Since data banks with technical informations are set up and the gathering initiated in an increasing number of institutions, especially for military or aerospace applications, this compatibility requirement must have the very first priority.

Lastly, the profits which may be expected from the outlined automatic diagnosis system are important, because it is basically designed for complex systems of high cost, characterized by multiple failure patterns, and important interactions between the external environment, the maintenance and the production control. Statistical pattern recognition like hereabove is probably the only approach to diagnosis in mechanical and non-purely electronic equipments.

While automated diagnosis is being implemented on operational systems connected to small embarkable computing units, the research is being carried forward about:

- diagnosis on the basis of the variations in time of certain parameters, i.e. the fluctuations in rotation speeds;

- sequential learning and diagnosis (see POKROWSKY[13], PAU[11]).

REFERENCES

(1) BECKER, P.W. Recognition of patterns, Copenhagen, Denmark, Polyteknisk Forlag, 1968.

(2) BENZECRI, J.P. Statistical analysis as a tool to make patterns emerge from data. Proc., 1968 Honolulu Conf. on pattern recognition, Academic Press, 1969.

(3) CORTINA, E., ENGEL, H.L., and SCOTT, W.K. Pattern recognition techniques applied to diagnostics. SAE rep. 7000407, Midyear meeting, Detroit, Michigan, 18-22/5/1970.

(4) GOARIN, R. Application de l'analyse des correspondances à l'étude de la fiabilité des composants électroniques, Congrès national de fiabilité, Perros-Guirec, September 1972.

(5) HANKLEY, W.J., and MERRILL, H.M. A pattern recognition technique for system error analysis, IEEE Trans. on reliability, Vol. R-20, No. 3, August 1971.

(6) KULIKOWSKY, C.A. Pattern recognition approach to medical diagnosis, IEEE Trans. Systems Science & Cybernetics, Vol. SSC-6, No. 3, July 1970.

(7) LOFTSGAARDEN, D.O., and QUESENBURY, C.P. A non-parametric estimate of a multi-variate density function, Ann. Math. Statist., 36, 1965, 1049-1151.

(8) PAGE, J. Recognition of patterns in jet engine vibration signals, IEEE Publ., No. 16 c 51, 102-105.

(9) PAU, L.F. Diagnostic statistique; synthèse des informations relatives à la fiabilité et à la maintenance d'un matériel aéronautique, L'Aéronautique et l'Astronautique, No. 34, 1972-2.

(10) PAU, L.F. Méthodes statistiques de réduction et de reconnaissance des formes, dr. thesis, Paris University, 1972.

(11) PAU, L.F. Sequential pattern recognition methods applied to technical diagnosis and maintenance, IMSOR, Technical University of Denmark, 1972.

(12) PAU, L.F. Statistical reduction and recognition of speech patterns, in: Machine perception of patterns and pictures, book, published by the Institute of Physics, London, as Conference series No. 13, 1972.

(13) POKROWSKY, F.N. On reliability prediction by pattern classification, Proc. 1972 Annual reliability and maintenability symposium, San Francisco, Annals of Assurance sciences, IEEE Catalog 72CH0577-7R, 367-375.

(14) TUKEY, J.W. Non-parametric estimation, II: statistical equivalent blocks and tolerance regions, Ann. Math. Statist., 18, 1947, 529-539.

(15) WATANABE, S., and LAMPERT, P.F. Evaluation and selection of variables in pattern recognition, in: Computers and information sciences, Vol. 2, N.Y., Academic Press, 1967, 91-122.

(16) YOUNG, H.W. Specifying the interface between design and test organizations, Inst. of electronic and radio engs., Conf. on automatic test systems, Proc. April 1970.

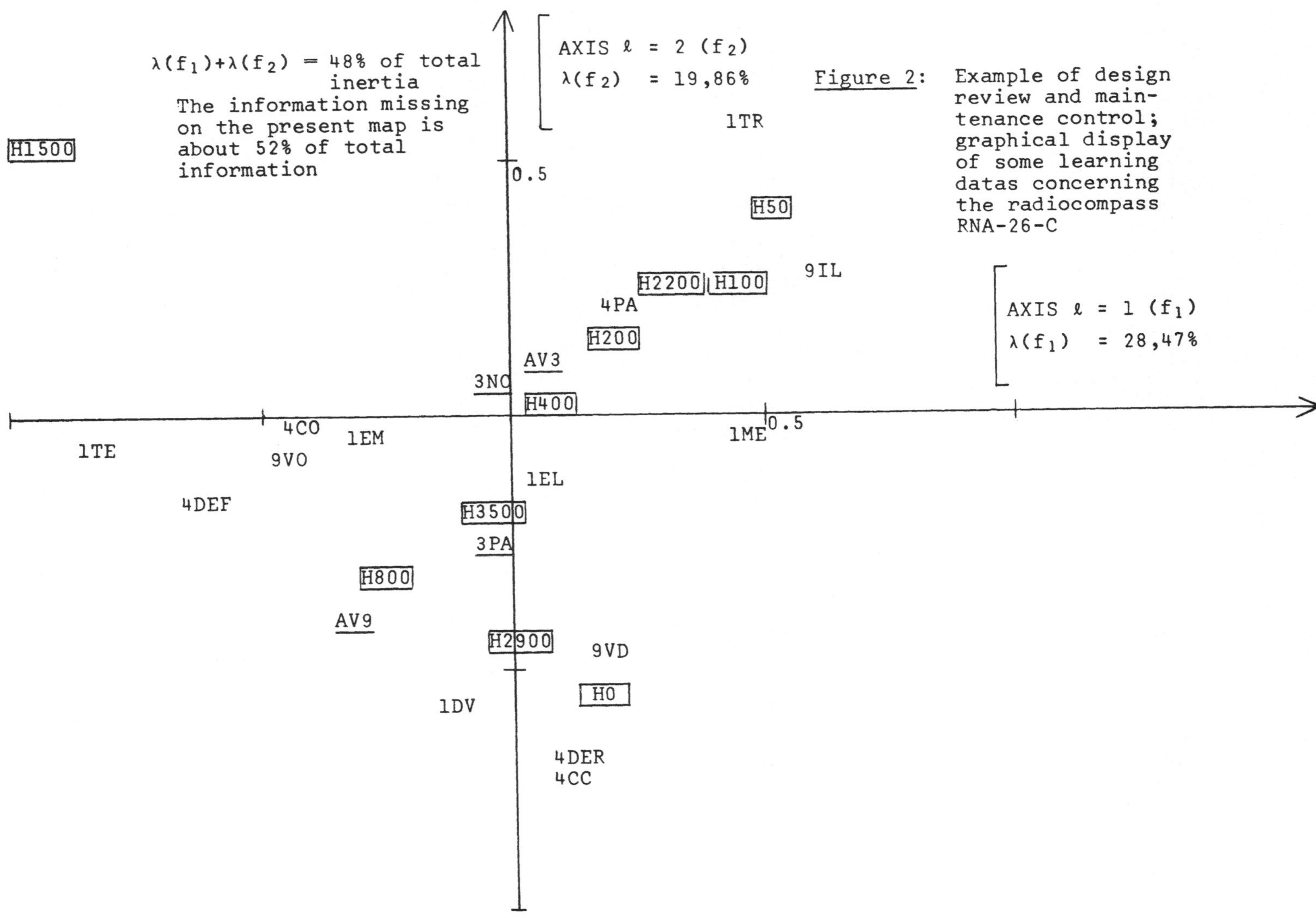

Figure 2: Example of design review and maintenance control; graphical display of some learning datas concerning the radiocompass RNA-26-C

Figure 3

Class c∈C of informations	Alternative i∈c	Interpretation
AV (type of aircraft)	AV3 AV9	Caravelle Fokker Friendship
H (TBO-intervals)	Hj*	Hj* is the TBO-interval j*∈J*; i.e. H400 means that there is an interval j* beginning at 400 hours; the next interval begins at 800 hours
1 (failed component)	1 EL	failures of non-active electronic components, i.e. resistors, ...
	1 TR	failures of active electronic components, i.e. transistors, ...
	1 EM	failures of electromagnetic components, i.e. relays, ...
	1 ME	failures of mechanical parts
	1 TE	failures of the elctrical supply system
	1 DV	miscellaneous failures of non-identified nature
3 (nature of operation)	3 PA	justified maintenance operations, because of failures of components
	3 NO	other maintenance operations: check, unjustified, trimming, ...
4 (diagnosis)	4 DEF	component out of service
	4 DER	badly trimmed component
	4 CO	bad electrical contact
	4 CC	short-circuit
9 (external implications)	9 VO	necessary maintenance of the VOR
	9 VD	badly trimmed VOR system
	9 IL	necessary maintenance of the ILS system

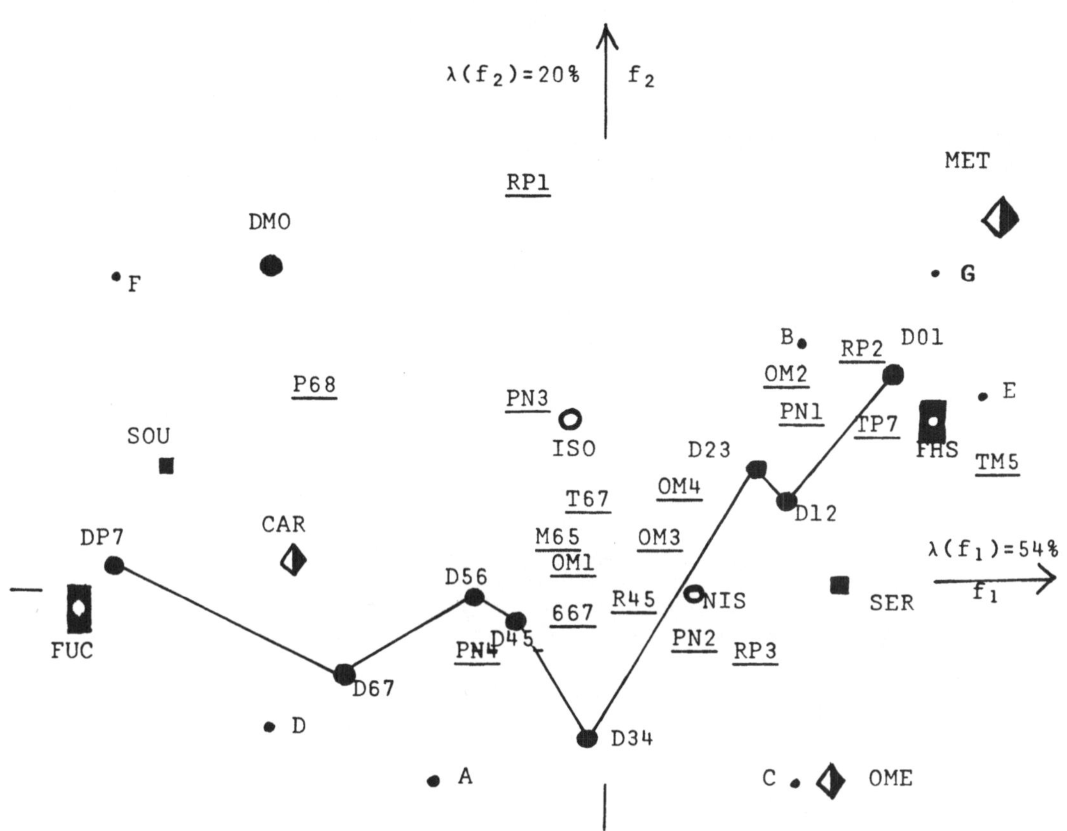

DMO : negative mean drift of electrical resistance at 1000 hours
D01,D12,D23,D34,D45,D56,D67,DP7 : Dmn indicates a positive mean
                    drift of n to m percent at 1000 hours
FHS,FUC : high-stability and common resistors , respectively
CAR,MET,OME : carbon film, metal film , metal oxyd resistors,resp.
ISO,NIS : isolated, non-isolated resistors , resp.
SOU,SER : welded,set connections , resp.
A until G : symbols for the manufacturers of resistors
M65,667,P68 : resistors manufactured before 1965,1966 or 1967 ,
                    1968 or later
PN1,PN2,PN3,PN4 : nominal effects as limited by 250,500 and 1000mW
OM1,OM2,OM3,OM4 : nominal resistance limited by 35Ω ,100kΩ ,300kΩ
TM5,T67,TP7 : test temperatures limited by 50° C , 75° C
RP1,RP2,RP3,R45 : ratio of actual to nominal effect , limited by
                    25 %, 50 %, 75 %.

<u>Figure 4 :</u>   Design review of common and high-stability
            resistors .

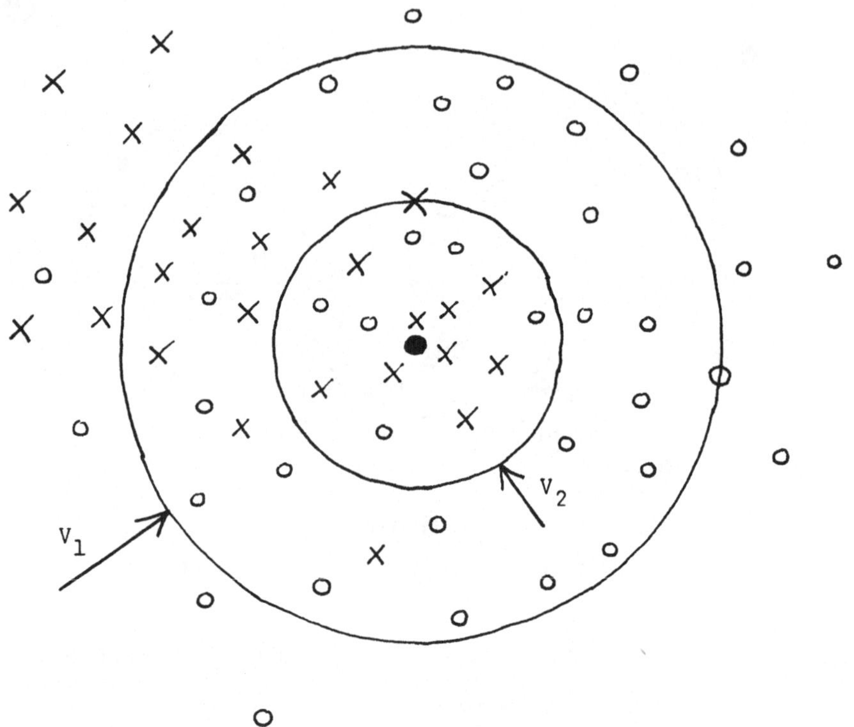

<u>Figure 5</u>: Generalization of the nearest neighbour rule

	Class d=1 (symbol 0)	Class d=2 (symbol x)
n_d	28	9
P_d	α	$(1-\alpha)$
N_d	38	25
V_d	2.500	0,529
$\dfrac{n_d\, P_d}{(N_d+1)V_d}$	0,287 α	0,654 $(1-\alpha)$

The unknown pattern belongs to:
- class d=1 if $\alpha > 0,692$
- class d=2 if $\alpha < 0,692$

Ein interaktives Verfahren zur teilautomatischen Auswertung von Luftbildern für Verkehrsanalysen

K. Wolferts

1. Aufgabenstellung

In den letzten Jahren nahm der Straßenverkehr in derart starkem Umfang zu, daß freies Fahren immer seltener möglich ist. Die Untersuchungen der verkehrswissenschaftlichen Forschungsinstitute haben daher vielfach zum Ziel, brauchbare Modelle für das Fahrverhalten im Kolonnenverkehr zu entwickeln und zu überprüfen, die sich über größere räumliche und zeitliche Bereiche erstrecken (mehrere Minuten bzw. einige Kilometer /9/, /1/).

Zur Gewinnung von Datenmaterial für empirische verkehrsstatistische Untersuchungen, speziell für Analysen des Fahrverhaltens in Kolonnen und Kfz-Pulks sowie zur Untersuchung von Fahrmodellen, wurden in den letzten Jahren photogrammetrische Verfahren entwickelt /3/, /2/, /21/, /1/, /16/. Diese Verfahren haben viele Vorteile, jedoch in allen Varianten einen gravierenden Nachteil: Die Datenerfassung mit manuellen Methoden ist langwierig, fehleranfällig und sehr aufwendig. Es soll daher versucht werden, mit vertretbarem Aufwand eine weitgehende Automatisierung der Erkennung, Klassifizierung, Zuordnung und Ortsmessung von Kraftfahrzeugen in Luftbildern zu ermöglichen.

Hierbei wird unter Erkennen das erstmalige Auffinden eines Fahrzeugs in einem Bild verstanden. Klassifizierung bedeutet die Einteilung als solcher erkannter Fahrzeuge in die Klassen Pkw, Lkw oder Lastzug in Abhängigkeit von der Fahrzeuglänge.

Mit Zuordnung wird der Vorgang bezeichnet, der in einem Bild bereits erkannte individuelle Fahrzeuge in den folgenden Bildern wiederfindet und die Bilder der Fahrzeuge einander richtig zuordnet.

Unter Ortsmessung wird die Bestimmung von Bildkoordinaten eines Fahrzeugpunkts (z. B. Fahrzeugmitte oder Mitte Vorderkante) verstanden (Abb. 3).

Aus den so gewonnenen Daten (Fahrzeuganzahl, Fahrzeugstandorte) können dann in einem Arbeitsgang in der Rechenanlage die daraus abgeleiteten Größen Abstände, Geschwindigkeiten und Beschleunigungen berechnet werden. Diese Werte müssen in zeitlich so dichter Folge gewonnen werden, daß die Ergebnisse sowohl als lokale (zeitbezogen auf einen Querschnitt) wie auch als momentane (ortsbezogen auf einen Zeitpunkt) Daten ausgewertet werden können.

2. Bisherige photographische/photogrammetrische Verfahren

Die bisher bekanntgewordenen Bildverfahren lassen sich in drei Schritte aufgliedern:

a) **Bildaufnahme,** die nach bekannten Verfahren der Photogrammetrie, z. T. mit modernem Instrumentarium, ausgeführt wird. Die Kammer wird entweder in Bildflugzeugen oder Hubschraubern eingesetzt oder sie wird auf Masten, Drehleitern, Häusern etc. aufgestellt.

Als Aufnahmegeräte werden vorwiegend 35-mm-Kleinbildkameras /2/, /16/, /5/, /9/, /1/ oder 70-mm-Rollfilmkameras /16/, /21/ mit elektrischem Filmaufzug und Kassetten mit Film für einige hundert Aufnahmen eingesetzt, seltener Luftbild-Meßkammern /3/ oder 16-mm-Filmkameras /21/. Die Bildmaßstäbe liegen zwischen 1 : 1500 und 1 : 24000, hauptsächlich jedoch zwischen 1 : 2000 und 1 : 8000, wobei kleine Maßstäbe nur für Zählzwecke Verwendung finden.

b) Die Datengewinnung aus den Bildern erfolgt entweder mit photogrammetrischen Meßgeräten oder mit (oft selbst gebauten) Rückvergrößerungseinrichtungen mit Koordinatenregistriermöglichkeit (Lochstreifen, Lochkarten, seltener Magnetband).
Das Institute of Transportation and Traffic Engineering of the University of California in Los Angeles (ITTE/UCLA) verwendet sogar einen Prozeßrechner in direkter Kopplung mit der Koordinatenregistriereinrichtung, nutzt den Rechner aber nur zur sofortigen Plausibilitätsprüfung und Fehlerkorrektur /16/. Der Prozeß der Datenerfassung wird von allen Anwendern als der zeitaufwendigste und fehleranfälligste Verfahrensschritt beschrieben.

c) Datenverarbeitung (Auswertung der Bilddaten, statistische Berechnungen)
Die oben genannten Verfahren werden teilweise für Zählungen und Dichtebestimmungen, aber auch für meßtechnische Auswertungen weiterverarbeitet. Die aus den Bildserien gewonnenen Daten liefern von den aufgenommenen Kfz die Positionen bzw. Abstände, Geschwindigkeiten, Beschleunigungen und Fahrzeuggrößen als Funktion der Zeit und/oder der Fahrstrecke. Die weitere Auswertung dieser Zwischenergebnisse wie die Entwicklung und Überprüfung von Modellen geschieht zweckmäßig durch den Verkehrswissenschaftler.

3. Forderungen an automatische Bildauswerteverfahren und Lösungsmöglichkeiten
Durch Bildabtastung und automatische Bildauswertung gewonnene Daten müssen die sichere Erkennung, Klassifizierung und Zuordnung der Fahrzeuge sowie die Messung der Fahrzeugpositionen in den einzelnen Bildern mit genügender Genauigkeit zulassen. Mit diesen Fragen im direkten Zusammenhang stehen die Parameter Bildmaßstab, Aufnahmehöhe, Bildformat, Auflösung und Genauigkeit des Bildabtasters.
Zur Frage der als ausreichend erachteten Genauigkeit ist nur bei Hoefs /9/ eine Angabe zu finden. Er fordert für Nettoweglücken $A^n < 20$ m einen max. Fehler der Beschleunigung von $|\Delta b| \leq 0,2$ m/s^2, was den zulässigen Fehler der Wegmessung auf $|\Delta s| \leq 0,08$ m/s^2 begrenzt. In dieser Größenordnung liegt auch das Beschleunigungsrauschen des Fahrzeugs, eine Schwankung der Fahrzeugbewegung mit einer Periode von ca. 10...20 s.
Die bisher bei verkehrstechnischen Untersuchungen angewandten Methoden (Lichtschranken, Pneumatische Schläuche, Radarmessungen) haben z. Z. erheblich geringere Genauigkeiten als

die photogrammetrischen Verfahren aufzuweisen. Von den bereits erwähnten computer-unterstützten Datenerfassungssystemen der UCLA werden bei Verwendung von 70-mm-Kameras und M_b = 1 : 16250 Lagegenauigkeiten von $\pm$ 0,9 m angegeben. Bei einem anderen Projekt dieses Instituts wurden Fehler angegeben, die bei M_b = 1 : 12300 bis zu 8 cm im Objekt erreichten. Die aus diesen Daten errechneten Geschwindigkeiten waren jedoch für weitere Auswertungen zu ungenau. Daher wählte man in einem neuen Versuch als Bildmaßstab M_b = 1 : 3000 und erreichte ausreichende Genauigkeit, für die Zahlenwerte jedoch nicht angegeben werden /16/. Authie et al. /1/ erreichen mit einem optisch-elektronischen Meß- und Entzerrungsverfahren Lagegenauigkeiten von $\pm$ 1 m und Geschwindigkeitsfehler von $\pm$ 10 %.

Döhler erhält aus Genauigkeitsuntersuchungen der photogrammetrischen Methode /3/ einige bemerkenswerte Ergebnisse: Der Fehler aufgrund der photogrammetrischen Meßgeräte ist zu vernachlässigen bzw. rechnerisch zu kompensieren; schwerwiegende Einflüsse ergeben sich im wesentlichen nur durch die Zentralperspektive aufgrund von Höhenunterschieden sowie durch Identifizierungs- und Einstellfehler. Da ein automatisches Verfahren bei der Aufnahme mit den gleichen Mitteln und Geräten arbeitet, bleiben deren Fehlerquellen also in der Hauptsache erhalten; es kommen die Fehler durch die Abtastung hinzu (Auflösung/Raster). Die Forderung an ein automatisches Auswertesystem lautet daher: Durch die Abtastung und das Verfahren zur Lokalisierung der Fahrzeuge darf die Genauigkeit, die mit den bisherigen photogrammetrischen Verfahren erreicht wird, nicht wesentlich beeinträchtigt werden.

Eine Bestandsaufnahme der bisher in der automatischen Zeichenerkennung erzielten Erfolge lassen es für die nächsten Jahre ausgeschlossen erscheinen, ein wirtschaftlich arbeitendes System aufzubauen, das Kfz-Erkennung, Klassifizierung, Zuordnung und Ortsmessung aus Luftbildern für große Bildmengen mit allen Nebenbedingungen durch ein vollautomatisches System mit vertretbarem Aufwand gewährleistet.

Wie die Untersuchung von Aufnahmen natürlicher Verkehrssituationen zeigt, enthalten die Abbildungen (Abb. 2) von Straßen außer den Fahrzeugen noch viele Störinformationen (Begrenzungs- und Haltelinien, Richtungspfeile, Helligkeitsunterschiede von Fahrbahnteilen nach Tiefbauarbeiten). Eine Abtastung in einem oder einigen Profilen, die parallel zur Fahrtrichtung liegen, und die Analyse nur dieser Profile, wie sie Döhler /3/ vorschlägt und mit Modellaufnahmen untersucht hat, führt daher nicht zum gewünschten Erfolg. Dieses Verfahren bedingt darüber hinaus eine erhebliche Vorleistung an zeichenerkennender Tätigkeit zur Festlegung der Lage der Abtastprofile.

Es wird daher ein Verfahren vorgeschlagen und auch untersucht, das die flächenhafte Bildinformation benutzt, dabei gleichzeitig die zu verarbeitende Informationsmenge und den Aufwand zur Erkennung und Identifizierung stark herabsetzt.

Das Hauptproblem der automatischen Bildauswertung für Verkehrsstatistik ist aufgrund der großen Datenmengen (einige 100 Bilder mit jeweils ca. 10 Fahrzeugen pro Auswertung) nicht das Erkennen von Fahrzeugen im Bild, sondern das Zuordnen bereits erkannter Fahrzeuge und deren Ortsmessung in den folgenden Bildern (pro Fahrzeug ca. 12 - 15 Aufnahmen im Abstand von 1 Sekunde). Hierzu erscheint die Korrelationsrechnung als geeignete Methode, die in vier verschiedenen Verfahren angewandt werden kann:

a) Die seit vielen Jahren bekannte optische Berechnung über die Fouriertransformation (/13/, /14/, /17/) benutzt die flächenhafte Bildinformation zur (bild-)parallelen Berechnung. Die Anwendung in diesem Spezialfall stellt jedoch erhebliche Probleme. Die Einzelfahrzeuge müssen in einem der zwei Bilder ausgeblendet werden, bevor sie zur Korrelation herangezogen werden, da sonst andere Fahrzeuge oder Umgebungsinformation verfälschte Korrelationsmaxima verursachen. Die Lage der Fahrzeuge mit der geforderten Genauigkeit optisch-elektronisch festzustellen, erfordert ebenfalls einen erheblichen Aufwand. Ein solches System benötigt zur Steuerung und Auswertung einen Spezialcomputer, der die dazu nötigen Apparaturen on-line angeschlossen hat und die Erkennungs- und Lokalisierungsvorgänge im Echtzeitbetrieb steuert und überwacht.

b) Die von den automatisierten photogrammetrischen Kartiergeräten bekannten elektronischen Analog-Korrelatoren /13/, /7/ sind für den Zweck der automatischen Verkehrsbildauswertung ebenfalls nicht ohne Schwierigkeiten zu verwenden. Hierbei müßte zusätzlich zu den optisch-mechanischen Baugruppen des Korrelators mit seinen Servoantrieben ebenfalls ein Spezialrechner in das System integriert werden, der ähnlich wie beim rein optischen Verfahren durch elektronische Berechnung und Steuerung die Bildteile ausmaskiert, die nicht gerade ein Fahrzeug enthalten. Gesteuert durch den optisch-elektronischen Korrelationsvorgang muß die Erkennung und Lageberechnung ebenfalls in Echtzeit im Prozeßrechner ausgeführt werden.

Neben den bisher aufgeführten direkten Bildauswerteverfahren bieten sich noch indirekte Verfahren an, bei denen die Bilder oder Teile daraus zuerst abgetastet und digitalisiert werden. Betrachtet man die zweidimensionale Grauwertverteilung der Bilder als Grauwertmatrizen, so bedeuten Spalten- bzw. Zeilenindex die Bildkoordinaten x und y, der Grauwert an der Stelle x/y entspricht dem Wert des Matrizenelements mit dem Spaltenindex x und dem Zeilenindex y. Aus den Grauwertmatrizen läßt sich dann mit rein rechnerischen, digital arbeitenden Verfahren unter der Verwendung von Universal- oder Spezialcomputern die benötigte Information gewinnen.

c) Die Berechnung der Korrelation durch digitale Fouriertransformation, auch unter Ausnutzung der als schnelle Fouriertransformation /12/ bekannten Verfahren, ergibt jedoch zu große Berechnungszeiten (einige Minuten), da immer über das ganze Bild mit einer Kantenlänge von 2^i Punkten transformiert werden muß (i ganzzahlig).

d) Die Berechnung der Korrelation nach statistischen Methoden unter Ausweitung auf zweidimensionale Verteilung. Hierbei läßt sich die Berechnung auf die Bildteile beschränken, die wirklich benötigt werden. Damit lassen sich erhebliche Zeiteinsparungen erreichen.

Dieses Verfahren d) wurde an dem im folgenden kurz beschriebenen System programmiert und es wurden ausführliche Untersuchungen damit angestellt.

4. <u>Das Karlsruher System zur automatischen Bildauswertung</u> /4/, /10/

In der Karlsruher Forschungsgruppe für Informationsverarbeitung und Mustererkennung wird seit einigen Jahren Grundlagenforschung auf dem Gebiet der automatischen Zeichenerkennung und Bildverarbeitung betrieben. Zu diesem Zweck steht der Forschungsgruppe ein Computer Control Data CD 3300 zur Verfügung. Der Rechner ist mit 32 k Kernspeicherworten à 24 bit, Lochstreifenein- und -ausgabe, Schnelldrucker, einem Magnetbandgerät (7-Spur) und zwei Wechselplattenspeichern (Kapazität zus. ca. 4 Mio Worte) ausgerüstet.

Zu diesen serienmäßigen Peripheriegeräten wurden in den letzten Jahren in der Forschungsgruppe eigene Geräte zur Bildabtastung und Auswertung entwickelt, angeschlossen und mit der notwendigen Betriebssoftware ausgerüstet. Hierzu gehört ein Flying-Spot-Scanner, der 23 x 23-cm-Filmnegative auf einer Fläche von ca. 20 x 20 mm mit einem Raster von 256 x 256 Punkten abtasten kann, was einer Auflösung von 75 μm entspricht. Dieser Abtaster kann neben der vollständigen systematischen Abtastung eines kompletten Bildes auch in anderen Abtastmodi betrieben werden (Einzelpunkte, Untermatrizen, Ausschnitte, Kontur-Erfassung usw.). Die Bilddateneingabe wandelt bei der hier verwendeten systematischen Vollabtastung die Grauwerte in 6-Bit-Zahlen um und transportiert sie zum Rechner. Damit lassen sich $2^6 =$ 64 Grauwerte pro Bildpunkt unterscheiden.

Zur visuellen Bild- und Zeichendarstellung und zur graphischen Dateneingabe wird unter Verwendung eines Großbild-Speicheroszillographen (Bildfläche ca. 21 x 16 cm $\approx$ DIN A 5 hoch) eine Displayeinheit benutzt, die über zwei Digital-Analog-Wandler in x-Richtung an 1500 und in y-Richtung an 2000 verschiedenen Punkten angesteuert werden kann. Die Informationsausgabe kann in drei verschiedenen Betriebsarten erfolgen:

1. normal wiederholend schreiben (wie beim normalen Oszillographen)

2. speichernd schreiben; eine einmal geschriebene Information bleibt auf dem Schirm lange (1 Std.) sichtbar.

3. "Write-Through": in einem Speicherbild wird sichtbar, aber nicht speichernd Information "angezeigt" (z. B. Fadenkreuz).

Schließlich läßt sich der ganze Schirm noch von gespeicherter Information löschen.

An dem Display befindet sich eine Rollkugel, mit der ein im "Write-Through"-Modus auf dem Bildschirm ausgegebenes Fadenkreuz in x- und y-Richtung verschoben werden kann. Die Koordinaten dieses Fadenkreuzes sind dem Rechner bekannt und können durch Drücken der Taste

"Store" abgespeichert werden. Es ist auf diese Weise möglich, in einem auf dem Display ausgegebenen Bild Koordinaten zu messen und dem Rechner einzugeben.

Ein Tastenfeld neben dem Display enthält außer der Store-Taste noch 31 freie Tasten, die durch ein Benutzerprogramm abgefragt werden können. Es ist damit möglich, verschiedene Programmzweige eines komplexen Programmsystems anzusteuern und so ein wirkungsvolles interaktives System Mensch – graphische Ein-/Ausgabe – Computer zu programmieren. Neben der Ausgabe von Punkten, Geraden, Kreisen, darauf aufgebauten geometrischen Figuren lassen sich durch ein Programm "Charaktergenerator" auch Schriftzeichen erzeugen sowie Bilder mit zwei Grauwerten (Schwarz-Weiß-Darstellung) speichernd ausgeben (siehe Abb. 2). Durch wiederholte nichtspeichernde Ausgabe von Teilen eines Bildes und photographische Überlagerung lassen sich auch Grauwertbilder als Photos erzeugen, ein allerdings langwieriger Vorgang (einige Minuten).

5. Verkehrstechnische Randbedingungen

a) Bildfolgezeiten und Bildmaßstab

Aus verschiedenen Quellen /5/, /16/, /67/ ist zu entnehmen, daß für Datengewinnung eine Zeitfolge von 1 sec oder kürzer erwünscht ist. Das hat im wesentlichen zwei Gründe: a) die mit den Daten durchgeführten Untersuchungen erfordern diese zeitliche Dichte, da die Reaktionszeiten von Kfz-Fahrern und die untere Grenze der gefahrenen Zeitlücken gerade ca. 1 Sekunde betragen, b) die auf 1 Sekunde bezogenen Werte für v und b ermöglichten starke Vereinfachungen bei weiteren Untersuchungen und Berechnungen.

Die Aufnahmen sollen deshalb mit genau und konstant 1 Sekunde Zeitabstand oder mit einer Zeitregistrierung ausgeführt werden, die die Messung von 1/1000 s ermöglicht. Damit wird der Fehler, der aus der Zeitregistrierung resultiert, bei etwa 0,1 % liegen.

Der gegenwärtige Hauptverwendungszweck von photogrammetrischen Verfahren für die Verkehrsanalyse liegt bei der Untersuchung des Fahrverhaltens in Pulks, in Kolonnen oder z. B. an signalgeregelten Verkehrsknotenpunkten. Damit sind Grenzen für die von einem Bild zu belegende Fläche bzw. für den Bildmaßstab vorgegeben. Aus der Aufgabe Pulkbeobachtung oder Stauraum vor Signalanlagen ergibt sich eine Mindestlänge von ca. 50 m Verkehrsweg, in dem beim Anfahren jeweils ca. 8 Kfz pro Spur auf einem Bild erfaßt werden. Bei Verwendung von 24 x 36-mm-Kleinbildformat entspricht das einem Bildmaßstab 1 : 1400, beim 70-mm-Format 1 : 700. In bezug auf maximale Verkehrsweglänge sind keine genau definierten Grenzen vorgegeben; mehr als 1000 m Verkehrsweg pro Bild erscheinen jedoch nicht mehr sinnvoll, was bei 70 mm einen Bildmaßstab von M_b = 1 : 14000, bei 23 x 23 cm 1 : 4350 entspricht.

b) Bewegungsverhalten der Fahrzeuge

Untersucht man die Veränderungen, die innerhalb des 1-Sekunden-Intervalls in der Kfz-Bewegung aufgrund des psychologischen Verhaltens der Fahrer und des physikalischen Fahrverhaltens der Fahrzeuge auftreten können, erhält man einige interessante Ergebnisse, die als Voraussetzungen in ein automatisches Verfahren eingehen können.

Bei einem mit konstanter Geschwindigkeit geradeausfahrenden Kfz benötigt man zur Bestimmung seines Weg-Zeit-Verhaltens nur zwei Messungen, z. B. zur Zeit $t = 0$ s und $t = 1$ s, um die weitere Fahrstrecke daraus zu berechnen. Der Weg des Fahrzeugs ist zwei Einflüssen unterworfen: 1) Lenkausschläge ändern die Fahrtrichtung und ergeben seitliche Abweichungen, 2) Betätigung von Brems- oder Gaspedal ergibt Verzögerungen oder Beschleunigung.

Beide Einflüsse wirken sich jedoch nicht in beliebigen Größen aus, sondern sind durch physikalische Gegebenheiten wie maximale mögliche Querbeschleunigung bis zum Schleudern bzw. Umkippen oder maximale Bremsverzögerung (Blockieren) bzw. maximale Beschleunigung (Motorleistung) begrenzt. Zusätzlich wirken physiologische und psychologische Einflüsse auf den Fahrer ein, der im normalen Fahrbetrieb die physikalisch möglichen Grenzen bei weitem nicht erreicht. So sind die aus Reifentests ermittelten maximalen Querbeschleunigungen ca. $5 \ldots 6 \ \text{m/s}^2$, dagegen liegen die für den Entwurf von Straßenkurven vorgegebenen Werte bei $2,1 \ldots 2,5 \ \text{m/s}^2$; im normalen Fahrbetrieb, beim Spurwechsel, Ausscheren, Abbiegen, Überholen werden $2 \ \text{m/s}^2$ praktisch nicht überschritten, da hier im allgemeinen sofortiges Gegenlenken erforderlich ist. Bei Beschleunigung und Bremsverzögerung sind Maximalwerte von $+ 2 \ \text{m/s}^2$ (z. B. in 14 s von 0 auf 100 km/h) bzw. von $- 6 \ \text{m/s}^2$ möglich (gesetzliche Vorschrift: Fußbremse mindestens $4,5 \ \text{m/s}^2$). Auch diese Werte werden im normalen Fahrbetrieb, vor allem im gebundenen Verkehr (Kolonnenfahren), nicht erreicht.

Errechnet man aus diesen Werten die in 1 Sekunde mögliche Abweichung des Fahrzeugstandorts von der Stelle, an der sich das Fahrzeug bei unbeeinflußter Fahrt befinden würde, für die Geschwindigkeiten zwischen 20 und 100 km/h, so findet man, daß die Geschwindigkeit hierbei praktisch keinen Einfluß hat:

Die Formel für den gefahrenen Weg s bei der Geschwindigkeit v unter Einfluß der Beschleunigung b lautet:

$$s = s_o + v \cdot t + \frac{1}{2} b \cdot t^2 \tag{1}$$

daraus folgt die aus der Beschleunigung resultierende Wegänderung gegenüber der mit konstanter Geschwindigkeit durchfahrenen Strecke

$$\Delta s = \frac{1}{2} b \Delta t^2 \tag{2}$$

Mit $\qquad \Delta t = 1$ s

und $\qquad b = 2 \ \text{m/s}^2$ bzw. $- 6 \ \text{m/s}^2$

erhält man so $\quad \Delta s = + 1$ m bzw. $\Delta s = 3$ m

Die Formel für den Querversatz s_q eines Kfz lautet:

$$s_q = r \cdot (1 - \cos \alpha) \tag{3}$$

wobei r der Radius und α der Zentriwinkel des Kreisbogens ist, auf dessen Umfang sich das Kfz bei Kurvenfahrt bewegt. Dieser Kreisbogen wird zwar nicht exakt gefahren (richtig wären Klotoiden-Abschnitte), ergibt aber brauchbare, auf der sicheren Seite liegende Näherungswerte. Wird in der Formel (3) der Radius ersetzt durch die Querbeschleunigung b_q

$$r = \frac{v^2}{b_q} \tag{4}$$

und

$$\alpha = \frac{v}{r \cdot t} \tag{5}$$

(im Bogenmaß) bzw. durch Einsetzen von (4) in (5) mit

$$t = 1\,s \text{ und } \alpha = \frac{b_q}{v} \tag{6}$$

so erhält man

$$s_q = \frac{v^2}{b_q}(1 - \cos \frac{b_q}{v}) \tag{7}$$

Untersucht man die für α vorkommenden Werte zwischen 20 und 100 km/h bei $b_q = 2,1$ m/s², so erhält man:

T a b e l l e   a

V =	20	30	40	50	60	70	80	90	100	[km/h]
v =	5,5	8,3	11,1	13,9	16,7	19,4	22,2	25	27,8	[m/s]
α =	0,38	0,25	0,19	0,15	0,126	0,108	0,05	0,084	0,076	[Bogenmaß]
α =	21,6	14,4	10,8	8,7	7,2	6,2	5,4	4,8	4,3	[°]

Bei Vorgabe einer Fehlergrenze von 0,1 % läßt sich für Winkel $\alpha < 22,6°$ der cos durch die Näherung

$$\cos \alpha \approx 1 - \frac{\alpha^2}{2} \tag{8}$$

ersetzen. Eingesetzt in (7) erhält man Querversatz mit

$$s_q = \frac{v^2}{b} (1 - 1 + \frac{1}{2} b_q^2) = \frac{b_q}{2} \tag{9}$$

Der Querversatz beträgt demnach für $b_q \leqq 2,1$ m/s² max. $\pm 1,05$ m.

Mit diesen Werten läßt sich nun ein Rechteck von 2,1 m Breite und 4 m Länge bestimmen, das unter normalen Fahrbedingungen als Erwartungs- oder Streubereich nach 1 s Fahrt definiert werden kann (Abb. 3).

Bleibt noch die Frage, wie viele Fahrzeuge in einem Bild maximal neu auftauchen können bzw. wie weit ein in einem Bild zum ersten Mal auftauchendes Fahrzeug sich vom Rand her in das Bild hineinbewegt haben kann.

Ausgehend von der Erfahrung, daß die Zeitlücke in 1 Sekunde im Normalfall nicht unterschritten wird, erhält man das Ergebnis, daß in einem Bild normalerweise ein , höchstens zwei Fahrzeuge abgebildet sind, die in dem vorhergehenden Bild noch nicht enthalten waren (Abb. 4).

Die Tiefe des Bereichs in einem Bild, in das ein neu abgebildetes Fahrzeug eingefahren sein kann, ist nur von der Geschwindigkeit dieses Fahrzeugs abhängig, die aber von der Geschwindigkeit vorausfahrender, bereits registrierter Fahrzeuge nicht wesentlich verschieden sein kann. Aus der Bildfolgezeit von 1 s erhält man die Tiefe dieses Bereichs, wenn man in Tabelle a die Geschwindigkeitszeile m/s als Längen in m liest und sie den Geschwindigkeiten in km/h zuordnet. Auf diesen Bereich ist die Suche von neu auftauchenden Fahrzeugen zu beschränken.

6. Teilautomatische Auswertung von Verkehrsbildern

Wie bereits angedeutet, ist eine vollautomatische Auswertung durch Erkennen und Klassifizieren von Fahrzeugen mit den üblichen Methoden der Zeichenerkennung wie Szenenanalyse, Mustererkennung oder ähnlichem aus Aufnahmen von beliebigen Verkehrssituationen nach dem heutigen Stand der Technik in der Zeichenerkennung mit wirtschaftlich vertretbarem Aufwand nicht möglich. Das wird auch noch für einige Jahre so bleiben. An dessen Stelle muß ein Verfahren treten, das unter Verwendung von Ausgangs- und Hilfsdaten, die durch einen Operateur angegeben werden, die reine Meß- und Zuordnungstätigkeit das automatisch arbeitende System ausführen läßt, während es die erstmalige Erkennung und Klassifizierung dem Operateur eines interaktiven Systems überläßt.

a) Die Zuordnung von Einzelfahrzeugen auf Folgebildern durch Korrelation

Begrenzt man in einem digitalisierten Grauwertbild ein Kfz durch Umbeschreiben eines Rechtecks, so stellt die innerhalb des Rechtecks liegende zweidimensionale Grauwertverteilung die Information Kfz dar (Abb.2d). Berechnet man die Korrelationskoeffizienten in einer zweidimensionalen Autokorrelation über dieses Fahrzeug und seine nähere Umgebung, so erhält man eine Verschiebungsmatrix der Autokorrelationskoeffizienten. Untersucht man diese Matrix nach topologischen Gesichtspunkten, erkennt man, daß um den Koeffizienten 1,000 der Deckungslage die Größe der Koeffizienten in einem großen Bereich nach allen Richtungen hin monoton abnimmt. Stellt man sich die gesamte Matrix als digitales Geländemodell vor (Abb. 5 a), so bildet der Korrelationskoeffizient der Deckungslage das Maximum eines Berges, der zwischen den Grenzen seines Monotonieverhaltens eine Breite von etwa 1...2 Fahrzeugbreiten und eine Länge von ebenfalls ca. 1...1,6 Fahrzeuglängen einnimmt. Innerhalb dieser 1,6 Fahrzeuglängen treten jedoch in ca. 20...30 % der Fälle 1 oder 2 Nebenmaxima auf, die z. B. durch Korrelation von Fahrzeugdach mit Motorhaube oder Kofferraumdeckel entstehen. Diese Nebenmaxima sind jedoch in ihrer Höhe längst nicht so ausgeprägt wie das Hauptmaximum und liegen in Fahrtrichtung etwa 1/3...1/2 Fahrzeuglängen vor oder hinter dem Hauptmaximum (ca. 1,50...2,50 m).

Genau das gleiche Verhalten wie bei der Autokorrelation zeigt sich bei einer Kreuzkorrelation eines Fahrzeugs aus Bild n mit dem Bereich um dasselbe Fahrzeug in den Bildern n + 1, n + 2 usw. Die Maxima erreichen zwar nicht mehr den Wert 1.000, sondern bei unseren Versuchen nur noch Werte zwischen 0,84 und 0,97, das charakteristische Verhalten des "Geländemodells" bleibt aber erhalten (Abb. 5a). Mit diesen Voraussetzungen läßt sich ein Algorithmus entwickeln, der automatisch von einem vorgegebenen Punkt auf einer beliebigen Stelle des "Hügels" entlang eines Gradienten den Gipfelpunkt sucht und damit praktisch die Lage eines aus Bild n vorgegebenen Fahrzeugs in Bild n + 1 auf eine Rasterweite genau automatisch bestimmt (Gradientensuchverfahren, Abb. 7).

Da, wie in 5 b) gezeigt, die Lage eines Fahrzeugs im <u>Normalfall</u> (keine extremen Beschleunigungen oder Richtungswechsel) sehr genau vorhergesagt werden kann, werden zur Ermittlung der tatsächlichen Lage im Mittel nur 2...4 Suchschritte benötigt, für die 12...24 Korrelationskoeffizienten berechnet werden müssen. Dieser Vorgang benötigt auf der CD 3300 bei einem Abtastraster von 14 cm in der Natur für einen Pkw etwa 1...2 Sekunden. In dieser Zeit ist die Identifizierung und die Messung enthalten (Abb. 8).

Sollte bei der Suche ein Nebenmaximum gefunden werden (aufgrund der in 5 b) gefundenen Werte nur möglich bei einer Bremsung des beobachteten Fahrzeugs mit $b \leqq - 1 \text{ m/s}^2$), läßt sich dieses aufgrund des geringen Wertes des Korrelationskoeffizienten ($< 0,65$) feststellen (siehe Abb. 5a re.). Eine zusätzliche Prüfmöglichkeit ist durch die Korrelation der über 5 x 5 Matrizen nach x und y abgeleiteten Grauwertsverteilungen gegeben. Die Berechnung der Ableitung sowie des kontrastverschärften Bildes ist in Abb. 6 dargestellt. Die 1. Ableitung eines Bildes ergibt ein Bild, das nur Konturen enthält (Abb. 2d). Dabei zeigte sich, daß die Maxima dann bei einem echten Gipfelpunkt zwischen 0,65 und 0,90 liegen (Abb. 5c), bei einem Nebenmaximum dagegen unter 0,38 (Abb. 5 d). Schließlich läßt sich als dritte Absicherung die Begrenzung des Erwartungsbereichs verwenden, da in über 50 % der Fälle dieses Nebenmaximum außerhalb des Erwartungsbereichs liegt.

Falls also eines oder mehrere dieser drei Prüfkriterien das Nichtauffinden des Hauptmaximums anzeigen, kann an anderer Stelle des Erwartungsbereichs mit der Suche neu begonnen werden. Führt dieser Vorgang mehrmals ohne Erfolg zum Abbruch, muß der Operateur am Bildschirm "helfend eingreifen".

b) Sonderfälle und Einflüsse des Bildwinkels

Es wird, besonders bei langsamen und damit auch dicht aufeinanderfolgenden Fahrzeugen, vorkommen, daß ein Fahrzeug vom Bildrand zerschnitten wird, d. h. es ist nur zu einem Teil, z. B. mit 1/2 oder 2/3, seiner Länge aufgenommen (Abb. 4 unten li.). Um hier Störungen auszuschalten und auch diese Teilinformation noch zu verwenden, wurde ein Verfahren entwickelt, das auch von dem als Muster für die Korrelation dienenden Bildausschnitt genau so viel abschneidet, daß sich bei der Korrelation in einer Randlage die Außenränder jeweils decken. Die so berechneten Korrelationskoeffizienten besitzen zwar nicht mehr die gleiche Signifikanz, da sie über kleinere Flächen berechnet wurden, sie reichen jedoch immer noch zur Lagebestimmung, solange dieses Abschneiden nicht mehr als 2/3 der ursprünglichen Information betrifft.

Zur Verringerung der Bildwinkeleinflüsse, d. h. der Bildänderungen, die wegen der Zentralperspektive beim fortlaufenden Durchfahren des Bildbereichs durch die Fahrzeuge auftreten (die Korrelationskoeffizienten können von 0,9 auf 0,7 abnehmen), wird nach jeder aufgefundenen Deckungslage die Musterinformation innerhalb des Bildausschnitts aus dem neuesten Bild genommen (ausgetauscht), so daß jede Korrelation zwischen zwei aufeinanderfolgenden Bildern ausgeführt wird. Damit wird der gesamte Bildwinkel in viele kleine Bildwinkel aufgeteilt, wodurch das Abnehmen der Werte der Korrelationskoeffizienten mit zunehmendem Bildwinkel verhindert wird.

c) Die Identifizierung neu aufgenommener Fahrzeuge

Korreliert man mehrere unterschiedliche Fahrzeuge nicht mit sich selbst, sondern mit Fremdfahrzeugen, so erhält man ein topologisch ähnliches Verhalten der Verschiebungsmatrix der Korrelationskoeffizienten, nur daß die Höhe der Maxima etwa zwischen 0,4 und 0,9 liegt (Abb. 5 b). Hält man sich einen Vorrat von etwa 5...10 "Musterfahrzeugen" als Bildausschnitt und korreliert diese auf Verdacht in dem Bereich, der in 5 b) (Tabelle a) durch die mittlere Pulkgeschwindigkeit vorgegeben wird, so hat sich gezeigt, daß in ca. 80 % der Fälle auch ein neu auftauchendes Fahrzeug gefunden und lokalisiert werden kann. Der so gefundene Bildinhalt wird danach innerhalb des Ausschnitts herausgenommen und als Muster für die Weitersuche verwendet. Kann mangels eines gut definierten Maximums eine Definition nicht mit Sicherheit vorgenommen werden, so muß auch hier wieder der Operateur am Display eingreifen und die Definition des Kfz vornehmen. Dieses neue Kfz kann zusätzlich in den Mustersatz aufgenommen werden, um die Neudefinition eines ähnlichen Fahrzeugs, das in späteren Bildern neu auftaucht, zu ermöglichen.

d) Die Berechnung des zweidimensionalen Korrelationskoeffizienten

Die Berechnung des Korrelationskoeffizienten K eines Bildausschnitts A mit einem Ausschnitt B gleicher Dimension eines anderen (oder desselben) Bildes geschieht nach der Formel

$$K := \frac{\Sigma(x - x_m) \cdot (y - y_m)}{\sqrt{\Sigma (x - x_m)^2 \cdot \Sigma(y - y_m)^2}} \tag{10}$$

Dieser aus der Statistik bekannte Korrelationskoeffizient ist invariant gegen affine Transformationen. Das bedeutet für diesen Fall, daß Pegelverschiebungen der Grauwerte durch Instabilität des Abtasters oder durch Änderungen der Beleuchtungsintensität von Bild zu Bild ohne Einfluß bleiben, genauso wie Änderungen der Gradation bzw. des Kontrasts durch Wechsel des Fahrzeugs auf einen andersfarbigen Untergrund.

In (10) bedeuten die x die (bei einem Ausschnitt von z. B. 20 x 40 Bildpunkten 800) Aus-

schnittspunkte A des Bildes AA, die x_m stellen den arithmetischen Mittelwert über die (800)
Punkte A dar. Entsprechend gehören die y und y_m zu den 800 Grauwerten des Bildausschnitts B
aus Bild BB.

Die Summation muß jeweils über den Zeilenindex Z (1...25) und über den Spaltenindex S
(1...40) ausgeführt werden. Da die Berechnung mit einem Ausschnitt aus Bild AA über
ca. 12...24 Ausschnitte des Bildes BB ausgeführt wird, ergibt sich eine sehr große Anzahl
an Rechenoperationen (ca. 10^5). Durch Umformen unter dem Gesichtspunkt, daß der Ausschnitt A
konstant bleibt, erhält man aus (10)

$$K := \Sigma x^2 * \Sigma y^2 - ((\Sigma x)^2 * \Sigma y^2 + \Sigma x^2 * (\Sigma x)^2)/n + (\Sigma x * \Sigma y)^2/n^2 \tag{11}$$

In (11) bedeuten $\qquad$ n = ZH x SB $\qquad$ (800 = 20 x 40)

$$x = \sum_{Z=1}^{ZH} \sum_{S=1}^{SB} A[Z,S] \qquad\qquad x^2 = \sum_{Z=1}^{ZH} \sum_{S=1}^{SB} (A[Z,S])^2$$

$$y = \sum_{Z=1}^{ZH} \sum_{S=1}^{SB} B[Z,S] \qquad\qquad y^2 = \sum_{Z=1}^{ZH} \sum_{S=1}^{SB} (B[Z,S])^2$$

Bei Verwendung dieser Form lassen sich die Ausdrücke mit x einmal berechnen und wieder
verwenden, nur die Ausdrücke mit y müssen für jeden der 12...24 Verschiebeschritte neu berechnet werden, was ca. 3×10^4 Rechenoperationen erfordert. Mit Anwendung der linearen
Indexfortschaltung konnte somit der Zeitaufwand auf ca. 20 % reduziert werden.

7. Genauigkeit und genauigkeitsbeeinflussende Parameter

Wie schon bei den praktizierten photogrammetrischen Verfahren sind auch bei einer automatischen Auswertung die Fehlerquellen dieser Methoden im wesentlichen vorhanden /3/. Durch
die automatische digitale Auswertung kommen jedoch einige neue Komponenten dazu, andere
verlieren an Einfluß.

So können die Fehler aus der Aufnahmekamera wie Verzeichnung der Aufnahmeoptik, Film-
schrumpf, Neigung zwischen Objekt- und Bildebene usw. entweder wegen zu kleiner Werte
vernachlässigt oder rechnerisch nach einer Kalibrierung korrigiert werden. Wird die Relativbewegung von Lichtquellen und abzutastendem Bild im Abtaster nicht mechanisch, sondern
elektronen- oder lichtoptisch erzeugt, so führt auch die Abtastung zu Bildfehlern, die aber
nach einer Kalibrierung des Abtastsystems rechnerisch korrigiert werden können. Die Wirkung
der Bewegungsunschärfen (Bildwanderung) läßt sich durch die Wahl kurzer Aufnahmezeiten
(z. B. 1/500 s) reduzieren, ist auf dem Bild nur zu etwa einem Drittel des theoretisch zu erwartenden Werts sichtbar und fällt aufgrund der gerasterten Abtastung auch nicht sehr ins Ge-
wicht. So führt bei der Belichtungszeit t = 1/500 s = 2 ms die Fahrzeuggeschwindigkeit v =
72 km/h $\hat{=}$ 20 m/s bei dem Bildmaßstab M_b = 1 : 2000 unter der Annahme eines Verschluß-

wirkungsgrads von 100 % zu einer theoretischen Bewegungsunschärfe von 20 μm und zu einer sichtbaren von 7 μm im Bild. Da normalerweise das Abtastraster erheblich größer ist, kann die Bewegungsunschärfe vernachlässigt werden.

Zur Zeitbestimmung der Einzelaufnahmen ist eine Messung der Absolutzeit unnötig, die Messung oder Registrierung der Aufnahmezeitpunkte relativ zur vorhergehenden Aufnahme muß dagegen sehr genau erfolgen. Bei Aufnahmeabständen von 1 Sekunde muß die Zeitregistrierung mit der Genauigkeit von 0,01 s erfolgen, was eine Auflösung von noch kürzeren Zeiten erfordert, um den durch die Zeitmessung verursachten Fehler für die Geschwindigkeitsberechnung unter 1 % zu halten. Untersuchungen, die im Rahmen einer anderen Arbeit /9/ ausgeführt wurden, zeigten, daß sich mit quarzgesteuerten, elektronisch ausgelösten Registrierkameras Zeitfolgen von 0,5 s mit einem mittleren Fehler von $\Delta t = \pm 0,001$ ms einhalten lassen, was eine zusätzliche Zeitregistrierung erübrigt.

Wie Döhler gezeigt hat /3/, können Unterschiede von Fahrzeughöhen je nach Abstand des Fahrzeugs vom Bildnadir (dem Fußpunkt des Lots vom Objektiv auf das Gelände) zu erheblichen Lagefehlern führen, wenn als Bezugspunkte Fahrzeugkanten gemessen werden. Dieser Fehler hat von allen Fehlerquellen den quantitativ größten Anteil, erscheint aber beim Korrelationsverfahren nur in stark vermindertem Anteil, da hier nicht einzelne Fahrzeugpunkte gemessen werden, sondern das Fahrzeug als ganzes (bzw. ein Bild davon) mit einem anderen, sehr ähnlichen Bild in die am besten übereinstimmende Lage gebracht und die Lageverschiebung relativ zueinander gemessen wird. Durch die digitale Abtastung kommt jedoch ein neuer, systematischer Fehler hinzu. Die Genauigkeit, mit der die einzelnen Bildpunkte erfaßt werden, ist durch die Rasterung vorgegeben, beim hier verwendeten Abtaster z. B. 70 μm im Bild, was bei einem Bildmaßstab von 1 : 2000 auf der Straße 14 cm entspricht. Da die durch das Korrelationsmaximum gefundene Relativbewegung ebenfalls in Rastereinheiten berechnet wird, enthalten die gefundenen Werte einen Fehler von $\pm$ 7 cm nur durch die Rasterung. Diese Streckenfehler gehen aber auch in die berechneten Geschwindigkeiten und Beschleunigungen ein. Diese Fehler lassen sich aber zum Teil wieder kompensieren. Aus dem Korrelationskoeffizienten mit dem Maximalwert und seinen 8 Nachbarn läßt sich eine Ellipsoid-Oberfläche berechnen, deren höchster Punkt dann nicht auf einen Rasterpunkt zu fallen braucht und einen erheblich genaueren Zwischenwert für die Relativverschiebung darstellt. Eine Untersuchung ergab für den angegebenen Fall einen Restfehler von $m_f \leqq \pm 5$ cm.

Bevor für eine Auswertung Bildmaterial aufgenommen wird, müssen aus den für die Genauigkeit gewünschten Werten und der in einem Bild abgebildeten Mindeststreckenlänge die voneinander abhängigen Größen Abtastraster, Bildmaßstab, Bildformat und Flughöhe bestimmt werden. Hierzu können folgende Formeln benutzt werden (die streng nur für lotrechte Aufnahmewinkel gelten /20/):

Abtastrasterweite x Bildmaßstabszahl   =   Rasterweite im Objekt

Bildformat (b) x Bildmaßstabszahl   =   Verkehrsweg pro Bild (Objektlänge)

$$\frac{\text{Bildlänge (b)}}{\text{Brennweite}} = \frac{\text{Objektlänge}}{\text{Flughöhe}}$$

$$\frac{\text{Bildfläche (h x b)}}{\text{Abtastrasterweite}} = \text{Zahl der Rasterpunkte}$$

Die gegenseitigen Abhängigkeiten der einzelnen Parameter sind in Abb. 9 als Nomogramme dargestellt. Die gestrichelten Linien zeigen als Beispiel die Werte der Parameter, die bei den Bildern dieser Untersuchung gelten.

Die Verwendung von Normalwinkelobjektiven wird empfohlen. Überweitwinkelobjektive sind wegen der großen Bildwinkeländerung und durch Umklappung verringerten Genauigkeit schlecht geeignet.

Abtastrasterweite und Bildmaßstabszahl sollen so gewählt werden, daß die Rasterweite 10...20 cm in der Natur beträgt. Genauigkeitsabschätzungen lassen dann einen mittleren Lagefehler von $|\Delta s| = 4...7$ cm und einen Beschleunigungsfehler von $|\Delta b| = 8...15$ cm/s^2 erwarten.

8. Vorschlag für ein interaktives System zur teilautomatischen Auswertung von Luftbildern für verkehrsstatistische Zwecke

Das beste "Zeichenerkennungssystem" ist bisher und wohl auch noch weiterhin ein geschulter, erfahrener Auswerter in Verbindung mit einer geeigneten Geräteausrüstung. Dieses "System" ist in der Lage, weitgehend unabhängig von Einflüssen wie z. B. Farbe, Beleuchtung, Schatten, Kontrast, Maßstab, Orientierung und anderen Einflüssen photographische Bilder mit einer relativ geringen Fehlerquote auszuwerten. Ein wirtschaftlich vertretbarer Kompromiß für die Aufteilung der Aufgaben auf den Automaten und auf den menschlichen Operateur geschieht am besten durch die Zusammenarbeit in einem interaktiven System Mensch - Computer.

a) Zur Bildaufnahme erscheint eine 70-mm-Rollfilmkamera mit automatischem, elektrischem Filmtransport und Rollfilmkassette für 30 m Film am besten geeignet. Bei Bildfolgezeiten von 1 s lassen sich mit den 500 Aufnahmen pro Kassette 8^m 20^s Verkehrsgeschehen aufnehmen. Das entspricht bei einer mitfliegenden Beobachtung einer Kolonne, die mit 72 km/h fährt, einem Weg von 10 km. Bei stationärer Beobachtung lassen sich mit einem Bildmaßstab von 1 : 2500 damit ca. 150 m Verkehrsweg erfassen, der bei einer Bruttozeitlücke von 2 s von ca. 250 Fahrzeugen passiert wird. Bei Verwendung eines Normalwinkelobjektivs mit f = 80 mm ergibt sich daraus eine Flughöhe von ca. 200 m. Falls man das Aufnahmeformat der Kammer verkleinern kann auf 45 x 60 mm oder gar auf 20 x 60 mm, was für die Beobachtungen von Straßen ausreicht, läßt sich die Zahl der Bilder pro Kassette um 33 % bzw. 200 % steigern. Auch 35-mm-Kleinbildkameras mit 17-m-Kassette ($\cong$ 450 Bildern im Format 24 x 36 mm) sind geeignet, jedoch wird die mit einem Bild zu überdeckende Verkehrsweglänge damit beim Bildmaßstab 1 : 2500 auf 90 m reduziert. Die Kamera muß über Verschlußzeiten von 1/500 s oder 1/250 s verfügen, um die Bildwanderung klein zu halten. Die Kamera muß über eine automatische Auslöseeinrichtung (quarzgesteuerter Intervallgeber) in Abständen von 1 sec ausgelöst werden. Am Rand der aufgenommenen Straße müssen Paßpunkte in genügender Anzahl und geeigneter Anordnung und Größe markiert werden, um die absolute Orientierung der Bilder berechnen zu können.

b) Der Bildabtaster kann ein separat arbeitendes Gerät mit Magnetbandregistrierung sein oder ein an den Verarbeitungsrechner angeschlossenes und von dort steuerbares Modell. Als Zeilenweite des Abtastrasters müssen Werte zwischen 30 und 60 μm erreicht werden, um das davon beeinflußte Filmformat, die Genauigkeit, den Bildmaßstab und damit den Filmverbrauch in vernünftigen Grenzen zu halten. Wird z. B. die Rasterweite im Objekt mit 10 cm gewünscht, die zu überdeckende Strecke mit 120 m, und steht eine 70-mm-Rollfilmkamera zur Verfügung, so muß der Bildmaßstab mit 1 : 2000 gewählt werden, die Rasterweite des Abtasters muß 50 μm betragen.

Zur rationellen Verarbeitung soll der Abtaster mit einer elektrisch gesteuerten Filmtransportvorrichtung ausgestattet sein. Ein Trommelabtaster kommt für Massenauswertungen also nicht in Betracht, eher ein Flying-Spot-Scanner. Ein an den Rechner angeschlossener Bildabtaster sollte auch vom Rechner aus steuerbar sein, um den Speicherbedarf und den Rechen- und Programmaufwand für die Auswertung zu reduzieren. Die vorkommenden Bildformate müssen mit einer Abtastung bewältigt werden können. Die Grauwertauflösung sollte 32 oder 64 Stufen ($\hat{=}$ 5 bzw. 6 Bit) betragen, mehr ist nicht notwendig.

c) Das Computersystem muß als Mindestausstattung folgende Bestandteile enthalten (Abb. 10).

1. Einen Digitalrechner (Universal- oder Prozeßrechner) mit Zugriffsmöglichkeit auf Teilworte (6-Bit-Zeichen oder 8-Bit-Bytes), Wortlänge z. B. 16, 18 oder 24 Bit (evtl. auch 12, 32 oder 36 Bit). Kernspeicherausbau ca. 32 k Worte. Eventuell bringt ein mikroprogrammierbarer Zentralprozessor Zeit- und Kostenvorteile.

2. Als Massenspeicher mit wahlfreiem Zugriff eine oder mehrere Magnetplatten mit einer Mindestkapazität von ca. 500 000 Zeichen.

3. Entweder einen Anschluß zur Steuerung und zur Datenübertragung eines Bildabtasters oder ein Magnetbandgerät, um die abgetasteten und auf Band gespeicherten Bilddaten einlesen zu können.

4. Eine graphische Bildschirm-Ein-Ausgabestation (z. B. Speicherbildschirm) mit Rollkugel- oder Lichtgriffel -Dateneingabe und/oder Filmbildprojektor mit steuerbarem Filmtransport und Rollkugel-gesteuertem Fadenkreuz.

5. Ein frei programmiebares Steuertastenfeld mit Anzeigelampen oder eine Schreibmaschine, um Programmsteuerfunktionen und Abfragen für den interaktiven Dialogbetrieb zwischen

Mensch und Maschine austauschen zu können.

6. Die Software soll in einer höheren Programmiersprache (ALGOL, FORTRAN) und in Assemblersprache (z. B. für Korrelation) geschrieben werden und miteinander verbunden werden können.

Ein Interruptsystem muß in Verbindung mit Kanälen die gleichzeitige Abwicklung von Ein-Ausgabe und internen Berechnungen ermöglichen.

Der Arbeitsablauf einer solchen automatischen Auswertung ist in Abb. 11 dargestellt.

7. Die meisten in wissenschaftlichen Rechenzentren vorhandenen Großrechner genügen diesen Anforderungen, falls sie Punkt 4 und 5 erfüllen. Diese beiden Sonderforderungen lassen sich jedoch durch die Kopplung eines kleinen Prozeßrechners (Satellitenrechners) mit vergleichsweise geringem Aufwand erfüllen.

9. Zusammenfassung

Zur Datenerfassung für Straßenverkehrsuntersuchungen werden neben herkömmlichen lokalen Meßverfahren photogrammetrische Methoden angewandt, die momentane Daten liefern. Werden sowohl momentane als auch lokale Meßwerte benötigt, steigt die Zahl der aufzunehmenden und auszuwertenden Bilder stark an, die Auswertung der Bilder ist nur noch unvollständig oder mit großem Personalaufwand möglich.

Eine vollautomatische Bildauswertung wird angestrebt. Sie ist aber für alle die Fälle, in denen photogrammetrische Verfahren brauchbar sind und auch verwendet werden, aus Gründen der Wirtschaftlichkeit, des derzeitigen Mangels an geeigneten Verfahren und der Vielfalt der vorkommenden Probleme in den nächsten Jahren noch nicht zu erreichen. Diese Arbeit befaßt sich daher mit der Aufteilung des Auswertevorgangs in automatisierbare Vorgänge und in solche, die einem Operateur in einem interaktiven System überlassen werden.

Für die Teilaufgaben Erkennen, Klassifizieren, Zuordnen und Ortsmessung von Fahrzeugen wurden verschiedene Verfahren vorgeschlagen und untersucht. Das Gradientensuchverfahren über zweidimensional verteilte Korrelationskoeffizienten wurde programmiert und mit verschiedenen Verkehrsaufnahmefolgen erprobt. Unter Zuhilfenahme der physikalisch gegebenen Grenzen der Fahrzeugbewegung hat es sich für die oben definierten Aufgaben sowohl unter dem Aspekt der geforderten Genauigkeit als auch unter wirtschaftlichen Gesichtspunkten als gut brauchbares Verfahren erwiesen.

Das Auffinden bzw. Erkennen erstmalig abgebildeter Fahrzeuge läßt sich mit diesem Verfahren zu etwa 80 % automatisieren. Die geforderte Genauigkeit für die Fahrzeugbeschleunigung von $|\Delta b| \leq 0,2 \ m/s^2$ läßt sich bei geeigneter Wahl der Parameter Abtastraster und Bildmaßstab erreichen.

Unterzieht man die Ortsmessungen jeweils eines Fahrzeugs einer Ausgleichung, läßt sich die Genauigkeit der errechneten Geschwindigkeits- und Beschleunigungswerte weiter verbessern bzw. die Parameter Abtastraster und Bildmaßstabszahl können größer gewählt werden.

Die erreichbaren Genauigkeiten liegen bei $|\Delta s| = 4...7$ cm bzw. $|\Delta b| = 8...15$ cm $\cdot$ s^{-2}. Als Verarbeitungszeiten sind Werte in der Größenordnung von 1...2 s pro Fahrzeug und Bild zu erwarten. Damit sind die Genauigkeiten der bisherigen manuellen photogrammetrischen Verfahren fast erreicht, die der sonst benutzten direkten Verfahren (pneumatische Schwelle, Lichtschranken etc.) sind übertroffen. Die Auswertung der Filmaufnahmen von 4 Minuten einspurig beobachtetem Verkehr auf einer Länge von 200 m bei einer mittleren Geschwindigkeit von v = 50 km/h (d. h. 300 Aufnahmen mit je ca. 6...7 Kfz) benötigt demnach etwa 30 Minuten Abtastzeit und 1 Stunde reine Rechenzeit (d. h. ohne Berücksichtigung der Wartezeit durch den interaktiven Ablauf). Das ergibt bei dichtem Kolonnenverkehr mit einer mittleren Bruttozeitlücke von 2 s ca. 1600 Kfz-Daten (120 Kfz mit ca. 13 Messungen pro Fahrzeug bei unbewegtem Aufnahmeort bzw. 6...7 Kfz mit 240 Messungen pro Kfz bei Verfolgungsaufnahmen).

Bisherige Verfahren benötigen für das gleiche Bildmaterial nur zum Ausmessen und Registrieren der Bilddaten ca. 15 Stunden /3/.

Die Fehlerquellen der manuellen Auswertung wie z. B. die Auswirkungen von Schlagschatten sowie die durch Unzulänglichkeiten des menschlichen Operateurs bedingten Identifizierungs- und Zuordnungsfehler sind damit weitgehend ausgeschlossen bzw. verringert.

Das angegebene Verfahren erschließt für die Erforschung des Fahrverhaltens im gebundenen Verkehr neue Möglichkeiten, da es erlaubt, große Datenmengen mit hinreichender Genauigkeit innerhalb eines vertretbaren Zeitraums zu beschaffen und auszuwerten.

Literaturverzeichnis

/1/ Authie, G., A. Giraud and M. Leglise   Economy with Accuracy in Assembling Traffic Displacement Data by Aerial Photograph. Australian Road Research 4, 3...11, 1972

/2/ Breuer, F. J.   Elemente des Verkehrsablaufs an kreuzungsfreien Straßenknoten. Straßenbau und Straßenverkehrstechnik 88, 1969

/3/ Döhler, M.   Straßenverkehrs-Untersuchungen mittels photogrammetrischer Verfahren und elektronischer Datenverarbeitung. Diss. TH Karlsruhe, 1966

/4/ Fink, B., R. Hartenstein, F. Holdermann, R. Schärf, M. Sties, W. Zorn   Beschreibung eines Computersystems zur Bildverarbeitung und einige Methoden zur automatischen Mustererkennung. Forschungsbericht aus der Wehrtechnik, Bonn 1970

/5/ Forbes, T. W.,
J. J. Mullin and
M. E. Simpson

Traffic Data Acquisition from air photos by modified
conventional methods.
Paper presented at Conference on Traffic surveillance,
Simulation and Control, Washinton D. C., Sept. 1964.
College of Engineering, Michigan State University, East
Lansing, Michigan

/6/ Gamer, J. B.

The Use of Photographic Method in Highway and Traffic
Engineering.
The Photogrammetric Record VII, Nr. 40, 473..474, London 1972

/7/ Hardy, J. W., H. R.
Johnston and J.M. Godfrey

An electronic correlator for the Planimat.
Zeiss-Mitt. Vol. 5, No. 3, 1969

/8/ Helava, U. U.,
J. A. Hornbuckle and
A. J. Shahan jr

Digital Processing and Analysis of Image Data.
Bendix Technical Journal 5, No. 1 (Image Data Processing)
Southfield, Michigan, 1972

/9/ Hoefs, D. H.

Untersuchung des Fahrzeugverhaltens in Fahrzeugkolonnen.
Diss. Uni Karlsruhe, 1972

/10/ Holdermann, F.

Preprocessing of Grey-scale Pictures.
Computer Graphics and Image Processing
Academic Press, USA, 66...80, 1972

/11/ Johnston, E. G. and
A. Rosenfeld

Geometrical Operations on Digitized Pictures
Picture Processing and Psychopictorics.
Academic Press, New York/London, 1970

/12/ Kazmierczak, H. und
F. Röcker

Digitale Korrelation zweidimensionaler Datenstrukturen auf
der Grundlage der schnellen Fourier-Transformation.
Forschungsbericht aus der Wehrtechnik, Bonn 1971

/13/ Kowalski, D. C.

A Comparison of Optical and Electronic Correlation Techniques.
Bendix Technical Journal, Detroit, Michigan, 1968

/14/ Krulikoski, S. J. and
R. B. Forrest

Coherent Optical Terrein-Relief Determination
Using a Matched Filter.
Bendix Technical Journal 5, No. 1 (Image Data Processing)
Southfield, Michigan, 1972

/15/ Lipkin, B. S. and
A. Rosenfeld

Picture-Processing and Psychopictories.
Academic Press, New York/London, 1970

/16/ Raudseps, J. G.

Automatic Detection of Vehicles in Aerial Photographs
of Highways.
Transportation Systems Center Cambridge, Mass., 1971

/17/ Röhler, R.   Informationstheorie in der Optik. Stuttgart 1967

/18/ Rosenfeld, A.   Picture Processing by Computer.
                          Academic Press, New York/London, 1970

/19/ Ruhm, K.   Traffic data collection and analysis by photogrammetric
                          methods.
                          Traffic Engineering and Control 13 (8), 337...341, 1971

/20/ Schwidefsky, K.   Grundriß der Photogrammetrie, 6. Aufl. Stuttgart 1963

/21/ Treiterer, J. and   Traffic Flow Investigations by Photogrammetric Techniques.
     J. I. Taylor   Highway Research Record No. 142, Highway Research Board
                          Washington, D. C., 1966

Die Untersuchungen zu diesem Thema wurden ermöglicht durch einen Forschungsauftrag des Bundesministeriums für Verkehr.

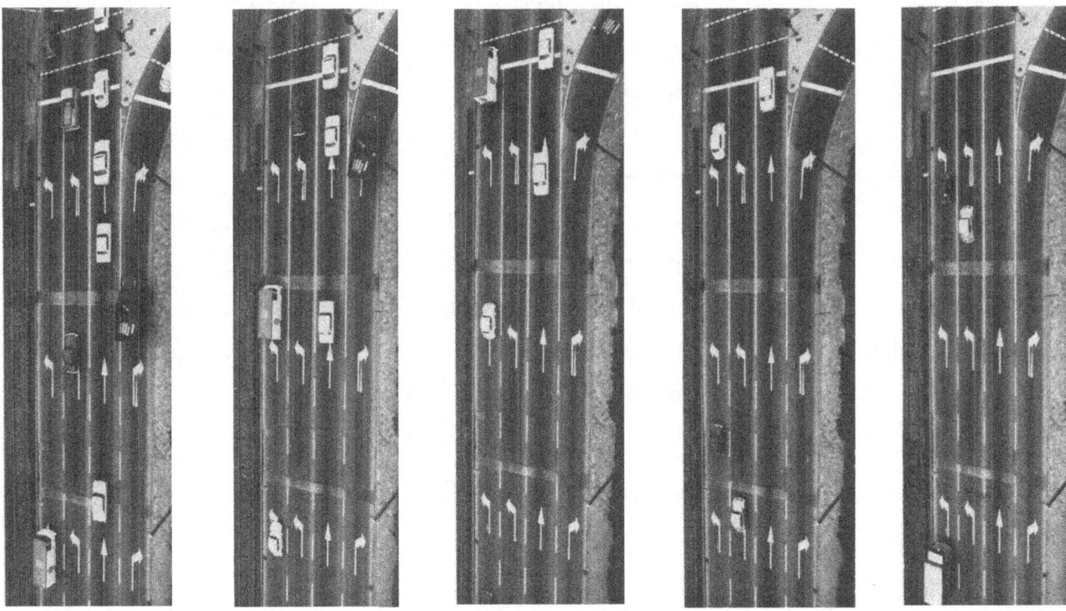

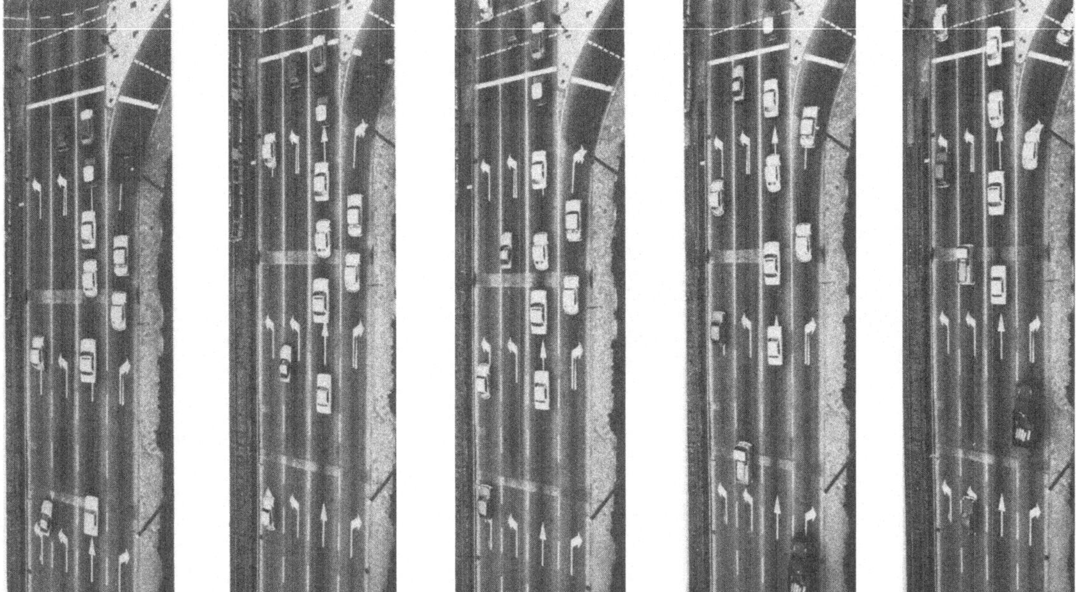

Abb. 1   Serie von 10 Folgebildern, im Abstand von je 1 Sekunde aufgenommen

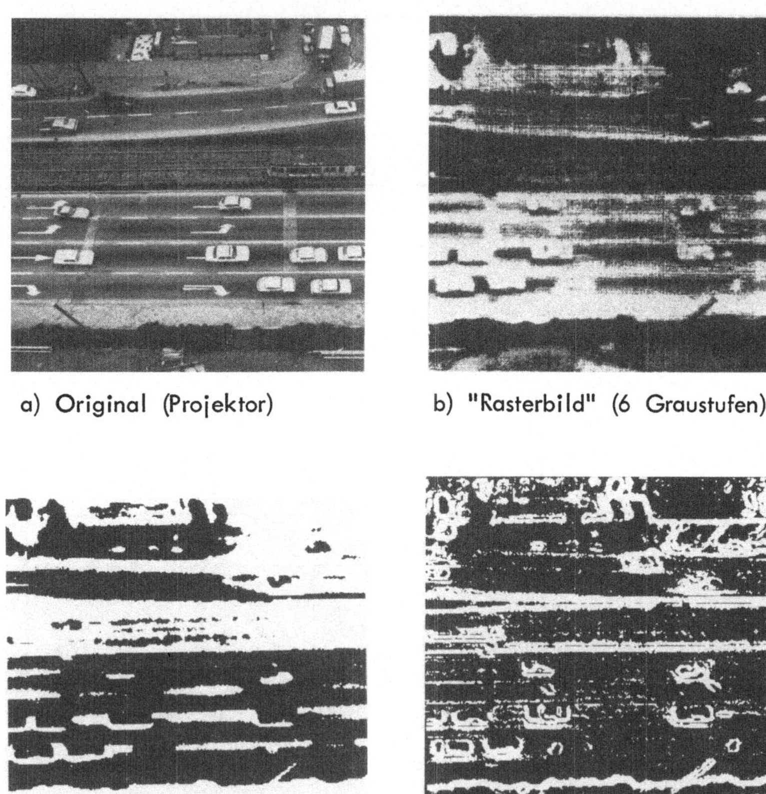

a) Original (Projektor)　　b) "Rasterbild" (6 Graustufen)

c) Schwarz/Weiß-Darstellung　　d) 1. Ableitung (Konturbild)

Abb. 2　Darstellungsformen von Bildern auf einem Display

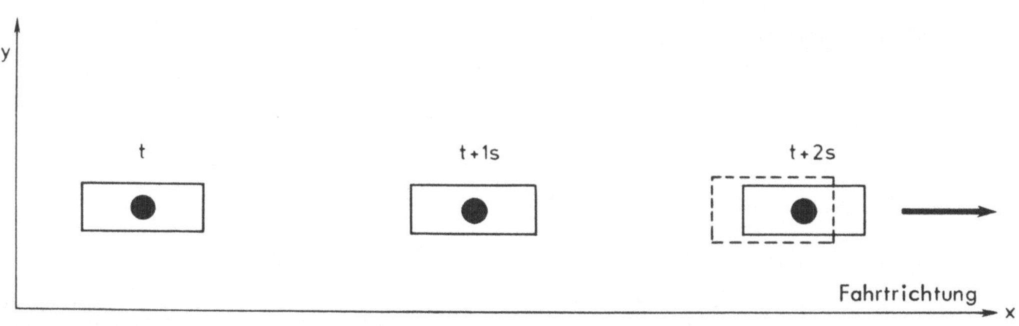

Abb. 3　Erwartungsbereich für t + 2 s bei Extrapolation aus t und t + 1 s

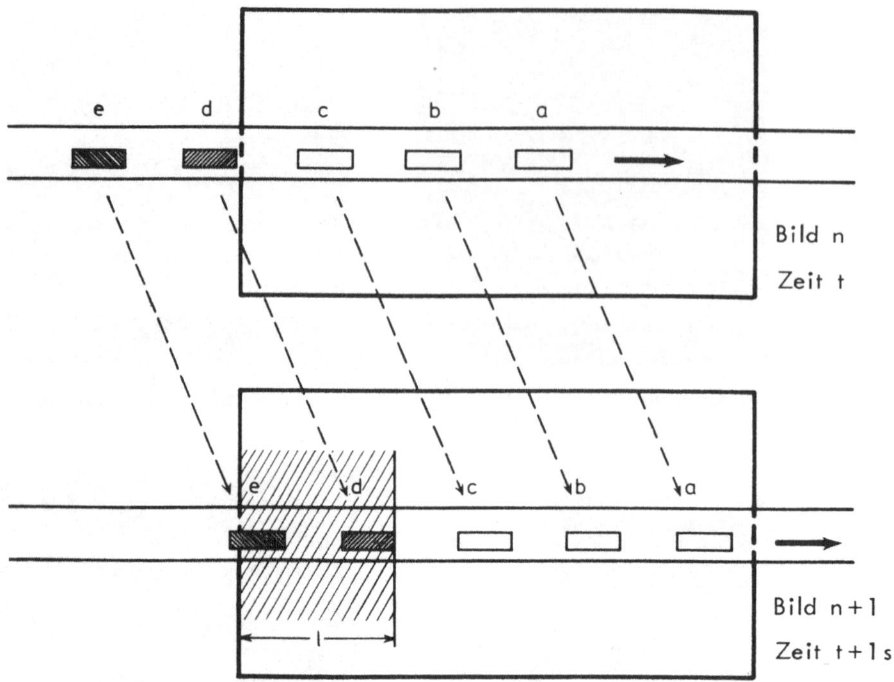

Abb. 4   Bereich l, der im Bild n + 1 neu abgebildete Fahrzeuge enthalten kann

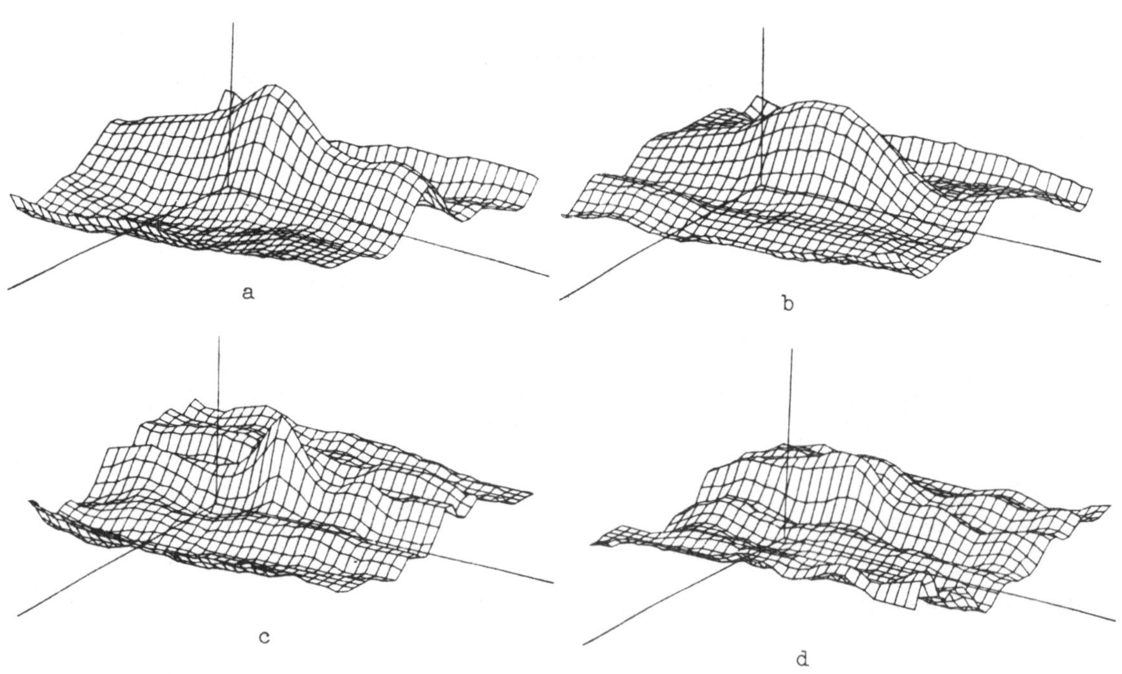

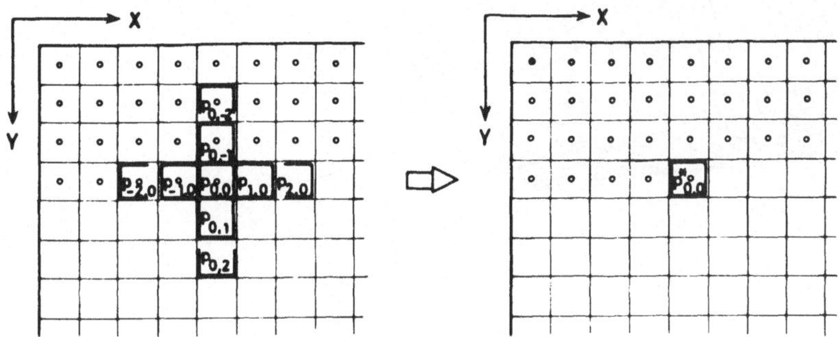

1. Ableitung : $p^* \triangleq p'$

$3 \times 3 : \quad p'^3_{0,0} = \frac{1}{2}\left(|P_{1,0} - P_{-1,0}| + |P_{0,1} - P_{0,-1}| \right)$

$5 \times 5 : \quad p'^5_{0,0} = \frac{1}{2}\left(|P_{2,0} - P_{-2,0}| + |P_{0,2} - P_{0,-2}| \right)$

2. Ableitung : $p^* \triangleq p''$

$3 \times 3 : \quad p''^3_{0,0} = \frac{1}{4}\left(P_{1,0} + P_{0,1} + P_{-1,0} + P_{0,-1} - 4P_{0,0} \right)$

$5 \times 5 : \quad p''^5_{0,0} = \frac{1}{16}\left(P_{2,0} + P_{0,2} + P_{-2,0} + P_{0,-2} - 4P_{0,0} \right)$

Kontrastverschärfung : $p^* \triangleq p^K = p - p''$

$3 \times 3 : \quad p^{K3}_{0,0} = P_{0,0} - \frac{1}{4}\left(P_{1,0} + P_{0,1} + P_{-1,0} + P_{0,-1} - 4P_{0,0} \right)$

$5 \times 5 : \quad p^{K5}_{0,0} = P_{0,0} - \frac{1}{16}\left(P_{2,0} + P_{0,2} + P_{-2,0} + P_{0,-2} - 4P_{0,0} \right)$

Abb. 6   Lokale Musterverarbeitung über 3 x 3 bzw. 5 x 5 Untermatrizen

Abb. 5   Topologische Modelle der Korrelations-Koeffizienten-Matrizen

a) Kreuzkorrelation mit Nebenmaximum

$MAX_H = 0,95 \qquad MAX_H = 0,52$

b) Kreuzkorrelation von 2 verschiedenen Pkw; MAX = 0,77

c) Kreuzkorrelation der 1. Ableitungen über

5 x 5 Untermatrizen; MAX = 0,82

d) Kreuzkorrelation der 1. Ableitung über 5 x 5 Untermatrizen

von 2 verschiedenen Pkw; MAX = 0,05

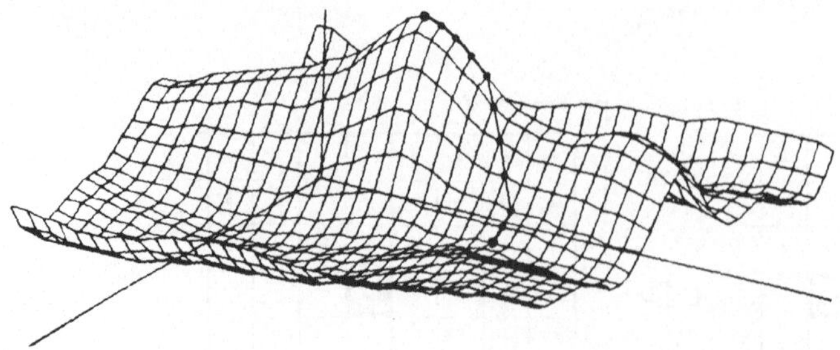

Abb. 7   Topologisches Korrelationsmodell mit Suchgradient

BILD 1/ 3 KREUZKORRELAT. 11.12.72 ZEILE 160 SPALTE 69. 21 * 38   ZEILE 159 SPALTE 54

IMAX	NSPN	NZEN									
1	54	159	-34	-31	-37	-103	-97	-101	-115	-108	-108
1	54	158	85	85	76	-34	-31	-37	-103	-97	-101
0	54	157	226	222	215	85	85	76	-34	-31	-37
0	53	156	383	366	359	235	226	222	85	85	85
0	52	155	539	490	466	422	383	366	263	235	226
0	51	154	641	558	507	619	539	490	491	422	383
3	50	153	615	518	440	744	641	558	717	619	539
3	49	153	717	615	518	847	744	641	814	717	619
3	48	153	801	717	615	929	847	744	887	814	717
3	47	153	838	801	717	956	929	847	902	887	814
4	46	153	810	838	801	914	956	929	852	902	887

IMAX NSPN NZEN   3 x 3 Korrelationskoeffizientenmatrix

Richtungsindex des Maximums IMAX:

0	1	2
3	4	5
6	7	8

Anordnung der letzten beiden 3 x 3 Korrelationskoeffizientenmatrizen:

0,810	0,838	0,801	0,717
0,914	0,956	0,929	0,847
0,852	0,902	0,887	0,814

Abb. 8   Kontrollausdruck der Maximumsuche auf Suchgradient

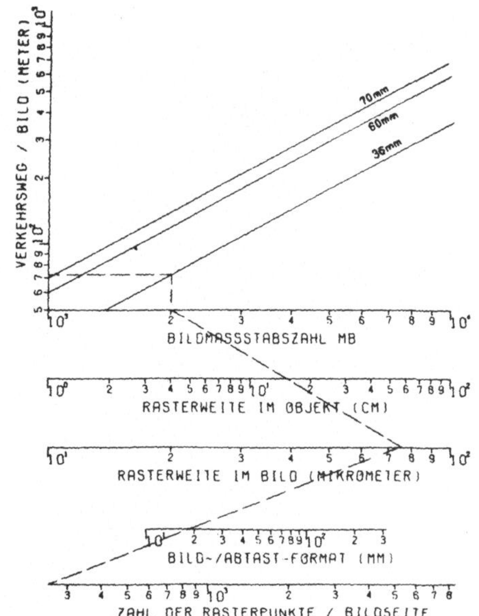

Abb. 9   Nomogramm der gegenseitigen
Abhängigkeit der Bildparameter

Abb. 10   Konfigurationsvorschlag zum System für teilautomatische Bildauswertung

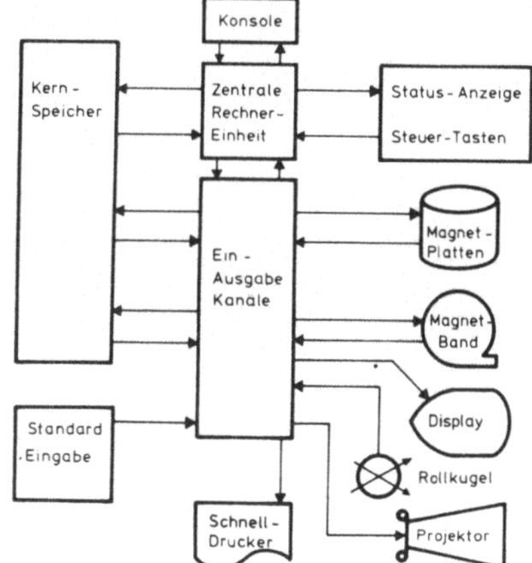

Abb. 11   Ablaufdiagramm des interaktiven Systems zur teilautomatischen Verkehrsbildauswertung

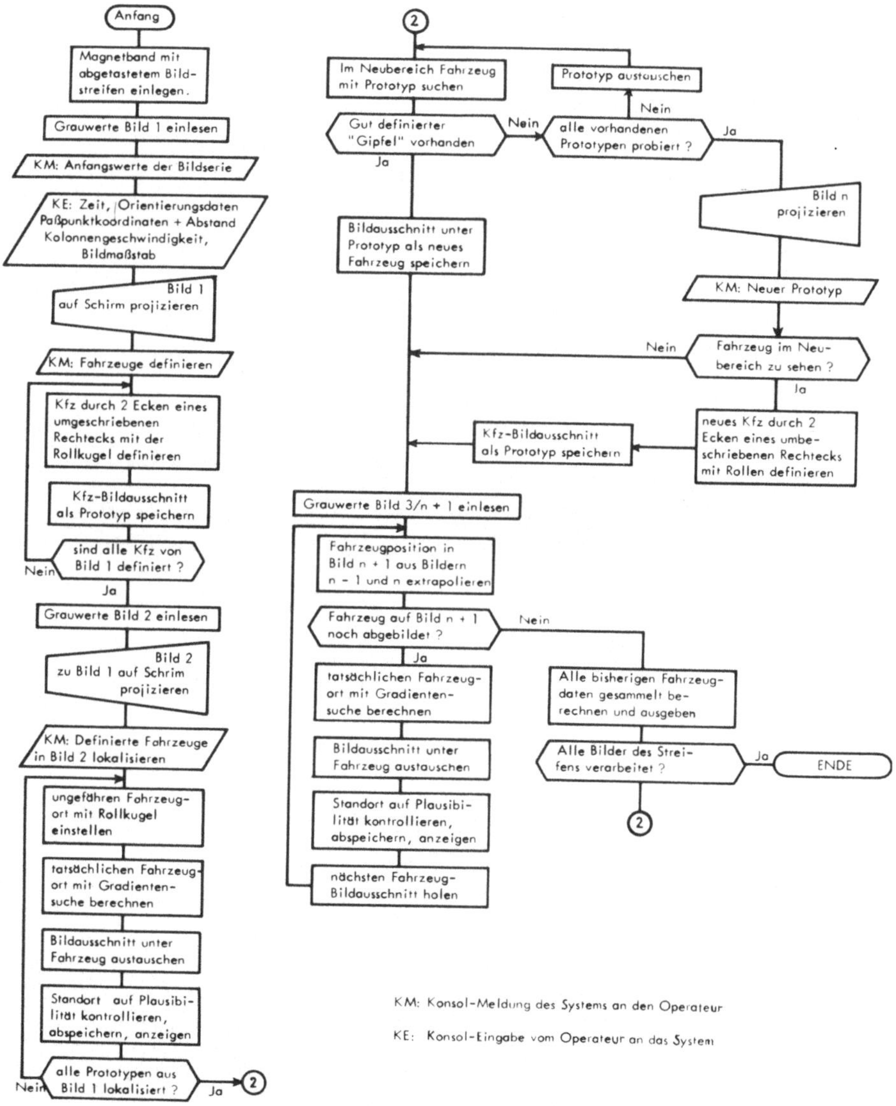

Interaktive Ortung und Identifizierung von Fischschwärmen

J.F. Böhme

Zusammenfassung

Dieser Bericht stellt ein interaktives adaptives Mensch-Maschine-System zur Ortung und Identifizierung von Fischschwärmen vor, das mit akustischen Sensoren arbeitet und das auf einem modernen Fischerei-Fangschiff installiert werden soll. Insbesondere werden die Arbeitsweise und die Organisation des Systems beschrieben. In einem Anhang wird die interaktive Entscheidungsprozedur zur Identifizierung vom wahrscheinlichkeitstheoretischen Standpunkt aus motiviert.

1. Einleitung

Auf der Brücke eines modernen Fischdampfers befindet sich der Jagdsitz des Kapitäns umgeben von mehreren Displays und Schreibern verschiedener Echolote. Diese Lote senden in horizontaler und vertikaler Richtung vom Schiff aus und in Schlepprichtung vom Fangnetz aus Schallstrahlen fächerförmig ins Meer und registrieren die Echos. Anhand dieser Aufzeichnungen und seiner Erfahrung entscheidet der Kapitän

1) an welchen Stellen relativ zum Fangschiff sich Fischschwärme befinden,
2) welche Sorten von Fischen zu erwarten sind,
3) ob ein Schwarm einen lohnenden Fang verspricht und schließlich
4) welche Manöver als nächste auszuführen sind. -

Das Ziel einer vom Ministerium für Wissenschaft und Bildung finanzierten Studie "Integriertes Fischfangsystem" war u.a., geeignete Geräte zu entwerfen, die diese Entscheidungen dem Kapitän abnehmen oder erleichtern können. Im Rahmen dieser Studie wurde ein interaktives adaptives Mensch-Maschine-System zur Ortung, Identifizierung und Auswahl konzipiert, das eine Lösung der Aufgabe liefert und das im folgenden erläutert wird. -

Die erwähnten Echolote (oder besser Sonar-Anlagen) sind die Sensoren und liefern für jeden Schallstrahl eine Zeitfunktion. Anhand dieser Signale und anhand von ozeanographischen Daten sowie von Informationen, die in der Fischereidatenbank gespeichert sind und

die über vergangene Fangergebnisse etc. berichten, müssen die gewünschten Entscheidungen gefällt werden. Prinzipiell beschreibt das Interferenzfeld eines geeignet akustisch angestrahlten Fischschwarmes diesen Schwarm vollständig. Zum Abtasten des Interferenzfeldes stehen aber nur die Hydrophone des benutzten Lotes zur Verfügung. Man erhält also, abgesehen von den zusätzlich zu beachtenden Umwelteinflüssen, keinen "Fingerabdruck" des Fischschwarmes, der eindeutig auf den Schwarm schließen läßt. Nicht einmal der Schluß auf die Fischart ist eindeutig möglich. Es müssen daher mehrere Indizien gesammelt werden, die man z.B. durch Aussenden verschieden modulierter Sendesignale und angepaßter Signalverarbeitung gewinnen kann. Anhand dieser Indizien muß mit Hilfe einer Art von Indizienbeweis z.B. auf die Fischart geschlossen werden. -
Die erläuterten Probleme legen es nahe, die Ortungs- und Identifizierungsaufgabe als ein statistisches Mustererkennungs- und Schätzproblem aufzufassen. Um die Entscheidungen zu optimieren, benötigt man eine genaue statistische Beschreibung der Echos in Abhängigkeit von Fischart und Umweltparametern. Eine ausreichende Schätzung dieser Statistik ist aus Aufwandsgründen nicht zu erhalten. Es bleibt also nur, die heuristischen Fähigkeiten des Menschen zur Konstruktion brauchbarer Verfahren auszunutzen.

2. Gründe für die Wahl des Systems

Für die Ortung und für die Identifizierung gibt es noch keine einfachen Rezepte, nach denen die zu fällenden Entscheidungen mehr oder weniger automatisch ausgeführt werden können. Die einzige zur Verfügung stehende Kenntnis über die Zuordnung der Echos zu Fischschwärmen ist die Erfahrung der Fischdampfer-Kapitäne. Ganz allgemein scheint ein vollautomatisches System zur Ortung und Identifizierung, das nur mit geringen mittleren Entscheidungsfehlern arbeitet, aus folgenden Gründen heute noch nicht zu verwirklichen zu sein:
1) Die Erfahrung der Fischdampfer-Kapitäne kann nur schwer derart formal ausgedrückt werden, daß sie unmittelbar für einen Entscheidungsautomaten verwendbar ist.
2) Die Menge der Informationen kann nur günstig mit assoziativen Speichermedien verarbeitet werden, solche sind aber heute in technisch einfacher Form noch nicht zu erhalten.
3) Der insgesamt benötigte Aufwand wird unverhältnismäßig groß sein. -
Jedoch ist heute für die Ortungs- und Identifizierungsaufgabe ein interaktives adaptives Mensch-Maschine-System mit vertretbarem Aufwand realisierbar. Ein solches System ist die Zusammenfassung eines

Rechners, der an die Lote angeschlossen ist, und des Kapitäns.
Zwischen beiden ist ein Display-Arbeitsplatz mit Lichtgriffeln und
Knopffeld das Kommunikationsmedium. Die Entscheidungen werden in
Zusammenarbeit von Mensch und Maschine ausgeführt, indem die asso-
ziative Speicher- und Entscheidungsfähigkeit sowie die Erfahrung des
Kapitäns zum Hypothesensetzen und die Rechen- und Verwaltungsfähig-
keit des Rechners zum Hypothesentesten günstig ausgenutzt werden.
Unter "adaptivem System" wird hier verstanden, daß der Kapitän und
die Maschine gemeinsam lernen, aus den Sensorsignalen Auskünfte über
Ort und Art der Fangobjekte zu gewinnen. Auf diese Weise kann die
Leistungsfähigkeit des Mensch-Maschine-Systems mit wachsender Zeit
verbessert werden. -
Nach Meinung des Verfassers sind noch keine einfachen und erfolgver-
sprechenden Verfahren bekannt, nach deren Prinzip man preisgünstige
Systeme obiger Art bauen könnte. Es wurde daher vorgeschlagen, einen
Prototypen zu realisieren, der möglichst flexibel hinsichtlich seiner
Signalverarbeitung usw. ist. Der Prototyp sollte auf einem Fischerei-
Forschungsschiff aufgebaut werden und zum Entwurf und zur Erprobung
von interaktiven Entscheidungsverfahren dienen. Sich als einfach er-
weisende Methoden können dann in weniger aufwendigen Geräten zur
Ausrüstung neuerer Fangschiffe implementiert werden.

3. Das Arbeiten mit dem System

Um wirkungsvoll fischen zu können, muß der Kapitän möglichst gut die
Situation unter Wasser in der Nähe seines Schiffes und seines Netzes
überblicken können. Diesen Überblick soll ihm der Operations-Display
(vergl. Abb.1) seines Arbeitsplatzes vermitteln. Im linken Teil des
Displays wird ihm ein Sonarbild gezeigt, das einen Horizontalschnitt
mit der Achse Netz-Schiff darzustellen versucht. (Sonarbilder besitzen eine geringe Auflösung, so daß ein Fischschwarm nur als eine
diffuse "Wolke" ohne scharfe Konturen zu erkennen ist.) Rechts oben
sind Längsvertikalschnitte vor dem Schiff und vor dem Netz und unten
rechts ein Quervertikalschnitt unterhalb des Schiffes abgebildet.
Striche, Marken und Text sind digital in das Bild eingefügt. Die
übrigen Informationen des Operations-Displays sollen dem Kapitän das
Manövrieren von Schiff und Netz erleichtern. -
Sei einmal angenommen,der Kapitän habe auf dem Horizontallotfeld eine
Wolke ausgemacht, von der er annimmt, sie stelle einen lohnenden
Fischschwarm dar. Dann setzt er mit dem Lichtgriffel eine Marke in
die Wolke. Daraufhin wird die Marke automatisch in Abhängigkeit von
den Schiffsbewegungen getrackt. Der Kapitän verfolgt den Weg und die

Entwicklung der Wolke eine Weile und möchte vielleicht dann den
möglichen Fischschwarm identifizieren. Er drückt den Knopf "Zeichnen"
des Knopffeldes und umzeichnet mit dem Lichtgriffel auf dem Horizontallotfeld das Gebiet, in dem der Schwarm zu erwarten ist. Ein Druck
auf den "Ausschnitt"-Knopf aktiviert einen zweiten Display, den
Identifizierungsdisplay des Arbeitsplatzes. Auf diesem Display erscheint dann das Bild "Vorauslotung horizontal" (Abb.2). Der Operations-Display behält sein Bild, denn der Kapitän muß sich ständig
über die Unterwassersituation informieren. Der Rechner hat nach dem
Befehl "Ausschnitt" um die gezeichnete Kurve das kleinste Rechteck
gelegt, das die Ausschnittdaten festlegt. Beim nächsten ausgesende-
ten Puls erscheint die gewünschte Vergrößerung des möglichen Schwarm-
bildes im linken kleinen Quadrat des Bildes "Vorauslotung horizontal".
Der Kapitän beobachtet jetzt die Ausschnitte von Puls zu Puls. Findet er ein Echo mit einer markanten Struktur, so berührt er mit einem
zweiten Lichtgriffel den Lichtknopf "halt". Ein Lichtknopf ist hier
ein umrandetes oder unterstrichenes Wort. Auf dem Identifizierungs-
display bleibt das Bild stehen und auf dem Operations-Display verändert es sich weiter. Berührung des Lichtknopfes "Hypothesensetzen"
läßt im rechten kleinen Quadrat des Bildes eine Liste von möglichen
Hypothesen erkennen. Der Kapitän setzt z.B. als erstes "Nachhall"
(kein Fischschwarm) und betätigt darauf "Hypothesentesten". Der
Rechner antwortet vielleicht mit "N" für nein. Die nächste Hypothese ist "Schwarm", der Rechner antwortet mit "J" für ja. Mögliche
weitere Hypothesen werden vom Rechner getestet. Dem Rechner ist es
auch möglich, mit "O" für "weiß nicht" zu antworten. Wenn "Vorschlag"
berührt wird, klassifiziert der Rechner den Echoausschnitt unter Berücksichtigung der letzten Hypothese des Kapitäns. Sollte der Kapitän z.B. aus einem Probefang wissen, welche Fischart zu erwarten
ist, kann er den Rechner über den Befehl "Lernen" und anschließen-
der Berührung des Namens in der Hypothesenliste belehren. -
Die Test-, Vorschlags- und Lernprozedur waren in diesem Beispiel
standardmäßig. Wünscht der Kapitän andere, insbesondere bei der Ver-
fahrensklärung, so kann er diese über den Befehl "nicht Standard"
wählen. Ein besonderes Verfahren würde benutzt werden, wenn der
Lichtknopf "Kontur" berührt wird. Nach der Instruktion "Zeichnen"
zeichnet der Fischer die vermutete Kontur des Schwarmes in den Ausschnitt. Dann wird für das Identifizieren des Schwarmes nur noch
diese Kurve ausgenutzt im Gegensatz zu anderen Verfahren, die i.a.
die volle Echostruktur des Ausschnittes benötigen und daher erheblich rechenaufwendiger sind. Mit "Notieren" kann sich der Fischer

den gezeigten Ausschnitt abspeichern und über "Notiertes" im rechten
Quadrat wieder ansehen, wenn über "periodisch" weitere Echos als
Ausschnitt im linken Quadrat zu sehen waren. Mit "Bewertung" nimmt
der Rechner eine Bewertung der Identifizierungsprozedur vor. "Mengenschätzung" liefert eine Mengenschätzung des Schwarmes nach bekannten heuristischen Methoden. Möchte man einen neuen Ausschnitt
z.B. aus dem Längsvertikalschnitt untersuchen, so berühre man den
Lichtknopf "neuer Ausschnitt" und hole sich auf die beschriebene Art
einen Ausschnitt aus dem Längsvertikalschnitt des Operations-Displays.
Es wurde weiter oben stillschweigend vorausgesetzt, daß der Kapitän
genügend a-priori-Kenntnisse über die im Fanggebiet zu erwartenden
Fische besitzt. Besitzt er diese nicht, so kann er über "Auskunft"
im rechten Quadrat mit der Fischerei-Datenbank kommunizieren und
sich die fehlende Information verschaffen. Dazu muß noch bemerkt
werden, daß der Kapitän auf zwei Echolotschreibern die Echostruktur
über einen längeren Zeitraum mit einem Blick übersehen kann, so daß
ihm zusätzliche Kenntnisse zur Verfügung stehen, um ihm das Hypothesensetzen zu erleichtern. Schließlich dienen die restlichen Licht-
knöpfe auf dem Identifizierungs-Display organisatorischen Zwecken.

4. Systemorganisation

Die Hardware des interaktiven Systems wird in groben Zügen durch
Abb.3 beschrieben. Organisatorischer Kern des Systems ist der Kommunikationsrechner. Alle anderen Geräte können als Perepherie zu
diesem Rechner aufgefaßt werden. Das System arbeitet (bis auf den
Überwachungslautsprecher) digital. Der Kommunikationsrechner ver-
waltet im Wesentlichen. Die Signale aus den Loten laufen direkt in
die Lotschreiber, in den Bildwiederholspeicher des Operations-Displays und den steuerbaren Zwischenspeicher. Diese Wahl muß getroffen
werden, um den Kommunikationsrechner nicht durch triviale Signalverarbeitung für andere Aufgaben zu blockieren. Die Lote sind in Abb.3
oben gezeichnet. Sie werden durch den Kommunikationsrechner wie alle
anderen Geräte gesteuert und geben digitale Signale aus. Die Schreiber arbeiten wie übliche Echographen. Der Operations-Display besitzt
eine 2-Gun-Röhre. Über das eine Ablenksystem werden die Echodaten
analog in Spiralablenkung abgebildet und über das andere vom Rechner
erzeugt die Striche und Symbole digital in kartesischer Ablenkung.
Dieser digitale Bildaufbau ist wegen der Lichtgriffeloperationen
notwendig. Der Identifizierungs-Display arbeitet rein digital und
wird vollständig über den Kommunikationsrechner beschrieben. Der auf
diesem Display dargestellte Bildausschnitt wird aus den Daten im

steuerbaren Zwischenspeicher vom Kommunikationsrechner aufgebaut.
Dieser Speicher enthält die Signale des Ausschnittes in maximaler
Genauigkeit im Gegensatz zum steuerbaren Bildwiederholspeicher, bei
dem man z.B. mit 4 bit Genauigkeit auskommt. Weitere Perepherie des
Kommunikationsrechners sind digitale Eingabestationen für ozeanogra-
phische und navigatorische Daten, eine Uhr (taktet das Gesamtsystem),
ein Lesespeicher (aus ihm wird zu Beginn der Arbeit die Systemüberwachung (s.u.) geladen), ein Sekundärspeicher (Fortsetzung des Kern-
speichers des Kommunikationsrechners) und eine Fernschreiberstation
(dient dazu, die Fischerei-Datenbank ständig zu aktualisieren und
Programmänderungen vornehmen zu können). Der Kommunikationsrechner
selbst muß im Real-Time-Betrieb arbeiten. Die einzelnen peripheren
Geräte sind mit verschiedener Priorität möglichst "gleichzeitig" zu
bedienen. Das erfordert Multiprogramming. Der Rechner sollte ein
schneller Prozeßrechner mit einer Wortlänge von mindestens 16 bit
sein. Der Identifizierungsrechner als peripherer Rechner ist ein
Rechner desselben Typs, nur ist er komfortabler in seiner Rechen-
fähigkeit ausgestattet. Als zusätzliches externes Rechenwerk ist
ein Feldtransformationsprozesser, mit dem man z.B. schnell die
Fourier-Transformation ausführen kann, an den Identifizierungsrechner angeschlossen. Sekundär- und Tertiärspeicher dienen zur Aufnahme
der Identifizierungsroutinen und -daten sowie der Fischereidatenbank.
Die zu klassifizierenden Echodaten erhält der Identifizierungsrechner
aus dem vom Kommunikationsrechner kontrollierten Zwischenspeicher. -
Die Software-Organisation wird durch das Funktionsblockdiagramm des
interaktiven Entscheidungssystems (Abb.4) beschrieben. Zentrale Ver-
waltung ist die Systemüberwachung. Diese kontrolliert die Kommunikationsverwaltung, die die Kommunikation mit dem Fischer überwacht.
Der Systemüberwachung untersteht weiter die Verwaltung der Daten der
Fischereidatenbank und der zum Identifizieren notwendigen Daten. Die
Systemüberwachung lenkt die Signalverarbeitung der Echodaten. Der
Signalprozessor enthält die Programmpakete Edition (Ausschnittbe-
rechnung etc.), Szenenanalyse (Normierung, Entstörung, Rasterung,
Mengenschätzung etc.), Rezeption (Berechnung eines niedrigdimensio-
nalen Vektors aus dem vorverarbeiteten Ausschnitt), Klassifikation
(Durchführung der statistischen Tests anhand der Vektoren) und Be-
wertung (Kontrolle der durch das Lernen erhaltenen Testalgorithmen).
Schließlich kontrolliert die Systemüberwachung die Datenstationen
und sämtliche Lote und führt in gewissen Abständen Funktionstests
der einzelnen Geräte durch.

Literatur

1) "Adaptive, Learning, and Pattern Recognition Systems".
   Eds. Mendel, J.S. and Fu, K.S., New York: Academic Press, 1970.

2) "Durchführbarkeitsstudie, Band 2 - Originalbeiträge".
   Arbeitsgemeinschaft "Integriertes Fischfangsystem",
   ERNO-Krupp-Seebeck. Bremen: ERNO, Januar 1972.

3) Whitney, A.W. and Blasdell, W.E.: "Study of Computer Graphics
   and Signal Classification Application". Techn. Rept., Rome Air
   Development Center, RADC-TR-148, September, 1970, AD 713 155.

Anhang: Motivierung der Identifizierungsprozedur

In diesem Anhang wird versucht, die Entscheidungsprozedur:
Hypothesensetzen des Kapitäns und Hypothesentesten bzw. Vorschlag
der Maschine in Abhängigkeit von der Hypothese (oder umgekehrt)
durch wahrscheinlichkeitstheoretische Überlegungen zu motivieren.
Das Entscheidungsproblem ist offensichtlich ein Mustererkennungsproblem. Als Muster sind dabei die zur Verfügung stehenden Informationen zu betrachten und als Musterklassen Mengen von Mustern,
denen man dieselbe Bedeutung (Nachhall, Hering o.ä.) zuordnet.

Zunächst seien einige Voraussetzungen erfüllt:
1) Das Mustererkennungsproblem läßt sich als wahrscheinlichkeits-
   theoretisches Problem deuten.
2) Die Beobachtungen des Kapitäns anhand des Bildausschnittes und
   der sonstigen ihm zur Verfügung stehenden Information lassen sich
   zu einer Variablen x zusammenfassen, die Werte aus einer Menge
   X annimmt.
3) Die Daten, die der Identifizierungsrechner aus dem Bildausschnitt
   erhält, können durch eine Variable y beschrieben werden, die Werte
   aus einer Menge Y annimmt.
4) I sei eine endliche Menge mit Elementen i, j, k und kennzeichnet
   die Namen der Musterklassen (also Bedeutungen).
5) Ein Wahrscheinlichkeitsraum $(X \times Y \times I, \Omega, p)$ beschreibt die Statistik der Muster ($X \times Y \times I$ Kreuzprodukt von X, Y, I; Ω σ-Algebra über
   $X \times Y \times I$; p Wahrscheinlichkeitsmaß über Ω).

Es wird also angenommen, daß sich die Merkmale der Musterklassen
durch bedingte Wahrscheinlichkeiten ausdrücken lassen und daß a-
priori-Wahrscheinlichkeiten über das Auftreten der Musterklassen
existieren.

Ein Mustererkennungsmechanismus entscheide mit Hilfe eines Zufalls-
generators, der durch eine Entscheidungsfunktion ε bestimmt ist:
Wenn a gemessen wird, ist $\varepsilon(i|a) \geq 0$ die Wahrscheinlichkeit dafür,
daß der Mechanismus i als Entscheidungsergebnis ausgibt, wobei
$\sum_i \varepsilon(i|a) = 1$ ist.

Fünf verschiedene Entscheidungsarten sollen betrachtet werden:
1) Der Kapitän entscheidet allein mit Hilfe einer Entscheidungsfunktion ε_1 aufgrund seiner Beobachtung x .
2) Der Rechner entscheidet allein mit Hilfe einer Entscheidungs-

funktion ε_2 aufgrund seiner Messung y .

3) Ein Supersystem entscheidet mit Hilfe einer Entscheidungsfunktion ε_3 aufgrund der Beobachtung x und der Messung y .

4) Der Rechner entscheidet mit Hilfe einer Entscheidungsfunktion ε_4 aufgrund seiner Messung y und der Kenntnis über die Entscheidungsfunktion ε_1 des Kapitäns sowie über dessen Entscheidungsergebnis i .

5) Der Kapitän entscheidet mit Hilfe einer Entscheidungsfunktion ε_5 aufgrund seiner Beobachtung x und der Kenntnis über die Entscheidungsfunktion ε_2 des Rechners und über dessen Entscheidungsergebnis j .

Im Fall 4) setzt der Kapitän eine Hypothese und der Rechner testet diese bzw. macht einen Gegenvorschlag in Abhängigkeit von der Hypothese und im Fall 5) ist es umgekehrt.

Als Fehlerwahrscheinlichkeiten findet man in den fünf Fällen

$$\bar{P}_1(\varepsilon_1) = 1 - \int_X \sum_i \varepsilon_1(i|x)\, p(dx, Y, i),$$

wobei $p(\cdot, Y, \cdot)$ Marginalverteilung bzgl. Y ist,

$$\bar{P}_2(\varepsilon_2) = 1 - \int_Y \sum_j \varepsilon_2(j|y)\, p(X, dy, j),$$

$$\bar{P}_3(\varepsilon_3) = 1 - \int_X \int_Y \sum_k \varepsilon_3(k|x, y)\, p(dx, dy, k),$$

$$\bar{P}_4(\varepsilon_4, \varepsilon_1) = 1 - \int_Y \sum_i \sum_j \varepsilon_4(j|y, i)\left[\int_X \varepsilon_1(i|x)\, p(dx, j|y)\right] p(X, dy, I),$$

wobei $p(\cdot, \cdot|y)$ ein Wahrscheinlichkeitsmaß unter der Bedingung ist, daß y gemessen worden ist und

$$\bar{P}_5(\varepsilon_5, \varepsilon_2) = 1 - \int_X \sum_j \sum_i \varepsilon_5(i|x, j)\left[\int_Y \varepsilon_2(j|y)\, p(dy, i|x)\right] p(dx, Y, I).$$

Man kann leicht nachweisen, daß im Fall 1) ε_1 die Fehlerwahrscheinlichkeit $\bar{P}_1$ minimiert genau dann, wenn gilt:
Für alle x aus X und alle i aus I ist

$$\varepsilon_1(i|x) = 0 \text{ genau dann, wenn } p(Y, i|x) < \max_i p(Y, i|x).$$

Mit der Kenntnis von $p(Y, \cdot|\cdot)$ kann also eine günstige Lösung ε_1 konstruiert werden. Ganz analog verhält es sich in den Fällen 2) bis 5).

Als minimale Fehlerwahrscheinlichkeiten ergeben sich dann

$$\min_{\varepsilon_1} \bar{P_1}(\varepsilon_1) = 1 - \int_X \max_i \left[P(Y,i \mid x) \right] P(dx, Y, I),$$

entsprechend $\min\limits_{\varepsilon_2} \bar{P_2}(\varepsilon_2)$,

$$\min_{\varepsilon_3} \bar{P_3}(\varepsilon_3) = 1 - \int_X \int_Y \max_k \left[P(k \mid x, y) \right] P(dx, dy, I),$$

$$\min_{\varepsilon_4} \bar{P_4}(\varepsilon_4, \varepsilon_1) = 1 - \int_Y \sum_i \max_j \left[\int_X \varepsilon_1(i \mid x) P(dx, j \mid y) \right] P(X, dy, I)$$

und entsprechend $\min\limits_{\varepsilon_5} \bar{P_5}(\varepsilon_5, \varepsilon_2)$.

Folgende Abschätzung ergibt sich unmittelbar:

$$\max_j P(X, j \mid y) = \max_j \int_X \sum_i \varepsilon(i \mid x) P(dx, j \mid y)$$

$$\leq \sum_i \max_j \left[\int_X \varepsilon_1(i \mid x) P(dx, j \mid y) \right] = \sum_i \max_j \left[\int_X \varepsilon_1(i \mid x) P(j \mid x, y) P(dx, I \mid y) \right]$$

$$\leq \int_X \sum_i \varepsilon_1(i \mid x) \max_j \left[P(j \mid x, y) \right] P(dx, I \mid y) = \int_X \max_j \left[P(j \mid x, y) \right] P(dx, I \mid y).$$

Nach Anwendung von $1 - \int_Y \ldots P(X, dy, I)$ auf den ersten, dritten und letzten Ausdruck der Ungleichungskette findet man für alle ε_1

$$(*) \quad \min_{\varepsilon_3} \bar{P_3}(\varepsilon_3) \leq \min_{\varepsilon_4} \bar{P_4}(\varepsilon_4, \varepsilon_1) \leq \min_{\varepsilon_2} \bar{P_2}(\varepsilon_2).$$

Entsprechend beweist man für alle ε_2

$$\min_{\varepsilon_3} \bar{P_3}(\varepsilon_3) \leq \min_{\varepsilon_5} \bar{P_5}(\varepsilon_5, \varepsilon_2) \leq \min_{\varepsilon_1} \bar{P_1}(\varepsilon_1).$$

In ($*$) z.B. gilt das Gleichheitszeichen rechts, wenn der Kapitän im Mittel seine Hypothese so ungünstig setzt, daß es der Maschine im wesentlichen nichts hilft, die Entscheidung des Kapitäns zu wissen. Das Gleichheitszeichen links gilt, wenn es dem Kapitän gelingt, seine Entscheidung im Mittel so gut zu treffen, daß es für die beste Leistung des Supersystems gleichgültig ist, für seine Entscheidung x und y oder i und y zu benutzen. Dieser Fall ist aber nur bei ganz speziellen Wahrscheinlichkeitsmaßen P möglich.
Zusammenfassend ergibt sich für die Identifizierungsstrategie:
Am günstigsten wäre es, mit Hilfe eines Supersystems zu entscheiden, was jedoch aus Aufwandsgründen ausscheidet. Bei vertretbarem Aufwand ist es günstiger,

a) <u>entweder</u> den Menschen an Hand seiner Beobachtungen eine Hypothese setzen und den Rechner diese Hypothese mit Hilfe seiner Messung testen bzw. einen Gegenvorschlag unter Berücksichtigung der Hypothese machen zu lassen,
als dem Rechner allein aufgrund seiner Messung die Entscheidung anzuvertrauen.

b) <u>oder</u> den Rechner vorschlagen und den Menschen den Vorschlag testen bzw. in Abhängigkeit von dem Vorschlag gegenvorschlagen,
als den Menschen allein entscheiden zu lassen.

Operations Display
Längsvertikal
Quervertikal
Horizontal
Netz
Schwarm m. Marke
Schwarm
Dichte Stb
Dichte Mitte
Dichte Bb
Menge
Datenfeld Füllgradmessung
Fisch - Visier
Hoch
Tief
Rechts
Links
Voraus
V_{SW}
V_{NW}
V_G
Schiff
Datenfeld

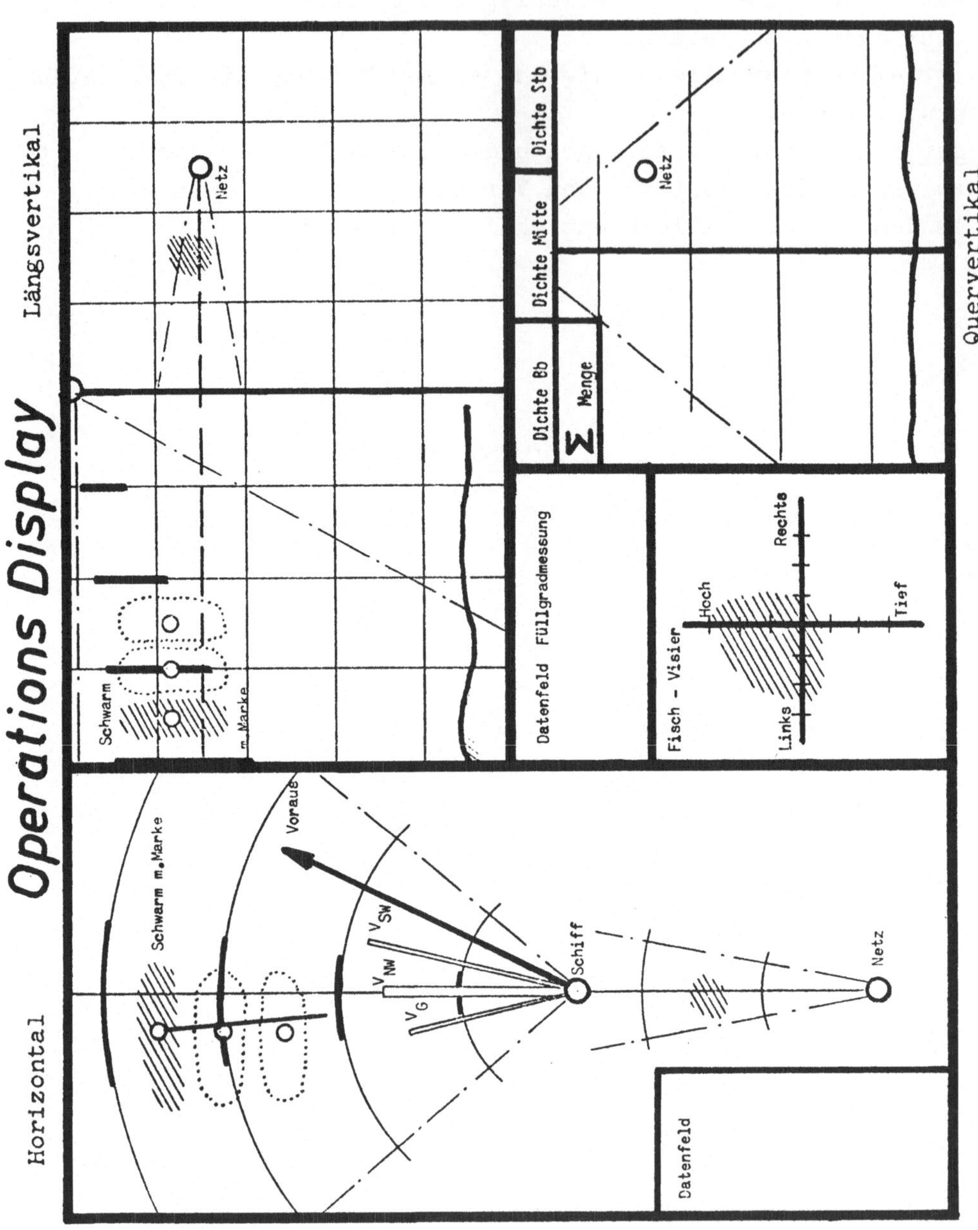

Abb.1

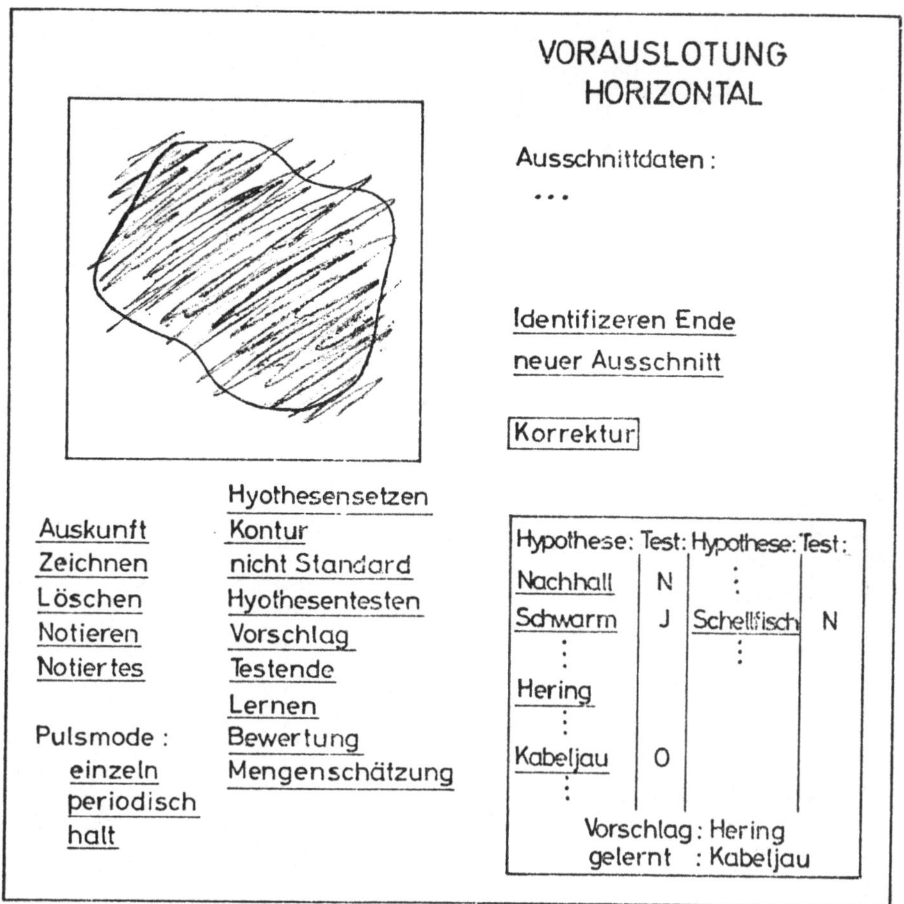

Displaybild „Vorauslotung horizontal"
des interaktiven Entscheidungssystems

Abb.2

Abb.3

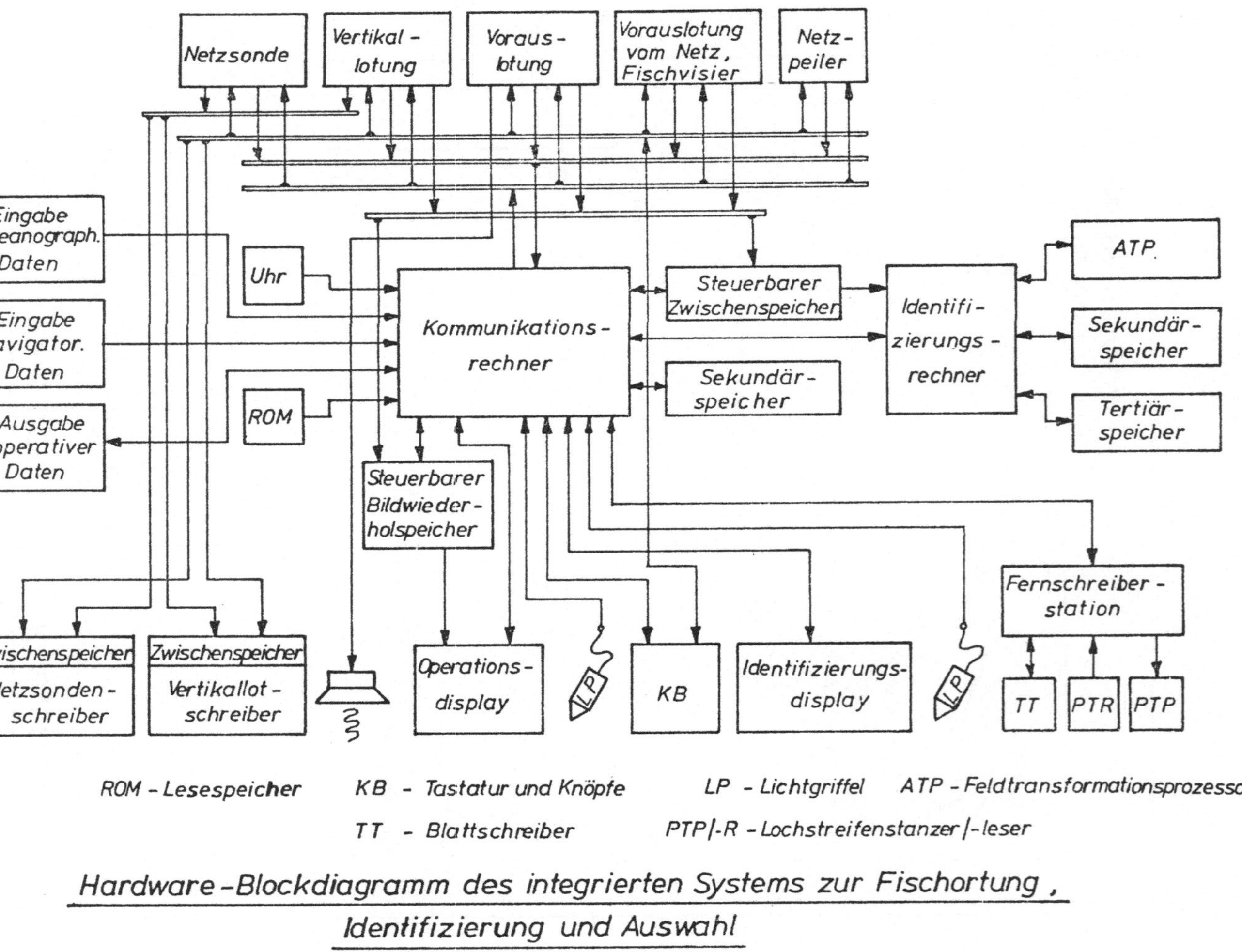

Hardware-Blockdiagramm des integrierten Systems zur Fischortung, Identifizierung und Auswahl

Bewertung
Klassifikation
Rezeption
Szenenanalyse
Edition
Datenverwaltung
Systemüberwachung
Kommunikationsverwaltung
Display-ausgaben
Hardcopy-ausgaben
Operateur
LP-Eingaben
KB-Eingaben
Sonardaten-eingabe-überwachung
Sonargeräte-überwachung
Fernschreiber-überwachung
Überwachung sonstiger Datenstationen
Funktionsblockdiagramm des interaktiven Entscheidungssystems

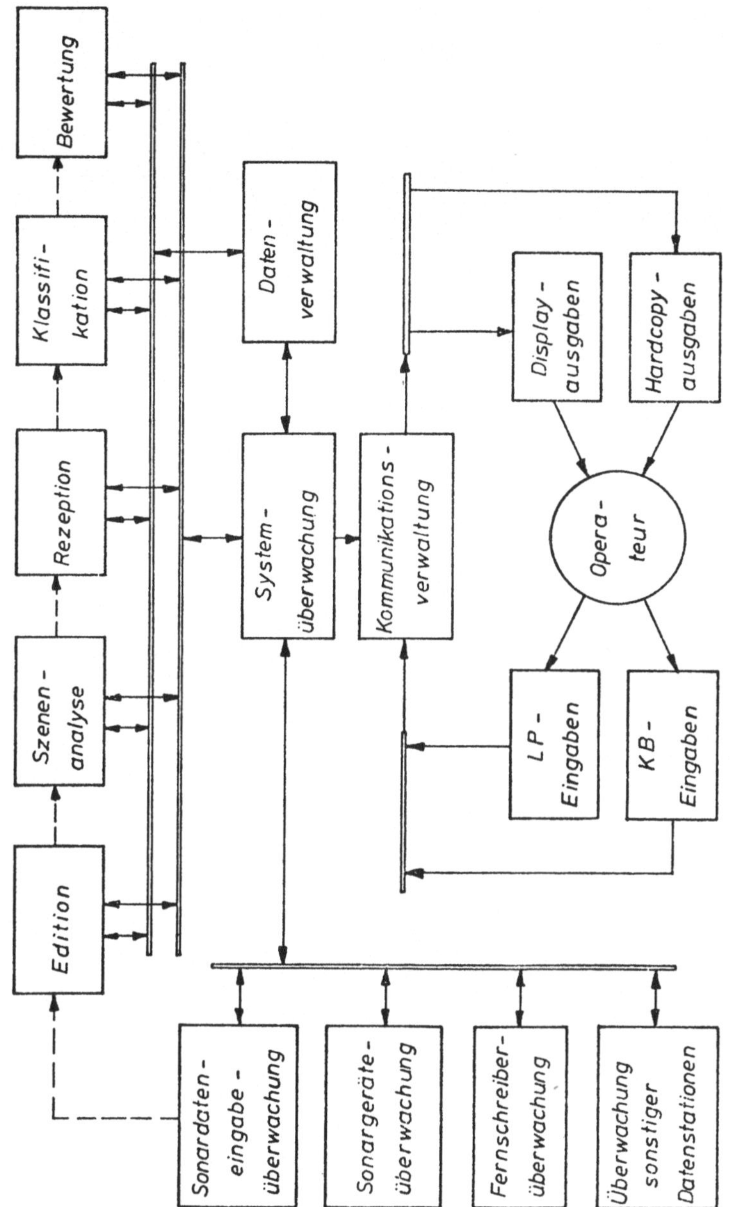

Abb.4

<u>NON-PURPOSIVE PERCEPTION IN COMPUTER VISION</u>

A. Rosenfeld

1. Introduction

Knowledge about the class of scenes being analyzed is extremely important, and often even indispensable, in designing computer programs to do scene analysis. This point has been stressed repeatedly by writers on the subject of scene anaylsis (see Rosenfeld [22-25] for references, as well as for the point itself). It has been contended that computer vision must be regarded as a purposive, goal-directed problem-solving activity. In spite of its title, the present paper does not take issue with this contention. Rather, the paper makes the complementary point that many "low-level" or "front-end" operations in human vision seem to take place almost independently of purposive factors. Moreover, these operations appear to be advantageous (under most circumstances), e.g., in that they combat the combinatorics of scene analysis: they make it unnecessary -- and indeed, perceptually impossible -- to examine more than a (relatively) few combinations of parts of a scene when searching for "objects" in the scene.

It appears to be useful to distinguish between perceptual and cognitive (here: "purposive") levels in vision (Narasimhan and Reddy [16]). "Recognizing a stimulus as a particular object appears to be separable from seeing the shape and surface properties of the object" (Beck [2], p. 144). "It is tempting to conclude that... perception is inevitably a constructive process which creates the world to suit the preceiver... Any such general conclusion is unwarranted, for it neglects the influence of what we shall call... literal perception" (Gibson [7], p. 210). Kanisza [11] has recently presented a set of demonstrations to the effect that the way in which objects are perceived depends on such factors as shape, contour, and color, rather than on the meanings of the objects. Some of these demonstrations are shown in Figure 1. He interprets his examples as showing that "autoch-thonous factors of perceptual organization" can override past experi-ence. An alternative interpretation by Beck [2, p. 144] is that past experience with formal or general properties of objects - surfaces, contours, etc. - can override past experience (or familiarity) with particular objects.

The remainder of this paper illustrates the concept of "non-purposive vision" with examples at two levels: edges, lines, and angles as visual entities; and the Gestalt laws of Organization, which govern the segmentation of a visual field into groups of such entities. Many other aspects of visual perception could also be discussed in this light -- e.g., illusions (nonveridical perceptions of slope, size, etc.); space and motion perception; perceptual models such as those of Dodwell [6], Julesz [10], and Sutherland [31]; or parallel vs. serial processing of visual information (for a recent review see Corcoran [3]). For a general review of the literature on form perception see Zusne [34].

2. Edges, lines and angles

The visual world tends to be seen as segmented at <u>edges</u> -- i.e., at loci of abrupt change in brightness, color, or texture. As Figure 2 shows, one can sometimes "see" edges where none are actually present, by extrapolation or inference from existing edges (see, e.g., Coren [4]). Note that when this happens, the region whose edges are partially present becomes "whiter" than the white background. It does not seem to be possible (except perhaps for unusual individuals) to produce this phenomenon when no edges at all are present; "seeing" objects on a blank surface is mental imagery, not perception.

The local brightness at an edge can influence the perceived brightness of an entire region. Figure 3 shows a computer-generated "pseudoedge" (Rosenfeld and Lee [27]) similar to those generated by O'Brien [17] and Cornsweet [5,20] using spinning drums or disks. Note that when the center strip is covered up, it can be seen that the two halves of the rectangle actually have the same brightness. The pseudo-edge phenomenon occurs even when the "edge" has a gap at its center; but it is weakened by gaps at the ends.

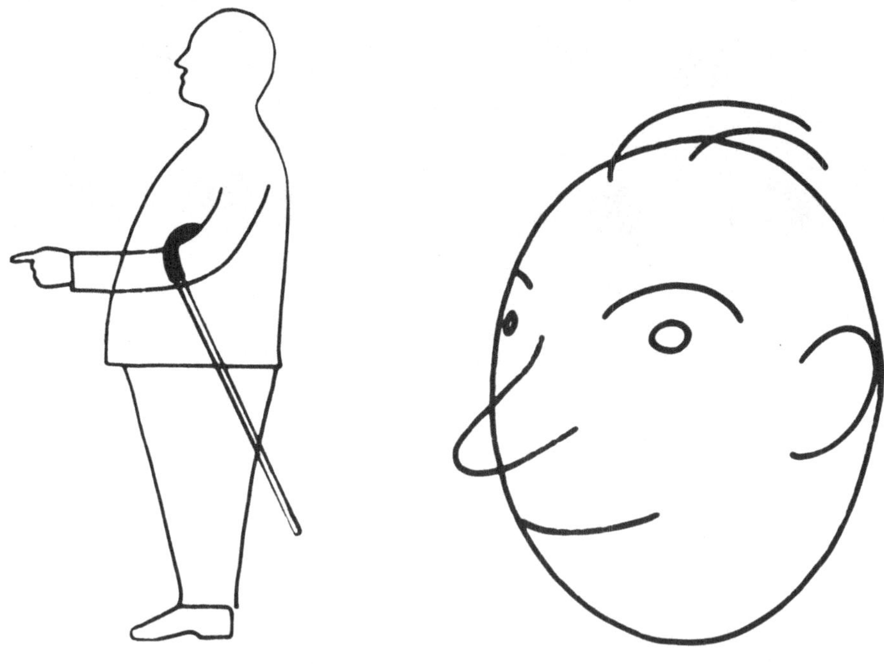

Figure 1. Perception of "impossible" situations. We see the arm, cane, nose, and knife blade as transparent. From Kanizsa [11].

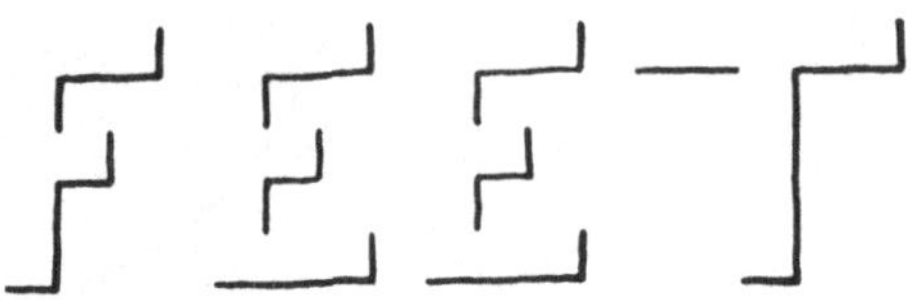

Figure 2.   "Inferred" edges.   From Coren [4], after

a)   Complete

b)   Gap in middle

c)   Gaps at ends

Figure 3.   "Pseudoedges".

A variety of types of edges can be detected by a four-step process of local property measurement, averaging, differencing, and nonmaximum suppression (Rosenfeld et al [9,29,30]). Figure 4 shows brightness averages, differences, and difference maxima for a cloud cover picture. It can be seen that suppression of nonmaxima is the key step that sharply localizes the edges; the differences have high values over a wide range on both sides of the edge (the width depending, of course, on the amount of averaging that was done). For computational expediency, unweighted averages over square regions are used here; Gaussianly weighted averages over rounded regions (Macleod [13]) would be more appropriate.

The simple first-differences used for edge detection in Figure 4 are not the only possible differencing operations (and probably not even the most plausible, from the visual systems modelling standpoint). One can also consider second-difference operators suitable for detecting lines, "streaks", or bars (Rosenfeld et al [29-30]; Macleod and Rosenfeld [14]). A recent application of such operators to the detection of ridges and ravines in an array of terrain elevation data (Peucker and Johnston [18]) is shown in Figure 5.

A method exactly analogous to that used for edge detection can be employed to detect curvature maxima ("angles") on digital curves (Rosenfeld and Johnston [26]). The method computes differences between average slopes, and suppresses nonmaxima (of the cosine of the difference). The resulting maxima, for a "chromosome" shape, are indicated by arrows in Figure 6; the x's in the figure indicate the positions of minima, which appear to be reasonable choices for points of inflection. On other recently investigated methods of segmenting a curve see (Langridge [12], Rosenberg [21], Ramer [19]).

The nonmaximum suppression step in all of these procedures insures that the results will be relatively isolated "events" (edges, lines, or angles). These results can thus be regarded as steps toward converting the (relatively) "continuous" visual input into a more discrete set of entities. Methods of singling out preferred combinations of these entities as objects ("figures" or "bodies") will be discussed in the next section. Meanwhile, it should be emphasized that the process of detecting the entities themselves is very little

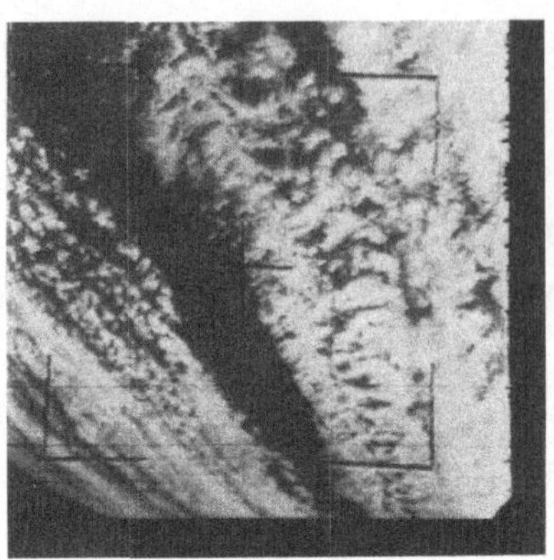

a_o) Original picture

$a_1 - a_6$) Averages over 2^k by 2^k neighborhoods, for k=1,...,6

$hd_1 - hd_6$) Horizontal differences corresponding to $(a_1 - a_6)$

$vd_1 - vd_6$) Vertical differences corresponding to $(a_1 - a_6)$

$ve_1 - ve_6$) Vertical edges (horizontal maxima on $hd_1 - hd_6$)

$he_1 - he_6$) Horizontal edges (vertical maxima on $vd_1 - vd_6$)

<u>Note</u>: All edge results have been multiplied by 2 for
        greater visibility on the output

Figure 4. Edge detection.

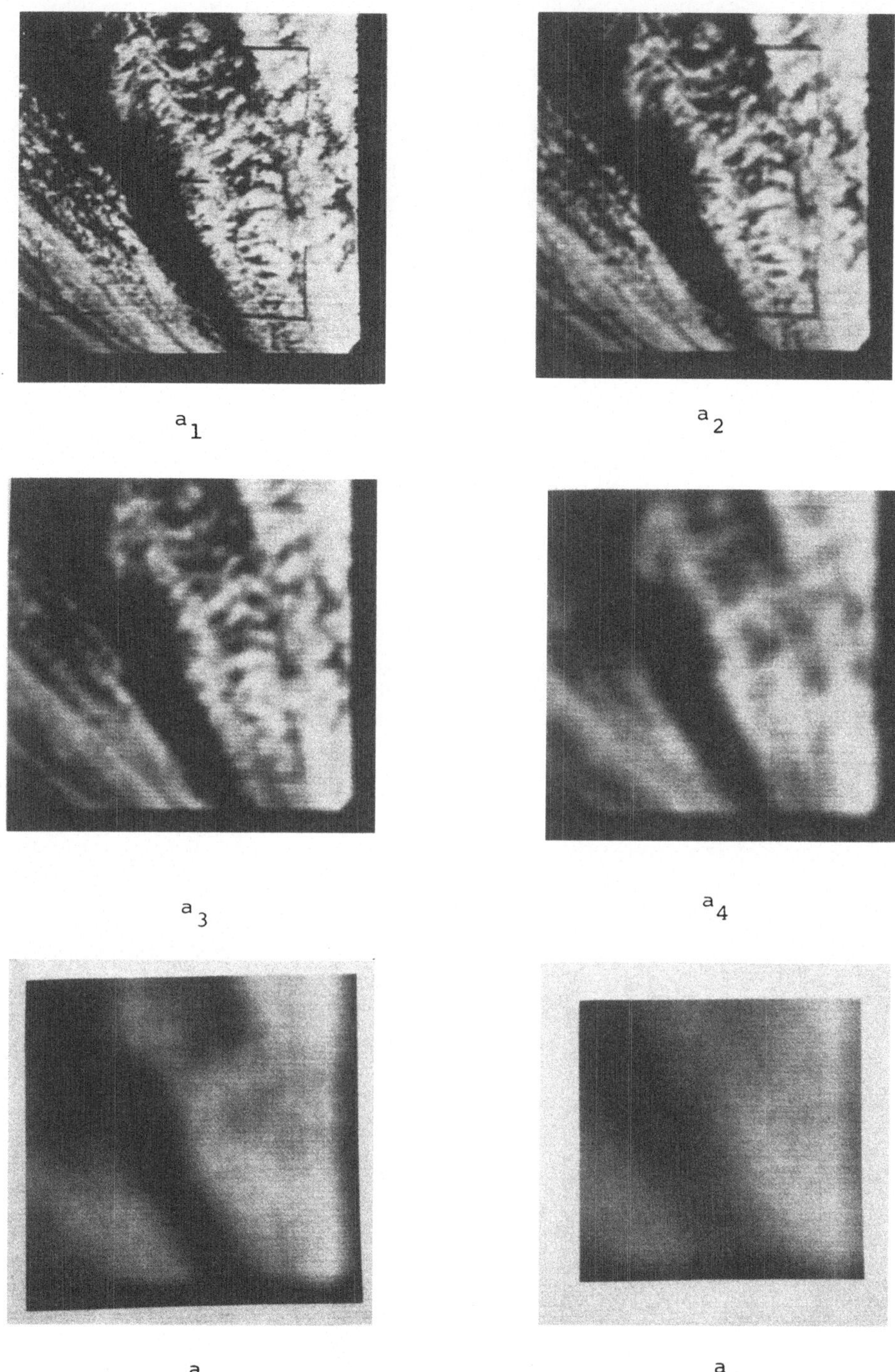

a_1

a_2

a_3

a_4

a_5

a_6

Figure 4. (continued).

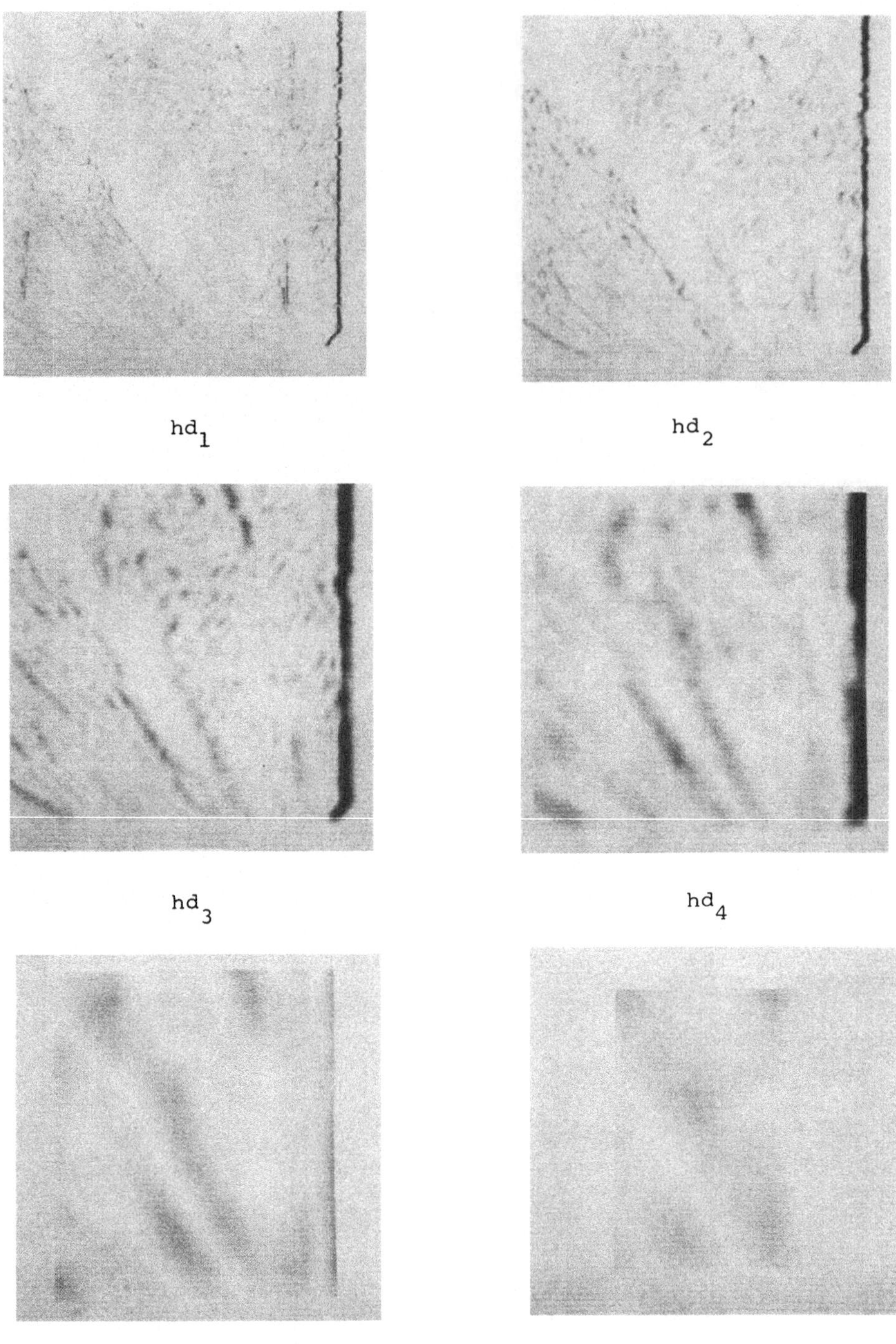

Figure 4. (continued).

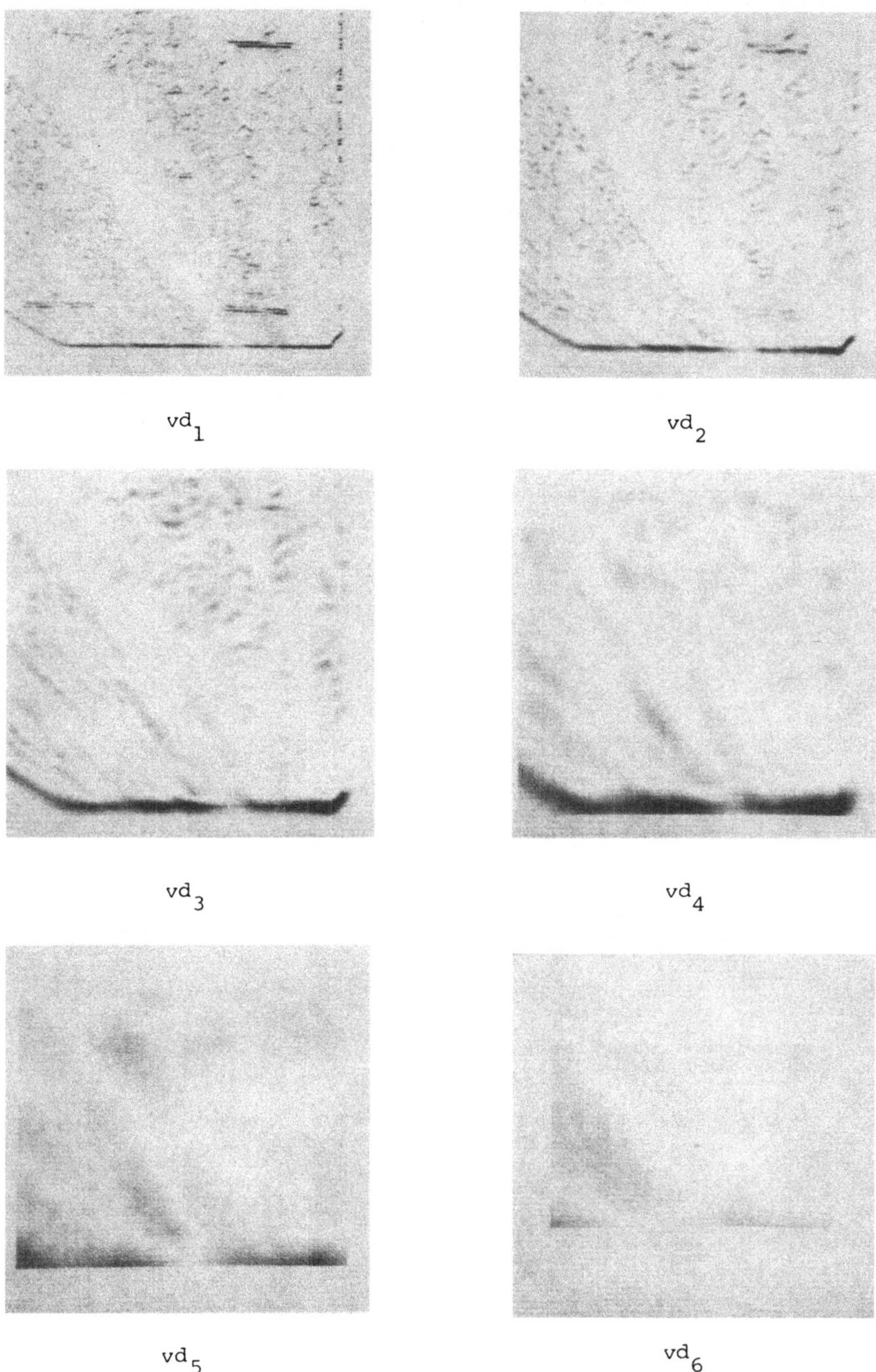

Figure 4. (continued).

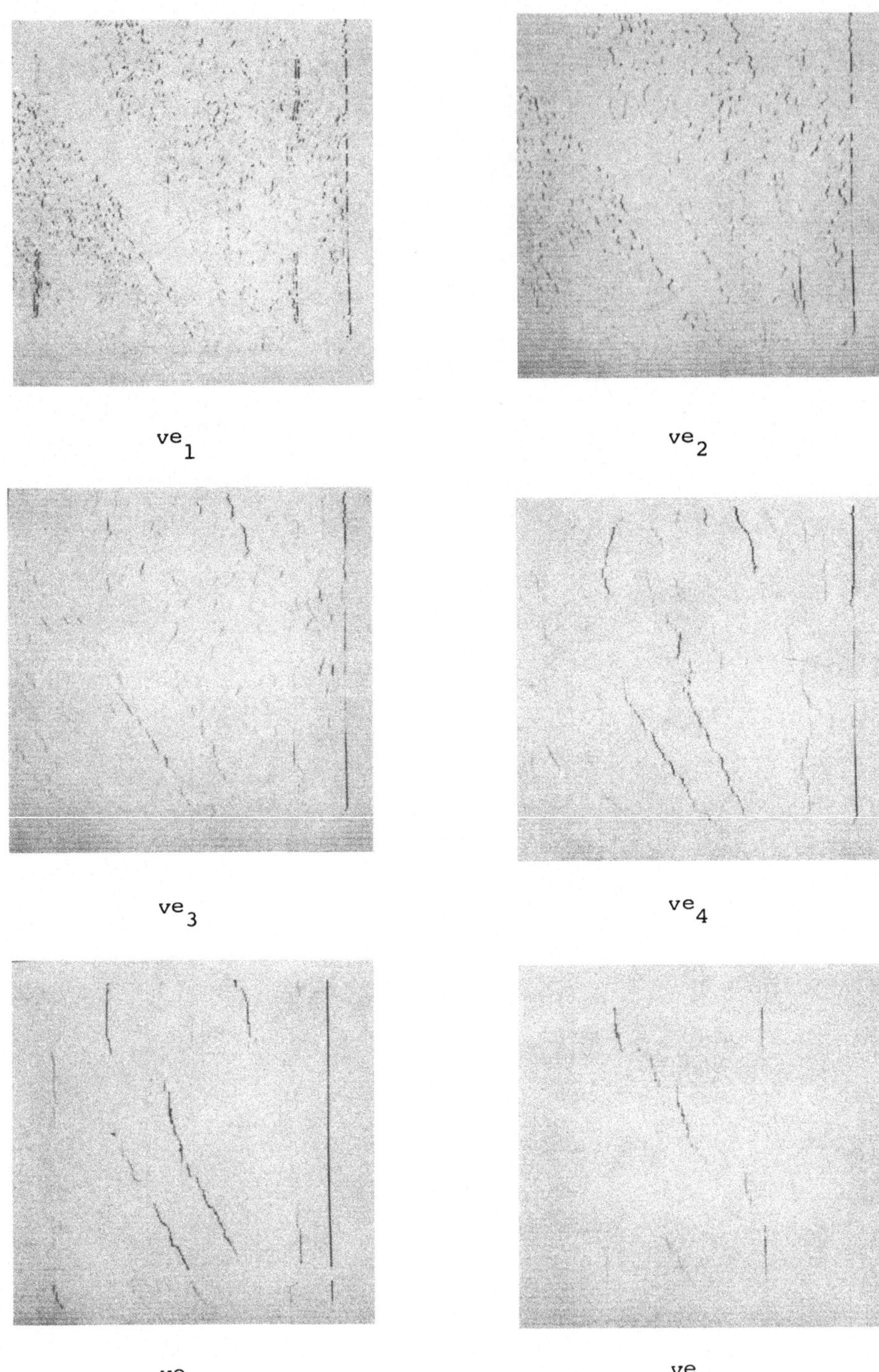

Figure 4. (continued).

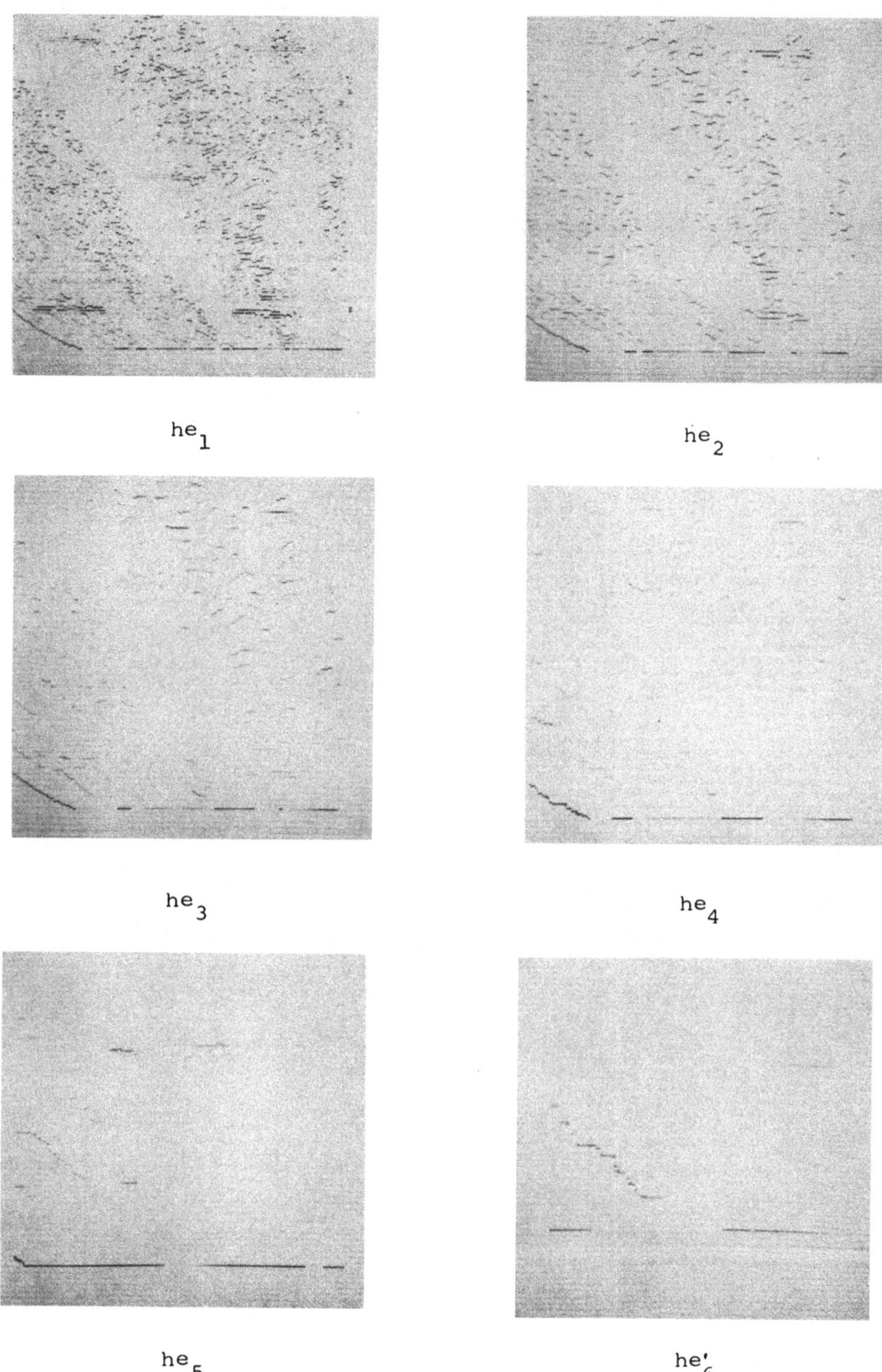

Figure 4. (continued).

a) Terrain elevations.

Figure 5. Line detection.

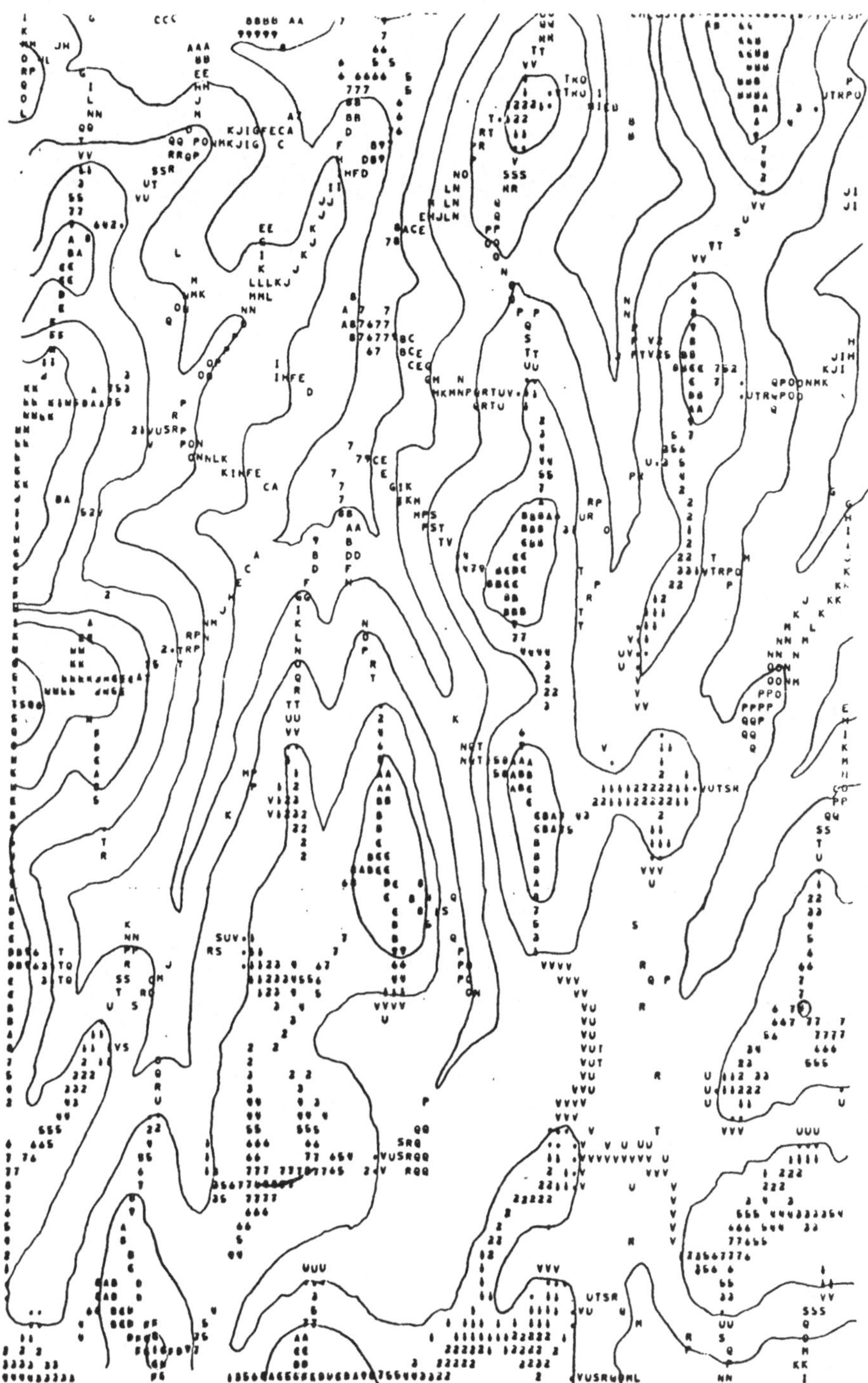

b) Ridges.

Figure 5. (continued).

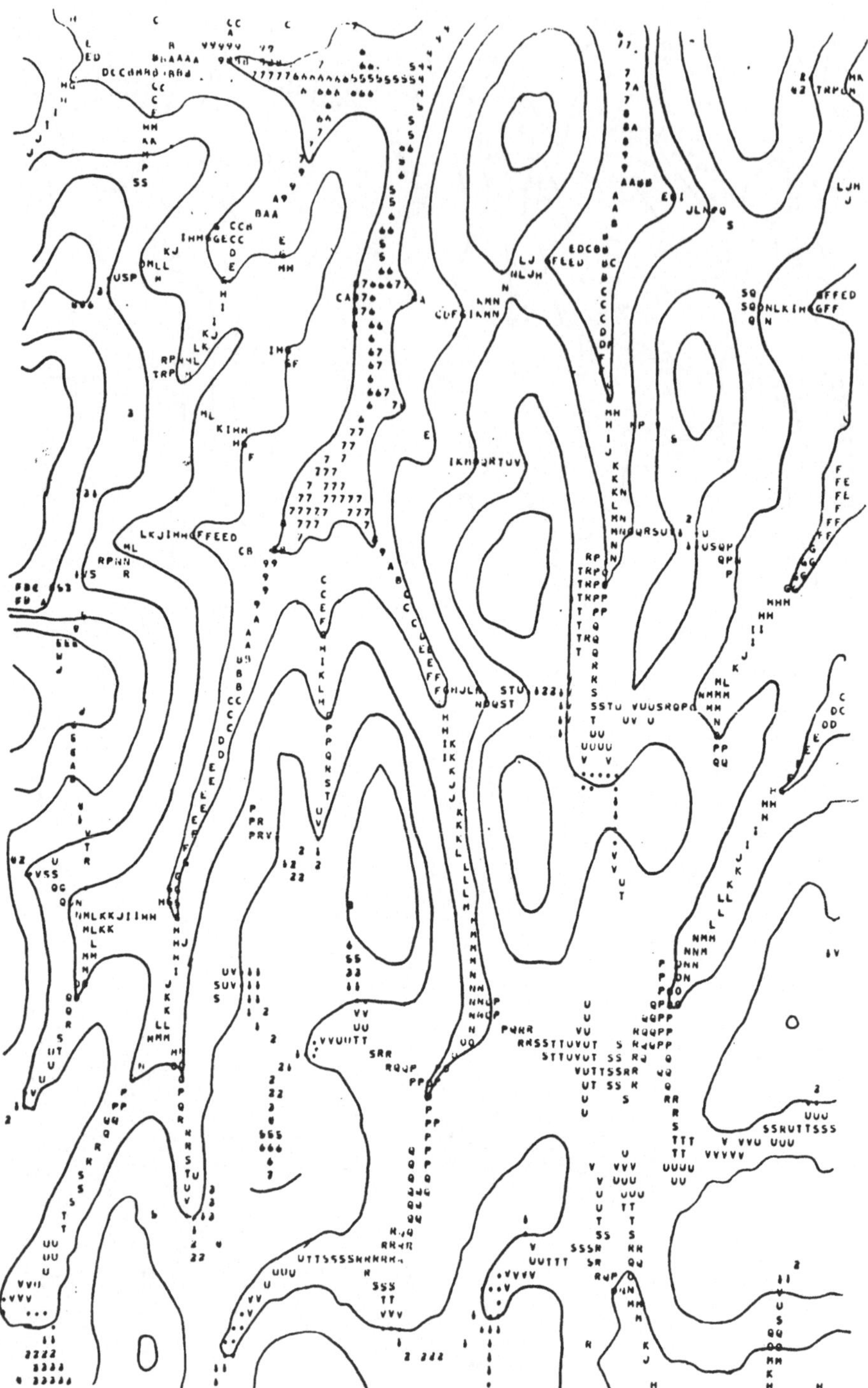

c) Ravines.

Figure 5. (continued).

influenced by purposive goals.

3. Objects

Gestalt psychology has demonstrated that one cannot see arbitrary subsets of one's visual input, or even arbitrary combinations of detectable entities such as edges or lines, as "objects". The Gestalt Laws of Organization describe various types of groupings of visual entities that are easy to see as units. These Laws are difficult or impossible to override by purposive effort (although when two laws conflict, such effort can determine which law governs the grouping). The examples given below are based in part on Wertheimer [32].

The **Law** of Similarity states that similar entities tend to group together (Figure 7). Here the similarity seems to be definable in terms of a small set of local properties such as brightness (or color) and slope; see (Beck [1]) for a recent review. There is evidence that the effectiveness of properties in producing similarity grouping corresponds to their effectiveness in directing one's attention to a peripheral visual stimulus. Note that the grouping phenomenon is a cause, rather than an effect, of attention.

According to the Law of Proximity, closely clustered entities tend to group (Figure 8). It is possible (Rosenfeld and Thurston [29]) that these groupings are seen as units because they excite spot (or streak) detectors in the visual system; for another explanation, involving a graph structure abstracted from the visual input, see Zahn [33]. The Law of Good Continuation states that when curves cross or branch, parts that smoothly continue one another are seen as belonging together (Figure 9). This too can be interpreted in terms of line or streak detectors.

By the Law of Closure, closed figures tend to be seen as units (Figure 10). A possible approach to explaining this phenomenon is that lines that "face" one another, or that meet at angles, are linked together, and that closed figures constitute clusters in the resulting graph structure (Rosenfeld and Lee [28]; for a very similar, and more comprehensive, model see Maxwell [15]). Lines that cross or meet at T-junctions can be interpreted as either linked or not linked; in this way, reasonable analyses of a variety of simple figures into parts can be obtained (Figure 11). The rules used here are somewhat analogous

Arrows = angles
X's = inflections

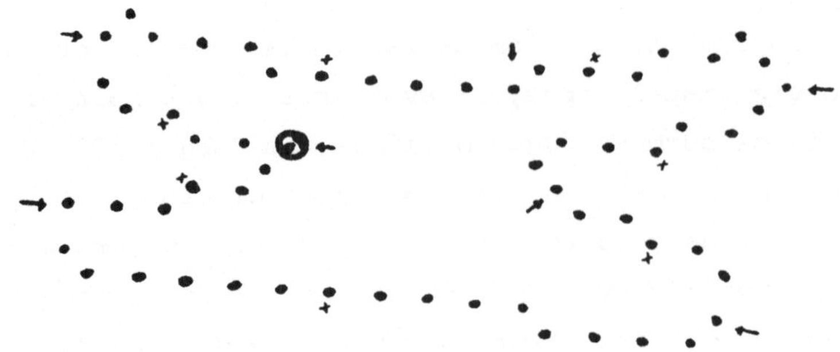

Figure 6. Angle detection.

(a)

Slope differences
produce grouping.

(b)

In their absence,
grouping is
negligible.

Figure 7. Similarity.
From Beck [1].

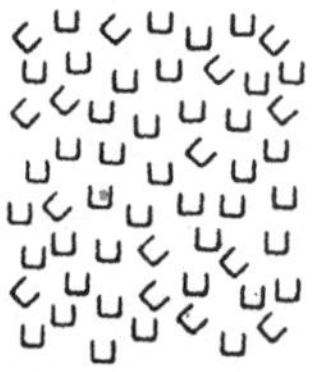

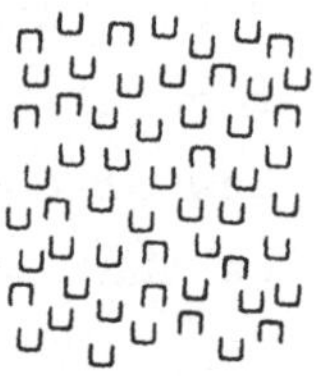

(a) The dots group naturally into 3's; any other
   grouping is virtually impossible to "see".

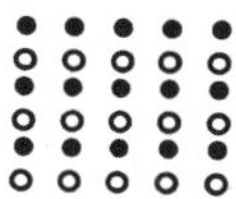

(b) Proximity vs. similarity: The dots can be
   grouped either by columns or by rows. From
   Wertheimer [32].

Figure 8. Proximity.

Figure 9. Good continuation. We see a smooth curve
          and a rectangular wave, not three closed
          figures. From Wertheimer [32].

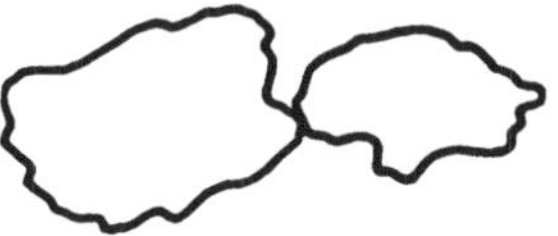

Figure 10. Closure. We see two closed curves, not a
           curve crossing itself. From Wertheimer
           [32].

to those used by Guzman [8] to link regions in a scene into "bodies",
using properties of the junctions at which the regions meet.

The laws that govern grouping can be interpreted as expressing
general properties of objects -- uniformity, compactness, smoothness,
opacity, etc. However, these laws do not reflect past experiences
with specific objects, as pointed out earlier. In particular, these
laws can easily override the effects of past experience. For example,
one does not "see" the E in Figure 11, even though an E is a very familiar figure. It is easy to hide or camouflage an object by extending or adding edges or lines in such a way as to create natural groupings that are incompatible with the object. A classic example is shown
in Figure 12. Even when one realizes that the hidden figures are present, this realization is on an intellectual rather than a perceptual
level: one does not "see" the E in Figure 11 even when aware that it
is there. Similarly, "THECAT" groups intellectually, but not perceptually; whereas "THE CAT" groups perceptually. The grouping laws are
valuable in reducing the number of combinations that must be examined
in attempting to analyze a scene into objects; but this has the consequence that most combinations become impossible to "see" as objects.

It should be pointed out, incidentally, that the apparent brightness of a region does not depend solely on the nature of the region's
edges, but is influenced by the way in which the region is grouped with
other regions. When the "Benussi-Koffka ring" shown in Figure 13 is
seen as a single unit, its brightness is seen as uniform; but when it
is seen as consisting of two halves, one on a black background, one on
a white background, the former half is seen as brighter than the latter
half. This effect weakens when the cuts in the ring are not seen as
extending the edge between the black and white backgrounds (Rosenfeld
and Lee [27]). A related demonstration, due to Benary and Wertheimer,
may be found in (Beck [2], plate 2, p. 44).

Figure 11. This can be seen either as two squares
or as a rectangle and a line, but not,
e.g., as an E and an I.

Figure 12. This is not seen as a W on top of an M.
From Wertheimer [32].

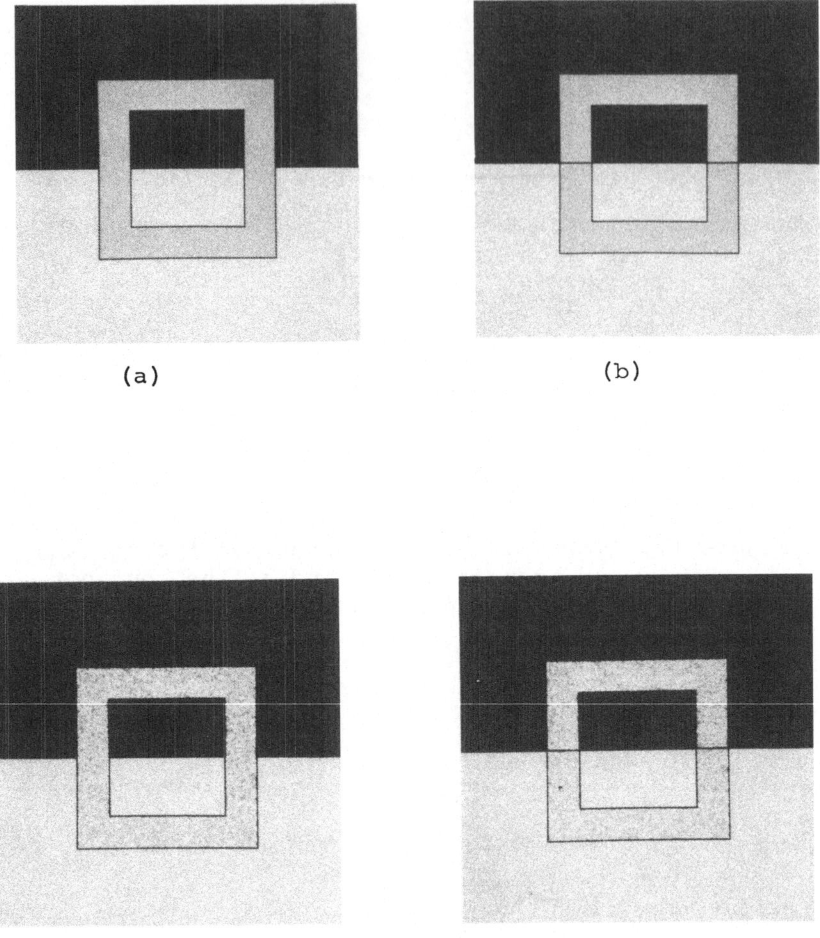

Figure 13. Benussi rings.

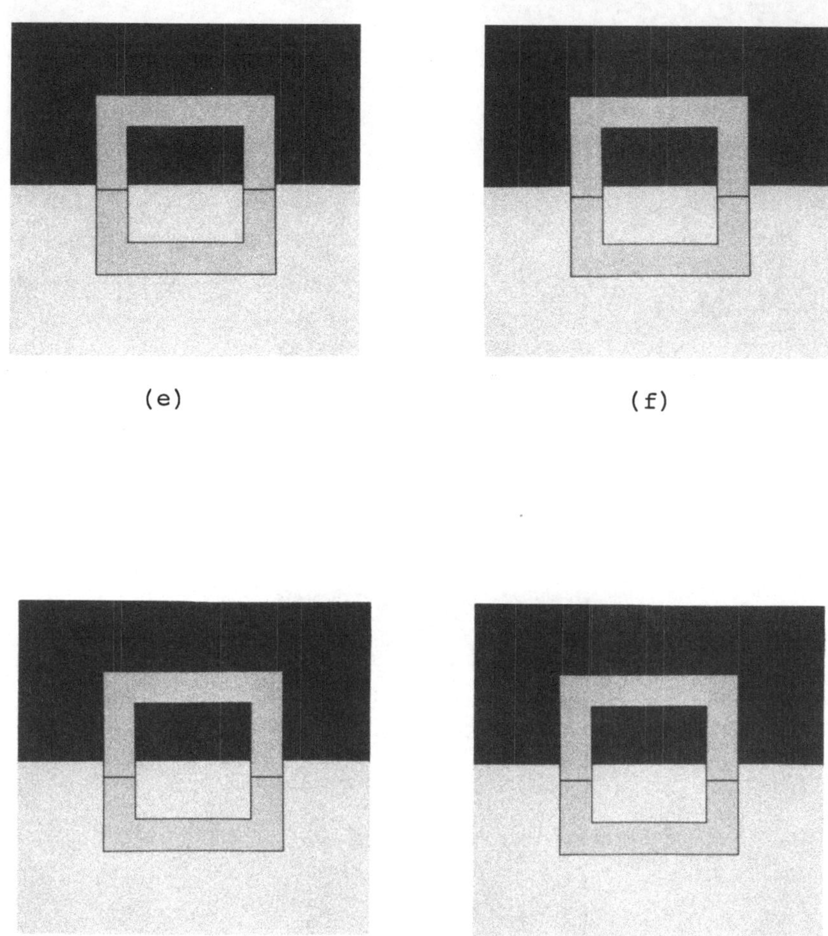

(e)   (f)

(g)   (h)

Figure 13. (continued).

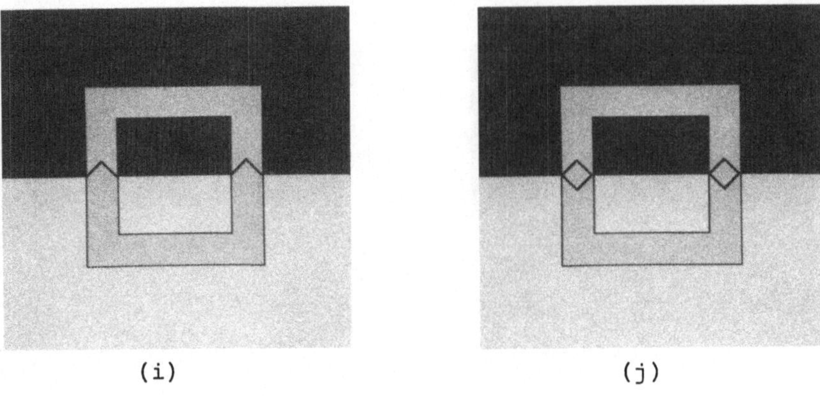

(i)   (j)

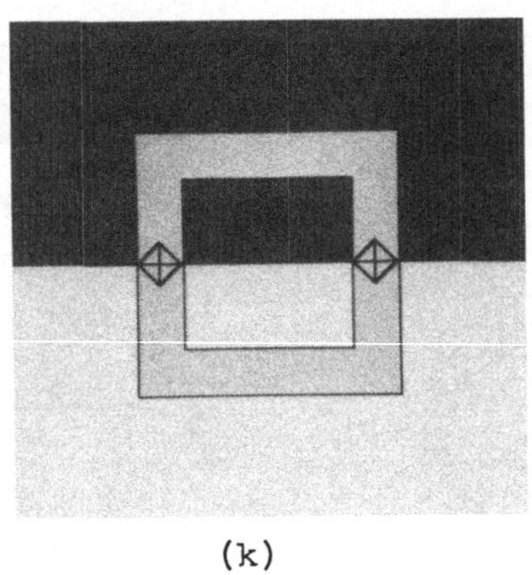

(k)

Figure 13. (continued).

REFERENCES

1. Beck, J. Similarity grouping and peripheral discriminability under uncertainty. *American Journal of Psychology 85*, 1-19 (1972).

2. Beck, J. *Surface Color Perception*. Cornell University Press, Ithaca, N. Y. (1972).

3. Corcoran, D. W. J. *Pattern Recognition*. Penguin, Baltimore, Md. (1971).

4. Coren, S. Subjective contours and apparent depth. *Psych. Review 79*, 359-367 (1972).

5. Cornsweet, T. N. *Visual Perception*. Academic Press, New York (1970).

6. Dodwell, P. C. *Visual Pattern Recognition*. Holt, Rinehart, and Winston, New York (1970).

7. Gibson, J. J. *The Perception of the Visual World*. Houghton-Mifflin, Boston (1950).

8. Guzman, A. Decomposition of a visual scene into three-dimensional bodies. *Proc. Fall Joint Computer Conf.*, 291-304 (1968). Also in Grasselli, A., ed., *Automatic Interpretation and Classification of Images*, Academic Press, New York, 243-276 (1969).

9. Hayes, K. C., Jr., and Rosenfeld, A. Efficient edge detectors and applications. TR-207, Computer Science Center, University of Maryland, College Park, Md. (1972).

10. Julesz, B. *Foundations of Cyclopean Perception*. University of Chicago Press (1971).

11. Kanizsa, G. Perception, past experience, and the 'impossible experiment.' *Acta Psychologica 31*, 66-96 (1969).

12. Langridge, D. J. On the computation of shape. In Watanabe, S., ed., *Frontiers of Pattern Recognition*, Academic Press, New York, 347-365 (1972).

13. Macleod, I. D. G. On finding structure in pictures. In Kaneff, S., ed., *Picture Language Machines*, Academic Press, New York, 231-256 (1970).

14. Macleod, I. D. G., and Rosenfeld, A. The visibility of gratings: a space-domain model. TR-205, Computer Science Center, University of Maryland, College Park, Md. (1972).

15. Maxwell, P. C. The perception and description of line drawings by computer. *Computer Graphics and Image Processing 1*, 31-46 (1972).

16. Narasimhan, R., and Reddy, V. S. N. Some experiments in scene generation using COMPAX. In Nake, F., and Rosenfeld, A., eds., *Graphic Languages*, North-Holland, Amsterdam, 111-122 (1972).

17. O'Brien, V. Contour perception: illusion and reality. *J. Opt. Soc. Amer.* 48, 112-119 (1958).

18. Peucker, T. K., and Johnston, E. G. Detection of surface-specific points by local parallel processing of discrete terrain elevation data. TR-206, Computer Science Center, University of Maryland, College Park, Md. (1972).

19. Ramer, U. An iterative procedure for the polygonal approximation of plane curves. *Computer Graphics and Image Processing 1*, in press (1972).

20. Ratliff, F. *Mach Bands: Quantitative Studies on Neural Networks in the Retina*. Holden-Day, San Francisco (1965).

21. Rosenberg, B. The analysis of convex blobs. *Computer Graphics and Image Processing 1*, 183-192 (1972).

22. Rosenfeld, A. *Picture Processing by Computer*. Academic Press, New York (1969).

23. Rosenfeld, A. Picture processing by computer. *Computing Surveys* 1, 147-176 (1969).

24. Rosenfeld, A. Progress in picture processing: 1969-71. *Computing Surveys 5*, in press (1973).

25. Rosenfeld, A. Picture processing: 1972. *Computer Graphics and Image Processing 1*, in press (1972).

26. Rosenfeld, A., and Johnston, E. G. Angle detection on digital curves. TR-197, Computer Science Center, University of Maryland, College Park, Md. (1972).

27. Rosenfeld, A., and Lee, Y. H. Some figure-ground effects in brightness perception. In TR-183, Computer Science Center, University of Maryland, College Park, Md. (1972).

28. Rosenfeld, A., and Lee, Y. H. A clustering heuristic for line drawing analysis. *IEEE Trans. C-21*, 904-911 (1972).

29. Rosenfeld, A., and Thurston, M. Edge and curve detection for visual scene analysis. *Ibid. C-20*, 562-569 (1971).

30. Rosenfeld, A., Thurston, M., and Lee, Y. H. Edge and curve detection: further experiments. *Ibid.* C-21, 677-715 (1972).

31. Sutherland, N. S. Outlines of a theory of visual pattern recognition in animals and man. *Proc. Royal Soc.* B171, 297-317 (1968).

32. Wertheimer, M. Principles of perceptual organization. In Beardslee, D.C., and Wertheimer, M., eds., *Readings in Perception*, van Nostrand, Princeton, N. J. (1958). Abridged from Wertheimer, M. Untersuchurgen zur Lehre von der Gestalt, *Psych. Forschung* 4, 301-350 (1923).

33. Zahn, C. T. Graph-theoretical methods for detecting and describing Gestalt clusters. *IEEE Trans.* C-20, 68-86 (1971).

34. Zusne, L. *Visual Perception of Form*. Academic Press, New York (1970).

Lecture Notes in Economics and Mathematical Systems

(Vol. 1–15: Lecture Notes in Operations Research and Mathematical Economics, Vol. 16–59: Lecture Notes in Operations Research and Mathematical Systems)

Vol. 1: H. Bühlmann, H. Loeffel, E. Nievergelt, Einführung in die Theorie und Praxis der Entscheidung bei Unsicherheit. 2. Auflage, IV, 125 Seiten 4°. 1969. DM 16,–

Vol. 2: U. N. Bhat, A Study of the Queueing Systems M/G/1 and GI/M/1. VIII, 78 pages. 4°. 1968. DM 16,–

Vol. 3: A. Strauss, An Introduction to Optimal Control Theory. VI, 153 pages. 4°. 1968. DM 16,–

Vol. 4: Branch and Bound: Eine Einführung. 2., geänderte Auflage. Herausgegeben von F. Weinberg. VII, 174 Seiten. 4°. 1972. DM 18,–

Vol. 5: Hyvärinen, Information Theory for Systems Engineers. VIII, 205 pages. 4°. 1968. DM 16,–

Vol. 6: H. P. Künzi, O. Müller, E. Nievergelt, Einführungskursus in die dynamische Programmierung. IV, 103 Seiten. 4°. 1968. DM 16,–

Vol. 7: W. Popp, Einführung in die Theorie der Lagerhaltung. VI, 173 Seiten. 4°. 1968. DM 16,–

Vol. 8: J. Teghem, J. Loris-Teghem, J. P. Lambotte, Modèles d'Attente M/G/1 et GI/M/1 à Arrivées et Services en Groupes. IV, 53 pages. 4°. 1969. DM 16,–

Vol. 9: E. Schultze, Einführung in die mathematischen Grundlagen der Informationstheorie. VI, 116 Seiten. 4°. 1969. DM 16,–

Vol. 10: D. Hochstädter, Stochastische Lagerhaltungsmodelle. VI, 269 Seiten. 4°. 1969. DM 18,–

Vol. 11/12: Mathematical Systems Theory and Economics. Edited by H. W. Kuhn and G. P. Szegö. VIII, IV, 486 pages. 4°. 1969. DM 34,–

Vol. 13: Heuristische Planungsmethoden. Herausgegeben von F. Weinberg und C. A. Zehnder. II, 93 Seiten. 4°. 1969. DM 16,–

Vol. 14: Computing Methods in Optimization Problems. Edited by A. V. Balakrishnan. V, 191 pages. 4°. 1969. DM 16,–

Vol. 15: Economic Models, Estimation and Risk Programming: Essays in Honor of Gerhard Tintner. Edited by K. A. Fox, G. V. L. Narasimham and J. K. Sengupta. VIII, 461 pages. 4°. 1969. DM 24,–

Vol. 16: H. P. Künzi und W. Oettli, Nichtlineare Optimierung: Neuere Verfahren, Bibliographie. IV, 180 Seiten. 4°. 1969. DM 16,–

Vol. 17: H. Bauer und K. Neumann, Berechnung optimaler Steuerungen, Maximumprinzip und dynamische Optimierung. VIII, 188 Seiten. 4°. 1969. DM 16,–

Vol. 18: M. Wolff, Optimale Instandhaltungspolitiken in einfachen Systemen. V, 143 Seiten. 4°. 1970. DM 16,–

Vol. 19: L. Hyvärinen, Mathematical Modeling for Industrial Processes. VI, 122 pages. 4°. 1970. DM 16,–

Vol. 20: G. Uebe, Optimale Fahrpläne. IX, 161 Seiten. 4°. 1970. DM 16,–

Vol. 21: Th. Liebling, Graphentheorie in Planungs- und Tourenproblemen am Beispiel des städtischen Straßendienstes. IX, 118 Seiten. 4°. 1970. DM 16,–

Vol. 22: W. Eichhorn, Theorie der homogenen Produktionsfunktion. VIII, 119 Seiten. 4°. 1970. DM 16,–

Vol. 23: A. Ghosal, Some Aspects of Queueing and Storage Systems. IV, 93 pages. 4°. 1970. DM 16,–

Vol. 24: Feichtinger, Lernprozesse in stochastischen Automaten. V, 66 Seiten. 4°. 1970. DM 16,–

Vol. 25: R. Henn und O. Opitz, Konsum- und Produktionstheorie. I. II, 124 Seiten. 4°. 1970. DM 16,–

Vol. 26: D. Hochstädter und G. Uebe, Ökonometrische Methoden. XII, 250 Seiten. 4°. 1970. DM 18,–

Vol. 27: I. H. Mufti, Computational Methods in Optimal Control Problems. IV, 45 pages. 4°. 1970. DM 16,–

Vol. 28: Theoretical Approaches to Non-Numerical Problem Solving. Edited by R. B. Banerji and M. D. Mesarovic. VI, 466 pages. 4°. 1970. DM 24,–

Vol. 29: S. E. Elmaghraby, Some Network Models in Management Science. III, 177 pages. 4°. 1970. DM 16,–

Vol. 30: H. Noltemeier, Sensitivitätsanalyse bei diskreten linearen Optimierungsproblemen. VI, 102 Seiten. 4°. 1970. DM 16,–

Vol. 31: M. Kühlmeyer, Die nichtzentrale t-Verteilung. II, 106 Seiten. 4°. 1970. DM 16,–

Vol. 32: F. Bartholomes und G. Hotz, Homomorphismen und Reduktionen linearer Sprachen. XII, 143 Seiten. 4°. 1970. DM 16,–

Vol. 33: K. Hinderer, Foundations of Non-stationary Dynamic Programming with Discrete Time Parameter. VI, 160 pages. 4°. 1970. DM 16,–

Vol. 34: H. Störmer, Semi-Markoff-Prozesse mit endlich vielen Zuständen. Theorie und Anwendungen. VII, 128 Seiten. 4°. 1970. DM 16,–

Vol. 35: F. Ferschl, Markovketten. VI, 168 Seiten. 4°. 1970. DM 16,–

Vol. 36: M. P. J. Magill, On a General Economic Theory of Motion. VI, 95 pages. 4°. 1970. DM 16,–

Vol. 37: H. Müller-Merbach, On Round-Off Errors in Linear Programming. VI, 48 pages. 4°. 1970. DM 16,–

Vol. 38: Statistische Methoden I, herausgegeben von E. Walter. VIII, 338 Seiten. 4°. 1970. DM 22,–

Vol. 39: Statistische Methoden II, herausgegeben von E. Walter. IV, 155 Seiten. 4°. 1970. DM 16,–

Vol. 40: H. Drygas, The Coordinate-Free Approach to Gauss-Markov Estimation. VIII, 113 pages. 4°. 1970. DM 16,–

Vol. 41: U. Ueing, Zwei Lösungsmethoden für nichtkonvexe Programmierungsprobleme. VI, 92 Seiten. 4°. 1971. DM 16,–

Vol. 42: A. V. Balakrishnan, Introduction to Optimization Theory in a Hilbert Space. IV, 153 pages. 4°. 1971. DM 16,–

Vol. 43: J. A. Morales, Bayesian Full Information Structural Analysis. VI, 154 pages. 4°. 1971. DM 16,–

Vol. 44: G. Feichtinger, Stochastische Modelle demographischer Prozesse. XIII, 404 Seiten. 4°. 1971. DM 28,–

Vol. 45: K. Wendler, Hauptaustauschschritte (Principal Pivoting). II, 64 Seiten. 4°. 1971. DM 16,–

Vol. 46: C. Boucher, Leçons sur la théorie des automates mathématiques. VIII, 193 pages. 4°. 1971. DM 18,–

Vol. 47: H. A. Nour Eldin, Optimierung linearer Regelsysteme mit quadratischer Zielfunktion. VIII, 163 Seiten. 4°. 1971. DM 16,–

Vol. 48: M. Constam, Fortran für Anfänger. VI, 143 Seiten. 4°. 1971. DM 16,–

Vol. 49: Ch. Schneeweiß, Regelungstechnische stochastische Optimierungsverfahren. XI, 254 Seiten. 4°. 1971. DM 22,–

Vol. 50: Unternehmensforschung Heute – Übersichtsvorträge der Züricher Tagung von SVOR und DGU, September 1970. Herausgegeben von M. Beckmann. VI, 133 Seiten. 4°. 1971. DM 16,–

Vol. 51: Digitale Simulation. Herausgegeben von K. Bauknecht und W. Nef. IV, 207 Seiten. 4°. 1971. DM 18,–

Vol. 52: Invariant Imbedding. Proceedings of the Summer Workshop on Invariant Imbedding Held at the University of Southern California, June – August 1970. Edited by R. E. Bellman and E. D. Denman. IV, 148 pages. 4°. 1971. DM 16,–

Vol. 53: J. Rosenmüller, Kooperative Spiele und Märkte. IV, 152 Seiten. 4°. 1971. DM 16,–

Vol. 54: C. C. von Weizsäcker, Steady State Capital Theory. III, 102 pages. 4°. 1971. DM 16,–

Vol. 55: P. A. V. B. Swamy, Statistical Inference in Random Coefficient Regression Models. VIII, 209 pages. 4°. 1971. DM 20,–

Vol. 56: Mohamed A. El-Hodiri, Constrained Extrema. Introduction to the Differentiable Case with Economic Applications. III, 130 pages. 4°. 1971. DM 16,–

Vol. 57: E. Freund, Zeitvariable Mehrgrößensysteme. VII, 160 Seiten. 4°. 1971. DM 18,–

Vol. 58: P. B. Hagelschuer, Theorie der linearen Dekomposition. VII, 191 Seiten. 4°. 1971. DM 18,–

Vol. 59: J. A. Hanson, Growth in Open Economics. IV, 127 pages. 4°. 1971. DM 16,–

Vol. 60: H. Hauptmann, Schätz- und Kontrolltheorie in stetigen dynamischen Wirtschaftsmodellen. V, 104 Seiten. 4°. 1971. DM 16,–

Vol. 61: K. H. F. Meyer, Wartesysteme mit variabler Bearbeitungsrate. VII, 314 Seiten. 4°. 1971. DM 24,–

Vol. 62: W. Krelle u. G. Gabisch unter Mitarbeit von J. Burgermeister, Wachstumstheorie. VII, 223 Seiten. 4°. 1972. DM 20,–

Vol. 63: J. Kohlas, Monte Carlo Simulation im Operations Research. VI, 162 Seiten. 4°. 1972. DM 16,–

Vol. 64: P. Gessner u. K. Spremann, Optimierung in Funktionenräumen. IV, 120 Seiten. 4°. 1972. DM 16,–

Vol. 65: W. Everling, Exercises in Computer Systems Analysis. VIII, 184 pages. 4°. 1972. DM 18,–

Vol. 66: F. Bauer, P. Garabedian and D. Korn, Supercritical Wing Sections. V, 211 pages. 4°. 1972. DM 20,–

Vol. 67: I. V. Girsanov, Lectures on Mathematical Theory of Extremum Problems. V, 136 pages. 4°. 1972. DM 16,–

Vol. 68: J. Loeckx, Computability and Decidability. An Introduction for Students of Computer Science. VI, 76 pages. 4°. 1972. DM 16,–

Vol. 69: S. Ashour, Sequencing Theory. V, 133 pages. 4°. 1972. DM 16,-

Vol. 70: J. P. Brown, The Economic Effects of Floods. Investigations of a Stochastic Model of Rational Investment Behavior in the Face of Floods. V, 87 pages. 4°. 1972. DM 16,-

Vol. 71: R. Henn und O. Opitz, Konsum- und Produktionstheorie II. V, 134 Seiten. 4°. 1972. DM 16,-

Vol. 72: T. P. Bagchi and J. G. C. Templeton, Numerical Methods in Markov Chains and Bulk Queues. XI, 89 pages. 4°. 1972. DM 16,-

Vol. 73: H. Kiendl, Suboptimale Regler mit abschnittweise linearer Struktur. VI, 146 Seiten. 4°. 1972. DM 16,-

Vol. 74: F. Pokropp, Aggregation von Produktionsfunktionen. VI, 107 Seiten. 4°. 1972. DM 16,-

Vol. 75: GI-Gesellschaft für Informatik e. V. Bericht Nr. 3. 1. Fachtagung über Programmiersprachen · München, 9–11. März 1971. Herausgegeben im Auftrag der Gesellschaft für Informatik von H. Langmaack und M. Paul. VII, 280 Seiten. 4°. 1972. DM 24,-

Vol. 76: G. Fandel, Optimale Entscheidung bei mehrfacher Zielsetzung. 121 Seiten. 4°. 1972. DM 16,-

Vol. 77: A. Auslender, Problemes de Minimax via l'Analyse Convexe et les Inégalités Variationnelles: Théorie et Algorithmes. VII, 132 pages. 4°. 1972. DM 16,-

Vol. 78 : GI-Gesellschaft für Informatik e.V. 2. Jahrestagung, Karlsruhe, 2.–4. Oktober 1972. Herausgegeben im Auftrag der Gesellschaft für Informatik von P. Deussen. XI, 576 Seiten. 4°. 1973. DM 36,-

Vol. 79 : A. Berman, Cones, Matrices and Mathematical Programming. V, 96 pages. 4°. 1973. DM 16,-

Vol. 80: International Seminar on Trends in Mathematical Modelling, Venice, 13–18 December 1971. Edited by N. Hawkes. VI, 288 pages. 4°. 1973. DM 24,-

Vol. 81: Advanced Course on Software Engineering. Edited by F. L. Bauer. XII, 545 pages. 4°. 1973. DM 32,-

Vol. 82: R. Saeks, Resolution Space, Operators and Systems. X, 267 pages. 4°. 1973. DM 22,-

Vol. 83: NTG/GI-Gesellschaft für Informatik, Nachrichtentechnische Gesellschaft. Fachtagung „Cognitive Verfahren und Systeme", Hamburg, 11.–13. April 1973. Herausgegeben im Auftrag der NTG/GI von Th. Einsele, W. Giloi und H.-H. Nagel. VIII, 373 Seiten. 4°. 1973. DM 28,-